A HISTORY *of* MODERN ITALY

A HISTORY *of*

MODERN ITALY

Documents, Readings,

& Commentary

by Shepard B. Clough & Salvatore Saladino

1 9 6 8

COLUMBIA UNIVERSITY PRESS   *New York & London*

Shepard B. Clough is Professor of History at Columbia University &
Salvatore Saladino is Associate Professor of History at Queens College,
C.U.N.Y.

To Rosa & Zina

PREFACE

In preparing this work it has been our aim to present to the reader something other than a collection of documents or an anthology of readings. A compendium of documents possesses something of history's vital quality, but such evidence of the past is available in great and varied abundance. Its very abundance requires selection, arrangement, and interpretation not readily possible for the reader unspecialized in the subject. On the other hand, a body of well-connected readings offering either a narrative account or a series of interpretations may well include original documentary evidence, but the bulk of the evidence forming the basis for the narrative or the interpretation is kept, as it were, away from the reader's eyes. By combining documents, commentary, and interpretive or narrative readings we have sought to effect a continuously flowing synthesis of the broad currents in modern Italian history while keeping before the reader the evidence on which our and others' commentaries are based.

We have selected those documents that seemed to us most representative and expressive of these currents, providing our own narrative or commentary when it seemed suitable and employing excerpts from works of outstanding scholars either to present an established interpretation or to convey the variety of views prevalent on the subject in question. There is no pretense of complete comprehensiveness. Some significant documents may well have been omitted either because their existence escaped us or because we found them unavailable for reproduction. And although we have striven for impartiality in the documents and interpretations presented, the story we have told is such that neither all our preferences nor those of others could receive full satisfaction.

We are grateful to the authors and publishers who have allowed us to reproduce portions of works under their copyright, duly noted in the work, and to the editorial and production staff of the Columbia

University Press, most particularly Miss Phyllis Holbrook, for all their assistance.

SHEPARD B. CLOUGH
SALVATORE SALADINO

P.S.   The reader should know that the plan for this work and the choice of a large number of the documents was a joint enterprise of the authors. Most of the actual work of editing and the writing of connecting commentaries was done by Professor Saladino. I acted largely as an editor at this stage of the undertaking.

SHEPARD B. CLOUGH

CONTENTS

Maps

PART ONE

THE RISORGIMENTO: THE IDEA AND ITS PRACTICAL EVOLUTION TO 1848

MAP 1
A topographical map of Italy

I. THE SEARCH FOR ORIGINS

To break into the continually flowing stream of history involves of necessity an arbitrary act and implies an abrupt change—the ending of one development and the beginning of another. Although such sudden mutations are seldom found in the annals of the past, the historian uses periodization for purposes of clarity, much as the playwright uses acts and scenes to make clear the progression of his story. In his selection of periods, the historian endeavors to begin with periods in which significant changes in government, in economics, in thought, and in social relationships were taking place.

The latter part of the eighteenth century seems to have been one of the times when profound alterations in the lives of the peoples of Western Europe were occurring. Some of these peoples had already joined small principalities into unified political states, and others, notably in Italy and Germany, had unification still before them. Most were experiencing some agitation for more representation in government, if not democracy itself. Nearly all were experiencing some economic development and especially an extension of the capitalist system, with industrialization on the not distant horizon. And many were witnessing the growth of a wealthy middle class which wanted changes that would further its members' interests, but which challenged many of the existing institutions and traditions then in existence.

Thus the end of the eighteenth century is a logical time to mark a break in modern European history. Especially appropriate is this period for breaking into the stream of Italian history, for this was a time fraught with change. It was the beginning of movements that led directly to the unification of the many Italian states into a single state in 1861 and thus to a profound alteration in the entire life of the Italian people.

The period of Italian history from sometime in the eighteenth century to actual unification has come to be known as the Risorgimento, or "resurgence." But historians differ over the nature of this resurgence and the forces that initiated it. This is not to be wondered at, for a strong attachment to history can lend excessive weight to remote antecedents, whereas indifference to this past often leads to "revolutionary" interpretations that view any historical movement under consideration as if detached from all prior developments. National pride may lead one to reject or de-emphasize the importance of foreign influences, while a studied cosmopolitanism often results in denial that there can be developments unique to one nation. Finally, personal preferences of an ideological or practical nature cannot but color both the search for origins and the evaluation of a movement's outcome.

The search for the origins of any historically important movement always entails the danger of viewing the past too sharply in the light of the movement being studied. Inasmuch as the Risorgimento led to a political fulfillment in the nineteenth century, it was almost inevitable that some writers would understand the preceding century largely as a preparatory or seeding period. The eighteenth century thus ran the risk of losing its own peculiar identity. Franco Valsecchi, a perceptive student of the Enlightenment—European as well as Italian—has examined this problem, and in the process raises some questions regarding the indigenous character of the eighteenth-century Italian reform movement, its relation to the general European Enlightenment, and its possible influence on the development of the national idea.

1. THE RISORGIMENTO AND THE EIGHTEENTH CENTURY

Franco Valsecchi, *L'Italia nel settecento, dal 1714 al 1788*. Milan: Arnoldo Mondadori, 1959, pp. 945–46, 954, 958–59, condensed. Courtesy of the author and the publisher. Our translation.

The eighteenth century is situated on the threshold of a new era—that of the Risorgimento—which marks the birth of modern Italy. As a consequence this century has felt the attractive force of the Risorgimento and recently has fallen within its orbit. In this sense one may say that the evolution of historical writing consists in the progressive assimilation of the history of the eighteenth century into that of the Risorgimento, or, in other words, in rendering the meaning of the eighteenth century in Risorgimental terms.

Liberal thinkers during the first half of the nineteenth century appeared already to acknowledge an intimate affinity of their thought with the currents of reform which in Italy preceded the French Revolutionary and Napoleonic crisis. The work of eighteenth-century Italian reformers, a work which was an expression of our needs, seemed to these thinkers to have exercised an innovating effect which was more intimate and profound, and more consonant with the nature of our country, than the influence which came from the outside with foreign [French] invasion. It is known how Manzoni [1] came to deplore

---

[1] Alessandro Manzoni (1785–1873), one of Italy's greatest novelists and an intellectual force in the creation of Italian national consciousness. Ed. note.

the coming of the revolution as a foreign intrusion which compromised the domestic evolution undertaken in thoughtful proportions by the reform movement. Scores of early nineteenth-century economists and political figures recalled the reforming tradition of the preceding century and concluded that the necessary premise for national emancipation was to be found in a higher level of intellectual and economic life: it is as if they were continuing along the same road as their eighteenth-century predecessors and toward the same goals, but with a new spirit and a clearer awareness.

However, as the Risorgimento movement acquired a more definite countenance during the nineteenth century with a more accelerated rhythm of events, with insurrections and wars, the angle of historical vision was altered. The struggle for liberty and independence was no longer seen as meshed with an activity—such as the eighteenth-century reform movement—developing under the aegis of dynastic absolutism and foreign domination. Attention was turned away from the movement of reform and toward another aspect of the eighteenth century: on the one hand, the more advanced political currents recalled the eighteenth century of Jacobinism and of the revolt against the Old Regime, and saw in this other eighteenth century the prelude and annunciation of a revolutionary regeneration; on the other hand, moderate liberal historiography, in examining the tumultuous events of eighteenth-century conflicts for European equilibrium and hegemony, tended to emphasize the first and decisive assertion of the Savoyard state of Piedmont-Sardinia, risen to the role of protagonist in the peninsula as the power on which "Italy's hopes" converged.

Historical criticism has traveled a long way since the nineteenth century; an impressive amount of work has gone into investigation and research, and a richer, wider, and more complex perspective of the eighteenth century has resulted. Full light has been shed on the play of economic and social forces, a play which earlier had remained imperfectly understood or hidden; the century's spiritual, philosophical, and religious evolution has been explored in its innermost folds and turns; the picture of Italy's national life has been divided into its various regional elements and it has been inserted within the framework of Europe. But the central theme of all these studies, their inspiring motive, has been always the Risorgimento; that is, the interpretation of the eighteenth century in function of the national rebirth, of the great national movement which dominated and filled the following century. The result was an emphasis on and thorough examination of eighteenth-century traces of the Risorgimento: emphasis on the developmental continuity that links one century with the other, and a search in the eighteenth century of the forewarning signs of the "imminent Risorgimento," of the rise and affirmation of national and unitary consciousness. As a consequence, the eighteenth century came to lose its own distinctive countenance and autonomy; it became absorbed by the great phenomenon of the Risorgimento in which it lost its own existence; and the problem of the eighteenth century was resolved and reduced to the problem of the origins of the Risorgimento. . . .

Thus, Italian historiography has addressed itself to the search for the origins of the Risorgimento with a systematic investigation bent on finding in the eighteenth century every symptom of developments to come. This investigation has produced considerable results; it has brought new elements to light and has raised new problems; it has produced a veritable "revision" of the history of the various aspects and periods of the eighteenth century. Nevertheless, this investigation appears vitiated by a fundamental flaw, which is: its original characteristic of trying to demonstrate a preconceived thesis; of aiming a priori to seek and find the Risorgimento in the eighteenth century, of anticipating motives, so to speak of "retracing" the eighteenth century according to the Risorgimental model, rather than studying this century from within, in its positive historical reality.

The debate revolves around . . . several fundamental points: the peculiarity, or "autochthonous" character, of the Italian reform movement in the eighteenth century; the new national appearance assumed by Italian politics as a consequence of the assertion of the Savoyard state; the manifestation of a national consciousness on the moral plane; and the manifestation of a demand for unity on the political and economic level. . . .

[But, in fact] the idea of nation remained a literary one in the eighteenth century. Its contact with political reality occurred only with the coming of the French Revolutionary shock and the Napoleonic experience. And the crossing from the literary to the political phase came only with the transformation of the generic cultural affirmation of Italianity into a well-defined political doctrine; that is, with the principle of nationality, which is the affirmation of the nation as the fundamental agglomerate of political society and as the necessary basis of the state. This is a conception which not only characterized the new phase of history in Italy but was affirmed as a principle of universal validity in Europe; it is linked to the new approach which the French Revolution gave to political problems, in contrast to the old dynastic conception of the state; and it resolves itself in the ideal of a new European order based on national states to be substituted for the old order of dynastic Europe. The principle of nationality has as its premise, therefore, a new conception of the state and of society. It is the conception of the state as an expression of the people, of society based on the fundamental equality of men. One cannot conceive of the new idea of nation without the new idea of democracy. To grasp the origins of the national idea one must look to the formation of the modern idea of democracy.

To be sure, the premises of this evolution [of the idea of democracy] are to be sought beyond the French Revolution, in Enlightenment thought and in the reforms which this thought brought into being. But even in this matter, may one speak of an autochthony, of a peculiar originality of the Italian reform movement? Italian thought during the Enlightenment experienced the imprint of the French center of irradiation, as did moreover the rest of the continent. Italian reform received its impulse from foreign princes: the great reforming centers of the peninsula—Milan, Florence, and Naples—were the seats of the new dynasties established in Italy, the Hapsburgs and the Bourbons.

Italian thought is distinguished within the European setting by its own characteristics which were an expression of particular Italian attitudes and historical exigencies. Princely initiative found an active and fruitful collaboration among elements of the local population from which it received a particular imprint; but this does not mean that the Italian reform movement was a whole unto itself. It means simply that Italy entered into the circulation of European thought and politics and brought with it its own contribution. Besides, this contribution was the work of an intellectual élite well informed and up to date with the currents of the century and in open disagreement with tradition, which it fought; it was aware of the backward state of the nation and wished to promote its development to European levels. In a certain sense it was an élite which represented European thought in Italy more than it did Italian thought in Europe.

[In the eighteenth century] there did not exist in Italy the conditions necessary for a renewal to occur from a domestic impulse rather than from foreign reflex. The necessary political conditions were lacking: beginning with Piedmont, the independent states were either still in the old phase of pre-Enlightened absolutism or, as Genoa and Venice, were old-fashioned aristocratic republics. As we have seen, reforms occurred only in the states subject to foreign rule, as was Milan, or to the new Bourbon and Hapsburg dynasties of Naples, Parma, and Florence. Necessary economic and social conditions were also lacking. Italy's economy was still prevalently agricultural; industrial development was meager, especially if we keep in mind the panorama of the whole peninsula, including the States of the Church and the Southern kingdom. The result was the absence of the new middle classes, those classes which were asserting themselves in other and economically more advanced nations. For this reason the Italian reform movement was not the expression of classes already mature and able to make their demands prevail; rather it was an intellectual fact promoted by intellectuals who came from the aristocracy, the clergy, or from a bureaucratic bourgeoisie tied to the old social order. It is because of this make-up that the Italian reform movement of the eighteenth century was lacking in radicalism; its make-up explains also the sense of balance which placed limits on the movement's action and thought, even in the struggle against the traditional order of things, and gave it an essentially conservative although enlightened character. For these reasons, Italian reformers opposed the Revolutionary developments, which they felt to be a foreign intrusion. The same reasons explain the appeal which eighteenth-century reform had on the nineteenth-century Risorgimental reform movement which was likewise influenced by the same élite intellectual and social characteristics.

In conclusion, the new fact to which may be traced the origins of the Risorgimento is not to be found in the "myth" of a literary and cultural stamp born with the Renaissance which from the Renaissance on accompanied the idea of Italian nationhood; it is to be found in the transformation of this generic literary idea into a well-defined political principle, the principle of nationality, of the state as a nation. In turn, this principle presupposed the principle of democracy, that is, the conception of the popular state substituted for the old dynastic conception.

It is during the Revolutionary and Napoleonic period that these principles acquired definite form and real historical effectiveness in Europe; and it is through the vicissitudes and struggles of this period that these principles permeated Italian life. Nevertheless, throughout the course of the eighteenth century there is evident in Italian life an evolution which not only prepared the ground to receive and assimilate the seeds of the new political conception but which also laid the bases for spiritual and political developments of a specifically national character, developments which found their expression in the Risorgimento.

There is a nearly universal consensus that the assertion of the need and possibility of an independent and united Italy was at first and primarily the work of men of letters rather than men of state. We shall dispense with the effort of tracing the antecedents of this literary-cultural assertion all the way back to Dante, Petrarch, and Machiavelli, and limit ourselves to significant eighteenth-century manifestations.

Giambattista Vico (1668–1744) is a giant of the Italian Enlightenment, for long scarcely appreciated save in Italy for the originality of his philosophical thought but recognized quite early by the men of the Risorgimento as a major influence in the shaping of their national attitudes. Emiliana Pasca Noether has examined this influence as one of the seeds of Italian nationalism; and although she avoids the extremes of the indigenous interpretation which tends to make of the Risorgimento a phenomenon purely Italian in origin, her emphasis on the Risorgimental importance of Vico's major philosophical work, *La scienza nuova* [The New Science], is not much lessened by her warning that "there must have been something in Vico besides the fact that he represented a wholly Italian philosophy in opposition to the French influence against which Italians rebelled with growing national feeling in the nineteenth century."

2. SEEDS OF ITALIAN NATIONALISM: GIAMBATTISTA VICO

Emiliana P. Noether, *Seeds of Italian Nationalism, 1700–1815.* New York: Columbia University Press, 1951, pp. 52–62, *passim.* Original footnotes omitted.

At first it is hard to discover just what in Vico may have influenced the intellectual preparation of the Risorgimento. His works appear to contain little that would appeal to an enthusiastic nationalist. No plans for a united Italy, no open condemnation of foreign rule, no exaltation of Italy above all other lands—Vico is seemingly quite content to be a subject of the Spanish crown. In a letter of 1744 to Cardinal Troiano Acquaviva, however, while explaining the subject of the *Scienza nuova*, Vico gives some indication of his feelings as an Italian. The philosophy of nations, he writes, "is now for the first time discussed by Italian talent . . . [and] written in the Italian language."

Still there must have been something in Vico besides the fact that he represented a wholly Italian philosophy in opposition to the French influence against which Italians rebelled with growing national feeling in the nineteenth century. And this something is revealed only when the hard outer shell of Viconian philosophy is cracked, exposing the kernel. The effort is worth making because then it is seen that in attempting to formulate the laws which regulate the course of humanity, Vico, though himself not a nationalist, anticipated many of the principles of nineteenth-century nationalism.

Nationalism, as it was understood by the nineteenth-century patriot, developed simultaneously with the newly found political consciousness of the dignity of man. Individual man thereby acquired a new conception of his rights and grew in his own estimation. Italian nationalists in reviewing their origins realized that almost a hundred years before Vico had said that "the world of civilized nations was certainly made by men." Man was the medium through which civilization had developed; hence "all sciences, all disciplines, and arts have been directed to perfect and regulate man's faculties." Man's importance could not have been more clearly stated.

At the same time that nineteenth-century nationalism exalted man and his activity, it tended to divorce allegiance to the sovereign from allegiance to the state, thus making the latter a mystical entity which transcended the existence of its citizens. But the citizens by being loyal to the state were in reality serving their own interests, for the state was a personification of themselves, their ancestors, and their descendants. The state therefore acquired human characteristics.

Vico had already noted this relationship between man and the state and had predicted that from the principles governing human nature would emerge the principles which regulated the history of the world. Searching for laws, he believed that by studying "certain principles of the humanity of nations from which, no doubt, have arisen all sciences, all disciplines and all arts" he would reach his aim. To complete the analogy between humanity and nations, Vico conceived the development of nations organically. As individual man goes through the inevitable life cycle of childhood, youth, and old age, so do nations. After which Vico proceeded to demonstrate that the development of nations followed directly upon that of man. . . .

One of the most powerful factors in nineteenth-century nationalism was a revived interest in a national language. This was so because language promotes like-mindedness and develops group consciousness. For Vico 150 years before, language meant even more than that. The study of language, or philology, was to Vico "not only the study of words and their history, but since to words are annexed ideas of things, above all the history of things, philologists must therefore deal with wars, peace, alliances, voyages, commerce, customs, laws and money, geography . . . chronology, and with any other matter related to man's existence on earth. In short, philology (in the Viconian meaning which is after all the exact meaning) embraces not only the history of languages and literatures, but also that of ideas and of deeds, of philosophy and of politics."

Being closely connected with man, language followed a development similar to all other human activity. At the beginning the masses of people were mute, uttering only quasi-intelligible sounds. The first human expressions were made for religious ceremonies. Known only to the few, they were veiled in mystery. The second period in the evolution of language was the heroic. Language was then oral, poetical, grandiloquent, and full of imagery. Not so restricted as the divine, it was, nevertheless, not used by the common people, but by their lords, the warriors whose brave deeds were often its subject. The third stage was the language of all—written, commonly understood, and simple. Language, moroever, represented for Vico a characteristic distinguishing one people from another. "As people through the influence of different climates developed individually," Vico believed, "similarly from these individual identities arose equally different languages."
. . . .

As I have pointed out already, Vico was not an Italian nationalist. His philosophy was a universal philosophy of "the natural law of nations." He did not concern himself with the political disunity of Italy in his times. So we find no reference to a united Italy being the third phase of Italy's cyclical development. It was the Italian nineteenth-century nationalists who realized that Italy's cyclical evolution had been interrupted by foreign interference. At a time when other states—France, Spain, and England—had been able to unite and suppress internal disturbances, Italy had become the battleground of foreign troops. Thereafter, completely deprived of its national entity, it had been reduced to a weak conglomeration of states incapable of concerted action. Since all nations went through similar cyclical developments, however, it was inevitable that Italy should become a national state.

To this argument Italian nationalists added the idea that Italy, perhaps more than other states, had a right to achieve nationhood because of the previous greatness of its inhabitants, for in all countries one of the main sources of nationalist pride is the boast that one's ancestors were highly civilized while other peoples were still digging for roots and living in caves. An earlier work of Vico, *De antiquissima italorum sapientia ex linguae originibus cruenda,* written fifteen years before the first version of the *Scienza nuova,* partly supplied the arguments for such boasts on the part of Italian nationalists. In it Vico determined that many centuries prior to Rome Italy had been the seat of an ancient civilization, rich in wisdom, which had rivaled if not equaled Greek philosophy.

Starting from the premise that Latin was closely related etymologically to the Etruscan and Ionian languages, Vico had determined that these peoples had reached a high degree of culture and wisdom much earlier than Rome. . . .

Vico thus proved to the satisfaction of Italian nationalists the existence of a pre-Roman Italic civilization, and the *De antiquissima italorum sapientia* became one of the sources of nationalist inspiration. It strengthened the belief of the nationalists in the inherent superiority of Italy and of its history which could be traced back to a people older and wiser than the Romans themselves, who in their time had spread civilization to the rest of the known world. But the Italian nationalists failed to realize that the *Scienza nuova* superseded this earlier work. In it Vico castigated the conceit of nations that believed to have been "the first to discover the principles of human life." Rather, one of Vico's most important principles was that all nations show like cycles of development. All must eventually attain the same degree of maturity, whether they have had contact with more advanced nations or not. As examples he cites the countries of the east and of northern Europe which had had little intercourse with western civilization, but whose history nevertheless showed a similar evolution.

Still, in proclaiming the equality of all men and all nations by virtue of their equal development, Vico had laid the basis for yet another nationalist tenet. If, as he believed, men and nations did go through like developments, though each produced indigenous customs and cultures and retained its individual "soul," then, the nationalists reason, each such homogenous group has a right to govern itself. Foreign domination must be abolished.

But all that man had ever accomplished or could hope to accomplish on this earth was possible only through the assistance of a Divine Providence. This proved to be another source of Viconian inspiration for the Italian nationalist, for it must not be forgotten that the Risorgimento had a religious overtone. In many instances it may have been directed against the political authority of the pope, but though anti-clerical, it was not anti-religious. With Vico, Italian nationalists might well believe that "lacking a provident God, there would not have been in the world anything other than error, bestiality, ugliness, violence, fierceness, rottenness, and blood, and perhaps through the great wilderness of the horrid and silent earth there would be no human race . . . the world of nations was ordained by God."

It seemed as though many of the aims and aspirations of the Risorgimento could find justification in Vico. Even the ideal of constituting Italy under a monarchical form of government could be justified by using Vico's test. Vico had defined monarchy as the best form of government men could attain. . . . Vico's monarchy was a liberal monarchy. Free republics fell, Vico believed, because everyone was more concerned with advancing his own particular well-being than safeguarding that of the nation. In order to save the nation "one man rose (such as Augustus in Rome) and through arms took control of public affairs." But to succeed he had "to have the support of the people. Monarchies therefore are by nature popularly governed . . . by laws through which the monarch gives his subjects equality; by the monarch's habit of humbling the powerful and safeguarding and freeing the masses from oppression; . . . and by keeping them satisfied and happy through providing the means of livelihood and leaving them their natural liberty." The people thus for Vico is not the forgotten group of society. Rather under a monarchy it would enjoy a privileged position.

Vico's ideas had few followers throughout the eighteenth century. What knowledge of them existed was limited to Naples where some of Vico's students kept his philosophy alive. Among these Antonio Genovesi, teacher at the University of Naples, economist, and philosopher, incorporated many Viconian concepts in his philosophical works. He passed on the knowledge to his pupil Giuseppe Maria Galanti who in turn was friend and adviser to Vincenzo Cuoco, one of the more important of the early nineteenth-century nationalist patriots. . . .

As Vico became known, the Italian patriots struggling for independence and unity realized that in Vico they would find philosophical justification for their aspirations. If they took the trouble to struggle with his often obscure phraseology, they would be rewarded with the elements of a nationalist philosophy. A nation, like a man, had its own distinguishing characteristics and a soul. It had, therefore, the right to govern itself. Language was all important and a part of a nation's heritage, closely connected with its history, customs, and philosophy. Nations went through cyclical developments and there was no earthly power which could impede the completion of a nation's development. In addition, Italian feelings of superiority were put on firmer foundations, than mere boasting, by reference to Etruscan and Ionian ancestors. Finally, monarchy was removed from the purely selfish sphere of the aggrandizement of the house of Savoy and proven to be the most beneficial form of government the free people of Italy could have.

II. THE REVOLUTIONARY AND NAPOLEONIC ERA

The French Revolution and the Napoleonic period are recognized by all—even by the protagonists of the indigenous development of Italian national consciousness—as having exerted an enormous influence on the evolution of Risorgimental thinking. This French influence can be viewed positively, as an encouragement to Italy's liberation from the various domestic and foreign shackles imposed by the Old Regime, or negatively, as in the case of Noether's reference to "opposition to the French influence against which Italians rebelled with growing national feeling in the nineteenth century."

In Italy, as elsewhere in Europe, the outbreak of the French Revolution produced a complex of reactions which do not lend themselves to a simple and uniform explanation. Champions of reform under the auspices of enlightened despots recoiled before the republican and democratic pretenses of Jacobinism. Others, and in a smaller number, welcomed Jacobinism as a logical practical conclusion of Enlightenment principles; while still others became confirmed in their earlier opposition to any reform whatever. In time, almost all active elements of Italian society began to react against the subjection of Italy to French exactions.

The consequences for Italy which derived from the revolution in France were felt even before Napoleon's descent upon the northern plains in 1796. It is not only a question of Jacobin-inspired conspiracies and risings, such as occurred in Naples, Turin, Bologna, and Palermo between 1792 and 1795, nor the consequent reaction by the governments of Piedmont, Naples, and the Papal States to the spread of revolutionary ideas. It is also the centuries-old fact that a divided Italy could not avoid becoming a party and a pawn in the international rivalries occasioned or accentuated by the French Revolution. When the war of the first coalition against revolutionary France began in 1792, Piedmont threw its lot with Austria; and Naples, deterred by the presence of a French naval squadron from doing the same that year, found the assurance of the British fleet enough to enter the war in 1793. Venice, Genoa, Tuscany, and the Papal States may well have preferred to remain neutral, but Austria's dominant position in northern Italy, in addition to the presence of the British fleet in the Mediterranean, made inescapable the involvement of all of Italy in the Revolutionary and Napoleonic Wars.

Out of this involvement and under the influence of French-imposed revolutionary laws and institutions, viewed either positively or negatively, there emerged the first coherent manifestations of political nationalism in Italy.

Among the earliest contributors to the current of conscious nationalism is Vittorio Alfieri (1749–1803), one of Italy's greatest dramatists. While other Italians were welcoming the French armies in 1796 and later as liberators, and under their auspices erected revolutionary republics all over the peninsula, Alfieri unburdened himself of fierce anti-French and patriotic sentiments, which are examined in the following selection from a work by Gaudens Megaro as "another example of the enormous influence of the French Revolution in arousing national sentiment."

3. VITTORIO ALFIERI, FORERUNNER OF ITALIAN NATIONALISM

Gaudens Megaro, *Vittorio Alfieri, Forerunner of Italian Nationalism.* New York: Columbia University Press, 1930, pp. 34, 100–2, 126–28, 148, *passim*. Footnotes omitted.

Alfieri spent most of his time between 1786 and 1792 in Paris, and though preoccupied with putting out a complete edition of his works, he had an opportunity to observe historic stages of the French Revolution. At first, when the Bastille was stormed, he was sympathetic towards the revolutionary movement, but, as it progressed, he became one of its fiercest opponents. Despite his own craving for liberty, he saw in the Revolution the deformation of all true liberal principles. To him there was no difference between the tyranny of one or the few and that of the many. One of his writings, *Il Misogallo* ("The Anti-Gaul," or "The French-hater"), is a work in prose and verse denouncing the Revolution and reflecting his antagonism to the French people. . . .

This furious and mordant attack on the French people and institutions by a single individual was dedicated to "The Past, Present and Future Italy . . . the August Matron, for so long the principal seat of all human wisdom and values, and now unarmed, divided, dejected, unfree . . . to Italy, which some day will undoubtedly rise again, virtuous, magnanimous, free and one." Alfieri insisted on the unity of Italy which nature had so well separated by definite boundaries from the rest of Europe.

He asserted that the sole basis of Italy's political existence—in any form whatsoever—is to be hatred of the French. Hatred, then, seems to be the basic element of national unity, according to Alfieri. He wrote:

The hatreds of one nation against another, having always been—for it cannot be otherwise—the necessary fruit of injuries reciprocally received or feared, cannot therefore be either unjust or base. On the contrary they are a very precious part of the paternal heritage; only such hatreds have wrought those true political miracles that are afterwards so admired in history. . . .

He himself would teach the Italians to abhor the French; to despise the French, the Italians would learn from the French themselves. From the happy mixture (the adjective is the poet's) of these two sentiments, hatred and contempt, Italy ought to begin to reveal more clearly her national characteristics. From his time on, Alfieri added, the word *Misogallo* would be synonymous with *Libero Italiano* (a Free Italian).

If Italy was to be one in hating with implacable hatred those ultramontanes who had caused and still were causing the most frequent and bloody harm to Italy, if her most sacred duty was to hate her natural and perennial enemies, it is clear that Alfieri was imbued with a strong sense of nationalism. Here Alfieri symbolizes a stage in the development of Italian nationalism. The oppression of the foreigner, at this time the French, called for their expulsion, the *sine qua non* of national independence. Love for Italy revealed itself in great part in hatred of the foreigner. There could not be hatred alone, however. There was need of a new orientation towards national ideals, of interior change, of a return to Italian traditions. The Italians could not afford to imitate; they had to create a new life through their own forces. Writing at a time when Italy was suffering the anguish of invasion, when the beneficent results of the Revolution were still obscure, the impulsive and contemptuous reaction of Alfieri is very significant. . . .

Scornful as Alfieri was of the Italians of his day, distant as a united Italy might appear to him, nevertheless he had great faith in the exceptional potential qualities of the Italians, and he cherished a fervent hope that the Italians of the future would be those fiery and enthusiastic freemen whom he so frequently idealized. His voice was not one of melancholy hope, it was not a mere wail and lamentation; it was a voice of courage. Instead of merely bemoaning the fact that the Italians were not what they once had been, he insisted that their capacities were still great and that their future could be a great one. If the Italians were to become free and united, they must have the will to be so. They must will to be great. The trouble with the French, according to Alfieri, lay in the excess of self-confidence, and with the Italians in the lack of it.

In the words of Alfieri, concluding his *Exhortation to liberate the Italians from the Barbarians:*

To think or to say that what has already been done by men cannot be done again by other men, especially in the same territory, is an absurd and demoralizing axiom; it is the usual and obtuse defense of timid and base minds, who affirm as impossible everything they themselves cannot do; and their warped vision does not permit them to see any further than one or two generations ahead of them.

His own axiom is this: "Virtue is the thing which more than any other is created by being praised, taught, loved, hoped and willed; nothing renders it more impossible than the infamous belief that it is impossible."

In addition to recognizing the geographical unity of Italy and the racial and linguistic similarities among Italians, Alfieri contributed to the growth of the Italian national spirit the ideas of sentiment, of will and of a mission. It is immaterial that the Italians did not become the leaders of a new European literature, as he had hoped. What is material is that he thought them capable of it and urged them to take a place of leadership in the world. It is immaterial that the basis of Italian nationalism was not hatred for the French. What is material is that the preaching of hatred implied a desire to see Italy free of foreign political and intellectual domination and dependent on its own initiative. Above all, the Italians had to possess a will, a feeling, a sentiment to become spiritually and politically one in the future. . . .

In Alfieri we find a development of ideas which historically prepare the way for modern Italian nationalism: hatred of tyranny, lay and religious; love of freedom, individual and national; and the praise of the ancients. In respect of his native Italy, Alfieri's hope was a united and independent country, founded on liberty, free of foreign intellectual influence, one, culturally and politically. This vision was complete in him and justifies the appraisal of him as the greatest forerunner of Italy's national political conscience.

Alfieri expected no benefit for Italy from the French influence generally manifest in the peninsula by the time he completed the *Misogallo* in 1798. There was tangible justification for his distrust of the French. In July 1797 much of northern and north-central Italy had been united by Napoleon when he fused the French-sponsored "Jacobin" Cispadane and Transpadane republics (centered in Modena and Milan respectively) into a "Cisalpine Republic" with a government of his own choosing. But the encouragement to Italian nationalism offered by this French-created republic was somewhat reduced by Napoleon's cession of Venice to the Austrians in the peace treaty of Campo Formio in October of the same year. Napoleon's disregard of Italian popular sentiment in refusing to allow the people of the Cisalpine Republic to choose their own government and in ceding formerly independent Venice to Austria for the sake of concluding peace, seemed to confirm much of Alfieri's criticism.

But even after these acts by Napoleon revealed that the French republic's primary concern was with French interests, some Italians still placed most if not all their hopes on France's benevolent influence, as did the Neapolitan revolutionists who erected the "Parthenopean Republic" in 1799, only to see it fall within five months in consequence of French military reverses. Among the Neapolitans who witnessed the rise and fall of their republic was a young lawyer, Vincenzo Cuoco (1770–1823), who in 1801 wrote *An Historical Essay on the Neapolitan Revolution of 1799* (*Saggio storico sulla rivoluzione napoletana del 1799*). This and later works helped place Cuoco in the forefront of those Italians who were becoming increasingly convinced that Italy's Risorgimento could come only through the efforts of the Italians themselves. Emiliana Noether's evaluation of Cuoco's role sets him in a direct line with Vico and Alfieri not only as forerunners but also as distinctly Italian forces in the formation of national consciousness.

4. VINCENZO CUOCO AND THE FORMATION OF ITALIAN NATIONALISM

Noether, *Seeds of Italian Nationalism, 1700–1815*, pp. 158–63, 165, *passim*. Original footnotes omitted.

Cuoco's analysis of the Neapolitan revolution's failure proceeds from the Viconian concept that each people develops individually. As it develops, it creates its own patrimony of laws, customs, and ideas. Consequently any revolution or change must occur within this national framework. In the days elapsing between the flight of Ferdinand IV and the entry of the French troops, Naples could have worked out its own salvation. The people were ready to follow a leader who would have spoken their language. No such leader appeared. Instead, a feverish attempt was made to superimpose a French structure on a Neapolitan base. The result was disastrous, for base and structure collapsed. If the republic had been established by the Neapolitans, and the constitution founded on the needs and customs of the Neapolitan people; if real benefits had been given to the people instead of fobbing them off with abstract terms, then perhaps the people, instead of turning against the novelties which they did not understand and did not trust, might have acted quite differently. The history of the republic might have been one of success instead of failure. . . .

The Neapolitan revolutionists had attempted to achieve overnight all the changes which France had effected in years. The result had been a "passive" revolution—a movement in which a few did everything while the bulk of the population stood sullenly aloof. If a revolution is active, that is, involves the participation of all, it usually succeeds. A passive revolution can only succeed if it guesses the wishes of the people and so gains their acquiescence. Lacking it, the Neapolitan patriots did not even take steps to win it. They were French in thought and sympathies, while the people remained Neapolitan. The leaders had spoken of liberty in terms of freedom of thought, press, and religion. For the masses, this liberty was an unimaginable good which could be understood only through tangible benefits—safety, comfort, lower taxes, increase of industry, and other immediate, visible improvements. In fact, the patriot leaders feared the people. Though speaking of liberty and reform, they were reluctant to share their power with them. No common interests existed and when the forces of Cardinal Ruffo appeared the people welcomed back the order they knew and understood.

To have succeeded, the Neapolitans should have restored the ancient privileges and removed the obstacles which long centuries of oppression had opposed to the natural rights of the people. All nations, no matter how corrupt or miserable, have traditions which deserve to be preserved; and all governments, regardless of despotism, possess some features which can be incorporated into a free state. These remains of past traditions and government practices are precious to the wise legislator and should form the basis of any laws. The old Neapolitan laws and customs contained remnants of the ancient republican form of government, and the new constitution should have relied on these.

Again and again Cuoco stresses the necessity of considering the historical background before making changes. A movement which disregards historical forces, he saw, was doomed to failure; the foundation of any constitution being the character of the nation itself. There could exist no ideal constitution suited to all men, as there was no garment or shoe fitting everyone. . . . To attempt to reform everything as the Neapolitan revolutionists had tried in 1799 was to risk destroying everything.

Thus from the failure of 1799, Cuoco drew the lessons he preached to later Italian patriots. The process of constitutional evolution must be slow and fundamentally educational. Cuoco's second tenet therefore was that the mass of the people must be educated to the ideals of unity and independence. The more ignorant people were the more difficult it was to rule them, for the fewer ideas they had, the stranger any innovation would seem to them. But before the masses could be educated the leaders must know the country, its resources, and its traditions. Though the leaders of the Neapolitan revolution had been learned men, they had lacked a thorough knowledge of the region they tried to rule. . . .

In Italy the specific problem of education was to create a public spirit. Cuoco returned often to this concept of public spirit, and it is clear that to him nationalism and public spirit were almost synonymous. How was public spirit to be created? First, by informing the people about their past. Second, by a careful and impartial consideration of other nations, which might appear great at first, but which under study might loom less large. Then one's national advantages would become evident. Third, by a just appraisal of conditions at home, neither over-praising, nor unjustly criticizing. . . .

The most difficult problem the Italians faced in the early years of the nineteenth century was to rebuild a feeling of national self-esteem. Depressed by centuries of political impotence, overshadowed by the economic and cultural advances of the national states, and dazzled by the French Revolution, Italians tended to minimize their own abilities. Cuoco sought to show them that they held within themselves the seeds of their regeneration, or, as he called it, virtues. Love of work was for him the only foundation of virtue. Work would restore to Italy the arts it lacked. Work would render Italians independent of foreign imports and increase the use of Italian products. The more

Italian things people used the more esteem or self-respect would develop. From this esteem and self-respect would grow love of country.
Once they had reached national self-consciousness, the Italians would
be ready to demand their independence. But unless they were prepared to fight for it, independence would not be forthcoming. The belief had grown that Italy was anyone's prey because its people were
militarily inept. Like Machiavelli and Giannone, Cuoco sought to persuade his countrymen that the *sine qua non* of political life was military strength. But this military strength had to be founded on justice.
It should not be turned to oppress other peoples or employed in inter-
necine struggles.

Cuoco had thus far given the Italians much practical advice. It was
not ignored, for the Risorgimento which was essentially a rebirth of
the Italian people adopted and followed all of Cuoco's principles. . . .

With Cuoco the cycle which had begun with Vico's *Scienza nuova*
was completed. During the eighteenth century Italy had developed
feelings of nationality which could lead only to political nationalism.
The French Revolution accelerated the process. In their reaction
against French hegemony, Italian nationalists turned to their past and
found sources of unexpected hope and justification. The eighteenth
century had prepared the ground for the Risorgimento. Vico's philosophy gave them assurance that all nations went through cyclical developments. Even a superficial application of his theory revealed that
Italy's cycle was ready to be completed. After centuries of political un-
importance, Italy was on the brink of attaining nationhood.

The sequence Vico-Alfieri-Cuoco suggests the negative aspects of foreign influence in the development of Italian nationalism, inasmuch as all three men
reveal in varying degrees and for various reasons a reaction to French intellectual or political hegemony over Italy. But there was also an aspect of this
hegemony which was positive at first, and with long-lasting effects. The
Napoleonic Kingdom of Italy, formed in 1805 out of another Napoleonic
creation (the Cisalpine or Italian Republic of 1797–1804) gave to northern
and central Italy the first experience with political unity since ancient times.
However unpleasant French rule eventually became, nothing could cancel
the lessons Italians learned of the desirable results to be achieved by unity,
even when this unity was incomplete and the creature of a foreign power.

The selection reproduced below from a work by R. J. Rath presents in
concise fashion the formation of the Kingdom of Italy, its accomplishments,
and the consequences of its ten years of existence.

5. THE NAPOLEONIC KINGDOM OF ITALY

R. John Rath, *The Fall of the Napoleonic Kingdom of Italy* (1814).
New York: Columbia University Press, 1941, pp. 13–15, 17, 21–22, 25–
26, *passim*. Original footnotes omitted.

In the spring of 1796, when Napoleon Bonaparte marched into the
plains of northern Italy at the head of his army of 38,000 men, a new
era began in the Apennine peninsula. Before Napoleon's astoundingly
rapid conquest, Italy, divided as it was into nine different sovereignties, each with its own political system and each with its own culture,
had been little more than a geographic expression; now it was to have
the first taste of political unity since the days of the Roman Empire.
During the period of the Napoleonic Empire, the nine parts were to
be reduced to three—the part annexed to France proper, the Kingdom
of Naples, and the Kingdom of Italy—each of them dependent upon
the central authorities in Paris.

The northeastern and north central parts of Italy, which are the
subject of our discussion, experienced several changes in their form of
government and territorial configuration before they were finally made
into the Kingdom of Italy. Immediately after Bonaparte's entry into
Italy in 1796, revolutionists in Modena, Ferrara, Reggio, and Bologna
created the Cispadane Republic; and the inhabitants of Milan, Mantua,
Bergamo, Brescia, and Crema were grouped together in the Transpadane Republic. In 1797, Napoleon combined these two infant republics
into one large trans-Alpine state, the Cisalpine Republic, and, at the
same time, gave the old Venetian territory situated between the Adige
and Po rivers to Austria as an indemnity for her loss of Belgium and
the Duchy of Lombardy.

The newly created Cisalpine Republic did not long remain undisturbed. In 1799, after the formation of the second coalition against
France, an Allied army overran northern Italy, overthrew the Republic,
restored the Austrian laws, and inflicted severe punishments upon the
supporters of the French. The next year the Hapsburgs were again
evicted from this territory when Napoleon, who had returned from
Egypt and had been made First Consul, defeated the Allied armies at
Marengo and decreed the re-establishment of the Cisalpine Republic.

In 1802, the Cisalpine Republic was transformed into the Italian
Republic, with Bonaparte as president and the Milanese Francesco
Melzi d'Eril as vice-president. After Napoleon became Emperor of
France in May, 1804, he decided to transform the Italian Republic
into a kingdom. . . . On March 17, [1805], a constitutional statute was
issued calling the French Emperor to the throne of Italy on condition
that the kingdom would be kept forever distinct from the Empire and
that on the conclusion of peace Napoleon would resign in favor of either his natural or adopted son. On May 26, amidst the joyful acclamations of the people, Napoleon was formally crowned king in the
Milanese cathedral.

When first created, the Kingdom of Italy included the territory that
had comprised the former Italian Republic. . . . Additions, however,
were soon made. The first of these was the city of Venice and the remaining Venetian territory on the mainland which had been taken
from Austria in the Treaty of Pressburg (December 26, 1805). . . .
In 1808 the papal March of Ancona and the papal Duchies of Mace-
rata, Fermo, and Urbino, and in 1810 the South Tyrol were united
with the kingdom. Thereafter no more territorial additions were made.

Very few of the different parts of the newly created Kingdom of
Italy had previously been combined in a single political entity. Prior
to the French Revolution they had been governed by diverse authorities. . . .

Although the various parts of the kingdom differed from each other
to a remarkable extent, as we have seen, Napoleon, nevertheless,
welded them together, like the other territories under his control, into
a highly centralized political unity directly under his own personal supervision. . . .

The situation that confronted the officials of Napoleon, in Italy as
well as in the other countries under the domination of the French
Emperor, was the creation of a new order, the making of which always causes dislocations and brings both good will and hatred for
those who do it. Before the Russian debacle in the fall of 1812, the
old political laws of Italy, the same as elsewhere, were destroyed, and
the country was moulded and broken and moulded anew. The last
vestiges of feudalism were wiped out. Justice according to the ideas of
the rising bourgeoisie was instituted; civil equality was established.
The adminstration was well ordered and energetic; the laws were

clear and just. The introduction of the French civil and commercial codes, the systematic and efficacious repression of brigandage, and the construction and repairing of roads and bridges helped to stimulate commerce and industry; whereas the direct intervention of French authorities in constructing canals and dams, in giving prizes for agricultural improvements, and in improving the existing irrigation system, encouraged agriculture. New primary and secondary schools were established, and the universities of Pavia, Bologna, and Padua acquired an importance which they had not had for centuries. The city of Milan especially profited from the changes. Prior to Bonaparte's Italian campaign, it was a provincial capital; now it was the center of a large, thriving, and pretentious kingdom and of a brilliant and pompous court life such as the city had never seen.

Reforms such as these were beneficial to the inhabitants of the Kingdom of Italy, and many Italians were well pleased with them. Other creations and policies of the new French masters, however, were burdensome and annoying and tended to produce a considerable amount of dissatisfaction. One grievance for many persons was the lack of political liberty in the kingdom. The council of state prepared the laws, the viceroy promulgated them, the senate registered them, the ministers made them applicable, and the prefects and vice-prefects enforced them throughout the kingdom. The presence everywhere of an arbitrary police curbed all opposition to the regime, and the omnipresent censorship effectively prevented any expression of discontent.

More exasperating were the heavy military and economic burdens laid upon the shoulders of the inhabitants of the kingdom. Napoleon never took pains to conceal from his viceroy that his interest in Italy was wholly confined to what the Italian people "could furnish him in money and men for his European wars." He admonished Prince Eugene to bear in mind that he was always to consider "*France above all*," and that he was to make Italy's interests inseparable from those of France.

Since Napoleon took such an attitude, it was to be expected that he made ever increasing demands for more Italian soldiers for his army. Beginning in 1801, each year brought about a new request for more men. By 1812 the Kingdom of Italy had furnished a total of 91,788 men to Napoleon's military forces. Of these, 22,000 were killed in the

Peninsular War. Twenty-seven thousand went with the viceroy and General Pino to Russia, scarcely 1,000 of whom returned to their native land. The Italians, the same as the Germans, the Dutch, the Poles, and other peoples under Napoleonic domination, had to shed their blood for causes other than their own.

The Italians also had to endure the same onerous economic burdens as other subjects of the French Emperor. Government expenses in the Kingdom of Italy slowly but steadily increased. . . . By October, 1813, the royal treasury was bankrupt, commerce and industry were in a wretched condition, and large numbers of people, especially in the mountain valleys of the Venetian departments, were on the verge of starvation. Thus, several months before the final defeat of Napoleon's armies and, with it, the overthrow of the French government in Italy, the Kingdom of Italy, like other countries under Napoleon's control, was in a state of almost complete prostration, and a considerable number of its inhabitants were crying for relief from the heavy exactions from which they were suffering.

III. RESTORATION AND REVOLUTION:
THE CONTINUING STRUGGLE FOR
POLITICAL LIBERTY AND
INDEPENDENCE, 1814–1831

The end of Napoleonic power in 1814–15 required a readjustment of affairs in Italy, as it did elsewhere in Europe; but it would be a mistake to think that the restoration period resulted in the complete undoing of all changes enacted since the French Revolution. The statesmen who assembled at the Congress of Vienna in 1814 did not try to obliterate everything that had happened in the preceding twenty-five years nor did they nurture the illusion that this was possible. Certainly they could not "restore" the minds of men, or undo all reforms effected in territories that had been annexed to or controlled by France, or eradicate all remnants of French institutions, like the *Code Civile*.

So far as "restoring" formerly ruling dynasties is concerned, the Congress of Vienna did a relatively thorough job, although the Italian states and dynasties that were restored should not be viewed as the caricatures frequently depicted under the influence of the ambiguous notion of "reaction." True, Piedmont was returned to the sway of the house of Savoy in the person of Victor Emmanuel I, an illiberal monarch not indifferent to administrative reforms or to hopes of creating a kingdom of Upper Italy. The house of Hapsburg-Lorraine returned to the Grand Duchy of Tuscany with Ferdinand III and to the Duchy of Modena with Francis IV, the first prince a liberal and enlightened man, the second enlightened but most illiberal politically and ambitious for territorial expansion and perhaps a royal crown. The Duchy of Parma went to the former empress of the exiled Napoleon, the Hapsburg Maria Louise, who governed with moderation, as did Marie Louise of Bourbon in the Duchy of Lucca. The moderating influence of the Cardinal Secretary of State Consalvi spared the Papal States from a severer reaction, but not even he could save these temporal domains of the Pope from a host of conflicting political and religious jurisdictions and from consequent maladministration. In Naples and Sicily the restored Ferdinand IV of Bourbon broke all the conciliatory and moderate pledges he had made upon his return; and in 1816, abolishing all vestiges of Sicilian autonomy and installing a rigidly conservative regime, he proclaimed himself Ferdinand I, King of the Two Sicilies. Lombardy and Venetia were constituted into provinces within the Austrian empire, thereby being denied any vestige of independence other than in routine local matters. Austrian rule was politically severe and fiscally burdensome but it had the virtues of being efficient and impartial in administration. Lastly, the territory of the former Genoese republic was annexed to Piedmont, making of the latter a more distinctly Italian state than it had been before the Revolution, but embittering many Genoese.

Clearly, the restoration of the old order was of varying degrees; but whatever the case, the overwhelming majority of Italians (rural, agrarian, and scarcely aware of liberal ideas and institutions) was for the moment not openly hostile to the old dynasties and the old ways. There were some significant exceptions: aristocrats, especially the Milanese, proud of their heritage and disgruntled by their subjection to foreign rule; members of the commercial and professional classes who yearned to regain the political ascendancy they had enjoyed during the Napoleonic period; army officers and public officials disaffected by reduction in rank or compulsory retirement designed to make way for "restored" colleagues; all those who remained attached to the political and social ideals proclaimed, if not always practiced, by the French revolutionaries; and lastly, the few who still thought of a united Italy.

Living under regimes that on the whole did not tolerate open political activity, this disaffected minority could express its views and plan for the future only in secrecy. Hence the rise and growth of secret political societies, principally the *Carboneria*, which spread from the South to the rest of Italy and in the North affiliated with the *Federati*, the *Guelfi*, and the *Adelfi*. The Carbonari and allied groups favored constitutional government and independence from foreign rule; some members espoused republican ideals and others possibly aspired to political unification. Cutthroats mingled with the most noble idealists. For approximately a decade, between 1820 and 1831, the Carbonari and kindred conspiratorial organizations held the main stage in Italy's struggle for political freedom. It is significant that the three main attempts they made against restored regimes occurred in the Kingdom of the Two Sicilies, Piedmont-Sardinia, and the Papal States, precisely in the three largest Italian states, not under Austrian rule or influence, and the ones with the most consistently illiberal governments.

The Neapolitan revolution which began in July 1820 was certainly inspired by the Spanish revolution of the earlier part of the same year, the two events sharing substantially the same causes, ideals, and initial Carbonari leadership. They also shared the same fate: failure, owing to divisions between moderate and radical factions, regional rivalries, and foreign intervention. In the Two Sicilies it was the conflict between the Carbonari and the more moderate Constitutionalists, between Sicilian autonomists and Neapoli-

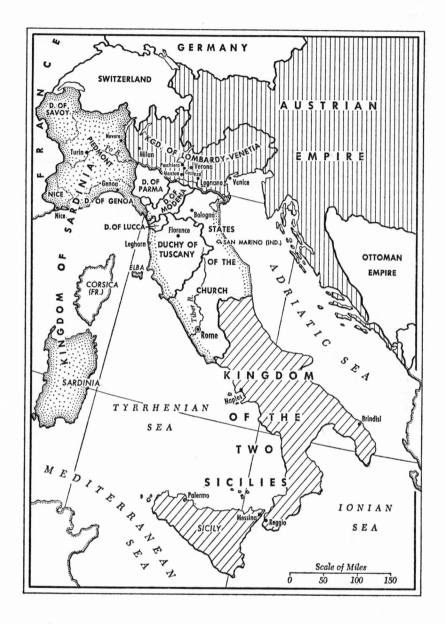

Map 2
The Italian states in 1815

tan centralists, and the intervention of Austrian troops which doomed the revolution by the spring of 1821. The Spanish revolution came to an end in 1823 when French intervention completed the work of dissolution engendered by moderate-radical dissensions within the revolutionary camp.

The Neapolitan revolution was near its end when the Carbonari promoted a rising in Piedmont. Trusting in the support of Charles Albert, a prince of a younger branch of the house of Savoy and heir presumptive to the throne, a group of military leaders seized the citadels of Alessandria and Turin, proclaimed a constitution, and spoke of independence and unity. Victor Emmanuel I abdicated; in the absence of his brother and immediate heir, Charles Felix, he appointed as regent his twenty-two-year-old nephew, Charles Albert, who on March 13 promulgated the constitution demanded by the revolutionists. For the next eight days the young regent's ambiguous behavior toward revolutionaries and royal relatives alike laid the basis for a controversy as to his actions and real intentions which has become a much disputed issue of Italian historiography. On March 21 Charles Albert fled the Piedmontese capital to eventual exile in Tuscany. He had earned the hatred of the revolutionaries, who considered him a traitor to their cause, and the distrust of the new king, Charles Felix, who for a time threatened to disown him as his heir to the throne. Charles Felix's resolute opposition and the intervention of Austrian arms ended the Piedmontese revolution by early April 1821; and so a rising full of liberal and nationalist ambitions came to an ignominious end, compromising princes and Carbonari but not stirring the masses, who felt little in common with aristocratic and secretive conspirators.

Between 1821 and 1831 the Carbonari continued to conspire in various Italian states; when, in the latter year, they registered another calamitous failure, in central Italy, they began rapidly to lose whatever following they had retained during the preceding decade. It was clear by 1831 that there was something inherently unproductive in the Carbonari's approach to the problem of redeeming Italy. The man who made the most searching examination of the deficiencies of Carbonarism and who offered a promising alternative was the Genoese Giuseppe Mazzini (1802–72). Reared under liberal influences by his parents, hostile to the Savoyard monarchy which had absorbed the formerly independent republic of Genoa, and of a nature so sensitive that as a young man he resolved always to wear black in mourning for the distraught state of his beloved Italy, Mazzini quickly moved from literary to political activity, seeking freedom in both fields and asserting that tyranny in one could not but be accompanied by tyranny in the other. He joined the Carbonari in 1827 and in 1830 was confined in the fortress of Savona as a subversive. Early in 1831 he exchanged imprisonment for exile, and repaired to Marseilles where he continued his political agitation. The failure of the revolution of 1831 in central Italy convinced him that Carbonarism had no future in Italy, and that it was necessary to chart a new course with a new organization.

In the following selection from his *Life and Writings* Mazzini explains the reasons for his joining the Carbonari and for his eventual disenchantment.

6. MAZZINI AND THE CARBONARI

Joseph Mazzini, *Life and Writings,* 6 vols. London: Smith, Elder, & Co., 1890–91, I, 14, 66–73, *passim.*

While studying the events of 1820 and 1821, I had learned much of Carbonarism, and I did not much admire the complex symbolism, the hierarchical mysteries, nor the political faith—or rather the absence of all political faith—I discovered in that institution. But I was at that time unable to attempt to form any association of my own; and in the Carbonari I found a body of men in whom—however inferior they were to the idea they represented—thought and action, faith and works, were identical. Here were men who, defying alike excommunication and capital punishment, had the persistent energy ever to persevere, and to weave a fresh web each time the old one was broken.

And this was enough to induce me to join my name and my labours to theirs. . . . [But] it was clear to me, after a defeat like that in the centre, that the only possibility of success left to us consisted in a complete reconstruction of the whole machinery of insurrection, out of youthful and unknown materials. . . .

Carbonarism appeared to me to be simply a vast *liberal* association, in the sense in which the word was used in France during the monarchies of Louis XVIII. and Charles X., but condemned by the absence of a fixed and determinate belief to lack the power of unity, without which success in any great enterprise is impossible.

Arising during the period when the gigantic but tyrannous Napoleonic unity was tottering to its fall, amid the ruins of a world; amid the strife between young hopes and old usurpations; and the dim foreshadowings of the people opposed to the records of a past the governments were seeking to revive;—Carbonarism bore the stamp of all these diverse elements, and appeared in doubtful form amid the darkness diffused over Europe at that critical period.

The royal protection it encountered at its outset, and indeed so long as there were hopes of using it as an instrument of warfare against imperial France, had contributed to give the institution an uncertain method of action which tended to divert men's minds from the national aim.* True it is that on seeing itself betrayed it had cast off the yoke, but preserving unconsciously some of its former habits, and above all a fatal tendency to seek its chiefs in the highest spheres of society, and to regard the regeneration of Italy rather as the business of the superior classes than as the duty of the people, sole creators of great revolutions. It was a vital error, but inevitable in every political body wanting a sound religious faith in a great and fruitful principle, supreme over all the changes of passing events.

Now Carbonarism had no such principle. Its only weapon was a mere negation. It called upon men to overthrow: it did not teach them how to build up a new edifice upon the ruins of the old.

The chiefs of the Order, while studying the national problem, had discovered that although all the Italians were agreed upon the question of independence, they were not so upon the question of unity, nor even upon the meaning to be attached to the word liberty.

Alarmed at this difficulty, and incapable of deciding between the different parties, they chose a middle path, and inscribed *Liberty* and *Independence* upon their banner. They did not define what they understood by liberty, nor declare how they intended to achieve it: the country, they said—and by the country they meant the upper classes —the country will decide at a future day.

In the same spirit they substituted the word *union* to that of *unity*, thus leaving the field open to every hypothesis.

Of equality they either did not speak, or in so vague a manner as to allow every man to interpret it according to his own views, as political, civil, or merely Christian equality.

Thus did the Carbonari begin their work of affiliation, without affording any satisfactory issue to the doubts and questions then agitating men's minds, and without informing those whom they summoned to the struggle what programme they had to offer to the people in return for the support expected from them.

And numerous recruits were enrolled from all classes; for in all

* Carbonarism was founded in the kingdom of the two Sicilies in 1811, with the approbation of the minister of police, Marghella, and of the king, Murat. It spread rapidly among the *employés*. In 1814, when prohibited by Murat, it demanded and obtained the protection of King Ferdinand, then in Sicily. Lord Bentinck received its advances with equal favour. Afterwards, when the re-establishment of the former form of government rendered it no longer necessary to the plans of the monarchy, severe persecutions were commenced against it.

there were numerous malcontents, who desired no better than to prepare the overthrow of the existing order of things; and also because the profound mystery in which the smallest acts of the Order were enveloped exercised a great fascination over the imagination of the Italians, always impressionable to excess. . . .

The society had, however, reached a degree of numerical strength unknown to any of the societies by which it was succeeded. But the Carbonari did not know how to turn their strength to account. Although the doctrines of Carbonarism were widely diffused, its leaders had no confidence in the people; and appealed to them rather to attain an appearance of force likely to attract those men of rank and station in whom alone they put their trust, than from any idea of leading them to immediate action.

Hence the ardour and energy of the youth of the Order—of those who dreamed only of country, the republic, war, and glory in the eyes of Europe—was entrusted to the direction of men, not only old in years, but imbued with the ideas of the empire; cold precisionists, who had neither faith nor future, and who, instead of fostering, repressed all daring and enthusiasm.

At a later period, when the immense mass of Carbonari already affiliated, and the consequent impossibility of preserving secrecy, convinced the leaders of the necessity for action, they felt the want of some stronger bond of unity; and not having a *principle* upon which to found it, they set themselves to seek it in a *man*—a *prince*.

This was the ruin of Carbonarism. . . .

They [the Carbonari] had no sincere faith in the constitutional form of government; they sneered at monarchy among themselves, yet nevertheless they hailed and supported it; at first as a means of acquiring strength, afterwards because the adoption of the monarchical system freed them from the responsibility of guiding the masses whom they feared and misunderstood; and at last because they hoped by baptizing the insurrection with a royal name, to soften Austria, and win the favour of some great power—either England or France.

It was for this reason they cast their eyes on Charles Albert in Piedmont, and Prince Francesco at Naples; the first a man of a tyrannical nature, and though ambitious, incapable of greatness; the second a hypocrite and traitor from the very beginning of his career. They offered the management of the destinies of Italy to each of these princes, leaving it to the future to arrange the irreconcilable views of the two pretenders.

Events, however, clearly proved that true strength is derived not from the mass, but from the cohesion of the elements by which the aim is to be achieved; and revealed the inevitable consequences of the absence of principles in those who place themselves at the head of revolutions.

The insurrections of the Carbonari were successful—they had no very grave difficulties to overcome;—but they were immediately followed by serious internal discord. The work of mere destruction once fulfilled, each Carbonaro fell back upon his own individual aims and opinions, and all were at variance as to what they had to create. Some had imagined themselves to be conspiring in the interest of a single monarchy; many were partizans of the French constitution, many of the Spanish; some were for a republic; others for I know not how many republics; and all of these complained that they had been deceived. . . .

Such did Carbonarism appear to me—a huge and powerful body, but without a head; an association in which not generous intentions but ideas were wanting; deficient in the science and logic which should have reduced the sentiment of nationality, pervading its ranks, to fruitful action.

Mazzini's doubts about the efficacy of the Carbonari and especially his distrust of their reliance on aid from princes and foreign powers seemed wholly confirmed by the failure of the 1831 revolutions in central Italy. These revolutions were inspired in part by the overthrow of Charles X in France and his replacement by Louis Philippe, whose Prime Minister, Jacques Laffitte, proclaimed in December 1830 the principle of nonintervention as official French policy. The Italian revolutionaries interpreted this official statement as safeguarding them from foreign and particularly Austrian intervention. One leader of the revolutionaries, Ciro Menotti, trusted also in the friendship and support of Francis IV, Duke of Modena, who seemed to aspire to a royal crown in central Italy with the aid of the revolutionaries and the support of France. But fearing that the revolution might lead to a republic and disillusioned of French support, the Duke of Modena had Menotti and his fellow conspirators arrested on February 3, 1831. A wave of insurrections spread throughout Modena, Bologna, Parma, and Reggio Emilia, and approached Rome itself. At this juncture, Louis Philippe assured Rome of France's support in safeguarding the Pope's temporal authority in the Papal States. Under the pressure of a threat of war from Austria if France insisted on its stand that there be no direct intervention of foreign powers in Italian affairs, Louis Philippe abandoned the cause of the Italian revolutionaries and accepted Laffitte's resignation. Thereupon the Austrians proceeded to march into central Italy and crush the revolutions.

News of this latest blow to Italian aspirations reached Mazzini while in Corsica on his way to exile in France. His response to the last major effort by the Carbonari was almost immediate. He wrote in his memoirs: "I at last determined to obey my own instincts; and I founded the Association of Young Italy (*La Giovine Italia* [*La Giovane Italia*]), with the following statutes for its basis."

7. GENERAL INSTRUCTIONS FOR THE MEMBERS OF YOUNG ITALY (1831)

Joseph Mazzini, *Life and Writings*, I, 96–97, 100–13, *passim.*

LIBERTY — EQUALITY — HUMANITY —
INDEPENDENCE — UNITY.

SECTION 1

Young Italy is a brotherhood of Italians who believe in a law of *Progress* and *Duty*, and are convinced that Italy is destined to become one nation—convinced also that she possesses sufficient strength within herself to become one, and that the ill success of her former efforts is to be attributed not to the weakness, but to the misdirection of the revolutionary elements within her—that the secret of force lies in constancy and unity of effort. They join this association in the firm intent of consecrating both thought and action to the great aim of reconstituting Italy as one independent sovereign nation of free men and equals. . . .

Young Italy is *Republican* and *Unitarian:*

Republican—because theoretically every nation is destined, by the law of God and humanity, to form a free and equal community of brothers; and the republican is the only form of government that insures this future.

Because all true sovereignty resides essentially in the nation, the sole progressive and continuous interpreter of the supreme moral law. . . .

Because our Italian tradition is essentially republican; our great memories are republican; the whole history of our national progress is republican; whereas the introduction of monarchy amongst us was coëval with our decay, and consummated our ruin by its constant servility to the foreigner, and antagonism to the people, as well as to the unity of the nation. . . .

Because, before you can induce a whole people to rise, it is necessary to place before them an aim, appealing directly and in an intelligible manner to their own advantage, and their own rights. . . .

Young Italy is *Unitarian:*

Because, without unity, there is no true nation.

Because without unity, there is no real strength; and Italy, surrounded as she is by powerful, united, and jealous nations, has need of strength before all things.

Because federalism, by reducing her to the political impotence of Switzerland, would necessarily place her under the influence of one of the neighbouring nations.

Because federalism, by reviving the local rivalries now extinct, would throw Italy back upon the middle ages. . . .

These principles, which are the basis of the association, and their immediate consequences, set forth in the publications of the association, form the creed of Young Italy; and the society only admits as members those who accept and believe in this creed. . . .

Both initiators and initiated must never forget that the moral application of every principle is the first and the most essential; that without morality there is no true citizen; that the first step towards the achievement of a holy enterprise is the purification of the soul by virtue; that, where the daily life of the individual is not in harmony with the principles he preaches, the inculcation of those principles is an infamous profanation and hypocrisy; that it is only by virtue that the members of Young Italy can win over others to their belief; that if we do not show ourselves far superior to those who deny our principles, we are but miserable sectarians; and that Young Italy must be neither a sect nor a party, but a faith and an apostolate.

As the precursors of Italian regeneration, it is our duty to lay the first stone of its religion.

SECTION 4

The means by which Young Italy proposes to reach its aim are—education and insurrection, to be adopted simultaneously, and made to harmonize with each other.

Education must ever be directed to teach by example, word, and pen, the necessity of insurrection. Insurrection, whenever it can be realised, must be so conducted as to render it a means of national education.

Education, though of necessity secret in Italy, will be public out of Italy. . . .

Convinced that Italy is strong enough to free herself without external help . . . in order to found a nationality, it is necessary that the feeling and consciousness of nationality should exist. . . .

The one thing wanting to twenty millions of Italians, desirous of emancipating themselves, is not power, but *faith*.

Young Italy will endeavour to inspire this faith,—first by its teachings, and afterwards by an energetic initiative.

SECTION 6

The colours of Young Italy are *white, red,* and *green.* The banner of Young Italy will display these colours, and bear on the one side the words—*Liberty, Equality, Humanity;* and on the other—*Unity, Independence.*

SECTION 7

Each member will, upon his initiation into the association of Young Italy, pronounce the following form of oath, in the presence of the initiator:—

In the name of God and of Italy— . . .

I, *A. B.*:

Believing in the mission entrusted by God to Italy, and the duty of every Italian to strive to attempt its fulfilment—

Convinced that where God has ordained that a nation shall be, he has given the requisite power to create it; that the people are the depositaries of that power, and that in its right direction for the people, and by the people, lies the secret of victory—

Convinced that virtue consists in action and sacrifice, and strength in union and constancy of purpose—

I give my name to Young Italy, an association of men holding the same faith, and swear—

To dedicate myself wholly and for ever to the endeavour with them to constitute Italy *one free, independent, republican nation.* . . .

Now and for ever:

This do I swear, invoking upon my head the wrath of God, the abhorrence of man, and the infamy of the perjurer, if I ever betray the whole or a part of this my oath.

IV. THE "MODERATE" APPROACH TO
INDEPENDENCE AND UNITY

Mazzini's call to the youth of Italy and to all noble spirits was a preeminently religious appeal for sacrifice on behalf of the fatherland. In the words of one historian, "Mazzini's propaganda is magnificent—but it is merely war." [1] It was war, but it was also something more. In fighting against Italy's "materialistic" and "Machiavellian" past and present, it also helped create a vision of a purer future. But both Mazzini's "war" and his vision of the future could not but disturb and alienate all those Italians who, although sharing his ambition for independence and unity, would not accept his republican and democratic hostility toward all princes and existing regimes. His call for popular insurrections under the leadership of his organization, and his insistence on a unitary rather than a federal Italian state, had the effect of further reducing the effectiveness of his appeal. However disinterested and elevated Mazzini's message may be judged to be, it was destined to be heard and heeded by only a select few. Under his direct guidance or as a result of his inspiration, these few engaged in insurrections in Piedmont (1833, 1834), in the Two Sicilies (1837, 1841, 1844), and in the Papal States (1843, 1845). Mazzini himself was forced into a life of prolonged exile; ejected from France in 1834 and from Switzerland in 1837, he found final and generous refuge in England, which became his second home and the scene of continuing literary and propagandistic activity on behalf of his ambitions for Italy. As an exile and outlaw with a death sentence awaiting him in Piedmont, he could not lead those self-styled moderates who preferred reform to revolution, sought the collaboration rather than the hostility of princes and foreign powers, and trusted more in material progress as an effective unifying force than in the gospel of moral rejuvenation and insurrectional activity.

The American historian Kent Roberts Greenfield was among the first to examine in detail the effort made by moderate liberal Italians, especially in Lombardy, to help create those progressive economic and social institutions which in their opinion had eventually to issue in political reforms and national unification. "A conspiracy in open daylight" is the phrase Greenfield

[1] G. F.-H. Berkeley, *Italy in the Making, 1815–1846* (Cambridge, England, At the University Press, 1932), p. 139.

has borrowed from Massimo d'Azeglio, a leader of the moderate cause, to characterize the political possibilities implicit in the movement of reforms championed by Lombard economic Liberals in a number of journals from 1815 to 1848. According to Greenfield, the Liberal Lombard journals [2] had a double effect: the engendering and adoption of practical measures for the material and social rehabilitation of Italy, and the dissemination of the usually implicit but clearly understood preaching that this rehabilitation could best be promoted by economic and political unity. The following selection is devoted to an examination of the fundamental assumptions underlying the work of the Lombard journals.

8. "A CONSPIRACY IN OPEN DAYLIGHT": ECONOMICS, LIBERALISM, AND NATIONALISM

Kent Roberts Greenfield, *Economics and Liberalism in the Risorgimento: A Study of Nationalism in Lombardy, 1814–1848*. Baltimore: The Johns Hopkins Press, 1934, pp. 266–68, 276–79, 296–97, *passim*. Original footnotes omitted.

Was there, behind all these enterprises in journalism, a statesmanlike purpose, a far-seeing patriotism? The difficulty of detecting the "philosophy" of this literature, the failure of the writers to identify themselves with a school of thought or a recognized body of doctrine, perhaps explains in part why their activity and the history of what it accomplished has received so little attention from historians of the Risorgimento. Did they see whither their efforts were tending? Was there, within the realm of the practical, a goal for the Italian nation towards which they were driving? If there was a "conspiracy in open daylight," when did it begin to be seen as such by the conspirators themselves?

It is evident at once that the Lombard journalists whose work has been reviewed were all animated by a conviction of progress, of a forward movement of European civilization, and that they therefore proceeded from a principle diametrically opposed to the maxim of "govern and change nothing" on which the policy of Austria was based. Civilization in Europe had received a new impulse; it was advancing and changing at an ever-accelerated rate: this is the great fact which the journals proclaimed on every page; and their writers insisted, with

[2] Principally the *Conciliatore* (1818–19), the *Annali universali di statistica* (1824–48), the *Politecnico* (1839–45), and the *Rivista europea* (1838–48).

increasing urgency, that the Italians could not afford to remain spectators of this movement. It was something inevitable; they could not
shut it out. They must adjust themselves to it without delay or suffer a
fatal loss.

But "progress" is a vague term; and it becomes necessary to sound
the writers of the time and determine, if possible, what it meant to
them, and what in their view adjustment to it implied for Italy.

In proclaiming the progress of "the century," the Lombard publicists believed that they were not influenced by a doctrine but announcing an inexorable fact. Giuseppe Pecchio, one of the collaborators of the *Conciliatore* expressed the idea when he wrote: "I laugh at
the despotism which wishes to repel liberty while this, in its despite,
comes in from every side by means of civilization. . . . If it fetters
the liberty of the press, truth enters through the universities. If it per-
secutes or imprisons a university professor, civilization comes in with
foreign commerce. If it adopts the prohibitive system to diminish this
inconvenience, the roads, the roads alone, suffice to put minds in contact in a ferment." . . .

The Liberal journalists proposed to introduce modern progress into
Italy by means of specific reforms. . . . But they were aware that the
new social order required something more fundamental than an
equipment of up-to-date institutions and implements; it required certain attitudes, a moral and intellectual re-education of the individual,
which was essential to its functioning and also essential to the resur-
rection of Italy.

What were the elements of the moral code on which this re-
education was to be based? Naturally the first was freedom. The journalists recognized freedom—freedom of contract; freedom of trade,
even of trade in landed property; freedom of the individual—to be
the basis of the new social order which they were ushering into Italy.
Hence their emphasis on enterprise, self-reliance, and thrift. They
manifested no enthusiasm for freedom in the abstract. That had been
the passion that obsessed a more naïve generation, who had sought
Liberty as an end in itself. Applied to politics, liberty had produced
the excesses and reactions of the French Revolution. Now they saw it
when applied to economic life producing the evils of unbridled indus-
trialism and inordinate commercial greed—the "spirito bancario," the
"speculative spirit," which they abhorred. The evils of *laissez-faire*

they proposed to temper by common-sense opportunism and by the inculcation of a sense of philanthropy. . . .

It was less to the idea of freedom than to the exercise of it that the journalists sought to educate their countrymen. Naturally individualists, without experience in either economic or political coöperation, the Italians must be taught not only to act but to unite. To this end the journalists never wearied of extolling "the spirit of association" as the essence of successful endeavor in modern life. The associations that underlay the sluggish functioning of Italian society had been either forced or conventional. In an era of freedom, Italians must learn the art of voluntary association. Only out of this spirit could the institutions of a new order arise. . . .

The practical nature of the means by which the development of the habit of association was sought is a key to the spirit of the moderate Italian patriots as opposed to the Mazzinian radicals. The ideal of association was in the air of Western Europe at the beginning of the century; but Mazzini's ecstatic teachings presented an apotheosis of Association, as a stern and beautiful emanation of the *Zeitgeist*, approaching the individual with a moral imperative, while the Moderates, without ceasing to hail it as inherent in the spirit of the age, envisaged it as a practical necessity. With joy they saw material interests and the interests of a rejuvenated Italy marching hand in hand, as if to the tune of some fundamental law of nature. . . .

The thought of the Lombard journalists may be summarized [thusly]. Progress is continuous and inevitable. It develops out of the needs of civilized living; it is the essence of civilization itself. In their time, a time of swift movement, the dominant needs of civilization were expressed in terms of economics and science. The Italians, caught in the onrushing stream, must be awakened to their true interests and re-educated to meet them—disciplined in the spirit of association, in the knowledge of science, in the exercise of social charity. In the acceptance of progress lay the hope of redemption for Italy.

This much they said. The rest they could not say. It was that if the Italian nation collected its forces to advance on the road of progress it was bound to become united and free. This idea was implicit in their philosophy, and it may well be suspected that it was the idea that made their words glow and gave the patriotic publicists steadfastness in their endeavor. It was too soon to speak of political institutions. These must be built up bit by bit as opportunity permitted. First, a national journalism; then steamships, railroads, factories, schools, and charities; then national scientific congresses and plans on a national scale for agriculture, technology, prison reform, poor relief; then a national railway net and a customs-league:—with these they had brought into view the necessity for the first step in political union backed by all the force of "the century." The political institutions they desired would inevitably arrive, as they had in France and England; they would come when a genuine community of interests had brought the nation to see in union and freedom not merely a dream but a necessity.

Greenfield alludes to the vigilance of Austrian censorship as a reason why the Lombard journals had to be circumspect in elaborating on the political implications of their campaign for economic and social reforms. Three explicitly political works appeared in the 1840s which avoided foreign and domestic censors by being printed either abroad in freer countries or clandestinely in Italy. These works, by the Piedmontese Vincenzo Gioberti, Cesare Balbo, and Massimo d'Azeglio, are fitting companions to the hundreds of articles appearing in the Lombard journals. It is true that most of the journalism examined by Greenfield was animated by secularist conceptions of social progress, derived largely from Enlightenment principles; whereas the ideas of the three Piedmontese writers noted above are not always in perfect harmony with these principles. But the books by the Piedmontese school and the Lombard journals together sum up the cause of the moderate approach to freedom, independence, and unity; and collectively they can be said to have succeeded in disseminating this cause to the point of aiding its triumph over both monarchical reaction and Mazzinian republicanism. It is understandable that Mazzini, among others, should have characterized Gioberti, Balbo, and d'Azeglio as being the unwitting corrupters of the younger generation of their day.

The moderation of the political *moderati* lay in their espousal of monarchical government limited by a fundamental statute or constitution; in their willingness to accept a federated rather than a unitary or centralized Italian state; and in their conviction that if the Italian states, severally or collectively, were ever to achieve independence from Austria—this aim they shared with Mazzini—its achievement could come to pass only or principally by diplomacy and the military might of princes rather than through popular insurrections. The political moderates thought of themselves as practical men, aiming at the possible and eschewing the impossible, however desirable the latter might be. But even the possible requires an effort in order that it become actual, and people do not attempt the possible unless they are persuaded that it is within their reach. To this end of persuasion, Gioberti, Balbo, and d'Azeglio wrote their works; subsequent events in Italy were to test the worth of their efforts.

Vincenzo Gioberti was born in modest circumstances in Turin in 1801. He was ordained a priest in 1825 and distinguished himself in theology at the University of Turin; as a young man he may have joined a secret society favoring Italian independence and unity but he never joined Mazzini's Young Italy, whose methods he repudiated after approving of them at an earlier time. In 1831 he became a chaplain at the Piedmontese court; two years later he was arrested for his agitation in favor of freedom for the Poles, but was released in the same year. After a brief exile in Paris, he moved to Brussels, where he lived in political obscurity until 1843, when the publication of his *Del primato morale e civile degli Italiani* [On the Moral and Civil Primacy of the Italians] gave him a political reputation which surpassed his already high prestige as a philosopher and theologian. Upon the establishment of constitutional government in Piedmont in 1848, Gioberti joined the Cabinet and eventually became Prime Minister, from December 1848 to February 1849. In the latter year he was sent to Paris on a special mission; because of disagreements with his government's policies he resigned but remained in Paris and died there in 1852.

Gioberti's *Primato* asserts the moral and civil primacy of the Italians, and explains this primacy largely as a function of the primacy of Rome, first imperial and later papal. Accordingly, this Italian primacy has as its political corollary the independence of Italy from foreign rule. In 1843 Gioberti saw federalism as the most practical avenue to and guaranty of this independence. Finally, the Pope, as Bishop of Rome, spiritual head of Roman Catholicism, and temporal ruler of a large Italian state, was seen by Gioberti to possess a special primacy within Italy which entitled him to be the head of the proposed Italian federation.

In terms of historical significance, the substance of Gioberti's argument in favor of Italy's privileged position is not so important as the reasons for presenting this argument in 1843. Gioberti's reasons for writing his work reveal more of Italy's state in the 1840s than does the truth or error of the asserted Italian primacy. His preferences for federalism and papal leadership were historically dead issues after 1848, when it became clear that the head of Roman Catholicism could not lead a war of liberation against Catholic Austria. In consequence, we have chosen from the *Primato* a selection in which Gioberti justifies the reasons for disseminating his ideas.

9. VINCENZO GIOBERTI ON THE MORAL AND CIVIL PRIMACY OF THE ITALIANS

Vincenzo Gioberti, *Del primato morale e civile degli Italiani*. Brussels, 1843 "Proemio" [Introduction], condensed. Our translation.

Man cannot avail himself of his forces and exercise appropriately his powers unless he is first aware of possessing them. Similarly, a nation cannot occupy in the world that rank which suits it unless it feels itself worthy of occupying it. In consequence, excessive modesty, although at times praiseworthy in private individuals, is always blameworthy in the public because it, so to speak, cuts the nerves necessary for virtue and magnanimous actions. A dignified and measured humility in individuals and a discreet and moderate pride in states would be veritable perfection in human affairs, if our nature were able to adjust itself to that middle path in which the greatest excellence is found. But, inasmuch as men almost always go too far in some degree, it is frequently opportune to push them in the direction opposite from the extreme to which they have gone, in order that the force of impulsion, coupled with the force of inertia may produce, almost as a mixed effect, the optimum desired temperament. By virtue of this consideration, when a people has reached the lowest depths of misery and civil degradation, when its spirit is depressed and its energies prostrate, it is not only excusable but also merciful counsel to attempt to reinvigorate it by using such language which under all other circumstances would be dangerous. . . . Therefore, if in order to raise the notion which this people has of itself and to infuse in its breast that courage necessary for virtuous and magnanimous action, one seeks to arouse in it the dormant spark of self-respect, this effort will not be censurable as unreasonable and unchristian, as it would truly be if such language were used in speaking to those who sin by boldness and arrogance. It is proper that in any case the reasons employed and the things said be true, both because the profession of truth must always come before other considerations, and because it is not lawful to adulate even those in misery; [besides] adulation never bestows valor on anyone. Consequently, whoever were to commend a degraded people for merits it does not and cannot have and were to attribute to it rights and privileges it does not possess would deserve to be censured. . . . But when a nation has received from God certain irrefutable prerogatives which it has forgotten, it is not only lawful but necessary to remind it of them in the most effective language, without fear that this comfort will induce it to go beyond the proper limits and think too much of itself. . . . In devoting my thoughts to this matter I thought it not inappropriate, in a work written earlier, to plead with my meager eloquence the privileges of the fatherland God has given me. . . . Nor did I have the slightest fear of rendering my compatriots excessively proud; for, inasmuch as Italy for the last several centuries has bent its knee before foreigners and has not thought itself fortunate unless following in their footsteps; and inasmuch as these [foreigners] although implored again and again on bended knee that they return whence they came beyond the Alps, have not deigned to give their assent . . . I did not fear that by calling Italy's attention to its hereditary decorum it would increase excessively its claimed rights and belongings. Verily, I frequently regretted that my pen was much inferior to the argument and that to many it might appear bold of the likes of me to dare to continue, with words, the enterprise begun with actions by the most sublime Pontiffs Gregory, Alexander, Innocent, and Julius, and continued by the marvelous intellects of Dante, Machiavelli, Pico, and Alfieri, whose great minds raised them above the humbleness of the private estate and gave them the right to be heard as town criers and as almost spontaneous monarchs of the nation. The teaching of these latter men, as it is relevant to my purpose, when reduced to a strict formula free of accessories which veil or mar the teaching, is precisely that which I discussed in the earlier work when I awarded to Italy a moral and civil primacy over all the peoples of the universe. But, inasmuch as I touched upon this point without developing it . . . it seemed to some of my countrymen that I had attributed to our common fatherland a boast which although desirable was more than could be hoped for; moreover, it seemed not in conformity with current ideas regarding the equality of peoples and contrary to the fact—manifest to many—of French predominance. Others, who did not expressly repudiate my notion, complained that I had not defined it with sufficient precision and with consideration of the fact that the primacy of a people (even when excluding, as I did explicitly, the matter of political predominance) can be understood in many ways, and that to speak of it in most general terms, as I have, is almost like saying nothing. Finally, still others, although admitting the right [of Italy's primacy] observed that present reality was against it and, therefore, judged my work as useless, in fact harmful. They reasoned that it is not very merciful to remind a fallen people of their lost dignity and to revive in them the grief of their having lost it and the desire to recover it, especially at a time when the satisfaction of this desire is prohibited by fortune. These latter think that I would have been wiser to consider whether or not it is possible in our day to restore Italy's ancient lordship; that if the suitable means for achieving this end were known, and were neither blameworthy nor fanciful, propose them; otherwise, be silent. Although these observations have been made known to me only by letter or in person, I believe it my duty to reply to them in print publicly, and this because of the kindness and love of Italy of those who made them as well as for the importance of the subject matter and the temper of our times which, in some respects, seem to me to be less adverse than the past to the beginning of the great enterprise of the Italian *risorgimento*. I shall show that if this [*risorgimento*] does not take place, the fault will be solely of the Italians; and that they have no reason to attribute their ills to Providence, because they have in their hands the remedy for the greater part if not for all of their ills, and that they can avail themselves of this remedy without a shadow of rashness or guilt. Reader, whoever you are, provided that you are an Italian, give me your benevolent attention. Do not fear that my argument will offend anyone by appearing harsh and injurious to governments or to any order of citizens whatsoever, by fomenting those seeds of hatred, of tumults and discords which unfortunately nestle among some of our fellow countrymen. . . .

The heavenly Father granted to each branch of the human family some special gift in order that it may not blush with shame in the councils of its brother peoples. This is true above all of Europe, to whose natural advantages are added the achievements of civilization; this Europe, which once consisted of a commonwealth of nations and potentates under a single head—and is destined to be such once again—is within its small confines a compendium of the world, and includes as much a variety of gifts, attitudes, offices, and fortunes as there are members constituting its Christian and political brotherhood. . . .

Therefore, if I plead for the prerogative of influence and honor which I contend belongs by firm right to my country, and even speak with some heat against those who would deny or usurp it, I do not believe that for this reason I am in the least lacking in my duty toward other nations. . . . For, if among the several sons of the same father one alone has the title and the honors of the first-born—title and honors which amount to a civil superiority in the kingdom and in the family, without prejudice or dishonor to the younger sons—then why cannot a similar privilege be admitted as rational and just in the society of nations? All the more so in the light of the fact that Italy's primacy is not absolute; it is restricted to the order of ideal things and leaves to other peoples a very large field in the ample circle of civil facts and rights. In this field each one of them can find a way to honorable primacy; in fact, as we shall see later, several of them do enjoy such primacy. . . . I add that I do not despair at all of receiving the approval of foreigners as well: I mean those who are wise and who judge with reason and not with their emotions. Because the primacy which I attribute to my country is not a vain haughtiness designed to stimulate the self-esteem of those possessing this primacy; it is rather an arduous and burdensome ministry conducive of the welfare of all. . . .

In order to proceed with my argument in an orderly manner, I shall begin with a definition of what I mean by the moral and civil primacy of Italy; then I shall proceed to a proof of its legitimacy, reviewing the various aspects of its civilizing activity in the double order of thought and action. In touching upon these main points it will be my aim to show that Italy alone possesses the qualities necessary to be the leader-nation, and that although in our own day it may have almost completely lost this leadership, it is within its power to revive it. I shall also refer to the most important conditions for this *risorgimento.*

Gioberti's work carefully avoided raising explicitly the problem of Italy's independence from Austrian domination, seeking by his silence on this problem to facilitate a freer circulation of his work in Italy than would have been the case had he assumed an openly anti-Austrian position. A year after Gioberti's *Primato* there appeared in Paris Cesare Balbo's *Delle speranze d'Italia* [The Hopes of Italy], a work dedicated to Gioberti and acknowledging his inspiration. Count Cesare Balbo was the son of Prospero Balbo, who had served Victor Emmanuel I of Piedmont as Minister of Education and of the Interior, from 1819 to 1821, and who had introduced some reforms in spite of stubborn resistance from most of the restored nobility. Cesare was born in Turin in 1789 and died there in 1853. As a young man he was much influenced by Alfieri, but this influence did not prevent him from serving in the administration of the Napoleonic Kingdom of Italy. After the Restoration Balbo entered the Piedmontese army and for a time was on friendly terms with Charles Albert, heir presumptive to the throne. The Piedmontese revolution of 1821 proved adverse to both prince and count; the former was obliged to go into foreign exile and Balbo, although opposed to the revolution, was sentenced to ten years of domestic exile in a remote Piedmontese community because of his friendly relations with the conspirators. During this period of enforced political inactivity Balbo devoted himself to historical writings, culminating in the *Speranze d'Italia* in 1844, written with the tacit approval of Charles Albert, King of Piedmont since 1831. In 1847 Balbo founded the newspaper *Il Risorgimento* in collaboration with Count Camillo Benso di Cavour; and the next year he was called by Charles Albert to assume the post of Prime Minister in the newly established constitutional government of the Piedmontese state. His government presided over the declaration of war against Austria late in March 1848, after the anti-Austrian risings in Lombardy and Venetia, but was obliged to resign in July 1848 over differences with Parliament on the question of how Lombardy was to be united with Piedmont. Balbo remained active in Piedmontese politics until his death in 1853.

In the *Speranze d'Italia* Balbo adopted Gioberti's federal solution to the question of Italy's unification; but whereas Gioberti was an emphatic Neo-Guelph [3] in the *Primato*, entrusting the leadership of the proposed Italian federation to the Pope, Balbo's Neo-Guelphism must be said to be largely nominal, willing to grant the Pope the honorary position of primacy among Italian princes but reserving for Piedmont effective leadership of the federation. Moreover, Balbo was explicitly in favor of ending Austrian influence in Italy, placing his hopes in some "great opportunity," which he saw principally in the eventual dissolution of the Ottoman empire. Balbo expected that this dissolution would make possible the compensation to Austria of some of Turkey's Christian provinces in exchange for Lombardy and Venetia, which he hoped would be united with Piedmont in a large kingdom of Upper Italy. He was opposed to attacks on the Pope and the Papal States, thus disagreeing with Mazzinians and other "immoderates," out of fear that these attacks would have a divisive effect on Catholic Italy and would be too dangerous for the probable reaction of the Catholic states of Europe. The moderation of Balbo's approach to unity and independence and his assertion that adequate moral and material preparation was necessary in order successfully to seize the great opportunity when it came, are the themes emphasized in the following selection from Balbo's work.

10. "THE HOPES OF ITALY"

Cesare Balbo, *Delle speranze d'Italia*, Paris, 1844. Second dedication to Vincenzo Gioberti, condensed. Our translation.

Sir and Friend, when you did me the favor of accepting my first dedication you expressed the generous fear that your name "might perhaps

[3] In Medieval Italy the Guelphs were a political party or grouping generally on the Popes' side in their struggle with the German emperors. Neo-Guelphism is a nineteenth-century attempt at reviving papal leadership in Italian affairs. Ed. note.

prejudice the work in the eyes of some people." But I predicted a graver and more certain prejudice, stemming from the fact that I had aimed at political moderation not different from yours. It is natural and unavoidable: one cannot walk straight in the center of a crowded road without striking, here and there, right and left, against blacks and whites.* Moreover, this is the beauty and the strength of true political moderation—that while the extreme sides have in mind but one opponent to fight and dislodge, we have two. Therefore (if you will allow me to put my name after yours in these matters), we have only reaped that which we sowed; we have only the war which we began. If we had not foreseen it we would have shown little understanding of human affairs; if we were now to marvel at it we would be guilty of inconstant judgment; if we were to halt or, worse still, to retreat, we would be of little heart.

In all countries where there are opposing sides (and they are to be found in our day everywhere, either in the open or hidden, manifest or latent) there are many who love the fatherland less than they do a fraction of it, less than their side or even their class; there are many who love their own side less than they hate their opponents; there are many who would change nothing and many who would change everything, and many who would have not only conservation or change but revolutions either backward or forward; and all of this less for the benefit of the fatherland than for their own gain of goods, of glory, or of vengeance. . . . However, in those countries where the sides or parties are in the open, where one may openly fight for or against them, without doubt the danger is least, and from this fact is derived the strength of the moderates. There the moderates can reveal the sincerity and virtue of their moderation by their words, their writings, and by their daily and public actions; they can distinguish themselves from all those weak, doubting, or doubtful men who are the impostors of the moderate side and the perversion of the virtue of moderation. . . . There [the true moderates] are recompensed for present injustices by the certain and not distant justice of posterity.

But it is not so in countries where the hidden sides exaggerate in that secretiveness which becomes natural and necessary to them.

---

* The analogy refers to political factions in late medieval Florence. The "blacks" represented the commercial and banking oligarchy; the "whites" on the whole represented the *popolo minuto* (the little people). Ed. note.

Under such a veil and shield there arise here and there those so-called defensive and offensive leagues which in fact are principally exclusive and which then turn hotly against anyone who does not join them and disdains them, against anyone who speaks clearly and openly. [In such places] there occur those "purges" which are always senseless even when conducted by the victorious side, more senseless when conducted while the struggle continues, and most senseless when there is not even an open conflict. . . .

Things are even worse in countries (such as Italy) where, repression and secretiveness being long-standing conditions, the extreme sides have both repeatedly failed in the enterprises they pretended to conduct on behalf of the fatherland. In that case, when their respective impotence is proved and demonstrated, they attribute it to the fatherland; then many of these to whom the fatherland has paid no heed arise to prevent it from giving heed to anyone else, and from either side many turn not only against whoever acts or speaks differently from them (a usual occurrence everywhere) but also against whoever does or says anything in any fashion (an exceptional occurrence manifested in these most unhappy countries); then there arises and grows not only the indifferent generation (another usual occurrence) but also the despairing generation (an exceptional occurrence and the worst of all). . . . In countries where repressed, hidden, and defeated sides are the rule, the men of despair multiply on both sides and even in the middle; and then they divide and subdivide in numerous genera and species. . . . All these hopeless ones then form a mass, a plurality, a generation fatal to the whole nation, which they encourage towards discouragement; it is especially fatal to whoever acts, writes, or speaks with the intent to encourage; and it is even more fatal to whoever encourages to moderate action, that is, immediate, continuous, and universal action. In such a country it is more beautiful than in any other to set oneself up strongly against the hopeless of the right and the left and even of the center.

And this, Sir and Friend, you have undoubtedly done in your book on the *Primato*. I hope to do the same, at times following in your steps and at other times daring to depart from you. And, therefore, it is not the dedication but the very title which may hurt my book; it is the word "hopes" which I have raised against all the hopeless in Italy. I confess that I raised this word with complete imprudence;

neither when I began nor as I continued [the work] did I think of the hopeless ones. When I began I addressed myself against those who find everything in Italy for the best and did not think of those who find everything for the worst. As I continued I addressed myself against those who have too much hope and did not think of those who have none. In this progressive era, in this time of universal industry I did not think there was anyone who despaired completely of a nation of more than twenty million people. How foolish I was! Now I perceive that these [hopeless ones] are many in number: there are some of high and highest station and some of low and lowest estate; some who are on the inside of power, and some on the outside; some who are whites and others who are blacks; in short, there are many. For these I should have entitled and written a book on the Fears and not on the Hopes of Italy; and by flattering in some the fear of the black menace, and in the others the fear of the white menace, I would have served all fears; I would have perhaps served those persecutions and those instruments of vengeance which are the sole and impotent industry of both despairing sides; at least I would have contributed to the universal sloth which is the usual offspring of reciprocal fears. It is a pity that I did not think of all of these and all of this in time!

But now there is no longer any remedy; the book is written and exists. It is a manifesto of moderate hopes, with its three chapters directed against those who would change everything and its ten chapters directed against those who would change nothing. . . .

It is my opinion that fifty and more years ago * Italy was progressing and changing too slowly, but in short it was progressing moderately. It is a fact to which I have referred several times, and it is in any case incontestable by anyone who has either a recollection of the preceding century or has read about it. Then, from outside Italy there came the two extreme parties, those who would change everything and those who would change nothing. Only the moderate party is native to Italy; and this is natural because Italy is an ancient land; among modern nations it is the first offspring of that civilization which above everything else is moderating in character. But, impelled from the outside, for many years (I shall not debate whether or not it is thirty or forty years) the two extremes alternated in predomination.

* Before the French Revolution of 1789. Ed. note.

However, it is undeniable that for the last ten or fifteen or more years there has been a resumption of slow changes (too slow and also too few in my opinion), but in any case real and moderate. Also undeniable is the increase of the side of moderation at the expense of the two extremes. . . . Even here, even in unhappy and subject Italy the generation of extremists is giving way; and after an extremist young Italy * there is rising a still younger moderate Italy.

And, therefore, in spite of current disadvantages and griefs, even here there can and must arise among the moderates a hope of a more or less distant and ultimate justice. Will they be heard? Will they succeed in deterring the fatherland from those two evil ways both of which lead to revolutions and therefore inevitably to crime, shame, and harm? In such a [happy] eventuality the moderates who live long enough may perhaps find themselves justified by grateful contemporaries as indicators of the right way. . . . But sooner or later, happily or unhappily, the justification of the moderates is certain even in Italy—that is, it will not fail those who will have assured themselves the attention of posterity. . . . And you, Sir and Friend, have already assured yourself this attention with your philosophical and political works and, if you will allow me to choose from your writings, principally with that *Theory of the Supernatural* whose necessary place in philosophy you have proved and with that book on Italy's future which opened a new career of political moderation to Italian writers. You are among the greatest and most generous [figures] of that Italian literature abroad which seems to me to be one of the nearest and most fruitful of Italy's hopes, and you yourself therefore are one of these hopes.

The third leading figure of the group of moderate Italian nationalists loosely characterized as "Neo-Guelphs" is Massimo d'Azeglio, born in 1798 in Turin the son of the Marquis Cesare Tapparelli d'Azeglio. After a brief military career he turned to painting and the writing of romantic historical novels. His interest in politics was promoted by frequent discussions with his first cousin Cesare Balbo, to whom he dedicated his tract *Degli ultimi casi di Romagna* [On Recent Events in Romagna], published clandestinely in Florence in 1846. The storm aroused by the appearance of this work obliged d'Azeglio to leave Tuscany, then the most tolerant of the major Italian states. In 1848 he joined in the war of liberation against Austria as an aide to the commander of the papal contingents participating in the war with

* A clear reference to Mazzini's Young Italy. Ed. note.

uncertain papal approval. After the calamitous end of this war (which is examined in the following chapter) and the abdication of Charles Albert of Piedmont, his son Victor Emmanuel II chose d'Azeglio as his prime minister in 1849 to follow a course somewhere between the extremes of Mazzinianism and reaction. D'Azeglio held his post until 1852 when he broke with Cavour and was then replaced by him. D'Azeglio remained politically active for the next decade, and died in 1866.

An examination of d'Azeglio's "On Recent Events in Romagna" makes it difficult to see how he can properly be included among the Neo-Guelphs. It is true that d'Azeglio shared Gioberti's and Balbo's strong hostility to popular insurrections and conspiratorial groups, preferring the "open conspiracy" of propaganda and peaceful agitation; all three men were attached to the federal idea, in varying degrees; and they all sought independence from Austria, although Gioberti had to be circumspect in expressing this preference in 1843. Moreover, it was possible to agree with Balbo's "Hopes of Italy" and still retain faith in a Neo-Guelph solution to Italy's national problems, in spite of Balbo's personal preference for actual Piedmontese leadership. But whoever agreed with d'Azeglio's severe indictment of the government of the Papal States in the "Recent Events in Romagna" could not easily be a Neo-Guelph; for although d'Azeglio did not favor the total destruction of the Pope's temporal authority, he did want it reduced, and he was prepared to acknowledge only a spiritual and moral primacy to the Pope. On the other hand, this attitude toward the Papacy did not put d'Azeglio in the camp of the "democrats" or the radicals, most of whom were pronouncedly anticlerical. Finally, whoever shared his strictures on the 1845 insurrection in Rimini (in Romagna) as "untimely and harmful" could not follow the banner of popular revolution. In short, those Italians who were persuaded by d'Azeglio's arguments against papal government and insurrectional activity had only one practical alternative remaining to them—follow the Piedmontese banner, provided the prince on the throne of the house of Savoy would heed d'Azeglio's warning that in the past princes and dynasties had fallen not because of "rebels, sectarians, and philosophers" but because they had lost that universal consensus which is the only lasting basis of authority.

11. MASSIMO D'AZEGLIO ON INSURRECTION AND PAPAL GOVERNMENT

Massimo d'Azeglio, *Degli ultimi casi di Romagna*, Florence, 1846, *passim*. Our translation.

Very few people and perhaps only those who were on the spot know the truth of the risings in Rimini of last September [1845]. It cannot be otherwise in an Italy where private correspondence does not dare and public journals do not wish to tell the truth. According to the news reported in the latter, copied by foreign newspapers and thus disseminated throughout Europe, a few hundred desperate men led by an individual sentenced to ten years in the galleys had disturbed the public peace and overthrown the papal authority in Rimini. Subsequently they dispersed into small bands throughout the Apennines and, fleeing before the bayonets of the Swiss [papal troops], they broke up completely within a few days. In leaving the city [Rimini] they committed disorders and thefts and thus earned the accusation of being disturbers of the peace, thieves, and scoundrels.

I judge the Rimini insurrection to have been untimely and harmful; I shall always judge as untimely and harmful such partial risings; and I shall add openly that for these reasons I consider them censurable, because a tiny minority does not have the right to judge whether or not it is advisable to drive its country into the great struggle for independence. [This minority] does not have the right to gamble on one throw of the dice the peace, liberty, and lives of an incalculable number of its fellow citizens and, what is more important, the honor and future of the whole nation. . . . But, if I believed—and I do believe—that its authors did not ponder over the impossible, untimely, and therefore unjust nature of their enterprise, this does not mean that they are to be considered thieves and scoundrels, as Italian and foreign newspapers have done. . . .

However small their importance, the events in Romagna are nevertheless an episode in the question of Italian independence. It is a question which the more fervently it is examined in secret hearts and conversations the more severely it is prevented from disclosure in free discussions and free demonstrations. It is a question which grows every day, and it has become kindled even in that part of the Italian people which, badly known, seems inert and unaware of itself. It is a question which must necessarily agitate every nation which has been robbed of its independence, of the heavenly inheritance left to it by the father common to all men. Finally, it is a question which can be compared to a great explosive mine dug beneath the whole of the peninsula; a mine which no one has the right to set afire without the consent of the many and much less for reasons of personal desires and sufferings. It is a general, necessary, and just question, one which all of us have, justly and virtuously, the right to treat. . . .

The aim of the Italians in all their risings from 1820 on—excepting the events of 1821 °—has been the elimination of local abuses and sufferings; it has been an isolated aim little mindful of neighboring and equally Italian peoples. If in several of these insurrections there was revealed the desire for a better reordering of the entire nation and for the driving of our common forces toward a common end, this desire always took second place, so to speak; and, as soon as it seemed that this desire could endanger the more pressing enterprise of local gain, it was completely silenced.

And thus, because of their egoism and the wretchedness of their purposes, the Italians have had what they deserved.

The aim of the recent rising, as of preceding risings, was wholly partial and, so to speak, provincial. We can see what success it had. Things ended as they necessarily had to; indeed, as they deserved to end.

The counsel that Italians should put the cause of the nation in first rank and that of its various parts in the second rank is not simply a counsel to entertain purposes more generous than has been the case in the past; it means to point to a consideration of pure interest; it means to indicate the only way which can sooner or later lead us first to the attainment of the good of all and then, as a necessary consequence, to the attainment of individual good. . . .

In fact, we in Italy may be of differing opinions on the best way of reforming the individual states and on the form of regime. This diversity issues naturally from the unequal degrees of suffering endured; but ask any Italian, from Trapani [Sicily] to Susa [Piedmont], whether or not it is useful for Italy to free itself from foreign domination and influence, and no one, thank God, will reply other than in the affirmative, no one will refuse to give his mind or his hand to this end. Even our princes would be denying their conscience and the honor of their dignity if they replied otherwise; among foreign nations, the independent ones would deny their principles and the subject ones their hopes and most cherished desires if they replied otherwise. . . .

If we consider carefully the present situation in Italy and all of Europe we can readily see whether or not it was possible for an armed rising to succeed.

° D'Azeglio appears to be referring to the fact that the 1821 Piedmontese insurrection aimed at Italian independence from Austria as well as at Piedmontese constitutional reforms. Ed. note.

At a time when peace and war are determined not by generous ideas or notions of national honor or ideas of justice but by calculations for the best employment of capital, while King Louis Philippe reveals himself as the preserver at all costs of that peace which he considers useful to France, is it possible to believe that for the sake of tenderness toward Italy he would abandon his system and put in jeopardy his most vital concerns by preventing Austria from hurling toward Italy two hundred thousand soldiers and two hundred cannons? And the agitators of Rimini, of the whole [Papal] State, of all of Italy, what have they to pit against these? Even against twenty pieces of artillery, not to say more, only cannon balls avail, not talk. . . .

Who, then, will prevent Austria from snuffing out in Italy the first spark of a fire which threatens nothing less than [Austria's] very existence?

If, in turn, the authors of the Rimini insurrection were to say, as they have said on similar occasions: *If we had not been alone and if all the other Italians had risen in mass?*

I reply: Whoever would practice affairs of state should have the most necessary of qualifications, and that is a sense of the practical, a vision of the world and of men as they really are and not as they perhaps should be; nor should such a person excuse his error after the failure of his enterprise by saying: *If the others had done . . . and should have done this or that.* In such a case those so accused could reply: *You did not ask us whether or not we wished to cooperate in the enterprise or thought it timely; and, not having given promise of our cooperation, you have no right to reproach us.*

But even if they had been consulted, the mass of Italians would have refused to rise in arms, because there exists among the masses, especially the Italian, that sense of the practical which at times is not found in individuals. . . . And if the Italian populace does not study politics, if it does read the newspapers, if it knows nothing of European interests and balance of power, still it does know that even if it were to succeed in freeing itself from the yoke of its local government, it would have accomplished nothing; disorganized and unarmed it would have to fight against a disciplined and armed Austria. . . .

I believe that with the foregoing reasons I have proved that the Rimini insurrection was untimely and useless, which is the same as proving that it was harmful besides. . . . [But] if fury and the inability to bear with their grievances impelled [the Rimini rebels] to engage in acts which must be judged as untimely and therefore as harmful and censurable, are we to pronounce upon them an absolute condemnation without mitigation?

At this point I thank God that at last I have discharged my bitter task of aggrieving the vanquished and the unfortunate, and that the moment has come instead to address myself to the victors, to those who do not suffer the distress of prison or the misery of exile, to those who are powerful and who enjoy fortune's every favor; and now I feel words coming to me more surely and more freely. . . .

Romagna and the entire Papal State seem tranquil, and one may say of them what was said of Poland: *L'ordre règne à Varsovie* *, but this tranquillity should not be mistaken for what it is not. The government of the Pope will achieve neither true nor lasting tranquillity with the establishment of new tribunals . . . created for the purpose of eliminating at least the great infamy associated with the former [ones]; the men and the methods are similar to those of before. It will not achieve tranquillity with the specter of imprisonment . . . or with the bestial manner used with political prisoners, who are treated as murderers and thieves and who are chained together, contrary to the customs of all civilized nations. . . . The papal government will not achieve tranquillity by increasing its guard of mercenary bayonets, as rumor has it that it intends to do now. It will achieve it with the justice, charity, and forgiveness it preaches and yet refuses to practice; it will achieve it by observing for once the holy law it teaches; it will achieve it by coming to those honest agreements which universal opinion asks of it. . . .

There is no princedom, no authority in the world which can stand on any base other than universal opinion or consensus. The only bond which prevents human society from dissolving is the idea of a right admitted by all. The [Holy Roman] Empire's rights in the Middle Ages and rule by divine right served as foundation-stones so long as the world had faith in them; now this faith is dead and no human power can revive it. The old faith in the former rights has been replaced by a new one: faith in rights common to all. As with all new

---

* "Order reigns in Warsaw"—ironic phrase used by the French to describe the subjection of the Poles after their unsuccessful and mercilessly repressed revolution against Russia in 1831. Ed. note.

believers, the first to embrace this new faith went to extremes and were fought by extremes from the other side. This is the history of our times for approximately the last sixty years. The two forces by which the world progresses, when in contrast to one another have followed the law of dynamics, according to which two divergent thrusts produce a diagonal median. The idea of rights common to all has been purified by the action of contrasting extremes and has by now become universal; it is an opinion held by all and, as we have said, opinion is the mistress of the world. . . .

As an ancient and ecclesiastical princedom the Papal State could still enjoy a great power, if it knew how to use it; if it knew how to follow the example of the English aristocracy, changing in time with public opinion, consenting to its honest requests, and admitting that at times it is prudent to grant something willingly in order not to be dispossessed of everything later and by violence.

But, on the contrary, neglecting that power which is his true power and the one exclusively his own as an ecclesiastical prince revered by Catholics the world over, he [the Pope] seeks support from the two powers most hated not only by Italian public opinion but by the opinion of all Christian civilization: two powers which by their ruinous action (and this will come sooner or later) will ruin him as well; and these are, mercenary troops at home and foreign troops from abroad. . . .

Foreign troops—that is, Austria's protection—assuredly keep him on his feet materially and violently; but, as do his mercenaries, the former prove that he cannot rely at all on his own subjects. In addition, they render him hateful to the Italians, who with every passing day become more inflamed with the desire for independence which they see harmed by the renewal of the Papacy's ancient guilt, which is that of calling the foreigner into Italy in order to use him against the Italians. Outside of Italy it is an ugly spectacle for honest men and devout Catholics to see Austria hold Romagna by the hair so that the Pope may practice the government pleasing to him. In consequence it happens that in Italy and outside not only Protestants or others opposed to Rome but the very Catholics most devoted to him, and priests as well, when not moved by private passions discard all regard for the Pope's temporal authority, preach that it is harmful to faith and religion, and would either eliminate it altogether or at least restrict it to small dimensions. In short, the two forces on which he would rely will not be able to help him at the first occasion of some grave disorder in the European balance of power, and everyone sees how many such disorders are near, if not imminent. If the two forces on which he relies will not then be able to save him, they are surely able and most effective now to deprive him of the true and only power which at all times and in all circumstances would be his surest defense, that of the consent of universal opinion.

PART TWO

THE RISORGIMENTO: POLITICAL
FULFILLMENT AND NEW
UNCERTAINTIES, 1848–1870

MAP 3
Italy at the time of unification, 1859–1870

V. THE DECLINE OF FEDERALISM
AND REPUBLICANISM AND THE
ASCENDANCY OF
PIEDMONT-SARDINIA

The political fulfillment of Italy's aspirations for unity came to pass during the eleven years from 1859 to 1870. But these eleven years of success had been preceded by eleven years of trial, opening with the enthusiastic expectations and bitter disillusionments of the revolutionary years of 1848–49 and closing with the first successful war of independence against Austria in 1859. Altogether, these twenty-two years constitute one of the most dramatic periods of Italian history. The process of unification—concluding a first stage in 1861 and its final stage in 1870—was a triumph for the moderates and a source of despair for those federalists and republicans who could not reconcile themselves either to a unitary state under Piedmontese hegemony or to monarchical institutions. Consequently, unification was achieved under something of a cloud or, to be more precise, a number of clouds. These included the unrelenting hostility of Mazzini and his more devoted followers toward monarchical and insufficiently democratic institutions, and the equally unrelenting hostility of the Papacy, despoiled of its temporal power and much of its properties by the makers of the united Italian state. As in the case of the war against Austria in 1866, unification was marred by something less than brilliant military feats. The newly united state had also to face grave economic and social problems, especially in the South; and it was troubled by disorders abetted by Bourbon and clerical opponents as well as by followers of Mazzini and Garibaldi. Finally, at the very moment of unity, Italy had to contend with a resurgence of regional animosities directed especially against triumphant Piedmont.

The traditional animosity or rivalry among the several Italian states had been a chief argument used by the federalists, who opposed the plan of a unitary or centralized Italian state. This was also the argument that made the Neo-Guelph solution of a federated Italy under the presidency of the Pope so plausible on the eve of the revolutions of 1848. Indeed, in tracing the immediate antecedents of these revolutions it is customary to begin with the accession of a new Pope in 1846.

So long as Gregory XVI sat on the papal throne there appeared to be little hope that the Pope would lead, and would be accepted as the leader of, a federation of Italian states. First, because Pope Gregory and his advisers seemed to have no liking for this project and, second, because so long as the government of the Papal States remained as d'Azeglio had described it in his indictment of 1846, liberal opinion in Italy would not accept leadership from papal Rome. The accession in June 1846 of Giovanni Maria Mastai Ferretti, Bishop of Imola, as Pius IX seemed to remove the substance of both obstacles. Pius IX was reported to have been much impressed by Gioberti's *Primato,* and the new Pope's liberal leanings seemed confirmed by the measures he enacted during the first year of his pontificate. Within a month of his accession he amnestied all political prisoners in his domains. The expectations aroused by this step were heightened in March 1847 when restrictions on the press were relaxed and the remaining controls entrusted to a commission composed predominantly of laymen. During the following June a *Consulta di Stato* [a consultative body] was established, stimulating much hope for eventual constitutional government. The extent of the implications seen in the Pope's acts can be gauged in part from Garibaldi's offer of his sword to the Pope for the liberation of Italy and from Mazzini's letter urging Pius IX to "unify Italy, your country."

The Pope's actions sparked much desired reforms elsewhere. Most importantly, in Piedmont, one of the three large and independent Italian states, King Charles Albert dismissed his ultra-conservative Minister of Foreign Affairs, Count Solaro della Margarita, in October 1847 and replaced him with the more moderate Count Asinari di San Marzano. At the end of the same month restrictions on the press were relaxed, whereupon many new journals were founded, including *Il Risorgimento,* of which Cesare Balbo and Cavour were cofounders. Symptomatically, in the Kingdom of the Two Sicilies, where no meaningful reforms were enacted or even promised, popular disaffection had recourse to insurrection. Although the September 1847 risings in Reggio and Messina were severely repressed, when Palermo rose successfully in January 1848, the rest of Sicily followed, and within days all the island save the citadel of Messina was in the hands of the revolutionaries. The events that followed in Italy during the next two months came at a precipitous speed. Toward the end of January Ferdinand II of the Two Sicilies, pressed by the victorious revolutionaries, made public the essential points of a constitution, to which he swore an oath on February 10. Two days later Charles Albert of Piedmont-Sardinia announced the draft of a moderately liberal constitution known as the *Statuto.* In Tuscany the grand duke granted a constitution on February 15.

Events moved even more rapidly after news of the February 22 revolution in Paris reached the other capitals of Europe. The Albertine *Statuto* was promulgated officially on March 4; four days later Charles Albert appointed a new Ministry led by the moderate Cesare Balbo and the democrat Lorenzo Pareto. Ten days later Pius IX granted the Papal States a constitution providing for a Chamber of Deputies and a Senate, but with reservations which excluded the parliamentary assembly from legislating on wholly or partially ecclesiastical matters and which entrusted the College of Cardinals with the right to veto any bill passed by the two Houses.

News of a revolution in Vienna on March 13 and the flight of Metternich led to even more radical events in Italy. On March 17 the Venetians rose against the Austrians and within days proclaimed a republic under the leadership of Daniele Manin and Nicolò Tommaseo. On March 23 Milan ended its heroic struggle of the "Five Days" with the expulsion of the Austrian garrisons and their retirement to a group of fortresses in eastern Lombardy and western Venetia called the Quadrilateral. The same day Cavour wrote in the *Risorgimento* that "the supreme hour of the Savoyard monarchy had come."

The war that Piedmont began against Austria on March 23, 1848, in the name of the liberation of Italy went well until May. The Piedmontese military effort was supported enthusiastically by volunteer groups from all over Italy as well as by regular contingents sent willingly or unwillingly by the heads of other Italian states. But in June and July Italian arms met several serious defeats. The factors that contributed to these reverses were Pope Pius' open disengagement from the national cause against Austria at the end of April, the withdrawal of the Neapolitan contingents in May, the growing suspicion among some Italians that Piedmont sought more its own aggrandizement in northern Italy than the unification of all of Italy, and an ill-coordinated and inept military command. In consequence, Piedmont signed an armistice with Austria in August obliging the former to evacuate its troops from Lombardy and Venetia. Bitter recriminations were directed against the Piedmontese government both by nationalists from the rest of Italy and by Piedmontese radicals who did not approve of what appeared to be purely dynastic concerns with territorial gains.

The cause of Italian liberation and unity under moderate auspices seemed to collapse rapidly. Faced with the imposition of a radical Ministry, the Pope fled Rome for a refuge in the Kingdom of Naples late in November and called upon the rulers of Europe to restore him to his full temporal authority. The Roman revolutionaries retaliated by proclaiming a republic in February 1849 and by entrusting dictatorial power in March to a triumvirate that included Mazzini. In February the Grand Duke of Tuscany, Leopold II, also fled his state, which fell under the control of another radical triumvirate. In Piedmont the moderates lost ground to men of the Left who were determined to renew the war against Austria. The moment seemed opportune for this step: in March 1849 the city of Venice was still resisting the Austrians besieging it; the Roman republic was rallying supporters from all over Italy, including an Italian legion led by Garibaldi; and the Hungarians had once again risen against the Hapsburgs. On March 20 the Piedmontese resumed hostilities with Austria; by March 23 they suffered a crushing defeat at

Novara, obliging Charles Albert to request an armistice. The terms Austria sought to impose on Piedmont were so onerous that Charles Albert decided on immediate abdication in favor of his son Victor Emmanuel and went into exile in Portugal.

Considered superficially, the war that began so auspiciously in the spring of 1848 and which foundered completely in the spring of 1849 marked the failure of a number of causes. With the eventual revocation or disregard of all but one of the constitutions granted in 1848 it seemed that hopes for liberal constitutional government in the peninsula had been completely dashed. The Pope's refusal to participate in armed conflict against Catholic Austria on behalf of Catholic Italy and the rivalries and suspicions engendered among the several Italian states during 1848 wholly discredited the federal solution—Neo-Guelph or otherwise—for the unification of Italy. The collapse of the Venetian and Roman republics proclaimed during the revolutionary year compromised the very idea of a republican Italy. And the failure of Italian arms to defeat Austria seemed to disprove the maxim that Italy could and should unify itself by itself (*"L'Italia farà da sè"*) and led to the realistic conclusion that Italy would have to seek foreign aid and foreign alliances in order to free itself of the most detested of foreign influences, Austria. But, in addition to this greater realism, something concretely positive had issued from an otherwise catastrophic political experience, and that was the ascendancy or, at least, the primacy of Piedmont. Its King, Charles Albert, had twice challenged the might of Austria, and its dynasty had the distinction of being the only one in Italy to retain and observe the constitution it had granted.

Excerpts from the 1848 constitution of the Kingdom of Piedmont-Sardinia are presented because of its intrinsic significance as the fundamental law of the Piedmontese state from 1848 to 1861 and, with minor modifications, of united Italy until near the end of the Fascist dictatorship; also because the constitution's provisions, although only moderately liberal, reveal one of the reasons why most Italian liberals of the period of unification came to look to Piedmont as the only Italian state worthy to lead the cause of independence and unity.

12. THE ALBERTINE CONSTITUTION (*STATUTO*) OF 1848

Gazzetta Piemontese, Vol. XVI, No. 674 (January 1–December 31, 1848). Our translation.

Article 1. The Catholic, Apostolic, and Roman religion is the sole religion of the state. All other forms of worship now existing are tolerated in conformity with the law.

Art. 2. The state is governed by a representative monarchical government. The throne is hereditary according to the Salic law.

Art. 3. The legislative power shall be exercised collectively by the King and two Chambers, the Senate and the Chamber of Deputies. . . .

Art. 5. The executive power is reserved to the King alone. He is the supreme head of the state; he commands all the armed forces on land and sea; he declares war, makes treaties of peace, of alliance, of commerce, and of other kinds, giving notice of them to the Chambers as soon as the interest and security of the state allow, and accompanying such notice with opportune explanations. Treaties entailing either a financial burden or changes in the territories of the state shall have effect only after the approval of the two Chambers.

Art. 6. The King makes all appointments to offices of the state; he issues the decrees and regulations necessary for the execution of the laws, without suspending or dispensing with the observance thereof.

Art. 7. The King alone has the power to sanction and promulgate laws. . . .

Art. 9. The King convenes the two Chambers annually; he may prorogue their Sessions and dissolve the Chamber of Deputies; but in the latter case he shall convene a new Chamber within four months.

Art. 10. The King and the two Chambers have the right to propose legislation, but all laws imposing taxes or approving the budgets and accounts of the state shall be presented first in the Chamber of Deputies. . . .

THE RIGHTS AND DUTIES OF CITIZENS

Art. 24. All subjects of the Kingdom are equal before the law, regardless of their rank or title.

All shall equally enjoy civil and political rights and shall be eligible to civil and military offices, except as otherwise provided by law.

Art. 25. All shall contribute without distinction to the burdens of the state, in proportion to their possessions.

Art. 26. Individual liberty is guaranteed. No one shall be arrested or brought to trial except in cases and in the manner prescribed by law.

Art. 27. The domicile is inviolable. No search of domicile shall be permitted except in cases and in the manner prescribed by law.

Art. 28. The press shall be free, but the law may suppress abuses of this freedom. However, Bibles, catechisms, liturgical and prayer books shall not be printed without the prior permission of the [local] bishop.

Art. 29. All forms of property without exception are inviolable. However, when legally ascertained public interest requires it, one may be obliged to give up such property wholly or in part, with just compensation and in conformity with the law.

Art. 30. No tax shall be levied or collected without the consent of the Chambers and the King. . . .

Art. 32. The right of peaceful assembly without arms is recognized, in conformity with laws that may regulate this right in the interest of public welfare.

This provision does not apply to assemblies in public places or in places open to the public. Such assemblies remain completely subject to police regulations.

THE SENATE

Art. 33. The Senate shall be composed of members appointed by the King for life; its number is not limited. . . .

Art. 35. The President and Vice-Presidents of the Senate shall be appointed by the King. The Senate shall choose its own Secretaries. . . .

CHAMBER OF DEPUTIES

Art. 39. The elective Chamber shall be composed of Deputies chosen from electoral constituencies in conformity with the law.

Art. 40. No Deputy shall be admitted to the Chamber unless he is a subject of the King, has reached the age of thirty, enjoys civil and political rights, and fulfills other requirements specified by law. . . .

Art. 42. Deputies are elected for a period of five years. Their mandate expires automatically at the end of this period.

Art. 43. The President, Vice-Presidents, and Secretaries of the Chamber of Deputies are chosen by the Chamber at the beginning of every Session and for its entire duration. . . .

Art. 45. Except for the case of *flagrante delicto*, no Deputy shall be placed under arrest while the Chamber is in session nor may he be brought before a court in a criminal proceeding without the prior consent of the Chamber.

Art. 46. No warrant of arrest for debts shall be executed against a Deputy while the Chamber is in session, nor for the three weeks immediately preceding and following such Session.

Art. 47. The Chamber of Deputies has the right to impeach the King's Ministers and bring them to trial before the High Court of Justice [the Senate].

PROVISIONS COMMON TO BOTH CHAMBERS:

. . . Art. 50. The offices of Senator and Deputy are without remuneration or monetary compensation of any kind.

Art. 51. Senators and Deputies shall not be held accountable for opinions expressed and votes given in the Chambers.

Art. 52. Sittings of the Chambers shall be public; but when ten or more members request it in writing, deliberations may be held in closed session. . . .

Art. 54. Deliberations are taken by majority vote.

Art. 55. All bills shall first be examined by the Committees each Chamber shall elect for preliminary consideration. After a bill is discussed and approved by a Chamber, it shall be transmitted to the other Chamber for debate and approval; thereafter, it shall be transmitted to the King for his sanction. . . .

Art. 56. If a bill is rejected by one of the three legislative powers [Chamber of Deputies, Senate, and the King], it shall not be presented again during the same Session. . . .

Art. 64. No one shall be a Senator and a Deputy at the same time.

ON MINISTERS

Art. 65. The King appoints and dismisses his Ministers.

Art. 66. Ministers do not have the right to vote in either of the Chambers unless they are members thereof.

They do have the right of entrance [to both Chambers] and the right to speak.

Art. 67. Ministers are responsible.

No law or act of the government shall go into effect unless signed by a Minister.

ON THE JUDICIARY

Art. 68. Justice emanates from the King and is administered in his name by such judges as he shall appoint.

Art. 69. Except for cantonal judges, judges appointed by the King shall be irremovable after three years of service.

Art. 70. Courts, tribunals, and judges currently existing are retained. The judicial organization may not be altered except by legislation.

Art. 71. No one shall be withdrawn from his ordinary legal jurisdiction. Consequently, no extraordinary tribunals or commissions shall be created.

Art. 72. Proceedings of tribunals in civil matters and hearings in criminal matters shall be public, in conformity with the law.

Art. 73. Binding interpretation of the laws is an exclusive prerogative of the legislative power.

GENERAL PROVISIONS

Art. 81. All laws contrary to the present Statute are abrogated. . . .

Given in Turin this day, the 4th of March in the year of our Lord 1848 and the 18th year of our reign.

Charles Albert
[*Countersigned* by seven Ministers of State]

The viability of the 1848 constitution was soon to be tested during the crisis following Charles Albert's abdication. His son and successor, Victor Emmanuel II (1820–78), found the Piedmontese Parliament so intractable in its opposition to the armistice concluded with Austria that he felt obliged to dissolve the Chamber of Deputies on March 30, 1849. The fact that no date was fixed for new elections raised grave doubts about the permanence of the recently established parliamentary institutions. When the elections were finally held, in July, the democratic factions of the Left, unreconciled to the armistice terms which provided for Austrian occupation of a number of strategic places in Piedmont and the reduction of the Piedmontese army to peacetime strength, won control of the Chamber. The Left's desire for renewal of the war against Austria was still strong: the Roman republic, led by a triumvirate which included Mazzini and defended by legions under the command of Garibaldi, had just been crushed by the intervention of French arms on behalf of the Pope's temporal authority; but the Venetians were still resisting under the incessant bombardment of Austrian cannons. Even after the capitulation of Venice in August 1849, the Piedmontese Left still refused to agree to the terms of the peace treaty concluded by the Piedmontese and Austrian governments in August. In November the Left succeeded in imposing a condition on the approval of the treaty to the effect that the treaty be accompanied by a law according Piedmontese citizenship to all émigrés from other Italian states (Lombardy and Venetia) which had formerly voted for union with Piedmont. This condition was unacceptable to the Austrian government and, by necessity, to the Piedmontese government as well. The latter, led by Massimo d'Azeglio since May 1849, saw no alternative other than to dissolve the Chamber once again.

Government and Parliament were now faced with a grave constitutional crisis. Contrary to all reality and reason, a majority in the Chamber of Deputies refused to accept the inescapable consequences of the fact that Piedmont, friendless and alone in Italy, could not resist the Austrian demands. Unable to govern with Parliament, King and government appeared to have no alternative but to govern without the assent of the elected assembly. Such a resolution to the political impasse would have meant the end of a meaningful constitutional regime; and when, on November 20, the day of the dissolution of the Chamber of Deputies, Victor Emmanuel II issued a proclamation to his people, some interpreted it as a *coup d'état*. In truth, no such *coup* was intended, or, if it had been considered, it was not executed. The facts are that the decree of dissolution fixed the date of new elections within three weeks and the convocation of the new Chamber within a month. Had a *coup* been intended, the elections could have been deferred constitutionally for four months, at most, or the meetings of the old Chamber could have been prorogued for an indefinite period. Fears of a *coup* stemmed, therefore, not from the procedure followed by the King, which was perfectly in accord with the *Statuto*, but from the severity of the language employed in the proclamation, which does contain an implied threat. In his proclamation of November 20, 1849 (*Proclama di Moncalieri*), Victor Emmanuel said: "I shall say nothing of the attacks detrimental to that prerogative [in the conduct of foreign policy] accorded me by the law of the state. But I have good reason to hold the Chamber to a strict accounting for its most recent acts, and with a sense of assurance I appeal to the judgment of Italy and Europe. . . . If the country, if the voters deny me their cooperation, hereafter the responsibility for future events will not be mine; and in the disorders that may arise they will be able to complain not of me, but of themselves." [1]

[1] For the full text of the Proclama, see Licurgo Cappelletti, *Storia di Vittorio Emanuele II* (3 vols.; Rome, Enrico Voghera, 1892–93), I, 85–88. Moncalieri is the name of the royal castle where Victor Emmanuel was staying at the time of the issuance of the proclamation.

The bluntness of the language with which the King appealed to the country over the heads of its representatives apparently helped convince a majority of Piedmontese voters that the country had no alternative but to accept without new conditions the treaty concluded with Austria. The general elections, dutifully held on December 9 as had been promised, resulted in a strong majority for the government's policies. Aided by the support of such moderate liberals as Cavour, the peace treaty with Austria was approved on January 7, 1850.

The King's and his Ministers' loyalty to constitutional government and the good sense of the voters had helped preserve the country's still young liberal institutions. The major internal threat to these institutions came from the factions of the prerevolutionary conservative Right, predominantly clerical or clerically inspired, that had not reconciled themselves to parliamentary government. Opposition to this clerical influence in politics and in the country at large occasioned the first major domestic reform attempted by d'Azeglio's Ministry. The reform in question goes under the name of the Siccardi Laws, which aimed at the abolition of privileged ecclesiastical courts and the right of ecclesiastical asylum. It was during the debate on these laws, early in 1850, that Cavour emerged as the effective leader of the government's majority in the Chamber. By October 1850 Cavour was admitted into the government and entrusted with the Ministry of Agriculture, Industry, and Commerce. Except for a brief period of six months during 1859, Cavour was to remain near or at the summit of power in Piedmont until his death in 1861.

Perhaps more than any other Piedmontese, it was Cavour, with his unswerving faith in moderate constitutional government, who helped preserve and strengthen liberal institutions in Piedmont. Without the safeguarding of these institutions, Piedmont would probably not have been able to rally the liberals from all over Italy; and without this rallying around Piedmont, the story of Italy's eventual unification would certainly have been different and the realization of unity itself probably much delayed.

13. CAVOUR, STATESMAN IN THE MAKING

Count Camillo Benso di Cavour was born in Turin in 1810, at that time a department in the French empire. He was the son of the Marquis Michele Benso di Cavour, Chamberlain to Prince Camillo Borghese, who was the husband of Napoleon's sister Pauline and governor of Piedmont. Prince Borghese held the child at baptism and gave him his own Christian name. Through his mother's family—the de Sellon—Cavour was related not only to the Protestant Huguenot aristocracy that had sought refuge in Switzerland after the revocation of the Edict of Nantes in France in 1685 but also to the Bourbon Legitimist branch of French aristocracy. Cavour entered the Piedmontese Military Academy at the age of ten and received a commission in the Corps of Engineers at sixteen. His father had intended that young Cavour follow a military career, but the young man's "Jacobin" ideas earned him the enmity of his patron, Prince Charles Albert. After the latter's accession to the Piedmontese throne in 1831, Cavour concluded that he had no future in military life and resigned his commission. In 1832 he sought to visit Lombardy, but was denied entry because the Austrian authorities considered him to be "a most dangerous individual." After extensive travels in England, France, and Belgium, Cavour settled down to the management of his elder brother's estates at Leri, where he introduced the newest farming methods of the day. He invested in banking and industry and in 1842 helped form an agricultural association in Piedmont, a group devoted to economic and political liberalism. In the mid 1840s, after additional travel in England, he wrote articles on the Irish question and free trade as well as a politically oriented article on Italian railroads. In 1847 he helped found the newspaper *Il Risorgimento;* the next year he entered the Piedmontese Parliament where, except for his defeat during the landslide victory of the radicals in January 1849, he was to remain without interruption until his death in 1861.

As long as Charles Albert remained on the throne of Piedmont, Cavour's political future remained clouded and uncertain. In 1832, the year after the unsuccessful revolutions in central Italy, Cavour wrote a letter to "an English friend" deploring conditions in Piedmont: "Pressed on one side by Austrian bayonets and on the other by papal excommunications. . . ." Eleven years later he still thought of Piedmont as "a sort of intellectual hell . . . where intellect and knowledge are considered infernal things by him who has the goodness of governing us." [2] Cavour's hostility toward the government of Charles Albert was based not only on the King's generally illiberal policy after his accession to the throne in 1831, but also on a personal antipathy the two men felt for each other. The following letter by Cavour is in a sense a brief and candid autobiography, written in October 1847, the month Charles Albert replaced the conservative Minister Solaro della Margarita with the more moderate Asinari di San Marzano.

A Brief Autobiography: Letter by Cavour to the Marquis
Léon Costa de Beauregard, in Champigny (Savoy)

Chiala, ed., *Lettere,* I, 112–16. Our translation from the original French.

You will find it strange that I am living in the country and that I take no steps to become connected with the government. According to you

[2] Luigi Chiala, ed., *Lettere edite ed inedite di Camillo Cavour* (6 vols.; Turin, Roux e Favale, 1883–87), I, 3, 49.

I should bestir myself to obtain a place and play a role on the political stage. Inasmuch as I am speaking to a friend such as yourself, I shall not in the least affect any false modesty, and I shall not say to you that I think myself incapable of serving king and country. I am perhaps mistaken, but I confess that I am not of this opinion. On the contrary I may deceive myself to the point of thinking that I possess as much ability and knowledge as most of the people who occupy the first ranks in politics. If I stand aside, it is for other reasons. It is because I am convinced that there exist between me and power certain obstacles which I could not surmount without sacrificing my personal dignity. Furthermore, it is probable that the sacrifices which I might be disposed to make would be in vain. It is a disagreeable situation, but I do not know how to change it. Perhaps you will judge matters as I do when I acquaint you in a few words with some details of my history. I was appointed a Court page at the age of thirteen and was the object of very marked favor on the part of the Prince of Carignano [the future King Charles Albert]. I responded very badly to this exalted predilection. Carried away by the ardor of youth and by the exaltation of beliefs which even now I do not disavow in their substance, I broke with the Court thanks to imprudent words which I uttered when I was graduated from the Military Academy. The prince treated me with excessive rigor. He denounced me to the King, Charles Felix, who, to my great astonishment, showed himself very tolerant toward me. Banished from the Court, I gave free rein to my opinions which, I confess, were very exaggerated. I spent six years in the Corps of Engineers, from the age of sixteen to twenty-one, without concealing my manner of thinking from anyone; however, I did not commit the least act or contract the least commitment contrary to the oath of loyalty I had sworn. When the prince acceded to the throne, one of his first acts was an act of severity toward me. He sent me to the fortress of Bard during a season of the year when there was no work to perform or workers to supervise. I bore with this exile, but at the end of eight months I obtained my father's permission to resign from the army and return to private life.

Since then I have always concerned myself with serious matters. Age and study have much modified my opinions but have not changed them. Fundamentally, I am now as liberal as I was at the age of eighteen in the sense that I still desire that which may bring the greatest good for humanity and the development of civilization. I am the same as I was upon graduation from the academy, still convinced that the world is drawn along by an inevitable march toward a new goal, that to wish to arrest the course of events means to arouse storms without hope of bringing the ship into port. But now I am persuaded that the only real progress is progress which is slow and wisely ordered. I am convinced that order is necessary for the development of society, and that of all the guarantees of order a legitimate power with profound roots in the history of the country is the best. Therefore, considering everything, I do not think I am more liberal than a great number of those who occupy the avenues to power.

Highly placed men have shared this view and, on a number of occasions, have sought to bring me into the government. But they have always found an invincible obstacle in the supreme will [of the King]. The Count of Pralormo who, as you know, was always persistent in his endeavors, tried several times to surmount this obstacle, without success.

That which happened many years ago would be repeated now and with greater reason. I was young then and without inconvenience I could have accepted a junior position. Now I could not or, if you prefer, I would not. Eight years ago I was very popular; now I no longer am at all. In the Agricultural Association I fought with energy against an extremely liberal party. The government supported the latter; it put me in the wrong, and at the same time I lost my position in the Association and the favor of the liberals. I have done nothing to reacquire this favor, so that, if the King were to give me an office, he would displease more people than he would satisfy. There is, therefore, no chance whatever that he should think of me; and if someone else were to present my name to him, he would have no reason for surmounting the repugnance he feels for me.

There you have it, my dear Léon: a sincere explanation. It will make my conduct less strange to you. I have devoted myself to agriculture. In order for it to have a real interest for me, I practice it on a large scale. Until now I have been rather successful. I have digressed from the usual road and have tried improvements of a new kind. . . . I have succeeded in establishing a discount bank in Turin. . . . I have created a vast plant producing fertilizers and chemical products which, I believe, has no rival in Italy. Finally, I flatter myself in thinking that I have contributed more than anyone else in building a magnificent rice mill. . . .

If I write to you of what I have done it is not to boast but only to prove to you that I am not a lazy person who, with the pretext of cultivating his lands, passes his days in sweet idleness. . . . If I remain in private life it is because I cannot leave it with dignity or in a way of being able to be truly useful to the country. . . .

I shall close by writing a few words on the events of the day. You surely know of the changes which have taken place in the Ministry. The new Ministers have as yet done nothing to indicate the road they intend to travel. While waiting, public opinion becomes impatient and more demanding every day. One cannot resign oneself to remaining behind Rome and Tuscany [where reforms had been enacted or announced]. . . . In fact, it is impossible to continue for long in being liberal on the other side of the Ticino [river bordering on Austrian-controlled Lombardy] and repressive on this side of the river. Foreign policy is one with domestic policy, and a sharp contrast between these two policies could not last for long. All sensible men feel this, no matter the shade of opinion they prefer. I believe the King himself is convinced of this. Consequently, I do not doubt that he is working toward some concessions. But, what they will be, and how they will be granted, this I cannot tell you. There is talk of a law on the press, of the abolition of exceptional [ecclesiastical] courts, and I do not know what else. . . .

In the meanwhile the public patiently distracts itself by shouting "Long live Pius IX" and by getting itself chased by the cavalry. I do not think that a serious [insurrectional] movement is probable or even possible; but the excitement is immense and repressive measures would have only a momentary success. The illness which troubles the country is serious. If one were to employ force, one would quickly reach the acute stage only to fall into a chronic state to which the least external shock or internal commotion could prove fatal.

14. CAVOUR AND THE ITALIAN PRIMACY OF PIEDMONT: AN ERA OF REFORMS

The external shocks Cavour feared were not long in coming. They came in Sicily in January 1848; in France the next month; in Vienna, Milan, and

Venice in March. Twice, in March 1848 and March 1849, Piedmont challenged the might of Austria and twice it met defeat. There followed the abdication of Charles Albert, who had ceded to the pressures of the Piedmontese Left and renewed a war which led to the destruction of his armies within three days. The constitutional crisis over the approval of the peace treaty with Austria, its subsequent resolution by the Proclamation of Moncalieri, and the victory of the moderates in the elections of December 1849 finally opened the way for Cavour's rapid ascent to power. Charles Albert's abdication had eliminated an insurmountable obstacle for Cavour; the fortunes of the Left had been depreciated by its unfortunate conduct of the war and its unreasonable opposition to the peace treaty; and so the day had come for Cavour and the moderate party.

Cavour's credentials as a moderate or, according to the terminology employed in Piedmontese parliamentary circles, as a liberal conservative had been certified during the hectic years of 1847–49. As cofounder of the Turin daily *Il Risorgimento* in December 1847 he shared and helped fashion the newspaper's program of domestic reforms and the independence of Italy from foreign domination. In January 1848 he used the pages of his newspaper to call for the establishment of constitutional government. When the *Statuto* was granted by Charles Albert, Cavour defended it against the criticisms of the Left, which preferred a more democratic document created by a popularly elected Constituent Assembly rather than by the King. In this defense Cavour revealed his moderation and his disagreement with the democrats, but his liberalism was confirmed in his own criticism of the *Statuto* for the provisions which gave the Catholic Church a privileged position and for the royally appointive character of the Senate. The first matter, Cavour argued, would violate the right of complete religious freedom; the appointive Senate, he feared, would be too subservient to the executive, as indeed it proved to be.

When elections for the newly established Chamber of Deputies were held in April 1848 under a restricted franchise based on wealth, which Cavour favored, he was returned Deputy from Turin, with a program calling for a "free and united Italy, and for our country [Piedmont] a genuine constitutional system in which the throne rests on the firm and large foundation of popular freedoms." He supported the first phase of the war with Austria, but, after the armistice of August 1848, he opposed its renewal. He lost his seat in the January 1849 elections, which were a triumph for the democrats, who in March led Piedmont to its second military defeat. Bitter over his country's defeat and his own exclusion from Parliament, Cavour accused Charles Albert of betraying the moderates in favor of the ultrademocrats whom he berated as "incompetent," "cowardly," "imbecile," and "demagogues." [3]

After his return to the Chamber in the elections of July 1849, Cavour supported the approval of the peace treaty with Austria as an inevitable neces-

[3] Letter of April 29, 1849, to the French Countess Anastasia de Circourt, his close friend and confidante. Chiala, ed., *Lettere*, I, 146–47.

sity. With the victory of the moderates in the December 1849 elections following the Proclamation of Moncalieri, Cavour rose rapidly in the councils of government. The approval in March 1850 of the Siccardi Laws depriving the Church of its special courts and the right of asylum—privileges considered to be inconsistent with the constitutional provision of equality of all before the law—marks the emergence of Cavour as one of the leaders of the Chamber. It also marks the advent of Cavour and Piedmont to the forefront of the Italian scene.

Excerpt from Cavour's Speech on the Siccardi Laws,
Chamber of Deputies, March 7, 1850

> Camillo di Cavour, *Discorsi parlamentari,* 11 vols. Turin: Tipografia della Camera dei deputati, 1863-72, I, 409.

[After citing with approval the reforms enacted in England between 1829 and 1846, Cavour concluded]: Timely reforms do not weaken authority, they strengthen it; they do not increase the strength of revolutionary spirit, they reduce it to impotence. (*Sensation in the Chamber.*) Consequently, I say to the Ministry: Imitate openly the example given by the Duke of Wellington, Lord Grey, and Sir Robert Peel. These are men whom history will proclaim as the first statesmen of our times. Proceed freely along the road of reform and do not fear that you thereby weaken the authority of the constitutional throne entrusted to you. If you so proceed you will strengthen this throne. Its roots will become so strong in our country that even if the revolutionary storm were to break out about us, it will be able not only to resist this storm but also to gather about itself all the living forces of Italy and lead our nation to that high destiny to which it has been called. (*Prolonged and loud applause from all benches. . . . All the Ministers shake the speaker's hand and several Deputies from the left congratulate him.*)

In October 1850 Cavour took the first major step toward the realization of his long-held ambition to be Prime Minister of Piedmont. The death in August of the Minister of Agriculture, Industry, and Commerce created a vacancy in the government; the post was entrusted to Cavour and he exploited it fully to implement his ideas on the advantages of free trade. Treaties of commerce and navigation were negotiated with France, England, and Belgium between 1850 and 1852 and were approved by Parliament, in spite of opposition from the protectionists of the conservative Right. The following speech in defense of free trade contains a classic exposition of Cavour's views on the intimate interrelationship between economics and politics, and particularly between economic and political freedom.

Cavour's Speech in Favor of Free Trade, Chamber of Deputies, April 15, 1851

Cavour, *Discorsi parlamentari*, II, 380–83, *passim*. Our translation.

Modern history, especially that of the last century, shows that society is clearly and inevitably moving along the road of progress. The laws which regulate this process have not as yet been determined by either the wisest philosophers or the most sagacious statesmen. But in the midst of so much uncertainty this much is sure: the course of humanity is directed toward two goals, one political and the other economic. In the political order humanity tends to modify its institutions in order to bring an ever increasing number of its members to participate in political power. In the economic order it clearly aims at the improvement of the conditions of the lower classes, toward a better distribution of the products of the soil and of capital. . . .

Two means are offered us in order to reach this goal [improving the conditions of the lower classes]. All systems conceived in modern times by the wisest and boldest intellects may be reduced to two. Some have faith in the principle of liberty, in the principle of free competition, in the free development of moral and intellectual man. They believe that with the ever-increasing realization of this principle there must follow an increased well-being for all and especially for the less affluent classes. This is the school of the economists. . . .

There is another school, professing absolutely different principles. It believes that the miseries of humanity cannot be relieved and that the conditions of the working classes cannot be improved except by restricting individual action ever more and by enlarging without limit the central action of government. This, gentlemen, is the socialist school.

We should not deceive ourselves: although this latter school has reached baleful and sometimes atrocious conclusions, it cannot be

denied that in its principles it possesses something attractive to generous and high-minded men. Now, the only way of fighting this school
which threatens to invade Europe is to oppose its principles with
other principles. In the economic as well as in the political and religious orders, ideas and principles are not fought effectively except
with other ideas and principles. Physical constraint is of little use.

Certainly, cannons and bayonets can repress theories for a time and
preserve the physical order. But if these theories make headway in the
intellectual sphere, then, gentlemen, believe me that sooner or later
they will be translated into effect and will triumph in the political and
economic order as well. (*Applause.*)

Now, gentlemen, I say that the strongest ally of the socialist
school—in the intellectual order, to be sure—is found in protectionist
doctrines. The latter derive absolutely from the same principles as the
former. These protectionist doctrines may be summarized as maintaining that it is the right and therefore the duty of the government to intervene in the distribution and employment of capital, that the government has the mission and authority to substitute its will, which it
considers more enlightened, for the free will of individuals. If this
contention were admitted as an unimpeachable truth, I do not know
how one could reply to the working classes and their self-appointed
advocates if they appeared before the government with the following
argument: You believe it your right to intervene in the distribution of
capital (if you permit me a barbarism), in the regulation of capital.
But why do you not intervene in the regulation of the other element
in production, wages? Why do you not organize labor?

In truth, I believe that if the doctrines of protectionism are admitted, there follows logically the necessity of admitting, if not all, at
least many of the doctrines of socialism. . . . I hope that the foregoing considerations have convinced [the Deputies of the Right] that
if the policy of the Ministry is frankly and openly liberal, it is also
conservative; conservative not of the rotten part of the social structure
but rather of those fundamental principles on which society and our
free institutions rest.

The genuinely liberal if not democratic overtones of the preceding speech,
coupled with repeated words of concern for the welfare of the lower classes,
constitute an important part of Cavour's plan to disassociate himself from
the more conservative men of the Right and to make overtures to the leaders

of the moderate Left. These overtures were directed principally at Urbano Rattazzi, the recognized leader of the moderate or Center Left. Rattazzi had been a member of several Piedmontese Ministries in 1848 and 1849 and in the latter year had been the most important member of the Ministry which had renewed the war with Austria. Cavour criticized this step and its proponents as cowardly and imbecile. But as Rattazzi moved away from the extreme or democratic Left toward the Center, and as Cavour approached the Center from the other direction, the two men came to an understanding known as the *Connubio* [the marriage], a name given sarcastically to the alliance of the two Centers by an opponent from the conservative Right, Count Thaon di Revel. The occasion which brought the *Connubio* into being was a domestic crisis over the press late in 1851 and early in 1852, following the December 1851 *coup d'état* which made President Louis Napoleon dictator of France. The democratic press in Piedmont was sharply critical of the French President, not only because he had subverted the French republic but because he was the man who in 1849 had intervened militarily to destroy the Roman republic led by Mazzini and Garibaldi. The Piedmontese government of Massimo d'Azeglio was desirous of retaining Louis Napoleon's professed friendship. Accordingly, it presented a bill on December 17, 1851, which dealt with press libels of foreign sovereigns and heads of government. The proposed law would authorize the Public Prosecutor to initiate legal action in cases of such libel and would have these cases heard before magistrates rather than before juries. The bill aroused fears in Piedmont that a conservative reaction was in the making and that the government had ceded to foreign pressure. In fact, a confidential dispatch by d'Azeglio to the Piedmontese ambassadors in France and England shows that such pressure had been exerted and that it had been peremptorily and proudly rebuffed.

Contrary to the desires of the Right, which wanted the proposed law to include provisions restricting freedom of the press on domestic matters, the law passed in February 1852 remained limited to comments by the press on foreign questions. This limitation was the work of Cavour, and during the three months following the approval of the law Cavour and Rattazzi consummated their political "marriage." Rattazzi supported the government loyally and Cavour succeeded in having Rattazzi elected President of the Chamber of Deputies. But this election alienated Cavour from the Prime Minister, d'Azeglio, who had become aware that Cavour had replaced him as the effective head of the government. The two men had a sharp altercation over the Rattazzi candidacy and, when the King refused to accept d'Azeglio's resignation, Cavour had no alternative but to present his own in May 1852. Soon after his resignation, Cavour confided to a friend that in time d'Azeglio, ailing from a wound received in 1848, would also have to resign, "and then we shall be able to form an openly liberal Cabinet."

Cavour did not have long to wait. In line with the program of domestic reforms initiated by his Ministry since 1849, d'Azeglio introduced in June 1852 a bill which made a civil ceremony a condition for a legally valid marriage. The bill was passed by the Chamber of Deputies with a large majority, but intransigent papal opposition, culminating in the withdrawal of the Papal Nuncio from Turin, moved Victor Emmanuel to withdraw his support from the proposed law. As a consequence, d'Azeglio's parliamentary position was so shaken that he decided to resign. Having become reconciled with Cavour, d'Azeglio designated the latter as his successor and as the only man capable of commanding a majority in Parliament. The King agreed to Cavour's designation as Prime Minister with much reluctance and only after Cesare Balbo's failure to form a more conservative government. Cavour received his appointment at the end of November and, on December 15, he presented the civil marriage bill to the Senate. The debate was bitter and the bill failed in the Senate by a single vote, 38 to 39. Supposedly because of the King's wishes, the government had chosen not to make the outcome of the vote a question of confidence. Nevertheless, Cavour delivered a strong speech in favor of the bill. This speech contains a classic statement of his famous concept of a "free Church in a free state."

*Cavour's Speech before the Senate on the Civil
Marriage Bill, December 16, 1852*

Cavour, *Discorsi parlamentari*, VI, 133, 139–41, 147–48. Our translation.

If the institution of civil marriage, if the separation of the marriage contract from the sacrament of marriage were directly contrary to dogma, then how could the Church tolerate it in France, in Holland, in Belgium, in England, and in almost all the states of the other hemisphere? . . . .

Many speakers oppose the law because they believe it will have the effect of weakening the religious sentiment of our people or else of weakening that reverence which we ardently wish shown toward the faith of our ancestors. They wish that the prescriptions of the Church receive at least the sanction of civil law [that is, that civil law make mandatory a religious ceremony]. But, gentlemen, at this point the question assumes much larger dimensions, because it is a question not merely of a law on civil marriage but of an entire system. It is a question of deciding whether or not it is in the greater interest of the state and of religion that civil authority give its sanction to the prescriptions of the Church. In short, whether it is more profitable for religion to be absolutely free or to have the aid and support of the civil authority.

If we were to admit the principle propounded by several speakers, especially by the Honorable Senator d'Azeglio [Roberto, brother of Massimo d'Azeglio, the former Prime Minister] and of the Venerable Archbishop of Vercelli, we would return to the old laws of the Middle Ages. If the interests of religion require that the civil power give its sanction to prescriptions regarding marriage, why not ask that the civil power give its penal sanction also to the other prescriptions of the Church, at least to the other external acts of [faith] which it prescribes? . . . .

Gentlemen, if you turn your minds back to the beginning of this century and consider the state of the Catholic religion almost everywhere in Europe at that time and compare it to the present, you will see that there has been an immense Catholic progress.

(*A voice:*) To be sure!

Cavour: I see Catholic progress in England, I see it in Holland and Belgium, I see it in many parts of Germany, and, finally, I see a great Catholic progress in France. It pains me to say it, but the only country where until now there has been little Catholic progress is Italy. (*Signs of approval from the galleries.*)

And, if there has been Catholic progress in England, Holland, Belgium, Germany, and France, it is to be attributed exclusively to the fact that in these countries Catholicism is absolutely separated from the civil power. And this progress is evident from the time that in many of these countries the principle of freedom of conscience was proclaimed and rigorously and widely applied. . . .

As I have already said, more than any other reform the nation desires the one on civil marriage. In order to satisfy this legitimate desire, the Ministry presented during the last months of the preceding Session a bill which was approved by the immense majority of the other Chamber. This bill met with intense opposition from a party which believes it neither timely nor possible to proceed with ecclesiastical reforms—even in matters exclusively within the province of the civil authority—without the consent of the Court of Rome.

I hasten to say that among those who opposed this bill there are many, for whom I profess the highest regard, who employed legal and fair methods. But there are many in the opposition party who were not content with legal opposition. With underhanded and fraudulent means they sought to arouse all kinds of opposition to this reform. Indeed, many members of this same opposition—with whom, I am sure, the first-mentioned do not agree—not only fought the marriage law reform but turned their attacks even against those political institutions which they believed to be instruments of the reforms they opposed.

. . .

I repeat that, with regard to reforms for which the agreement of the Holy See is perhaps indispensable, it is not possible to deceive ourselves that agreement can be reached unless first we enact all those reforms which are absolutely in our power to enact.

Far from being an obstacle to agreements with the Court of Rome, the proposed law is in fact an indispensable preliminary to them. For this reason, all those who are sincere in wishing to arrive at such agreements should give their favorable vote to the proposed law.

Cavour's plea to the Senate did not prevail. After its defeat in the Senate, the civil marriage bill was withdrawn, but the hostility between the clerical Right and the government persisted. Cavour sought to strengthen his parliamentary base in October 1853 by having Rattazzi, leader of the Center Left, admitted to the government as Minister of Justice. In November Cavour decided to ask the King to dissolve the Chamber and hold new elections. In the ensuing electoral campaign he employed all the government's influence and prestige in favor of progovernment ("ministerial") candidates, thus helping to establish the practice of governmental interference in elections which was to become a permanent feature of Italian political history. Cavour won a stable majority and proceeded with his program of reforms.

Early in 1854 Parliament approved a law abolishing all duties on wheat and other grains and thus instituted complete free trade in these commodities. Although the measure was unpopular with many large landowners, Cavour considered its passage a major triumph. A severer test of his political skill and popularity developed in 1854 with the introduction of a bill abolishing all religious congregations not engaged in preaching, teaching, or the care of the sick. The bill provided for the confiscation of the property of the suppressed congregations and the devolution of this property to a fund under state control. In addition, all other ecclesiastical bodies possessing property were to be taxed progressively and their contributions were to be added to the fund. In turn, the fund would defray the cost of pensions to members of the suppressed congregations as well as the allowances to poor parish priests previously supported by the state treasury.

The bill was presented in November 1854. It had the support of the entire Left and a good part of the moderate Right, but it met with great resistance from the conservative Right and from virtually the entire Piedmontese episcopate. Cavour defended the bill as a relief for the treasury and a spur to the economy by its elimination of property held in mortmain. Cavour's arguments, as well as the more radical arguments motivated by hostility to the

Church, led the Deputies to give the bill a large majority in March 1855. But opposition in the Senate and the King's wavering support put the government's majority in jeopardy. Victor Emmanuel II had lost his mother, his wife, and a brother within a month, from January to February 1855, and apparently became persuaded that he was suffering from an "evident divine punishment." Consequently, he urged the government to accept a compromise whereby the bill would be withdrawn on condition that the bishops make a contribution of nearly a million lire, thus freeing the state treasury of the burden of supporting poor parish priests. Cavour refused to accept the compromise and offered his resignation, which the King accepted on April 28, 1855.

Much more than the career of one man was at stake. The King's attitude threatened alienation of the liberals from the monarchy. Such an eventuality not only would put the entire constitutional order in danger but would discredit Piedmont in the eyes of all Italian liberals, with the effect of undermining Piedmont's Italian primacy and the hopes of many nationalists that Piedmont would lead the future struggle for independence and unity. This, at least, was the fear shared by many. Cavour wrote to Massimo d'Azeglio on April 29 that the latter prevail upon the King "to ward off the danger of a sordid intrigue of priests and bigots ruining the country." [4] D'Azeglio had already sought an audience with the King to persuade him to reject the bishop's compromise and retain Cavour in power. But when denied access to the Court he had recourse to a letter full of anguish and pleading, a letter which d'Azeglio subsequently described as having helped put the ship of state on its right course once again.

It is difficult to evaluate the influence of d'Azeglio's letter on the King's eventual decision to ask Cavour to return to office. Apparently Victor Emmanuel was persuaded that Cavour was indispensable and that the ultraclerical party had gone too far. Upon his return to power Cavour, on his part, made the King's position easier by agreeing to some moderating amendments to the congregations bill, which was then passed by the Senate and approved by the Chamber of Deputies in its amended form at the end of May. In July Pope Pius IX issued a papal allocution which condemned the congregations law and excommunicated all those who had proposed, approved, or sanctioned it. The issuance of this religious penalty was but a signal of an ever-growing conflict between the Papacy and most of the men who were eventually to lead Piedmont in its role as unifier of Italy.

Wittingly or unwittingly, this role had been assumed in the fall of 1854, precisely at the time of the introduction of the congregations bill. Piedmont had then begun negotiating a treaty of alliance with England and France with a view to its entry into the Crimean War against Russia. It was the prospect of this participation which weighed so heavily in the decision to resolve the congregations question in a manner satisfactory to Parliament and the active liberal forces in the country.

[4] Chiala, *Lettere*, II, 108–9.

15. PIEDMONT IN THE CRIMEAN WAR: THE ASCENDANCY OF FOREIGN POLICY

Apart from the desire to redeem Piedmont's military reputation, much damaged by the defeats of 1848–49, the reason for the determination of the Piedmontese government to play a role in the Crimean War was the desire to achieve the status of the leading Italian power. This could best be done by participating in a successful war on the side of two major European powers, England and France, and with the exclusion of Austrian participation. The implicit and necessary assumption in any step leading to Piedmontese primacy in Italy was the eventual elimination of Austrian influence in the peninsula. From the purely Piedmontese point of view Austrian influence in Italy was not only a constant reminder of the Piedmontese failures of 1848–49 but also a constant threat to truly independent Piedmontese policies both in foreign and domestic affairs. Inasmuch as Austrian influence was also the greatest barrier to the independence and unification of all of Italy, it developed that Piedmont's anti-Austrian attitude coincided perfectly with the cause of Italian unification. Had this coincidence of interests not been so complete, it is doubtful that Piedmont would have risked two wars in 1855 and 1859 solely for the sake of Italian unification. Furthermore, had Piedmont not successfully established a reputation of being a liberal and reforming state, it is even more doubtful that it could have rallied the support of liberals and even democrats all over Italy.

Toward the end of 1854 England and France invited Piedmont to join them in a treaty of alliance and participate in the Crimean War. The Piedmontese Foreign Minister, General Giuseppe Dabormida, insisted on a number of conditions directed against Austria: specifically, that Piedmont be treated as an equal at the eventual peace conference, that the Italian question be debated at the conference, and that the allied governments press Austria to end the confiscation of the property of political refugees from Lombardy who had been given asylum in Piedmont. Fearing to antagonize Austria, whose aid they still hoped for in the war, England and France rejected these conditions. Inasmuch as Cavour was willing to enter into the alliance without any conditions, Dabormida resigned; Cavour took his place as Foreign Minister in January 1855 and immediately signed the treaty.

When the treaty was presented to Parliament for debate and approval in February 1855 it was opposed, ironically, by both the extreme Left and the extreme Right on the grounds that Piedmont had yielded to foreign pressure and that, given the presumed likelihood of Austrian participation in the war on the side of the Western alliance, Piedmont would find itself fighting side by side with Austria. Furthermore, the extreme Left argued that Piedmont needed to save all its forces in defense of the cause of Italian unity and not to fight for the sake of Turkish interests and possibly on the side of Austria. This last eventuality was feared by the Left as a step in the possible abandonment of Piedmont's espousal of Italian independence. Cavour replied that in joining the alliance the government had acted freely and in the interests not only of Piedmont but of all Italy. The following excerpts from a speech of February 6, 1855, make clear both the open and unspoken reasons which moved Cavour to enter the Crimean War.

Cavour's Speech to the Chamber of Deputies Justifying the Alliance with England and France and the Projected Participation in the Crimean War, February 6, 1855

Cavour, *Discorsi parlamentari,* IX, 90–91, 111–12, 115–17. Our translation.

Gentlemen, first of all the government considered whether or not the war being fought in the East was of real interest to our country, whether or not we had a material political interest in taking part in it and in cooperating with the aims that the Western powers sought to achieve. We did not have much difficulty in concluding that Sardinia was highly interested in the aims of the present war. In fact, gentlemen, if the present war were to end happily for Russia, if it were to bring the victorious eagles of the Czar to Constantinople, clearly Russia would thereby acquire absolute dominion in the Mediterranean and an irresistible preponderance in the councils of Europe.

Well, gentlemen, either of the two consequences would have to be considered as fatal to the interests of Piedmont and all of Italy. . . .

It is my opinion that if Russia were to acquire an irresistible influence in the councils of Europe, our country, our institutions, our nationality would run a most grave risk. The history of the last forty years shows you that Russia has always exercised its very great influence in fighting all liberal tendencies and in repressing every effort at popular emancipation. . . .

It is said that Austria is allied with these two nations [England and France]. And what of it? . . . . If it were ever to happen that in the course of events our flag were to find itself not far from that of Austria, I would say that it is Austria that will have changed its principles, not us.

But perhaps the Honorable Deputy Brofferio [Angelo, a leader of the democratic or extreme Left] and those who maintain that our accession to the treaty must bring with it a change in the policies of our country, think that we have given in to solicitations, counsels, invitations, and pressures from foreign powers. . . . I believe it my duty to declare forcefully that we have entered into the alliance . . . with our principles and beliefs unchanged, without disavowing any of our past actions nor any of our future aspirations. . . .

Is our joining the alliance injurious or useful to Italy? This is the point to resolve, the question to answer. I believe I can reply without hesitation that our joining the alliance is most useful to Italy. . . .

Gentlemen, I believe that the principal condition for the improvement of Italy's fortunes—the condition that stands above all others—is to improve its reputation, to see to it that all the peoples of the world, governors and governed alike, acknowledge its good qualities. To do this two things are necessary: first, to prove to Europe that Italy has enough civil virtue to govern itself regularly under a regime of liberty and that it is able to adopt the most perfect forms of government yet known; second, that its military valor is equal to that of its ancestors.

Your conduct during the past seven years has rendered this service to Italy: it has shown the world in the clearest fashion that Italians know how to govern themselves with wisdom, prudence, and loyalty. It is now up to you to render it an equal if not greater service. It is up to our country to show that the sons of Italy know how to fight with valor on the fields of glory. And I am certain, gentlemen, that the laurels our soldiers will earn in the East will profit more the fortunes of Italy than have the efforts of all those who have sought to achieve its regeneration with declamations and writings.

Cavour's Assessment of the Paris Peace Congress

After Parliament's approval of the treaty in March 1855, Cavour had his way and Piedmont entered the war with an expedition of 15,000 men to the Crimea. But Cavour's political position at home was not strong. He barely survived permanent exclusion from the government at the end of April 1855 over the congregations bill and had been recalled to office unwillingly by the King because no effective substitute was available. The war was not popular in Piedmont, and a military defeat in the Crimea could easily have been Cavour's political undoing. Fortunately, the Piedmontese expeditionary corps acquitted itself well in the battle of Chernaia on August 16, 1855, a victory which Cavour considered as washing away the stain of the disaster of Novara in March 1849. But the news of Sebastopol's fall to the Western allies in September made him unhappy at first because the Piedmontese had not participated in this success and because he feared that it might mean the rapid end of the war. Cavour wanted the war to continue in order to achieve even greater military successes and to make Austria's position more difficult. In fact, Austrian diplomacy succeeded in putting itself in a most difficult situation during the Crimean War. On the one hand, Austria was indebted to Russia for the latter's help in crushing the Hungarian revolt of 1849; on the other hand, it could not favor a major Russian victory and the consequent dismemberment of the Ottoman empire. Such a victory would jeopardize Austrian interests in the Balkans and upset the delicate balance of power in the area. Finally, the longer the war lasted the greater Piedmont's favor with the Western powers would be, whereas Austria's continued neutrality, in spite of a vague alliance with England and France, would diminish Austria's favor with all the belligerents. It was to Austria's interest to have the war end as quickly as possible and to exclude Piedmont from any important role at the eventual peace conference. To these two ends Austria pressed Russia to agree to end the war early in 1856 and, on the other hand, persuaded England and France to limit Piedmont's participation to those phases of the peace conference which pertained solely and specifically to Piedmont. Were such a limitation to stand, there would be little for Piedmont to do or say at the peace conference; and Cavour's principal aims for entering the war, that is, the extraction of some territorial concessions for Piedmont in northern Italy and the presentation of the Italian question before a world forum would all come to naught.

The Peace Congress ending the Crimean War was convened in Paris toward the end of February 1856. During Cavour's earlier visit to Paris in December 1855 Napoleon III had asked him to write down "that which you believe I can do for Piedmont and for Italy." When the Congress was convened, one thing the French emperor did do was to facilitate Piedmont's participation on equal terms with Austria and all the belligerents. But he was not able to persuade Austria to cede Lombardy and Venetia to Piedmont in exchange for the Danubian principalities of Walachia and Moldavia or to agree to any other territorial changes in Italy in favor of Piedmont. The other assistance Napoleon was able to give was to assure the discussion of the international and domestic conditions of the Italian states—the Italian question—but only after the signing of the peace treaty with Russia on March 30, 1856. In short, as the following letters demonstrate, the Peace Congress and the war it concluded brought neither Piedmont nor Italy any material gains. But the willingness of the French and English representatives to denounce the misgovernment of the Papal States and the Kingdom of the Two Sicilies and Napoleon's growing conviction that only war could persuade Austria to accept changes in the Italian peninsula, all confirm Cavour's judgment that something positive had been accomplished.

LETTER TO URBANO RATTAZZI, MINISTER OF THE INTERIOR, FROM PARIS, APRIL 9, 1856. Chiala, *Lettere*, II, 214–15. Our translation.

The Italian question was discussed at the Congress in yesterday's session. Walewski [French representative at the Congress] was clearly embarrassed in speaking of the papal government and was very weak in his replies to the energetic protests of Buol [Austrian representative]. He was much more explicit with regard to Naples and spoke of its government with sharp criticism. . . .

Clarendon [British representative] was most energetic, with regard to both the Pope and the King of Naples. He called the government of the former the worst that has ever existed; as for the latter, he characterized it as Massari * would have done. . . .

At the end of the session I said [to Clarendon]: "My lord, you can see that there is nothing to hope for from diplomacy. It is time to employ other means, at least as regards the King of Naples." He replied: "We must do something about Naples and soon." . . . .

Something must be done. Italy cannot remain in its present condition. Napoleon is convinced of this, and if diplomacy is powerless, let us have recourse to extralegal means. Although I am moderate in my opinions, I am rather favorable to extreme and bold means. I believe that in this century boldness is frequently the best policy. It profited Napoleon; it may profit us as well.

CAVOUR'S LETTER TO GENERAL ALFONSO LA MARMORA, COMMANDER OF THE PIEDMONTESE EXPEDITIONARY CORPS IN THE CRIMEA, FROM PARIS, APRIL 13, 1856. Chiala, *Lettere*, II, 221–23. Our translation.

If the positive and material results of the Congress are zero, I do not thereby believe that one can say that the Congress was fruitless. It is a fact of great importance for France and England to have acknowl-

* Giuseppe Massari (1821–84), Neapolitan subject very critical of the Bourbon government in the Two Sicilies. Ed. note.

edged in an explicit and open manner that conditions in Italy are very bad and that Europe's interest requires that they be improved. Also very important is the acknowledgment that this improvement cannot be realized except by the aggrandizement of Piedmont. . . .

All the French generals speak to me with praise for you and our soldiers. We have gained much from the point of view of military prestige. This is something which will be very useful to us.

LETTER BY CAVOUR TO THE DEPUTY MICHELANGELO CAS-TELLI, FROM PARIS, APRIL 1856. Chiala, *Lettere*, II, 227. Our translation.

I cannot go into details but I assure you that we have no cause for complaining of the emperor. France wanted peace; he had to make it; and therefore he had to ask for Austria's cooperation. Consequently, he could not treat Austria as an enemy power. Rather, up to a certain point he was forced to treat her as an ally. In such circumstances he could not use threats regarding the Italian question. Only exhortations were possible. These were employed and were without effect. Buol * proved unmovable in big as well as in little matters. Although this tenacity is to Italy's damage at present, it will end up as an advantage in the future. The emperor is most irritated by it and does not hide the fact. The other evening he said to me: "Austria does not wish to cooperate in anything. She is ready to make war rather than agree to the cession of Parma to you. Now, at this moment I cannot present her with a *casus belli;* but never fear, I have the premonition that the present peace will not last long."

The emperor proposed that Austria take the Danubian principalities in exchange for Lombardy and Venetia, and in my presence said to Clarendon: "It is the only reasonable solution to the Italian problem." This is enough to prove the emperor's good intentions and also the need not to irritate him with epigrams that are useless and which may do great harm.

* Buol-Schauenstein, Austria's representative at the Congress. Ed. note.

VI. THE WARS AND REVOLUTIONS OF NATIONAL LIBERATION

16. THE RALLYING OF NATIONAL PUBLIC OPINION

Cavour's concern with the need not to irritate Napoleon derived from the fact that Italians of democratic persuasion saw the failure of the Paris Peace Congress to accomplish anything positive for Italy as proof of their contention that nothing could be hoped for from the man who had crushed both the Roman and the French republics. This contention was expressed in print and the French emperor was not long in learning of it. It was Cavour's task both to prevent the emperor from being annoyed by Italian criticism of his policies and at the same time to exploit this criticism to Piedmont's and Italy's advantage. Cavour's resolution of the problem was a clear restatement of the views of Cesare Balbo and Massimo d'Azeglio: Italian radicalism was the product of the repressive regimes which existed in the peninsula; only moderate and constitutional government could succeed in mitigating and containing this radicalism within the limits imposed by the need for order; and only Piedmont had succeeded in establishing this kind of government. Consequently, all those who wished to avoid revolution in Italy would have to promote the making of Piedmontese constitutionalism hegemonic throughout the peninsula. But to make this thesis convincing Cavour had to prove that the Piedmontese cause was not provincial and limited to a corner of the peninsula. He had to show that moderates throughout Italy were prepared to rally around Piedmont. In short, he had to show that the cause of Italian nationalism was disposed to follow a moderate course and the Piedmontese banner.

In this enterprise help came from an unexpected quarter. Daniele Manin, formerly an ardent republican and the leader of the Venetians in 1848–49 during their heroic struggle against the Austrians, announced in 1855 his willingness to submerge his republican preferences for the sake of unification. Within a year Garibaldi made the same sacrifice. And on August 1, 1857, the Italian National Society was born with the Venetian Manin as its president, Garibaldi of Nice soon to become vice-president, and the Sicilian Giuseppe La Farina as secretary.

The following excerpts from a recent study by Raymond Grew present an assessment of the important role played by the Italian National Society in the creation and direction of a national public opinion in Italy during the years immediately preceding unification.

An Assessment of the Importance of the Italian National Society

> Raymond Grew, *A Sterner Plan for Italian Unity: The Italian National Society in the Risorgimento.* Princeton: Princeton University Press, 1963, pp. x–xi, 473–74. Original footnotes omitted.

Above all [the Society] was a movement of opinion. Its formation was the most dramatic sign that republicans were turning to Cavour, that nationalists would accept unification under Piedmontese monarchy, that the era of Mazzini was really over. Because it drew increasingly close to Cavour and even claimed to be an instrument of his policy, the history of the National Society becomes an important measure of what Cavour's policy really was. Nearly every argument about the nature of Cavour's nationalism or about the skill and intent of his political manipulations rests in some part on one's views of the Society.

From 1857 to 1862, the Society published a newspaper, first a weekly, then a daily. Its circulation was national, for even before the war of 1859 it was smuggled across the borders into the petty states it sought to eliminate. The Society had, in addition, connections with other influential newspapers; it published a number of pamphlets which were distributed in thousands of copies, and its committees issued hundreds of manifestoes. It was the Society, more than any other agency, which developed and broadcast the dominant ideas of the "high" Risorgimento. In the National Society one finds the ideology of the Risorgimento in practice, the set of ideas—just below the level of political theory—in terms of which Italian nationalists conceived the unification they were bringing about.

Organized through local committees across the Peninsula, the Society's membership provides an indication of who Italy's monarchical nationalists were, where they were numerous and how they were effective. . . .

Without the National Society, or some agency to accomplish what it did, Italy could hardly have been united in the middle of the nineteenth century. This proposition can be roughly tested even in the concrete realm of the events themselves. Would Piedmont have been willing to run such risks without the assurances the Society and its propaganda provided that she had a following throughout the Peninsula? Would Cavour's dispassionate designs have been sufficiently trusted outside Piedmont to prevent dissension to the point of disaster in 1859 and 1860? Would the war of 1859 have been clearly enough a national one to hold France in check and to keep British sympathy? Would revolution have spread so far so safely? Would the provisional regimes of 1859 have gained so easily the aura of popularity? Without the appearance of agreement the Society presented, could Garibaldi have been used effectively by the moderates or Cavour have triumphed over him? Would the plebiscites have been risked or the elections so open as they were? It seems unlikely.

Certainly, Italian unification without the National Society would not even have seemed a national experience shared by patriots everywhere. The Society allowed thousands of politically conscious Italians who would otherwise have felt excluded to have a part in making Italy. Without its guidance, their desire for change might have erupted in isolated bursts, been dissipated and lost as a political force.

It gave Cavour invaluable aid by providing apparent popular sanction for his policies, while at the same time serving as the guarantor to nationalists of Cavour's patriotic intent. The SNI [Società nazionale italiana] may even have acted as something of a pressure on Cavour, pushing him to a more nationalist policy; certainly it provided him with a useful justification abroad. If Cavour seems not to have relied very heavily on the Society, its effects are apparent in his expectation of greater popular sacrifice than there was in central Italy in 1859, in Naples and the Marches in 1860.

The desire for a unified nation, an abstraction only tenuously attached to more specific programs, became the central theme of Italian political life. If the changes unification brought benefitted primarily one fraction of Italians, that was disguised as a few became the voice of a nation.

The National Society stood as the most striking evidence contemporaries had that Italians did want unification—evidence which its propaganda made more impressive. More than 4,000 men, perhaps twice that number, joined the Society from 1857 to 1864. This means that nearly everyone in Italian life who could vote or could influence those who voted must have had some contact with the SNI, some exposure to its ideas; a sizable number of the politically significant were moved to join the Italian National Society. It was largely in the Society's terms that the Risorgimento was understood by the respectable core of Cavourians who were indispensable to its success.

One man who found it impossible to reconcile himself with Cavour and the monarchy was Mazzini, the symbol incarnate of republicanism. In 1857 Mazzini left the safety of his London exile and returned to Piedmontese territory, where a sentence of death awaited him if caught by the authorities. There he led in the planning of a great conspiracy designed to raise the people of the Two Sicilies against the Bourbons and a supporting conspiracy in Genoa. Both enterprises were initiated early in the summer and both came to a calamitous end. But even in failure, Mazzini caused Cavour grave difficulties. The Piedmontese conservatives held Cavour and his Minister of the Interior, Rattazzi, responsible for Mazzini's activities. Rattazzi was especially vulnerable because of his radical past, and his alleged weakness in preventing Mazzini's conspiracies played a role in the victory of the conservatives during the elections of November 1857. Cavour found himself obliged to sacrifice Rattazzi, whose resignation was accepted by the King on January 13, 1858. The next day there occurred an event which almost shattered the cause of moderation and, by consequence, the cause of rallying national and international opinion around Piedmont's Italian primacy.

On January 14 Felice Orsini (formerly a long-time follower of Mazzini but in 1858 no longer among his disciples) hurled several bombs at the carriage bearing Napoleon III and his wife to the Paris Opera. The emperor and the empress escaped serious injury; scores of bystanders were less fortunate. The reasons for the attempt were Orsini's rage at Napoleon's role in the destruction of the Roman republic in 1849 and his alleged obstruction of the cause of Italian independence. It has also been suggested that Orsini sought to frighten Napoleon into doing something for Italy, but this speculation does not face the fact that had Orsini's attempt on Napoleon's life succeeded, the help desired from the French emperor would have been made impossible.

Orsini's act endangered not only Cavour's hopes for French aid in an eventual war against Austria but also the entire cause of political moderation in Italy. The emperor's demand, after the attempt on his life, that the Piedmontese government restrict freedom of the press in order to curb those newspapers that seemed to subscribe and incite to political assassination ("theory of the dagger") placed Cavour in a most difficult position. Were he to accede, or even appear to accede, to this demand he would jeopardize the support of many liberals and certainly of those Italian democrats and republicans who were beginning to turn toward the Piedmontese monarchy. Cavour refused the French request that he suppress the Mazzinian newspaper *Italia e Popolo,* arguing that such a step was unconstitutional. Victor Emmanuel, in turn, was outraged by Napoleon's threat that unless Piedmont corrected its ineptitude and weakness in dealing with anti-French agitation, Napoleon would feel obliged to abandon his plans to help the cause of Italian independence and reconcile himself with Austria. The Piedmontese King instructed his special envoy to Paris, General Enrico Morozzo della Rocca, to deliver the following message: "Say to the emperor in the language you think most appropriate that this is not the way to treat a faithful ally; that I have never tolerated violence from anyone; that I follow always and without stain the road of honor; and that for this honor I am answerable only to God and my people. [Say to him] that for 850 years we have carried our head high and that no one shall make me lower it; and that with all this, I wish nothing more than to be his friend." [1]

Napoleon may have been impressed by the proud tone of the Savoyard's message. He was probably more impressed by the fact that within eight days the Piedmontese government presented Parliament with a bill providing penalties for conspiring against the life of foreign sovereigns and heads of government and for encouragement by the press of political assassination. The bill also imposed restrictions on the selection of juries. The Left attacked the bill as an act of submission to Napoleon, and the Right appeared to gloat on the fact that the government's previously liberal policies had brought it to this pass. Indeed, the parliamentary committee chosen to examine the bill reported for its rejection. It is a tribute to Cavour's power of persuasion that he was able to have the bill passed in both Chambers by large majorities. His reasoning was clear and simple: the Italians could not solve the Italian question by themselves alone; they needed the aid of foreign powers. Such powers could not be antagonized by conspiracies and incitation to political assassination from an intemperate press. Consequently, the proposed bill, whose moral and political propriety he asserted, should be passed. These points are implied or made explicit in the following speech, which is famous for Cavour's violent attack on the Mazzinians and his revelation of a plot against the life of Victor Emmanuel.

Cavour Defends His Policies and Attacks the Mazzinians:
Speech of April 16, 1858 before the Chamber of Deputies

Cavour, *Discorsi parlamentari,* X, 467–68, 472–77, *passim.* Our translation.

At the beginning of this year the political horizon did not seem

[1] Chiala, *Lettere,* II, 300–1, note.

dark . . . and then there came the attempt of January 14. This attempt produced an immense commotion in France, not only among its rulers but also among the entire nation. . . .

It was therefore natural that the French government should seek ways to prevent the repetition of such acts, and to this end it . . . addressed itself to all neighboring and friendly powers for measures to prevent the repetition of this misdeed. . . .

While we [the Piedmontese government] were discussing projects and measures most suitable for reaching the goal we sought in agreement with the French government, a tribunal in Turin announced the acquittal of the newspaper *La Ragione*, which had been tried for publishing an article deemed by the Public Prosecutor to be an apology of the attempt of January 14.

This acquittal made a most grave impression in the country and abroad. (*Signs of agitation.*) We had to be much concerned with the acquittal both because of the effect it produced and because of the consequences that could follow from it. After due examination of the political situation we decided to present . . . a bill for the punishment of conspiracies, for the better definition of the crime of defending and justifying regicide, and for a reform in the selection of the semestral jury list.

I wish to speak with complete frankness. I say to you that our decision was influenced chiefly by two political considerations. At this point, gentlemen, I enter into the most delicate and thorny part of my speech and for this reason I have need of all your indulgence. (*Signs of attention.*)

After 1831 there was formed in and outside Italy a sect which, motivated by ardently patriotic sentiments, sought the achievement of independence. Owing to the absolute absence of freedom in Italy and because of the sect's generous proposals, manifested with uncommon intelligence, it was able to attract to its ranks a large part of bold Italian youth. This sect is Young Italy. Even before 1848 it had lost a part of its following because of the failure of its efforts. And when the era of reforms began in Italy, another part of its following sided and united with the party which believed that it could achieve the betterment of the nation's lot through peaceful means. Nevertheless, when the events of 1848 occurred its following was numerous.

I shall not repeat here the story of the part this sect played in the events of that time. I do not wish to begin a debate over past events, nor do I wish to engage in recriminations. I shall limit myself to expressing my firm conviction that the opposition of this sect to King Charles Albert contributed substantially to the sad results of our military efforts. (*Signs of approval.*)

However it may be, when that epoch of glory and misfortune came to an end, when in 1849 all the old regimes were reestablished in Italy, when the sect had to abandon all Italian provinces and withdraw abroad, it found itself if not diminished in ranks certainly much more gloomy and embittered in spirit and resolved upon the most sinister enterprises.

And, in fact, gentlemen, this sect was seen to change its doctrines little by little and proclaim as legitimate those means which before 1848 had inspired a just horror among the sectarians themselves. . . .

Consequently, after the events of Milan [1853], after some other attempts no less foolish and no less criminal, we see this sect in its writings getting closer little by little to theories justifying more explicitly the practice of political assassination. . . .

It is a great harm for Italy to have people abroad able to say: There is in that country a sect which professes the doctrine of political assassination. But what is more serious and painful, gentlemen, is the fact that these wretched doctrines find in the peninsula a soil in some way prepared to receive them. . . .

Well, gentlemen, we thought that inasmuch as there is a sect which professes the doctrine of political assassination, inasmuch as there are people who, perhaps because of the fault of others, are inclined to apply these doctrines, we thought that in the interest of Piedmont and all of Italy it was necessary (*much emphasis*) that in the sole Italian state governed under a regime of liberty there should be heard the strong voice not only of the government but also of the nation as represented by Parliament, and that this voice protest solemnly and energetically against the villainous doctrine of political assassination. (*Strong signs of approval from all sides of the Chamber.*)

This is the first political motive which led us to present the bill before you.

Gentlemen, there is another motive, even more painful than the first. (*Signs of attention.*)

After the attempt of January 14 this government received information from various parts of Europe that the sectarians, stimulated by the event in Paris, were more impassioned than ever, and that there was talk in their conventicles not only of resuming their execrable work but of extending it to other heads of government. It was no longer a question of the Emperor of France alone; it involved a sovereign of much more immediate interest to us.* (*Sensation in the Chamber.*). . . .

In considering the consequences which might follow in the event of our failure to take appropriate measures, it did not escape us that a reaction could occur if the country came to know that under a Ministry which called itself liberal nothing had been done to strike at an infamous doctrine threatening the life of our King. Gentlemen, the masses are not always reasonable. And when for legitimate reasons they are repeatedly aroused, a profound and uncontrollable reaction could develop not only against us but also against the entire liberal party. (*Very good!*)

This, gentlemen, is the second political consideration that prompted us to present the bill before you.

I believe that no one can construe this bill as resulting from foreign pressure. No one can construe it as anything other than an action conforming with sentiments of dignity and duty. No, there was no pressure; or, if there was, it was the kind of pressure before which the most honest men must bow: the pressure of our conscience. (*Very good! Bravo!*)

Cavour's terrible charge against Mazzini and his party could not go unanswered. The great "apostle" replied to the Piedmontese Prime Minister with equally terrible language, and in so doing revealed the chasm dividing the two approaches to independence and unity. If ever there had been a chance of reconciliation between the two men and the views they espoused, Cavour's speech and Mazzini's reply diminished this chance to the point of extinction. Cavour profited from the exchange and with him profited the cause of a moderate monarchy moderately united. But something was lost by the alienation of those two men, and this loss was not to benefit the subsequent course of Italian history.

* Cavour had received information from the Swiss government that an attempt was being planned on his life and that of Victor Emmanuel. Ed. note.

Mazzini's Reply to Cavour's Accusations, June 1858

Giuseppe Mazzini, *Politica* (Vol. LIX of *Scritti editi ed inediti*. Edizione nazionale.) Imola: Paolo Galeati, 1931, XX, 289–90, 295, 320, 331–32. Our translation.

Sir,

For a long time I have known you to be much more devoted to the Piedmontese monarchy than to our common fatherland; a materialist worshiper much more of *fact* than of any sacred and eternal principle; a man of intellect more astute than profound; a promoter of under-handed parties and, because of patrician temperament and innate tendencies, adverse to liberty. But I did not believe you to be a slanderer. You have now shown yourself to be such. In your speech of April 16 you have slandered, for the sake of a grievous end, an entire party that by your own admission is devoted to national independence and unity. . . .

By the use of obscene libels from foreign police you have exhumed to your own discredit the charge of the theory of the dagger, a theory unknown to Italy. Knowing that lies could increase the votes in your favor, you have declared to the Chamber that the proposed liberticide law was intended to protect the life of Victor Emmanuel, allegedly threatened by us. And cowardly, you hurled this accusation as nothing more than a political device in order possibly to free yourself from the stain of submissive surrender to the emperor of France. Therefore, if before this I did not like you, now I despise you. Until now you were only an enemy, now you are a base and unbecoming enemy. . . .

Do you take us for villains and madmen? To whom and to what could the death of Victor Emmanuel ever profit? He reigns but does not rule. His indifferent but not tyrannical temperament may earn him the reproof of persons who remember what solemn duties he could but does not care to discharge; hatred for him, never. I believe him to be better than his Ministers, and I regret only the fact that this is not saying much. We would loathe as an assassin whoever were to kill him. . . .

In the meanwhile, in order to gratify a foreign despot, you mutilate the freedom of the state . . . you stamp on the forehead of the only Italian people representing before Europe the seed of our future the shame of an alliance with the man who killed freedom in his own country and who in Rome mowed down the flower of our youth. . . .

Sir, between you and us here is an abyss. Ours are two radically different programs. . . . We represent Italy; you represent the old, greedy, and timid ambition of the house of Savoy.

Above all, we want national unity; you seek only territorial aggrandizement for the royal domains in northern Italy. You oppose unity because you despair of conquering and dominating it.

We believe in the initiative of the Italian people; you fear it and seek all ways to prevent it. . . .

We believe that once the nation comes into being it should be free to choose the institutions to govern it. You deny national sovereignty and make acceptance of the monarchy an overriding condition for any help in the enterprise. . . .

We worship one faith, the NATIONAL FAITH; one principle, the republican and popular PRINCIPLE; one policy, the bold and continuous expression by word and deed of Italian RIGHTS. You bend your knee before force, before the treaties of 1815, before despotism, to anything, so long as it is supported by *big battalions.* You have neither morality nor faith.

We accuse you; you slander us.

Italy will judge between you and us.

Italy's final judgment is not clear or is as yet undelivered. The immediate judgment was unfavorable to Mazzini, as is shown by the growth of the Italian National Society. Even more immediate was the judgment given by Napoleon III. Pleased by the attitude of the Piedmontese government, Napoleon forgot the threats he had made to Victor Emmanuel at the beginning of the year, and in July 1858 took the first concrete step toward the realization of his promise "to do something for Italy." This step took the form of a secret meeting between the emperor and Cavour at Plombières, in eastern France. From the agreements reached at Plombières there was to come within a year the second Piedmontese war against Austria and the beginning of the revolutions of national liberation.

17. THE SECOND WAR AGAINST AUSTRIA AND THE REVOLUTIONS OF NATIONAL LIBERATION

At Napoleon's invitation, Cavour met secretly with him on July 20, 1858 in Plombières, a resort in the Vosges Mountains. There the two statesmen discussed what Napoleon "could do for Piedmont and Italy" and after an eight-hour colloquy agreed on the following points: Piedmont was to provoke Austria into declaring war by promoting agitations in Austrian-protected Massa-Carrara; Austria's "aggression" would justify French support of Piedmont in expelling the Austrians from all Italy; a Kingdom of Upper Italy would be formed under the house of Savoy; the Pope would retain Rome and its environs; a portion of the Papal States and all of Tuscany would be formed into a central Italian Kingdom; the Kingdom of the Two Sicilies was to remain undisturbed; and the resulting four Italian states were to form a federation under the presidency of the Pope. In repayment of French aid, Piedmont was to cede Savoy to France and the possible cession of Nice was left open for future consideration. There was also considered the possible marriage of Victor Emmanuel's daughter, Clotilde, to Napoleon's cousin, Prince Jerome Napoleon.[2]

The Plombières agreement put Cavour in a state of exaltation at the prospect of a second war against Austria. This prospect received signal confirmation on January 1, 1859, when Napoleon, at a New Year's reception for the diplomatic corps, said to the Austrian ambassador in Paris, Baron Hübner: "I regret that our relations with your government are not so good as formerly. [But] I pray you to tell the Emperor [Franz Joseph] that my personal feelings toward him are unchanged."[3]

Within nine days of Napoleon's foreboding remarks to Baron Hübner, Victor Emmanuel delivered a speech before the Piedmontese Parliament which further aggravated the portent of Napoleon's words. This speech is especially important because it was prepared with the emperor's approval and editorial assistance.

"Italy's Cry of Anguish": Victor Emmanuel's Speech to the Piedmontese Parliament, January 10, 1859

Cappelletti, *Storia di Vittorio Emanuele II*, II, 6. Our translation.

Senators, Deputies:

The new year begins under troubled skies. Nevertheless, you will set about your parliamentary duties with customary dispatch.

Comforted by the experience of the past, we go forward with resolution toward future eventualities.

This future will be happy, our policy being based on justice and on the love of freedom and of the fatherland.

[2] Chiala, *Lettere*, II, 321–27; cf. Antonin Debidour, *Histoire diplomatique de l'Europe, 1814–1878* (2 vols.; Paris, F. Alcan, 1891), II, 178.
[3] Debidour, *Histoire diplomatique*, II, 185.

Although small in territory, our country has acquired prestige in the councils of Europe because it is great for the ideas it represents and for the sympathies it arouses.

This condition is not free of danger because, although we respect treaties incurred, *we are not indifferent to the cry of anguish directed toward us from so many parts of Italy.*

Strong in our internal harmony and trusting in our rights, prudent and decided we await the decrees of divine Providence.

In a letter of January 11, 1859, Cavour explained to the Piedmontese Minister in Switzerland that the true meaning of the King's speech was to place Austria in an impasse from which it could not escape except by recourse to war. "We must not announce war as our policy. We must not even show that we want it. But we must show that it is the inevitable consequence of Austrian policy." [4]

Cavour knew that the English government was much annoyed with him for forcing it to choose between its earlier sympathy for the Italian cause and its current tendency to favor Austria as a check to Russia. But he trusted in French support and, to a lesser extent, in that of Russia. Depite Piedmontese participation in the Crimean War against it, Russia was more hostile to Austria than to Piedmont and held Austria guilty of ingratitude for not helping in the war after Russian assistance to Austria helped crush the Hungarian revolution in 1849. Cavour also informed his representative in Switzerland that in the event Austria were to receive the support of Prussia, everything would have to be done to bring Switzerland into the war on Piedmont's side.

Cavour's confidence in France's support seemed confirmed when a few days later Prince Jerome Napoleon, cousin of the emperor, came to Piedmont to sign a treaty incorporating the principal points of the Plombières agreement and to prepare for his marriage with the Piedmontese Princess Clotilde. Although the treaty remained secret, the marriage was public and its implications were obvious. A law authorizing the Piedmontese government to negotiate a loan of 50 million lire and the not too secret recruitment of volunteers from all over Italy made even clearer by February and March 1859 what Piedmont's intentions were. The corps of volunteers, eventually known as the *Cacciatori delle Alpi* [Alpine Chasseurs] was put under the command of Garibaldi, whose offer of services was accepted by Cavour and who was given the rank of major general in the Piedmontese army. Never able to reconcile himself with Mazzini, Cavour found it easier to work with the less doctrinaire Garibaldi. This most fruitful collaboration was another indication of the success of the Italian National Society—of which Garibaldi was the vice-president—in persuading many Italians to abandon at least for

[4] Chiala, *Lettere*, III, 9–12.

the moment their personal political preferences for the sake of the common cause.

Suddenly the prospects for the Piedmontese and Italian cause became very dark. The British government made an attempt to reconcile Piedmont and Austria in order to prevent a war which in the event of an Austrian defeat could disturb Europe's balance of power too much in favor of France and Russia. Failing in its efforts at reconciliation, England promoted the calling of an international Congress and a program of general disarmament. Cavour acceded unwillingly to England's proposals. But Austria seemed intent on humiliating Piedmont and insisted both on the exclusion of all Italian states from the projected Congress and on immediate Piedmontese disarmament. Cavour's spirits were immediately revived when, on April 23, Austria sent Piedmont an ultimatum requesting a reply within three days to the Austrian demands that Piedmont return its armed forces to peacetime status and disband all Italian volunteer units. In substance, this ultimatum fulfilled the provision of the Franco-Piedmontese treaty conditioning French assistance on Austrian aggression. On the day the ultimatum expired, April 26, Cavour informed the Austrian representative that Piedmont had accepted the British disarmament proposals, that he had nothing further to add, and that responsibility for future events would fall on Austria's shoulders. It was a clear enough rejection of the Austrian demands. The second Piedmontese war against Austria had begun. But this time Piedmont was not "to go it alone"; it had the brief but effective help of a major power and the longer and also effective help of a large number of Italians. In spite of the heartbreaks and uncertainties to come during the next year and a half, the road to independence and unity had finally been found.

On April 27, the day after Piedmont's break with Austria, the Florentines rose against their grand duke and forced him to leave his domains. Piedmont immediately assumed a protectorate over Tuscany and reappointed its ambassador in Florence, Carlo Boncompagni, as its Commissioner for Tuscan lands. Following upon the victory at Magenta over the Austrians early in June, the duchies of Parma and Modena also rose against their princes and expressed their desire for union with Piedmont. Piedmontese Commissioners were sent to both states, and the same was done in Romagna, where a rising had occurred upon the withdrawal of the Austrian garrison from this portion of the Papal States. Underlying all these risings was to be seen the work of the Italian National Society and the secret encouragement of Cavour.

If Piedmont were able to retain control over all these lands the result would be a far greater Kingdom of Upper Italy than Napoleon had bargained for at Plombières. This and other considerations weighed heavily on Napoleon's decision to agree to an armistice with the Austrians. The awful slaughter at the battles of Magenta and Solferino and an epidemic of typhus among the troops made the war increasingly unpopular in France, where Catholic opinion's concern for the safety and temporal power of the Pope grew with the Franco-Piedmontese successes. Austria's strong positions at the fortresses of the Quadrilateral (Peschiera, Mantua, Verona, and Le-gnano) had yet to be faced and tested, and the prospect of greater slaughter was not inviting to Napoleon. Furthermore, Napoleon had to consider the import of two developments on the international scene. A new government in England led by Palmerston showed signs of concern with any further growth of French influence in Italy. Prussia's mobilization of 400,000 men on the Rhine posed a threat to both France and Austria, for although Prussia's intentions were not clear, the threat was real enough to influence the French and Austrian emperors' decision to conclude an armistice early in July 1859. News of the armistice was a shattering blow to Cavour, who apparently lost his senses when he learned of its conditions.

The Armistice of Villafranca and the Agony of Cavour: Documents and Interpretations

> Cappelletti, *Storia di Vittorio Emanuele II,* II, 82–90, *passim.* Our translation.

(Armistice Terms and Peace Preliminaries Agreed upon by the Emperors Napoleon III of France and Franz Joseph of Austria at Villafranca, July 11, 1859.)

"The two sovereigns favor the creation of an Italian Confederation. This Confederation shall be under the honorary presidency of the Pope.

"The Emperor of Austria cedes to the Emperor of the French his rights to Lombardy, with the exception of the fortresses of Mantua and Peschiera. . . . The Emperor of the French shall transfer the ceded territories to the King of Sardinia.

"Venetia shall be a part of the Italian Confederation; *however, it shall remain under the crown of the Emperor of Austria.*

"The Grand Duke of Tuscany and the Duke of Modena shall be returned to their states, and shall grant a general amnesty.*

"The two Emperors shall request the Holy Father to introduce indispensable reforms in his states."

The [French] Emperor had Victor Emmanuel read these terms in the presence of Prince Napoleon. When the King saw that their con-

* The Duke of Parma is not mentioned in this article. This was done deliberately after the Emperor Napoleon expressed the desire that the Duchy of Parma-Piacenza be united with Piedmont. . . .

tents were so different from what the Emperor had indicated on July 8 [when a simple truce in hostilities had been decided] he could not control his indignation and said that he would continue the war alone. The Emperor answered in this fashion: "Do as you like. But take care, instead of one enemy you may find two facing you." Victor Emmanuel thought about it for a while; then, with that good sense natural to him, he at once assessed the harm that Italy would incur if he were to have a falling out with France. He said to the Emperor: "Whatever Your Majesty's decision may be, I shall always be most grateful for what Your Majesty has done for the independence of Italy. I beg you to believe that you can count on my loyalty on any occasion." . . . .

When Cavour heard of the armistice preliminaries of Villafranca he felt a terrible blow which nearly deprived him of his senses. He ran immediately to the Piedmontese Headquarters at Monzambano exclaiming that he could not so easily resign himself to the Emperor's *great betrayal.* . . .

An eyewitness * narrates the following account of the events of the next day [July 11, the day of the agreement on the armistice terms and peace preliminaries]: "Cavour and his secretary returned to Villa Melchiori [the royal residence]. By now he knew that *the great sacrifice* had been consummated. . . . General Della Rocca tried to calm him, but it was in vain. His exasperation aroused the pity of all present. His face was burning red; his manner, usually simple and natural, now revealed in the violent gestures to which he abandoned himself the indignation which deprived him of all self-control. . . . The conversation between the King and his Minister lasted approximately two hours and was most stormy. I heard it said that Cavour's first words were anything but respectful for the Emperor of the French. He counseled Victor Emmanuel immediately to reject the peace conditions and to withdraw his troops from Lombardy, leaving Louis Napoleon to extricate himself as best as he could from the difficult situation in which he would then find himself (?). Cavour bluntly told his sovereign that Italy's interests had been betrayed and that the royal dignity had been brutally outraged; and he did not refrain from counseling him to abdicate. They say that during the entire conversation the King showed a calm and a coolheadedness of which few had thought him capable. He tried in all ways to calm his exasperated Prime Min-

* Count Carlo Arrivabene, military correspondent for the English *Daily News.*

ister who, spurred by anguish, seemed to have lost his reason. . . . It was asserted and generally believed at Monzambano that the fury which had possessed Cavour manifested itself in expressions sufficiently disrespectful to have obliged the King to turn his back to Cavour."

[Cappelletti adds the following in a note]: M. A. Canini wrote in his *Briciole di storia* that when the King saw the Count so agitated, he said to him: "Calm yourself, calm yourself. Remember that I am the King." The Count, besides himself with anger, is supposed to have replied: "I above all know the Italians. I am the true King." And Victor Emmanuel, in the same tone: "But what are you saying? *You say that you are the King? You're a knave.*" *

Cavour's fury lasted several days. But even while threatening violently to become a revolutionary, he managed to retain enough sense of balance to take measures that were eventually to help assure Piedmont the permanent acquisition of those central Italian states which according to the provisions of Villafranca should have been restored to their expelled princes. The following excerpts show that the clever statesman had not succumbed completely to his mental distraction.

CAVOUR'S LETTER TO GENERAL ALFONSO LA MARMORA, COMMANDING GENERAL OF THE PIEDMONTESE ARMY, JULY 16, 1859. Chiala, *Lettere*, III, 109–11. Our translation from the original French.

The Emperor arrived yesterday [in Turin]. . . . I had to receive him at the station with my colleagues. He shook my hand but said not a word.

I thought it proper not to attend the dinner. In the evening he had me called to him. He told me he did not want us to separate in discord. . . . He justified the peace exclusively on the basis of military considerations. According to him he would have needed 300,000 men to take Verona and he did not have them. I did not debate the matter. I limited myself to some observations on the sad fate of the countries abandoned to their former sovereigns: Modena, Tuscany, and Romagna. The Emperor assured me that he would plead their cause before the [projected] European Congress; that while waiting for the

* The passage in italics was spoken in Piedmontese dialect. Ed. note.

Congress we had only to prevent the old dynasties from returning. This declaration is in complete conformity with the King's order which I sent to you by telegraph [the day before]. I beg you to execute the order with latitude. Allow the Tuscans, the Modenese, and the Romagnols [in the Piedmontese army] to leave. Urge them to do themselves honor [in preventing the return of the expelled princes]. If we prevent the restorations before the Congress opens much will have been gained. Farewell.

TELEGRAM BY LUIGI CARLO FARINI, PIEDMONTESE COMMISSIONER IN MODENA, TO CAVOUR, JULY 15, 1859. Chiala, *Lettere,* III, 109. Our translation from the original French.

Please note that if the Duke [of Modena], trusting in agreements of which I have no knowledge, were to make any attempt [to return] I shall treat him as an enemy of the King and the fatherland. I shall not allow myself to be driven out by anyone, even if it were to cost me my life.

TELEGRAM BY FARINI TO CAVOUR, JULY 16, 1859. Chiala, *Lettere,* III, 112. Our translation from the original French.

I am still waiting for your instructions. While waiting, honor and necessity will dictate them to me. I shall not compromise the government, but neither shall I compromise the future. We can still save everything. [Cavour replied the next day and informed Farini that he was no longer Prime Minister.]

CAVOUR'S TELEGRAM TO FARINI, JULY 17, 1859. Chiala, *Lettere,* III, 112. Our translation from the original French.

The Minister is no more; the friend shakes your hand and applauds the decision you have taken.

Upon Cavour's insistence, General Alfonso La Marmora, an old friend and a colleague for nearly ten years in the Piedmontese government, agreed to head the new Ministry, with Rattazzi at the important Ministry of the Interior. The most urgent task facing the new government was the execution of the Villafranca armistice conditions. In accordance with these provisions, the

Piedmontese Commissioners in the central Italian states were recalled, but these states were nonetheless saved for Piedmont and for Italy by the action of a number of men who were to become Cavour's political heirs after his death in 1861.

In August 1859 Baron Bettino Ricasoli induced a popularly elected assembly in Tuscany to vote the deposition of the house of Hapsburg-Lorraine and a declaration of preference for union with Piedmont-Sardinia. In Modena, Luigi Carlo Farini resigned as Piedmontese Commissioner and assumed a personal dictatorship. Under his auspices a popular assembly deposed the Modenese duke in August and voted for the annexation of the Duchy to Piedmont. In September, Marco Minghetti, a Bolognese who had sat in the Piedmontese Parliament, guided the people of Romagna to vote for the annexation of their territory to Piedmont. By November, all the central Italian states save Tuscany were grouped together under the collective name of Emilia with Farini as dictator and with the Piedmontese *Statuto* as its Fundamental Law. A defensive military league was established between Emilia and Tuscany; the command was given to General Manfredo Fanti, a Modenese who was another recruit from the Piedmontese Parliament and who had a long revolutionary past. Garibaldi was chosen as his second in command.

All these measures were pleasing to Piedmont but also embarrassing. For the Piedmontese government openly to accept and implement the annexations voted by the popular assemblies of central Italy would have been too blatant a violation of the armistice terms. In the light of almost inevitable international repercussions, it would have been especially dangerous for Piedmont to occupy the papal territory of Romagna. And had Garibaldi been allowed to execute his project of invading the papal state of the Marches, there would most surely have been intense foreign reaction. In consequence, after definitive peace treaties were signed at Zurich on November 10, 1859, Garibaldi abandoned his project of invasion of the Marches and resigned his command.

The tripartite treaties of Zurich among France, Austria, and Piedmont provided for the implementation of the Villafranca armistice terms. The only significantly new provisions were the payment of 60 million lire by Piedmont to France to help cover the costs of the war and an additional 100 million lire as reimbursement of a like sum that France had paid Austria for assuming Lombardy's public debt. Also new was the suspension of any decision on the restoration of the deposed central Italian rulers. The treaty's terms left many issues unresolved, and the failure of La Marmora's government to cope successfully with these issues seemed to prove the indispensability of Cavour's return to office.

Toward the end of 1859 and the beginning of 1860 significant changes in the international situation and in Piedmontese domestic politics facilitated Cavour's return to power and the resumption of his policies. Napoleon decided on closer relations with England and on a virtual break with the

Papacy. The signs of this change in French foreign policy were the replacement of Walewski as Foreign Minister with Edouard Thouvenel, who was notably anticlerical, and the semiofficial publication in Paris of a work, *The Pope and the Congress*,[5] which advocated the restriction of papal temporal power to the region of Lazio (Latium). Napoleon's change of heart served Cavour well, inasmuch as the latter was willing to pay the price of the emperor's support—cession of Savoy and Nice—whereas the La Marmora-Rattazzi government seemed to be seized by doubts and hesitations. Rattazzi, who was the strong man in the government, sought to avoid making the cessions promised in the January 1859 treaty of alliance with France by counting on English support against further French territorial aggrandizement in Europe. To this end, and to weaken Cavour's power in Parliament, Cavour's former partner in the *Connubio* of 1852 played the dangerous game of trying to rally the extreme Left around himself by using Garibaldi, who was unalterably opposed to the cession of Nice—his birthplace. But Napoleon's decision in favor of more cordial relations with England destroyed the basis of Rattazzi's foreign policy, while his definitive and bitter break with Cavour undermined the government's domestic position. Cavour was incensed by reports of Rattazzi's intrigues against him. But he was even more distressed by La Marmora's apparent complicity in these intrigues, and he denounced the latter as being no longer "either a political or personal friend." [6] No government could remain in power long with Cavour in the opposition. On January 16, 1860, the La Marmora-Rattazzi Ministry resigned and the King most reluctantly requested Cavour to form a new government.

Once again in office, Cavour used all his political and personal influence on the British government to agree to Piedmontese annexation of the central Italian states provided the annexations were preceded by affirmative plebiscites in the states in question. Napoleon's support of these annexations was assured by a secret treaty in which Cavour agreed to cede both Savoy and Nice to France, on condition of subsequent approval by the Piedmontese Parliament. On March 11–12, 1860, at the time of the signature of this treaty, universal manhood suffrage plebiscites were held in the central Italian states on the question of "Union with the constitutional monarchy of Victor Emmanuel or a separate kingdom." Truly, the choice offered was not large, for it excluded the alternatives of a republic, a federation, or any solution other than the one specified. The results were overwhelmingly, almost unanimously, in favor of union. Then, seizing the opportune moment, Cavour ordered general elections for March 25 in the now unified Kingdom of Northern and Central Italy. The result was a great victory for the Cavourians, and this victory assured the government that Parliament would approve the treaty ceding Nice and Savoy to France. In spite of Rattazzi's op-

[5] The reference is to a projected European Congress to discuss the Italian question. The full Congress never took place.
[6] Chiala, *Lettere*, III, 167–73, *passim*.

position and Garibaldi's resignation from the Chamber in protest against the treaty, the cession was approved in May and June by large majorities in both houses of Parliament. Cavour's predictions made in a letter of January 7, 1860, that within a brief time the unitary principle would triumph "from the Alps to Sicily" had been partially borne out. The new Italian state did not yet stretch to Sicily, but in less than a year this too would come to pass.

The eventual acquisition of the Kingdom of the Two Sicilies and of all the papal territories save Lazio was to be an accomplishment most gratifying to Cavour and to the moderate nationalists who followed his lead. But it was not achieved without much acrimonious division among the soon-to-be-united Italians, and it laid the basis for many future bitter debates on how and for whom Italy had been united.

As early as the spring of 1860, after the plebiscite in Romagna approving the annexation of this papal province to Piedmont, the Pope carried out the threat he had made in a letter to Victor Emmanuel and pronounced the major excommunication against all those who had supported and participated in the separation of Romagna from the States of the Church. On the other hand, Garibaldi, the man who would have despoiled the Church of all its temporal power, was not much better disposed toward Cavour. And it was Garibaldi who more than any other single individual was to contribute to the unification of the South with the North. Various episodes in the conquest of the Two Sicilies by Garibaldi and his "thousand" volunteers were to assure that united Italy would be born amidst irreconcilable divisions.

18. CAVOUR, GARIBALDI, AND THE THOUSAND

Garibaldi was already a famous figure even before his conquest and liberation of the South. He was born in Nice in 1807. As a youth he followed his forebears' calling of the sea but soon fell under the sway of Mazzini's apostolate for a united and republican Italy. This persuasion and his participation in a Mazzinian conspiracy forced him into exile in 1834. He went to South America where he fought in the rebellion of southern Brazil and in the Uruguayan civil war of the 1830s and 1840s. He returned to Italy in 1848, distinguishing himself in the first war against Austria and particularly in the defense of the Roman republic against the French expeditionary corps in 1849. Forced into exile once again he lived briefly on Staten Island in New York and then resumed his career as a ship's captain. He returned to Italy in 1851 to live on the island of Caprera, off the Sardinian coast. During the 1850s he became convinced that Italian unification required the military might of the house of Savoy and reconciled himself to monarchy, abandoning his former republican preferences. His adhesion to the Italian National Society in 1857 confirmed this change, and his acceptance of the rank of major general in the Piedmontese army in 1859 removed him further from his Mazzinian past. He participated in the war against Austria as head of the Alpine Chasseurs and reported a number of victories, further increasing his military prestige and popularity. In September 1859 he was made second in command of the forces of the central Italian states but in November he was persuaded to resign this post and to abandon his plan for an incursion into the papal province of the Marches. His former tolerable relations with Cavour turned for the worse late in 1859 and early in 1860. In December he broke with the Cavourian-dominated National Society and formed an abortive rival organization, the *Nazione Armata* [The Nation in Arms]. In January 1860 he lent himself to Rattazzi's efforts to weaken Cavour's parliamentary following, and when, once again in power, Cavour contracted the treaty ceding Nice and Savoy to France, Garibaldi made his dramatic protest against Cavour's policies by resigning from Parliament. Prevented by royal interdict from making any assaults on the remaining papal territories, Garibaldi sought new fields of action.

The way was being prepared for him by others, principally the Sicilian exile Francesco Crispi, who had been a leading participant in the Sicilian revolution of 1848. After the failure of this revolution, Crispi sought refuge in Piedmont, only to be expelled in 1853 by Cavour's government. As an exile in London, Crispi became Mazzini's collaborator, which fact made him more than ever suspect to Cavour. Toward the end of 1859, with Cavour out of office, Crispi sought the aid of Rattazzi in a venture to raise the Sicilians against the Bourbon dynasty. Rattazzi appeared to show interest in Crispi's plan but, owing to his own precarious political position, was not able to give the kind of encouragement and tacit approval Crispi desired.[7] Cavour's return to power in January 1860 seemed to foreclose the possibility even of indirect help from the Piedmontese government. Cavour wanted no quarrel with the Bourbon government of the Two Sicilies and its European supporters at a time when he was preoccupied with the plebiscites and the treaty of cession with France. Besides, any enterprise involving Garibaldi's collaboration with Mazzini's supporters was bound to arouse an almost automatic negative reaction in him. In fact, early in April 1860, after Crispi brought news to Garibaldi in Turin that the Sicilians had risen and that he should lead an expedition to their aid, the latter went to the King, with whom he had for long been on better terms than with Cavour. Garibaldi requested that he be entrusted with a brigade of the Piedmontese army for the Sicilian expedition. Victor Emmanuel consulted Cavour and then refused both his approval and support for Garibaldi's enterprise. Cavour apparently feared an understanding between Garibaldi and Mazzini, and a joint venture not in Sicily but somewhere in the Papal States. Such an eventuality would have been disastrous at this juncture to Cavour's delicate balancing of international and domestic affairs. He feared especially to antagonize Napoleon, with whom he was negotiating for the withdrawal of the French garrison from the Papal States. He was also concerned with reputed Garibaldian and

[7] Francesco Crispi, *Memoirs of Francesco Crispi*, (3 vols.; London, Hodder and Stoughton, 1912–14). Translated by M. Prichard-Agnetti from vols. I to III of T. Palamenghi-Crispi, ed., *Memorie e documenti* (5 vols.; Milan, 1911–14), I, 116–19.

Rattazzian intrigues against him. Some of these fears are expressed in the following letter.

CAVOUR'S LETTER OF APRIL 24, 1860, TO LUIGI CARLO FARINI, FORMER DICTATOR OF EMILIA AND CAVOUR'S MINISTER OF THE INTERIOR. Chiala, *Lettere,* III, 240–41. Our translation.

I arrived in Turin yesterday evening after a visit to Spezia and a day's stay in Genoa. In the latter city I found much agitated sentiment owing to Garibaldi's intrigues. The Mazzinians are nestling themselves around him [Garibaldi] and are raising their heads once again. . . .

Guglianetti is much preoccupied by Rattazzi's intrigues. It seems that Miglietti [a Deputy of the Right!] is in league with him. . . . In truth, the cup of power is overflowing with gall. . . .

Cavour was disabused of his erroneous impression of a concerted Garibaldian-Mazzinian intrigue by a letter from Giuseppe La Farina, the secretary of the National Society and a most devoted Cavourian. La Farina informed Cavour that he had spoken with Garibaldi of the Sicilian expedition, that Garibaldi wished to work with La Farina, and that there was no agreement between the Mazzinians and the Garibaldians. On the contrary, there was a pronounced discord. La Farina also made an oblique reference to the failure of the "cases" to arrive in Genoa. The cases in question contained rifles sent from Modena for use by the National Society in support of an eventual expedition to Sicily.

The cases arrived in Genoa on April 24, the same day La Farina wrote to Cavour, but on the twenty-eighth there also arrived in Genoa news that the Sicilian revolt had collapsed. Garibaldi ordered the projected expedition abandoned, only to order it again into execution when a few days later it was confirmed that the first news had been misinterpreted because of the garbling of a coded telegram. The insurrection had indeed been suppressed in Palermo but it continued in the provinces. This was enough encouragement for Garibaldi to embark his Thousand volunteers in Genoa and leave for Sicily on May 6. In five days Garibaldi reached western Sicily and landed at Marsala. Two days later, May 13, he assumed the dictatorship of Sicily in the name of Italy and Victor Emmanuel; but Sicily had yet to be won. A hard-fought victory at Calatafimi on May 15 opened the way to Palermo. Joined by several thousand Sicilian volunteers, and aided by a rising within the city, Garibaldi took the capital at the end of May. Late in July another major victory, at Milazzo, obliged the Bourbon forces to abandon all Sicily save for several fortresses. An almost impossible enterprise had succeeded, and almost immediately a debate began as to whether Cavour had obstructed or facilitated Garibaldi's venture. The following documents and interpretations shed some light on the merits of the opposing sides in the debate.

TELEGRAM BY CAVOUR TO A. MATHIEU, GOVERNOR OF CA-GLIARI, ISLAND OF SARDINIA, MAY 7, 1860. Chiala, *Lettere*, III, 245. Our translation from the original French.

Garibaldi has embarked for Sicily with 400 volunteers on two ships of the Rubattino Company. If he enters any port of Sardinia, arrest the expedition. I authorize you to employ if necessary the squadron under the command of Admiral Persano.

LETTER OF MAY 7, 1860, BY CAVOUR TO THE MARQUIS ALES-SANDRO D'ASTE (CAPTAIN IN THE PIEDMONTESE NAVY) AT PALERMO, SICILY. Chiala, *Lettere*, III, 245–46. Our translation.

The night before last, two ships of the Rubattino Shipping Company, the *Piemonte* and the *Lombardo*, left Genoa illegally with General Garibaldi and a number of individuals on board intent, it appears, to reach Sicily.

The two ships were not furnished with the necessary papers or, at least, these papers were not in order.

In addition to the foregoing, which is transmitted for your information, I add that you must remain foreign to all that may occur in their attempt to land, and you must not interfere in the matter in any way.

TELEGRAM BY CAVOUR TO A. MATHIEU, GOVERNOR OF CA-GLIARI, MAY 8, 1860. Chiala, *Lettere*, III, 246. Our translation from the original French.

Do not arrest the expedition on the high seas; only if it enters a port.

LETTER BY CAVOUR TO COUNT CARLO DI PERSANO, REAR ADMIRAL, LA MADDALENA (NAVAL BASE OFF THE SARDIN-IAN COAST), MAY 14, 1860. Chiala, *Lettere*, III, 248–49. Our translation.

When I was assured that General Garibaldi intended to land on a Roman shore, I sent an order to the Governor of Cagliari to have the expedition arrested.

Now that the General is in Sicily and the ships on which he embarked destroyed,* it is no longer the case to recall previous instructions but rather to provide for the eventualities which may result from the bold General's attempt. . . .

I do not believe that the King of Naples is about to adopt extreme measures against us as a result of Garibaldi's venture. Nevertheless, it is better to be ready for every eventuality. For this reason I invite you to transmit to me in a restricted and confidential manner your views as to what is to be done in the event the King of Naples were to declare war.

CAVOUR'S LETTER TO BARON BETTINO RICASOLI, GOVERNOR GENERAL OF TUSCANY, MAY 16, 1860. Chiala, *Lettere*, III, 250. Our translation.

Garibaldi has landed in Sicily. It is very lucky that he did not execute his intentions of attacking the Pope. We cannot stop him from making war on the King of Naples. It may be a good or a bad thing, but it was inevitable. Had we tried to restrain Garibaldi by force he would have become most dangerous within the country. What will happen now? It is impossible to predict. Will England help him? It is possible. Will France hinder him? I do not think so. And we? We cannot support him openly, neither can we restrain individual efforts on his behalf.

We have therefore decided not to allow new expeditions to leave from the ports of Genoa and Leghorn, but not to prevent the sending of arms and munitions so long as this is done with some discretion. I am aware of the inconveniences of the ill-defined line we are following, but I do not know how to define another line with less grave and dangerous inconveniences.

CAVOUR'S LETTER TO COLONEL EFISIO CUGIA, CHIEF OF STAFF, IVth CORPS IN BOLOGNA, MAY 17, 1860. Chiala, *Lettere*, III, 251. Our translation.

Garibaldi's expedition is a most serious matter. Nevertheless, I believe that we neither could nor should have prevented it. It was openly

* The ships were beached. Ed. note.

favored by England and weakly opposed by France. Many of our most devoted friends supported it. Should I have put myself in opposition to them? It would have been a mistake which would have created the greatest difficulties in the country. . . .

You can rest assured, if necessary we shall take energetic and extreme measures against the Mazzinians.

Cavour's fear that the Mazzinians would try to capture the Garibaldian expedition for their own purposes were heightened by the presence of Crispi as Garibaldi's chief lieutenant in Sicily. To offset Crispi's influence on the General, La Farina, also a Sicilian and the secretary of the National Society, was sent by Cavour to Palermo early in June to promote the immediate annexation of the island to Piedmont. But Garibaldi was opposed to immediate annexation because his aim to free Italy of all foreign influence—meaning the French in the Papal States and the Austrians in Venetia—required that he retain dictatorial control of Sicily as his secure base of operations. Consequently, when La Farina became too pressing in the demand for annexation and tried to discredit the Mazzinian Crispi, Garibaldi had La Farina unceremoniously expelled from the island early in July.

Soon Cavour was to meet yet another setback in his plans to limit Garibaldi's influence in the South. He had hoped to use his agents in Naples to promote an insurrection there, thus justifying the intervention of Piedmontese troops and the immediate annexation of the northern half of the Two Sicilies. But Garibaldi's victory at Milazzo persuaded Cavour that it was not possible to prevent the General's crossing the Straits to the mainland. Nevertheless, the Prime Minister still insisted on the need to prevent the liberation of Naples by the Garibaldians. The following excerpts reveal Cavour's reasons for fearing Garibaldi's success and his appreciation of the services the General had rendered Italy.

CAVOUR'S LETTER TO THE MARQUIS SALVATORE DI VILLAMARINA, SARDINIAN MINISTER TO NAPLES, JULY 30, 1860. Chiala, *Lettere,* III, 300. Our translation from the Italian version. The original was in French.

It is highly desirable that the liberation of Naples not be accomplished by Garibaldi. If this were to occur the revolutionary approach would take the place of the constitutional monarchical party. If the Dictator were to arrive victoriously in the capital of the [Neapolitan] Kingdom, revolution and anarchy would be planted there, and this would have a very bad effect on Europe. Add to all this his mad design to go to Rome, despite and against France. That would be the complete ruin of the Italian cause. It is therefore necessary that a national movement occur in Naples before Garibaldi's arrival.

CAVOUR'S LETTER TO AN "INTIMATE FRIEND," AUGUST 9, 1860, ON THE GREATNESS OF GARIBALDI. Chiala, *Lettere,* III, 321–22. Our translation from the original French.

It would be very much to my taste to convene Parliament and engage in a great parliamentary battle. But I am convinced that even if I were to save my prestige I would lose Italy. Now, my dear friend, I say to you without exaggeration that I much prefer to lose my reputation and see Italy united. And to unite Italy in the present circumstances we must not pit the King and Garibaldi against each other. Garibaldi has a great moral power; he exercises an immense prestige not only in Italy but above all in Europe. I believe you are wrong when you say that we are placed between Garibaldi and Europe. If tomorrow I were to enter into a contest with Garibaldi, it is probable that I would have the majority of the old diplomats with me, but European public opinion would be against me. And public opinion would be right because Garibaldi has rendered the greatest services possible for any single individual. He has given the Italians confidence in themselves. He has proved to Europe that the Italians know how to fight and die on the fields of battle in order to reconquer their fatherland. . . .

We must not fight with Garibaldi except in the event of two hypotheses: (1.) if he were to try to drag us into a war with France or (2.) if he were to go back on his program and proclaim a political system other than the monarchy of Victor Emmanuel. So long as he remains loyal to his own banner ["Italy and Victor Emmanuel"] we will have to get along with him. This does not mean that it is any less desirable for the Neapolitan revolution to be accomplished without him. But if, in spite of all our efforts, he were to deliver the continent as he has delivered Sicily, we will have no choice but to take him into account, and very much so. That will take us into a war with Austria. I realize that this eventuality is considered with apprehension, but I believe that its dangers are being exaggerated. Every time that our soldiers have had a real desire to fight, they have beaten the Austrians.

A sharply contrasting interpretation of the early months of the expedition
of the Thousand is given by Tommaso Palamenghi-Crispi, Francesco Crispi's
nephew and editor of his memoirs.

An Anti-Cavourian View of Garibaldi's Expedition to Sicily

Francesco Crispi, *Memoirs*, I, 237–44, *passim*. The passage reproduced
below consists of comments by Tommaso Palamenghi-Crispi.

The news of the departure of the Thousand for Sicily had caused
much surprise. The Sardinian government itself was amazed when it
became known that a handful of men had set out to conquer a State
that was defended by sea by the strongest navy in Italy, and by land
by a numerous and well-disciplined army. . . . But the country in
general, and especially the youth of the nation, in whom ideas of liberty and of nationalism were fomenting hotly, saw only the heroic
beauty of the action, and knowing little of the true state of Sicilian
matters, anticipated not bloody defeat but splendid victory.

When the news of the successful landing became known, and was
quickly followed by that of the victory at Calatafimi, where on the
open field the Thousand had defeated regular troops three times as
numerous as themselves, a great flame of enthusiasm swept the peninsula. The impulse to hasten thither, to have a part in the glory, to help
in some way, seized one and all, for all now knew that the time had
come when Italy would indeed be made.

The Sardinian government was also quick to perceive this fact.

Revolution was shaping national destinies, and Count Cavour's
chief anxiety was for the security and prestige of the Piedmontese
monarchy. Diplomacy could ignore these events, for the "non-inter-
vention policy" had been accepted by the whole of Europe. England
would certainly not be opposed to a popular uprising in Italy—she
who had encouraged Italy to fight her own battles against her oppressors. Louis Napoleon could not bring back as enemies those very
troops whom, but the year before, he had brought as comrades to the
Italians on the battlefields of Lombardy. But how about history? History would declare that the domination of the House of Savoy, of that
small country at the foot of the Alps, had spread throughout Italy not

by virtue of its own policy and prowess, but thanks to the strength of the people, directed by the revolution.

Personally also the haughty minister, conscious of his own worth, and proud of having forced this aged Europe to observe the fluttering in the breast of the sleeping beauty, about to awake—proud of having constrained the powers to accept the liberation of Lombardy, and furthermore of having prevented them from offering any resistance to the annexation by Piedmont of the small states of Central Italy—personally also Count Cavour must have experienced bitter humiliation on seeing the fruit he had believed to be still unripe about to be boldly gathered by the hand of another.

The state of Cavour's mind may therefore be easily imagined when the first fabulous news (the adjective is his own) reached him in Turin very shortly after the occurrence of the great events. He had not prevented the expedition—it would perhaps be more exact to say he had been unable to prevent it—but he had used every means in his power to persuade Garibaldi to relinquish it. For a year the General's friends among the Sicilian emigrants had been urging him to postpone the action in Sicily for an indefinite period, and even as late as the fifth of May several persons had repaired to Villa Spinola at Quarto to seek to dissuade him. But when he was once on his way, and the probability of success immediately became apparent, could Cavour still persist in his disapproval? It would have been impossible indeed. Public sentiment became suddenly so inflamed by this triumphant audacity, and it so thoroughly roused the spirit of chivalry in Victor Emmanuel himself, that had Cavour not consented to support the undertaking he would have been forced to retire from government. He therefore lent it his support by openly tolerating enlistment, removing the ban of confiscation from the supplies of arms, offering no opposition to the sailing of ships from Genoa with volunteers, and granting various other favours. But although forced by the good conduct of the revolution to lend it his support, he had not relinquished any of his early animosity against it. Nevertheless, the moment had arrived when monarchy and revolution must cease to look askance at each other and join hands, for revolution was creating for monarchy what monarchy was incapable of creating for herself—Unity.

Cavour's animosity was indeed unjustifiable.

No one had any right to doubt Garibaldi's sincerity when he landed at Marsala with the Italian flag and in the name of Victor Emmanuel. Better than any one else Cavour was acquainted with Garibaldi's personal devotion to the King; he knew of the letter the leader of the Thousand had despatched to the sovereign on setting out from Quarto, and was aware of his long-established conviction that the great majority of the people were not in favour of a republic, and his consequent declaration that he would contribute neither morally nor materially towards its establishment. Cavour was, moreover, aware that since 1849 Mazzini and Garibaldi had not been on good terms.

Nor could he doubt the monarchical sentiments of Garibaldi's Lieutenants. . . . Crispi he knew only through police reports, which in all countries reveal only the darkest side. Had he taken the trouble to sift the truth of these reports he would have discovered an ardent patriot and a man of sterling characterisics in this Sicilian exile who was expelled from Piedmont in 1853, and forced to leave Turin at the beginning of 1860. . . . But he listened only to Giuseppe La Farina, who probably described his fellow-countryman as a rabid Mazzinian, perhaps even as an implacable anarchist, and certainly as an enemy against whom all means were justifiable.

Cavour was equally unjust to Mazzini.

As long as the period of dark conspiracy against the existing order lasted, that is, conspiracy against those foreign governments that oppressed and those national governments that from prudence or weakness endured oppression—as long as the persistent propaganda for the principles of nationalism was based upon the republican ideal—the resentment against the formidable conspirator felt by men who judged the Italian problem by other standards, and with different sentiments, may easily be accounted for. But when, moved by the joy of seeing Italy delivered from the foreigner, and united, Mazzini publicly and privately renounced his prejudice, and in no ambiguous language, saying: "I will freely accept unity under the King. . . . The dream of my life has ever been Unity!"—when it became manifest that, if a people in whom consciousness of their rights had been awakened had risen up in their pride of nation to achieve liberty, this praiseworthy action was due precisely to that persistent propaganda, then Cavour's attitude towards Mazzini ought to have become unbiassed and more just. But, on the contrary, he continued to regard Mazzini as the enemy. *Mazzinian* still remained a term of opprobrium, and stamped a man as dangerous, and the anti-Mazzinian phraseology of the conservatives, which had been formed during the long years of preparation, retained all its significance, all its strength. Mazzini therefore had much to suffer during the year 1860. The monarchical party continued to hate him; the ex-republicans who had sacrificed their early principles that Italy might be made were forced to drop him in order to avoid the accusation of insincerity. Had Cavour possessed a more generous spirit, instead of allowing him to be hunted like a beast of prey, he would have recognised the services Mazzini had rendered, the results of which were shining with so pure a light at that very time. He might even have been able, had he seized the solemn moment when Mazzini declared he would create no division by "talking republic," to hold him to these sentiments, and attach him definitely to that Italian monarchy which was being established by the suffrage of the entire nation. Thus the great epic of Italian Unity would have been enacted without the renewal of the story of Saturn in connection with one of its greatest workers.

Count Cavour's human weakness found a pernicious ally in Giuseppe La Farina.

The individuality of this other Sicilian exile who, although once a republican, became an important and ambitious supporter of the Count's policy, must not be overlooked. It would be unfair to deny that La Farina possessed both genius and patriotism combined with a strong will, but there can be no doubt that these qualities were tarnished by his unbounded presumption and foolish vanity. . . .

Count Cavour, who was no longer either able or willing to disregard the events that were succeeding each other with such amazing rapidity in Sicily, arranged with La Farina—who probably supplied him with information tinged with his own personal estimate of men and things—that the latter should be placed by Garibaldi's side to control him, to direct matters according to his own wishes, and make absolutely sure of Sicily for Piedmont. In a word, he was to catch up with events that had not waited upon Cavour's convenience.

But if the plan was a daring one, the choice of an instrument could not have been worse. . . .

La Farina immediately set about conquering both Garibaldi and Sicily. . . . Garibaldi consented to receive Count Cavour's envoy, inquired somewhat ironically concerning his journey and the state of his health, and then listened absent-mindedly enough to what he had to say, frequently interrupting him to assure him that everything was progressing favourably, and that his services were not needed. In the end he dismissed him coldly, and a moment later the General was entertaining Crispi with an account of the interview.

Cavour's Gratitude to Garibaldi

In spite of Victor Emmanuel's injunction not to cross the Straits, Garibaldi moved from Sicily to the mainland late in August. According to some accounts, the royal disapproval of an invasion of the mainland was intended for public and diplomatic consumption only; in fact the enterprise had the King's secret blessing. Aided by popular risings in Calabria and Apulia, Garibaldi made rapid progress toward Naples, which he entered with a few followers on September 7. Fearing a Garibaldian attack on the papal territories of Umbria and the Marches and the consequent danger of Garibaldi's encounter with the French garrisons, Cavour decided to order the Piedmontese army to move into these two areas. In his communications to the French government Cavour attempted to justify this invasion of papal territory as the only way of preventing Garibaldi from extending his revolution throughout all of Italy. Garibaldi seemed to confirm Cavour's argument by issuing a proclamation on September 17, 1860, to the people of Palermo in which he announced his intention of crowning the King of Italy in Rome. The General endeared himself even less with Cavour by suggesting to Victor Emmanuel that he dismiss his Prime Minister. In substance, the King's reply was to assume personal command of his troops fighting in the papal provinces and thus face Garibaldi with the prospect of having to war against his King if he insisted on marching to Rome. Cavour, on the other hand, turned to Parliament and secured approval of a bill authorizing the government to accept annexations of the former papal and Bourbon lands in the event these annexations were approved by popular plebiscites.

Although Crispi and Mazzini opposed immediate annexation of the southern provinces to the Piedmontese-dominated Kingdom of Northern and Central Italy, Garibaldi finally agreed to it. His decision was prompted by a number of factors: his desire to avoid further division among the Italians at so crucial a moment; the effect of royal pressure on him; a certain eagerness on Garibaldi's part to be finished with the whole business; and Cavour's willingness to treat generously the volunteers who had rallied to Garibaldi's Army of the South. The specific issue in question regarding the last point was the recognition the regular Piedmontese army would grant to officer ranks Garibaldi had given to volunteers in his Army of the South. The following letter by Cavour to Farini, Minister of the Interior accompanying the

King, shows not only his determination to deal fairly with Garibaldi's followers but also his inability to reach any compromise with Mazzini.

CAVOUR'S GRATITUDE TOWARD GARIBALDI: LETTER TO LUIGI CARLO FARINI, OCTOBER 8, 1860. Chiala, *Lettere*, IV, 34–35. Our translation.

In my opinion, the King must show himself inexorable toward Mazzini [whom Cavour believed to be intriguing with Garibaldi] and his avowed or secret followers: [But] we must be generous toward all those who have fought. If Garibaldi's army acclaims the King, it must be treated well. It is a question of fighting against the demands and pedantries of the regular military. A supreme necessity of state requires that you not give in. Woe to us if we were to show ourselves thankless and ungrateful toward those who have shed their blood for Italy. Europe would condemn us, and in our country there would occur a tremendous reaction in favor of the Garibaldians.

I have had a most spirited discussion with Fanti [General Manfredo Fanti, Minister of War] on this point. He spoke of the army's needs and demands. I replied that we were not in Spain and that in our country the army obeyed.

I do not thereby mean that we must retain all the ranks given by Garibaldi or by others on his behalf. Heaven forbid that such an absurd idea should enter my head. But on the other hand we cannot do as Fanti wishes and send all the Garibaldians home with a simple gratuity. . . .

I would not compromise on this point. Rather than assume the responsibility for an act of black ingratitude, I shall prefer to go bury myself at Leri [his estate].

I have such contempt for ungrateful people that I feel no anger toward them and forgive their slanders. But, by God! I could never bear the justified accusation of being thankless for services such as the conquest of a kingdom of nine million people!

Toward the end of October plebiscites were held in Sicily and the Neapolitan provinces on the question: "The people wish to be one and indivisible under the scepter of the house of Savoy." The favorable reply was almost unanimous. Garibaldi's task in the South was done. He had only to surrender his dictatorial authority to the King and say farewell to his "citizen-soldier" volunteers. Garibaldi asked the King that his comrades in arms of the Army of the South be welcomed into the royal army. This request was to be met only in small part. Another request, that he be appointed the King's lieutenant in the South for a year was rejected completely. Thereupon the General refused all offers of decorations, rank, titles, and money, and early in November left Naples for his home on the island of Caprera. But he was not to remain there long; and his frequent departures from this place of self-imposed exile were to mark several major episodes in the history of Italy for the next decade.

The early months of 1861 saw the fall of the last remnants of organized Bourbon resistance to Piedmontese arms and the holding of elections in all Italy save for the papal state of Lazio and Austrian-controlled Venetia. Symptomatically, the Legislature chosen at these elections of January 1861 was numbered consecutively after the preceding seven Legislatures of the Piedmontese Parliament, so that what in fact was the first Legislature of United Italy was counted technically as the eighth since the creation of the Piedmontese Parliament in 1848. Equally revealing was the fact that when, on March 14, 1861, the Italian Parliament approved a law proclaiming Victor Emmanuel King of Italy, it acceded to his request that in homage to his house he retain the number "II" rather than assume the number "I," regardless that logic required him to be styled the "first" King of Italy. These seemingly trifling matters were generally regarded as mere distractions at a time when the achievement of the fondest hopes of the Risorgimento had finally and so swiftly come to pass. It was time for general jubilation and not for carping and petty differences over who had done what, or more, for the common cause. But these differences were to appear before united Italy was less than a month old. They have not stopped appearing ever since.

VII. THE UNITED KINGDOM OF ITALY, 1861–1870

19. THE UNRECONCILED: THE POPE, MAZZINI, AND GARIBALDI

The official proclamation of the Kingdom of Italy in March 1861 marked the beginning of a united Italian state; it did not mark the end of old divisions nor did it ward off the beginning of new ones. During a debate toward the end of March, Parliament affirmed the necessity that Rome be the capital of Italy, and Cavour announced his famous formula of a free Church in a free state. Parliament approved the formula for Cavour's solution to the Church-state question; but the reconciliation with the Papacy, toward which Cavour had devoted much attention and negotiation since the fall of the preceding year, had already come to nought. Cavour had offered the Church complete freedom from any state interference in the conduct of its spiritual ministry and guarantees for much of its properties in exchange for the Papacy's renunciation of its claims to temporal authority. After some apparently promising progress, the negotiations were broken off, and the breach was made official by a protest from the Cardinal Secretary of State Antonelli, made public on April 15, 1861.

Papal Protest to the Proclamation of the Kingdom of Italy, April 15, 1861

Isaia Ghiron, ed., *Annali d'Italia,* 3 vols. Milan: Ulrico Hoepli, 1888–1890, I, 22–23. Our translation.

A Catholic King, forgetful of all religious principles, contemptuous of all rights and trampling on all laws, after having little by little despoiled the August Head of the Catholic Church of the greater and more flourishing part of his legitimate possessions, today assumes the title of *King of Italy*. With this act he seeks to place a seal on the sacrilegious usurpations he has already accomplished and which his government has already declared it seeks to complete at the expense of the patrimony of the Holy See.

Although the Holy Father has protested solemnly against every new enterprise which offended his sovereignty, it is nonetheless obliged today to make a new protest against the act by which there is assumed a title whose aim is to legitimize the iniquity of so many preceding acts.

It would be superfluous to recall the sacred nature of the Church's patrimony and the Sovereign Pontiff's right to this patrimony: it is an incontestable right recognized at all times and by all governments. And from this right it follows that the Holy Father can never recognize the title of *King of Italy* which the King of Sardinia confers upon himself, because such a title injures the rights and sacred property of the Church. He not only cannot recognize this title but he protests once more in the most absolute and formal manner against such a usurpation. . . .

Not for the first time, nor for the last, Mazzini found himself in agreement with the Pope in their common condemnation of the men who had fashioned the newly united Kingdom. The motives of the two condemnations were radically different, but the disturbing effect of the censures were to be felt in Italy for decades to come. The following excerpts from Mazzini's writings were prepared in 1861, thirty years after his founding of Young Italy.

Mazzini's Assessment of the Unification of Italy, 1861

Joseph Mazzini, *Life and Writings*, I, 53–54, 267–69, *passim*.

I did not then [1831], and do not now believe, that the salvation of Italy can ever be accomplished by monarchy; that is to say, the salvation of Italy such as I understand it, and as we all understood it a few years since—an Italy, one, free, and powerful; independent of all foreign supremacy, and morally worthy of her great mission.

Nor have recent events induced me to alter this conviction. The Piedmontese monarchy would never have taken the initiative of an Italian movement if the man of the 2d of December [Louis Napoleon] had not offered the assistance of his army, and Garibaldi, with five-sixths of the republicans, their cooperation. . . .

All that the Piedmontese monarchy can give us—even if it can give so much—will be an Italy shorn of provinces [Nice and Savoy] which ever were, are, and will be, Italian, though yielded up to foreign domination in payment of the services rendered; an Italy the abject slave of French policy, dishonoured by her alliance with despotism; weak, corrupted, and disinherited of all moral mission, and bearing within her the germs of provincial autonomy and civil war.

Even now, while I write, the misgovernment inherent in the monarchical institution is rapidly preparing the way for a crisis of *separatism* in the south—the south which, at the opening of the new life, was intoxicated with the grand idea of unity and Rome. . . .

The potent and unanimous voice of the Italian people has proclaimed to all literary theorists that our *Utopia* of thirty years since was, in fact, a prophetic intuition of their wants and aspirations, of their hidden life, and of their future. The free vote of the Italian people has solved the problem, and declared them *Unitarian* at every cost, and this under circumstances the most unfavourable. They have sacrificed every other right to this great aim, overcoming with admirable perseverance the fears and hesitations of the monarchy, and resisting all the suggestions and temptations offered by their foreign ally, and his timid or venal supporters, in order to win them over to his plan of a confederation, which would have condemned them to perpetual weakness.

The decision of the country, therefore, might appear to exempt me from the necessity of adding another page upon this subject.

But the systematic misgovernment of the sect of men but yesterday disbelievers in the possibility of national unity, who are nevertheless called upon by the monarchy to organize and direct it at the present day; the stupid pertinacity with which these men strive to substitute the imperfect expression given to the life of a fraction of Italy thirteen years ago * to the manifestation of *collective* national life now invoked by the country, may cause the popular mind—I will not say to retrocede towards the former state of things—but at least to vacillate

---

* The Piedmontese *statuto,* or constitution, wrung from Charles Albert by revolution in 1848, and very hastily framed to suit the immediate exigencies of the case.—*Translator's Note.*

in a dangerous manner as to the course indicated by a true instinct of the Italian mission.

The Nation is a *new fact*, the only fitting expression of which is a NATIONAL PACT, dictated by an Italian constituent assembly in Rome; the organization of a citizen army from one end of the country to the other; an Italian policy freed from all foreign protection or influence; a war boldly undertaken for Venice; and a government representing not a mere *coterie*, but the whole people, without other exception than of those adverse to the unity of their country.

Garibaldi Accuses Cavour of Provoking a Civil War

Mazzini's reference to the incipient crisis of separatism in the South and his strictures against the "systematic misgovernment" of Italy's new rulers found an echo in the views being expressed by Garibaldi, who had returned to Turin early in April to attend the sessions of the Chamber of Deputies, to which he had been elected from Naples. Cavour feared that Garibaldi's appearance in Parliament was designed to force the government into some hostile move against Austria. This impression was heightened by a speech in which Garibaldi seemed to criticize both King and Parliament. To free himself of the charge of this alleged criticism, Garibaldi addressed a letter to the President of the Chamber denying the charge, but then proceeded to give substance to the allegation by adding: "The deplorable state of the Army of the South and the abandon to which my valorous comrades-in-arms have been unjustly relegated have truly moved me to contempt for those who have been the cause of so many disorders and so much injustice." If this was not a direct indictment of King and Parliament, it certainly was a not very veiled criticism of the government chosen by the King and supported by Parliament. Cavour himself admitted that the Minister of War, General Fanti, had moved with "exasperating slowness" with regard to the treatment of the officers in Garibaldi's former Army of the South. Equally disturbing was Garibaldi's proposal that a National Guard be created. This proposal was feared by many as intending to create a military organization to rival the regular army.

On April 18, 1861, Garibaldi appeared in the Chamber of Deputies dressed not in his uniform of a general in the Italian army but in the red shirt he had worn as leader of the Thousand. Before Garibaldi presented his proposal for a National Guard, Baron Bettino Ricasoli asked the government for a statement on the measures it intended to take regarding the Army of the South and spoke of a "dangerous dualism" in the country. Garibaldi began his speech by denying any intention on his part of promoting a "dualism" between himself and Cavour. But the thought of the cession of

Nice to France weakened his initial restraint and he added that he could never extend his hand "to him who had made me a stranger in Italy." Then, with all restraint gone, he delivered an awful indictment against Cavour.

GARIBALDI'S SPEECH IN THE CHAMBER OF DEPUTIES, APRIL 18, 1861. *Atti del parlamento italiano,* Sessione del 1861, *Camera dei deputati, Discussioni,* I, 577–78. Our translation.

Garibaldi: In speaking of the Southern Army I should above all narrate its very glorious history. The prodigal deeds it performed were obscured only when the cold and unfriendly hand of this Ministry made its evil effects felt. (*Commotion and agitation.*) When, for love of harmony and horror of a fratricidal war provoked by this very same Ministry. (*Most lively protests from the ministerial bench. Violent interruptions in the Chamber.*)

(*Many cries from the right and center:*) To order! To order!

The President [Rattazzi]: I pray the Honorable General Garibaldi. (*Noises drown out his voice.*)

Cavour: (*With emphasis.*) It is not permissible that he should insult us in this fashion! We protest! We never had such intentions. (*Applause from the Deputies and the galleries.*) Mr. President, see to it that the government and the nation's representatives are respected! Call him to order! (*Interruptions and comments.*)

The President: Silence. It is the prerogative only of the President to maintain order and regulate the debate. Let no one disturb the proceedings with calls to order. [This was a most direct rebuff by Rattazzi to Cavour.]

Crispi: I request to be heard on a point of order.

Garibaldi: I thought that after thirty years of service to my country I had earned the right to say the truth before the people's representatives.

The President: I pray the Honorable General Garibaldi to express his opinions in terms which are not offensive to any member of this Chamber and the persons of the Ministers.

Cavour: He said that we provoked a fratricidal war! This is hardly an expression of opinion! (*Interruptions and various comments from all benches.*)

Garibaldi: Yes, a fratricidal war! (*Most lively commotion in the*

Chamber and the galleries. . . . The sitting is suspended for a quarter of an hour.)

All efforts at reconciliation in the Chamber failed. But within the week the two antagonists met at the King's insistence and effected a measure of reconciliation in his presence. Some evidence that Garibaldi had come to understand Cavour's policies better is provided by a letter of May 18, 1861, in which Garibaldi appears to accept Cavour's argument that the cession of Nice was an inevitable sacrifice for the sake of Napoleon's support. Garibaldi added : "Let Victor Emmanuel be Italy's arm and you its brain, Count; and together form that powerful whole which is the only thing lacking to Italy today. I shall be the first to shout in Parliament for that dictatorship which is indispensable in times of great need. . . . Trusting in your superior ability and your firm determination to do the best for the fatherland, I shall await the happy voice that once again will call me to the field of battle." [1]

But the voice in which Garibaldi had acquired renewed confidence was never to call him again. Within three weeks of Garibaldi's letter, Cavour's voice was forever stilled, after a physical agony of seven days completed the work of more than a decade of spiritual and physical exhaustion on behalf of a cause he had served so well. Cavour died of a cerebral hemorrhage on June 6, 1861, two months before his fifty-first birthday and on the eve of what appeared to be a promising solution of the Roman question.

20. THE ROMAN AND SOUTHERN QUESTIONS

The phrase "Roman question" is one of the more ambiguous terms in the history of modern Italy. In the most general sense it means the problems arising out of relations between Church and state in Italy from the period of unification to the Lateran Agreements of 1929. Historically and more concretely, the question can be divided into at least three distinct phases: the period between 1859 and 1861, when the Church lost most of its temporal domains to the expanding Piedmontese state; the decade from 1861 to 1870, full of national and international complications on how to acquire Rome and how to confiscate and then dispose of Church properties; and the period between 1870 and 1929, which saw relations between the Kingdom of Italy and the Papacy move slowly from bitter hostility toward eventual reconciliation.

During the first half of 1861 Cavour appeared to be moving toward the successful conclusion of the first phase. The securing of diplomatic recognition of the Kingdom of Italy by many of Europe's major powers meant their *de facto* acceptance of the end of papal temporal power everywhere in Italy save for the region of Lazio. At the time of his death, Cavour was negotiat-

[1] Ghiron, ed., *Annali d'Italia*, I, 38–40.

ing with Napoleon for French recognition of the Kindgom of Italy and the withdrawal of French troops from Rome, on condition that Italy be reconciled with the Pope and the remaining papal territory be guaranteed from attack by "regular or irregular troops." After Cavour's death and in homage to him, Napoleon proceeded to recognize the Kingdom of Italy even before the fulfillment of the specified conditions, but he insisted on these conditions before evacuating his garrisons from the remaining papal possessions in Lazio.

A "Last Attempt" To Solve the Roman Question Peacefully

The new Prime Minister, the Tuscan Baron Bettino Ricasoli (supported by a parliamentary group known as the *Destra Storica* [Historical Right]) was anxious for a rapid solution of the Roman question because he feared intemperate attempts by the "action now" party and because the remaining papal state was rapidly becoming a hotbed of Bourbon reactionary conspiracies intended to raise the neighboring Neapolitan provinces against the Italian government. But Ricasoli's imperious manner seemed unsuitable to the times. This manner served him well in 1859 when he had helped save Tuscany for Piedmont but not so well during his brief tenure as Prime Minister (June 1861–February 1862). Ricasoli was devoted to Cavour's policies, but he lacked the latter's flexibility in trying to execute them. He also lacked Cavour's considerable charm, and those who called Ricasoli "the iron baron" did not necessarily mean it as a compliment. Some indications of the new Prime Minister's character shine through the formal language of the following letter regarding France's assistance in solving the Roman question.

LETTER BY RICASOLI TO COSTANTINO NIGRA, ITALIAN AMBASSADOR IN PARIS, SEPTEMBER 10, 1861. Ghiron, ed., *Annali d'Italia*, I, 170–75, *passim*. Our translation.

Your Excellency will have noted from the latest communications I have had the honor to exchange with you how incessant and always more grave are the preoccupations of His Majesty's government regarding the Roman question. . . .

There is virtually no domestic problem of which Italian public opinion does not relate the origins to the lack of the capital, Rome. No one believes that it is possible to establish a satisfactory administration of the state until the center of this administration is transferred to Rome—equidistant point to the two ends of the peninsula. The logic of national unity is a sentiment which today prevails among Italians, and this logic does not allow for unity to be cut in half by the existence in the heart of the Kingdom of a state which is foreign, and hostile besides: because, it must be said that the country's legitimate impatience to possess its capital is stirred by the behavior of the Roman Curia regarding Neapolitan affairs. . . .

Given the incontestable right of Italians to have Rome as the capital of the nation; given, as a consequence, the Italian government's inescapable duty to achieve this end; in the light of unanimous public opinion; and in order to avoid grave disturbances and ill-considered attempts—which are always deplorable even when forestalled and repressed—the government has decided to make a last appeal to the Pontiff's mental uprightness and goodness of heart to reach an agreement on the basis of the following conditions: on the one hand, complete freedom of the Church, the Italian government abandoning any and all involvement in religious matters; on the other hand, renunciation of temporal power.

Your Excellency will find enclosed a copy of the letter which, by express order of His Majesty, I have addressed to His Holiness Pope Pius IX on this matter. Your Excellency will be pleased to communicate this document to the government of His Majesty the Emperor of the French [for transmittal to the Pope]. . . . The absence of all diplomatic relations between the Italian government and the Holy See prevents us from transmitting it directly to the Holy Father. . . .

While Your Excellency will have care to express to the government of His Imperial Majesty how complete is our confidence in its benevolent dispositions and in the efficacy of its intervention in this most important matter, Your Excellency will also explain that if this last attempt were unfortunately to fail, [our] Majesty's government would find itself enveloped by the gravest of difficulties. . . .

The effects of a [papal] rebuff may be more easily predicted than calculated. But it is certain that the religious sentiments of the Italians would be greatly shaken; and the country's impatience, contained until now by the hope of a solution more or less near, would become most difficult to hold in check. . . .

It may seem to some that it is contrary to usage, to tradition, and perhaps even to customary reverence that the letter addressed to the Sovereign Pontiff should be signed by me rather than by His Majesty our King. There are two reasons for this deviation from generally accepted practice. First of all, as Your Excellency surely knows, in other situations analogous to the present one His Majesty has written personally to the Pope and either received no reply or received one of a kind offensive to his royal dignity. In the light of such precedents it was impossible for us to expose the dignity of our sovereign to a new danger of offense. Furthermore, it seemed to His Majesty's government that, on an occasion in which it addresses itself respectfully to the Sovereign Pontiff in the name of the Italian nation, the one who is the customary interpreter of the deliberations of the executive power and who, especially when Parliament is not in session, represents the nation should also be the one to interpret the nation's wishes and sentiments.

Ricasoli's efforts to reach an agreement with the Papacy and with France were a total failure. When Napoleon refused to transmit Ricasoli's proposals to the Pope, Ricasoli made them public in Parliament in order to bring them "before the conscience of Italy and all of Europe." This act testified to the failure of his diplomacy. It did not strengthen him in Parliament, where he had lost the support of the Cavourian Marco Minghetti, his former Minister of the Interior, and failed to acquire that of Rattazzi. The latter had thoughts of supplanting Ricasoli and therefore refused the post Minghetti had vacated. Rattazzi was a confidant of Victor Emmanuel and Napoleon III, and both these rulers found the "iron baron" far too haughty for their tastes. Moreover, Ricasoli was not especially popular in the country, where Action Committees (*Comitati di provvedimento*) were being formed for daring enterprises either against Austria or against Rome. During a debate in February 1862 on the legality of these committees, Ricasoli defended their constitutional propriety, and thus found himself abandoned by the Right without securing the support of the Left. Upon Ricasoli's resignation at the end of February, a new government was formed by Rattazzi, who thus finally realized his ambition to be the King's chief Minister. But Rattazzi's nine months in power were to be most troubled, and the principal cause of these troubles was the government's indecision on how far to promote or restrain the action of volunteer groups intent on taking Rome by force.

At first it seemed that Rattazzi and the King would find it easier to work with Garibaldi than had been possible for either Cavour or Ricasoli. In part to distract popular attention from Rome, Rattazzi and the King formulated an ill-defined plan for the raising of the oppressed nationalities in the Austrian empire and the taking of Venetia while Austria was involved in its Balkan troubles. Accordingly, Garibaldi was charged with the promotion of exercises in target practice all over Italy—a thinly disguised subterfuge for the gathering of volunteers for action in the Balkans. But when, in May 1862, some of these volunteers appeared to be on their way to invading Venetia, they were arrested and detained with some violence, arousing Garibaldi's ire and Rattazzi's disavowal of any anti-Austrian venture. Whatever understandings there may have been between Garibaldi and the government were now shattered. Garibaldi went to Sicily—the scene of his greatest triumph—and raised the banner of "Rome or Death."

The following address by Garibaldi shows how the Roman question was inextricably tied to the conditions of the South, and how once again the two "questions" pitted Garibaldi against the government and thus raised the specter of civil war.

Garibaldi vs. *Napoleon: Address to the People of Palermo, July 15, 1862*

Ghiron, ed., *Annali d'Italia*, I, 241. Our translation.

People of Palermo,

The master of France, the traitor of December 2, he who shed the blood of our Parisian brothers, occupies Rome under the pretext of protecting the person of the Pope as well as religion and Catholicism. Lies! Lies! He is moved by lust, by prey, and by infamous thirst for power. He is the first to feed brigandage; he has become the chief of brigands and assassins.

People of the Vespers,* people of 1860, it is imperative that Napoleon evacuate Rome. If necessary, let there be another Vespers.

Upon receiving news that volunteers from all over Italy were gathering in the vicinity of Palermo and that Garibaldi had formed a "Roman Legion" with the motto "Italy and Victor Emmanuel—Rome or Death," the King issued the following proclamation to the country.

Royal Proclamation against Rash Agitation To Take Rome by Force, August 3, 1862

Ghiron, ed., *Annali d'Italia*, I, 245–46. Our translation.

At a time when Europe renders homage to the good sense of our country and to its rights, it grieves my heart to see that inexperienced

---
* Reference to the Sicilians' massacre of their French masters on Easter Monday, 1282. Ed. note.

and misled youths—forgetful of their duty and of the gratitude they owe our best allies—make signs of war in the name of Rome. . . .

Faithful to the Constitution and the oath I have sworn, I held high the Italian banner made sacred by the blood and glorious valor of my people. Whoever violates the laws and infringes upon the freedom and security of the fatherland by erecting himself as judge of its destinies does not follow that banner.

Italians! Beware of blameworthy impatience and rash agitation.

When the hour for the completion of the great enterprise comes, the voice of your King will make itself heard.

Every call which does not come from him is a call to rebellion, to civil war.

The responsibility and full weight of the law will fall on those who do not heed my words. Acclaimed King by the nation, I know my duties. I shall know how to preserve the dignity of the Crown and of Parliament in order to have the right to ask for justice for Italy before all Europe.

Victor Emmanuel
[*Countersigned* by all his Ministers]

The royal proclamation did not have its intended effect. Garibaldi's followers continued to increase in Sicily, and preparations were made for a crossing to the mainland and a march on Rome. On August 17, after a report by the Ministry branding Garibaldi a rebel, the King ordered the declaration of martial law in Sicily. Three days later the same measure was adopted for the Neapolitan provinces. But neither these measures nor the surveillance of the Straits of Messina were enough to prevent Garibaldi from landing over two thousand volunteers on the mainland late in August. There followed a brief encounter between the Garibaldians and the regular army at Aspromonte, in southern Calabria. A dozen men were killed and among the over forty wounded was Garibaldi himself—"wounded by an Italian bullet!" he is said to have exclaimed bitterly. Popular resentment at plans to try Garibaldi for rebellion forced the government to abandon this course and grant him and most of his followers a general amnesty at the first suitable occasion, which came in October with the marriage of one of the King's daughters to the King of Portugal. This gesture of leniency was not enough for the government to regain its popularity, nor did it please Napoleon who, after the latest Garibaldian enterprise, was less willing than ever to withdraw his garrisons from Lazio. Attacked for different reasons by both the Left and the Right in Parliament, Rattazzi decided to resign early in December before the Deputies could vote him out of office.

A new government was formed by two Cavourian lieutenants, Luigi Carlo Farini as Prime Minister and Marco Minghetti as Minister of Finance. All Piedmontese were deliberately excluded from the Cabinet, giving rise to another manifestation of political regionalism in united Italy. This anti-Piedmontese gesture was but a mild expression of regionalism in comparison to the intermittent rebellion and civil strife plaguing the South since the time of unification. And when Minghetti replaced the ailing Farini as Prime Minister in March 1863 he was soon to have before him a report which acquainted him in full detail with the awesome problems of the Southern question—a question fully as portentous as the unresolved problem of how to acquire Rome.

One reason why Minghetti had resigned from Ricasoli's Ministry in September 1861 was his opposition to the administrative centralization which the Tuscan baron sought to impose on united Italy. In March 1861 Minghetti and Farini had cosponsored with Cavour a bill for administrative decentralization providing for self-governing communes, provinces, and regions, with considerable autonomy and initiative allotted to the regions. Fearing that any measure of regional autonomy would perpetuate those local differences and interests which had made unification so difficult, Ricasoli preferred and began the implementation of a centralized structure by extending the Piedmontese administrative system to all of Italy. One consequence of centralization was regional reaction to real or imagined Piedmontese predominance in state administration. Nowhere was this reaction more intense than in the South. A grave socioeconomic crisis, fanned by Bourbon-clerical intrigues and Garibaldian discontents, erupted into a protest called "brigandage" by those who found it easier to ascribe the whole complex problem to "brigands" than to search for less facile explanations. One of the first acts of the Farini-Minghetti Ministry was to secure the appointment of a parliamentary commission to study the Southern question. The commission presented two reports to the Chamber of Deputies in secret session on May 3 and 4, 1863. One report was prepared by Giuseppe Massari, Deputy of the moderate or Center group and a redoubtable opponent of the Bourbons; the other report came from Stefano Castagnola, Deputy of the Left. The Massari-Castagnola reports have become the classic exposition of the brigandage problem in the South in the 1860s.

Excerpts from the Massari-Castagnola Parliamentary Reports on Brigandage in the Neapolitan Provinces, May 3–4, 1863

Ghiron, ed., *Annali d'Italia*, I, 328–80, *passim*. Our translation.

The primary causes of brigandage are the predisposing ones, and first among these is the social condition. The economic status of the peasant precisely in those provinces where brigandage has reached the highest proportions is quite unhappy. . . . The tiller of the soil has no bond which ties him to the land. His condition is precisely that of the totally propertyless; and even if his wages were raised, his economic status would not thereby improve. . . .

[Futhermore] although the feudal system has been extinguished by the progress of civilization and by prescriptive laws, it has nonetheless left a heritage which is not yet wholly destroyed. . . . The barons are no more but the tradition of their abuses of power and overbearing manner has not yet been erased, and in several of the localities we have named the present landlord still represents in the eyes of the peasant the ancient feudal lord. The peasant knows that his efforts bring him neither well being nor prosperity. He knows that the fruits of the soil watered by his sweat will not be his. He sees and feels himself condemned to perpetual misery, and the instinct for revenge rises spontaneously in his soul. When the opportunity comes he does not let it pass. He becomes a brigand, that is, he seeks to acquire by force that well being and prosperity which another's force prevents him from achieving, preferring the fruitful discomforts of a brigand's life to honest but ill-rewarded labor. In this guise, brigandage becomes misery's savage and brutal protest against age-old injustices.

But perhaps the predisposing cause of brigandage deriving from unhappy social conditions—from misery and poverty—would not have the terrible efficacy which in fact it does were it not powerfully supported by another cause of the same kind, that is to say, the Bourbon system. Misery alone would perhaps not produce so many pernicious effects were it not connected with other evils which the inauspicious Bourbon rule created and left in the Neapolitan provinces. These evils are: the careful nurturing and expansion of ignorance; the accrediting and diffusion of superstition; and especially important, the absolute lack of confidence in law and justice. The thousands of men whom the Bourbon government butchered on the block or caused to suffer in prisons, galleys, or exiles were not its most unhappy victims. The executioner's ax and the gallows were neither the greatest nor the most cruel forms of punishment used by the Bourbons. They endeavored with all their power to commit the most nefarious of parricides, that of depriving a whole people of its consciousness of justice and honesty. Ferdinand II * in particular brought to this stubborn enterprise

* Reigned from 1830 to 1859. Ed. note.

an industry and intelligence which were truly infernal. . . . Famished for absolute rule, little did he care that he ruled over a desert, so long as he ruled. . . . His long and baleful reign was a permanent brigandage against the most sacred property right—that of honesty—and against the most precious prerogative in the life of nations—morality. . . . This apostolate of immorality and injustice, coming as it did from the heights of a throne, could not but have its effect on the miserable poor. . . . We have it told and repeated to us by many honorable and authoritative men that these people have no sense of justice; they have no faith in it; they do not believe in it. . . .

Furthermore, that the absence of roads should promote and assist brigandage is so self-evident that it is hardly necessary to prove it. Even this deplorable absence was one of the elements of the Bourbon system and the result of a preconceived design. The Bourbons had magnificent roads built in the vicinity of Naples in order to deceive foreigners and thus acquire the appearance of a civilized government. In this guise they realized their goal: a mask of civilization in Naples and a totally unveiled barbarism in the provinces. . . .

These were the conditions of the Neapolitan provinces at the time of the political changes of 1860. At this point we are naturally led to discuss the proximate and immediate causes of current brigandage, for it is well to remember that the ones we have been discussing up to now are only the general predisposing causes of this cruel scourge. . . .

Among the proximate and immediate causes of brigandage there are enumerated both those which were inevitably inherent in the nature of things and those which derived from the dubious aims of the dispossessed dynasty. . . . Foretelling the destiny which awaited him, and faithful to the customs of his family and his father's dictates, Francis II * prepared insidiously to disturb the peace of those provinces which he had not known how to retain by courage and bold works. The first seeds of brigandage were sown during the last days of Bourbon rule. . . . During the months of July and August 1860 . . . the ranks of reaction were secretly prepared . . . in the hope of stifling the national movement as had been done in May 1848. Old functionaries were confirmed in their offices . . . ; the troops were authorized to sack and pillage; jails and galleys were deliberately left with little supervision. . . . Before abandoning Naples Francis II

* Son of Ferdinand II; reigned from May 1859 to February 1861. Ed. note.

issued a decree which immediately opened the jails to many and to others soon thereafter. It was a completely premeditated design for reaction. . . . The peasantry everywhere was incited and urged to join with the Bourbon troops and gendarmes. At Castelmorone, at Piedimonte, Caiazzo, and Casolina the volunteers in [Garibaldi's] Southern Army had to fight against armed peasants. . . . A certain Giorgi, in the company of an officer of the Bourbon army, harangued a group of peasants with these words: "Francis II wishes to make an end of these *gentlemen* who do you harm. He charged me to say to you that he will give you all their wealth and houses. I am also charged by the Pope to bless you and absolve you of your sins." Everyone knows that in local slang *gentleman* means whoever has a suit of clothes, whoever possesses anything.

Now, the words referred to above reveal clearly the Bourbon plan of effecting a restoration by means of a war between the classes, by inciting the passions and grievances of the poor against the rich or well to do, of the proletariat against the property owner. . . .

The reasons why brigandage continues to exist and has not ceded before the heroic constancy and indomitable valor of our soldiers are clearly revealed by the events of the last two years. This is a painful responsibility which belongs to no single political party and which, at the same time, belongs to all. . . . Errors were committed by [Garibaldi's] dictatorial government as well as by the four Royal Lieutenancies and succeeding administrations. . . . The rapid succession of men and governing bodies had the effect of increasing the sense of uncertainty and political oscillation. . . . These uncertainties and oscillations seemed all the larger in the eyes of a people who, because they had suffered much, hoped for much, and who could not understand and could not be expected to understand why the miraculously rapid work of destruction had to be followed by such a slow process of rebuilding. People who are accustomed to seeing evil done instantaneously cannot but find it inexplicable and intolerable that there should be so many inevitable delays in the doing of good. . . .

New and strong nourishment to brigandage was provided by corruption in communal and provincial administration, by justice not always administered fairly, by the weaknesses of mayors, and by inadequate police forces. Aid to brigandage came also from the clergy. . . . Naturally, we do not mean the entire clergy, but that part of it

which sacrificed religious principles to worldly interests . . . and gave
its hand to all the enemies . . . of the peace and integrity of the Italian nation. . . . During last December a preacher spoke the following
words from the pulpit of one of Naples' most crowded churches: "*Our
brothers the brigands* have been victorious in various parts of Italy, as
they will always be victorious because they fight against a usurping
King. May the Madonna grant us the miracle of seeing the usurpers
chased from our Kingdom." . . .

All incursions by brigands from papal territory are promoted and
equipped by Bourbon committees to be found here and there outside
our state and acting in concert with committees within our land.
There are committees in Marseilles, in Paris, and at Malta; they
abound in Rome and in locales closer to our borders. The committee
of the town of Alatri [in Lazio] is directed and presided over by the
bishop of that diocese. . . . The leaders of these committees who re-
side in Rome are open members of Francis II's court. . . . Francis II
is therefore aware of all these machinations and not only tolerates but
wishes it that his cause be represented and served by bandits and
marauders.

Senator Ferregui, Solicitor General of the Court of Cassation in
Naples, has told us that the root of brigandage is in Rome. So long as
that root is not removed, brigandage will not be extirpated. Senator
Niutta, President of the same Court, told us that the principal support
of brigandage comes from Rome. The illustrious Luigi Settembrini
told us that the principal inspiration comes from Rome because it is
from Rome that, in addition to money, there comes the idea that
there, in Rome, is to be found the King of the Two Sicilies, who one
day may return.

Rome and the South—the two problems were inseparably bound together;
and although the Italian Parliament could do very little to solve the Roman
question, it was able to take measures to "solve" the Southern question.
Three months after the presentation of the Massari-Castagnola reports, Parliament passed and the King signed a law for the repression of brigandage in
the South. The law provided for Draconian measures, including the suspension of all constitutional guarantees, the introduction of trial by courts martial, and the summary execution of armed suspects. However justified this
policy of repression may have been, it hardly addressed itself to the socioeconomic causes of the phenomenon of brigandage so masterfully exposed
by Massari and Castagnola. An equally fierce repression was mounted in

Sicily where, in addition to conditions roughly analogous to the ones defined in the parliamentary reports dealing with the Neapolitan provinces, there was the added problem of massive draft evasion. Whatever the faults of Bourbon rule, it had had for the Sicilians at least one merit: unlike the united Italian administration, the Bourbons never imposed military conscription on the people of the island. Parliament's approval of the severe treatment of the Sicilians so disgusted Garibaldi that in December 1863 he decided to resign his seat in the Chamber of Deputies in order not to be even an "indirect accomplice in crimes which are not mine."

21. THE COMPLETION OF UNIFICATION: THE ROAD TO VENICE AND ROME

While the Italian government was engaged in repressing intermittent rebellion in the South—a task whose cost in lives has been estimated as greater than the losses incurred in all the preceding efforts at national unification [2] —it also continued with its efforts to solve the Roman question. The almost universal opinion of the country was that the South could not be permanently pacified so long as Rome remained in alien hands. Following the lines laid down by Cavour in his negotiations with Napoleon, Minghetti concluded an agreement with France in 1864 known as the September Convention. This agreement provided for the gradual evacuation of French troops from papal territory on condition that Italy guarantee the integrity of the remaining papal state and that, as a pledge of this guarantee, Italy transfer its capital from Turin to another city. The Convention was unpopular in Piedmont, especially in the capital city of Turin where serious riots and scores of dead and wounded occasioned Minghetti's fall from office.

A new ministerial combination was formed by the Piedmontese bloc of General Alfonso La Marmora, Giovanni Lanza, and Quintino Sella. It presented the September Convention for Parliament's approval with the assurance that it did not involve any renunciation of national aspirations—meaning Rome—thus trying to dispel the fears that the projected transfer of the capital from Turin to Florence meant the abandonment of hopes that Rome would become the capital. But, in fact, one of the underlying assumptions of the Convention was precisely that Rome would not become the capital of Italy unless and until a reconciliation was reached with the Pope. The prospects of such a reconciliation became less and less likely as time wore on. In December 1864 Pope Pius IX issued his encyclical *Quanta Cura* and the companion *Syllabus of Errors*, both documents condemning in substance nationalism and the basic liberal principles guiding the founders of the Italian state. Specifically censured was the practice of civil marriage. As if pointedly to rebuff the Pope, the Italian Parliament passed a series of laws during

[2] Denis Mack Smith, *Italy: A Modern History* (Ann Arbor, The University of Michigan Press, 1959), p. 75.

the first four months of 1865 which provided for the further centralization of
Italian administration under Civil and Penal Codes uniform for all Italy. Besides giving the national legislature authority to regulate all aspects of communal and provincial administration, these codes contained a provision for
obligatory civil marriage. Pressed by a grave fiscal crisis, the government
was moved to present in 1866 a bill for the suppression of monastic orders
and the expropriation of their properties. The eventual approval of this bill
made relations between Italy and the Papacy more difficult than ever.

The following excerpt from a work on Italian economic history presents
the background to the fiscal crisis and its connection with the perennial sore
of the Roman question.

Fiscal Needs and Relations with the Church

Shepard B. Clough, *The Economic History of Modern Italy*. New York:
Columbia University Press, 1964, pp. 42–43, 47–49. Original footnotes
omitted.

The War of Unification against Austria had cost nearly 400 million
lire—89 million for the conduct of the war, 145 million for three-fifths
of the Lombard-Venetian debt, 100 million to France for another part
of the Lombard debt which France had paid Austria, and 60 million
to France for part of its cost of the war. . . .

In March 1861, Count Bastogi, Leghorn banker and Minister of
Finance . . . proposed and got accepted the principle that United
Italy should assume the public debts of the predecessor states—a sum
that amounted to about 2,400 million lire. . . . Furthermore, there
was the Herculean task of bringing together the budgets of the prior
states into a national budget, for budget practices varied widely and
estimates of both receipts and expenditures were almost impossible to
make with any degree of accuracy. No one knew, for example, how
much tax evasion there was; only an oracle could have forecast what
military expenditures would be to cope with brigandage, or to keep
an army at fighting trim for fear of international complications; and
even a supernatural power would have been hard pressed to know
how much the founding fathers would pay out for public works, especially railroads.

How difficult budgeting was—or at least achieving any semblance
of a balance—can be gathered from the fact that in 1861 the deficit

for the year was expected at first to be 268 million, and was ultimately 505 million. In 1862 the deficit at the beginning of the year was expected to be 319 million, but turned out to be 400 million, which was almost twice receipts; and in 1863 the deficit was 382 million. In fact for the four years 1861–65 deficits amounted to 2,178 million, or to 47 per cent more than receipts.

The desperateness of the treasury's situation was such in these early years that recourse was had to borrowing. Indeed, from 1861 to 1865 the public debt rose by 2,660 million or more than the total amount of the public debt of United Italy in 1860. . . . The rising public debt had led the statesmen of the day to search arduously for new sources of revenue. Unfortunately receipts from the taxes just discussed were slow to attain the volume needed and consequently recourse was had to what many considered measures of desperation. These were: (1) the seizure and sale of those properties belonging to religious orders and the Church which were not used for religious purposes; (2) the sale of the domain of the state, that is, certain properties belonging to the state; (3) the sale of state railways to private companies; and (4) the instituting of the *Corso Forzoso,* that is, declaring the paper money of the banks of issue to be no longer convertible into gold or silver.

The question of the state's seizing the property of religious orders and of the Church had . . . been an issue since the French Revolution and had been partially carried out in Piedmont (1855). With the unification of Italy relations between Pius IX and the state became more tense than ever. . . . Nevertheless, when the Piedmontese laws pertaining to religious orders and the Church were extended to Italy (from 1860 to the law of August 21, 1862), they were not applied rigorously. For the moment no monasteries or convents were suppressed in Sicily, Tuscany, Emilia, or Lombardy and many were allowed to continue in Umbria, the Marches, Naples, and Piedmont. In fact, there were still 2,400 religious houses with 47,000 members, and the income of monasteries, bishoprics, and of religious chapters was estimated to have been 50 million, although many parish priests lived in real poverty. Also, both the state and local governments spent millions every year for religious purposes.

As time went on Pius' position against the new state and its principles became more adamant and in his encyclical *Quanta Cura* and in the accompanying *Syllabus of Errors* (1864), he condemned nationalism, liberalism, and everything else which undermined his temporal position. On the other hand, the Italian parliament began to give less consideration to religious issues and to think more of the wealth to be obtained by expropriating the property of religious orders. Finally, after a long parliamentary struggle and in the excitement generated by the War of 1866, the laws of July 7, 1866, and of August 15, 1867, were passed.

These laws provided for the suppression of monastic orders and the seizure of their property; the expropriation of much of the real property of the Church not used for religious purposes; and an extraordinary 30 per cent tax on other ecclesiastical property except that of parishes and of a few other organizations engaged strictly in matters concerned with religion. In all, property estimated to be worth 1,700 million was taken.

The considerable sum thus acquired was placed under the control of a department known as the Domain of the State, which had in addition to Church properties, the iron mines on the Island of Elba, forests, mineral springs, arsenals, some irrigation canals, and common lands, especially sea swamps and mountain tops. The whole thus administered from 1860 to 1882 had a total value estimated at 1,928 million.

To turn this vast holding into funds which could be used to pay the debts of the state was not so simple as might be imagined. So far as land was concerned, the law prescribed that it should be sold in small lots in order to satisfy the land hunger of the peasants and to get more intensive cultivation. Desirable as this may have been, it meant that not much land could be put on the market at any one time for fear of driving the price down and that purchasers had to be given terms in which to make payments (usually fifteen years) because they had little capital. Sidney Sonnino in an official investigation of the sale of ecclesiastical lands contended that the rich got the lion's share. At public auctions the poor were scared away. Futhermore, there was some antipathy to the purchase of land previously held by religious orders or the Church because of fear that titles to the property might some day be successfully contested by former owners or because of religious scruples. And, in fact, there were serious disturbances over the issue, particularly in Palermo in 1866.

Military "Victory" and Domestic Insurrection: Venetia and Palermo

The Palermo insurrection of September 1866 was but another disturbing aspect of what should have been Italy's proud moment of a second victory over Austria. With Rome still beyond its reach, the Italian government decided early in 1866 that it could not lose the opportunity offered to it by Prussia for a common venture against Austria and the prospective acquisition of Venetia. The agitation for a rapid completion of unification was difficult to contain: a discontented Garibaldi, a resurgent Mazzini, a troubled South—all these factors weighed heavily in the decision to risk the fortunes of war once again. A great victory not only would increase Italy's prestige abroad but, perhaps more important, it would raise the country's confidence in itself and solidify its still fragile institutions.

A treaty of alliance against Austria was signed by Italy and Prussia in April 1866, and although Austria made it known in May that it would be willing to cede Venetia to Italy as the price for its neutrality in an eventual Austro-Prussian war, General La Marmora refused the offer as contrary to the country's honor and pledged word. At the beginning of hostilities during the second half of June, La Marmora assumed the post of Chief of Staff of the army and relinquished the premiership, which was entrusted to Ricasoli. Victor Emmanuel had nominal command of the army, but the actual field command was exercised by La Marmora with 12 divisions and General Enrico Cialdini with 8 divisions. Garibaldi responded to a royal summons and assumed command of a corps of volunteers eventually numbering 40,000. The combined Italian land forces in the Italian theater of operations numbered approximately 260,000, exactly double the Austrian strength in the area. On June 24, four days after Italy's declaration of war, Italian arms met with defeat at Custoza, scene of the Piedmontese defeat in 1848. The extent of this second reversal at Custoza was not serious but owing to the division of field command, confusion of plans, and poor staff work, the import of the defeat was overestimated and a general withdrawal was ordered. On July 20, the ineptly commanded Italian war fleet suffered a defeat in the Adriatic, near the island of Lissa. Two days later the Prussians, previously victorious at Sadowa (Königgrätz), decided to conclude a truce with the Austrians and began negotiations for peace without Italian knowledge or participation, in clear violation of the Italo-Prussian alliance. It seemed like Villafranca all over again. A series of victories by Garibaldi's volunteer corps in the Tyrol had saved the honor of Italian arms, but the Austro-Prussian armistice made it impossible for the regular Italian forces to redeem themselves. Unable to fight alone, Italy had to agree to an armistice with the Austrians under terms which assured Italy the acquisition of Venetia, but which forced it to abandon any claims to the Tyrolean areas conquered by

Garibaldi and to other Italian-speaking areas in the North and Northeast. These areas were eventually to be known as the "unredeemed provinces" (*Italia irredenta*), and Italian agitation for their acquisition from Austria was to poison relations between the two countries for the next fifty years.

Italy acquired Venetia under the provisions of the October 1866 Austro-Italian peace treaty of Vienna; but coming on the heels of military defeat, this acquisition was further marred by Austria's insistence that its cession of Venetia be accomplished indirectly, from Austria to France and from France to Italy. While the country was rejoicing as best it could over the dubious conditions of its acquisition of Venetia, there occurred in Palermo an insurrection of wide proportions that proved to many the need to acquire Rome and further restrict the political influence of the Church in Italy.

REPORT OF SEPTEMBER 24, 1866 BY GENERAL RAFFAELE CADORNA, ROYAL COMMISSIONER AND MILITARY COMMANDER IN SICILY. Ghiron, ed. *Annali d'Italia*, II, 347–54, *passim*. Our translation.

For some time rumors had been circulating in Palermo and surrounding communes of grave and imminent disorders, of large armed bands scouring the neighboring countryside, and of a projected attempt to break into the city to attack the garrison and take over the government.

An intense gunfire was heard from the north and south of the city from three to four o'clock on the morning of the 16th of this month. . . .

The insurgents advanced from all sides and, owing to their large numbers in the center of the city as well as to the activity of those hidden there the night before, fighting took place in almost all quarters of the city. . . .

By three o'clock in the afternoon the bands were masters of the city, except for the fortress of Castellamare, the prison, the Treasury building, the royal palace, and the City Hall, all of which remained in control of the troops. . . .

In brief, until the morning of the 20th—when three battalions led by General Masi arrived—all efforts of the few forces then available * . . . were aimed at holding firm [in the royal palace] against

---

* The garrison of the city and province of Palermo at the time consisted of 3,196 men, including a battery of artillery. Ed. note.

the threats and attacks of the bands, which pushed their daring to the point of demanding that we treat with them, as if the government could ever have recognized them as belligerents.

On the evening of the same 20th a battalion of Bersaglieri led by General Masi made a brilliant charge along the Avenue Vittorio Emanuele, but military necessity obliged it to return to the royal palace thereafter. However, on the morning of the 21st the attack was resumed and the City Hall position [previously lost] was taken. In the meanwhile, some units of the Longoni and Angioletti divisions were arriving. These units invested the northern and southern extremities of the city with [relief of] the royal palace as their objective. After several violent encounters with bands of malefactors they succeeded in putting them to flight. Communications were reestablished with the center of the city, and from that point on the anarchy was decisively crushed.

Inasmuch as the causes and origins of this disorder are matters which preceded my arrival here—and on which I am therefore not called to judge—I shall abstain from any evaluation regarding them. . . .

Nevertheless, I am obliged to say that the action of friars and nuns much influenced the promotion of the lamented disorders. It is clear even from preliminary investigations that their money was the principal resource that put up and maintained the armed bands with arms and munitions. Several friars took part in the fighting side by side with the rogues. These squads were entrenched principally in convents. The greatest resistance came from squads in the convent of the Stigmatics: the nuns assisted in the fighting and encouraged the rebels to fire upon the troops. In the light of this and other facts, public opinion demands the suppression of these citadels of reaction.

The law of July 1866 suppressing "these citadels of reaction" had not yet gone into full effect at the time of the insurrection in Palermo, but there is no doubt that the provisions of this law had much to do with monastic and clerical support of the insurrection. In an effort to reach some accommodation with the Papacy, Ricasoli's Ministry presented a moderate bill in January 1867 which in effect made for a total separation of Church and state: the state would relinquish all its rights over pontifical and diocesan religious acts in Italy, but at the same time the proposed law would abolish all remaining special privileges of the Church, eliminating Catholicism's position as the state religion and affirming the complete equality of all religions before the law. The bill provided also for the final liquidation of confiscated monastic and diocesan property by means of a monetary payment by the Church of 600 million lire. There was much agitation in the country over the bill's provisions: some thought them too lenient toward the Church while others thought them too harsh. Ricasoli's efforts to contain this agitation by prohibiting all public assemblies and demonstrations led to an adverse vote in the Chamber, which was then dissolved. The resulting elections of March 19, 1867, left Ricasoli's position sufficiently precarious for him to resign in April.

Inasmuch as Ricasoli's fall was occasioned by strong opposition from the Left, the King turned to his confidant Urbano Rattazzi, a man of the moderate Left, to form a new government. But the unfortunate Rattazzi, who had lost power in 1862 after only nine months in office, was once again to have a very short tenure in 1867, and for the same reason—indecision on how far to encourage Garibaldi in a venture to take Rome by force.

Sometime in September 1867 Garibaldi conceived or accepted the idea of promoting an insurrection in the Roman provinces and then assuring its success by leading a force of volunteers from Italy into the papal city. The enterprise did not remain secret—if ever it was—for long. Garibaldi himself virtually made it public with an announcement on September 16 calling on the Romans to "go forward, break your irons on the hoods of your oppressors; there will be many Italians on hand to share your glory." Five days later Rattazzi had an announcement issued to the public warning it of violations of the September Convention with France and reminding all Italians that no one was above the law. And, in fact, on September 24 Garibaldi was arrested, but three days later he was freed and allowed to return to his home on the island of Caprera. This was but one of the many gestures of indecision characteristic of Rattazzi at this juncture. While appearing to oppose a violent seizure of Rome—in order not to alienate Napoleon—he allowed the arming of volunteers with weapons from the National Guard. He apparently hoped that if a popular rising were to occur in Rome, he would be justified in allowing free play to the volunteers and perhaps even in intervening with regular troops. But the Garibaldians moved into papal territory before the outbreak of the planned popular insurrection. Strong French protests to the Italian government weakened Victor Emmanuel's support of his Prime Minister, and Rattazzi resigned on October 19. Two days earlier Garabaldi had escaped from Caprera and on October 23 he crossed from Italian into papal territory to assume command of his volunteers. Alarmed by French threats, Victor Emmanuel chose a new Ministry whose three leaders were, or were soon to be, members of the Royal Household: General Marquis Senator Luigi Federico Menabrea, First Aide-de-Camp, as Prime Minister; Marquis Senator Filippo Gualterio as Minister of the Interior; Count Senator Luigi Guglielmo Cambray Digny, Master of Ceremonies of the Royal Household, as Minister of Finance. Secure in the support of these devoted servants of his dynasty—all three Senators—the King, master of the government as he had never been since the advent of Cavour, issued a proclamation which disowned Garibaldi's venture.

Royal Proclamation Condemning the Invasion of Papal Territory, October 27, 1867

Ghiron, ed., *Annali d'Italia*, III, 114–16. Our translation.

Scores of volunteers incited and seduced by the work of a certain party [probably an allusion more to Mazzini than to Garibaldi] have violated the frontiers of my state without my authorization or that of my government.

The respect which all citizens owe the laws and international agreements sanctioned by Parliament and by me make for an inexorable debt of honor in the present grave circumstances.

Europe knows that the banner raised in lands near mine, on which there is written the destruction of the supreme spiritual authority of the head of the Catholic religion, is not my banner.

This enterprise places our common fatherland in grave danger. It enjoins me with the imperious duty both to save the honor of the country and not to confuse two different objectives in one or two absolutely distinct causes.*

Italy must be protected from the dangers it may incur. Europe must be convinced that Italy is faithful to its commitments and that it neither wishes to be, nor can it be, a disturber of public order.

A war with our ally [Napoleon] would be a fratricidal war between two armies which fought for the same cause.

Entrusted as I am with the right to make war and peace, I cannot tolerate any usurpations of this right.

I trust, therefore, that the voice of reason will be heard and that the Italian citizens who violated this right will withdraw immediately behind the lines of our troops.

The dangers which disorders and ill-considered enterprises may create among us must be exorcised; the authority of the government and the inviolability of the laws must be maintained.

* A not too clear reference to the difference between the aim to acquire Rome peacefully, and in accordance with international agreements, and the attempt to take Rome by force and perhaps attack the Church as well. Ed. note.

The honor of the country is in my hands, and the country will not deny me the confidence it had in me in its darkest hours.

When spirits are calmed and public order completely restored, my government, in agreement with France and in accordance with the expressed wishes of Parliament, will try faithfully and with every effort to find a useful arrangement which may put an end to the grave and important question of the Romans.

Neither Napoleon nor Garibaldi heeded Victor Emmanuel's assurances and pleas. At the end of October French troops returned to Rome, whence they had left at the end of 1866 in accordance with the September Convention. Garibaldi, on his part, continued his march into papal territory. On November 3, after holding his own against papal troops, Garibaldi met defeat at the hands of French soldiers using rapid-fire weapons (*chassepots*). The end of the battle of Mentana cost Garibaldi 150 dead, 240 wounded, and 1,765 prisoners. He himself was taken prisoner by Italian authorities on November 5, while on his way to Leghorn and Caprera. Quite contrary to the severe language of the royal proclamation, Garibaldi was released toward the end of the month and allowed to return to his home. On December 5, 1867, an official royal act amnestied him and all his followers for their latest enterprise on behalf of Rome. But this act did not spare the government severe censure in Parliament. The Left was alarmed by the predominance of royal placemen in the government, nor did the King's repeated assertions of his royal prerogatives in the proclamation of October 27 escape the attention of those who believed that the King should reign but not rule. Characterized by many Deputies as reactionary, the Menabrea-Gualterio-Cambray Digny Ministry was upset on December 22, 1867, by a vote of 199 to 201. The King refused to accept Menabrea's resignation. After a crisis of nearly three weeks Menabrea and Cambray Digny were reconfirmed in office, but Gualterio was sacrificed to make way for Carlo Cadorna, an old Cavourian who was more acceptable to the Left as Minister of the Interior.

General Menabrea remained in office the whole of 1868 and most of 1869. It was an exceptionally long tenure, characterized by a courageous but unpopular policy of high taxation, including the introduction of the grist tax,[3] and an equally unpopular policy of domestic repression against the continuing brigandage in the South and repeated disturbances inspired by republicans in Romagna. The Left, and especially the republican and socialistic elements on the extreme Left, branded the government as reactionary. Garibaldi specified this charge in a letter addressed to his electors in the Gallura area of northeast Sardinia who had returned him to Parliament.

---

[3] A tax on the grinding of food grains, to be collected by the mill operator, and popularly known as the "tax on the food of the poor."

*Garibaldi Recalls His Republicanism and Attacks the Government:
Letter of December 24, 1868*

Ghiron, ed., *Annali d'Italia*, III, 161–65, *passim*. Our translation.

Never have I been placed in a more perplexing circumstance than by
my election as Deputy from Gallura. I am pitted between the affection I bear for these dear and attractive people, whom I would serve
with my life, and the repugnance I feel in being near a government
which could be called a "negation of God," as a distinguished Englishman [Gladstone] called the government of Naples before 1860.

Although old republicans in principles and deeds, I and my friends
accepted the monarchy in good faith, and asked of it nothing other
than that it improve the conditions of our poor people, that it maintain the people's dignity against tyrants and against the people's
Vampire of a thousand years [the Pope]. I leave it to you to decide
what has been obtained from this government.

Tolerant by nature, I am averse to use harsh language toward anyone. I would have been the first to support respect for a government
promotive of the good, no matter the government's political denomi-
nation. But is the government which today rules Italy a government
for the good?. . . .

What can one expect from a government which is good for nothing
except to act as a tax collector, as a squanderer of public monies, and
finally as an agent of a foreign tyrant? In truth, this government's behavior during the recent events in the Roman provinces was a series
of betrayals. . . .

On November 3 a government I am ashamed to call Italian not only
abandoned and did not assist a handful of young men fighting at
Mentana but also robbed them of their weapons, munitions, and
bread. . . .

This handful of young men, I say, deprived of all things necessary
to a soldier, nevertheless fought at Mentana for half a day against two
armies and for a while was master of the field of battle. . . .

My loving friends, I have thought that you would not be indifferent
to my kind of representation, which is more revolutionary than parlia-

mentary. And I hope that you are persuaded of the fact that a body's members cannot be healthy when the heart is sick. Wherefore I am convinced that I served the cause of Gallura on the banks of the Tiber—there, where the sick heart of the Italian fatherland is to be found.

You well know how the immunity which is the privilege of a Deputy is respected in Italy:* This immunity is not, therefore, the incentive that leads me to accept the mandate with which you seek to honor me. Rather, it is the love I bear for these attractive people, who are satisfied with my little worth and whom I shall serve very badly but with all my soul.

Garibaldi's reference to his republican principles and his explicit denunciation of the King's government were but one symptom of a growing disenchantment with Victor Emmanuel. The King's determination to rule as well as reign was evidenced by his appointment of General Menabrea and others personally loyal and devoted to him. Twenty years of parliamentary tradition, especially under governments led by forceful personalities such as d'Azeglio, Cavour, and Ricasoli, had tended to erode the King's constitutional prerogatives. Victor Emmanuel's intention to reassert these prerogatives was not limited to public proclamations, such as that of October 27, 1867. His retention of Menabrea in spite of an adverse vote in the Chamber in December of the same year was another sign of the King's resolution. An even more forceful earnest of his purposes was provided in July 1869, when he vetoed a bill approved by both houses of Parliament granting rights of citizenship to all Italians living in provinces not yet united with Italy. The King's veto was prompted by fear of international complications, for it was clear that the bill's provisions were aimed at the inhabitants of papal territory. But this interposition of the royal will before the expressed wishes of Parliament's majority was a most unusual step whose import could not be obscured by the substantive wisdom of the royal veto. There was no question of constitutional impropriety: the *Statuto* was explicit in granting the King the right of veto. But parliamentary tradition ran against the exercise of this right, and Parliament appeared determined to uphold a tradition which was tending toward parliamentary supremacy.

A serious constitutional crisis was developing. It came out into the open in November 1869 when Giovanni Lanza, Cavour's heir as leader of the moderate Right, was elected President of the Chamber of Deputies in opposition to the government's candidate. Menabrea felt obliged to resign. There fol-

* Allusion to the fact that Deputies had been arrested in spite of parliamentary immunity, as in his own case and that of three Deputies of the extreme Left after Garibaldi's attempt to march on Rome in August 1862. Ed. note.

lowed a crisis lasting over three weeks during which the King's desire to retain Menabrea and assert his right to choose his Ministers was obstructed by the Chamber's clear preference for Lanza. The latter, in turn, refused to form a new government unless the King accepted a program of economy in the armed forces and agreed to the dismissal of Menabrea, Cambray Digny, and Gualterio from the Royal Household. These three men were, in fact, the King's most trusted personal advisers. To admit, however indirectly, that even the selection of the Royal Household fell under parliamentary control was to allow a precedent which could eventually deprive the King of most of his effective political power. Victor Emmanuel resisted as best he could. He turned to General Senator Enrico Cialdini, who proved unable to form a Ministry; he threatened to abdicate, with no effect. Having reconciled himself to the loss of his personal advisers, the King finally accepted Lanza's demand for economies in the military establishment. Lanza's accession to office thus marked a turning point in Italian constitutional development. It also marked the beginning of a program of balanced budgets, economy, and administrative efficiency. Lanza promised to examine every budget with a "miser's lens"; Quintino Sella, his Minister of Finance and second most important man in the government, spoke of "economies to the bone." But before their three and a half years in office were far along, Lanza and Sella had to face the last episode of the Roman question during the unification period.

This episode began in July 1870, when France and Prussia went to war. Pressed by military needs, France evacuated its troops from papal territory early in August and later that month sent Prince Jerome Napoleon to Italy with the offer of complete Italian freedom of action in Rome in exchange for an alliance and military help against Prussia. Lanza and Sella opposed the alliance; the King, ever mindful of Napoleon's help in the war of 1859 and his own word never to abandon the emperor, favored assisting France. But popular opposition to war and the program of economy in the armed forces put war out of the question. After a threat to resign, Lanza's and Sella's will prevailed over the King's knightly sense of honor. When the government was attacked by those who deplored its economies in the military establishment, Sella replied with characteristic bluntness by saying that to maintain a large army and navy Italy would have to dispose of great financial resources, which it did not have.

The wisdom of Italy's decision to remain neutral became apparent after the French military disaster at Sedan on September 2, 1870. The next day a group of Deputies from the moderate and extreme Left addressed a plea to Lanza: "The catastrophe announced today indicates for the government the easy accomplishment of its duty: immediate occupation of Rome." This thought had not escaped the government, but before acting it preferred to make a last attempt at reconciliation with the Pope and peaceful acquisition of Rome. The following letters exchanged between Victor Emmanuel and Pius IX show the nature of the effort and the reasons for its failure.

A Last Appeal by Victor Emmanuel to the Pope: The King's Letter to Pius IX, September 8, 1870

Cappelletti, *Storia di Vittorio Emanuele II*, III, 434–36. Our translation.

Most Blessed Father,

With the affection of a son, the faith of a Catholic, the loyalty of a King, and the soul of an Italian, I address myself once again to Your Holiness' heart as I have done at times in the past.

Europe is threatened by a whirlwind full of dangers. Availing itself of the war which desolates the heart of the continent, the party of international revolution grows in impudence and audacity. It prepares, especially in Italy and in the provinces governed by Your Holiness, the last offenses against monarchy and the Papacy.

Most Blessed Father, I know that the greatness of your soul will never be inferior to the greatness of events. But as a Catholic and Italian King I am by disposition of Divine Providence and the will of the nation the custodian and guarantor of the destinies of all Italians. As such I feel it my duty to assume before Europe and all Catholicism the responsibility for the maintenance of order in the peninsula and the security of the Holy See. . . .

I deem it an indeclinable necessity for the security of Italy and the Holy See that my troops, already on guard at the frontier, go beyond the frontier and occupy those positions indispensable for the safety of Your Holiness and the maintenance of public order. . . .

My government and my forces will limit themselves absolutely to actions which preserve and safeguard the rights of the Roman populations. These rights are easily reconcilable with the inviolability of the Supreme Pontiff, his spiritual authority, and the independence of the Holy See. . . .

Your Holiness will permit me once again to hope that the present moment, as solemn for Italy as for the Church and the Papacy, may prove fruitful for that spirit of benevolence—which has never been extinguished in your soul—toward this land which is your fatherland as well. I hope also for the fruitfulness of those feelings of conciliation I have always sought with untiring perseverance to translate into reality in order that, by satisfying the nation's aspirations, the head of Catholicism may be surrounded by the devotion of the Italian people and retain on the banks of the Tiber a glorious seat independent of all earthly sovereignties. . . .

I pray Your Holiness to impart unto me your apostolic benediction and I affirm once again my feelings of profound respect for Your Holiness.

Victor Emmanuel

The Pope's Rejection of the King's Appeal: Pius IX's Reply to Victor Emmanuel, September 11, 1870

Cappelletti, *Storia di Vittorio Emanuele II*, III, 436. Our translation.

Your Majesty,

Count Ponza di San Martino has delivered to me a letter which it pleased Your Majesty to write to me. But this letter is not worthy of an affectionate son who boasts of professing the Catholic faith and who glories in his kingly loyalty. I shall not go into the letter's particulars because I do not wish to renew the pain which a first glance at it caused me. I thank God for allowing Your Majesty to fill with bitterness this last period of my life. As for the rest, I cannot accept the requests made in your letter, nor can I adhere to the principles it contains. Once again I appeal to God and into His hands I put my cause, which is wholly His. I pray Him to grant Your Majesty much grace to free your soul from all perils, and to allow you to partake of the mercy you need.

Pius PP. IX

On the morning of September 12, the day after the Pope's reply, Italian troops under General Raffaele Cadorna crossed the frontier into the Papal State. The Pope ordered the commander of papal troops defending the city of Rome to offer only the token defense necessary to establish that an act of violence had been committed by the Italian government and to negotiate a surrender as soon as the gates of Rome were pierced. The gates were pierced on September 20, the day after the above-mentioned papal order, and the whole city was surrendered, save for the Vatican palaces and the castle of Sant'Angelo. A plebiscite was held on October 2 in the Roman provinces:

133,681 votes were cast in favor of annexation and 1,507 voted against. When the results of the plebiscite were presented to Victor Emmanuel in his capital at Florence, he commented: "The arduous enterprise is finally accomplished, the fatherland is made."

VIII. JUDGMENTS AND EVALUATIONS
ON THE RISORGIMENTO

Benedetto Croce, contemporary Italy's most famous philosopher-historian, has noted that with the acquisition of Rome in 1870 many Italians felt that the best part of their lives had been lived and that after the "poetry" of Italy's "heroic" fulfillment of its unitary idea there could not but come the "prose" of ordinary existence. It was virtually inevitable that there should follow a debate on precisely what had been accomplished with the achievement of unification; equally inevitable were the questions on what had not but could have been wrought.[1] Raymond Grew's work on the Italian National Society [2] refers repeatedly to the fact that one of the Society's greatest achievements was its success in persuading many Italians to sacrifice the immediate realization of particular political and economic institutional preferences for the sake of the overriding imperative of unification. But, once completed in 1870, this unification which Croce has called the masterpiece of nineteenth-century liberal-nationalism had to mean the end of the uneasy truce on partisan policies and methods. And, just as the history of the thirty years covered by the next part of this work is essentially an account of the eruption of partisan ideologies and approaches from the cover imposed by the patriotic truce of the 1850s and 1860s, so is the recent historiography on the Risorgimento period essentially a manifestation of the desire to abandon the hagiography of earlier historians in favor of more searching and sometimes more partisan interpretations.

Among the first writers to seek a reorientation in Risorgimental historiography was Piero Gobetti. As a young man of twenty-five Gobetti wrote a work [3] that pictured the Risorgimento as a revolution that had failed because it had been led by mediocre men and not by heroes. The liberal historian Adolfo Omodeo replied to Gobetti by arguing that the latter's thesis was part of an old "satanic-luciferian prejudice" which made rebels more worthy and good than conservatives. Omodeo accused Gobetti of loving revolution

[1] Benedetto Croce, *Storia d'Italia dal 1871 al 1915* (13th ed.; Bari, Laterza, 1964), pp. 2–3.

[2] Raymond Grew, *A Sterner Plan for Italian Unity* (Princeton, N.J., Princeton University Press, 1963).

[3] Piero Gobetti, *Risorgimento senza eroi* (Turin, Edizioni del Baretti, 1926).

for its own sake, "as if nothing good and great can be accomplished unless it is explosive; as if the sound continuation of the past and the development of its traditions within us were of no merit." [4]

The failure of the "heroic" minority which led the struggles of the Risorgimento was examined with greater profundity and ideological awareness by Antonio Gramsci, founder of the Italian Communist Party. While in a Fascist prison from 1926 to shortly before his death in a hospital in 1937, Gramsci kept voluminous notebooks full of historical and theoretical observations. His commentaries on the Risorgimento reveal that he shared Gobetti's view of the Risorgimento as a revolution that had failed (*rivoluzione mancata*). Gobetti attributed this failure to the unheroic nature of its leaders and to the lack of popular initiative, the latter owing to an unenlightened public opinion and retarded economic denvelopment, whereas Gramsci emphasized the economic retardation, whose effects he synthesized into the motto that the Risorgimento was an agrarian revolution that had failed. He compared the Risorgimento with the French revolution of 1789; and to the question of why the French revolution was a popular movement whereas the Risorgimento was not, his reply was that the latter was led and accomplished by an "heroic" minority whose principal goal was the prevention of an agrarian revolution rather than a struggle against the enemies of unification. Gramsci considered this attitude on the part of the moderates to be a perfectly logical defense of their economic interests; he was much more critical of the Party of Action—Mazzinian and Garibaldian in inspiration—for its failure to promote a policy which reflected the desires of the masses, and especially the peasantry, for thoroughgoing socioeconomic reforms. His final judgment was that the Party of Action failed in this respect principally because it was essentially "an organ of agitation and propaganda in the service of the moderates." [5]

A contemporary Italian Marxist historian, Giorgio Candeloro, pays homage to Gramsci's "precious guidance," but he warns that Gramsci's thought should not be applied in a simplistic manner for the solution of all the complex questions facing the student of history. He accepts Gramsci's thesis that the Risorgimento was a bourgeois revolution that failed to reach its historical fulfillment because it did not realize a revolutionary transformation in the countryside, as did the French revolution. But in a subtle way Candeloro appears to modify Gramsci's position by noting that although the state that came out of the Risorgimento was certainly dominated by the bourgeoisie, the structure and policies of this state favored the subsequent development of bourgeois society "within certain limits." Candeloro is precisely Marxist in his contention that the subsequent development of bourgeois society also meant the development of its internal contradictions.[6]

[4] Adolfo Omodeo, *Difesa del Risorgimento* (2d ed.; Turin, Einaudi, 1955), pp. 439–40.

[5] Antonio Gramsci, *Il Risorgimento* (Turin, Einaudi, 1949), pp. 65, 72–73.

[6] Giorgio Candeloro, *Storia dell'Italia moderna* (3 vols.; 2d ed., Milan, Feltrinelli, 1956–60), I, 10, 14, 389.

Rosario Romeo, another contemporary Italian historian, has subjected Gramsci's thesis to a searching criticism which concludes with the assertion that Gramsci's position is essentially anachronistic. Given the historical circumstances surrounding the Risorgimento, an agrarian revolution would have been impossible because of international and domestic reasons: the major European powers would not have permitted a Jacobin revolution in Italy, and the gulf that separated the urban masses and the countryside in Italy would have prevented this revolution even if the foreign obstacle had been removed. Furthermore, argues Romeo, even if one were to grant the possibility of such an agrarian revolution, it is still to be proved that this "alternative course" would have been more "progressive" than what actually took place. Romeo remains convinced that, in fact, because of the consequent effect of fragmentation in landholding, an agrarian revolution would actually have been unprogressive in its effect on the development of agricultural capitalism.[7]

The Marxist interpretation of the Risorgimento has been loosely called materialistic. But there is another "materialistic" interpretation which appears to reduce Italy's unification to the material fact of joining together a number of separate political states. It is against this other kind of materialism that Luigi Salvatorelli, another distinguished historian, has addressed his most severe criticism. The following brief excerpt from his writings makes clear the central problem as he sees it.

22. THE PROBLEM OF THE RISORGIMENTO: MATERIALIST OR SPIRITUAL CONCEPTION

Luigi Salvatorelli, *Pensiero e azione del Risorgimento,* 6th ed. Turin: Einaudi, 1960, pp. 13–16, *passim.* Reproduced by courtesy of the author and the publisher, Giulio Einaudi, Editore. Our translation.

Precisely what is meant by the Italian Risorgimento, and above all what is it that "rises anew": what is its relation to modern European history, of which the Risorgimento is the Italian equivalent? In what measure is it political, ethical, or cultural in character? Is it a purely indigenous product or does it reveal foreign causes and influences, and of what kind and degree? When does it begin and when does it end? These are all questions of which some have been treated with persistence and resolved, especially in recent times, with a dogmatic certainty not always conforming to the soundness of the treatment; but they have not been examined systematically as a whole. In this respect

[7] Rosario Romeo, *Risorgimento e capitalismo* (Bari, Laterza, 1959), pp. 21–30, *passim.*

there is a difference with the Renaissance, which in recent decades has been discussed precisely as a conceptual whole and on a European-wide plane. The Risorgimento, on the other hand, has continued to be considered as a fact of almost purely Italian concern. Whatever one may think at present of this last point, it is certain that for us Italians the Risorgimento is a capital part of our history—a history of yesterday that projects its shadow on today, hovering between past and future. The interest occasioned by the problem is seen immediately in the contrasting evaluations of the various forces operating in the Risorgimento, of their development, and even of the results of the Risorgimento itself. In these judgments we note oscillations which at times lead even to the complete overturning of formerly held positions; and these oscillations are due not only to differences in thought and to alternations in historiographical approaches but also to political contingencies and practical considerations. . . .

There is an ingenuous representation of the Risorgimento—widely and unwittingly diffused—which would reduce it to the formation of the Kingdom of Italy between 1859 and 1861 and its completion in 1866 and 1870. Such a conception of the Risorgimento eliminates the "problem": we have only to recite the litany of how the various parts of Italy were annexed to the Savoyard kingdom of Victor Emmanuel II. This would be an account of a series of external events: battles, military occupations, treaties, plebiscites, parliamentary votes, and royal decrees. Nevertheless, if we subject this ingenuous conception to rational analysis we find that it comes to an interpretation of the Risorgimento as a purely political-territorial fact of state. In philosophical terms this interpretation may be said to lead to materialistic positivism; in political terms, to monarchical absolutism. In fact, during the Fascist period the thesis was propounded that the process of the Risorgimento consisted in the absorption of the various Italian states or regions by the Savoyard kingdom of Sardinia; and that, therefore, the earlier formation of this Sardinian kingdom constituted the prologue—the only prologue—of the new Italy. . . . In fact, the Savoyard monarchy's role and manner of participation in the Risorgimento were of capital importance; but if the Risorgimento is summed up as the enlargement of the Savoyard monarchical state into the kingdom of Italy, it means that the Risorgimento is reduced to the external aggregation of the various regions of Italy to Piedmont-Sardinia, in short, to the material fact of annexations. But then in such a case the annexations do not conclude an historical process; they do not represent the manifestation of the will of the country; rather, they are reduced to a pure act of power. In this fashion one denies to the Risorgimento national, popular, and spiritual elements; and in consequence no true difference exists any longer between the formation of Italian unity and any foreign conquest whatever.

Accordingly, we may safely put aside this ingenuous conception, which is revealed as being intrinsically invalid . . . we add here only . . . two considerations. The first is that the territorial or Savoyard conception is unable to comprehend within itself a whole series of episodes which are undoubtedly "Risorgimental." If the Risorgimento is reduced purely and simply to the territorial formation of the Savoyard kingdom of Italy, then what place can there be in it for the Neapolitan revolution of 1820 or the one in central Italy of 1831, both of which aimed simply to transform the domestic institutions of some Italian states? The same may be said of the several risings in Romagna between 1840 and 1846 or of the risings in the kingdom of Naples between 1821 and 1848. In addition, the entire Mazzinian activity, which although unitarian was also republican, would clearly run the risk of figuring as "anti-Risorgimento"; indeed, such a representation of Mazzinianism was the ultimate and most secret hope of the supporters of the Savoyard-territorial theory, one of whom had occasion to speak of "republican leprosy." Furthermore, even a large part of the revolutions of 1848 as well as the immediately preceding insurrections aiming at reforms would remain outside the threshold of the Risorgimento. The other consideration is that from the beginning of the use of the term "Risorgimento" in reference to a specific period of Italian history and, more precisely, as an indication of the new destiny of our country, the term has never been employed in a purely territorial-state sense. From Bettinelli to Carducci, from Alfieri to Gioberti, from the Jacobin patriots to Santarosa, from Mazzini to Cavour, all—whether using the specific term or an equivalent to express the same concept—have understood the Italian Risorgimento as a fact, or better, as a process of a spiritual character, as an inner and complete transformation of Italian life, as an affirmation of national and individual autonomy.

PART THREE

PROBLEMS AND POLICIES OF THE
UNITARY STATE, 1870–1900

IX. THE FRAGMENTATION OF POLITICS AND THE FALL OF THE RIGHT, 1870–1876

If we adopt Salvatorelli's definition of the Risorgimento as an "affirmation of national and individual autonomy," then it must be said that the Risorgimento continued beyond 1870, because the autonomy of the newly formed Italian state was not yet secure at that date, while the autonomy or liberty of the individual required an even greater affirmation during the following thirty years. In essence, the meaning of the period from 1870 to 1900 is to be found precisely in the problems and proposed solutions arising from the need to preserve Italy's newly found unity and the liberty of its people in the face of grave foreign and domestic dangers. The most immediate danger stemmed from the forceful acquisition of Rome, permanently alienating Pope Pius IX from the Italian state. As long as this alienation continued, Italy had to face the double prospect of foreign efforts at restoring the Pope's temporal authority, and domestic divisions between Italians who were concerned for the Pope's ancient prerogatives and others who would treat him simply as the spiritual head of one of several religious faiths. Equally as urgent as the solution of the Roman question was the need to establish the fiscal stability of the Italian state. The governments of the Right led by Giovanni Lanza (1869–73) and Marco Minghetti (1873–76) tried desperately to balance the budget by administrative economies and a host of new consumer or indirect taxes, among which the most unpopular was the *macinato* tax imposed particularly on the grinding of wheat and to a lesser degree on other cereals. This tax on "the food of the poor" was exploited by the liberals and radicals of the Left as proof of the partisan, class nature of the Right; and, inasmuch as the tax fell more heavily on the wheat-consuming regions, which were in the South, it occasioned a revival of regionalism in politics, giving more fuel to the protagonists of the ever-present Southern question. Economic and social issues were coming increasingly to the forefront now that the great political question—unification—had been solved.

The common desire to achieve unification had held the Right and Left together, however much these two branches of Italian liberalism may have disagreed on the methods best suited to realize the common goal. Even such outspoken democrats and former republicans as Garibaldi and Crispi had come to agree that "monarchy unites us, a republic would divide us." But with the acquisition of Rome the cement that held moderates, progressive liberals, and democrats together was dissolved, and each group and sub-group began to promote its special causes. A political fragmentation became inevitable, and inasmuch as the Left championed the more popular causes —lower taxes, wider suffrage, educational reforms, greater personal liberty, and more governmental concern for the South—it was only a question of time until any weakness on the Right would bring the Left to power, even with a limited franchise based on wealth. Moreover, the Right was inherently weak, because many of its leaders were not unalterably opposed to the causes espoused by the Left. The former simply wished to move more slowly and cautiously in order not to endanger the stability of the newly formed state.

The first issue that revealed the weakness of the Right's position came with the passage of the Law of Papal Guarantees. The bill was adopted in the Chamber by a margin of votes—185 to 106—which is deceptively large but in fact is small in the light of the governmental majorities customary in Italian politics of the day.

The Lanza-Sella Ministry, which had decided on forceful acquisition of Rome in 1870, was mindful of the foreign and domestic repercussions following from this act. In order to attenuate their effect, the government offered and hoped that the Pope would accept a number of guarantees regarding his person and his office. Pius IX's refusal to accept these guarantees made of them a purely unilateral and unnegotiated act; but although the Pope proceeded to announce himself a "prisoner in the Vatican," the substance of the Law of Papal Guarantees of 1871 was in fact enjoyed by him and his successors, making possible a slow accommodation between the Church and the Italian state during the following half century.

23. EXCERPTS FROM THE LAW OF PAPAL GUARANTEES, MAY 13, 1871

Raccolta ufficiale delle leggi e dei decreti del Regno d'Italia, 2d Series, XXXI (1871), 1014–22. Our translation.

TITLE I. PREROGATIVES OF THE SUPREME PONTIFF
AND OF THE HOLY SEE

Article 1. The person of the Supreme Pontiff is sacred and inviolable.

Art. 2. Any attempt against the person of the Supreme Pontiff and the provocation to commit such an attempt shall be punished with the same penalties as established for similar offenses against the person of the King. . . .

[However] discussion of religious matters shall be entirely free.

Art. 3. The Italian government attributes the Supreme Pontiff with sovereign honors within the Kingdom. . . .

Art. 4. An annual income of 3,225,000 lire is endowed and reserved for the Holy See. . . .

Art. 5. In addition to the endowment mentioned in the preceeding article, the Supreme Pontiff shall retain the use of the apostolic Vatican and Lateran palaces with all buildings, gardens, and lands thereto appertaining, and also the villa of Castel Gandolfo with all its appurtenances. . . .

Art. 6. During the vacancy of the Pontifical See, no judicial or political authority shall for any reason hinder or limit the personal liberty of the cardinals.

The government shall see to it that assemblies of the Conclave and of ecumenical Councils are not disturbed by external violence.

Art. 7. No public official or agent of the police authority [of the Italian state] shall, while in the performance of the duties of his office, enter the palaces and places of the Supreme Pontiff's customary or temporary residence, or those places where a Conclave or ecumenical Council is assembled, unless authorized to enter by the Supreme Pontiff, the Conclave, or the Council.

Art. 8. Papers, documents, books, or registers of a purely spiritual character deposited in pontifical offices or Congregations shall be free from the legal processes of visit, search, or seizure.

Art. 9. The Supreme Pontiff shall be entirely free to fulfill all the functions of his spiritual ministry; to this end he may have affixed to the doors of basilicas and churches of Rome all such notices deriving from his ministry.

Art. 10. All ecclesiastics in Rome for the purpose of taking part in the promulgation of acts pertaining to the spiritual ministry of the Holy See shall not on this account be subjected to any interference, investigation, or control by the civil authorities. . . .

Art. 11. Envoys of foreign governments accredited to the Holy See shall be entitled within the Kingdom to all the prerogatives and immunities appertaining to diplomatic agents according to international law. . . .

Art. 12. The Supreme Pontiff shall be free to correspond with the episcopacy and with the whole Catholic world, without any interference from the Italian government. . . .

Art. 13. Within the city of Rome and within the six subsidiary sees outside the city, the seminaries, academies, colleges, and other Catholic institutions established for the education and training of ecclesiastics shall continue under the sole control of the Holy See, without any interference from the educational authorities of the Kingdom.

TITLE II. RELATIONS BETWEEN THE STATE AND THE CHURCH

Art. 14. All special restrictions upon the exercise of the right of assembly by members of the Catholic clergy are abolished.

Art. 15. . . . . Bishops shall not be required to swear loyalty to the King.

Major and minor benefices may be conferred only upon Italian citizens, except in the city of Rome and the subsidiary sees. . . .

Art. 16. The *exequatur* and *placet regio* and all other forms of government authorization for the publication and execution of acts by the ecclesiastical authorities are abolished.

But unless otherwise provided by a special law mentioned in Article 18, all acts disposing of ecclesiastical property and providing for appointments to major and minor benefices shall remain subject to the *exequatur* and *placet regio,* except for cases regarding the city of Rome and the subsidiary sees.

The provisions of the civil law regarding the creation and management of ecclesiastical institutions and the sale of their property remain unchanged.

Art. 17. In matters of spiritual discipline there shall be no appeal from decisions of ecclesiastical authorities, nor shall civil authorities recognize or grant any coercive execution of such decisions. . . .

However, all acts of the ecclesiastical authorities shall have no effect if contrary to the laws of the state or to public order, or if they prejudice the rights of individuals; such acts shall be subject to penal laws if they constitute an offense.

Art. 18. A future law shall provide for the reorganization, preservation, and administration of the ecclesiastical property within the Kingdom.

Art. 19. All existing regulations contrary to this law are abolished.

The debate that accompanied the passage of the Law of Papal Guarantees reveals that Parliament and country were divided into at least four camps regarding the law's provisions: the moderates of the Right, most of whom supported the law because they hoped that the considerable privileges it accorded the Pope and the Church would make possible a reconciliation between Church and state, and the opposition, which fell into three different camps. The "clericals" thought the law did not afford the Pope sufficient freedom of action; the "radicals" opposed granting the Church any special considerations at all, and favored total separation between Church and state by treating the Catholic Church in exactly the same way as all other confessions; and the "jurisdictionalists," who also favored a "nonconfessional" state but were opposed to the surrender of any of the state's rights to interfere in religious matters.[1] The moderates prevailed because their approach seemed best calculated to calm domestic disquiet and foreign concern for the Pope's freedom and security.

24. QUINTINO SELLA OF THE RIGHT DEFENDS HIS POLICIES

With the Roman question hopefully on its way toward a slow solution of mutual accommodation between Church and state, Quintino Sella, the stronger of the two men in the Lanza-Sella combination, addressed himself to the problem of fiscal stability. A man of considerable gifts and wide intellectual interests, Sella was accused of being obsessed with balancing the budget, regardless of the taxes and other fiscal burdens he was thereby obliged to impose on the poor. His promise to balance the budget in 1870 had gone unfulfilled, largely because of the need to reverse his program of "economy to the bone" even in the military. The unsettled international situation during the Franco-Prussian War, the seizure of Rome, and the resulting Italian fear of foreign efforts to restore to the Pope his temporal domains made it necessary to increase rather than diminish military expenditures. In March 1872 Sella, as Minister of Finance, informed the Chamber of Deputies that a deficit of 200 million lire required the imposition of new taxes and the raising of existing ones. Urbano Rattazzi, leader of the Left and Prime Minister for two brief periods in the 1860s, reminded Sella of his unfulfilled promise to balance the budget, whereupon Sella replied in a speech that, in its sharp rebuttal of many criticisms directed against him from the Left, marked a definitive end to the truce between the two sides of the Chamber.

[1] Cf. Gaetano Arangio-Ruiz, *Storia costituzionale del Regno d'Italia, 1848–1898* (Florence, G. Civelli, 1898), pp. 253–54.

Sella's Speech in the Chamber, March 18, 1872

> Quintino Sella, *Discorsi parlamentari*, 5 vols. Rome: Tipografia della Camera dei deputati, 1887–90, IV, 145–77, *passim*. Our translation.

It has been said: In 1870 you promised to reduce expenditures, you promised the famous economies to the bone, the reduction of the army budget to 130 millions. You promised an immediate balancing of the budget and the end of nonconvertibility of banknotes. . . .*

[But] as is usual with the opposition, it denies you the means for doing something, or it gives you only a little piece, and then says to you: You made promises and you did not keep your word. . . .

It is so unnecessary for me to remind you that the political situation has changed so radically since 1870 that it seems to me to be really a waste of time for all of us . . . to compare the situation as it was then with what it is today. [It is a waste of time] to attribute the larger military budget to a failure on my part to keep my word, or to reproach me for failing to meet the budgetary deficit with the means I then presented. Remember this most happy deficit is the result of the fact that we have assumed the Roman budget. You all know the happy reason why we now have this difference in budgetary conditions.

It is also very odd that reproach should come from those benches (*pointing to the left*) which have always shown themselves so solicitous for the success of events which we have had the good fortune to accomplish [the acquisition of Rome].

It was said to me: You should have foreseen. But of all people, Honorable Deputy Rattazzi, should you be the one to criticize others for lack of foresight? I admire your courage. (*Laughter at the right.*)

Rattazzi: I request the floor to speak on a point of personal privilege. . . .

Sella: The Honorable Rattazzi also said: You speak of economy and then you increase the personnel in the Finance Ministry. . . . It

---

* Reference to the *Corso Forzoso*, that is, the freeing in 1866 of Italy's banks of issue from the obligation of paying out gold or silver for their banknotes. Ed. note.

seems to me that if I increase the treasury receipts by an increase in personnel you should praise rather than criticize me. . . .

The Honorable Deputy Rattazzi also said to me: You promised a balanced budget and then you abandoned it. I have abandoned nothing, Honorable Deputy Rattazzi. We have had this great and most happy change of things [the acquisition of Rome] for which I should like to be able to take credit, and now I am here to propose a balanced budget to the Chamber. It is precisely for this reason that I torment you with the proposal to continue the nonconvertibility of paper currency. . . .

Gentlemen, let us put aside the minor differences we may have had. Let me ask: Does the great party [the Right] which had the courage to face unpopularity by voting taxes, does it—considering the matter as a whole—have much reason for regretting what it did? According to me, this party could well lead the nation to the Capitol to thank the gods. . . .

When I think how things were going during the preceding decade . . . in 1861 we borrowed 500 million, another 700 million in 1863–64, from 1864 to 1865, 425 million in loans and 150 in obligations on the public domain. In short, we were moving at the pace of about 400 million a year. . . .

Now, what has been the pace since 1871? Putting minor matters aside, we see, it is true, that we took 130 million of paper from the Bank, but we reimbursed 75 million in interest-bearing loans. . . . I do not at all deny that there may be things to be changed and improvements to be introduced. I am hardly so naïve a soul as to come before you and say that we live in the best of all possible worlds. But, gentlemen, when some come here and stigmatize everything that has been done, it seems to me that this is not a fair thing, and I would dare say that it is not patriotic. . . .

Branca: I request the floor to speak on a point of personal privilege.

Sella: . . . . because, in the final reckoning, what was done was done by the Italian Parliament, by the legal representation of the country. . . .

The Honorable Deputy Branca has said: You have too much intelligence (thank you for the compliment) to make such serious mis-

takes. Your hidden aim is to create a network of great financial monopolies. [United] Italy should have been of economic benefit for all
but you wish to limit this benefit to the few. You aim at a monarchy
surrounded by a banking aristocracy. . . .

I reply to the Honorable Deputy Branca and to those who have expressed ideas similar to his that our purpose is not to create monopolies, not the benefit of the few but the benefit of all, which we believe to be able to reach much more expeditiously in the manner we
have adopted. Our concept is really that of a monarchy surrounded by
an aristocracy, but by an aristocracy of great services to the country
and of virtuous industry. (*Bravo! from the right.*) Accordingly, it
seems to me that the ideas which we follow are not undeserving of
the confidence which we ask of you. . . .

I believe that although there are extreme groups in the Chamber
today—there may be one on this side (*pointing to the right*); it seems
to me that there is one on that side also (*pointing to the left*) which
treats our opponents not at all better than it does us—it seems to me
that in substance two great parties have become clearly delineated: on
one side the Left with a part of the Center-Left, on the other side the
Right with the Center. We do not hesitate in stating that we wish to
become ever more united essentially with the latter groups, which
have supported us and especially splendidly during our presentation
of the budget, and that it is essentially of them that we ask for explicit
confidence. (*Approval from the right.*). . . .

The Honorable Deputy Rattazzi says: You do not show respect for
Parliament. . . . Really, it does not seem to us that we deserve this
reproach of lacking in respect for Parliament. Our belief is that the
welfare of the country lies only with Parliament, and I do not think
that we need the Honorable Deputy Rattazzi to teach us this.

He spoke of an apathy which he attributes to us. Apathy? What
apathy? But gentlemen, when I look at the country I see that never
has it been more industrious. Or is it that you desire that there always
be agitation in the streets? Is this what you mean? (*No! No! from the
left.*). . . .

Apathy in Parliament! But what has happened? (*Whispers from the
left.*). . . . During the past weeks there was some apparent languor
but as soon as the debate began on the budgetary proposals now be-

fore us and so close to our hearts, look about you, gentlemen, where is this apathy? It is simply not there. (*Various comments*.). . . .

Then we are accused of a grave inconsistency, an inconsistency which is almost morally offensive. It is said: You had declared that you would acquire Rome by moral means; therefore, when it became necessary to breach the gates of the city by force, you should have resigned.

But Honorable Deputy Rattazzi, to whom should we have resigned our office? (*With emphasis*.) To those who led Italy to Mentana? (*Bravo! Good! from the right. Rumblings and commotion from the left*.)

Sella's reference to Garibaldi's defeat at Mentana in 1867 at the hands of French troops while the latter was attempting to take Rome by force was a stinging reminder that this unfortunate event was generally blamed on Rattazzi who, as Prime Minister at the time the Mentana enterprise began, failed both to halt the enterprise or assure its success. The whole of Sella's speech was a proud assertion of what was best in the Right: fiscal responsibility, courage in the face of necessary but unpopular measures, and a political program which, although not democratic, was consistently and coherently liberal in the classical sense of the word. But not all of the Right had Sella's firmness and indifference to unpopularity. If he did not seem especially to mind the reputation of being the most hated Minister of his or any other day in Italy, some of his colleagues on the Right appeared more susceptible to the pressures of public opinion. So long as Rattazzi lived and stood as the figure around whom the Left and the Center-Left could rally, the Right, fearing his advent to power, rallied around Sella and Lanza. But almost immediately after Rattazzi's death early in June 1873, the Right abandoned Lanza and, more particularly his Finance Minister, Sella, whose financial measures were voted down on June 25 by a vote of 157 to 86. The Ministry's fall had been determined by the opposition of a part of the Right, led by Marco Minghetti, and that of virtually the entire Left, now led by Agostino Depretis. After the resignation of the Lanza-Sella government, Sella logically advised the King to designate a Ministry of the Left, but his colleagues did not share this view and the mandate was entrusted to Minghetti. The latter attempted a *connubio*-style coalition with the moderate Left but when its leader, Depretis, demanded the Ministry of the Interior for his party, the negotiations collapsed and the whole Right, fearful of the Left's rise to power, rallied around Minghetti. For the next thirty-two months Minghetti was to preside over the last long-term government of the Right that Italy was to have during the nineteenth century. Indeed, during this period of nearly three years the liberal or moderate Right was to undergo so thorough a fragmentation of its forces that after its fall in 1876 it never again regained its sway over Italian politics.

Minghetti was unlike Sella in many ways, and the points that divided these two leaders of the Right divided many of their followers as well. Sella was anticlerical, politically a liberal, but in economics not a doctrinaire believer in *laissez faire;* Minghetti was quite moderate on the Church-state question, politically a conservative, and a believer in classical economics. But however much Minghetti may have differed from his predecessors at the Right, he was, rightly or wrongly considered their heir and so had to assume the burdens of their unpopularity as well as the prestige of their achievements. Most unpopular of all were the Right's fiscal policies aiming at a balanced budget through high taxation and administrative economies.

25. MARCO MINGHETTI OF THE RIGHT ATTEMPTS TO DIVIDE THE LEFT

Minghetti gave candid expression of his essentially conservative political and economic views in a speech of April 22, 1874, much of which was in reply to the opposition program presented by Francesco Crispi, one of Garibaldi's chief lieutenants in the conquest of Sicily and a leader of the democratic or radical Left. Crispi had called for universal suffrage, administrative decentralization, an elective Senate, the abolition of the grist tax, and the establishment of a fiscal structure based on a proportionately assessed land tax. This program was not shared completely by the moderate wing of the Left opposition as led by Depretis, and Minghetti's speech was an obvious attempt to divide the Left by appealing for the support of its moderate wing. The speech is significant also because a reference to the inevitable "transformation" of parties constitutes one of the first expressions of a concept recognizing that the terms of the old dialectic between the "historic Right" and the "historic Left" of the unification period were no longer historically meaningful. Out of this recognition there was to come the practice of "transformism," a practice which aimed at the formation of parliamentary majorities from all sectors of Parliament, regardless of nominal party labels and past political attitudes.

Minghetti's Speech in the Chamber, April 22, 1874

> Marco Minghetti, *Discorsi parlamentari*, 8 vols. Rome: Tipografia della Camera dei deputati, 1888–90, VI, 87–91, *passim.* Our translation.

The Honorable Deputy Crispi has presented a program whose clarity and moderation I acknowledge. He has expressed a complex of ideas which although indicative of his opposition to the government nonetheless shows that his opposition remains within the limits of our Constitution.* . . .

I acknowledge willingly that these ideas have a certain value, but I must say that I cannot accept them because they seem untimely to me. I admit the propriety of constitutional reform, for I am not idolatrous of the Constitution to the point of thinking it immutable. . . . But only when the entire opposition in the country shares the Honorable Deputy Crispi's views, only when its supreme and real desire becomes that of reforming the *Statuto* and nothing other than reforming the *Statuto*, I believe that only then will the time have come to think of proceeding with it. (*Good! Good! from the right and center.*)

I do not fail to appreciate that popular suffrage should and may be enlarged in proportion to the growth of education and prosperity in the country, in proportion to the growth of the number of citizens able to give their votes usefully. (*Agitation to the left.*). . . .

Gentlemen, I am not an admirer of universal suffrage. Indeed, when I look at some of our European neighbors [France?], when I see the effects it has produced there, I confess that I feel a certain dismay, and I would not wish that my country experiment with something that has not yet been tested by the experience of others. (*Good! from the right. Rumblings from the left.*). . . . I do not know what consequences [universal suffrage] might produce; I am not sure that a party which we all fear might not thereby become master of the situation.† (*Very good! Bravo!*)

At any rate, I do not deny that these proposals may some day become practical; but in my view they are not practical today. Therefore I declare in my name and in the name of the government over which I have the honor to preside that I shall fight them. . . . I believe that if democracy were to triumph before it became educated and disciplined . . . if government were reduced solely to a predominance of numbers, I believe that democracy would begin with the subversion

---

* Crispi's program was moderate in comparison to his republican past; the reference to the Constitution was a pointed reminder that there was an opposition at the extreme Left and extreme Right which did not accept the monarchy or the Albertine *Statuto*. Ed. note.

† Most likely a reference to the clerical party, whose triumph in France with the advent of Marshal MacMahon to the presidency in 1873 raised great fears in Italy that France might support efforts to restore the Pope's temporal authority. Ed. note.

of all that still remains of noble institutions and would then end—as all unrestrained power has always ended—by killing itself. (*Bravo!*)

I cannot agree that elective local officials should replace all the existing agents of the central government. The Honorable Deputy Crispi knows only too well the conditions of the provinces and communes freed barely ten years ago from a blind tyranny, to think that it is possible to leave them to their own resorts without any guidance and supervision from the central government. . . .

As for a reform of the tax system according to the Honorable Deputy Crispi's views, I reply that I could discuss the matter with him . . . if I had the good fortune to be able to come before you with a budgetary surplus. But so long as we have a deficit we can consider not even a reduction of existing taxes, much less a repealing of any of them. . . .

But if the Honorable Deputy Crispi has expressed the views of one part of the Left . . . there is another part which it seems to me is not disposed to accept all of the program he has presented. . . .

When His Majesty honored me with the mandate to form a new Ministry, it seemed to me that the time of great political questions being ended—I mean the great questions regarding independence and unity—it should be possible to come to an understanding on other matters and thus form a great parliamentary majority. . . . I seemed to feel a current in the country that indicated that the time had come for a change within the parties which had been in contention until then. For, you see, I cannot accept that kind of immobility, of rigidity, which the Honorable Deputy Corbetta [Eugenio, of the Right] prescribed for political parties. They too become modified and evolve according to the times. Although faithful to their principles, nevertheless they become transformed in the face of new problems. . . .

26. POLITICAL REGIONALISM, NORTH VS. SOUTH

Minghetti's appeal for a political truce, to serve as a prelude and condition for the "transformation" of the parties which had issued from the struggle for independence and unity, went unheeded. On May 24, 1874, Minghetti's Ministry was overturned by one vote, 166 to 165, on a bill that declared null and void all private legal instruments, such as loans and property transfers, unless a registry tax be paid. Inasmuch as nonregistering of private legal in-

struments was more common in the South than in the North, the issue acquired a strong regional aspect, with the Left, strongest in the South, making much of this issue during the general elections which followed upon the
King's refusal to accept Minghetti's resignation. These elections were
marked by bitter attacks against the Right, especially after what seemed like
the arbitrary arrest of a number of republican leaders early in August 1874.
The Left's successes at the polls emboldened it to continue with its attacks
on the "misgovernment" of the Right and more especially on a bill authorizing the government to employ such extraordinary public safety measures as
preventive arrest, the denial of release on bond, and the detention of persons
in penal settlements (*domicilio coatto*) by administrative rather than judicial proceedings. The debate which accompanied the presentation of this
bill raised the regional, or North-South issue, with an intensity reminiscent
of the hectic days of the 1860s.

Speech by Francesco Crispi before the Chamber of Deputies, June 10, 1875

Francesco Crispi, *Discorsi parlamentari*, 3 vols. Rome: Tipografia della
Camera dei deputati, 1915, II, 242–61, *passim*. Our translation.

The campaign against the southern provinces and Sicily in particular
did not begin today [in the Chamber]. It began last year in several
northern newspapers. I am convinced that these newspapers did not
express the views of that party which worked for the unity of Italy
. . . and which shares with us the honor of having achieved that state
of things that makes it possible for us to speak in this Chamber here
in Rome.

The limiting and localizing of the question [of public order] to the
South would produce two blameworthy consequences, one political
and the other social.

Gentlemen, it is bad to divide Italy into two parts, even if only
morally. . . . It is not patriotic to suppose even in the slightest that
the morality of the people in the South is inferior to the morality of
those in the North of the peninsula. . . . Contempt of one province
for another would be a sign of our decadence and could be the cause
of very great harm.

In coming to the second consequence, I say that the social harm
which derives from localizing the question is this: if we consider the

evil to be limited to Sicily, we shall not succeed in curing it; we shall only apply remedies which will render it more knotty. There comes immediately to mind this question: Is there a social question of public order? Does the incidence of criminal acts in one province rather than in another reveal evidence for the belief that some parts of Italy are more sick than others? Gentlemen, I deny this flatly. . . .

I must avow, although with great pain, that the incidence of criminality throughout the Kingdom has increased excessively. . . . In 1869 . . . the number of homicides consummated or attempted throughout the Kingdom was 2,083; in 1870 it was 2,303. But what an increase is coming! In 1871 . . . there were 4,866 homicides; in 1872 they declined somewhat to 3,921. In 1873 and 1874 . . . the number of homicides was almost stationary. In 1873 there were 3,270 and during the first nine months of 1874 there were 2,564 of them.

Let us proceed to highway robberies, another great evil we must point to because it is the one that has served as the pretext for the law we are debating. Throughout the entire Kingdom 1,161 highway robberies were committed in 1869; in 1870, 995; in 1871 they increased to 4,373. . . .

The total number of thefts and other crimes against property, including highway robbery, is 80,124 for 1871 and 88,079 for 1872. (*Sensation in the Chamber.*)

(*A voice:*) God help us!

Crispi: So much for Italy as a whole. [After citing additional statistics Crispi concludes:] Considering the ratio between regional population and the number of crimes committed . . . you can readily see that the extreme part of Italy [Calabria, Sicily, and Sardinia] accounts for a greater number of crimes. . . .

We have the duty to investigate the real reasons for this rising number of crimes throughout the whole Kingdom. It is the Ministry which should have given the answer to this question, but we too can give it, and we must.

What is the reason for this excessive number of crimes?

Gentlemen, remember that the economic conditions of the country have not improved since 1869. After 1869 we have had, above all, the terrible grist tax, which is a tax on hunger, and an ever-increasing rise of all other taxes that hit indirectly the poorer classes of society. Add to this the decrease of natural products in proportion to the rising population, the decrease of domestic industrial products, and the consequent rise of consumer prices. . . . Finding themselves in economic straits because of unemployment or low wages, the workman and the peasant do not go to the Stock Exchange, they take to the road, they ransack houses and demand at the point of a knife that which governmental improvidence once more prevents them from securing legally. . . .

What is the remedy for all this?

There is a general remedy applicable to the whole country. I insist that the remedy must be general, in spite of the special needs of certain provinces. This remedy rests with the executive authority, gentlemen, and above all with appropriate legislation. And even more than with legislation, it rests with a tax system which is more equitable, less vexing, less fiscally oriented, of a kind which does not render the people desperate.

It is a mistake to think that there is need for special [security] measures and that these measures are necessary only in those provinces with which you have been concerned.

No, gentlemen, on this we do not agree. If crimes in Sicily had increased for reasons peculiar to the place . . . then explain to me why this terrible crime rate is not to be found there before 1860 . . . when brigandage was unknown there, when even the very word was unknown? . . .

In 1844 there were 87 homicides in all of Sicily . . . in 1850, 95 . . . in 1851, 107 . . . in 1852, 115. . . . As for highway robbery, there were 11 cases in all of Sicily in 1850, 17 in 1851, and 85 in 1852. The latter is the highest figure I find for the whole period. . . . Under the previous [Bourbon] government the number of serious crimes was quite small and there is no comparison whatever between today's crime rate and that of the period before 1860.

You will understand from all this that neither the nature of the place, nor the special instinct of the population, nor the moral and economic condition of the island is the cause of the crimes which have been ever-increasing in our own times. Gentlemen, the cause is in your laws and in your government.

For fifteen years Sicily has been lacking a truly free government. . . . It has been under martial law three times, and four or five times under a regime of extraordinary laws. . . . Now, gentlemen, can you expect a part of the country that for fifteen years has been governed with martial law, penal settlements, and punitive parole to be in a normal state? Can you expect that the morale of this part of the country, its heart, the soul of its people be calm and tranquil when you have incited them, when you have made them vexed and irritated to the point of convincing them that you are their enemies rather than the government of liberty and reparation? (*Very good! from the left.*)

In spite of bitter opposition from the Left, the extraordinary public safety measures were passed early in July 1875. At Lanza's insistence and as a concession to the Southerners, a parliamentary commission was created to inquire into the condition of Sicily, a question which had rallied all factions of the Left but had not strengthened the Right. Minghetti's position was further weakened by the issue of state management of railways. In 1865 the rail lines owned by the state had been sold to private companies to relieve the mounting pressure of deficits. This sale pleased the economic liberals found on both sides of the Chamber, and especially on the Left, many of whose members were opposed to further strengthening of what they considered an already too strong and all-pervasive state authority. When early in March 1876 Minghetti's government presented a proposal for state ownership of all rail lines, it was faced with the opposition not only of almost the entire Left but also of a strong group of predominantly Tuscan Deputies from the Right who broke with the government because of their economic liberal prejudices against state management of such an important part of the country's economy. This Tuscan group entered into relations with the moderate Left and caused the fall of Minghetti's government precisely at the time when it was able to announce with great pride that the budget had finally been balanced. It is ironic that the Right should have fallen at the moment of its achievement of a goal toward which it had striven for nearly a decade. But this goal had engendered too much unpopularity, and it helped reveal that the Right was no longer an homogeneous body, if ever it had been. The subsequent rise of the Left to power has been called the "parliamentary revolution of 1876"; and although the term "revolution" is too strong a description for the moderate program with which Agostino Depretis presented his government of the Left in 1876, it does properly emphasize the country's expectation of new things it hoped would come from the first long-term administration of the Left Italy was to have since its unification.

X. THE ADVENT OF THE LEFT AND THE BEGINNING OF THE DEPRETIS ERA, 1876–1881

The more than ten years between 1876 and 1887 during which Agostino Depretis dominated Italian political life are customarily called the era of "transformism." This much used and abused term is employed to describe the practice of disregarding the old party labels of Left and Right in fashioning a stable parliamentary majority. Depretis did not invent the practice. Cavour had had his "*connubio*" with Rattazzi of the Center-Left; Giovanni Lanza of the Right had come to power in 1869 with the votes of much of the Left; and during his three years in office Minghetti had openly courted the support of the moderate wing of the Left led by Depretis. Finally, it was a dissident group of the Right which assured Minghetti's fall in 1876, thus opening the way for the Left's advent to power. What distinguished Depretis' transformism is, therefore, not its novelty but its openness and its candid acceptance of the fact that with the completion of Italy's unification, the "historic" Right and Left had lost most if not all of their reasons for existence as distinct parties, and that the time had come for a "transformation" of political life on the basis of new issues and problems. These new issues were: franchise reform, a more equitable tax structure less vexing to the poorer classes, greater concern with the problems of the South, administrative reorganization, and greater regard for individual rights. It has been suggested already that the Left did not have a monopoly in its support for many of these reforms; furthermore, the Left itself was by no means unanimous on how far these reforms were to be pushed. In fact, the Left of 1876 was not much more homogeneous than the Right it had displaced. What is commonly called the party of the Left was actually a coalition of at least four distinct groups: a number of moderates, led by Depretis, who wanted a limited extension of the franchise, administrative decentralization, the abolition of the grist tax, and some educational reforms; a group of democrats, led principally by Crispi, who wanted universal suffrage; a small but more radical faction composed of republicans and vague socialists; and a number of regionalists, chiefly Southerners, who may have had something in common with one or another of the three preceding groups but who were held together by their opposition to what they considered the excessively Northern orientation of the Right. In fact, what kept the whole Left together more than any other factor was not unanimity of views but a strong desire to displace the Right in power. Consequently, it was almost inevitable that once in power, the various factions of the Left should reveal the many differences dividing them. The practical result of these differences was the realization that the leaders of the Left could remain in power only by following a moderate program acceptable to the more progressive factions of the Right. This fact, in substance, is the cause and meaning of "transformism." The political purists of the day were distressed by the blurring of party labels engendered by transformism. Their ideal of a distinct two-party system modeled after the English system of a conservative and a liberal party in neat opposition was a theoretical preference which had no basis in the realities of Italian political life of the day. And it was the purists' attacks on transformism that made of this perhaps inevitable practice something unseemly and corrupt. Their attacks were directed most particularly against Depretis, who proved to be the most successful practitioner of transformism and who was Prime Minister longer than any other figure in nineteenth-century Italy.

Depretis (1813–87) was born in Lombardy. After a career in political journalism he served in the Piedmontese and later the Italian parliaments without interruption from 1848 to the time of his death. In 1859 he was one of Cavour's Prefects in Lombardy and the next year Garibaldi chose him as his Deputy-Dictator for Sicily. In Parliament he sat at the Left from the very beginning of his career. After Rattazzi's death in 1873, Depretis became the leader of the new or "Young Left," whose program of a "democratic monarchy" he presented in a speech to his constituents of Stradella in October 1875. It was with this famous "program of hope" that he came to power in 1876. The speech which follows is a paraphrase of his Stradella program, and it was given in March 1876 upon the presentation of his Ministry to the Chamber of Deputies. His appeal to the moderates on both the Left and the Right is an unmistakable sign that the practice of transformism was already on its way to becoming a permanent feature of Italian political life.

27. DEPRETIS PRESENTS THE PROGRAM OF THE LEFT BEFORE THE CHAMBER OF DEPUTIES, MARCH 28, 1876

Agostino Depretis, *Discorsi parlamentari*, 8 vols. Rome: Tipografia della Camera dei deputati, 1888–92, VI, 257–69, *passim*. Our translation.

Gentlemen, not too long ago I had a natural occasion publicly to explain my political views not only on the dangers arising out of an excessive concern with stability but also on the fundamental ideas held by the political party to which I am honored to belong. At that time [Stradella speech of 1875] I presented, specified, and circumscribed within its practical limits the program of the constitutional opposition; today it becomes a governmental program.

The essential points of this program are shared by the men who have undertaken with me the task of giving the public administration a new direction. A long period of testing assures me that my colleagues who fought along with me in the ranks of the opposition will remain faithful to this program. I trust that, at least with regard to the general tendency and reviving spirit of this program, it will meet with the approval also of those Deputies who joined us in the formation of a new majority. . . .

If I am not mistaken, this new majority came together because of two chief causes: a sense of repugnance felt at the prospect that government and Parliament should allow themselves to be distracted, for dubious and perhaps irritating reasons, from the supreme task of bringing the financial question to a good end; and the desire that greater care should be exercised in consulting the country and in preserving the honesty and dignity of parliamentary institutions. (*Very good! from the left.*). . . .

Our first and supreme task will be the removal of even the most distant doubts regarding the honest, loyal, and full implementation of representative institutions. (*Very good! Good! from the left.*) To this end, we shall endeavor to present as quickly as possible a reform of the franchise law. . . . But in order to assure the honest and spontaneous expression of public opinion . . . it will be necessary to keep the often repeated promise of restoring to provincial and communal bodies the free management of those interests which the law has entrusted to their representation. (*Good!*) It will be necessary to put an end to the interference of the central government in institutions of local interest. . . .

The absolute independence of the judiciary is the first postulate for honest political institutions. (*Good!*) We of this Ministry shall make every effort to eliminate all undue governmental interference with this supreme office [the judiciary] which is the guarantor of public peace and social honesty. (*Very good!*). . . .

Questions regarding ecclesiastical policy cannot be discussed in a few words. The Chamber's past debates on this theme gave the opposition sufficient opportunity to present its ideas, which are shared by a considerable number of the honorable colleagues sitting in other sectors of the Chamber. It is our pressing duty to declare that in this, as in all other matters, our government will not be aggressive. No spirit of hostility, but also no illusion of reconciliation. (*Lively approval from the left.*). . . .

Gentlemen, it is a most ancient opinion that ignorance is the mother of all forms of servitude. Consequently, we believe it to be our strict duty that, as soon as the demands and bonds of daily life allow, we should resume consideration of the theme of compulsory popular education. (*Very good! from the left.*). . . .

As for foreign policy, it is our view that the foreign policy of our governments during the recent past has been rendered easy by reason of the great events which have occurred in Europe. Europe has understood even better than ever that united Italy is a solid guarantee of peace and tranquillity. Consequently, we shall try to conduct our relations with foreign governments with a prudence not less than that employed by our predecessors. Nevertheless, we neither wish nor can forget that in order for Italy to hold the high place assigned to it by its past, its geographic location, and the number of its people—a high place it has not always enjoyed—it must seek in the sympathy of civilized peoples that safety which it has already achieved from the consent and interest shown by governments. . . .

Our military establishment is founded on the same general principles as those adopted by the major part of Europe's great powers, and it is much advanced toward the practical realization of these principles. We propose to resume this interrupted effort, to complete it and perfect it. With equal confidence we shall continue the task of transforming the naval establishment. . . .

Gentlemen, all of you feel that the grave problem of the railways deserves the most thoughtful consideration. . . . We declare at the very outset (*signs of attention*) that we cannot lend ourselves to the redoubling of the government's responsibility and the burdens of the administration by assuming the management of the railways. (*Very good! from the left.*) However important this management may be from the military and political points of view, nevertheless it carries with it the difficulties and complications of a veritable industrial operation. We could agree to temporary state management of a part of our railways only if it were an unavoidable necessity—and this has not been proved as yet—and only on a temporary basis. (*Signs of commotion at the right.*). . . .

I do not hesitate to say that from 1870 on Italy's financial situation has been moving toward a progressive improvement to which new taxes and the natural development of older ones contributed. But, allow me to say that the financial situation has improved also by reason of peaceful times and because of the truly heroic forbearance of the Italian people.(*Very good!*). . . .

We shall not forget that exacting care in collecting taxes and thrift in expenditures are the two fundamental rules of good financial operations. Our administration will not abandon these rules. We propose to waste not even a lira of the state's receipts, and no new expenditures will be allowed without taking steps to see to it that these expenditures are covered by receipts. (*Approval from the right.*)

I am indeed happy to see that the basis of my party is becoming larger . . . (*Signs of commotion.*). . . .

Everyone must certainly know that no tax has yet been found that is paid willingly; but there is need for evident justice in all taxes, and especially in those cases which most nearly reach the highest possible burden, as in the grist and income taxes. (*Very good! from the left.*) It is imperative that the harshness of tax laws be free of the slightest appearance or even shadow of fiscal sophistry. (*Lively approval from the left.*). . . .

It has been said that the government is not a political party. We, on the other hand, say that a party is not a government. (*Good! from the left.*) Honored by the confidence of our august Sovereign, we stand before you, gentlemen, as a government of the whole country. (*Very good! from the left.*) We intend to govern with the ideas and support of our party, but in the interest of all. And to the many who must help us in the administration of the state we say frankly that we are disposed to accept the cooperation of all men no matter the party to which they belong, of all honest, loyal, and capable men who fulfill the duties of their office, obey the laws, and see to it that they are obeyed. (*Bravo! Good!*). . . .

You will surely understand that all these ideas and duties I have spoken of must be subjected to that law of prudence, development, and gradualism which prevails over every practical achievement. Gentlemen, we feel the weight of the enormous difficulties [facing us]; we feel the duty of meeting the country's expectations with exceptional industry; but even more we feel the dangers which issue from haste and impatience. However, it seems to us that after coming to power only yesterday, after having been excluded from power for so long . . . no one should expect from us such rashness as to present as immediately and practically solved the many questions we face on this our advent to the arduous office we have accepted. (*Very good! from the left.*)

We trust in the patriotism of our old friends who, after having learned the art of perseverance even without the comfort of hope will now learn how to find patience in victory. (*Very good! from the left.*)

28. DIVISIONS WITHIN THE LEFT

The program expounded in Depretis' speech was clearly of the Left, although moderate and eclectic enough to be acceptable to much of the Right. Furthermore, the language, style, and mood of his speech were very much of the Right; and this capacity to express the program of one part of the Chamber in a language pleasing to the other was one of the secrets of the mastery this already old and tired man was to exercise over Parliament for the next decade. But there was another source to his mastery, and this derived from the fact that in the parliamentary elections of November 1876 Depretis' Minister of the Interior, the Sicilian Baron Giovanni Nicotera, employed all the resources of the state to defeat the Right, which he reduced to a mere 90 seats whereas the number of "Ministerials" was increased to 418. Prefects and other officials of the state's administration were transferred en masse or retired from office, and those who were retained were employed as electoral agents of the government. All kinds of promises were made to assure the election of the government's canditates: schools, postal and telegraph offices, lighthouses, decorations, and jobs were offered with a free hand to the constituents of friendly candidates, whereas the opposition was harried in a most unseemly fashion. The Left's landslide victory, secured by these manipulations and by the general desire for electoral and fiscal reforms, not only shattered the Right but also assured that the Left's internal divisions would soon come to the fore.[1] So long as the Left had been in the opposition its various wings had buried their differences for the sake of the unity indispensable for victory and power. Once in power these differences

[1] Cf. Arangio-Ruiz, *Storia costituzionale*, pp. 298–300.

could be hidden no longer; and only the supple maneuvering of a Depretis, who was moderate enough to be acceptable to the moderates of the Right and old and conciliatory enough to assuage the rival factions in his own party, could keep the Left in power for the next decade.

After the elections of November 1876 one possible troublemaker for Depretis' government, Crispi, was made President of the Chamber; but the chief source of division within the Left was Nicotera, whose manner was as haughty and autocratic toward his colleagues of the Left as toward his opponents on the Right. His conduct of the elections of 1876 appeared to aim not only at the defeat of the Right but at the creation of a personal following, apparently with the aim of eventually replacing the aged Depretis. When, in December 1877, Depretis found it necessary to rearrange his Ministry, he replaced Nicotera with Crispi at the Interior. But Crispi was at this post less than three months when, in March 1878, he was forced to resign in consequence to newspaper charges, inspired by Nicotera, that Crispi's second marriage had been bigamous. The new King, Umberto I, who had succeeded his father, Victor Emmanuel II, upon the latter's death in January 1878, was reported to be much disturbed by the charges against the Minister of the Interior; and when the Chamber of Deputies elected Benedetto Cairoli as its president in preference to the government's candidate, the King had no choice but to accept Depretis' resignation and entrust Cairoli with the formation of a new government.

The Left was now divided into at least five parliamentary factions, each bearing the name of its leader. There were followers of Depretis, of Nicotera, of Crispi, of Cairoli, and of Giuseppe Zanardelli. These factions existed only or largely in Parliament; not one of them had an organization of local clubs throughout the country; none was wholly or even largely homogeneous in its views. The most that can be said with precision is that the Cairoli-Zanardelli combination was more democratically inclined than the Depretis-Nicotera coalition. Crispi was *sui generis*—a special case unto himself. When asked one day whether he was a Mazzinian or a Garibaldian, he replied in the negative to both questions. Asked what he was then, he answered, "I am Crispi." [2]

Apart from the very real and significant personal differences among its leaders, the Left was divided over the question of how far and how fast to move in the realization of the program which had brought it to power. The factions led by Cairoli and Zanardelli thought the speed too slow and the distance traveled too short. But in fact some reforms had been achieved during Depretis' two years in power. The reorganization of the military establishment had begun; religious oaths were abolished in criminal and civil proceedings; a law was passed regarding conflicts of interest rendering certain persons ineligible to sit in the Chamber of Deputies; the rate of taxation for lower incomes was reduced; a parliamentary inquiry into the conditions of agriculture was voted; lower elementary education was made free and com-

---

[2] Francesco Crispi, *Scritti e discorsi politici, 1849–1890* (2d ed.; Turin-Rome, Roux e Viarengo [189?]), editors' preface, p. ix.

pulsory; religious instruction in public schools was made optional and was to be conducted during special hours; the first steps were taken toward the abolition of the death penalty; imprisonment for debt was abolished; and women were recognized as having the right to act as witnesses for public and private legal instruments.

This is not an unimpressive list, but it was marred by the fact that the grist tax had not been abolished, nor had the promised franchise reform been enacted. Very little had been done in the way of administrative decentralization, and personal freedoms had not been made more secure than they had been under the Right. In fact, Nicotera had been free in prohibiting the assembly of republicans and members of the Socialist International; and Pasquale Mancini, Minister of Justice, had severely restricted the right of release on bond.

The accession of the Cairoli–Zanardelli Ministry in March 1878 promised the country a more democratic orientation in governmental policy. Cairoli was a member of a celebrated family of patriots that had given the lives of four sons in the struggle for Italian independence. Cairoli himself had been a Mazzinian conspirator against Austria and had shared his master's republican preferences. He had served with Garibaldi's Alpine Chasseurs during the Franco-Piedmontese-Austrian War of 1859; had followed Garibaldi to Sicily, where he was seriously wounded; and at the age of forty-one had been a volunteer in the war of 1866. Zanardelli, a Lombard, as was Cairoli, had a past also full of patriotic achievements. He participated in the revolution of 1848 and served as Cavour's agent in Brescia in 1859. Never a republican, he always remained a progressive liberal of the most scrupulous and unimpeachable honesty in public and private life. In economic views he was also liberal and, because of this tendency, he had resigned as Depretis' Minister of Public Works in 1877 rather than agree to any measure of state operation of the railways. His participation in Cairoli's government as Minister of the Interior was a pledge to the country that personal and political freedoms would be respected with the utmost regard. The speech reproduced below is especially notable precisely because its strictures on electoral manipulation and the violation of basic freedoms were aimed particularly at Nicotera, Zanardelli's own colleague on the Left.

The Views of the Progressive Liberal Left: Zanardelli's Speech to His Constituents of Iseo (Lombardy) on November 3, 1878

> Giuseppe Zanardelli, *Discorsi parlamentari*, 3 vols. Rome: Tipografia della Camera dei deputati, 1905, I, 94–97, 104, 121, *passim.* Our translation.

For many years I and my colleagues in the liberal opposition have fought against a policy of resistance and constraint, against restrictions on the freedom of individuals and associations, against distrust of the movement and free contest of ideas and the development of individual and local initiative. We have fought against the idea (whether propounded or practiced) that would convert the government into a partisan political party.

It was therefore our duty not to do that which we criticized in others. Taking the government to be a power and not a party and considering that an administration must have the essential characteristic of protecting the interests of all instead of being biased and partisan (*Good!*), I thought it my duty to practice the most calm impartiality. (*Very good!*). . . .

Although I had to resist the impulses of my soul and certain legitimate sympathies, in elections I have always practiced and preached a rigid neutrality. (*It is very true!—Applause.*) In fact, all equilibrium of contending parties is upset when, in electoral contests, the government becomes an instrument for the preservation of its own power. This is especially true where, in a highly centralized country as ours still remains, the government intervenes directly with the whole of the functionaries, affairs, and interests with which it is entrusted, with prodigal restraints imposed on one side and favors granted to the other. On the contrary, inasmuch as the vote of a political election should serve precisely as a judgment delivered upon the government, the latter should not interfere with this judgment, which it should await quietly and respectfully; it should not deprive the Deputy of his independence by protecting his candidacy and thus making him feel that he has been chosen by and for the government. (*Very good! Very true! Right!*)

Honest elections are essential to free institutions; and therefore every government that truly wishes to apply these institutions is obliged to respect and in no way disturb the honesty of elections. And even some administrations of the Right did not fail to guide their actions according to this rule. I remember that when I held the office of Royal Commissioner in the province of Belluno, while the Honorable Bettino Ricasoli was Minister of the Interior, I received from him not a single word in the sense that the government should exercise the least influence on the elections then scheduled in Venetia. (*Bravo! Good!*)

Besides, the government of the Left had no need whatever to engage in such interference. A gust of public opinion is worth more than any interference or pressure in determining the outcome of elections. (*Applause.*). . . .

There is another freedom which I am conscious of having preserved in its entirety, and that is the freedom and privacy of the telegraph services*. . . . I have literally never intercepted a single telegram. (*Bravo!*) There have been telegrams bearing exaggerated or false news which could have seemed alarming and therefore dangerous, spreading rumors of nonexistent demonstrations or disorders. I chose not to prevent the transmission even of these. Because, in fact, when it becomes known that the government does not obstruct the transmission of any news, the public becomes watchful and gives an appropriate reception to news spread by exaggerating reporters who, in repeating their actions, end up by discrediting themselves. (*Bravo!—Applause.*). . . .

Therefore, you see that just as for the telegraph services so for the press and the right of assembly and association, freedom can frighten only those who depict it in their imagination as something horrible and baleful. . . .

The rights of the individual must remain beyond the reach of any parliamentary majority whatsoever. (*Very good!*) A law, so long as it remains a law, may not be dispensed with by a majority; it may no more be violated by a vote than by force; otherwise, a government sure of its majority could put itself above all laws. (*Applause.*). . . .

And now, without any ado, I take a big jump and come to the suffrage law. . . . On the first day of the Chamber's reconvocation I shall present a bill for franchise reform. The liberal party assumed this commitment a long time ago; it must fulfill it as soon as possible. (*Very good!*). . . . Italy is a country of 28 million people but it has only 605,000 voters. It means that we have 2 voters for every 100 inhabitants, whereas France has 26, Germany 20, and England 8. . . . But what bases, what limits are to be assigned to an extension of the franchise? . . . . In my view, apart from qualifications of age and possession of civil rights, the only other condition for voting should be a level of education sufficient to assure that whoever is to have the right to vote should possess an understanding of the vote he is about to cast.

---

* This is another caustic reference to Nicotera who, as Minister of the Interior, had violated the privacy of the telegraph services in 1877. Ed. note.

Zanardelli's speech could not please the radical elements of the democratic and extreme Left who clamored for unrestricted universal suffrage; nor was it any more pleasing to the authoritarians to be found on both the Left and the Right. But it was a veritable calamity for Zanardelli and Cairoli that, on November 17, within fourteen days of the speech, King Umberto was to be the target of an attempted assassination in Naples. Cairoli was traveling in the royal carriage; as the would-be assassin, Giovanni Passanante, made a second thrust with his dagger toward Umberto I, Cairoli shielded his King with his own body and received a wound in the leg. But there were not enough Deputies who would shield Cairoli and Zanardelli from the accusation that their excessively permissive policy in matters of public order was the principal cause of the assassination attempt and other disorders plaguing the country. Virtually the whole Right went on the attack when, on December 3, 1878, the Chamber began its debate on the government's domestic policy. More damaging was the criticism that came from the Left. Depretis was mild in his censure, but Crispi was less tolerant. He raised the complex theoretical question of whether "prevention" or "repression" was the best policy for the preservation of domestic order: prevention of illegal acts by timely restriction of public freedom or repression of such acts only after clear manifestation that the acts were in the process of occurring.

Crispi Helps Upset a Government: Excerpts from His Speeches of December 5 and 7, 1878

Crispi, *Discorsi parlamentari*, II 312, 319, 322, 325. Our translation.

Gentlemen, we should have no illusions. The political conditions of our country are most serious. Italy is at present in what is perhaps the most critical situation it has yet faced. . . .

Why is Italy in such a disquieted state? Why are we uncertain of our future? Gentlemen, several disorders have taken place lately in our country. An event has occurred which seemed impossible in Italy! This misdeed could have been possible and I would have understood it if it had taken place in 1859 and in 1860, when passions were high, when five princes had been dispossessed, and when we, working for freedom, unity, and the monarchy, raised that throne which is the glory of the country and the security of the nation. (*Good! Bravo!*)

But today, with a loyal and young King who has barely begun his reign and whose actions are marked only by honesty, virtue, and love of country, how and why could this crime have been committed today? Give me the reason.

Fortunately, the King's life was saved, and happy is the man who was able to offer himself in order to achieve such a high duty. (*Bravo!*) You will not blame me if I envy this act; it is the only envy possible by those who are patriots and his [Cairoli's] friends. (*Bravo!—Applause.*)

The King's life was saved, but the country's institutions were shaken precisely because of the uncertainty which prevails in all our souls. If our institutions are not in danger, no one will be able to say to me that they have the same moral stability they possessed before November 17. . . .

I asked the Ministry [two days ago] the reasons for the social illness that we feel and the remedies which should be applied. The Honorable Minister Zanardelli replied with the presentation of three kinds of idea. First of all he recalled the disorders which took place during the sixteen years of government by the Right, adding that in the light of the fact that our opponents neither knew how nor were able to prevent these disorders, it should not be surprising if he too had not learned how during his ten months in power.

As for the power of government to deal with such disorders, he discharged all his responsibility onto the shoulders of the Minister of Justice.

Last, he recalled English practice in these matters, and thus concluded that his inertia belongs to a good school. . . .

You said that you have deferred the members of the Barsanti circles * to the judicial authorities, and you have perhaps done the same for the [socialist] Internationalists. But you have not told me what you will do if the judicial authorities free these individuals as they did in 1872 when they freed those who attended a republican congress at the Argentina [theater in Rome]. . . .

The Honorable Minister Zanardelli thinks that in our country the judicial authorities are sufficient safeguard against all eventualities. He therefore abdicates to his colleague, the Minister of Justice, those powers which the law has attributed to the Minister of the Interior. The Minister of the Interior in Italy has the ultimate authority over the police power. He must know that he is the Minister of the Interior only on condition that he safeguard the public peace; and when this

* Republican groups named after the soldier Pietro Barsanti, executed in 1870 for inciting his fellow soldiers to rebellion. Ed. note.

public peace is shaken or compromised, he is the one responsible. This high office is entrusted to this Minister by the law of 1865. He exercises his office by means of Prefects, Deputy-Prefects, police chiefs, and all the other agents spread about the Kingdom. According to Article 9 of this law, it is the duty of the Minister of the Interior not only to preserve public order but, especially, to prevent the commission of crimes. Now, the Honorable Minister Zanardelli did not have the courage to assert that he is the chief of police of the Kingdom.

Zanardelli (*Minister of the Interior*): It was not necessary to say this.

Crispi: I am happy that now you do not deny this fact [of being the chief of police], but you did not say so in your speech, and perhaps you feared for your popularity. (*Rumblings and lively interruptions at the extreme left.*)

Zandardelli: Yours is a language of the Right; go sit at the right.

President: Do not interrupt. I beg my Honorable colleagues to be silent.

Crispi: If they think they can frighten me, they are mistaken!! (*Rumblings.*)

President: Unless the debate proceeds with calm, I shall adjourn the sitting.

Crispi: Gentlemen, I can understand that sitting next to you [at the left] I am an inconvenience. . . . (*Interruptions by the Deputy Mazzarella.*)

President: Honorable Deputy Mazzarella, I call you to order.

Crispi: . . . but unfortunately I have nowhere else to sit. Here I have been and here I shall stay. Everyone thinks according to his lights, and the opinion I hold against this Ministry burdens me more than the disapproval directed against me by those who are convinced that the present government is on the right road.

Gentlemen, when one is in power it is necessary above all not to fear unpopularity. Whoever does not fear it, whoever knows how to face it, serves the country better than those who allow themselves to be dragged along by disorderly demonstrations. (*Bravo! Very good!—Commotion on the extreme left.*) These intemperate outbursts, this fight against me, give the wrong to those who oppose me, and they do not make the government any stronger. (*Bravo!—Interruptions; rumblings.*) The Ministry will find itself in such a position that, even if it were to want to, it would not be able to control the violence of its friends, who are dragging it where perhaps it does not wish to go. (*Lively signs of approval.*)

Very well, it is for this reason above all that I shall vote against it.

The Cairoli-Zanardelli government was overturned on December 11 by a vote of 263 to 189. The reasons for its fall included not only the concern aroused by the attempt on the King's life but also considerations of foreign policy. Crispi's mention of disorderly demonstrations referred in part to the growing activity of a group of Irredentists who wished to "redeem" the Italian-speaking territories still under Austrian rule—the provinces of Trent and Trieste. Inasmuch as Crispi had become a protagonist of an alliance with Germany and possibly with Austria, he logically concluded that the government's toleration of Irredentist demonstrations was contrary to the national interest. A firm anticlerical, Crispi and most other Italian political leaders had feared since 1870 that the powerful French clerical party would support some desperate effort to restore the Pope to his former temporal domains. This fear was heightened by the election of Marshal MacMahon to the French presidency in 1873; and although this ultra-conservative president did not actually take any step in favor of the Pope, the fear remained. In May 1877 MacMahon became involved in a serious constitutional crisis over the issue of whether the French Ministry was responsible to Parliament or to the president. While the outcome of this crisis remained in doubt, the Italian government under Depretis sent Crispi, then President of the Chamber, on a tour of consultation with the governments of the major European powers. Bismarck of Germany offered Italy an alliance against France; but the victory of the republicans in the French elections of October 1877 and the election of a new Pope, Leo XIII, in 1878, seemed to reduce the urgency of this alliance and, owing to the opposition of Depretis' government, Crispi's efforts came to nought.

This failure to provide Italy with a strong ally was especially important when after the end of the Russo-Turkish War of 1877–78, a congress was convened at Berlin in June 1878 with the aim of reducing the gains Russia had achieved at Turkey's expense. Cairoli was then in power, and he and his Foreign Minister, Count Senator Luigi Corti, concluded that Italy's weak diplomatic position made necessary a policy of "clean hands," meaning disinterest in territorial or other material acquisitions. In consequence, Cairoli's government had to suffer the attacks of those who pointed out that whereas England had acquired Cyprus and Austria was allowed to occupy Bosnia and Herzegovina, Italy had lost a golden opportunity to extract concessions from Austria regarding the unredeemed provinces in return for Italian acquiescence to Austria's occupation of Bosnia-Herzegovina. Corti's diplomacy has been damned generally as inept, and Cairoli's admission to his constituents that although his government's diplomacy may not have been "able," at least it had been "honest," exposed him to the characterization of being "incapable but honest."

Among the most bitter critics of Cairoli's foreign policy were the Irredentists, who made an explosive appearance on the Italian scene in 1878. The republican antecedents of many of the Irredentist leaders, such as Matteo Renato Imbriani, were another reason for Crispi's hostility to them. He, the former republican who had become an ardent supporter of the monarchy in the 1860s, could not tolerate Zanardelli's acquiescence to Irredentist demonstrations. These considerations of foreign policy were only vaguely implied in Crispi's speeches (the preceding excerpts); but they weighed heavily in his opposition to Cairoli's government, which fell as much from weakness in foreign policy as from an allegedly over-liberal domestic policy.

The parliamentary weakness of the Right precluded its succession to the fallen Cairoli. Depretis was once again called to office, but the divisions within the Left were so numerous that he lasted less than six months, and when Cairoli succeeded him in July 1879 he lasted only until November. Then, by a combination which Crispi called "most hybrid," Cairoli and Depretis composed their differences. Cairoli became Prime Minister and Minister of Foreign Affairs, and Depretis chose the key Ministry of the Interior. It was a form of internal transformism within the Left, and it kept the government in power for nearly two years until, in May 1881, the unlucky Cairoli was upset by another crisis in foreign policy. No one other than Depretis could form a new government, and by means of several ministerial combinations he remained in power uninterruptedly until his death in 1887. The last six years of the Depretis era were to mark the definitive triumph of transformism and the beginning of the social question.

XI. THE TRIUMPH OF TRANSFORMISM AND THE BEGINNING OF THE SOCIAL QUESTION, 1881–1887

The crisis that brought Cairoli down in May 1881 resulted from France's announcement of a protectorate over Tunisia, where Italian investments were considerable and the number of Italian settlers greater than those from France. In spite of this material Italian interest, at the time of the Congress of Berlin French diplomacy succeeded in gaining German and English support for French control over Tunisia. Bismarck found it useful to divert France's attention away from revenge against Germany and toward colonial expansion, while England preferred to have France involved in Tunisia and thus possibly reduce French competition in Egypt. Cairoli's diplomacy once again proved inept; and Parliament's mood after the French announcement was so hostile to the government that Cairoli chose to resign before an adverse vote could force his retirement. This refusal to face an indictment of his policy has been judged by some as being unconstitutional, and in fact it did make the solution of the resulting political crisis unusually difficult. Sella, the most authoritative representative of the Right, attempted to form a coalition government with moderates of the Left; but the prospect of the Right's return to power so alarmed the factions of the Left that they momentarily buried their differences and assured the designation of Depretis as the new Prime Minister. But the Depretis who returned to power in 1881 was no longer the bearer of the "happy program" of 1876. There was a sort of sad resignation in the speech with which he presented his new government to the Chamber in June 1881. The magic of the "parliamentary revolution" of 1876 was gone; its place had been taken by the practical everyday necessities of politics; and the pressure of these necessities overrode party distinctions, thus making transformism a supreme political imperative.

29. THE END OF THE "HAPPY HOPES": DEPRETIS' SPEECH BEFORE THE CHAMBER OF DEPUTIES, JUNE 2, 1881

Depretis, *Discorsi parlamentari*, VII, 689–92, *passim*. Our translation.

I do not come before you today, as I did five years ago, full of happy hopes and to announce a new parliamentary era. I come with a strong resignation and with the most precise determination of one who has given himself to the performance of his duty. . . .

In thinking of the question of electoral reform, I repeated to myself the manly exhortation of "Either with this, or on it." * (*Good! from the left.*) Yes, gentlemen, the most important part of the program of this administration is precisely the electoral reform law. . . . It is our duty to keep the chief promises made by the various past governments of the Left, and we shall do our duty. . . .

Gentlemen, I touch upon another grave question. All of us here feel the duty of devoting our most assiduous efforts to our patriotic armed forces, which are the national representatives of fraternal discipline, of respect for the laws, and of devotion to King and country. You will understand that my remarks on military expenditures will have to be brief and, I hope, clear and precise. (*Signs of attention.*). . . . All of us know that the ordinary budget † of the War Ministry has risen during the few years from 1877 to 1880 from 165 million lire to 180 millions. It is also known that during this brief period the extraordinary expenditures increased notably. Proportionately speaking, increases in expenditures for the navy were no less great. . . .

Now, we can announce to the Chamber and the country that the progressive improvement of our finances and credit—following rationally and necessarily from the fiscal system adopted a few years ago—allows us to provide with greater efficiency for this great national need. We shall be able to devote the larger part of the budget's

* The reference is to the injunction for bravery with which Spartan mothers sent their sons off to war: return alive with your shield or lying dead on it. Ed. note.

† The *ordinary* budget covered annually recurring expenses and the *extraordinary* budget was for nonrecurring expenses, such as wars and capital improvements. Ed. note.

surplus to ordinary and extraordinary military expenditures, and we
trust that Parliament will follow the same practice in subsequent fiscal
years. . . .

A few words on our foreign relations and then I will have ended.
(*Signs of attention.*) Gentlemen, we shall always keep in mind that in
our foreign relations Italy will always maintain friendly relations with
the other powers. These relations will be strengthened on the basis of
justice and reciprocal respect, and Italy will make every effort to reconcile its duties toward the family of nations with those it has to
itself.

Italy is the last country to enter the society of great powers; it came
into being as an element for order, harmony, and peace. It shall remain as such; it asks for itself nothing other than peace with dignity.
(*Very good! from the left.*) Nor, you can be sure, shall we forget that
in times of passion and distrust the great interests of state are best
safeguarded only with that serene and patient calm which accompa-
nies the consciousness of being in the right. (*Very good!*)

It was truly a resigned speech, and the lukewarm reception accorded by the
Chamber indicated that the hurt of the colonial defeat suffered at the hands
of France was still very much alive. Depretis' reference to the need to
strengthen the armed forces was another indication of strained relations with
France, but the reference to budgetary surpluses could not but prove irritating to some members of the Chamber. The budget had in fact shown small
surpluses during the early years of the Left after 1876; but, when in 1879
the first step was taken in fulfilling the Left's promise to abolish the grist tax,
these surpluses were put in jeopardy. By 1884, when the whole of the grist
tax reached its scheduled gradual repeal, military expenditures put a heavy
pressure on the budget, whose precarious position was masked by the "financial prestidigitations" of Depretis' Treasury and Finance Minister, Agostino Magliani. Magliani's accounting manipulations were in time to be
called sarcastically a "happy finance" because they tended to hide the less
than happy economic realities facing the country. These realities came to be
known as the "social question," and it is significant that one of the first men
to raise this question in Parliament was the Tuscan Baron Sidney Sonnino
(1847–1922), who sat not at the left but at the center-right in the Chamber.

The growing concern with the social question was another dissolving element affecting the old party alignments. Apart from the issue of the grist
tax, on whose repeal the Left had been by no means unanimous, the Left
and the Right were not irremediably divided on socioeconomic questions.
The bulk of these two parliamentary coalitions was composed of men with

middle-class origins; their primary divisions had been essentially political, particularly on the question of how to unify Italy. The disappearance of this question in 1870 marked the beginning of the dissolution of the two coalitions of Right and Left, and although the latter managed to make a show of unity after 1876 for the sake of keeping the Right out of power, it was already obvious how divided the Left really was. The championing of the social question by elements from the center and right of the Chamber could not but divide the Left even more. This continuing division made transformism more necessary than ever.

It was Sidney Sonnino of the Center-Right faction who persistently drew the attention of Parliament to the social question in 1880, the year he first entered the Chamber after acquiring a reputation as an economist and publicist on social questions. His maiden speech of June 9, 1880, was made in favor of a bill on workmen's compensation, which had the support of Minghetti, Luigi Luzzatti, and Pasquale Villari, all from the moderate Right. Sonnino asserted that the life and health of workmen constituted an interest superior to the rights of private property and to the demands of "frantic industrial competition." It was the kind of speech that could easily have come from the benches on the extreme left.

The bill Sonnino proposed and defended had no immediate outcome; he was more immediately successful with a resolution of July 7, 1880, calling on the Chamber to support the government in its bill to abolish the remaining portions of the grist tax and to consider new and more equitably distributed taxes to meet the budgetary needs resulting from the proposed abolition of the whole grist tax. That a Deputy from the Center-Right should support a government of the Left was another indication of the workings of transformism.

30. THE CENTER AND THE RIGHT RAISE THE SOCIAL QUESTION: SONNINO'S SPEECH OF JULY 7, 1880, ON SOCIAL JUSTICE FOR THE PEASANTRY

Sidney Sonnino, *Discorsi parlamentari*, 3 vols. Rome: Tipografia della Camera dei deputati, 1925, I, 5–6, 8–11, 20–21, *passim*. Our translation.

I am in favor of the bill proposed by the government and here, in brief, are the reasons. In the first place, I believe the grist tax to be excessively burdensome on some classes of the population. Even more important, it is so odious as to make it a serious cause for discontent. Therefore, for political and economic reasons, I think it urgently necessary that it be repealed. . . .

Gentlemen, until now we have too long forgotten the conditions of the farming class in our country. They move one to pity: in half the Kingdom conditions are worse than in any other part of Europe. What these conditions are will be revealed to you by your Commission of Inquiry into Agriculture, assuming . . . a report will ever come from that Inquiry.* (*Very good!*) Ill paid, ill housed, ill nourished, and crushed by excessive labor under the most unhealthy conditions, to counsel the peasant in a large part of Italy to be thrifty is an irony. (*Good!*) All assertions by the law which declare him to be free and equal to all other citizens are a bitter sarcasm. For him, who knows nothing of the world outside his village, the name of Italy means conscriptions, it means taxes, it means the overbearing behavior of the wealthy classes. From the day he first heard of that name, he has seen his conditions worsen in every way. (*Good!*). . . .

The tax collector and the military policeman, these are the only propagators of the religion of the fatherland among the brutalized masses of our peasantry. It is with tax bills, with punitive parole and penal settlements, with freedom for usury, with the overbearing behavior of the wealthy classes, with political inequality, and with *de facto* inequality before the law—it is with all this that the peasant is taught that Italy is the great common mother that watches with loving care over all her children, without distinction or preference. (*Bravo!*). . . .

I say that our tax structure is directed completely against the interests of the peasants and that its effects are made even more harmful by the way it is applied. . . . In the Southern provinces, where the peasants are generally concentrated in large villages, excise duties weigh most heavily on them. There are a number of such essentially rural communities where nothing or almost nothing is collected from the surtax on land, which would be borne by the rich landowners, and where the greater part of communal tax receipts comes from consumer taxes. In some other Southern communities, and especially in Sicily, there is a preferential application of the tax on draft animals instead of that on cattle. Why? Because mules and donkeys, which are taxed by 8 or 5 lire, belong to the peasants, whereas cows and oxen—entire herds—are either exempt or taxed by a few lire, and this

---

* A masterful report did come out, in fifteen volumes, between 1881 and 1885, but its recommendations went largely unheeded. Ed. note.

because they belong to the landowners. (*Very good!*) And all this is done under the mantle of the law! And with these practices, which vary according to the locality, the peasants end up by paying for expenditures (or the fruits of expenditures designed to find jobs for the sons of the well-to-do rural and urban classes, or for the construction of buildings, monuments, fine roads, theaters, beautifying enterprises, or for other luxury expenditures) all of which are undertaken for the exclusive use and benefit of the latter [well-to-do] classes. . . .

Gentlemen, unfortunately we have (if you permit me an expression perhaps a little too absolute in meaning) in certain parts of our country legalized with our institutions and our theories the oppression of one class by another. Under the mantle of the law and of doctrines, we have covered up a process of exploiting our own fellows. And while on the one hand we do this, on the other hand and with singular contradiction we push this brutalized and embittered peasant to go to school in order that he may acquire a clearer and fuller awareness of his degradation, of the legalized oppression of which he is a victim; in order that he may equip himself with that degree of education which, making him in his own eyes the moral peer of the more prosperous, will make absolutely intolerable the enormous differences in the material conditions of life. (*Bravo! Good!*) But this is not all.

We make a soldier of the young peasant who suffers hunger every winter, who works in the rice fields, who sleeps in one room with all his family—father, mother, brothers, and sisters all in one bed. We make of this young man a soldier; we teach him *esprit de corps,* which is a spirit of brotherhood; we teach him honor, the sense of his own dignity; we teach him to defend these treasures at the risk of his life; we permit him to lead the life of a human being and accustom him to certain comforts; and above all we show him the immense strength that comes from union in association, from the subordination of individual wills for the sake of the common good, from discipline. And after all this, we send this man back to his squalid dwelling; we send him back to a life of hardship and misery, to work in the rice fields, to sicken from pellagra because he eats only maize, to fall ill of malignant fever from sleeping out in the open at harvest time. In short, we send him back to live, in one form or another, that brutal life which is the lot of millions of our peasants. And then we expect that from all this there should not be born the seeds of rebellion, seeds which develop, multiply, and little by little undermine the foundations of our society!

Yes, let us build schools; yes, let us educate our peasants; but we should also provide in some fashion for the improvement of material conditions. At least let us refrain from making them worse; let us show that we have the good will to help them.

Our state has thought of the working classes only when there has been need of imposing a general or broadly based tax. I am convinced within the most inner depths of my being that only when we shall have given the vote to everyone, only when we shall have introduced universal suffrage in that fashion and with those procedures which allow the voting peasant to have a full and clear awareness of the act he performs, only then will there be a serious change in the tendency of our legislation, which today burdens the poor rather than the rich, the agricultural class more than other classes. (*Bravo! Bravo! Very good!*) Allow me to say that this goal will not be reached with the [franchise] reform offered by the Ministry's latest proposal. This proposal seems to have been studiously prepared with the purpose of excluding altogether any representation of the agricultural classes. But now I return to the argument which concerns us most immediately today.

The question of repeal of the grist tax is already compromised in Italy. We are no longer dealing with a virgin situation. Other speakers have pointed this out; accordingly, I shall pass over this matter. Those who are opposed to repeal of the tax on the grinding of wheat should not, last year, have supported repeal of the tax on the grinding of inferior cereal grains. It would be indeed an enormous injustice to wish to limit the benefit of repeal of the tax on bread to one part of Italy's working classes.

And in this matter one should not brand with the charge of regionalism whoever invokes the right of equal treatment of all parts of our country. In this case the regionalist is the one who wants the inhabitants of certain provinces only to enjoy the first tax reductions. (*Very good! Bravo! from the left.*) All of you know that certain Italian provinces gain little or nothing from repeal of the tax on the second grinding.* This is so because in these provinces almost no use is made of inferior grains. . . .

* The grist tax repeal effective in 1880 covered only the inferior cereals, such

The social question in Italy is essentially an agricultural question. Let us take steps now, in these moments of calm and tranquillity. During the early years of our *risorgimento* as a nation we had to repress energetically a veritable social war, as was the case of brigandage in the Neapolitan provinces: a real war, with several thousand dead in combat and executions.

De Zerbi [Rocco, of the Right]: This is blasphemy! Brigandage was not a social war.

Sonnino: It was a harsh necessity. But let us take steps in time: let us eliminate the seeds of hatred and divisions in the future. Because, if a numerous class—indeed, the most numerous in our society—were to become convinced that our institutions are directed only to its harm, if it were to become convinced that its only defense lies in its own strength, and if it were to acquire a full awareness of its strength, then, gentlemen, it might well be too late to take remedial steps. (*Good! Bravo! from the left.*)

The foregoing speech by Sonnino is one of the earliest and most penetrating documents on the conditions of the agricultural classes in Italy. In his references to the conditions of Southern Italy, Sonnino, a Tuscan, spoke like a Southern regionalist. His indictment of the overbearing and callous attitude of the well-to-do classes was severe enough to do justice to a doctrinaire socialist. It was even more impressive because it came from a reforming aristocrat of the Center-Right whose scholarly studies on Southern agriculture gave special weight to his revelations. Sonnino's speech, one of his most effective during his long political career, raised the problem in a manner so direct and explicit as to make impossible any further neglect of the social question. It also tied this question inextricably to the one of suffrage reform.

On no issue were the Left and the Right so internally divided as on the reform of the electoral law. Sonnino of the Center-Right wanted not only universal manhood suffrage but also proportional representation and suffrage for women. Depretis and Zanardelli of the Left wanted the suffrage limited to those possessing an education of at least the fourth grade of elementary school; Nicotera, also of the Left, wanted this qualification to include all grades of elementary school; Crispi, on the other hand, favored limiting educational qualifications simply to the ability to read and write, and also favored provincial electoral colleges, whereas the first two leaders of the Left were willing to settle for smaller multiple-member constituencies. The extreme Left, led by Garibaldi, Cavallotti, and others, asked for nothing less

as corn, which were ground twice and which were consumed predominantly in the North. Wheat, consumed most generally in the South, did not benefit from the partial repeal of 1880. Ed. note.

than complete universal suffrage, as did Sonnino. Whereas almost the entire Right favored a reform granting suffrage to all who paid direct taxes and, in addition, to members of the armed forces regardless of tax status.

In 1881 and 1882 two electoral laws were passed, the first providing for an enlarged electorate and the second for multiple-member constituencies. The electorate was enlarged to include all citizens who paid a direct tax of at least 19.80 lire a year or had completed the fourth grade of elementary school; members of the armed forces were eligible to vote after two years of service and with the possession of educational proficiency equal to that required by regimental schools. The number of eligible voters was thus increased from 621,896 in 1879 to 2,049,461 in 1882, plus 94,734 from the military contingent. The percentage of the population eligible to vote increased from 2.22 in 1879 to 7.09 in 1882. Of all voters eligible in 1882, 1,338,737 qualified on the basis of education, while 710,724 did so on the basis of taxes paid. The country was divided into 135 constituencies: 35 were to elect 5 Deputies each; 36 were to elect 4 Deputies each; 61 were to elect 3 Deputies each; and 3 constituencies had 2 seats allotted to each.[1]

The general elections held in October 1882 on the basis of the new laws did not produce any very extraordinary results. The extreme Left doubled its representation but the overwhelming majority of the seats went to men bearing moderate labels. There were rumors of all kinds of electoral arrangements implemented during the elections and, in fact, as Arangio-Ruiz points out, now that the issues of the grist tax and electoral reform were out of the way, except for personal likes and dislikes there was very little to divide the moderates of the Right and of the Left. This almost total disappearance of programmatic differences between Right and Left made the 1882 elections a signal affirmation of the reality of transformism. Minghetti of the Right announced in October 1882 that the Left's program, as presented by Depretis, was also that of his party. Within several months Minghetti validated this assertion by confirming it in open Chamber, and Depretis proceeded courteously to welcome the Right's offer of collaboration.

31. TRANSFORMISM IS OFFICIALLY CONFIRMED: MARCO MINGHETTI'S SPEECH TO THE CHAMBER OF DEPUTIES, MAY 12, 1883

Minghetti, *Discorsi parlamentari*, VIII, 264, 267–68, 272–74, 276–77, *passim*. Our translation.

Yesterday the Honorable Deputy Nicotera raised the banner of the old or historical Left against the old or historical Right. . . . In truth, I could cite some examples when, because of internal dissensions, a

[1] Cf. Arangio-Ruiz, *Storia costituzionale*, pp. 361–73, *passim*.

part of the Left not only found it not unpleasant to have the support of the Right but even asked for it. I said that I do not want to harp on the past, and I shall keep my word. But I ask: Today, do these old labels indicate the same differences as existed in the past? . . . .

At the beginning of our existence as a nation our task was so great that, this fact notwithstanding, we were able to divide into two parties. Our aim was one but the means for reaching it were absolutely different. Some wanted to achieve the unification of Italy by means of spontaneous popular initiative. Impatient with any delay, they hoped that enthusiasm would be enough to conquer our independence in its entirety. We, the others, wanted conversely to make sure of the present, to prepare our forces, to prepare for the future by means of alliances, and to reserve always for the government the direction and initiation of matters of public welfare.

These two parties fought openly, and at the time they had a reason for existing. Another reason for party distinctions was occasioned by the quest for a balanced budget and the stabilization of our public finances. It cannot be denied that there was a party which was convinced that the excessive raising of taxes not only would fail to achieve this desired end but would also destroy the vital economic forces of the country. The other party, on the other hand, thought the gravest sacrifices to be necessary, urgent, and inevitable. Very well, we fought against each other and we won. If you wish, we harried the taxpayer with imposts, but we saved Italy's finances, its credit, and its honor. We left you with a state of things which allowed you to achieve that in which you glory.

But today, where is the banner, where is the principle that divides us? . . . .

Gentlemen, every time it proves impossible to answer these ideas with valid objections, someone replies with an ambiguous word, transformism. . . . What do you mean by transformism? Do you mean that men and parties do not always remain immobile but, rather, change their ideas and sentiments according to circumstances, public needs, changing times and places? If this is the case, allow me to say that transformism is the general law of all living things. There is no plant, no animal, no human being that is today the same as it was yesterday. And if—in order not to digress from our theme—we ourselves examine the ideas we held ten years ago, we will find many changes

in our judgments; and those who most inveigh against transformism
will be the first to acknowledge that they are different from what they
were.

I repeat, in this sense transformism is a general law, because that
which is not susceptible to transformation is dead. (*Interruptions from
the left.*)

With regard to this matter two days ago I said a phrase that
seemed to displease the Honorable Deputy Nicotera. I said that government is the greatest of transforming environments, because when
men reach the power of government they find themselves in the midst
of difficulties which did not face them before. They are forced to fight
against unforeseen necessities; they feel a responsibility much greater
than they felt before. Accordingly, they modify their views and are
more cautious in their actions. Gentlemen, this is what I said, and no
more. . . .

If, on the other hand, transformism is understood to mean the renunciation of ideas and principles which one still holds; and if this renunciation is made for secondary reasons or reasons of gain; in such a
case I would repudiate both the word and the idea of transformism
with all the strength of my soul. . . .

How is it, then, that this sort of entente [between Right and Left]
has come to pass? It has occurred for the following reasons: the laws
which in the past were the occasion for our contests have now been
approved; the political direction taken by the President of the Council
[Depretis] is one which I favor. What has been the result of all this?
It has attenuated the differences between us and has brought the similarities to the forefront. This is a natural course, and whoever accom-
modates himself to it is not properly the object of reproach. . . .

There are some men who entertain a strange notion of the President
of the Council. They believe—to use an expression of the sixteenth
century—that his aim is to enjoy the benefits of the day, to maneuver
among the various parties and exploit the contending passions, always
to have recourse to expedients in order to prolong as much and as
easily as possible the life of the government. They think that when
finally his rule comes to an end he will want to be able to repeat the
only too proverbial Italian saying: Dead am I, the world is at an end.

I hold a totally different notion of the Honorable President of the
Council. I believe that the Honorable President of the Council

Depretis—who is an old and proved patriot, an old and proved servant of the house of Savoy—after having opened both gates to democracy now feels the need to establish a strong and stable government supported by the compact majority of this Chamber, a government which will preserve inviolate the country's institutions and which will proceed with a sure and measured step along the road of civilized progress. . . . If that is the intention of the Honorable President Depretis—and I do not doubt it—I feel it my duty to offer him my loyal support.

Depretis cordially accepted Minghetti's offer, but noted with regret that not all were inclined to believe and accept the "peace" concluded between the two parliamentary factions. Among the men of the Left most convinced that there could not and should not be peace between Left and Right was Crispi. He considered the *connubio* between Depretis and Minghetti as an attempt on the part of the Right to infiltrate and demolish the Left. Toward the end of 1883 Crispi was joined by four other leaders of the Left—Cairoli, Zanardelli, Nicotera, and Baccarini—in the formation of the "Pentarchy," which was devoted to combating Depretis' inclination toward and dependence on the Right. The Pentarchy had no success against Depretis, principally because of the fear that his fall could mean the return of the Right to power. Consequently, for the next four years Depretis remained in office by virtue of several reshufflings of his government, ceding his office in 1887 not to political opponents but to death. In April 1887, four months before his death, Depretis was obliged to rearrange his government once again, this time because of the repercussions over the destruction of an Italian column of about 500 men at the hands of the Ethiopians. This last of the eight ministries led by Depretis included Crispi at the Interior and Zanardelli at Justice. Its importance lay in its decidedly "leftish" composition and, above all, in Crispi's return to the government after an absence of more than nine years. The era of Depretis had ended, and the troubled years of the Crispi period had begun.

XII. THE CRISPI PERIOD, 1887–1896:
DOMESTIC AND FOREIGN CRISES

The thirteen years between 1887 and 1900 were among the most troubled in modern Italian history. Francesco Crispi held the reins of government for approximately half of this period and he imparted to these years the feverish and active quality that was so essential to his nature. The problems which became acute during his tenures of office were not all of his making. Some derived from causes quite independent of his actions, but most of them were rendered more difficult by the nature of the man whom King and Parliament had called upon to deal with them. The first important problem resulted from Italy's increasingly strained relations with France, a country Italy had feared until 1877 because of possible French support of efforts to restore the Pope's temporal authority. The victory of the republicans in the French elections of 1877 reduced this fear; but after 1881, when France proclaimed its protectorate over Tunisia, Italy's thwarted ambitions in North Africa had the effect of adding hatred to fear. In response to these strong feelings and in the realization that France had been able to outplay Italy in the contest for influence in North Africa because of Italy's weak diplomatic position, Depretis decided reluctantly to conclude a defensive alliance with Germany and Austria in May 1882. This Triple Alliance had been accepted by much of the Italian Left, but it was even more welcome to the Right and was thus one of the reasons for Minghetti's willingness to support Depretis after 1882. The five-year Alliance signed in 1882 specifically excluded any hostile intentions toward England; it was directed principally against France, which pleased Crispi, who was decidedly anti-French and who had been a protagonist of an alliance with Germany as early as 1877. Italy would have preferred an alliance with Germany only, but Bismarck's insistence on Austria's participation was a fixed condition the Italian government had to accept or else forgo any agreement whatever.

Participation in the Triple Alliance had a number of effects on Italian domestic politics. Some elements of the Left viewed the Alliance as a turn by Depretis toward more conservative policies, a presumption that pleased much of the Right but outraged the extreme Left and more especially the Irredentists who viewed an alliance with Austria as the death of their ambitions to redeem the Italian-speaking territories still in the Austrian empire. Another effect was the increase in Italy's military expenditures made necessary in part by the obligations incurred in the Alliance. This effect—also displeasing to much of the Left and the extreme Left—meant a return to unbalanced budgets. But perhaps the most important result of the Alliance was the further strain imposed on Franco-Italian relations.

After a number of unpleasant incidents between Italians and Frenchmen in Italy, Tunisia, and East Africa—where Italian shipping interests had begun to establish colonial outposts since the late 1860s—Crispi decided in February 1888 to break commercial relations with France. There followed a tariff war with disastrous results for Southern Italian agricultural exports to France. This event deepened the economic difficulties the country was undergoing, difficulties which were connected with the world-wide economic dislocation characteristic of the late 1880s. It was unfortunate for Crispi that he should have come to office in difficult times, but in his own view he was a man made for such times, although many critics charged that most of the problems he had to face were of his own making. By his own assertion Crispi was a man of destiny. He announced this presumed fact in a speech of opposition to Depretis on March 4, 1886, a year before he settled his differences with Depretis and became his Minister of the Interior: "Place there [pointing to the Ministers' bench] a man of energy; but not a man who bends and gives way; not a man who, in order to assure himself a majority, needs to reward the Deputies who, in turn, have to reward the voters. Place there a man with a sure program around which men of conviction and confidence may rally. . . ." There is little doubt as to the identity of the man Crispi had in mind, but the only "sure" program he possessed was colonial greatness abroad and a policy of stability at home which, if necessary, would be achieved by repressive measures. But colonial adventures and domestic repression proved ineffective against the discontent ever rising in the country, and one of the signals of this discontent was the appearance and expansion of the socialist movement.

The following excerpt from a work by Ernest Lémonon, a French student of Italian social and economic history, is a concise summary of the rise of Italian socialism.

32. ITALIAN SOCIALISM: THE SIGNAL OF THE ERUPTION OF THE SOCIAL QUESTION

Ernest Lémonon, *L'Italie économique et sociale, 1861–1912.* Paris: Felix Alcan, 1913, pp. 257–59, 261, 263, 338–39, 342–47, *passim.* Our translation.

Italian socialism was born in Naples where, in 1867, Mikhail Bakunin * founded a circle that was the first Italian section of the [Social-
ist] International. . . . In 1869 the Neapolitan section of the International already numbered 600 members. The press had contributed
strongly to the dissemination of socialist ideas . . . but Garibaldi's
adherence to Marxist doctrines was also one of the most powerful
causes for their dissemination in the peninsula. . . . But it is necessary also to keep in mind that Garibaldi . . . was not a revolutionary.
He was an idealistic Socialist. . . .

From the very beginnings of socialism in Italy one notes a twofold
tendency, still existing today. The International was clearly revolutionary; Garibaldi and his friends were, on the other hand, reformists
desiring to improve the fate of the working class by legal means. . . .
[But] from its beginnings and in spite of Garibaldi's prudent wisdom,
the Italian socialist movement has moved in the direction of revolution: the efforts of Bakunin and his friends were aimed in the direction of overthrowing the existing social order. . . .

The revolutionary ferment that Bakunin and his disciples spread
throughout the Italian working classes developed very quickly. The
movement which, as we have seen, was born in the South, spread to
northern Italy. Sections of the International were formed in Turin and
Milan, and at the beginning of 1870 more than thirty periodicals defended international socialism in Italy. Garibaldi's followers joined the
International en masse, as did a large number of mutual aid societies
and cooperatives. . . . It is estimated that in 1871 the International
numbered 10,000 members [in Italy]. These members came from
different environments and social conditions. There were many "intellectuals" from the bourgeoisie or the nobility among them; the rest
were urban workers or peasants. . . .

During its first few years of existence Italian socialism attempted to
carry out a great number of revolutionary outbursts. . . . In 1872
there was held at Rimini the first congress of the Italian sections
joined into a national federation. The secretary of the federation was
Andrea Costa, at the time one of Bakunin's most ardent disciples.
. . . The congress was marked by the break with Marxism, and also

* Mikhail Bakunin (1814–76), Russian anarchist and revolutionary. One of the
leaders of the First International Workingmen's Association founded in 1864, he
fought with Karl Marx for control and was expelled in 1872. Ed. note.

by the joining of the Italian sections to the International Alliance of Socialist Democracy, a *very clearly revolutionary* secret association just founded by Bakunin. . . .

Little by little a large number of Socialists repudiated anarchism's theories and practices and rallied to legalitarian socialism, whose foundations were being laid by Enrico Bignami and Osvaldo Gnocchi Viani. It was the electoral law of 1882 that determined these conversions. This law provided for an appreciable extension of the right to vote and tripled the number of voters. Until then the Socialists' tactic in elections had been abstention. In 1874 only one Socialist candidate had contested the elections, Enrico Bignami . . . and his candidacy had as its aim only a protest against the government's repression and violence. Bignami was not even of age to be a candidate! . . .

After the passage of the 1882 electoral law, certain Socialists—the extreme left of the International as led by [Enrico] Malatesta—argued in favor of continuing the old tactic of not participating in elections. But the right wing of the party favored the contrary point of view and finally won out. . . .

In elections of 1882 the Socialist party presented ten candidates . . . who altogether received 49,154 votes, that is, about 4 per cent of the votes cast. A greater number of Socialist candidates contested the elections of 1886, 1890, and 1892, but the results did not correspond to the efforts made. In the 1882–86 Legislature the Italian Parliament numbered but 4 Socialist Deputies. . . . In the 1886–90 Legislature the Socialists were represented by Costa (Imola), by the journalist Alcibiade Moneta (Mantua), and by Dr. Musini (Borgo S. Donnino). The number of Socialists rose by 2 in the 1890–92 Legislature; it reached 10 in the 1892–95 Legislature, 12 in the 1895–97 Legislature, 16 in the 1897–1900 Legislature (with 8.9 per cent of all votes cast), and 32 in the 1900–4 Legislature (13 per cent of the vote). . . .

It was not until 1891 that the Socialists organized themselves into a real political party at a congress in Milan. [On May 1 of the same year] Filippo Turati, a wealthy lawyer from Milan, and Anna Kuliscioff, a Russian revolutionary, had founded a review—*Critica Sociale*—which exercised a profound influence on the socialist movement. One hundred and fifty workingmen's associations, many of them of recent origin, were represented at the congress.

The following year a new congress held at Genoa fixed in a precise manner the road Italian Socialists were to follow. The party decided to lead a life of its own and to break definitively from the anarchists.* From this moment on socialism and anarchism in Italy were to be two distinct terms. But soon another question arose. Could the party ally itself with other political groups in the conduct of its parliamentary activity? Very lively discussions arose and contradictory resolutions were adopted. At the congress of Reggio Emilia [1893] it was decided that the Socialist party could not cooperate with any other party; but at the Parma congress of 1895 the Socialists proved less intransigent and specified the cases in which an alliance [with other parties] could take place.

33. THE CRISPIAN MANNER

One of the reasons for the change in Socialist tactics between 1893 and 1895 was the heightening of the repressive policy Crispi had adopted as early as 1888. In that year Crispi had reacted to the growing number of Socialist, anarchist, and Irredentist demonstrations by proposing a bill that would require all promoters of public assemblies and processions to secure the approval of the authorities twenty-four hours before the intended event. The bill had the support of Zanardelli, Minister of Justice from the moderate Left, and of Sonnino from the Center-Right. Only the extreme Left offered strong opposition to it. In constitutional terms this bill was perfectly appropriate and apparently an innocuous measure of public order. But much depended on the discretion with which the authorities would employ the power the bill gave the government. Zanardelli as Minister of Justice provided a strong assurance that the government would use its power with restraint; but the key Ministry of the Interior was held by Crispi himself, and when the first important test of the government's sense of discretion occurred early in February 1889, Crispi revealed a manner his opponents defined as authoritarian.

In February 1889 serious disorders occurred in Rome because of the actions of several thousand workers unemployed on account of a crisis in the construction industry. Crispi accused the promoters of these disorders of at-

* The expulsion of the anarchists at the Genoa congress of August 1892 marked the triumph of the Marxists in the Italian Workingmen's [Socialist] Party and the adoption of a resolution setting forth the basic Marxist principles of class struggle and socialization of the means of production and distribution of wealth. The resolution distinguished between agitation for immediate reforms in the conditions of the working classes (eventually known as the "minimum program") and preparation for the "conquest of power," later known as the "maximum program." Ed. note.

tempting to provoke a social revolution: "Do you know what some of them were shouting? And I do not mean the honest workmen, because honest workmen are not guilty of the vandalistic scenes of yesterday. (*Very good!*) The fault is of those who mixed among the workmen in the guise of defending their interests. They were shouting long live the social revolution! Very well, gentlemen, I have given orders that from today on, and for as long as the agitation lasts, there are to be no assemblies in all of Italy. In that way the matter will come to an end. (*Good! Bravo!—Prolonged applause from the centers and the right.*)" [1]

The source of the applause in the Chamber was symptomatic. Approval came from the Right, but none from the Left. This fact guided Crispi to practice a little transformism of his own when, during the next month, he recomposed his Ministry with a slight inclination toward the Right. But the latter was not sufficiently mollified, especially because Crispi insisted on retaining the Ministry of Foreign Affairs as well as that of the Interior. His conduct of the two most important posts in the government exposed him to charges of personal and dictatorial government, and even the historian Arangio-Ruiz, who was of moderate inclination, had occasion to write: "He spoke only of himself, of his system, of his ideas. He drew the fundamental ideas of his policies not from the country, much less from Parliament or from a party, but from his own brain. All the credit was his, and he was without fault." [2]

Neither the Left nor the Right could for long tolerate Crispi's real or alleged authoritarian manner. Even less tolerable was Crispi's notion that the best way to prevent disorders in the country was to prohibit all public assemblies. And for the men of the Right Crispi's least tolerable characteristic was his incapacity to be forgiving and respectful of his old antagonists at the right side of the Chamber.

Crispi's Angry Outbursts Bring About His Fall:
Speech of January 31, 1891

Crispi, *Discorsi parlamentari*, III, 619–20. Our translation.

The Honorable Deputy Bonghi [Ruggero, of the Right] spoke at length yesterday and uttered some bitter words with regard to my policies. The Honorable Deputy Bonghi was a member of the government from October 1874 to March 1876. Respect for the dead obliges me not to examine the government of that time. I could reply in such a manner as to prove to the Chamber how the present public adminis-

[1] Crispi, *Discorsi parlamentari*, III, 259.
[2] Arangio-Ruiz, *Storia costituzionale*, p. 446.

tration, the present finances, are in appreciably better condition than they were then. (*Laughter; comments.*) I could say something more; I could say that in those days you had neither army nor fleet (*Very good!*) and that you are responsible for a foreign policy which was servile toward foreigners [France].

Muratori [Angelo, of the extreme Left]: Very good!

(*The Honorable Minister of Public Works, Senator Finali* [Gaspare, of the Right], *rises and leaves the Ministers' bench. Lively applause from the right and center; shouts of* Viva Finali!)

Di Rudinì [Antonio, of the Right] (*Most agitated.*): You should be ashamed of yourself! We served only the policy of our country and the King! You should be ashamed of your words! (*Most lively agitation and commotion. The President repeatedly rings the bell.*)

(*Voices from the right:*) Vote! Vote! Vote! . . . .

Crispi: We are going back to the old days. Believe me, I am ill at ease here at my place. (*Rumblings.*) I am ill at ease here, and with all my soul I hasten a vote which may free me; but I must say what I feel. (*Very good! from the left.*). . . . Your vote will tell the world whether Italy wants a strong government or whether it wishes to return to those governments which with their hesitations and uncertainties led to the discredit of our country. (*Good! Bravo! from the left. Agitation; commotion.*)

Crispi had his wish to be free. By a vote of 186 to 123 the Chamber relieved him of his burdensome "place" on the same day. Within two weeks, on February 6, 1891, the combined forces of the Right and dissident anti-Crispians of the Left formed a new government which once again confirmed the parliamentary necessity of transformism. The Sicilian Marquis Antonio Di Rudinì, of the Right, assumed the posts of Prime Minister and Minister of Foreign Affairs; the Sicilian Baron Giovanni Nicotera, of the Left, went to the Ministry of the Interior. But the Rudinì-Nicotera combination had an almost insoluble problem to face: how to balance a budget in which extraordinary military expenditures could not be met by ordinary receipts. Giuseppe Colombo, Minister of Finance, and of the Right, suggested reducing the size of the army. His proposal met with no support among his colleagues in the government and he resigned in April 1892. The government proposed an increase in the tax on indirect inheritances and requested full powers for two years in order to reform the administrative structure of the country with a view to economies. The Left under Zanardelli and Crispi remained silent, apparently not desirous of returning to office in such difficult times. The major attack on the government came from Giovanni Giolitti, of the Center-

Left, who had served as Crispi's Minister of the Treasury for twenty-one months between 1889 and 1890. Highly skilled in financial and administrative matters by long service in public administration, Giolitti proposed "many and important reforms" in the administration of the state. Giolitti's attack shook the government sufficiently for it to be overturned by an adverse vote of 193 to 185.

In May 1892 the Piedmontese Giolitti was chosen to replace Di Rudinì and Nicotera who, with Crispi, had constituted five years of Sicilian rule over Italy. Giolitti's Center government lasted from May 1892 to November 1893, and it proved to be a bad beginning for the man who was to dominate Italian political life during the first fourteen years of the coming century. Giolitti had to face a number of problems in addition to the thorny financial question of unbalanced budgets: an enormous scandal involving excessive and fraudulent circulation of banknotes by the Bank of Rome, one of Italy's six banks of issue; the killing of a number of Italian workers at Aigues-Mortes, in southern France; and the insurrectional state of Sicily, where leagues (*Fasci*) of peasants and workers agitated for a rapid solution of their economic grievances. Giolitti's involvement in the Banca Romana scandal and his unwillingness to use extreme measures to repress the *Fasci siciliani* brought about his downfall. King and country turned to Crispi once more, in spite of the fact that he too was suspected of improper acts in the bank scandal. It seemed that only a strong hand could deal with the disturbed conditions of the country and especially Crispi's native Sicily.

The nature of Sicily's problems toward the end of the century has been examined by two English writers, Bolton King and Thomas Okey, from whose work the following excerpt is derived.

34. CRISPI'S REPRESSION OF THE SICILIAN DISTURBANCES OF 1893–1894

Bolton King and Thomas Okey, *Italy Today*. London: Nisbet & Co., 1909, pp. 83–86.

The first troubles came in Sicily. The island was suffering from a depression in all its chief productions—wine, lemons, sulphur—and though it was not quite the most miserable part of Italy, there were special circumstances that made it the most uneasy. The proud impatience of the people, the old antagonism to the mainland, an absentee landlordism forgetful of its duties, the local tyranny of cliques which abused local government for party and personal ends, kept Sicily ripe for agitation. In 1891 Socialism made its first appearance, and the Socialists organized a network of unions (*fasci*) among the downtrodden peasants. The members of the *fasci* knew or cared little about Socialism. Practically, the organization was a kind of Land-League, and was in fact a security against violence. The *fasci* were founded and controlled by men of the middle class and a few young nobles; they were religious, almost clericalist, in their tone; they opened schools and aimed at developing cooperative societies and popular libraries; in their club-rooms sometimes hung a crucifix, and by the side of Karl Marx and Mazzini were portraits of the King and Queen. In the troubled times that followed, their leaders always tried, and often managed, to keep order, and it was only a few of the worse organized *fasci* that had any hand in the disturbances.

But the richer classes, trained by generations of unpunished tyranny, saw their power threatened. No longer would the landlords grind the faces of the peasant-farmers; no longer would the local cliques spend the rates for their own benefit. All . . . the band of landlords and middlemen, of officials and police, took fright. They refused work to members of the *fasci;* the police, unable to discover illegalities, invented them; every demand for higher wages was prosecuted as "a strike with violence"; the Sicilian Deputies had the ear of the Government, and hounded it on to flood the island with soldiers and put down the *fasci* with a strong hand. Collision inevitably resulted. Early in 1893 the peasants of Caltavuturo, thinking, probably with reason, that there was jobbery in the letting of the communal lands, went out one day in mass to dig them; they were met by a company of soldiers, who without provocation fired on them and killed several. Giolitti promised that the soldiers should be prosecuted, but nothing was done, and feeling grew bitter through the island. Here and there the people were stung to violence. The police tried to break up the unions by legal or illegal means, and towards winter the people began to despair of peaceful remedy. In December the spirit was growing dangerous. Again and again some crowd, in protest against communal misgovernment and local taxes, hissed the Syndic or occasionally attacked the town-hall; the soldiers fired, generally without any aggression from the crowd, the people retaliated with stones, till the street was strewn with dead and wounded men, and the people fled, to be arrested in batches and sentenced to savage penalties. Altogether in those days nearly 100 of the people and one soldier were killed.

Meanwhile Giolitti had tried at first to shut his eyes to the trouble that was threatening, then made a feeble attempt to please both sides. He left the police a free hand in their evil work, and flooded the island with soldiery, but he seems to have hoped that the officers, who all through behaved better than the civil officials, would act as peace-makers, and he put pressure on the local authorities to repeal the communal duties on corn. Naturally, he contented nobody, and the richer classes throughout the country called for Crispi, as the one man who had strength to stamp the sinister portent out. Crispi seems for a moment to have thought of conciliation and he planned drastic agrarian laws. But Crispi's head never long kept cool, and he readily believed the stories of conspiracy that the police invented. Convinced that only strong repression could save the island from revolution, he disgraced free Italy by a brutal coercion, that well-nigh rivalled the doings of Austrians or Bourbons in the old days. For seven months Sicily was under martial law. In many places people of all classes were arrested in mass; the press was gagged; cooperative stores, belonging to the poor, were dissolved and their effects seized. The procedure of the military courts was often a farce of justice; the evidence was generally such as no decent court would have listened to; and though the young officers, who were the only counsel allowed to the defendants, manfully did their best, they were browbeaten by the presiding generals. The Central Committee of the *fasci* were charged at first with conspiring to sell the island to France or Russia. The charge was made on the report of a police-officer, who had "metaphysical certainty" of its truth, but no evidence; and though it was enough to convince Crispi, it was too flimsy even for a military court. They were sentenced, none the less, because, among other offences, they "advocated the moral and material emancipation of the labourers." By June there were over 1800 Sicilians sentenced to the horrors of the semi-penal settlements on the islands (*domicilio coatto*).

King and Okey's indictment of Crispi's methods is severe but no more severe than some speeches made in the Italian Chamber. In attempting to defend his policy in Sicily and in Carrara, where agitation on the part of marble workers was met with martial law as in Sicily, Crispi developed the thesis that all these disturbances were the work of Socialist and anarchist agitators in league with clerical elements. In this fashion Crispi lumped together all the groups for which he had a special aversion and thus justified the use of 40,000 troops in Sicily and thousands of others in Carrara. He replied to charges that he had exceeded his authority in declaring martial law in the disturbed areas by reminding his critics that the King had undisputed powers to declare war and make peace. When Renato Matteo Imbriani, an Irredentist leader of the extreme Left, asked, "And where is this war?" Crispi replied in February 1894: "It no longer exists because we suffocated it. At one time it did exist and it could have spread everywhere. We have snuffed it out." He replied to another charge by asserting: "Gentlemen, it has been said—and very inopportunely—that to the demands of starving people we answered with bullets. No greater slander than this can be addressed against honest men. . . . The blood which has been shed in the rebellious communes falls on the consciences of those who rebelled against the law." [3]

Either because it approved of his policies or because it feared for an insoluble crisis in the event Crispi were overthrown, Parliament continued to support his government until the fateful days of early March 1896 when, stunned by the news of the destruction of the Italian forces in Ethiopia, Crispi's policy of colonial adventures finally brought an end to his political career.

35. COLONIAL ADVENTURES AND THE FALL OF CRISPI

Excluded from Tunisia by France and unwilling or unable to share dominion in the Sudan with England, Italy found her colonial aspirations limited to the East-African areas adjoining the Red Sea. In 1890 the ports of Massawa and Assab and the interior city of Asmara were constituted into the colony of Eritrea. The year before an Ethiopian king, *ras* Menelik, had usurped the throne of the King of Kings of Ethiopia upon the death of Emperor John. Menelik had long been supplied and armed by Italy in the course of a policy that aimed at pitting rival Ethiopian chieftains against each other. His advent to the imperial throne appeared to be a major success for Italian colonial policy, especially after the signing of the Treaty of Uccialli between Italy and Menelik in May 1889 in which Menelik seemed to acknowledge an Italian protectorate over Ethiopia. But in 1890 Menelik repudiated this alleged acknowledgment by arguing that the Amharic and Italian texts of the Treaty of Uccialli differed in phrasing and led to different interpretations. Quite apart from the problem of Menelik's original interpretation of the treaty in 1889, by the next year he appeared to feel sufficiently secure, especially because of encouragement and some military assistance from Russian and French interests, to declare his independence of Italy. For the next five years Italy hesitated between a policy of colonial retrenchment and one of expansion toward Ethiopian territories. This hesitation afflicted Crispi

[3] Crispi, *Discorsi parlamentari*, III, 691, 702.

himself, although it was his government which had signed the Treaty of Uccialli in 1889; but there can be very little doubt of Crispi's long-range views on colonial matters. These views were stated forcefully in a speech of 1888, the year after he formed his first government.

Crispi on the Necessity of Colonial Acquisitions: Speech of May 12, 1888, in Reply to Demands that Italy Withdraw from East Africa

Crispi, *Discorsi parlamentari*, III, 75–76. Our translation.

Gentlemen, Italy arrived far too late in the family of great powers. She had the honor of discovering America but did not have the strength to impose her dominion there. . . .

Colonies are a necessity of modern life. We cannot remain inert and allow the other powers to occupy by themselves the portions of the world as yet unexplored. If this were to occur, we would be guilty of a great crime toward history because we would thereby close forever the avenues to our ships and the markets to our products. (*Good!*)

Since 1860 Italy has been in a state of continuous economic progress, and the day may come when we shall have need of easy and secure markets. We shall not have them except by unfurling our flag on all the seas of the world.

Someone has thought to ask us: But what will you do at Massawa? What material profit, what benefit shall we have after the expenses and dangers we have undergone?

Gentlemen, in the public shops benefits are not counted in lire and cents. Great nations have the need to assert themselves in the various parts of the world for the protection of their commerce and for the performance of that civilizing mission in whose triumph we are obliged to participate. (*Bravo!*). . . .

I said that we begin today [in colonial endeavors], and we would begin very badly if at the first setback [as at Dogali in 1887] * we were to flee from the places we have occupied. (*Very good! Bravo!—Lively signs of approval.*) We would give a very poor show of ourselves if we were to tire so easily and fail in perseverance.

* Site about 18 kilometers to the west of coastal Massawa, Eritrea, where Ethiopians destroyed in January 1887 an Italian column of over 500 men attempting to penetrate into the interior. The defeat shook Depretis' position and led to the admission of Crispi into the government. Ed. note.

This policy of looking only to material interests is too bourgeois. (*Good! Bravo!*) There is something much greater: it is the dignity of the fatherland and the interests of civilization. (*Very good! Bravo!*) We are at Massawa, and we shall stay.

The impending disaster for Italian arms in Ethiopia resulted precisely from the fact that Italy did not stay in Massawa. It sought to expand southward, toward the province of Tigre in northern Ethiopia. The consequences of this ill-conceived and ill-directed expansion came to a conclusion with the Italian defeat at Aduwa on March 1, 1896. The fatal progression of events leading to Aduwa is recounted in the following excerpt from the work by Arangio-Ruiz.

Prelude and Conclusion of a Colonial Disaster in 1896

Gaetano Arangio-Ruiz, *Storia costituzionale*, pp. 522–24. Our translation.

When the XIXth Legislature began [in June 1895] the war in Tigre had already begun and Italian arms had distinguished themselves in several victories. . . . Parliament, and especially the Chamber of Deputies, was enthusiastic. The government went before the Chambers happily and took full advantage of the news. When General Baratieri [Oreste, Governor of Eritrea] returned to Italy for a rest, he was made the object of such clamorous praise for his heroism that he was almost taken to the Capitol to be crowned with a laurel wreath.

Nevertheless, there was still doubt that with the end of the rainy season the war in Eritrea would begin again. A sizable part of the Chamber of Deputies had strong fears that a policy of expansion would produce many calamities, and Crispi accepted the justness of these remonstrances, promising to remain within the limits desired by the Assembly. Parliament's summer recess was decided on the basis of this understanding.

But when Parliament was reconvened on November 21, Baratieri had already advanced with rapid marches up to Debra-Ailat and had declared the annexation to Eritrea of all the territory he had occupied. Although fortune had smiled upon his boldness, a lively debate developed in the elective Chamber, where the preoccupations of many found expression. But the government showed such confidence and assurance that, on December 3, 267 Deputies voted in its favor as against 131, with only 3 abstentions.

But in Africa things were going quite otherwise. . . . Two thousand soldiers, including Italians and native levies (*Ascari*) sent as an advance corps under the command of Major Toselli, were destroyed at Amba-Alagi by an overpowering force of Shoans * under the command of *ras* Makonnen. The garrison of Makallè,† commanded by Major Galliano, was besieged.

It is easy to imagine the pain felt by the country and the Chamber of Deputies. The government's few critics reproached Crispi and his majority for the ease with which the complete reassurances had been offered barely seven days before. Nevertheless, the government did not become discouraged. It reassured the Chamber, although less amply than before, and asked for 20 million lire, which was granted after the approval of a resolution by Torrigiani [Marquis Filippo, of the Right] in which the Chamber reaffirmed its opposition to an expansionist policy and expressed its confidence in the government. . . .

With an army of 30,000 men Menelik went to the camp of his *ras* [tribal or princely chieftains] and assumed command of the entire Ethiopian army. Strong fears were roused in Italy because, one by one, all assurances given or implied by the government were now seen as coming to nought. In order to avoid a sharp debate in the Chamber the government prorogued the Session on January 12 [1896], thus assuming an awesome responsibility. On the 26th of the same month Eritrea was declared to be in a state of war.

In the meanwhile Baratieri was preoccupied in Eritrea for the besieged garrison of Makallè, whose prospective destruction either by hunger or enemy arms would have pained Italy much. He managed to have the garrison freed [by surrender with honors of war and the right to retire to the Italian lines] and without suing for peace, but with the result that the barbarian army, led by the Emperor, was able to advance up to Aduwa, where it assumed formidable positions without any attack on its flanks from Italian arms during its march.

General Baratieri had 20,000 or 25,000 men under his command; he

---

* Shoa: a province in central Ethiopia. The defeat of Amba-Alagi occurred on December 7, 1895. Ed. note.

† In Tigre province, northern Ethiopia. Ed. note.

asked for more, and 10,000 were sent to him. But the uncertainties of the situation in Africa, the inactivity of Italian arms, and the fact that Parliament was closed, all had the effect of keeping the country in a state of great tension. The government itself had a certain lack of confidence in Baratieri's performance and it ordered General [Antonio] Baldissera to go to Massawa as secretly as possible in order to assume the military command of the colony. But it was too late!

On the last day of February General Baratieri—because of lack of supplies or because he read in some telegram from the government an incitation to action or because he entertained confidence of victory—consulted his staff officers, of whom all except Major Salsa favored an attack. Baratieri thereupon chose the next day for a decisive battle. The army was divided into three operational columns, one each under the command of Generals Albertone, Dabormida, and Arimondi; a reserve fourth column was put under the command of General Ellena.

Difficult terrain, unknown roads, divided columns, and very superior enemy forces *—all of these factors converted the battle of March 1 into an enormous defeat. Italian artillery made a carnage of the Abyssinians, who were strong in number and courageous. Divided and encircled, the Italian columns lost 8,000 men in dead and wounded. Generals Dabormida and Arimondi were killed, General Albertone and more than 2,000 officers and men were taken prisoners. The withdrawal of the survivors took place in such a disorderly fashion as to lead to charges of cowardice, which were nurtured by ungenerous dispatches from Baratieri, who had been the first to retreat, in order, as he said, that the colony might not lose its commander and not suffer additional harm.

With the news of the enormous disaster there took place a general outburst of indignation in all Italy. Grave disorders occurred in several cities. Public opinion manifested itself clearly, unanimously, and clamorously in favor of immediate and complete withdrawal from Africa and for the dismissal of the Ministry. More than a hundred Senators, including many who were not accustomed to bothering themselves with parliamentary activity, came to Rome and, meeting in a private gathering, approved a resolution requesting a new govern-

---

* The Ethiopian forces in the battle of Aduwa were estimated to exceed 80,000 as compared to 14,500 men under Italian command. Ed. note.

ment. Some of Crispi's friends advised him to resign in order to prevent an outburst in the Chamber and commotions in the streets. . . .

The government tendered its resignation and the King hastened to accept it. When the Chamber met on March 5 it had only to hear Crispi announce his resignation and the King's acceptance. Contrary to unchanging custom, this announcement was met by most lively applause, with shouts of "long live the King" from both sides of the Chamber, and with loud exclamations, interruptions, and shouts.

The era of Crispi had come to an inglorious end not altogether fitting for a man who had devoted about fifty years of his life to Italy's cause as he saw it. There was something almost indecent and certainly cruel about the way he was reviled and allowed to die in penury in 1901, particularly when one considers that much of the criticism and neglect inflicted upon him came from men many of whom had composed his large parliamentary majority for more than six years. Crispi may have represented some of the worst features of Italian life, but no one can effectively deny that in him Italy had often seen its very best.

XIII. THE PARLIAMENTARY REGIME
IN CRISIS, 1896–1900

Crispi's resignation had come about because of the country's revulsion against his adventurous policy abroad and his repressive measures at home. The government that succeeded him was led by Marquis Antonio Di Rudinì of the Right, who presided over a conglomerate representation ranging over both sides of the Chamber. The most pressing tasks facing the new government were the liquidation of the African enterprise and the restoration of domestic tranquillity. The African troubles were concluded by retrenching to the colony of Eritrea and through negotiations for the freeing of Italian prisoners held by the Ethiopians. Concessions were made to domestic unrest by making communal mayors elective, by economizing on military expenditures, by an amnesty of all those arrested during the troubles of 1894, and by placating Sicily with the appointment of a civil commissioner for the island and with repeal of the customs duty on the exportation of sulphur. Finally, a new approach in foreign policy was adopted by concluding a treaty on commercial navigation with France in October 1896.

Early in 1897 Di Rudinì decided to hold general elections to acquire a more cohesive following than the one offered by the heterogeneous majority that had supported him more as a reaction to Crispi than as an expression of real confidence. The extreme Left (Socialists, Republicans, and radical Democrats) increased in strength, but the Chamber remained otherwise unchanged in composition, and thus promised to continue in its uncertain support of Di Rudinì's government. The resulting ministerial instability accentuated already existing doubts concerning the future of Italy's parliamentary institutions.

In 1893 Ruggero Bonghi, a noted leader of the Right, had written an article (*L'ufficio del Principe in uno Stato libero* [The Office of the King in a Free State]) in which he called upon the King to exercise his office of moral superintendence over the country above and beyond the limits of parliamentary government. Six years before, in December 1887, Crispi, who had changed from republicanism to strenuous defense of royal prerogatives, had told the Chamber how much he was pained by those who would make a tyrant of Parliament and a slave of the King's Ministers. In May 1895 Sidney Sonnino, then Crispi's Treasury Minister, spoke of parliamentary de-

generation and decadence; and in January 1897 he wrote an unsigned article
in which he offered to solve the problem of ministerial instability by "a return to the Constitution." This famous document expressed the view that
Italian political life had degenerated because of a shift from constitutionally
or royally directed government to government under the mercy of parliamentary majorities. Inasmuch as the Constitution (the *Statuto*) entrusted
the executive power to the King and inasmuch as it also gave him the initiative in appointing Ministries, the government's responsibility should be primarily and chiefly to the King and not to Parliament.

36. SONNINO'S "TORNIAMO ALLO STATUTO" [LET US RETURN TO THE CONSTITUTION]

Un Deputato [a Deputy], "Torniamo allo Statuto," *Nuova Antologia*,
CLI (January 1, 1897), 12, 14–15, 23–24, 27–28, *passim*. Our translation.

The questions at issue are two, not one, however much they are intimately connected. From the elective Chamber's progressive usurpation of the executive power there have followed not only the confusion of functions between Ministry and Parliament (most signally the
Chamber of Deputies) and the deplorable intervention of the government in elections but also the effective usurpation on the part of the
Ministry of powers reserved exclusively to the King. The latter's role
has been reduced to one of negation and inaction, and the executive
power has come to be considered as being legally and actually in the
possession of the Ministry, and not the King.

The elective Chamber has succeeded in exceeding its functions and
in invading the powers of the Crown by means of a doctrine which
has converted the King's Ministers into Ministers of the Chamber; that
is, it has submitted them to direct dependence on changing parliamentary majorities.

In a country such as ours where the intervention of the state, already so widespread, is invoked to an even greater extent, we cannot
now effectively deprive the Chamber of the powers it has usurped and
thus restore the health of the entire parliamentary machinery until we
free, in part, the Ministers from their direct dependence on the Chamber and restore to them the old and original characteristic of [being]
Ministers of the King. . . .

Having become almost independent of the King, and having arrogated to themselves all real and effective functions, today's governments (and I do not speak of this or that Cabinet) now would become independent of the Chamber as well by denying the latter any right of interference in the executive power. . . .

In its desire to impose its will too far, the Chamber has succeeded in nullifying itself. It has sought not only to legislate but also to govern all by itself, and now it has fallen into the power of any man who by organizing some local clique, by rallying around himself the representatives of some large region, by managing street demonstrations, or by any other means or expedient is able to acquire political power for himself. . . . In seeking ever more to master the executive power, the Chamber has found itself instead made a servant of the Ministry, that is, of that group of men which has secured power by any means and which, with the myriad forms of electoral intimidation and corruption, can dispose of the majority at its pleasure. . . .

I hasten to the conclusion of my discourse by summarizing the ideas to which I have referred until now.

Two great social and political forces are growing and being organized in Italy, and both have tendencies and aspirations which are revolutionary with regard to representative and liberal monarchy. On the one hand we have socialism which, in the name of equality, would suppress all individual liberty. Reasoning that free competition (over-exaggerated by the doctrinaires of the "laissez-faire" school of economics) may in fact be an obstacle to the development of the human personality and to the individual freedom of the greater number of people, the socialists end up by suppressing altogether all personal freedom by making the state sole owner of the means of production and sole distributor of the fruits of labor, and thus in fact tend toward a despotic bureaucracy, toward the tyranny of mandarin rule.

On the other hand we see clerical organizations taking gigantic steps in the name of the most elevated ideals of human society and on behalf of order and the conservation of past social traditions. But in fact these organizations, which are the enemies of freedom of conscience and thought, actually tend toward the most intolerant obscurantism and toward the repression of disorder by suppressing progress and every movement of the human spirit.

In the face of these dangers the liberal state every day demolishes ever more thoughtlessly its defenses. . . . I wish that my voice could rally all men of good will, liberals and conservatives alike, in order that we might organize a great party which, for the sake of fighting effectively both socialism and clericalism, would propose as its immediate program the delimitation of the various powers of the state and the development of the functions of the Crown, restoring to it the rights sanctioned in the fundamental pact voted by those plebiscites which constituted the Kingdom of Italy.

I do not in the least intend to move toward any form of caesarism or unrestrained or uncontrolled autocratic government, nor to any form of despotic or absolute government. We want the liberal and representative monarchy of the *Statuto*, with a monarch who is an effective and active prince, and not one who is delivered blindfolded into the hands of a "mayor of the palace" who goes by the name of President of the Council of Ministers.

The elective Chamber and the appointed Senate should cooperate actively in legislating. In addition, they should always inspect, discuss, and check the actions and policies of the government by means of votes cast on the performance of responsible Ministers as well as on the bills and budgets they present. But they [the Chambers] should exercise neither directly nor indirectly, by means of one or more of their delegates, that executive power which is within the exclusive competence of the King. He, in his turn, is subject to the laws, as are all other powers and persons; but he participates in the making of these laws with his right of initiative and sanction.

It was not my intention in this essay to make allusions or accusations against the present or past governments. I intended to point out and analyze a transformation that has been developing in our institutions and that has seemed to me to be one of the principal causes of their progressive decadence. This transformation has been expressed in a formula, "The King reigns but does not rule," which is in open contradiction with the Constitution's will and the nation's expectations for the preservation of free institutions in Italy.

The document reproduced above reveals that in politics Sonnino was a liberal of early nineteenth-century vintage; but on social questions he was capable of being as critical as any socialist, in spite of his strictures against the consequences of socialism's tendency to create a despotic bureaucracy of mandarins. Sonnino shared socialism's concern with the social question, the nature of which he had analyzed long before socialism became a significant force in Italy; but he could not share socialism's revolutionary implications and, even less, the doctrine of violence which was practiced no matter how often it was renounced by socialist congresses. The events which put the entire parliamentary regime into a state of crisis during the last three years of the nineteenth century stemmed from the concern aroused in the minds of Sonnino and others that the revolutionary implications of Italian socialism were about to become explicit. These implicit dangers may have been exaggerated, but to those who believed in them they were very real.

37. THE END OF THE CENTURY: CRISIS AND DENOUEMENT

In April 1897 King Umberto was the target of a second unsuccessful attempt on his life. Throughout the rest of the year unrest increased all over the country, and it became especially serious early in 1898 when food prices rose sharply owing to bad harvests and the effects of the Spanish-American War. Di Rudini's government, based as it was on a conglomerate coalition which depended on the support not only of elements of the Right but also of much of the Left and the tolerance of the extreme Left, appeared unable to decide on a fixed course. It practiced some repression of socialist groups, with the result that it alienated much of the extreme Left while not sufficiently satisfying the Right, which accused the government of weakness and hesitation. The decision to reduce the import duty on wheat by 33 per cent produced similarly dubious results. The duty reduction did not prevent a further rise in the price of bread and thus did not allay the discontent of the extreme Left, but it did antagonize the large wheat-growing interests in the country.

Late in April 1898 food riots broke out throughout the peninsula. Di Rudini reacted by suspending all import duties and by calling a new class of conscripts to arms. On May 6 Florence was put under martial law after the occurrence of disorderly street demonstrations; the same measure was taken in Naples on May 10. But the worst demonstration by far happened in Milan. On May 6 some Milanese attacked the central police offices of the city, whereupon they were met with gunfire by police agents and army units. The next day a general strike was proclaimed and barricades went up all over the city. Milan was put under martial law, but it was not until May 9 that the city was restored to order by cavalry charges and artillery fire. It is a generally held opinion that the repression of the Milanese riots was unnecessarily violent. Only two police officials were killed during the four days of rioting while, according to official reports which some consider too modest, 80 civilians were killed and 450 were wounded. There is very little evidence to support the contention that the Socialists and Republicans either planned an insurrection or incited the demonstrators, many of whom were women and children. But it seems that the government really feared the beginning of a social revolution. This fear explains the unfortunate telegram of congratulations sent by Di Rudinì to General Fiorenzo Bava Beccaris, the military commander of Milan under whose orders artillery had been used against the demonstrators. Di Rudinì actually praised General Bava Beccaris for helping save the whole country. Even more unfortunate than this telegram were the decoration and personal letter King Umberto sent Bava Beccaris for his "great service rendered to the country's institutions and to civilization." These were signs of a veritable panic quite unjustified by the reality of events. And the signs were multiplied by mass arrests of Republicans, Socialists, and clericals; by the dissolution of their organizations and the seizure of their newspapers; and by the generous employment of courts martial and severe sentences.

The government had clearly gone too far. Its severities disgusted much of the Left and also helped make martyrs of arrested Republicans and Socialists, some of whom were subsequently elected to Parliament even while still in prison. Nor did the government assure itself the support of all men on the Right who were anxious for the preservation of public order. In fact, it was Sonnino, a man of the Center-Right, who helped upset Di Rudinì's government in June 1898.

Sonnino Helps Upset Rudinì's Ministry:
Speech in the Chamber of Deputies, June 16, 1898

Sidney Sonnino, *Discorsi parlamentari*, II, 539–41, *passim.* Our translation.

A man who for a number of years has shown that he does not understand the grave danger which his love affair with subversive parties has meant for the public welfare, such a man does not have the right to ask for a vote of full confidence. Even less does he have the right to ask for extraordinary powers. He conducted this love affair first as leader of the opposition and then as head of the Ministry; he has subordinated all the governmental program he had professed to the sole end of remaining in power. (*Good!—Laughter.*)

A man who for two years, in times as grave as the present, has not known how to guide his governmental actions by any other or higher goal than that of fighting the preceding government [led by Crispi], such a man cannot in truth parade himself as a standard bearer of harmony.

Until a month ago it was proper to ask every day whether the Honorable President of the Council Di Rudinì and his financial advisers were not leading us headlong blindly toward political and social revolution. And now, solely because the insurrectional attempts were well repressed by the military, these same men lay claim to being considered as the only legitimate champions of order. They find it strange that there are some who hesitate to entrust them with the most absolute confidence in the future.

It is necessary today, as it was yesterday, not to look only at the passing moment but to look firmly to the future. We should not allow a spirit of vengeance or personal resentment or an ill-conceived desire to change policy to lead us onto a road of blind reaction without an exit. Agreed, it is necessary to tighten the screws of the machinery of the state (*interruptions from the extreme left*); it is necessary to slow down its movement in order never to allow the brakes to be wrung out of our hands; it is necessary to notice dangers in time and to prevent violent shocks. But we must do this by proceeding always toward the same radiant ideals of orderly freedom, civilized tolerance, and political education of the people that fifty years ago inspired the patriots who gave us a free and independent fatherland.

The policies followed today by the Honorable President Di Rudinì give us no more confidence in the road he is following than they did yesterday. In order to avoid charges of inconsistency he will soon return to his first loves and his first mistakes; or, because of an impatient desire to dispel distrust of his past and in order to rehabilitate himself in the eyes of the conservatives, he will have to become violent in order that he may appear strong. . . .

(*A voice from the left:*) This is true.

Sonnino: . . . . The rule of liberty prevails only where the law rules supreme, even in the case of a severe and stringent law. Where arbitrary rule prevails there can be license for slaves, subject to the caprice of a vizier, but not a life of free men and no healthy development of civil liberties. (*Bravo!*)

I fear for the future of our representative institutions not because I fear the severity of existing or future laws (when these are intended to shield us from the stupid attacks of revolutionaries) but because I fear the aggravation of the illness of parliamentarianism, an illness which borrowing now the banner of freedom and then the banner of authority, ends up in a confusion of powers. From this confusion there follows in practice the exaltation of the hybrid and expansive power of the Minister or Chancellor—a power unknown in the *Statuto* but which has become the chief danger of our institutions. (*Good! Bravo!*) This is so because the new "mayors of the palace" draw strength from the supposed consent of majorities created and mustered by them for the purpose of overwhelming the enlightened and serene will of the Sovereign, while, on the other hand, they avail themselves of the prestige of the Crown for their own uses and purposes in order to influence the free judgment of Parliament in the legitimate exercise of its most essential functions. (*Applause.*). . . .

I summarize and conclude. Precisely because we are men of order, precisely because more than ever before we wish to see the great mass of the members of the moderate Liberal party united in one group for the better defense of constitutional liberties, precisely because we desire to return quickly to normal conditions, we cannot accept the Honorable President Di Rudinì's permanence in power as a fundamental dogma and point of departure for all discussions.

Two days later, on June 18, 1898, Di Rudinì resigned as Prime Minister, to be succeeded by General Luigi Pelloux, who was the first general to rise to this office since the fall of General Luigi Menabrea in 1869. Like Menabrea, Pelloux came from Savoy, the ancestral seat of the royal house; but unlike Menabrea, Pelloux had sat always at the left, from the time he entered the Chamber of Deputies in 1880 to the time he was made a Senator in 1896. He was also the first Senator to become Prime Minister since Menabrea. Pelloux had served as Minister of War under Di Rudinì of the Right (1891–92, 1896–97) and under Giolitti of the Center-Left (1892–93). As commander of an army corps in the Bari area he had refrained from proclaiming martial law during the disturbances of May 1898. All these extraordinary qualities and antecedents made Pelloux the apparently ideal choice as head of a government designed to pacify the country with a policy of moderation and restraint. But, as Benedetto Croce has pointed out, some occult transformation occurred in this man who at first renounced the use of extraordinary police measures, ended the state of martial law prevailing in several provinces, reduced the sentences of many political prisoners, and promised the creation of a more equitable tax structure. By February 1899 his policy of pacification suffered a fatal blow at his own hand with the introduction of a bill for additional measures regarding public safety and the press. The vicissitudes that accompanied the efforts first to have the Chamber pass the bill and then, failing in this more normal course, to have its provisions enacted by decree, occasioned the eruption of a constitutional crisis whose gravity and

consequences are examined in the following excerpt from a work by Bolton
King and Thomas Okey.

The Failure of Rule by Decree

Bolton King and Thomas Okey, *Italy Today*. London: Nisbet & Co.,
1909, pp. 101–7.

In 1898 he [Pelloux] promised to use only the existing law for purposes of repression, but in the following February he introduced the
Bill whose troubled history has made the gravest constitutional crisis
of United Italy. Its more important provisions proposed to empower
the Prefects or police to forbid meetings in the open air or in places
open to the public, and empower the Government to suppress any association, "whose object was to subvert by overt acts (*per vie di
fatto*) social order or the constitution of the State." The Bill was met
by very cogent objections. It was urged by many, even of those who
agreed with its principles, that it was unwise to stir up angry controversy, when the more important of the powers contemplated in the
Bill were already possessed by the Government, or, at all events, had
been exercised by it for years past. Under the Italian law both the
right of public meeting and the right of combination were on a very
unstable footing. Charles Albert's Statute recognized no right of public meeting in the open air or in places of public resort. The Law of
Public Security, by requiring the promoters of a public meeting to
give twenty-four hours' notice of it to the authorities, seemed tacitly to
recognize the right. But the Government had, at all events since 1890,
held that this provision gave them the right to prohibit beforehand
meetings which had illegal ends in view, and Nicotera and Crispi and
Di Rudinì had acted freely on this interpretation, the first even for-
bidding meetings to protest against the Triple Alliance. The right of
combination was not mentioned in the Statute, but it had long been
practically recognized, and the Penal Code, by providing against
criminal associations, implicitly admitted the legality of those which
were for lawful ends. But a clause of the Code, which punished for
"exciting to hatred between different social classes in a manner dangerous to the public peace," was capable of great latitude of interpre-

tation in the hands of judges, who wanted to use it against the Socialists or any labour movement. No doubt there were good arguments
for putting the law on a clear footing; but Liberals felt that it were
better that restrictions of liberty should rest on an arbitrary stretching
of the law than on the law itself. They dreaded that under a reactionary Government, and with judges only too amenable to its pressure,
the new law would be easily turned into a weapon against labour,
that every trade-union and cooperative society and chamber of labour
would be at the mercy of the Government and the local cliques of
employers who had its ear. Besides, the country was quiet again; it
was folly to waste on an odious and unnecessary Bill time that was so
urgently needed for financial and social reforms; and sensational legislation tended to make Europe think that Italy was on the verge of
revolution, discredited the country, and frightened foreign capital. For
several months the Bill was suspended, but in the summer of 1899 Pelloux finally broke from the Left, and in June the Bill, made yet more
stringent by a Parliamentary Committee, came again before the
Chamber. Then, for the first time in the history of the Italian Parliament, it was met by determined obstruction. There had been disorderly scenes in previous Parliaments, but now the Extreme Left
fought with a dogged and persistent use of obstructionist tactics. The
Government grew impatient, and on June 22 announced that unless
the Bill were passed within a month, its provisions would come into
effect by royal decree, though they were to be submitted to Parliament at some unspecified future date. When the threat failed to daunt
the obstructionists, Parliament was prorogued on the last day of June,
and the *decreto-legge* came into effect on July 20.

The *decreto-legge* was defended on the ground that in the face of
obstruction it was the only means of giving effect to the wishes of the
majority of the Chamber. But it was flatly unconstitutional. It is true
that it was not the first of its kind. Still the principle was entirely subversive of Parliamentary government, and so conscious were the ministers of its illegality, that they tried to postpone its promised discussion by Parliament, and hoped to appease public opinion by a fuller
amnesty for the *Fatti di maggio*.* But in February 1900 the Court of
Cassation at Rome, for once showing independence, decided that the
decreto-legge had merely the status of a Bill before Parliament, and

* Reference to the disturbances of May 1898. Ed. note.

had therefore no legal effect. The whole unconstitutional structure collapsed, and the Ministry was compelled to bring the Bill afresh before the Chamber. Public opinion had declared more and more against it, and now it was opposed not only by the Extreme Left, but by nearly all the Constitutional Left * and by the Di Rudinì section of the Right. In the first division on the Bill the Government had a majority of only 27. Amendments poured in; the Extreme Left obstructed by interminable speeches, and the first clause was still under discussion, when the majority attempted to checkmate the obstructionists by moving to appoint a Committee to draft new Standing Orders, and give at once provisional effect to their recommendations without further reference to the Chamber. That more stringent Standing Orders were necessary was acknowledged by all parties, including the Extreme Left. But it was intolerable that the Chamber should abdicate all voice in making them, and the unlucky motion only gave the obstructionists a new opportunity. There were angry scenes between Deputies and the Chair; the opposition refused to be conciliated by some nominal concessions of the Government; and on March 29 Signor Colombo, the President, put the amended motion without allowing further discussion, and in a scene of confusion declared it carried. The Constitutional Left protested against the illegality; the Extreme Left next day hissed the President out of the Chamber. But neither he nor the majority would draw back, and four days later the two Lefts and a few members of the Right walked out of the Chamber in protest, and the new Standing Orders were approved by the remaining Deputies. Parliament was prorogued for six weeks, and the Government, satisfied with their victory or despairing of further success, demonstrated the futility of their policy by withdrawing the *decreto-legge*.

The new Standing Orders contained nothing that would have been very dangerous to minorities under an impartial President, and to an Englishman the opposition to them may seem exaggerated. The more stringent of the rules empowered the President to name a disorderly member or, in extreme cases, to suspend him for eight days; and in the case of an unduly protracted debate to ask the Chamber to limit

* As distinguished from the "Extreme Left," which made a principle of its opposition to the Constitution because the fundamental Statute had never been presented to the people for approval, rejection, or amendment in 1848 or thereafter. Ed. note.

the length of speeches or to move the closure. In another Parliament there would have been nothing unfair in this. But in a Chamber, where the President was chosen by a party vote and was generally more or less the tool of the Ministry, these powers were unsafe. The Extreme Left, with Colombo's rulings fresh in their memory, believed that it was a question of life or death to them, that it threatened their existence as a Parliamentary party. When the Chamber met on May 15, and Colombo tried again to act on the new Orders, they twice shouted him down, and the sitting broke up in confusion, while they sang Garibaldi's Hymn and shouted insulting epithets. Next day the President resigned, and the Ministry decided to dissolve Parliament and appeal to the country. Sonnino, who all through was the influence behind the scenes, had persuaded himself that the Extreme Left would be extinguished at the new elections. Probably few shared his illusion. The country woke to a sudden interest; the Extreme Left was the only party with an electoral organization ready at hand, and the elections resulted in the triumphant increase of their party and the moral defeat of the Ministry. It came back with a small and unstable majority, and on the actual votes polled it is doubtful whether in the country it had a majority at all.* The wiser men in the Cabinet, including the Premier, recognized their defeat, and were willing to compromise. Their cooler followers realised that the crisis was becoming a very dangerous one. Signor Gallo, the new President, proposed that the Standing Orders of April 3 should be tacitly shelved for new ones, and the Extreme Left concurred, on condition that the clauses for suspending members and limiting the length of speeches were abandoned. It seems that everything was in train for a settlement, when the rank-and-file of the Right, supported by part of the Cabinet, revolted, and refused to come into any arrangement which ignored the April Standing Orders. This made Pelloux' position impossible, and he resigned on June 18. A new Cabinet was formed by Signor Saracco, a member of the less extreme Right, whose appointment marked a policy of conciliation towards both the Lefts. Signor Villa, the new President, had fresh Standing Orders drafted, which were unanimously accepted by the Chamber, though Sonnino and the irreconcilables of the

* Signor Torresin gives the Ministerialist vote at 663,000; that of the Constitutional Left at 271,000; that of the Extreme Left at 331,000. Another estimate gives: Ministerialist vote, 611,000; Constitutional Left, 304,000; Extreme Left, 345,000; and a few thousand Independent votes. [Authors' note.]

Right abstained from voting. The new Orders allowed the President to suspend a disorderly member for any period not exceeding eight days, but omitted the clauses that empowered the Chamber to limit the length of speeches or move the closure.

The crisis closed to the general relief, and not even the assassination of King Humbert a few weeks later seriously disturbed the political quiet.

PART FOUR

THE GIOLITTIAN ERA, 1901–1913

XIV. ITALY MOVES TO THE LEFT

The elections of 1900 and the consequent resignation of Pelloux's Ministry appeared to indicate that the country wanted a more liberal policy in domestic affairs. But it was agreed that it was not possible to embark immediately on such a policy unless a measure of tranquillity were first restored in Parliament and the country at large. The man chosen to accomplish this restoration was the President of the Senate, the aged Giuseppe Saracco. Although a man of the Right, Saracco's views were moderate enough to secure him the support of all wings of the Liberal party, all being anxious to second his program of return to normal parliamentary government. But a general strike in Genoa at the end of 1900 proved that Saracco's government was either unwilling or unable to effect those changes in domestic policy which the Left and extreme Left thought necessary for a genuine national reconciliation. Abandoned by the Liberals of the Left (the Constitutional Left) and never supported by the extreme Left, Saracco's government was forced to retire in February 1901. The Left, led by Giuseppe Zanardelli and Giovanni Giolitti, censured the government for violating the right of association by dissolving the Genoese Chamber of Labor (*Camera del Lavoro*) in December 1900. The Right was equally displeased because, after this dissolution led to the calling of a general strike, the government panicked and permitted the Chamber of Labor's reconstitution. The new King, Victor Emmanuel III (1869–1947), who had succeeded his father to the throne after Umberto I's assassination on July 29, 1900, decided to choose his first Prime Minister from the Left, even though the Center and Right together still commanded a numerical majority in the Chamber. The most notable leader of this majority was Sonnino, who was still tainted with the reputation of being the evil genius behind Pelloux's Ministry. Sonnino's reputation freed the new King to experiment with the Left.

Although Zanardelli was chosen as the new Prime Minister, he assumed no portfolio for himself; and the key Ministry of the Interior, usually reserved for the Prime Minister, was entrusted to Giolitti, thus indicating that the latter was virtually a co-equal with his nominal superior. It is this fact that justifies speaking of the Giolittian era as beginning in 1901.

When, in June 1903, Zanardelli's government was weakened by Socialist charges that the Minister of the Navy was guilty of favoritism toward the steel interests, Giolitti chose to resign. Unsure of his parliamentary support and mortally ill, Zanardelli resigned in October of the same year. Giolitti succeeded him as Prime Minister and remained in office until 1905. He was again Prime Minister from 1906 to 1909 and from 1911 to 1914.

For ten and a half of the thirteen years preceding the outbreak of the First World War Giolitti was at or near the top of Italy's political scene. During these years he sought to temper the extremist tendencies of the country's political life by pursuing a program of political and economic concessions to the lower classes and to the parties claiming to represent them. This is the famous or infamous Giolittian program of national reconciliation or political "domestication." The best statement of this program was made by Giolitti himself in a speech of February 1901 (see pp. 246–51 below). But in order to understand the portents of this speech and the eventual evolution of Giolitti's program, it is necessary to have some notion of the economic transformation Italy was to undergo during the Giolittian period. The following excerpt from a work by Rosario Romeo, a leading member of the post-Second World War generation of Italian historians, makes clear the nature and scope of this transformation.

38. THE ECONOMIC FOUNDATIONS OF THE GIOLITTIAN ERA

Rosario Romeo, *Breve storia della grande industria in Italia*, 2d ed. Bologna: Cappelli, 1963, pp. 52–55, 57, 71–75, *passim*. Our translation. Reproduced by courtesy of the author and the publisher, Casa editrice Licinio Cappelli.

The depression in Italian economic life that began with the commercial crisis of 1887 lasted until 1898 and was attended by a drastic reduction in production, by financial crises, by distress among the lower classes, and by domestic disorders. With the disturbances in Milan during 1898, this depression seemed to lead the country to the extreme point of a social crisis of great proportions. Nevertheless, signs of recovery—limited to industry—were noticeable as early as 1896; and this recovery was in time to lead to the great economic expansion of the first fifteen years of the new century, that is, during the so-called "Giolittian era." As we have seen, the several decades before 1896 had witnessed a process of increased commercialization of the Italian economy. The infra-structure of modern economic plants and productive processes had been created in several parts of the country; a more solid financial structure had finally issued from the great banking crises [of the 1890s] and from the reorganization of the banks of issue, thus assuring a greater monetary stability which now made it possible for industry to have a surer basis for calculating its costs and proceeds and greater guarantees in its accumulation of savings. This complex of conditions was the result of developments in Italian economic life during the three or four decades after unification, and it made it possible for our productive structures to participate advantageously in the phase of high prices which began in world economy at the end of the depression [in prices] extending from 1874 to 1896. Except for the serious crisis of 1907, this new period of expansion lasted until the First World War. In earlier times, Italy's economy had not been able to extract much profit from the stimulus provided by international markets because a large part of Italy's productive economy had been only weakly tied to international markets. Then Italy had been like an economic island against whose shores broke the waves issuing from the world markets. Now, on the other hand, these waves, acting in the form of ever-rising prices, had a profound effect. They put in motion a mechanism which affected industrial production first and then became extended to a large part of the entire economy of the country.

The confirmation of what has just been said is found in the statistics of foreign trade. If we take the volume of imports and exports for the years 1888–89 as being equal to 100, we find that the following three-year period in fact shows a modest increase in exports side by side with a general decline in imports. The export indices for the latter period reach 113 for industrial raw materials, 107 for foodstuffs, and 108 for industrial manufactures. Not only is this a quite modest increase —obtained by means of further reduction in the already very modest domestic consumption—but it is also distributed among the various sectors of the economy with little significant variation. If, on the other hand, we look at the period 1894 to 1897—which is the time when the new industrial expansion began—we see that whereas export of semi-finished goods positively drops to an index of 93 and that of raw materials and foodstuffs rises to 117 and 121 respectively, export of finished industrial products registers a very strong surge forward, reaching an index of 163. The increase in this last form of exports is related to the analogous course of imports, which continue to drop to very low levels in all sectors of the economy except for the importation of industrial raw materials, which reaches an index of 115. Consequently, an increase in raw material imports as well as in manufactured exports reveals a growth in industrial activity, and this during a period when the other sectors of economic life were still dominated by the depressed state of the preceding years. Beginning with 1899, the expansion spread from industry to all the other sectors of economic life, with results which are made clearly evident by a few essential facts. National income, which in 1895 was 61,423 million lire of 1938 value, rose constantly during the following years and reached 92,340 million lire in the five-year period of 1911–15. Industry's contribution to the gross national private product rose from 19.6 per cent in 1895 to 25.0 per cent in 1914, while agriculture's contribution decreased from 49.4 per cent to 43.0 per cent. Annual savings quintupled during this same period, and the effect of this increase is seen especially in the growth of investments in productive plants and equipment. These investments amounted to 3,520 million lire (1938 value) in 1895; in 1914 they amounted to 10,346 million, after having reached the high of 11,692 million in 1911. And for the first time since unification there occurred, correspondingly, a general improvement in living conditions, as revealed by the substantial increase of per capita income from 1,886 to 2,458.

These are the data that justify speaking of the "Giolittian era" as the period which marked a decisive transformation of our country's economic life and which finally realized a veritable "industrial revolution." We must now examine more concretely the characteristics and motive forces of this revolution, and at the same time indicate its limits.

In the first place, a profound transformation took place in the industrial sector, which assumed an increasingly important place in the country's productive structure. The production index of the manufacturing industries as calculated by the Central Institute for Statistics shows a jump from 29 in 1896 to 54 in 1914. . . . In 1895 the production of capital goods constituted only 28 per cent of the whole industrial production, but in 1907 it rose to 43 per cent and in 1913 to 47 per cent. At the beginning of the period being considered, the value of metallurgical production represented only 3.1 per cent of total manufacturing production; in 1914 it reached 5.2 per cent. The machine industries contributed 13.3 per cent of the value of manufacturing production in 1895; in 1914 they rose to 21.6 per cent. During the same period the total value of all manufacturing production increased from 1,597 million to 3,711 million, while that of metallurgy rose from 49 million to 193 million, and that of the machine industries from 212 million to 802 million. Further, if we examine the important complex of agricultural-manufacturing industries—that is, the foodstuff and beverage industries, the textile industries, and tobacco manufacturing—we find that in the period 1891–95 they accounted for 74.2 per cent of the whole manufactures, but by 1911–15 they had dropped to 59.2 per cent. Conversely, the extractive-manufacturing industries, such as the machine, metallurgical, mineral, and others, rose from 19.8 per cent to 30.6 per cent of the total. The displacement of emphasis in favor of heavy industry is thus clearly evident.

These developments would not be understandable without an awareness of the new relations being established during these two decades between banking and industry. Immediately after the banking crisis of 1894 culminating in the collapse of the Credito Mobiliare and the Banca Generale, Crispi's government turned to the German government and German financial circles. It was a time of very bad relations with France and of a decided orientation of Italian foreign policy toward the Triple Alliance. Crispi asked for German help in creating a new great bank to replace the two that had collapsed and which would defend Italian state securities against speculations being conducted against them on the Paris exchange. The result was the creation of the Banca Commerciale with capital and personnel of German origin. At first this bank had a capital of 5 million, which rose quickly to 20 and later to 130 million. In time the Banca Commerciale was joined by the Credito Italiano, the Banco di Roma, and the Società Bancaria Italiana . . . . The appearance of these new great banks of ordinary credit radically altered the features of the Italian financial market. . . . These were banks created after the German model of the mixed bank, and they operated both in the area of ordinary credit as well as in that of investment credit in medium- and long-term loans. . . .

Several of the most important characteristics of the Italian "industrial revolution" are already revealed by the foregoing rapid review. The general paucity of capital gave the banks a particularly important role in industrial initiative. This same scarcity of capital at the same time established the foundations of a process of financial concentra-

tion which anticipated and frequently interfered with modern industry's needs for technical concentration, and this process was accelerated by the gravity of the 1907 crisis. The preceding expansion had
reached dizzying heights, especially in some sectors of the economy.
. . . True, the crisis was world-wide; but in our country it had long-
range consequences and in certain respects lasted until the war,
whereas elsewhere the crisis was by then practically overcome. Given
the difficult conditions in which industry found itself, it was obliged
more than ever before to lean on the banks, with the result that the
already burdensome ties of dependence became stronger. At the same
time many sectors of the economy began to experience a veritable
crisis of overproduction and all that came in its train. . . .

Without doubt, the most important reason for the crisis is the then
limited nature of the Italian domestic market. The dimensions of demand in the domestic market were limited above all by the modest sum
of the goods and services produced and consumed in a country, such as
ours, of mediocre productive capacity and low per capita income.
Nevertheless, this domestic market had certain [special] characteristics
which contributed to making difficult a parallel development of demand with respect to supply. From 1899 onward real wages for industrial labor improved, and they rose from an index of 76 for the aforementioned year to 100 in 1909. During the following three-year period
they declined, but in 1913 they once again rose to 100. Although we
cannot say that the purchasing power of the working masses remained
stationary, and much less that it declined, it is nevertheless true that
improvement from the very low initial levels was quite slow. And this
is true even if we emphasize the fact—more than is usually done
—that the contemporaneous development of the industrial revolution
with that of a powerful labor movement avoided in Italy those more
dramatic forms of open exploitation of workers which in other countries are characteristic of the early phases of industrialization. This
fact, however, had the effect of reducing the dimension of profits accumulated by industrial activity and, therefore, the rapidity of economic development. If, in spite of this, the general level of industrial
wages remained so low, the explanation is to be found in the existence
of a vast reserve of agricultural labor whose very presence limited the
bargaining power of the working masses. This is a fact of fundamental
importance, and it shows why in spite of the progress it achieved, the

industrial revolution of the Giolittian era did not succeed in giving Italy a predominantly industrial character. In short, it shows how the weight of a backward agricultural situation continued to weigh upon the country even up to the eve of the war.

In fact, the relations between industry and agriculture, and the effects on these two fields of the protectionist system begun in 1887, constitute one of the great themes of political and economic debate in Giolittian Italy. Free traders, Radicals, Southerners, and some Socialist groups were unanimous in pointing to the harm done agriculture by the disproportionate emphasis found in the tariff structure. Agriculture was obliged to buy at high prices the industrial products of domestic industry and at the same time its interests were sacrificed as a consequence of the closing of many of its foreign markets in retaliation against the reduction of Italian industrial imports. Certainly, the protective tariffs erected in defense of cereal and sugar-beet growers were not sufficient compensation to agriculture for the advantages accorded industry. On the contrary, this protection offered to agriculture served only to increase the proceeds of its most backward branch, or to stimulate the formation of one of the largest and least justifiable monopolies—that of the sugar interests. The frequently cited figure of wheat yield per hectare * always produced a great effect, serving almost as a capsule expression of the general backwardness of our agriculture. Even as late as the eve of the war, this figure reached an average of barely 10 to 11 quintals,† as against 21 to 23 quintals for England and Germany, and 23 to 26 quintals for Belgium and the Netherlands. In fact, the figures of Italy's wheat yield per hectare are a national average and of little meaning. They are the result of adding the average of 14 to 19 quintals for the Po Valley to that of 3 to 5 quintals for several southern regions. But a fact does emerge from these figures and it is that Italy's rural classes were still tied to a very modest standard of living and consumption. In consequence, Italian agriculture was not in a position to furnish adequate income to the too numerous population living from it. And the phenomenon of an excessive and unproductive labor supply in agriculture continued to exist in marked proportions, in spite of the enormous emigration abroad

---

* A measure of land surface equal to 10,000 square meters or 2.471 acres. Ed. note.

† A quintal is equal to 100 kilograms or 220.46 pounds of weight. Ed. note.

mainly from the most backward agricultural regions, and in spite of
the fact that agricultural population declined from about 65 per cent
of the total in 1861 to 42 per cent in 1901. Without a doubt, the existence of such a large market of peasant consumers tied to the low
and extremely variable incomes common to agriculture, was one of
the major obstacles facing several Italian mass-consumer industries,
and above all the cotton textile industry. And the poverty of agriculture as a whole also limited the expansion of certain industries turning
out producer's goods, such as chemical fertilizers and agricultural
machinery.

The all too slow improvement of Italy's economic conditions at the turn of
the century occasioned a number of labor disputes, including a strike by
Genoese port workers in February 1901. It was this strike and the vacillating reaction to it by Saracco's government that prompted Giolitti to make
the speech with which he returned most actively to the political forefront in
Italy after the eclipse of his political fortunes in 1893. Pressed by the shipping interests, the Prefect of Genoa sought to break the strike by dissolving
the local labor organization (*Camera del Lavoro*) after receiving the government's permission to take this step. The general strike that followed in
Genoa and Saracco's immediate capitulation to the strikers permitted Giolitti
to raise the whole problem of the reasons for disputes between management
and labor and the role the government should play in these disputes. The
speech which follows is generally regarded as one of the most explicit and
important statements on this problem.

39. GIOLITTI'S PROGRAM FOR A REORIENTATION
OF DOMESTIC POLICIES: SPEECH OF
FEBRUARY 4, 1901

Giovanni Giolitti, *Discorsi parlamentari*, 4 vols. Rome: Tipografia della
Camera dei deputati, 1953–56, II, 626–33, *passim*. Our translation.

The question now before Parliament, regarding the events in Genoa, is
one which concerns the highest questions of law and domestic policy.
Above all it touches upon the relations between the government and
the working classes, and it concerns the limits of the government's
competence in disputes between capital and labor. The greater part of
our social peace depends on the resolution of these questions.

Unfortunately there still persists within the government and among many of its representatives the tendency to view as dangerous all associations of workingmen. This tendency is the result of a scant understanding of the new economic and political currents that have become manifest for some time in our country as in all civilized countries; it reveals that we have not yet understood that the organization of workers walks hand in hand and step by step with the progress of civilization.

The tendency to which I have referred produces the deplorable effect of making enemies of the state out of the working classes, which see themselves constantly regarded with diffidence rather than benevolence by the government, in spite of the fact that the latter should be instead the impartial guardian of all classes of citizens. . . .

It is said that in their very constitution [the] Chambers of Labor have assumed a hostile attitude toward the state. But this is an inevitable consequence of the government's policy! How can you expect someone to be a friend of the state when he sees himself systematically persecuted by it? (*Bravo!—Good! from the left—interruptions from the right.*)

The government has but one duty, that of applying the law to these associations as to all others. If these associations are remiss, the government must be firm in its action. . . .

Saracco (*President of the Council*): This is what was done! (*Comments.*)

Giolitti: But so long as they do not violate the law, so long as they exercise a legal right, the intervention of the state is not justifiable. . . . The principal reason why Chambers of Labor are opposed is this: their activity tends to raise wages. I can understand that low wages should be an interest of the industrialists; but of what interest can it be to the state to help keep the workingman's wages low? It is a mistake, it is a veritable prejudice to believe that low wages promote the progress of industry. A badly nourished workman is always weaker physically and mentally. Note that the countries where high wages prevail are at the head of industrial progress. (*Bravo!*)

We praise our peasants' excessive frugality as a grand thing, but this praise is but another prejudice. Believe me, he who does not consume does not produce! (*Comments.*)

When the government intervenes in order to keep wages down, it commits an injustice, it commits an economic and a political error. It commits an injustice because whenever it takes the side of one class against another it becomes remiss in its duty to be absolutely impartial toward all citizens. It commits an economic error because it disturbs the economic law of supply and demand, and this law is the only legitimate regulator of wage levels as it is of all other goods. Finally, the government commits a grave political error because it makes enemies of the state out of those classes which in fact constitute the majority of the country. Only if it remains completely alien to the disputes between capital and labor can the state perform a useful role of peacemaker and sometimes even of conciliator. These are its only legitimate functions in this matter.

Some have said, almost as if to point to a scandalous situation, that the strike in Genoa was a political strike. This is veritably ingenuous. Whoever knows something of the labor movement, especially in northern Italy, knows perfectly well that the workers have understood the intimate and indissoluble connection which exists between economic and political questions. The working class knows perfectly well that from a reactionary government it can expect nothing but persecution, either in disputes with capital over the defense of workers' interests or with regard to the entire tax structure. No reactionary government will ever adopt the concept of tax reform in favor of the less affluent classes; and whenever there are pressing fiscal needs a reactionary government will increase the price of salt, the levels of excise duties on grains or on other consumer goods. But never will it propose a special tax on the richer classes. (*Bravo!—Approval from the left.—Comments.*) Consequently, there is no reason to be surprised if, even independently of the wishes of the participants, these strikes assume a character similar to the one revealed by the strike at Genoa. . . .

For a long time efforts had been made to prevent workers from organizing. Whoever has knowledge of the conditions of our country as well as those of other civilized countries must be convinced that this is impossible. The illegitimate resistance of the state against these efforts would have the sole result of giving these organizations a political end. But in themselves these organizations do not have and must not have any but an economic end. . . .

A very serious indication of our domestic conditions was provided us by the general elections of last year. Nine hundred thirty thousand

votes were cast for the constitutional candidates of all political grada-
tions, whether opponents or supporters of the government: the candidates of the popular parties received 335,000 votes. Consequently, if
the seats had been distributed in proportion to the votes received, the
extreme Left would today possess 134 seats. Two more general elections conducted under the same premises as the last, and assuming a
distribution of seats proportionate to the votes received, and the extreme Left becomes the majority. (*Exclamations.—Lively comments.*)

There are two other factors, perhaps even more important, which
we must take into account. There is above all that mass of voters
which does not participate in elections because not only does it not
recognize our institutions, it does not even recognize the unity of our
country.* Then there is the immense mass of illiterates, who constitute
the poorest, most discontented, and most impressionable of all classes.
From this class, which is the great majority of the country, there will
emerge the new phalanxes of voters, because they will qualify for the
vote either by reason of age or by increased education. It will be these
phalanxes which will determine the future of our political parties.

In my opinion there are only three true political parties: the Socialist, the clerical, and the constitutional. Now, I ask a very serious question: Which of these three parties will exercise the greatest influence
over this mass of future voters? The clergy has the advantage of a
great force, one of the forces which most moves the world, and that is
religious sentiment. But this is not enough, and so *Christian Democracy* has been organized. It has taken to heart the workers' material
interests as well as their spiritual needs; it has organized rural savings
banks, local workers' organizations, schools, and recreational centers.
And all this most recent movement has just received the approval of
the highest religious authority in the world.

Now we come to the Socialists. I have no need to tell you the nature
of their activity. They promise greater well-being and greater dignity
to the disinherited classes; they organize the proletariat and assume its
leadership and defense in all cases of dispute involving the interests of
the masses. The Socialists, however, have a great weakness. Many of
the promises they make are impossible of realization, and the more intelligent and honest among them even admit that these promises are

---

* This is a reference to the general abstention of Catholics in politics and to the
Papacy's refusal officially to recognize the Kingdom of Italy. Ed. note.

for the distant future. (*Oooh!—Comments.*) But inasmuch as they know that it is experience which educates a people, the Socialists have had the cleverness of doing all they could to remain distant from practical experience and from assuming administrative responsibilities. As a result, their influence at present is greater than it should be, according to my view of things; but it would be blindness to deny that they have made progress.

Now, the government, which represents without distinction all the constitutional parties, what has it done to rally the working classes around itself? Italy is one of the countries with the lowest average wages in the world, but it is the first in tax burdens on the prime necessities of life. Consider the sufferings of a man who has 2 or 3 lire a day to support himself and his family and who must pay excise duties, a tax on grain, a tax on salt, a tax on kerosene, and bear the consequences of the entire protectionist tariff system with the resultant enormous rise in the price of all that is necessary to life! (*Approval at the left.*). . . .

For years we have preached that the tax structure is not viable, that it is not equitable, that it is not just. And yet we do not bring ourselves to do something about it, as if unaware that if the day comes when grave events will force us to take some steps in this regard, it will then be necessary to grant much, very much more than would suffice today. (*Approval.*)

In the light of this lack of action on the part of the government, why should we be surprised if the extreme parties, the Socialist and the clerical, make headway in the country? (*Murmurings.*)

(*A voice from the extreme left:*) And what about the Republicans?

Giolitti: Very well, if you wish I shall say the popular parties. (*Comments.*)

The consequences of this governmental inaction may be quite different in the different parts of Italy. Wherever economic distress is less pressing and political education more advanced, the popular parties may achieve a measure of political power by means of the ballot box; but where economic distress is more pressing the danger is greater and more immediate because in these places it is difficult to advise people to be patient. . . . And if timely steps are not taken, you can be sure that even the extreme parties will be overwhelmed, because it is a waste of time to speak of evolutionary * improvements to people who are hungry. (*Approval from the left.—Animated comments.*)

The Italian people do not have revolutionary tendencies. Because of a long tradition, the Italian people tend to trust their government. And perhaps no other people have for centuries suffered such grave evils with so much resignation. A period of true social justice emanating from the government and the ruling classes would rally the affection of the people toward our institutions. . . .

We are at the beginning of a new period in history; anyone who is not blind sees this. New popular currents are entering our political life, new problems appear every day, new forces rise with which any and all governments must come to an accounting. And the very confusion which prevails among the parliamentary parties shows that the questions which now divide us are no longer those of the past. (*Comments.*)

The rising movement of the lower classes becomes ever more rapid every day. It is an irresistible movement because it is common to all civilized countries and because it is based on the principle of the equality of all men. No one can deceive himself into believing that the lower classes can be prevented from conquering their share of economic and political influence. The supporters of existing institutions have one duty above all, and that is to persuade the lower classes, by means of acts, that they have much more to hope for from existing institutions than from dreams of the future,† (*Good!—Comments.*) that every one of their legitimate interests will find effective defense in existing political and social institutions. (*Good! from the left.*)

Whether the advent to prominence of the lower classes is to be a new force for conservation, a new element for prosperity and greatness, or whether it is to be a whirlwind which will overthrow the fortunes of the fatherland, depends principally on us, on the attitude which the constitutional parties assume in their relations with the lower classes! (*Most lively approval and applause from the left.— Rumblings to the right.—Many Deputies congratulate the speaker.*)

* A reference to the preachings of the evolutionary socialists as distinguished from their revolutionary colleagues. Ed. note.

† "Sogni dell'avvenire"—dreams of the future—was a favorite phrase of socialist propaganda. Ed. note.

Giolitti's speech was an unmistakable appeal to the more moderate elements on the extreme Left to rally with the Liberals of the Left in the common program of a great social transformation. It was also an explicit announcement that Giolitti, Zanardelli, and other Liberals of similar persuasion were offering their candidacy for political leadership in Italy. When, ten days after this speech, Victor Emmanuel III entrusted the government to the Zanardelli-Giolitti combination, the parties of the extreme Left, and especially the Socialists, had to decide whether to support the new government for the sake of desirable reforms in the immediate future or to remain with their eyes forever fixed on "dreams of the future." The Radical party, consisting of democrats, most of whom had once been republicans, was the most moderate and numerous of the parties comprising the extreme Left; and although it had not altogether freed itself from a certain antipathy for the monarchy, it did not have strong prejudicial reasons for refusing to participate in His Majesty's government. The least powerful of the parties on the extreme Left was the Republican and, for reasons intrinsic to its principles, it could not join the royal government, although individual Republican Deputies might give it their support. But the problem was ideologically most vexing for the Socialists, whose parliamentary representation had risen from 16 to 32 during the 1900 elections and who held almost exactly one third of the 95 seats on the extreme Left.

At its formative Congress in Genoa in 1892 the Italian Socialist Party had rid itself of the anarchist element in its antecedents and adopted a clearly Marxist position. The next year the party announced the propriety of participating in parliamentary activity not as an end in itself but as a means toward achieving the party's revolutionary ends. In 1895 the National Council of the party proceeded to adopt a tactical or "minimum program" of reforms to be realized in the immediate future, in contradistinction to the "maximum program" of a wholly collectivized society, which remained the fixed but more distant goal of the party. The minimum program included: universal suffrage; pay for members of Parliament; guarantees of all the public freedoms; initiative and referendum; the eight-hour day; nationalization of the railroads, mines, and shipping; collective bargaining legislation; a single and progressive tax on incomes and inheritances; limitation of women and child labor; educational and other socioeconomic reforms.

The repressive measures employed by the governments of Crispi, Di Rudinì, and Pelloux during the mid- and late 1890s moved the Socialists to make common cause with the other parties on the extreme Left and, during the battle of parliamentary obstructionism in 1899 and 1900, even with the Liberals of the Left led by Zanardelli and Giolitti. In the elections of 1900 the Socialists engaged in electoral agreements with the Republicans and the Radicals with the purpose of throwing their combined support to those candidates of the extreme Left who had the greatest chances of victory. This tactic was successful enough to merit confirmation at the Socialist party congress of September 1900, but it also raised the fundamental question of how far the Socialists should go in cooperating with bourgeois parties. The advent of the Zanardelli-Giolitti Ministry in 1901 raised the even greater question of whether the Socialists could become "ministerials," that is, participate in a bourgeois Ministry or even support it.

For the Radicals the problem of deciding whether to support the new government was not as difficult as it was for the Socialists. Zanardelli had offered posts in the government to two Radical leaders, Giuseppe Marcora and Ettore Sacchi; and although they had refused the offer because their demand for a pledge to reduce military expenditures had not been met, they had nonetheless assured the government of their benevolence. Most Socialist Deputies were inclined to do the same, but they were aware that the intransigent or revolutionary current within their party would view such support of a bourgeois Ministry as a betrayal of socialist ideology. The editor of the Socialist periodical *Critica Sociale*, Filippo Turati, one of the most influential leaders of the Socialist Deputies in Parliament, sought to persuade his readers that the immediate choice before the extreme Left, and the Socialists in particular, was not between evolution or revolution but between a liberal government promising reforms and a possible return to the repressive regimes of the preceding decade. But in opting for the liberal Zanardelli-Giolitti Ministry, Turati's *Critica Sociale* clearly indicated in the editorial reproduced below that he and his followers had made their choice in favor of evolutionary or "reformist" socialism.

40. THE EXTREME LEFT RALLIES TO THE ZANARDELLI-GIOLITTI MINISTRY

Editorial, "Ministerialismo," *Critica Sociale*, April 16, 1901, pp. 113–14. Our translation.

It is important that we understand each other well on this matter. The so-called "ministerialism" of the extreme Left has prompted the all too easily comprehensible and furious anger of Italian reactionaries, who rightly interpret this "marvelous cunning" of the subversive parties—to use the language of the *Gazzetta di Venezia*—to constitute the sole obstacle to the former's return to rule the roost. Until now this rule of the public welfare has coincided only too well with the reactionaries' private interests. Besides, in their eyes a government which does not assume an attitude of open and violent opposition to the lower classes, which does not every morning dissolve a political club of a peasant league, which permits people to breathe, move, and talk, which does not devote all its efforts to make the people hate it—such a government is a disaster for the country's basic institutions. The only institutions they know are handcuffs, prisons, and penal settlements; they neither recognize, nor respect, nor conceive of other institutions.

Consequently, the furious anger of the reactionaries cannot surprise anyone; but it may appear more strange that mutterings of ill-humor should be manifest here and there even in our own ranks.

It would seem that for some of our friends the attitude assumed by the extreme Left is nothing but the result of a momentary opportunism which is painful to acknowledge and of which we should free ourselves as soon as possible. We, on the contrary, are convinced that this attitude is (as Ferri * said in his address of the 14th in Milan) the inevitable consequence of things. . . . As Ferri put it so well in his speech to the Chamber on March 7, the Zanardelli Ministry is principally if not exclusively the fruit of two years of efforts on the part of the extreme Left. In substance, it is the offspring of the obstructionist battle in Parliament. In contempt of the aroused Italian conscience, Italian reaction was intent on the covert suppression of the parliamentary regime, on crushing labor's right to organize, and on eliminating the popular franchise. But in attempting to realize these aims it broke its horns against the resistance of the extreme Left, and this resistance had the support of the people and was sanctioned in the elections of June 1900. . . .

But if the victory of the extreme Left was a formidable victory on the battlefield, it was not and could not be the end of the war. The fall of Pelloux, the accession of Saracco, and the election of a new President of the Chamber who vindicated the right of free speech in Parliament, were but signs and effects of an armistice during which the forces of the two armies could have time to regroup and resume the struggle. The truce was quickly broken by the Genoese workers. The question of labor's right to organize had been the secret motive and soul of the battle of obstructionism in Parliament, and this question rose anew with the political strike in Genoa. Now that the two

* Enrico Ferri, noted sociologist and criminologist, joined the Socialist party in the 1890s and played an important role as the editor of the party's leading newspaper, *Avanti!* Ed. note.

armies were nearly equal in strength, they assaulted each other and they crushed between them [Saracco's] government of truce which, with the resumption of hostilities, had exhausted its mission.

The outcome of the struggle remained uncertain. . . . In the face of the reactionary coalition in the Chamber—assisted by the Senate, the bureaucracy, and organized castes of parasites—there appeared a liberal and reforming coalition composed of three distinct bodies: the government with its supporters on the Left; the three groups on the extreme Left; and the country, which wants reforms and freedom. When we say "the country," we mean the combative forces of proletarian and *petit-bourgeois* origin which reflect the interests of the great majority of producers and which decided the outcome of the battle of parliamentary obstructionism. The result has been a state of unstable equilibrium; and if just one of the three above-mentioned bodies deserts or wavers, our battle is lost. . . .

The present equilibrium of the two contending sides keeps the legislative assembly in a state of paralysis, and the problem cannot be resolved except by an appeal to the country. The struggle in Parliament preordains the struggle at the polls. The stakes of the game are simply these: Who will "make the elections"? Will they be made by the country or by a government which allows the country to assert its will and its interests; or, on the other hand, will they be made by the oligarchies, armed perhaps even with a new and more restrictive electoral law or with truncated lists of eligible voters? . . . .

This is not the time to sit as impassive and inert judges of the Ministry's actions; it is time to cooperate toward a common end in which each of the participating elements has his corresponding share of responsibility. The inertia or mistakes of just one of these elements will compromise the result of the efforts of all. But, in this enterprise the prevailing interest and therefore the greater duties are of the Socialist party. As representative of the working classes it is this party which was the protagonist and the most concerned in the battle of parliamentary obstructionism. Now that the issue is the reaping or the losing of the fruits of this battle, the role of the Socialist party is the same as before. . . .

Thus understood, the question of ministerialism goes beyond the matter of the men who are in office and the confidence we may place in them; it becomes a question of general political tendencies in whose practical application the extreme Left and the popular parties are integral and indispensable elements. . . . If the Socialists wish to be a political party rather than a group of politicians and demagogues; if the minimum program is not just a feint; if the organization of workers and the class struggle are not just electoral verbiage; if, in short, we attach importance to the substance of things and not to their appearance, then we must make a very clear and decisive choice between the two tendencies that are in dispute. And we must make of the proletarian masses that believe in us the decisive force of a decisive victory.

The views held by Turati, Leonida Bissolati, and others who believed in evolutionary socialism prevailed sufficiently to permit the Socialist party to give its support to Zanardelli's Ministry. This support tended to make the government adopt a neutral position in disputes between capital and labor, thus arousing opposition from the Right and Center in Parliament. Twice, in June 1901 and March 1902, this bloc in the Chamber threatened the life of the Ministry, and only the votes of the whole extreme Left saved the government on both occasions. The opposition was especially concerned with the wave of strikes sweeping Italy after the advent of the new Ministry. In comparison to a little over 400 strikes and nearly 90,000 participants in 1900, in 1901 there were more than 1,600 strikes with a total of over 400,000 participants. Early in 1902 the government was obliged to use the military to operate the gas works of Turin, and on February 24 it militarized the rail workers to prevent a strike in this service. The necessity of this severe measure to safeguard so vital a service seemed to put in question the wisdom of the government's permissive attitude in preceding strikes. Zanardelli's government had already been shaken by a reference, in the Royal Address to Parliament of February 20, to the need for a divorce law. The next day the government's candidate for the presidency of the Chamber was defeated by a majority of blank ballots; and although the King rejected Zanardelli's subsequent resignation, the threatened strike of the railwaymen left the Prime Minister no choice but either to abandon his office or to take firm measures. The whole situation seemed opportune for an attack on a grand scale from the opposition. This attack was delivered on March 13, 1902, by Sonnino, the acknowledged leader of the conservative opposition. His principal target was Giolitti who, as Minister of the Interior, was held to be chiefly responsible for the government's attitude toward labor agitation. But Sonnino's speech also reveals that in his view the interests represented by the Center and the Right had to assume their share of responsibility for the problems of the day.

41. SONNINO ATTACKS THE "GIOLITTIAN MANNER" AND CHASTISES THE CONSERVATIVES: SPEECH IN THE CHAMBER OF DEPUTIES, MARCH 13, 1902

Sidney Sonnino, *Discorsi parlamentari*, III, 66–78, *passim*. Our translation.

Sonnino (*signs of attention*): The parliamentary situation has changed profoundly from the time the Chamber was adjourned last December. And the first open manifestation of this change occurred with the vote of February 21 for the election of the President of the Chamber.

During the two long months of vacation in their provinces the Deputies became more clearly aware of the country's real conditions and of the accelerated movement with which we are going down a precipitous decline. But the government, aware of nothing, lived in tranquillity and bliss. It entrusted its safety and that of the state to the extreme parties' evident interest not to create too serious troubles and embarrassments for the government and to maintain at least the external appearances of public order, in order not to endanger the political life of such a tolerant guardian. The government's blissful certainty of the results of its policy was so perfect and complete, so free of all doubt and hesitation, that it inserted in the Royal Address opening the new Session words of strong satisfaction for the supposedly achieved pacification of the country!

Only four days later 30,000 railwaymen were militarized, a whole class of soldiers was recalled from terminal leave, and the conscription of a new class was ordered ahead of schedule. I would like to believe that the government will explain why the serious and imminent dangers which suddenly menaced public order on February 22—and only such dangers could justify the measures taken—could not have been foreseen forty-eight hours before. It is strange that, in returning to the Chamber [after the King had rejected the government's resignation] the government did not immediately feel the appropriateness of giving us some news and explanation regarding this entire matter. It is as if nothing had happened. . . .

You have proceeded in all things from day to day without any general plan; you have sought always to surmount only the difficulties of the moment; you have had recourse to any and all expedients, you have compromised any and all precedents and any and all principles of normal government, for the sole purpose of gaining immediately the votes and praises of the extreme parties. (*Comments and approval.*). . . .

From the day you first took hold of the rudder of the ship of state we have seen constituted and accomplished a vast organization of the working classes. This organization has as its precise aim to oppose the other classes of society; its form and tendencies are political; its declared intention is to achieve the exclusive rule of the proletariat and the ruin of the existing political and social institutions of the state.

And in the meanwhile hatred and rancor are being disseminated with a free hand among the working classes . . . . (*Rumbling and interruptions from the extreme left.*) hatred and rancor not only against this or that Ministry, not only against this or that political figure, but rather against all that the principle of authority personifies, against all the well-to-do and cultivated classes, against all that represents property or capital. What painful prospects for internal peace we have before us this coming spring and summer in the countryside of a large part of Italy! . . . .

Last June, in the midst of an increasing agitation among the masses roused by those whose especial aim is to regiment them for political purposes, we had occasion to see the government itself incite to strike. This it did by solemnly praising and itemizing the supposed results already achieved by strikes and by denouncing before the Chamber the landowners of this or that province. . . .

Every time that a Chamber of Labor intervened in a local strike and there were threats—even if only verbally—to enlarge the scope of the disturbances, we saw the public authorities hurriedly enter the dispute in order to bring pressure to bear on the landowners or the industrialists and make them give in. (*Oh! Oh! from the extreme left.*)

(*Voices from the right:*) It is true! It is true! . . . .

Sonnino: It is shouted that the right to strike must be free, because it is labor's weapon, whether labor is organized or not. (*Interruptions.*) Of course! And it is precisely because we want the state to remain impartial in disputes between capital and labor, it is precisely because we think that ordinary strikes in each private industry must remain completely free (in those cases where the workers have not voluntarily consented to restrict this freedom for a fixed period of time or a specified form of work) that we cannot permit strikes in those primary public services which are constituted as privileged monopolies. . . .

To our conservatives of all shades I should like to say: Are you convinced . . . in the innermost recesses of your conscience that at the proper time you have always done all that was in your power to do to solve, or at least to move toward a solution of, many of those social questions whose danger of embitterment for you and for the country is now apparent? (*Interruptions.*) Have you always heeded those who in the past warned you of these dangers and urged you to eliminate the reasons or pretexts for eventual agitation? Have you always given proof, by means of prompt action, that you yourselves entertain those sentiments of social solidarity which now you would wish to have rooted in the souls of the poorest classes? . . . .

Now I say to the various parts of the great constitutional party, and without distinguishing between liberal-conservatives and progressives: In the face of the dangers which threaten the peace and prosperity of the country, their precise duty is to reunite their scattered forces into a *fascio* for the purpose of coping with the present situation in a manly and bold fashion. (*Bravo!*) By now it is useless to lull oneself with the deception that if we ignore the danger it will go away. The revolutionary wave becomes larger every day; it is necessary to become aware of this current, to dam it up, and to direct its flow so that its blind and devastating force may in time be transformed into a motive force for progress and civilization. (*Good!*)

After all, what substantial and profound differences of principle are there between the Right, the Center, and the Left on the most important and urgent economic, social, financial, and administrative problems of the day? I see none. (*Comments.*). . . .

Now, among the more serious reproaches which can be addressed to the present Ministry is that it has always striven with all its might to divide the constitutional elements of the country, whereas its chief duty is precisely that of pacifying and uniting. (*Oooh!—Comments.*)

It is for this reason, and because it has shown no foresight at all, because it has remedied nothing in a coherent and lasting fashion, because, on the contrary, it has made the domestic situation more profoundly grave and acute—it is for these reasons that I judge the Ministry's continuation in power to be a danger for the country and that I hope that the Chamber, consistent with its vote of disapproval of February 21, will wish to deny it its confidence. (*Bravo!—Most lively applause from the center and the right, shouts from the left.—Many Deputies congratulate the speaker.—Rumblings in the press gallery.*)

XV. THE FRUITS OF THE "GIOLITTIAN MANNER"

Sonnino's warning to the conservatives of all shades that they had their share of responsibility was consistent with his whole political past. In the 1880s he had been among the first to raise the issue of a great social question, especially as it existed in the South, and none could deny the genuineness of his concern for the lower classes. But his contention that no issue of substance divided the Right, Center, and Left factions of the Liberal party was not shared by the Left; and it was precisely this disagreement within the Liberal party that had prompted Zanardelli and Giolitti to look to the extreme Left for support. Sonnino viewed this move to the left as aimed at destroying the Liberal party. Giolitti, on the other hand, understood it as the only way to prevent the party from being crushed by the extreme forces of revolutionary socialism and reactionary clericalism. Guided by this conception of Italy's political realities, Giolitti offered the Socialist leader Turati a post in the Ministry he formed late in 1903 after Zanardelli's resignation. Turati declined the offer, pleading that his acceptance would not be understood by the masses and would divide his party.

In fact, the Socialist party was already sharply divided and would become more so in the coming years. The moderate, reformist, or evolutionary wing had carried the day at the Rome congress of the party in 1900; it triumphed again at the congress of Imola in 1902; but in 1903 it lost control of the party's leading newspaper *Avanti!* to Enrico Ferri, who had undergone many ideological fluctuations and who, after a phase of moderation, had returned to a revolutionary position. Another disturbing sign for the moderates was the growth of revolutionary syndicalism within the party. Inspired by the writings of Georges Sorel and influenced by anarchist doctrines of violence never wholly eradicated from the Socialist party, the syndicalists went on the attack and accused the "ministerial" Socialists of playing the game of the bourgeoisie. Early in 1904, the syndicalists, led by Arturo Labriola, imposed their will on the regional Lombard congress of the party held at Brescia. Their "intransigently revolutionary" position and their antimonarchism boded ill for unity. It was the foreboding of these events which prevented Turati from accepting Giolitti's invitation.

Giolitti also made an offer to the Radical leaders Marcora and Sacchi.

They too refused, but their eventual support of the government was assured when Giolitti accomplished the election of Marcora to the presidency of the Chamber in 1904. Giolitti's parliamentary base was made even more firm by his inclusion of two men of the Center-Right in his Ministry: Luigi Luzzatti at the Treasury and Tommaso Tittoni at Foreign Affairs. It was a bit of political transformism, for which Giolitti was censured by some of the extreme Left. But Luzzatti's and Tittoni's willingness to serve with Giolitti was more indicative that some conservative Liberals had moved toward his position than that he had accepted theirs.

Giolitti's position was stated in a speech of December 1, 1903, in which he presented his government to the Chamber. The program he expounded included a promise to continue the policy of "maximum freedom within the limits of the law" and the implementation of the following proposals: commercial treaties with a number of European countries aimed at the reduction of tariff barriers; the reduction of service charges on the public debt; nationalization of the railways; the introduction of a form of "reasonable progressive taxation"; a comprehensive program for the economic recovery of the South, including reforestation and soil conservation projects, state aid for rural credit institutions, a reduction of local taxes, and various public works; a general reform of elementary education and proposals for the improvement of the lot of schoolteachers; and a group of social reforms including the abolition of penal settlements, the strenghtening of the Fund for Workers' Disability and Old Age Pensions, a compulsory weekly day of rest for all workers, and the promotion of cooperative societies.

Within two days Giolitti spoke again in defense of his program and in rebuttal to the criticisms directed against the manner in which he had fashioned his Ministry. Portions of this speech are presented below.

42. GIOLITTI DEFENDS HIS PROGRAM OF REFORMS AND REPLIES TO HIS CRITICS: SPEECH OF DECEMBER 3, 1903

Giolitti, *Discorsi parlamentari*, II, 762–68, *passim*. Our translation.

Giolitti: Honorable gentlemen, I begin by noting with great satisfaction that in this elevated and important debate no one has challenged the government's program on its fundamental points. I shall refer to partial criticisms later on; now I observe that not even the extreme Left found any fault with the program's general approach.

The chief criticisms were directed against the way the Ministry was formed and against its composition. The Honorable Deputies Barzilai [Republican] and Bissolati [Socialist] spoke of the appeal I made to a leader of the Socialist party, the Honorable Deputy Turati. The Honorable Deputy Barzilai called this appeal a *beau geste*. Inasmuch as the Honorable Deputy Barzilai has said that I am altogether lacking in geniality, it seems contradictory for him to attribute a grand gesture to me. (*Laughter.*) And in fact it was not at all a gesture; it was a very serious proposal, because I am convinced that if I could have conferred with the Honorable Turati, together we would have found a number of problems of interest to the whole country for whose solution we could even have fallen into step together for quite some time. (*Comments.*) I do not know why we in Italy cannot do what has been done in France. . . .*

Colajanni [Napoleone, Republican]: France is a republic!

Giolitti: But the Honorable Deputy Turati did not raise the prejudicial question † [against the monarchy]! (*Good!—Comments.*) Now I ask you, what laws and what social measures approved in France could not be approved under the liberal Italian monarchy? (*Approval.—Comments.*)

(*A voice from the extreme left:*) The point is that they are not being approved!

Giolitti: And it is precisely because I wanted to show that we could do as they do in France that I turned to the eminent person whom I named. . . .

(*A voice:*) He'll be made a cardinal! (*Lively laughter.*)

Giolitti: I believe that in the Socialist party there is a rank higher than that of cardinal. (*Laughter.*)

Subsequently, I had very friendly conversations with the Honorable Deputies Marcora and Sacchi [leaders of the Radical party] and for the sake of history I must note that it was not the first time a Prime Minister turned to these two distinguished colleagues of ours. When the Honorable Deputy Zanardelli formed his Ministry [in 1901] he treated with them. I hoped to be luckier than he because I attributed great importance to their participation in the government. I wish now to make a formal declaration that although I did not have the good fortune of securing their participation in the government, I shall not change a single line in my program. (*Good!—Comments.*)

* This is a reference to the French Socialist Alexandre Millerand's participation in the "bourgeois" Ministry of René Waldeck-Rousseau (1899–1902). Ed. note.

† "La questione pregiudiziale": opposition in principle to monarchical institutions. Ed. note.

And now I turn to the way in which the political crisis was solved. Yesterday the Honorable Deputies Barzilai and Bissolati said to me that in the light of the refusal of the Honorable Deputies Marcora and Sacchi to participate in the government, I should have refused the King's mandate to form a Ministry. I begin by observing that my predecessor, who is a master in constitutional practices, did not follow this road. Although he was unhappy in failing to secure their collaboration, the Honorable Deputy Zanardelli formed his government because he was of the firm conviction that it was his duty to do so. Besides, I note another fact, and it is this: the two persons most competent to judge in this matter, the Honorable Deputies Marcora and Sacchi, told me themselves that it was my duty to form the new government. Clearly, it would have been more convenient for me to refuse the King's mandate. Those who know me well know that I do not hold to this or any other office. By refusing I would have avoided many griefs and, as has been said, I would have performed a grand gesture. But I did not have the right to make this grand gesture. With the Chamber closed I did not have the right of delivering the government to the minority. Had I done so the majority of the Chamber would have been justified in considering me as remiss in my duties. (*Bravo!—Good!*) I thought that above all I should concern myself with the program I would present to the Chamber.

Now, the Honorable Deputy Lucchini [Angelo, from the Center] has maintained that programs count for very little and it is men who count for everything. I am convinced that the country does not share his opinion. The country is interested in knowing how its interests are going to be treated, and not so much in knowing whether this or that man sits on the Ministers' bench.

(*Voices:*) It is true! It is true!

Giolitti: Consequently, you shall judge us by our deeds. Parties are formed by men who agree on a certain program, and all of us in the Chamber are in unanimous agreement on the program we have presented. . . .

(*A voice from the left:*) There are no longer any parties.

Giolitti: Parties exist around ideas.

Varazzini [Savino, Socialist]: There is only one party now.

Giolitti: I do not think it is a misfortune to have one's ideas shared by many. Suppose that the Honorable Deputy Varazzini's power of persuasion were to convert all of us to socialism, would such an eventuality render him unhappy? (*Laughter.*)

The Honorable Deputy Maggiorino Ferraris [from the Center] has admitted that my mandate to form the new government was in order, but he said that I should have invited members of the majority's Committee to participate in the government. Yesterday I permitted myself to interrupt him and ask him how this Committee had been constituted. After a day's reflection on this matter I still have not been able to learn who constituted this Committee. I have even been left with this doubt: Did the Honorable Deputy Ferraris belong to this Committee? (*Lively laughter.—Interruption from the Honorable Deputy Maggiorino Ferraris.*). . . .

The Honorable Deputy Barzilai should keep this question in mind: If someone had come to this Chamber three years ago with the program I have now presented, how many would have supported it? Very few, I believe. Can he complain of the fact that the progress of our liberal ideas has been so great that a program of freedom is now accepted by almost everyone? (*Bravo! Good!—Interruptions.*)

Lucchini [Center]: Whatever program you presented would have been well received.

Giolitti: I said that the fundamental aspects of the program have been opposed by no one. The chief criticisms of it were on this point, that it is too vast. . . . And yet I have not found a single speaker who has pointed to a single item he would like eliminated. The truth is that a great number of problems have accumulated which have long required a solution, and this is not our fault. I believe that the country has the right to ask that Parliament make up for lost time and that it solve questions whose solutions have been promised for many years. (*Bravo!*) We are determined to achieve this end, and if the Chamber will not follow us in this active enterprise, we shall relinquish the responsibility of government to others.

It is clear that at this moment the problems uppermost in importance are the economic ones. In fact, one can say that the true and substantial political questions of the day are all tied to the economic question. This fact was admitted by all speakers and above all by the representative of the Socialist party, the Honorable Deputy Bissolati, who spoke to us principally of class interests. The true power of the Socialist party lies in that it addresses itself to matters of interest, not to matters of simple appearances or matters of form. . . .

[With regard to matters of form] the Honorable Deputy Barzilai is displeased with me because I said that the Republican party has no reason for existing. . . . But his quotation of my words was not completely accurate. I said that it was my object to show that under a regime of freedom and reforms the Republican party had no reason for existing because any and all progress may be achieved under prevailing institutions. I now add a comment which the Honorable Deputy Barzilai will probably admit as true. If we were not able to prove that under our present institutions it is possible to achieve all the progress which the country requires, in such a case, the party to gain from this failure would be not the Republican but another party most distant from it. This latter party * has no representative in the Chamber but in the country at large it is much stronger than the Republican party. If the country were ever to become disgusted with existing institutions and were to feel that it could not reach the goals to which it aspires, on such a day it would not turn to the Republicans. It would turn to the opposite extreme. (*Very good!—Comments.*) On such a day I believe it would be impossible to argue that freedom no longer runs any risk in Italy.

Mirabelli [Roberto, Republican]: This is political astrology.

Giolitti: Honorable Deputy Mirabelli, please believe me when I say that I engage in far less political astrology than you do. (*Lively laughter.*)

The Deputies who spoke in the name of the extreme Left yesterday said that even their opposition could be of use to the government. I admit that this may be true but only in this sense: that their opposition and their energetic action have the effect of urging the majority toward intense and fruitful efforts. Let us hope that, in the interest of the fatherland we all love with the same intensity of affection, these efforts come to pass. (*Bravo!—Lively and prolonged applause and approval from the left.—Many Deputies congratulate the speaker.*)

Giolitti's failure in 1903 to induce the Socialist Deputies to collaborate in his program of reforms was a disappointment to him. He had hoped that with

---

* This is a reference to the clerical party. Ed. note.

his offer he could have effected a clear-cut separation between the moderate and revolutionary wings of the Socialist party. He did not succeed in this, but the Socialists almost realized his ambition as a consequence of the general strike which broke out in September 1904. Five months before, in April, the Socialist congress of Bologna witnessed the success of the revolutionary wing and of Enrico Ferri. The resolutions adopted at the congress attempted to mask the defeat of the moderates by speaking of "party unity," but nothing could hide the fact that Ferri's "integralists" and Labriola's syndicalists had beaten the reformists led by Turati and Bissolati. The first fruit of this victory was reaped in September 1904. The syndicalists chose the pretext of some bloody encounters between peasants and police in Sicily and Sardinia to proclaim a general strike in Milan. The strike spread throughout the country and paralyzed all activity for five days. Giolitti kept his nerve and decided that the best policy was to do nothing and wait until the strike wore itself out, as indeed it did. Several weeks later, he decided that the time had come to teach the Socialists a lesson. Instead of acceding to their demand that Parliament be convened, he chose to leave the final judgment of his policies to the country and called for new elections. The country's judgment proved unfavorable to the Socialists, whose representation dropped from 34 to 29; the extreme Left as a whole lost approximately 13 of the more than 100 seats it held before the election, and several explicitly Catholic Deputies made their first appearance in the Italian Parliament. It was in part because he feared this sort of popular reaction and in part because he was unalterably opposed to the excesses concomitant to a general strike that Turati wrote a stinging denunciation of his extremist comrades in the Socialist party.

43. THE GENERAL STRIKE OF 1904 AND THE "HOUR OF RESPONSIBILITY": THE MODERATE SOCIALISTS INDICT THEIR EXTREMIST COLLEAGUES

Editorial, "L'ora delle responsabilità," *Critica Sociale*, September 16–October 1, 1904, pp. 273–77, *passim*. Our translation.

It is not yet easy to make a final assessment of the good and the harm done the cause of democracy and the working classes by the political general strike. For five days it kept half of Italy in a state of agitation which to many seemed the "grand maneuver" preceding eventual and not too distant civil wars. It is our view that this strike produced an unquestionable good, one which is quite alien to the strike's intrinsic aims and to the predictions of its promoters and participants. The strike's useful result is that it made many things clear and evident. . . .

It is our view that not only all Socialists but also a great number of the Deputies of the extreme Left hold the following principles in common:

1. General strikes for *economic* purposes are intrinsically absurd. This has been proved so many times that it is useless to repeat the arguments.

2. *Political* general strikes as manifestations, protests, or warnings cannot be rejected or condemned absolutely. . . .

3. General strikes are a two-edged sword to be used with extreme care in most exceptional circumstances. They cannot be raised to the level of a normal means in the struggle of the working classes. . . .

Now, it is clear that these or similar principles did not guide the men (their names are known) who from the headquarters of the Chamber of Labor and from the seats of the stadium in Milan imposed on the recent general strike its meaning and rules. As Garzia Cassola shows in the following pages, they succeeded in making the strike appear to be their exclusive victory. These men have brought to Milan from the congress of Brescia * their theory of the stone thrown into the social machinery, causing this machinery to stop and break down. They have brought to Milan the prodigies of the act that is supposed to resolve all problems, and the mirage of the liberating *coup de main*. . . . They solemnly promised in their assemblies the fall of the government, proclaiming that unless this came about the strike should not under any circumstances come to an end. And they aroused the shouts and imprecations of the crowd—already in part intoxicated with the poison that had been spread—against whoever warned of the fraudulent folly of these proposals. But within a few hours—what an agreeable spectacle of helotism!—these individuals ate the arrogant promises they had made on the eve of the strike. Shouted down in their turn by the defrauded and disillusioned masses, these individuals had recourse to jesuitical subterfuges and attempted to mask their retreat by insisting that the strike had been but a first experiment at mobilizing the working masses, an experiment to

* Reference to the regional Lombard congress of the Socialist party held at Brescia early in 1904 under the dominance of revolutionary syndicalists. Ed. note.

be resumed "for wider ends" on a future occasion. On this future occasion, it would not be only the government or the existing form of government that would be swept away, but much more. As one of their more renowned speakers said, "We would then overthrow the puppets and the whole puppet show." And in that document worthy of a madhouse and that bore the name of supplement to the *Avanguardia* * and "Bulletin of the Chamber of Labor," they described their ephemeral personal orgy as "the dictatorship of the proletariat"!
. . . .

That it proved possible—too easily possible—for a Chamber of Labor to be the passive object of a brief uproar, and that fortunately the results were not too damaging and not permanent, is one problem. Quite another is the problem which the Socialist party as a whole must face. And this is so because, if we look at the facts we must admit that the leaders of the strike in Milan, the preachers of redemptive violence, the apologists of the conquered and conquering "crowd" who seek to return the arduous and complex efforts of the proletarian army to the pitiable and primitive exploits of the mob—these men are also legitimate children of the Socialist party. They are at the head of one of its Sections; indeed, of that single official Section in which—pitiable joke!—they would constrain as in a penal settlement all the Socialists of Milan. They publish their own newspaper, which profits from the prestige and aegis of the Italian Socialist Party even if it is for the purpose of destroying and vituperating this same party. And in all justice we must acknowledge that in this newspaper not a single fig leaf of modesty hides their beliefs and aims. More than one of our comrades in the old guard fraternize with them in the bivouacs of an allegedly common battle. Others among our comrades made use of them as decisive allies in order to rise to the highest ranks of the party. And at the congress of Bologna [in April 1904] they [the syndicalists] were able, by means of persons serving as their proxies, to divide among themselves the seats of the Executive Committee of the party. Consequently, if yesterday they spoke and acted in the name of the Italian Socialist Party, and if they do the same tomorrow, they did and will do so with perfect right. . . .

The general strike is a crossroad, and this crossroad has put in ques-

* Publication edited by the syndicalist leader Arturo Labriola. Ed. note.

tion not only the whole activity of the Socialist party but also the whole of socialism. On the one side we have the way which educates the awareness and solidarity of the proletariat. It is the way of resistance, cooperation, and administrative and political activity; it is study, propaganda, conquest of offices, laws, and practices, all of which are productive of those intellectual, technical, and moral forces that strengthen the proletariat in the daily class struggle. It is the way through which the working class and its representatives and its influence will penetrate gradually and intensely those political positions that until yesterday were reserved for the men, representatives, and exclusive influences of the bourgeoisie. It means an ever-improved qualification for the direct management of economic and political society; it means the preparation and safeguarding of governmental institutions that are openly democratic and boldly reforming. It is the effective and judicious class struggle, measured and civilized in its means, and coordinated with the potentialities of a general economic development. It is, in short, a revolution prepared and assured by evolution.

On the other side we have the blinding of proletarian consciousness with the illusion of an invincible force which is presented not as a potential but as an actuality, and which in fact barely exists, if at all. There follows contempt for voters, for Parliament, and for legislative reforms, the latter being considered as frauds which strengthen and assure the continued class rule of the bourgeoisie. There follow also the exaltation of immediate and total conquest of power; the mirage of proletarian dictatorships achieved in the streets and by means of street demonstrations; the necessary abandonment of all patient efforts at positive preparation and building; unrestrained and savage class struggle, destructive of all economic forces and periodically interspersed with convulsions and bloody reactions; inevitable disintegration and crushing of all proletarian organizations; the promotion of restrictive, coercive, and immobilizing legislation; the impossibility of any form of democratic government; increasing misery, physical and moral; and the entrusting of the revolution to the thaumaturgical efficacy of miracles.

Between these two roads there is not a single point in common. One road travels straight to socialism by means of arduous steps; the other meanders through a worsened *status quo* and ends up in reaction. It is impossible to find a way out through an intermediate path. The Socialist party cannot but make its choice. . . . The hour of responsibility has sounded for all. . . .

Giolitti was determined that the Socialists and others who had participated in the general strike should not have an opportunity to escape their responsibilities. Accordingly, he requested from the King authorization to dissolve the Chamber of Deputies and call new elections. The announcement embodying this decision also took advantage of the occasion to summarize the government's achievements during its first year in power and to emphasize its determination to continue along the path of reforms.

44. GIOLITTI ASSESSES HIS FIRST YEAR IN OFFICE

Report of October 18, 1904, Requesting that the King Dissolve the Chamber of Deputies and Call New Elections

Giolitti, *Discorsi parlamentari*, II, 1206–13, *passim*. Our translation.

Your Majesty,

On December 1st of last year the Ministry appeared before Parliament with the program it intended to follow and asked the Chamber of Deputies for an immediate and explicit vote of confidence. Two days later the Chamber of Deputies gave its approval with a majority of 167 votes.

At that time the program was criticized by many as too vast and too full of promises. We are pleased to note that after less than a year all the promises that lay within the government's power to fulfill have been kept and that the activity of the legislature developed even more rapidly than was indicated in our program.

In six months of parliamentary activity we have approved in normal fashion all the budgets of the state and, in addition to a great number of laws of secondary importance, also the following: laws providing for the economic transformation of the region of Basilicata, for the economic and industrial revival of Naples, for the transformation of communal debts in the continental portions of the South, and for the prompt construction of the aqueduct in Apulia. In addition, Parliament approved a radical revision of the law on charitable institutions for the purpose of safeguarding the patrimony of the poor and its allocation to purposes in keeping with the times. It revised the law on public health by intensifying efforts at curing malaria and pellagra and by asserting for the first time the duty of employers to provide better housing conditions for land workers. Measures were taken on behalf of elementary education and elementary schoolteachers with a generosity unknown in all previous legislation, the state contributing 8 million lire a year. The right to compete for public-works contracts was extended to cooperative and agrarian societies. The executive power was deprived of the right to alter the rolls of permanent employees in public administration, and this right was reserved to the legislative power. Many millions were spent for the great improvement of the conditions of the permanent employees in the postal and telegraphic services, in the services of the Finance, Treasury, Foreign Affairs, and Public Works ministries, as well as for the personnel of the state libraries, the judiciary, the prison system, and the junior ranks of the army. A social insurance fund was established for communal employees; the Fund for Workers' Disability and Old Age Pensions was strengthened; pensions were established for workers in the state tobacco monopoly; and provisions were made for the veterans of the wars of independence and for the survivors of Mentana. Measures were taken for putting the finances of the City of Rome on a sound basis, and we kept the old promise of connecting the Trastevere and Termini railroad stations [in Rome]. By means of two agreements with France we provided for the protection of our workers in that country and for the construction of the Cuneo-Ventimiglia-Nice railway line. We established a rational four-year plan of public works; we introduced in our penal legislation the sound principle of suspended sentence, and we began a radical reform of the prison system by introducing work in the open and by transforming reformatories from places of punishment into places of education and rehabilitation. Finally, in relation to commercial treaties we took steps to eliminate fraud in the production and sale of wines, to favor the expansion of the wine and citrus fruits industries, to regulate coastal shipping, to improve the fishing industry and the conditions of fishermen, and to promote those industries that use salt and alcohol.

If to this enormous legislative effort already completed we add a number of other items, it will readily be seen how baseless is the accusation made against us (at times with the utmost levity) to the effect that the government has been lacking in effective action for reform. We have negotiated commercial treaties with Germany, Switzerland, and Austria-Hungary and are well along the way in our negotiations with Russia. We have converted the 4.5 per cent rent to 3.5 per cent; we have converted the Roman municipal debt; and we have introduced new and rigid practices in the auditing of state accounts. The absolute necessity of these practices is proved every day by the very fact of the abuses they eliminate. Finally, we have presented a bill that establishes the guidelines for the state's management of those railways which are removed from private management. . . .

These last few years have proved that a regime of freedom benefits the workers more than any other class and that from this regime they have gained very great material and moral benefits. The Ministry is convinced that true prosperity and social peace can be had only by advancing the well being of the lower classes. Accordingly, it will keep its policy unchanged, trusting that the working classes will have a sufficiently clear understanding of their true interests and of their dignity so as not to allow themselves to be oppressed by selfish tyrannies which spring from below.

This program of maximum freedom is opposed strenuously by the extreme parties; but the government is determined to remain faithful to it because it has unlimited confidence in the good sense of the Italian people, to whom history has taught that in demagoguery and in reaction it has two equally dangerous enemies. . . .

Italy has entered a new period in its economic and political life. . . . It is an essential duty of the government to support this progressive movement by identifying and coordinating all of the country's energies. Thus, under the auspices of those institutions which gave us the unity of the fatherland, independence from the foreigner, and maximum freedom, Italy will achieve social peace and that highest degree of civilization, prosperity, and greatness which all those who love the fatherland desire.

It is with these aims in mind that we submit for your signature the decree dissolving the Chamber of Deputies and convening the voters for the coming November 6th, and for the 13th in those constituencies where a second ballot may be necessary.

XVI. APOGEE AND DECLINE OF THE
GIOLITTIAN ERA, 1906–1913

The elections of 1904 marked a decline in the parliamentary strength of the extreme Left; although small, the decline was significant because it indicated an arrest in the growth enjoyed by the extreme parties during the preceding decade. Giolitti had indeed taught them a lesson, and in this he had been aided by the appearance of several Catholic Deputies in Parliament. The Papal prohibition of 1874 (*Non expedit*) against Catholic participation in Italian politics still stood in principle, but the tacit approval given its violation in 1904 foreshadowed its partial repeal in 1905. Another index of change in the country's mood occasioned by the general strike of 1904 was the severity of attacks directed against Giolitti in the Senate and Chamber for his alleged faults in pursuing a domestic policy of which the strike was pictured as an inevitable fruit. Struck by an attack of influenza and nervous depression early in 1905, Giolitti chose to resign in March. He was succeeded by Alessandro Fortis, formerly a Republican and a Radical, whose government rested on the same majority that had upheld Giolitti. Fortis managed to execute Giolitti's planned nationalization of the railways in 1905, but fell from office in February 1906 over a commercial treaty with Spain that favored the manufacturing interests of the North while injuring the wine producers of the South. Giolitti reasoned that as a defender of the commercial treaty he could not return to office, and so he decided not to obstruct the designation of Sidney Sonnino as the new Prime Minister.

Sonnino held office from February to May, 1906; and during this first of his two "Ministries of one hundred days" (the second came in 1909–10) he attempted to enact a program of widespread reforms designed to reinvigorate the old Liberal Right and to prove to the masses that they could expect more solid reforms from this wing of the Liberal party than from its left wing. Sonnino even practiced his own version of transformism by inducing a Radical, Ettore Sacchi, and an independent Radical, Edoardo Pantano, to join the government. Also remarkable was the decision of the Socialist Deputies to support Sonnino in order to see what his government could accomplish. Their support was of brief duration. Denounced by the Executive Committee of their own party and aroused by Sonnino's refusal to allow an immediate debate on an encounter between strikers and police in Turin early in May, the Socialist Deputies not only abandoned their support of the government but resigned from the Chamber. Giolitti's decision that the time had come to end Sonnino's experiment doomed the government within days. By the end of May, Giolitti was once again in office and, supported by a coalition of the Liberal Left and Center, he remained in power for an extraordinarily long period, until December 1909. Absent from office during 1910 and early 1911, he resumed power in March of the latter year and held it until March 1914. The first of these three-year terms marks the apogee of the Giolittian era; the second, although full of considerable accomplishments, contains the seeds of dissolution of Giolitti's mastery over the Italian scene.

The following report summarizes exceptionally well the accomplishments of Giolitti's longest single period in office and justifies calling this period the golden years of his era.

45. THE APOGEE OF THE GIOLITTIAN ERA: MINISTERIAL REPORT OF FEBRUARY 8, 1909, REQUESTING ROYAL APPROVAL FOR THE DISSOLUTION OF THE CHAMBER OF DEPUTIES

Giolitti, *Discorsi parlamentari*, II, 1214–16, *passim*. Our translation.

Your Majesty!

. . . . The Ministry unanimously recommends to your Majesty the dissolution of the Chamber of Deputies and the consultation of the country on next March 7 for the first ballot and on the 14th where a second ballot is necessary.

The Legislature that has now come to an end has brought to completion reforms of truly exceptional importance in almost all branches of legislative activity. In execution of the program presented by the government before the last general elections [1904], the state assumed the management of the principal rail networks, including 13,200 kilometers of rail previously managed by private concerns. By purchasing the Southern railways the state became proprietor of all the principal rail networks. Two subsequent laws authorized the expenditure of 910 million lire for the proper reorganization of the rail lines that had been nationalized. The beneficial effect derived from this improved state of the railways is now being seen in our success in meeting the needs of a traffic that has increased beyond all expectations.

In the financial field we achieved the memorable conversion of our public 5 per cent bonds (gross) to 3.75 per cent. By 1912 these will become 3.50 per cent titles (net). This was an exceptionally serious operation because it involved securities valued at 8.5 billion lire. As a result of this conversion the Treasury achieved a saving of 20 million lire a year, and from January 1, 1912, it will profit from an additional equal sum. After this operation . . . the state's credit reached its highest point, with resulting benefit to the public economy by reason of lower interest rates for capital needed by industry and commerce.

Also in the field of public finance we note the following: reduction of the tax on kerosene by 50 per cent and the assurance of another reduction in the near future as a result of the commercial treaty with Russia; reduction in postal rates; assumption by the state of many expenditures which weigh on the provinces and the communes; redemption of the telephonic lines previously operated by private industry; . . . reduction of stamp taxes on promissory notes and of the tax on secured loans.

Public works projects, which so greatly promote the development of national wealth, were given a strong stimulus. We note the following: the law of July 12, 1906, authorizing the construction of supplementary rail lines in Sicily; the laws which authorized construction of railways and many other public works in Basilicata and Calabria; the law of July 14, 1907, for new port facilities which was the most complete law ever voted by the Italian Parliament in this field; the law of July 12, 1908, which authorized the construction of new railways with an estimated expenditure of 600 million lire; and the bill for internal water transportation already submitted to the Chamber and to be resubmitted to the new Chamber.

Systematic reforms of the public services also figured large in our legislative efforts. We note changes in the judiciary system: a law regulating the operation of the magistracy and fixing the legal tenure and other rights of magistrates; a law reordering the offices of court clerks and secretaries as well as the operation of administrative justice. We note also the law on the legal status of secondary schoolteachers and of civil service employees; a law for the furtherance of elementary school education; a bill on university professors already submitted to the Chamber and to be resubmitted to the new Chamber; a law reorganizing the services in the fine arts; a bill already approved by the Chamber safeguarding our artistic heritage; numerous laws on the reorganization of various services in the navy; . . . a new law on recruitment for the army; and a law appropriating funds for extraordinary military expenditures in defense of the state. . . .

The past Legislature's activity was even more intense in the field of social reforms. A comprehensive body of laws has assured all workers a weekly day of rest; the Fund for Workers' Disability and Old Age Pensions has been strengthened and put on a more solid footing; night work in bakeries was abolished; laws regulating women and child labor were improved; conditions of labor in rice cultivation were improved; two laws were passed greatly facilitating and subsidizing the construction of low-income housing; the rehabilitation of prison convicts was made easier and more speedy; low-interest loans were made more accessible . . . to communes for the construction of aqueducts and other public health installations; a bill was presented to help solve the very grave problem of abandoned children; . . . and two parliamentary inquiries were ordered on the conditions of land workers in the South and Sicily, as well as of miners in Sardinia. The results of these inquiries will make it possible for us to take effective measures on behalf of such large groups of workers.

Finally, during the course of the past Legislature a large number of laws were passed to meet special needs in several regions of the country. . . .

This rapid sketch of the more important laws voted by Parliament shows how worthily it has rewarded the country's trust. As a whole these laws are the reflection of a policy of peace, freedom, work, and social justice. We believe that this policy should be continued with ever increasing firmness and vigor so that our country may more rapidly approach that goal which was and is the ideal of all who love Italy. That this ideal may be reached by persevering along the road we have followed is proved in an evident fashion by the great progress Italy has made during the last few years.

The numerical results of the 1909 general elections proved to be a mixed blessing to Giolitti. Although his supporters remained a strong majority in the Chamber, the extreme Left showed a recovery from its losses in 1904 and rose to 110 seats, indicating that the favorable trend in its fortunes, interrupted in 1904, had been resumed. The elections also marked the appearance of over twenty Deputies who were associated with Catholic electoral organizations. The victories of both the extreme Left and the Catholics were portents of future difficulties for Giolitti. Not that he favored the disappearance of the parties of the extreme Left, nor that he was opposed to open Catholic participation in politics. The existence of the extreme Left had served him well as a threat with which to persuade the Liberals to enact his program of reforms; and the entry into Parliament of Deputies inspired by Catholic teachings should not have disturbed Giolitti. He, after all, had preached the need of inducing all elements in the country to participate in the moderating practices of parliamentary life in order to keep them from embarking on less moderate avenues of political expression. But a too rapid growth of the extreme Left on the one hand and of the political Catholics on the other would have the effect of diminishing that center coalition which was Giolitti's mainstay. Thus, the not too clear indications given by the elections, the bitter debate in the new Parliament over state contracts with subsidized shipping companies, and the somewhat unfavorable reaction in the Chamber's committees to Giolitti's proposal for a progressive tax on income and real estate seemed to persuade him that the time had come for another vacation from office. Accordingly, Giolitti resigned early in December 1909.

The formation of a new government was entrusted to Sonnino, who, in this second of his two "Ministries of a hundred days," did not repeat his earlier beckoning to the extreme Left. But inasmuch as the support of the Right and the Center-Right was not enough to assure the government a majority, Sonnino had by necessity to welcome the votes of the Giolittians. This fact made him a prisoner of the latter; and when in March 1910 they turned against him, Sonnino decided to resign without waiting for an explicit vote of no confidence. Giolitti apparently thought the time unsuitable for his return to power. He chose, instead, to promote the accession of Luigi Luzzatti, a noted economist and many times a Minister in preceding governments. Luzzatti formed a coalition government including men from his own Right as well as from the Giolittian Left and even two Radicals from the extreme Left.

Luzzatti's principal achievements during his one year in office were a temporary solution of the shipping question and, far more important, the reorganization of elementary education. This second measure removed elementary education from the control of small municipalities, whose financial resources were so meager as to make compulsory education a myth, and entrusted it to provincial councils. The state also increased its allowances for construction of school facilities and more adequate pay for teachers. Luzzatti also proposed a liberalization of the suffrage law, but, fearing that universal manhood suffrage would benefit the Socialists and the Catholics most particularly, he insisted on the literacy requirement and on making voting compulsory for all eligible voters. This stand jeopardized the Radicals' support of the government, and Giolitti, apparently ready to return to power, outbid Luzzatti by coming out in favor of eliminating the literacy requirement. When the two Radical Ministers decided to resign, Luzzatti's government was faced with no alternative other than to join them.

In March 1911 Giolitti formed his last prewar government. Once again, as in 1903, he offered a post to a leading Socialist. This time it was not Filippo Turati but Leonida Bissolati, the first editor of the party's newspaper *Avanti!*, one of the earliest Socialist Deputies in Parliament, and a leader in the reformist or evolutionary wing of the party. Bissolati refused the offer, as had Turati, and pleaded the same cause: the party was not ready to participate in power. Bissolati persisted in his refusal, even after an audience with the King; but this audience aroused the intransigents in the Socialist party, who could not forgive Bissolati his willingness to confer with the King. These elements in the party were not at all assuaged by Bissolati's refusal —scandalous to proper Court etiquette—to don a frock coat for the audience and by his going to the palace in street clothes.

Failing to lure the Socialists into the responsibilities of power, Giolitti turned to the Radicals, who by now had become accustomed to office and who offered Giolitti three of their leaders. The rest of the government was substantially the same as under Luzzatti, but its political orientation was clearly more to the left. This fact is revealed by the two essential points made in Giolitti's program speech of April 6, 1911. He called for an extension of the right to vote for all males who had reached the age of thirty and for all who had performed their military service, thus eliminating the literacy requirement for the overwhelming majority of adult males. He also proposed that, in order to promote the welfare of the lower classes, the state acquire a monopoly of life insurance and allot the revenues accruing from this service to the Fund for Workers' Disability and Old Age Pensions.

Clearly Giolitti's program of 1911 represents an overture to the extreme Left, and, after his slight bending toward the Right following the general strike of 1904, he was once again prepared to rely on the support if not the active collaboration of the whole *Estrema*. There were a number of indices which seemed to justify his judgment of the situation. The Socialist party had experienced a series of radical changes since the triumph of its revolutionary wing at the Bologna congress of 1904. The irreconcilable differences between the revolutionaries and the reformists had been papered over by an "integralist" resolution at the Rome congress in 1906; but in 1908 the reformists had triumphed at the Florence congress, and they had repeated their triumph at Milan in 1910. Giolitti may have been unnecessarily candid when he said, in a speech of April 8, 1911, that the Socialists had "relegated Karl Marx to the attic"; he may even have made the mistake of not distinguishing between the Socialists who sat in Parliament and the rank and file of the party; but he was certainly correct in judging that the leaders of the party and especially its Deputies in Parliament were on the whole no longer devotees of revolutionary socialism. He was certainly right in thinking that the Radicals had been "domesticated" into a governmental party, in spite of the anti-Giolittian diatribes of a few of their more independent colleagues. In short, if it were possible to assure the support of most of the extreme Left in favor of a program of reforms sufficiently advanced to merit the *Estrema's* benevolence but not so radical as to alienate the fundamentally bourgeois liberals of the Left, it should be possible to achieve a grand political realignment producing roughly a system of two internally homogeneous and opposing blocs, if not a perfect two-party system: a progressive bloc ranging from the Liberal Center-Left and Left to the extreme Left, and a conservative bloc including the Center-Right and the Right.

A serious obstacle to the implementation of this political realignment was Giolitti's reputation of being an unscrupulous manipulator of elections and political offices. Charges of political corruption were made against him by men from all political quarters, but one of the most devastating indictments of the "Giolittian system" came from the Socialist historian Gaetano Salvemini in his work *Il ministro della malavita*. Salvemini's ideas are prominent in the excerpt below, which is an exceptionally well-balanced account of this much-criticized "system" and which is derived from A. William Salomone's pioneer and authoritative study of the Giolittan era.

46. AN ASSESSMENT OF THE GIOLITTIAN SYSTEM

A. William Salomone, *Italy in the Giolittian Era: Italian Democracy in the Making, 1900–1914*, 2d ed. Philadelphia: University of Pennsylvania Press, 1960, pp. 108–10. Original footnotes omitted. Published originally as *Italian Democracy in the Making: The Political Scene in the Giolittian Era, 1900–1914.* Philadelphia: University of Pennsylvania Press, 1945.

. . . With good or questionable motives, through praiseworthy or reproachable methods, Giovanni Giolitti seemed to have conciliated and continued to conciliate antagonistic or indifferent masses of people and currents of Italian life within the great organism that was the Italian nation.

But it was precisely in that question of motives and methods that the opponents of Giolittian politics found the rallying points for their attacks on the entire Giolittian scheme of things. It was here that the elements of opposition to Giolitti fused—the purely political being sometimes inextricably intermingled with personal (psychological, spiritual, moral) antipathy to the man as a politico, as a type, as a symbol. Personalities as different and constrasting as Gaetano Salvemini, Arturo Labriola, Ettore Ciccotti, Napoleone Colajanni, Carlo Altobelli, Innocenzo Cappa, Leonida Bissolati, Mario Missiroli, Tancredi Galimberti—men of all classes and all political creeds were in agreement that *Giolittismo* as a method of government must be uprooted. What were the chief characteristics of this so-called Giolittian method or system? Both his contemporaries and historians still diverge widely in their emphasis on the various characteristics involved, but in one thing they are in accord: the basis of the system lay in the Machiavellian ability and shrewdness (*abilità* and *furberia*) of the keen Piedmontese. Said Barzilai: "One of the defects he possesses in a notably greater proportion than all others is his tendency to rule and work upon the vices rather than upon the virtues of men." Filippo Meda saw Giolitti as "the exponent of that political realism which may sometimes be offensive to moral idealism, but which is, nevertheless, a necessary product of the parliamentary regime."

Essentially an honest and upright man to whose personal integrity even his bitterest enemies repeatedly paid homage, Giolitti came to be associated with the use of a system of electoral pressures, tamperings, even occasional violence (what Italians called *pressioni e brogli*) that had caused him to be characterized by Gaetano Salvemini, in an outburst of moral indignation, "Minister of the Underworld" (*Il Ministro della mala vita*). The epithet stuck and was sometimes used and twisted out of all meaning by people who liked to heap all the sins, real and imagined, of Italian public life upon Giolitti's shoulders. Electoral corruption, decried in their day by such critics of the parliamentary system as Mosca, Turiello, and Pareto, was obviously neither an Italian invention nor a Giolittian monopoly. What was perhaps essentially Italian was the condition of the amorphous, passive, and, until 1912, disfranchised masses of the agricultural proletariat in the South who for centuries had suffered every form of injustice and oppression at the hands of the local oligarchies—wrongs not yet righted even after fifty years of political unity. In his highly moral and ethical crusade for the economic, social, and civic betterment and enlightment of the South already studied in connection with his Socialist activities, Gaetano Salvemini found in a man like Vito De Bellis, the ministerial candidate of the Apulian district of Gioia del Colle in the elections of 1904 and 1909, the symbol of an evil all could understand. Salvemini said in 1910: "Vito De Bellis is not a man: he is a symbol, a representative individual, an institution. He is *Giolittismo.*" The historian described minutely the preparations for the elections, the use of coercion (the *mazzieri* were electoral hooligans who used *mazze* or clubs to intimidate voters), bribery, fraud, even the show of public force, in order to insure the victory of the ministerial candidate. By his moral campaign Salvemini himself assumed the force of a symbol, that of the anti-Giolittian par excellence, and it was natural that in the general elections of 1913, when he offered his own candidacy in the district of Molfetta, he should have been fought tooth and nail by the ministerial henchmen whose idol was, on this occasion, an antimonarchist, Pietro Pansini a Republican. This election of Molfetta gained the widest notoriety through its having been covered by one of Italy's greatest newspapermen, Ugo Ojetti, of the Milan *Corriere della Sera*.

Vito De Bellis and Pietro Pansini, however, were by no means the only ministerial protégés, nor were Gioia del Colle and Molfetta or Bitonto, in Apulia, the only southern districts where electoral *Giolittismo* was practised. The Italian parliamentary debates after the three Giolittian elections of 1904, 1909, and 1913 are replete with the most varied charges of ministerial abuses and interference in electoral contests. In April 1907, for example, the Syndicalist newspaper *Propaganda* (Naples) featured the underground acts of one "Peppuccio" Romano, reputed to be a Government protégé whom the paper accused of being the chief of the Camorra in the city of Aversa, the head of the *mala vita* of the entire Terra di Lavoro, a buyer of votes, a seller of communal council and parliamentary seats. On May 26, 1907 Luigi Federzoni, the Nationalist journalist, writing under the pseudonym of "Giulio De Frenzi" in the *Giornale d'Italia*, Sonnino's organ, attempted to expose what he called the feudal methods and the electoral oppression of the Government's policy in the same Neapolitan region. These articles were naturally greedily seized upon by the whole anti-Giolittian press and were noised about the country and in the Chamber of Deputies.

On May 25, 1909 the old leader of the *Fasci siciliani,* the Sicilian Socialist deputy De Felice-Giuffrida, gave the Chamber a minute exposé of Giolittian methods on his own island. De Felice divided electoral Giolittianism into two periods: that of preparation, during which prefects were given their instructions, communal councils were dissolved, local chieftains rallied; then came the period of action, when the *ministeriali* were assured of their victory through the application of all available methods of coercing voters. Citing examples from the Sicilian districts of Paternó, Licodia, Licata, Castelvetrano, De Felice remarked: "Thus you, Honorable Giolitti, a fellow citizen of Massimo

D'Azeglio who made Italians in Piedmont, come to make Italians in Sicily!" The Republican Colajanni, also a Sicilian, half-seriously complained that it was unjust for Giolitti to show such partiality by applying his electoral methods only to the south of Italy, and he reproached the Prime Minister for his failure to foster the true principles of *italianità* where they were most needed. Salvatore Barzilai, in turn, stressed the point that Giolitti took his good wherever he found it; in the North he depended upon the support of the democratic forces, won over by favoritism of all kinds; in the South he depended upon the local oligarchies. The lack of political principles to animate his legislative programs made such ambiguity necessary for Giolitti, according to Barzilai. As a result, Giolittian majorities in the Chamber were personal followings rallied around a man rather than true political groupings held together by common beliefs and ideas. The result of this system had been [according to Barzilai] an estrangement, a widening of the gulf between Parliament and the life of the country. . . .

The sense of political estrangement to which the Republican Barzilai referred was unwittingly promoted by Giolitti in 1911, when he decided that the time had come for Italy to secure its strategic position in the Mediterranean by occupying Turkey's nominal possessions of Tripolitania and Cyrenaica in North Africa. This decision appeared to signify a radical change in his views on foreign policy. Giolitti opposed Crispi's "adventurism" in the 1890s and joined in the nearly unanimous demand to "get out of Africa" after the defeat at Aduwa in 1896. But after more than a decade of domestic progress and diplomatic realignment, Italy began to recover from the sense of humiliation and incapacity occasioned by that defeat. Giolitti became convinced that "historical necessity" demanded that the central portion of North Africa should not fall under the control of any power but Italy; that the diplomatic situation was favorable to Italy's ambition in the area; and that the favorable moment should be seized lest it be irrevocably lost. But his conversion to imperialism—however limited and guarded this conversion may have been and however motivated by his notion of "raison d'état"—could not but cause discomfiture in the ranks of his supporters on the Left and the extreme Left. It also jeopardized his program of domestic reform, not only by reason of his weakened position among the groups favoring reform but also because Italy was neither sufficiently prosperous economically nor stable politically to conduct two competing programs of reform at home and expansion abroad. It is generally agreed that the Italo-Turkish or Libyan War of 1911–12 marks the beginning of the dissolution of the Giolittian system.

The war for Libya was begun in 1911, after more than a decade of diplomatic preparation aimed at securing the support or benevolent neutrality of
the major European powers. This meant that Italy had to improve its relations with France, strengthen its friendly ties with England, cultivate
Russia, and at the same time not alienate its allies in the Triple Alliance.
Crispi's hostility toward France had made Italy too dependent on the Triple
Alliance as the only escape from total isolation. Even if Italy had had no
ambitions in North Africa it would have been likely that in time it should
choose to improve its relations with France simply not to be too dependent
on Germany and Austria-Hungary. The first step in this direction was taken
in 1896 when, while renewing its alliance with Germany and Austria-
Hungary, Italy also recognized France's hegemony in Tunisia. Two years
later, the tariff war with France was brought to an end, and in 1900 a number of important Franco-Italian agreements were reached, all marking a significant change of attitude in Italian foreign policy. The following passage
from a work by Benedetto Croce summarizes with exceptional clarity the
import of developments in Italy's foreign policy during the following
decade.

47. FOREIGN POLICY DURING THE GIOLITTIAN ERA

Benedetto Croce, *Storia d'Italia dal 1871 al 1915*, 13th ed. Bari:
Giuseppe Laterza e Figli, 1964, pp. 251–57. Our translation.

Italy's new attitude in foreign policy revealed a self-confidence the
like of which the country did not feel in domestic policies and administration, where discontent and criticism are always promotive of improvement. Foreign policy became more resolute and enterprising because Italy now possessed the necessary strength, and for this reason
its attitude was less pompous and noisy and more productive than in
the days of Crispi, when this strength was lacking. The needs for expansion, for new territories and colonies, for economic penetration in
the Balkans and the Near East had lost the quality of plans and aspirations held by a few individuals and had become part of national
consciousness. These needs were asserted not only by those youths
who in those days frequently assumed the title of "nationals" or "nationalists" but, before them, even by some authoritative Socialists, including Antonio Labriola himself, who was the man who had sys-
tematized Marxist Socialism in Italy and who now applied to the

question of expansion the same ardor which earlier he had shown for the class struggle.

Prinetti * had continued Visconti Venosta's † policy toward France, and in 1901 and 1902 two conventions were signed with the latter. These agreements committed Italy to support France's expansion in Morocco in exchange for French support of Italy's designs in Tripolitania and Cyrenaica. Italy also promised to remain neutral in the event France were the victim of aggression or in case it had to go to war because of a direct provocation and the defense of its honor and security. Statements made by Prinetti to the chamber [1901], the courtesies exchanged between the President of the French Republic and the Duke of Genoa at Toulon [1901], and later the King's visit to Paris [1903] and President Loubet's exchange visit to Rome in 1904, all had the effect of prompting the French press to write even of the existence of a "de facto alliance" between the two countries. In 1906, during the Algeciras Conference ‡ at which Italy was represented by Visconti Venosta, Italy did not support Germany's claims. Instead, it contributed to the outcome favorable to France, by which the latter was recognized as having a position of preeminence in Morocco.

Relations with England continued to be cordial. In 1904 an agreement was signed between the two countries regarding East Africa where, in 1905, Italy's colony of Somaliland was reorganized by reducing the functions of the Benadir Company § strictly to agricultural and commercial matters. The government assumed political sovereignty in the area after an agreement with the Sultan of Zanzibar and in 1908, with the gradual submission of the tribes in the interior, an act of Parliament provided for the new administration of the colony. As proof of friendship England in 1902 repealed the regulation which forbade the use of the Italian language in Malta, and in 1907 King Edward VII met with the King of Italy at Gaeta.

In 1903 the Czar of Russia had to postpone his intended visit to the

* Giulio Prinetti, Foreign Minister from 1901 to 1903. Ed. note.
† Emilio Visconti Venosta, Foreign Minister in 1863–64, 1866–67, 1869–76, 1896–98, and 1899–1901. Ed. note.
‡ Conference of European powers held at Algeciras, Spain, to mediate conflicting Franco-German claims in Morocco. Ed. note.
§ In 1898 the Italian government had ceded the administration of its Somaliland possessions to a private company, the *Società anonima commerciale italiana del Benadir*. Ed. note.

King of Italy because of the bad reception Italian Socialists threatened to give him and because of fears entertained by the Czar's police. The visit was made in 1909 at Racconigi, and on this occasion agreements were concluded with Isvolsky, who accompanied the Czar as his Foreign Minister. Italy agreed to the eventual opening or neutralization of the Straits and, in return, Russia agreed to Italy's eventual occupation of Tripoli. Agreements were reached also on the territorial integrity of the Ottoman Empire and on Balkan questions, in which latter connection Italy and Russia committed themselves to support the principle of nationality and not to treat on new questions with Austria-Hungary without the participation of both Italy and Russia.

In 1902 the Triple Alliance was renewed for the fourth time; but Italy's policies toward France, England, and Russia had aroused bad humor and distrust in German circles to the point that Bülow [the German Chancellor] had to take remedial measures. In a speech to the Reichstag on January 8, 1902, he tried to attenuate the gravity of the situation by asserting that the Triple Alliance did not prohibit its component members from having good relations with other powers and by making the humorous comparison with "a happy marriage, in which the husband should not appear displeased if his wife has an innocent dance with another man, because the important thing is that she not betray him." Bülow had to have recourse to other remedial measures after the visit of the French President, Loubet, to Italy, and to yet others when, after Italy's behavior at the Algeciras Conference, there were cries in the German press and assemblies that Italy's "dancing" was no longer without threat to marital fidelity. More measures had to be taken when, after the end of the Conference, the German Emperor William sent a famous telegram to the Austrian Emperor, Francis Joseph, in which he called Austria-Hungary a "faithful ally," thus implicitly excluding Italy from this praise. The German Emperor's Ministers issued a number of statements in which they sought to make of the telegram an expression of purely personal and private opinions, but they were not able to negate its impolitic effect. Besides, even in Italy there were questions as to how it would be possible for Italy to fight on the side of Germany and Austria-Hungary in the event of war.

Italy's real and intrinsic differences were with Austria-Hungary, with whom relations became and remained bad in spite of partial and passing accommodations. When Victor Emmanuel III made his tour of visits to the sovereigns of Europe after his rise to the throne, he went to St. Petersburg and Berlin in 1902, but he did not go to Vienna, remembering that his father's visit to that capital twenty years before had not been returned. As early as 1900 an agreement had been concluded between the two countries by Visconti Venosta regarding the *status quo* in Albania, and, in the event that this condition could not be preserved, Austria-Hungary and Italy agreed to assure the autonomy of this area. In 1902 Austria-Hungary committed itself in a declaration not to oppose an eventual Italian intervention in Tripolitania and Cyrenaica, and in 1904 it was the first to propose the appointment of an Italian general to the high command of the gendarmerie in Macedonia. But the rivalry between the two countries in the Balkans, and the claims which Italy put forward to boundaries it considered necessary and to the Italian-speaking territories in the Austro-Hungarian Empire, proved to be two interrelated, incoercible and incurable causes for differences between the two countries. The exclusion of Italian teachers from the University of Innsbrück in 1903 occasioned anti-Austrian demonstrations in Rome and elsewhere which the Italian government curbed with vigor. In 1905 the President of the Italian Chamber of Deputies, Marcora, spoke of "our Trentino," thereby provoking a diplomatic incident in which Italy refused to give Austria the satisfaction it demanded, limiting itself to expressions of regret over the matter. Once again Bülow had to smooth over the difficulty. In 1908 there arose a conflict of interests with Austria-Hungary over the Balkan railways. The latter favored one line, whereas Italy, in agreement with French, Russian, and Serbian bankers, favored another. The Austrians accused the Italians of encroachment in the Balkans, where an Italian company was building the port of Antivari and a rail line, while another company held the tobacco monopoly in Montenegro. Italian commercial agencies were operating in Durazzo and Scutari [Albania]; in the latter city there was also an Italian bank, and an Italian company held the concession for navigation on the Bojana River and the Lake of Scutari. The difference over the railway lines was eliminated by the revolution in Turkey and the advent of the Young Turks to power. These events removed the railway dispute from contention, but this same revolution led Austria to declare its annexation of Bosnia-Herzegovina contrary to the terms of the Treaty of Berlin of 1878. This annexation was a grave matter for Italy and for all of Europe, and a general war appeared imminent. Austria-Hungary massed troops in the Trentino and agitation in Italy became most intense. In the Italian Chamber, Alessandro Fortis [Prime Minister in 1905–6] said that it was impossible for Italy to bear much longer Austria-Hungary's armaments against her, that Austria-Hungary was the only power that threatened Italy, and that, ironically, it was an ally of Italy. The speech was received with acclamations, and the Prime Minister [Giolitti] as well as all the other Ministers—except for the Foreign Minister, who could not but remain rooted in his seat—gathered around the speaker to offer him their congratulations. Practically speaking, Italy was the loser: the promise of an Italian university for Trieste which had been flashed before the Italians was not kept. Austria-Hungary asserted that by the terms of the Triple Alliance it did not owe Italy any compensation for the annexation of Bosnia-Herzegovina * because, in annexing these two provinces, it had renounced its claims to the district of Novi Pazar [in southern Serbia]. On this latter point Austria-Hungary concluded a convention with Italy in December 1909 to the effect that if ever it were obliged to occupy Novi Pazar either permanently or temporarily, the provisions for territorial compensation in favor of Italy would be enforced. There ensued renewed protests of loyalty to the Triple Alliance by all three of its members, but the continued incidents which followed showed that the true state of feelings was otherwise. The Italian government subsidized the Italian-speaking population of Trieste against the Slavic element, assuring the victory of the former in municipal elections. In November 1909, on the occasion of presenting the flag to a new regiment of cavalry in Brescia, General Asinari di Bernezzo—who had fought against the Austrians at Custoza in 1866 —pointed to "the hills bathed by the blood of our heroes, behind which are the unredeemed lands awaiting the hour of liberation." In 1910 the *Pro Patria* association was reconstituted in Trieste and the National League celebrated its twentieth anniversary there. An army of tourists from Trieste was received with joy and emotion in Milan. Rome elected a Deputy born in Trieste; the mayor of the capital, Ern-

---

* One of the compensations Italy had hoped for in exchange for Austria's annexation of the two provinces was precisely an Italian university in Trieste.

esto Nathan, who was also grand master of the Masonic lodges and vice-president of the "Dante Alighieri" society, made a speech in which he called Trieste a "daughter of our common mother, Rome." In appearances the Dante Alighieri society was devoted to safeguarding and disseminating the Italian language, but in fact its purpose was irredentist. The country read with palpitating heart books, being published by writers of history, which contained new investigations on the persecutions, trials, and executions which Austria had wreaked upon Italian patriots; and these heroic and painful memories were thus revived by Austria's recent acts in the unredeemed lands. And yet, the Triple Alliance continued to exist, and, its expiration approaching, preparations were put under way for its renewal. Why and how should it be canceled? While speaking in the Reichstag in 1908, Bülow had referred to a remark made to him one day by an Italian diplomat, Nigra, to the effect that "Italy could not but be either an ally or an enemy of Austria-Hungary." Inasmuch as Italy could not by itself alone fight against the combined forces of Austria-Hungary and Germany, to renounce the alliance would have been the signal for a general war in Europe. And this was, in fact, the war which was being prepared in some obscure fashion; the war of which everyone was talking but in whose occurrence no one believed because even the thought of the massacre and ruin which it would entail was such a monstrous thing. Consequently, this war appeared as something impossible and mad in a world of intelligent and practical people. Besides, in the worst of hypotheses one could always count on the socialists, who would prevent it by means of their international organization; or one could count on the bourgeoisie, which would not dare to make war precisely out of fear of the socialist International. And so, in Italy as in the rest of Europe, people lived and worked and prospered, moving about tranquilly over a ground which had been thoroughly undermined.

Confident that the diplomatic preparation of the preceding ten years assured Italy the support or benevolent neutrality of the major European powers, Giolitti decided in 1911 that "historical necessity" obliged Italy to move into North Africa. The resulting war with Turkey lasted a year (September 1911–October 1912) and assured Italy's sovereignty over Tripolitania and Cyrenaica (Libya) and the occupation of the formerly Turkish Dodecanese Islands in the Aegean Sea. The domestic repercussions of this war were felt within a year, during the general elections of October–November 1913. These elections were conducted on the basis of a new law passed in 1912, which increased the number of eligible voters from 3,319,207 to 8,672,249, thus establishing virtual universal manhood suffrage. The principal issue in the elections was the Libyan War, its conduct, and its consequences. The parties of the Right had supported the enterprise and could be expected to give their votes to candidates who would support Giolitti's continuation in power. But the extreme Left was sharply divided by the war: a small group of Republicans had favored it and in 1912 were expelled from the party because of this stand. More serious was the division among the Socialists. The most moderate among them, led by Leonida Bissolati and Ivanoe Bonomi, reconciled themselves to the war as a national necessity and thus fell victim to the intransigents in the party who, influenced by the revolutionary vehemence of young Mussolini, decreed their expulsion at the party congress of Reggio Emilia in July 1912. This congress marked the end of the moderates' sway over the party; even Turati, emotionally and ideologically closer to Bissolati than to the revolutionaries, was led by his opposition to the war to make common cause with those same revolutionaries he had so often and so severely censured. As a result of the Libyan War Giolitti lost most of his influence over the Socialists; on the other hand he could not for long count on the Right, whose favorable attitude on the Libyan War would not likely be extended to include Giolitti's domestic policies. Fearful that the opponents of the war, particularly the Socialists, would capitalize on the internal unrest resulting from increased financial burdens, Giolitti or some of his lieutenants apparently reached an agreement with Count Ottorino Gentiloni, president of the Catholic electoral organizations. This so-called Gentiloni Pact assured Catholic support to those Liberal candidates who pledged themselves to certain conditions, most especially to oppose an expected divorce bill. After the elections, Count Gentiloni revealed that Catholic support had been given to 330 candidates and that over 220 of these had been successful. Inasmuch as 33 "Catholic Deputies" [1] had been elected, the remainder must have been Liberals of various shades, whose total number reached 310, 62 less than in the previous Legislature. The Radicals raised their representation from 51 to 70; the Official Socialists increased from 25 to 51; Bissolati's newly formed Reformist Socialist Party rose from its original 13 to 23; the Republicans declined from 23 to 17; and the Nationalists, contesting their first election as a party, won 6 seats.

The electoral successes of the extreme Left, in spite of the Gentiloni Pact, indicated a trend if not a flight to one pole, while the election of six Nationalists pointed to the other extreme. Although slight in number both in Parliament and the country, the Nationalists were influential in certain circles of Italian society. Their appearance on the political scene as a party of the ex-

---

[1] During the elections the *Non expedit*, or papal prohibition against Catholic participation in Italian politics, had been lifted in 330 constituencies. After the elections the *Osservatore Romano*, noting the reported success of over 30 "Catholic Deputies," reaffirmed Pope Pius X's injunction of 1905 that there be no Catholic Deputies, only Deputies who were Catholics.

treme Right is a sign that the Giolittian program of moderation was destined to face opposition from the intransigents at both extremes of the political spectrum. Had Italy not participated in the First World War or had the consequences of this war not been so severe, it is possible that the Giolittian manner would have been able to cope with its old enemies as well as with the new ones. But the war radically changed the terms of Italian political life, and one factor in this change was the Nationalist party. This party is particularly important for what it contributed to Fascist ideology and thus deserves some examination of its antecedents and the currents of opinion it represented.

The following excerpt attempts such an examination, with special emphasis on the fundamental differences distinguishing the Nationalist Right from the "Old Right" that had helped fashion Italian unity in the nineteenth century and, although opposed to the Left on a number of passing issues, shared with the latter the fundamental belief in parliamentary government.

48. THE "NEW RIGHT": AN IDEOLOGY OF EXTREMISM

Salvatore Saladino, "Italy," Hans Rogger and Eugen Weber, eds., in *The European Right: A Historical Profile*. Berkeley and Los Angeles: University of California Press, 1965, pp. 231–44, *passim*. Courtesy of the publishers.

Disoriented by their experiences during the Pelloux period, the heirs of the Old Right either engaged in ineffectual opposition to Giolitti or, as did Sonnino in 1903, came around to accepting Giolitti's judgment that the most effective way of preserving the essence of liberal institutions was to convince the masses that the state was not their enemy but "the impartial guardian of all classes of citizens." This conversion of part of the Old Right to the views of a man of the moderate Left was not without precedent in the nineteenth century but it did mean that a programmatic or ideological opposition from the Old Right to Giolitti's views was no longer politically meaningful. Most of Italy now seemed to have moved to the Left, and into the vacuum that resulted on the Right there moved a new formation, with Enrico Corradini as its principal spokesman.

Corradini had become politically conscious during the days of Italy's defeat in 1896, an event which shocked him out of his individualistic theories of art and esthetics into a concern for the greater human entity, the nation. He had experienced the influence of d'Annunzio, then the leading representative in Italy of art for art's sake, and the champion of the artist's prerogative to unrestricted freedom; but after Aduwa Corradini moved away from the d'Annunzian preoccupation with physical and intellectual sensuality and converted the latter's literary elitism into a political position. This conversion was best expressed by Corradini in his drama, *Giulio Cesare* (1902), where he glorified Caesar as the veritable personification of the genius of the Roman empire. The identification of national greatness with one man—an empire builder—became a fixed point in Corradini's thought and helps explain his admiration for Crispi, a would-be empire builder. It also helps explain Corradini's hostility toward Giolitti, who replaced Zanardelli as prime minister in 1903, the same year Corradini founded the periodical *Il Regno,* in which most of the basic doctrines of the Nationalist movement were first expressed. . . .

Il Regno was not only antisocialist but antidemocratic as well; it was systematically antiparliamentarian, which gave it a sense of affinity with revolutionary Socialists and Syndicalists. It asserted the moral value of social struggle, of war, and of imperial conquest. *Il Regno*'s articles emphasized the importance of foreign over domestic affairs; in the latter sphere they exalted the growing industrial and commercial expansion of Italy as a source of national pride and pointed to large-scale emigration as a drain on the nation's human and spiritual resources. Above all other men in Italy's recent past they glorified Crispi: "The last great statesman Italy has had . . . a statesman in the heroic sense of the word." In short, the formative Nationalism of the *Il Regno* period was a denunciation of all the qualities characteristic of "bourgeois" society in the pejorative sense of the word: pacifist, unheroic, cautious, and practical, which were precisely the qualities held up to scorn by the d'Annunzian vogue of heroic daring and heroic pleasure. . . .

The evolution of Corradini's thought between 1905, when his association with *Il Regno* ended, and 1910, when he helped form the Nationalist party, is not clear in its details although it is precise enough in general outline. . . .

As late as 1908, Corradini . . . was still preoccupied with socialism as the great antagonist. He then asserted that, although human existence was indisputably collectivist in nature, it was not collectivist in a socialist sense. Socialism made the individual the measure of all things while real life—that is, nationalist collectivism—wanted to transcend the individual to produce greater organisms or greater essential forms. Nationalism was therefore "the doctrine of those who view the nation as the greatest unit of collective life, as a truly and literally greater individual being." Corradini was aware that such a doctrine exposed him to the argument of the internationalists that a community of nations would logically constitute an even greater organism. He defended himself by arguing that "struggle is life," and if nations came into existence to end struggle within, they could continue to live only by engaging in struggle without: "internal peace for the sake of external war." It followed for Corradini that nationalism had necessarily to be imperialistic, for imperialism was the recognition of "the useful function of war." He denied the doctrine of the inviolability of human life on the ground that such a doctrine was a form of "individual egoism" that lived parasitically on the altruism of the collectivity. "Rationally speaking, the individual has no more importance than a drop of water with respect to the sea," and although war would be incomprehensible for the sake of the individual, it was a necessity for nations. "All the world is imperialistic," asserted Corradini, "either internally or externally; and today there is a proletarian imperialism which goes by the name of socialism."

With this assertion Corradini revealed that as early as 1908 he had taken the first tentative step toward the identification of revolutionary socialism as the domestic imperialism of the proletarian class. He was not yet prepared to offer an alliance to this class on the terms that if it would end its divisive imperialism at home it could join the Nationalists in their imperialism abroad. That offer was to be extended shortly before World War I when Corradini definitively adopted the doctrine of Italy as a proletarian nation, thereby asking the revolutionary Socialists to convert their class struggle at home into an imperialistic struggle on behalf of their proletarian nation. But as early as 1908 Nationalists and revolutionary Socialists already had at least one attitude in common, and that was the hostility they shared toward the prevailing regime or ruling class: "In the midst of these herds of sheep and clever little men who constitute in Italy the so-called ruling classes, give me one hundred men who are ready to die and Italy is renewed." This call for a hundred heroes to dispatch the "greedy and inept

clienteles we have on our necks," was made by Corradini; it could just
as easily have come from some of the more individualistic revolutionary socialists. . . .

Encouraged by the influx into their movement of not only Irredentists but also of those Republicans, Socialists, Syndicalists and Liberals who were discontened with Italy's position in the world, the Nationalists called a congress in Florence in December, 1910. The
congress discussed every significant aspect of Italy's internal and international situation, including relations with other political groups, the
problem of emigration, military preparation, Irredentism, and foreign
policy in general. Corradini was a leading speaker, concerning himself
particularly with emigration, the southern question, and the proletarian nature of Italian imperialism. The three topics were intimately
related in Corradini's mind: mass emigration, especially from the
south, was a necessity so long as Italy had no colonial empire to
which it could send its sons and both still retain their allegiance and
profit from their labor. Without colonies Italy's emigrants were
doomed to exploitation for others' benefit, playing the role toward the
host countries which the Socialists said the proletariat played vis-à-vis
the bourgeoisie: their work was everything and they were nothing.
Corradini reasoned that Italy was materially and morally a have-not
or "proletarian nation," and that the role of Nationalists was to do for
all of Italy what the Socialists had done for the proletariat. He asserted that what he preached was a "national socialism" in contrast to
proletarian socialism—"our teacher and adversary"—that told the
workers that their solidarity should be not with the Italian nation but
with the workers of the world. He explained: "It is necessary to nail
into the brain of the workers the fact that it is to their greater interest
to be in solidarity *with their employers* and *above all* with their nation,
and to the devil with solidarity with their comrades in Paraguay and
Cochin-China." Corradini thus expressed clearly and openly his developing concept of a "national egoism" that transcended the egoism of a
class and would alter the internal struggle of classes into an international struggle between proletarian and affluent nations.

A month after the congress of December, 1910, Corradini, aware of
the attraction the concept of Italy as a proletarian nation could have
for Italian Socialists, continued to develop it in a long speech he repeated in a number of important Italian cities. Having decided at the

congress to convert the Nationalist movement into a party, it became necessary to engage in active proselytizing, seeking converts in all quarters. After some hesitation the Republicans had been made welcome at the congress and in the party by eliminating an earlier reference to defense of established institutions. Corradini's speech of January, 1911, openly courted the Socialists by repeating that "Nationalism wishes to be for the whole nation that which socialism was for the proletariat alone . . . [that is] an attempt at redemption. . . ." Such a redemption could come only through the creation of a national consciousness from which the individual citizen would derive a sense of duty and discipline that would render the nation able to perform its role. The nation's role was identified as expansionist and, inasmuch as "nations do not acquire, they conquer," this role meant war, and war meant necessarily the subordination of the individual to the national interest.

This insistence on war as the supreme national act and on the consequent need to subordinate the individual to the nation did not have the approval of all the Nationalists at the Florence congress. Liberal and democratic elements attracted to nationalism because of patriotism and irredentist feelings apparently did not share Corradini's views on expansionist imperialism and totalitarian government. This was attested to by the composition of the managing board of the *Idea Nazionale*, a weekly that began publication on March 1, 1911. . . .

The program with which the *Idea Nazionale* began publication on March 1—a date deliberately chosen to commemorate the Italian defeat at Aduwa in 1896—made clear that the weekly was determined to channel the Nationalist movement in an illiberal, antidemocratic, and imperialistic direction. It proposed to recapture the genius and greatness of imperial Rome; to reinvigorate the authority of the state against the dissolving action of parties and classes; to fight against the corruption of parliamentarianism and Masonic democracy as well as against socialism, the one bourgeois and the other proletarian, but both antinational; to promote class solidarity in order to achieve greater collective well-being by political and economic competition with other nations; and to defend both the monarchy and the Church as traditional institutions making for national solidarity. . . .

For the sake of the superior interests of the nation, the Nationalists were prepared to recognize and respect the historical utility of such traditional institutions as the Church and monarchy; but, individual exceptions aside, the Nationalists did not mean thereby to be irrevocably committed to any one national institution, for that would render the whole of the nation subservient to a part and would be a denial of their major pragmatic premise that the parts of the nation justified themselves only in their service to the whole.

These views were generally accepted by the group of Nationalists who rallied around Corradini and the *Idea Nazionale,* and it was this group that triumphed at the two subsequent party congresses, at Rome in December, 1912, and at Milan in May, 1914.

Between the first congress of 1910 and that of 1912 came the Italo-Turkish or Libyan War. At first it appeared to be a major success for the Nationalists, then it led to some internal disorientation, and finally it became a source of greater strength. . . .

The Libyan War should have been the occasion for an immediate and sustained rise in the stock of the Nationalist party, but this did not happen—for two reasons: first, as nearly everyone had become imperialist, including Giolitti, many argued that there was no longer any need for a Nationalist party that made agitation for imperialistic expansion its chief reason for existence. Second, the Nationalists had represented the Libyan War as a "stroll in the sun" toward "the promised land." When the stroll slowed down to the standstill of a long and costly campaign of gradual conquest and the promised land proved to be a delusion, popular reaction turned against the party that had fostered expectations impossible to realize. At that point the Nationalists . . . ran the risk of political extinction, from which they were saved by developments in the Republican and Socialist parties. Both political groups had a minority that supported the Libyan War as a national necessity in spite of the Republicans' abhorrence for any royally supported enterprise and the doctrinaire opposition of the Socialists to imperialistic wars. The consequence was that both minorities were expelled from their respective parties in 1912 and, especially important, the Socialist congress of July, 1912, led to the triumph of the revolutionary intransigents led by Benito Mussolini. This triumph not only secured Mussolini a place on the party's Directorate but also led to his editorship of the party's principal newspaper, *Avanti!;* from its pages he inveighed for two years against the evils of the Giolittian parliamentary regime and against those members of his own party who had collaborated with the great "Domesticator" in dampening the revolutionary fervor of the working classes.

The Nationalists could not expect any immediate and direct gain from the victory of the extremists, especially in the Socialist party; but the long-range consequences were in their favor. Divided as they were in ideological positions, the extremists of Right and Left were united in their common hostility to the Giolittian system and in their common preference for violence, internal or external. This preference had already moved a number of Syndicalists to recognize how much they had in common with the Nationalists. Angelo Olivetti, a theorist of syndicalism, supported the Libyan War as a desirable experience in violence and as a concrete expression of his ideas: "Syndicalism abhors the pallid conventual equality of which collectivism dreams, and serves instead as a prelude to the formation of combative and conquering elites, unleashed in the assault toward wealth and life." From a common root in the elitist doctrines of Mosca and Pareto there had evolved the antithetical concepts of proletarian and national elites, and it was Corradini's signal achievement to have effected an explicit synthesis of the two in his doctrine of Italy as a proletarian nation obstructed in its development by the "plutocracies" of the world.

An article written by Corradini in November, 1912, a month before the second Nationalist congress, referred to the Libyan and Balkan wars as a struggle by proletarian nations against a common enemy, "European plutocracy." And for Corradini the most plutocratic of European nations was democratic and Masonic France. This article was but a prelude to the campaign he and his followers unleashed at the party's congress in December, 1912, against democracy and Freemasonry, which they condemned as egalitarian, pacifist, and internationalist. This condemnation, though reducing the party's ranks because of the withdrawal of those who could not accept it, rendered it more homogeneous, as Corradini and Federzoni had wished. The latter, in addition, achieved in this way a personal success in his long campaign against the Masons. There were other gains from the action of the congress: it eliminated at least one barrier in securing support from conservative Catholics, to whom Freemasonry was an outrage, and it brought the Nationalists still closer to the revolutionary Socialists who, under Mussolini's guidance, had openly insisted on the expulsion of Masons from the party as early as 1910. Mussolini's hostility to Freemasonry was based essentially on the same arguments the Nationalists employed. Both nationalism and revolutionary socialism were in agreement in demanding the exclusive allegiance of all their followers and could not tolerate any sharing of loyalties, particularly with an organization that was too pacifist and democratic or too bourgeois.

The Nationalists, if not the Socialists, showed an immediate gain from their anti-Masonic stand. In the general elections of November, 1913, Federzoni and Luigi Medici del Vascello were elected deputies from Rome, the city where the Masonic issue was most intensely fought and whose mayor, Ernesto Nathan, grand master of Italian Freemasonry, resigned as a consequence of the defeat of the candidates he had supported. Six Nationalists entered parliament in 1913, and this success persuaded the party of the wisdom of its tactic in progressively disassociating itself from other political formations.

Having broken definitively with the democratic parties at the congresses of 1910 and 1912, the Nationalists moved toward the completion of their self-imposed political isolation by turning against the liberal or moderate groups in the country. Corradini prepared the way with a speech he delivered in a number of important cities in December, 1913. He analyzed the results of the general elections of the preceding month and concluded that they confirmed the decadence of the liberal parties, especially as led by Giolitti. This decadence was revealed by liberalism's failure to perform its historic role, which was to promote class solidarity at home and international greatness abroad. Consequently, reasoned Corradini, it was the duty of the Nationalists to do what the liberals had failed to do. In order to carry out their self-appointed role as sole redeemers of Italy on both the national and international scene, the Nationalists, assembled at the Milan congress of May, 1914, adopted a resolution obliging all members of the party to end their association with other parties, specifically the Liberals. The future official theorist of Fascism, Alfredo Rocco, registered a personal triumph by having the congress accept his views on the incompatibility of nationalism and liberalism in both political and economic doctrines, and the congress openly came out in favor of economic protectionism.

With their last prewar congress, the Nationalists completed the formulation of their basic doctrines that revealed how radically the movement differed from liberalism of the Right as well as of the Left and how much it had in common with the positions of the extreme Left. The successes of the extreme Left during the elections of 1913, and a victory of Mussolini's revolutionary wing at the Socialist congress of April, 1914, suggested that the country was moving away from Giolitti's moderate course and that his program of domesticating the extremists into constructive political forces had met with a serious setback.

PART FIVE

THE FIRST WORLD WAR AND THE
ADVENT OF FASCISM, 1914–1922

MAP 4
Political Italy after the First World War

XVII. A NATION DIVIDED: NEUTRALITY OR INTERVENTION, 1914–1915

The destructive effects of the First World War were destined wholly to undo the program of social reform and political stabilization that had animated the Giolittian era. Giolitti cannot be held entirely responsible for this undoing. In fact, he opposed strenuously Italy's intervention in the war precisely because he was convinced that the country could not undergo the shock of a major conflict without irreparable damage to its political and economic institutions.

But, unwittingly, Giolitti himself had facilitated Italy's eventual participation in the general European conflict by his decision to go to war with Turkey over Libya in 1911. He had not engaged in this war with a light heart. War and foreign adventures were alien to his nature, and it was only because he feared that the occasion offered by Turkey's domestic weakness and a favorable international situation might not occur again that he conquered his fears of aggravating Europe's international tensions and disrupting his domestic program. But the Libyan War and the subsequent prolonged campaign of pacifying the tribes in the conquered areas were not only a drain on Italy's resources and the cause of bitter domestic disputes, they also aggravated tensions in the Balkans. Encouraged by Turkey's defeat at the hands of Italy, a Balkan coalition of Bulgaria, Serbia, Greece, and Montenegro tried its hand at further dismemberment of the Turkish Empire in October 1912. The two Balkan wars that followed are intimately related to the outbreak of general war in 1914, and in this sense the war for Libya can be viewed as a factor contributing to the European war in which Giolitti sought desperately to keep Italy neutral. He failed in this endeavor; a principal reason for this failure derived from his weakened grip on domestic politics.

In fact, when general war broke out in Europe in 1914 Giolitti was not in power, even though the elections of 1913 had returned a sizable majority of Giolittian supporters. But this majority was made unstable owing to the restlessness of the Radicals, the most moderate or "domesticated" of the parties on the extreme Left and an important part of Giolitti's parliamentary coalition. One of the fixed positions in the ideology of the Radical party was devotion to the laic state and a thinly veiled anticlericalism. Rumors of Giolitti's collusion with Catholic electoral organizations gave strength to the arguments of those Radicals who were restless under Giolitti's tutelage. It was these disaffected Radicals who assumed control of the party at a congress held early in 1914, and when, on February 3, the congress approved a resolution calling on the three Radical Ministers in Giolitti's government to abandon their posts, it became clear that not only the Radical party but the whole governmental coalition was in a state of crisis. Early in March the Radical group in Parliament heeded the congress' injunction and disassociated itself from the government. Two days later, March 10, Giolitti's Ministry resigned in spite of the fact that it still commanded a majority in Parliament.

The almost universal explanation offered for this resignation was that Giolitti did not wish to face the mounting economic distress and labor agitation resulting from the strains of the Libyan War. Equally general was the feeling that Giolitti could and would return to office whenever he thought the moment opportune. This moment was not to come during the next six years, with the result that Italy went to war in 1915 contrary to the views of the man who remained the unquestioned leader of Parliament's majority.

This political anomaly and the fact that for nine months, between August 1914 and May 1915, Italy experienced an anguishing debate on whether to intervene in the war or remain neutral had the effect not only of dividing the country but also of pitting Giolitti and a majority in Parliament against a minority whose desire for war led it wittingly (or unwittingly) to discredit the whole of parliamentary institutions. If war were to come, it would have to come against the objections of Parliament's majority, and this triumph could be achieved only at the cost of insisting that at certain moments a minority or élite group understood the country's interests better than the majority of its elected representatives. Such reasoning was perfectly coherent when it came from the Nationalists, who had no confidence in parliamentary or majority rule; but when it came from men and parties previously and otherwise devoted to representative government, it meant that the issue of neutrality or intervention in the war ceased to be purely a question of foreign policy and became a determining factor in altering the country's political institutions.

The man who brought Italy into war on the side of the Entente powers in May 1915 was Antonio Salandra, a leader of the Right and a member of several governments from 1891 to 1910. He was more conservative than Sonnino, under whom he had served during the latter's two "Ministries of a hundred days" in 1906 and 1910. In fact, it was Sonnino's unwillingness to expose himself to a third fruitless try at leading Italy that led to Salandra's designation in March 1914 as Giolitti's successor. Giolitti himself recommended Salandra to the King, and unfriendly critics reasoned from this that Giolitti had deliberately chosen as his successor a man so weak in Parliament and so unlikely to gain the support of the extreme Left that he would remain in power only as long as Giolitti instructed his followers to support the new government. In substance, Salandra himself shared this view, and he too believed that Giolitti would return to power in not too long a time. But the outbreak of war in the summer of 1914 altered the prospects of these otherwise plausible predictions.

On August 3, 1914, Salandra's government announced that Italy would remain neutral in the general war unfolding in Europe. The substantive reasons for this decision were: Italy's deficient military preparation; concern with the aftereffects of serious anarchist, Republican, and revolutionary Socialist disturbances in central Italy during the "Red Week" in June 1914; and, above all, the feeling that the Italian people wanted peace and would not accept a war on the side of their nominal ally, Austria. The two technical reasons justifying Italy's refusal to participate in a war on the side of its allies in the Triple Alliance were: first, Austria had decided on war against Serbia without prior consultation with Italy, as required by Article VII of the Triple Alliance; second, Austria's declaration of war on Serbia and Germany's declaration of war on Russia and France freed Italy of its obligations to its allies, Article II of the Alliance being specific on the defensive nature of the Alliance.

The country and its leaders were almost unanimously in favor of the declaration of neutrality, and, given Giolitti's private and public approval of the government's stand, Salandra was politically safe in the course he adopted. But almost immediately the issue arose as to whether neutrality was to be a permanent course or simply a point of departure. Inasmuch as war on the side of Austria was viewed as unthinkable, the alternatives open to Italy were limited to continued neutrality or eventual intervention on the side of the Entente. For nine months the country engaged in a debate on whether to extract some territorial compensations from Austria as the price of Italy's continued neutrality or to side with the Entente for the sake of ideological preferences and the hope that at the end of a victorious war Italy could acquire its unredeemed lands and complete its unification. The leading protagonists of these alternative courses were Giolitti, in favor of compensated neutrality, and Salandra and Sonnino, who had little hope that Austria could be persuaded to cede the unredeemed lands to Italy and who, therefore, eventually chose to commit Italy to the Entente. But beside this purely territorial concern there was the fact that many interventionists, including Salandra, viewed Italy's participation in the war also through its effect on domestic politics. Salandra saw the war as the supreme opportunity to revitalize the "historical Right" which, having led the struggle for unification in the nineteenth century, would now have the honor and prestige of bringing this struggle to its completion. And inasmuch as Giolitti was the champion of continued neutrality, a successful war could not but undermine his sway over the country's political life. These and other considerations are adumbrated or made explicit in the excerpts reproduced below from the memoirs of the two protagonists.

49. SALANDRA STATES HIS CASE FOR INTERVENTION IN THE WAR

Antonio Salandra, *L'intervento* (1915): *Ricordi e pensieri*. Milan: A. Mondadori, 1930, pp. 15–18, *passim*. Our translation.

By the end of 1914 two currents of opinion had gradually formed and become pronounced in the country, which had received with almost unanimous favor the declaration of neutrality. * One current was for remaining indefinitely in the position of spectators in the enormous conflagration; the old alliance being broken in fact if not in law caused the other current to favor intervention as quickly as possible on the side [the Entente] that had become reputed to be the only one suitable to Italian sentiments and interests. . . . Those who spoke and wrote—that is, the active minorities which in every great country carry along with them the mentally inert majority—became divided between *interventionists* and *neutralists*. These two currents were nurtured by reasons, passions, recollections, and connections of varied nature, and in their ranks there met political groups that until then had been inspired by contrasting idealities. And so, Nationalists and Freemasons had fervently adopted the cause of intervention, whereas irreligious socialism joined with political Catholicism in propounding the cause of absolute neutrality.

It was the arduous but indeclinable duty of the government to consider the situation and the interests of the country with courageous serenity, to set a goal for itself, and to prepare the means for its realization. After the first battle of the Marne (September 1914) and after the Russian invasion of East Prussia was arrested at Tannenberg and the Masurian Lakes, both sides in the war were stripped of their illusions about a quick end to the conflict. Time was necessarily in favor of the Entente which, although much less prepared at the outbreak of war, was richer in men and means; but these had to be pre-

---

* Perhaps the only leading political figure who favored immediate intervention on the side of Austria and Germany was Sonnino. He adopted this position because of his belief in a rapid victory of the Central Powers and because he felt that Italy was bound to honor its obligations under the Triple Alliance. After the declaration of neutrality he gradually moved in the direction of intervention on the side of the Entente. Ed. note.

pared and brought into the field. Meanwhile, no one, not even the most tenacious neutralists dared maintain that, while the hurricane of war raged not far from its borders and agitated the seas surrounding it, Italy could remain idly at rest and disinterested in the development and outcome of the world conflict. Everyone understood that the war would lead to a profound change in international relations and that an historical crisis was developing in which we could not avoid becoming involved. This conviction naturally aroused the inner patriotic passion of the men in charge of the government, although it was our duty to master this passion and control its expression. We thought, we felt that perhaps never again for generations and centuries would the occasion arise for completing the task of the Risorgimento by acquiring those frontiers which nature had given to the Italian people and by establishing supremacy on our seas. Consequently, as I have shown,* we chose our perilous but inescapable path and we prepared to follow it. But although we [of the government] had committed ourselves to each other,† as long as was possible we abstained from committing ourselves with others because we could not exclude the possibility that unexpected events and new conditions might arise to modify the decisions we had reached. We had reached these decisions fully aware of their enormous gravity and without pretensions of infallibility. Therefore [by the end of 1914] we still retained full freedom of action while preparing for intervention, which we thought inevitable in the spring of 1915.

It was clear to Salandra and Sonnino that intervention in the war on the side of the Entente for the sake of acquiring the Italian-speaking territories in the Austrian Empire could be achieved only after the country had been reasonably persuaded that it was impossible to acquire these territories by negotiations with Austria. These negotiations were conducted by Sonnino between

---

* Reference to the first volume of Salandra's memoirs: *La neutralità italiana, 1914*. Milan: A. Mondadori, 1928. Ed. note.

† Reference to Salandra's statement in *La neutralità* that by the end of 1914 the Italian government, Salandra and Sonnino in particular, had decided on intervention on the side of the Entente. Sonnino had joined Salandra's government as Foreign Minister in November 1914, after the death the month before of Marquis Antonino Di San Giuliano, who had served as Foreign Minister under Giolitti (1911–14) and had agreed to retain this post under Salandra when he formed his government in March 1914. San Giuliano's presence in Salandra's Ministry was one of the reasons for Giolitti's confidence in the government's foreign policy during the first three months after the outbreak of the European war. His death marked the beginning of Giolitti's estrangement from the government. Ed. note.

December 1914 to April 1915 without any real confidence that Austria could be persuaded to make the requested territorial cessions. There were others, principally Giolitti and his parliamentary majority, who were convinced that a strong, well-intentioned government could bring these negotiations to a successful conclusion and thus spare Italy the horrors of war.

Technically, Italy's request for territorial cessions from Austria was based on Article VII of the Triple Alliance, which provided that if either Italy or Austria modified the *status quo* in the Balkans, the Ottoman coasts, and the islands in the Adriatic and Aegean seas by a temporary or permanent occupation, this occupation could take place only after an agreement between the two powers based on the principle of reciprocal compensation. Italy maintained that Article VII had been violated by Austria's action against Serbia without Italy's prior approval, and as early as July 25, 1914, San Giuliano raised the question of Austrian compensation to Italy. His negotiations had no outcome because Austria would recognize the principle only on condition that Italy observe its obligations to the Triple Alliance. On December 9, 1914, Sonnino resumed the suspended negotiations with Austria, which continued until April 1915, although by March it was clear that Italy's demand for immediate cession by Austria of the territories eventually agreed upon was an insurmountable obstacle to any agreement.

Article VII had served as the technical basis for Italian territorial demands. The substantive basis for the demands was simply that if Austria did not accede to Italy's requests, Italy would consider the Alliance dissolved and would resume its "full freedom of action." In brief, this meant that Italy could then commit itself to the Entente powers, if it so desired. Convinced that not even German pressure and the good offices of the German ambassador extraordinary to Italy, Prince Bernhard von Bülow, would ever induce Austria to accept Italy's demands, Salandra and Sonnino turned to the Entente and by April 26, 1915, reached an agreement known as the Pact or Treaty of London.

50. THE PACT OF LONDON, APRIL 26, 1915

R. Ministero degli affari esteri, *Trattati e convenzioni fra il Regno d'Italia e gli altri Stati.* Rome: Tipografia del R. Ministero degli affari esteri, 1930, XXIII, 284–92, *passim.* Our translation from the original French text.

Article 1. A military convention shall be concluded immediately between the General Staffs of France, Great Britain, Italy, and Russia. This convention shall fix the minimum of the military forces that Russia shall employ against Austria-Hungary in order to prevent the latter from concentrating all its efforts against Italy, in the event that Russia were to decide to devote its principal effort against Germany. . . .

Art. 2. On its part, Italy undertakes to employ the whole of its resources in the pursuit of the war jointly with France, Great Britain, and Russia against all their enemies.

Art. 3. The fleets of France and Great Britain shall give their active and permanent cooperation to Italy until the destruction of the Austro-Hungarian fleet or the conclusion of peace. . . .

Art. 4. In the treaty of peace Italy shall obtain the Trentino, the Cisalpine Tyrol with its geographical and natural frontier (the Brenner frontier), as well as Trieste, the counties of Gorizia and Gradisca, all of Istria up to the Quarnero and including Volosca and the Istrian islands of Cherso and Lussin, as well as the small islands of Plavnik, Unie, Canidole, Palazzuoli, San Pietro di Nembi, Asinello, Gruica, and the adjoining islets. . . .

Art. 5. Italy shall also receive the province of Dalmatia in its present administrative boundaries. . . .

Note. The Adriatic territories enumerated below shall be assigned by the four allied powers to Croatia, Serbia, or Montenegro.

In the Upper-Adriatic, all the coast from the bay of Volosca on the frontiers of Istria up to the northern frontier of Dalmatia, including the littoral which at present is Hungarian, and all the coast of Croatia, with the port of Fiume. . . .

Art. 6. Italy shall receive full sovereignty over Valona, the island of Saseno, and surrounding territory sufficiently extensive to assure the defense of these points. . . .

Art. 7. If Italy obtains the Trentino and Istria in accordance with the terms of Art. 4, also Dalmatia and the Adriatic islands within the limits specified in Art. 5, and the bay of Valona (Art. 6), and if the central part of Albania is reserved for the constitution of a small autonomous and neutralized state, it shall not oppose the partitioning of the northern and southern parts of Albania among Montenegro, Serbia, and Greece, should that be the wish of France, Great Britain, and Russia. . . .

Italy shall be charged with the representation of the Albanian state in the latter's foreign relations. . . .

Art. 8. Italy shall be acknowledged as possessing total sovereignty over the Dodecanese Islands it occupies at present.

Art. 9. France, Great Britain, and Russia recognize in general terms that Italy is interested in maintaining the balance of power in the Mediterranean and that in the case of total or partial partitioning of Asiatic Turkey it should obtain an equitable share in the Mediterranean region adjoining the province of Adalia. . . .

Art. 11. Italy shall receive a share of any eventual war indemnity corresponding to its efforts and sacrifices. . . .

Art. 13. France and Great Britain recognize in principle that, in the event they were to increase their colonial domains in Africa at the expense of Germany, Italy would be able to claim some equitable compensations, notably with regard to the regulation in its favor of questions concerning the frontiers of the Italian colonies of Eritrea, Somaliland, and Libya and adjoining French and British colonies.

Art. 14. Great Britain undertakes to assist in the immediate conclusion, under equitable conditions, of a loan of at least £50 million to be issued on the London market.

Art. 15. France, Great Britain, and Russia shall support such opposition as Italy may make to any proposal tending to an introduction of a representative of the Holy See in any negotiation for peace or for the resolution of questions raised by the present war.

Art. 16. The present arrangement shall remain secret. Italy's adherence to the declaration of September 5, 1914 [committing the Entente governments not to conclude a separate peace] shall alone be made public, immediately after the declaration of war by or against Italy. . . .

With regard to Articles 1, 2, and 3 of this memorandum which provide for military and naval cooperation among the four powers, Italy declares that it shall enter the field as soon as possible and no later than a month after the signature of these presents.

The signature of the Pact of London by the plenipotentiaries of the four contracting powers was climaxed by an exchange of telegrams among the various Heads of States, two between the King of Italy with President Poincaré of France and Czar Nicholas of Russia. Although the Pact has been judged not to belong in the category of treaties in the technical sense of the term, and therefore neither ratified by the constitutional organs of the countries where applicable nor undersigned by the Heads of States involved, it was recognized to be a binding commitment among governments and a moral commitment by the Heads of States as expressed in the exchange of telegrams. This moral commitment apparently played an important role in King

Victor Emmanuel's decision to retain Salandra in power in mid-May 1915, when the Giolittian majority in the Chamber rebelled at the prospect of entering the war.

Early in May rumors began to circulate in Italy that the government had renounced the Triple Alliance—as in fact it had on May 4—and that an agreement had been concluded with the Entente. Additional rumors to the effect that Germany had persuaded Austria to make new concessions to Italy for the sake of its continued neutrality all had the effect of intensifying the already bitter disputes between neutralists and interventionists. A test of strength between the two groups and their leaders was in the making. This test and its eventual outcome is described in the following excerpt from Salandra's memoirs.

51. "THE RADIANT DAYS OF MAY" *

Antonio Salandra, *L'intervento* (1915). Milan: A. Mondadori, 1930, pp. 220–25, 227, 229, 260–63, 265–71. Our translation.

The political groups prepared to support the government at the decisive moment were still the same. Their vigor and following had been increased by their innermost conviction of the war's inevitability, by propaganda which aroused national sentiment, as well as by aversion to ever more apparent foreign interference. But the traditional cadres of Italian politics were in large part upset by unexpected events, with the result that new and at times overwhelming forces were released. Furthermore, these cadres appeared distorted by the parliamentary environment in which they were accustomed to live and recognize each other. It is true that the Nationalists, a young group, remained firm and fervent at their battle stations. Their moment had come and they knew how to exploit it. The same can be said for interventionist groups on the other side of the political spectrum: the Reformist Socialists and the greater part of the Radicals, who belonged to Freemasonry. The same, also, for a group of even more remote origins—that of the dissidents from Official Socialism. This last group included persons actuated by either vigorous patriotic sentiments or high culture, or even by subversive ideas that had made them seem dangerous the year before. Now they were of substantial use as a small but bold and active group which, mixing with the masses, made

* The phrase "radiant days of May" was used frequently by the interventionists during the war and after to indicate their triumph in May 1915. Ed. note.

them seem divided and thus succeeded in producing a notable effect of agitation and intimidation.

Only of the Liberals, who constituted the largest political group and who had exhausted themselves and destroyed their unity by reason of having governed the state, alone, for so many years, could it not be said that they favored one side or the other. We of the government and our friends in Parliament and outside proclaimed ourselves Liberals, and such undoubtedly we were, at the moment of becoming the principal actors responsible for intervention. The groups of the Center and the most notable leaders of neutralism also called themselves Liberals. But, good God, allow me to write, after fifteen years, not as a participant in the events but as an historian, that the latter group did not feel or did not understand that all the reasons for their conduct, however sincere and valid, had to bow before the indelible tradition of Italian liberalism, which was the tradition of the Risorgimento. By breaking this tradition during the period of neutrality and, what is worse, by keeping it broken during and after the war, they deprived the already old trunk of liberalism of its most vital fluid. They were among those most responsible for its fall. But it is best not to tarry with regrets and to return to the calm of history.

The forces in the other camp, that of neutralism, were anything but contemptible. The imminence of the decision induced those of these forces which had remained latent to express themselves; it obliged them to act and to discard the caution imposed upon them by the less than popular cause they had to defend against an increasingly intense and fervent propaganda which penetrated, if not the most dense, certainly the most sensitive strata of Italian society. In spite of reports coming to me from a number of sources, I do not believe that there was a real neutralist plot. But those tendencies having a common end were known to each other and were not lacking in intermediaries. They established more intimate contacts and organized themselves —not in a formal fashion but, as a matter of fact, more by the force of circumstances than by the will of specific persons—around a center and a leader: the center, Parliament; the leader, the major parliamentary figure of the day, the Honorable Giolitti.

Nos numerus sumus: this could have been the claim of the Italian Socialists. Their numerical strength had been demonstrated in the

elections of 1913 and had certainly not diminished thereafter. But in the most solemn moments of history it is not numbers which decide or direct the destinies of people. As I have already said, the most elevated, cultivated, courageous, and active elements of the [Socialist] party had chosen the interventionist cause, but their number was not large. The organized mass of Socialists continued to adhere to the absolute neutrality proclaimed and constantly reaffirmed by its leaders.
. . .

Catholic opinion was against intervention, although this opinion was uncertain and badly defined in its effects. But let us be clear: when I say Catholics I do not mean the very great majority of Italians who observe the national religion but who are at the same time firm in their patriotic sentiments and in their political opinions, if they have any. I mean that minority which, although not huge, was growing and becoming notable by reason of social conditions and relations, and which for a long time although inactive had remained politically organized around the Vatican. For several years this minority had been organizing and operating with an autonomy from the supreme hierarchies that was necessarily imperfect, and it had introduced itself into the political arena and the daily press. These Catholics had never denied the fatherland or its aspirations, nor would they ever do so later. But at the outbreak of the war they had experienced an explosion of pro-Triple Alliance sentiment, occasioned more than anything else by their obsession with Freemasonry, which was active in the other camp. But they had quickly corrected themselves and adhered to neutrality without further ado, even acknowledging that some future eventuality might make it impossible to remain neutral. But they could not resign themselves to the actual triumph of interventionism and thus were drawn logically to [Giolitti's] formula of *parecchio*,* through which the nation's aspirations appeared reconcilable with the preservation of peace. When, during the last weeks, the struggle was joined between intervention and the *parecchio* thesis, [these Catho-

* On January 24, 1915, Giolitti wrote a letter to a friend in which he expressed the belief that *parecchio* (a little less than "much") could be obtained from Austria by way of negotiation and thus Italy could remain neutral in the war. Actually, Giolitti had written *molto* (much), not *parecchio*, but the latter word was substituted by the editor of the Roman newspaper *Tribuna*, in which the letter was printed on February 1. The letter soon became famous as a statement of Giolitti's *parecchio* thesis. Ed. note.

lics] were forced to withdraw their support from the government, with which until then they had maintained friendly contacts and relations. . . .

It would be contrary to truth to limit neutralist sentiments to Socialists and Catholics. On the contrary, great was the number of people who had not allowed themselves to be carried away by the feelings and reasons that had led the government to its final decision. It would not be honest to say without further ado that these people were not good Italians. They belonged neither to socialism nor to political Catholicism. If obliged to assume a political label, they would have called themselves Liberals. But they nevertheless recoiled from the long and arduous war because of one or more of the following reasons: an innate need of the quiet life; legitimate family reasons; prediction of enormous economic difficulties; excessive evaluation of the enemy forces we would have to challenge and scant confidence in our military and moral resources, accompanied by a low estimate of the soundness of our state and its institutions. . . .

Determined to prevent the government from taking the last steps to war, Italian neutralism was given active stimulus and aid by foreign elements. In the end these elements proved to be not the least of the reasons for its discredit and its less than honorable defeat.

The greater the pressure of time, the more Villa Malta [private residence of von Bülow in Rome] intensified its work and multiplied its contacts which, although cautious, could not remain concealed. The operations were directed by Prince von Bülow, a man not at all lacking in shrewdness and propriety but whose inescapable position led him to reveal himself and attract public attention. His Austrian colleague, Baron Macchio, was of little or no use to him. . . .

In reality these two men expected little from us [Salandra and Sonnino]. All their hopes rested on Giolitti who would force us either to continue our negotiations with Austria or to overthrow us, eliminating at least Sonnino, of whose *raideur* von Bülow much complained. Macchio had already expressed the opinion that Sonnino and I proposed either to present the Chamber with an accomplished fact or fall gloriously. Abandoning its earlier caution, even the Berlin and Vienna press appealed openly to Giolitti.

The hopes of the two embassies were strengthened by the appreciably heightened agitation among the Deputies. I received repeated notices of the evident neutralist insurrection in the Chamber. Interventionist countermanifestations were not lacking, as for instance that of the Reformist Socialists who had accused Giolitti of being "guilty of illicit interference and perfidious pressure on the responsible powers of government." Giolitti was irritated and broke his silence, protesting, by means of a letter to the *Tribuna*, against the intolerant attitude shown to an opinion he had expressed not of his own initiative but because he had been *called*. In fact, he had been called by the King on the evening of May 9 after his [Giolitti's] arrival in Rome, but contrary to what his followers would have the public believe he had not been invited to come to Rome. Nevertheless, it must be acknowledged that the great majority of the Deputies present in Rome was rallying around its old leader. There were more than 300 of them, an extraordinary number considering that the Chamber was closed, and their number was increasing every day. It was said at the time that on his advice a plan to convene an extra-legal meeting in the Chamber had been abandoned. Instead, the Giolittian chieftains, most of them former Ministers, organized a new kind of demonstration: they encouraged visits and the sending of letters and telegrams of support and, in order to avoid a crowd in his house, the deposit of visiting cards with the doorkeeper of his residence on Via Cavour. Every method of persuasion was employed. . . .

According to a probably incomplete account given me, 283 Deptuties thus demonstrated their support of Giolitti's position, without counting the Socialists who, although working apparently independently, worked in the same direction. . . . In any case, they constituted more than an absolute majority of the Chamber. . . .

The agitation in Rome became general and difficult to contain when, on the evening of the 12th Gabriele d'Annunzio arrived there after his triumph at Genoa and his speech at the Quarto.* In the meanwhile Genoa had become a hotbed of interventionism. He was met at the Rome station by an immense throng which according to newspaper accounts ranged from 60,000 to 100,000 persons. Certainly, there were many. This throng accompanied him in triumph to the Hotel Regina where he spoke to the people and celebrated the glory

---

* Site in Genoa where on May 5 d'Annunzio had delivered a speech commemorating Garibaldi's departure with his Thousand for the conquest of Sicily in 1860. Ed. note.

of Rome and the memory of the Thousand. He was not too aggressive in this first speech but he did say: "Today the anguish of all Italy is turned toward Rome where for three days the smell of treason begins once again to suffocate us." This allusion was understood and underscored far more than his magnificent historical recollections. . . .

I was consequently much concerned for the public order. Because of the small number of police available I could not contain the demonstrations, nor could I use the troops, who were being prepared for other purposes. Indeed, I did not want to suppress these demonstrations, because they served not so much to defend the government as to propagate in the country the feeling of coming events and prepare it for them. I did not forget that the war was being imposed upon us by overriding ideals and interests of which the masses in general were little aware. . . .

It was not possible to continue for long under such circumstances. The scheduled date for Parliament's reconvening—the 20th—was too distant. By the time this date was reached passions in the country would have been more aroused than ever, and unavoidable and deplorable acts and events would probably have occurred in the meanwhile. As far as I was concerned there was no question—as some advised—of submitting our decisions to the Chamber for its approval. After having received repeated votes of confidence, which had been interpreted by the public as granting full freedom of action to the government, we had made irrevocable decisions and these had been ratified by the Sovereign. Parliament had only to draw its conclusions. But, rallying around a leader, the majority of the Chamber gave proof that it disagreed with the government. Within eight days we would have to undertake a probably turbulent and dangerous debate, and no matter how it might end, it would have the effect of further agitating and weakening the country and embitter its dissensions precisely at a time when harmony was the uppermost consideration.

Besides, there were urgent considerations of international politics to keep in mind. . . . Sonnino wrote to me: "It is my impression that Barrère, Rodd, and Giers,* all feel that we are trying to make game of them or that, at least, we shall allow ourselves to be outplayed in the Chamber. . . . It is my impression that the Entente, aware of the agi-

---

* The three men mentioned were the French, British, and Russian ambassadors, respectively. Ed. note.

tation in Parliament, no longer has faith in us or, at least, no longer trusts our strength, and will therefore take some rash step to compromise the situation irreparably before the 20th or before our opponents [the neutralists] are able to change it." . . . .

Bissolati and I made an estimate of the probable vote in the Chamber. Bissolati was pessimistic: according to him no more than about 70 Deputies were sincerely in favor of war; at voting time the number might perhaps reach 150. Even the most optimistic estimates led to a slight majority in either direction, which meant a schism on such a great question, and one to be avoided at all costs.

Truly, it was an anguishing moment, but it was necessary to be resolved. There was no point in engaging in futile consultations and discussions. I passed a sleepless night considering various hypotheses and solutions, and I reached a conclusion which I did not communicate in advance either to the King or to my colleagues in the government. The next day, Thursday the 13th, I convened the Council of Ministers for the afternoon. We decided unanimously to resign and formulated the following explanation for our step: "In consideration of the fact that the government's course in international policy lacks the harmonious consent of the constitutional parties—a consent made necessary by the gravity of the situation—the Council of Ministers has decided to present its resignation to His Majesty." It was not difficult to persuade my colleagues in the government to take this step. Several of them were discouraged and perplexed. . . .

Our resignation and the explanation we gave for it placed the responsibility on the shoulders where it belonged, that is, on the Honorable Giolitti and his friends. I logically suggested to the King that he address himself first of all to Giolitti, leader of the majority. A French writer called me a "beau joueur." This praise is deserved only if by play is meant not a sleight of hand cunning but rather a clear appraisal of a situation and the decision to face it promptly and in time.

Salandra had indeed outplayed Giolitti. By placing the final decision in the hands of the King, Salandra surmounted the obstacle of a hostile majority in Parliament. The King was morally committed to the Pact of London and to war; and, according to a speech by Salandra in November 1918, rather than fall short of this commitment the King was prepared to abdicate. This prospect of a grave institutional crisis in time of war, and the probably violent reaction on the part of the more determined interventionists in the event the neutralists were to succeed in keeping Italy out of the war, weighed heavily in Giolitti's eventual conclusion that he had lost the game. The interventionists of the extreme Left, among whom Mussolini was prominent,[1] threatened "either war or revolution"; the interventionists of the extreme Right coined their own motto: "either war without or war within." When, on May 16, 1915, the King rejected Salandra's resignation, the newspaper expressing the views of the Nationalists announced triumphantly that "the King had saved Italy," thus making explicit the fact that it was the King's will which proved to be the insurmountable obstacle to Giolitti's cause of continued neutrality.

Giolitti's version of the events that led Italy to war is summarized in the following excerpts from his memoirs, published six to eight years before Salandra's two volumes on La neutralità and L'intervento.

52. GIOLITTI DEFENDS HIS STAND IN FAVOR OF NEGOTIATED NEUTRALITY

Giovanni Giolitti, Memoirs of My Life. Translated from the Italian by Edward Storer. London: Chapman, 1923, pp. 388–94, 396–401, passim.

Early in the autumn [1914] a campaign against me was started in the ministerial press. Among other things, it was alleged that the government had been forced to declare for neutrality owing to the unprepared state of the army and navy, for which my various governments were responsible, and that I had done nothing to replenish the military stores exhausted by the war in Libya.

The former of these accusations, which, despite its absurdity, was repeated in the Chamber, was easily disproved by Signor Tedesco, former minister of Finance, in a speech he made on December 4th, in which he cited figures that admitted of no discussion and stopped the mouths of my accusers. . . .

As regards the second accusation, namely, the failure to replenish military stores after the Libyan war, I at once wrote to Spingardi, who had been minister of War at the time and had already given assurances in this matter to parliament. Although Spingardi did not wish

---

[1] At the outbreak of war in 1914 Mussolini had favored absolute neutrality. But in October he changed his position to one of watchful neutrality, and when this new attitude was rejected by the party's leadership he resigned as editor of the leading Socialist newspaper Avanti! On November 15 he founded his own newspaper, Popolo d'Italia, and announced his stand openly in favor of war on the side of the Entente. Ten days later he was expelled from the Socialist party.

to engage in discussion at the time, he later—shortly before his death—asked to be heard by the committee of enquiry instituted by the government to ascertain the responsibilities for the Caporetto disaster. His detailed report of what was done after the Libyan war entirely refuted the unjust attacks referred to. . . .

These accusations having been disposed of, another attack from the same quarter was launched. This time it was a rumour that I intended to overthrow the ministry and to form another under my own premiership with a programme of absolute neutrality. Of this report I was informed by letters from friends (the latter including Peano, Malagodi and Colosimo). My reply to these letters was a declaration to the effect "that to oppose the ministry would be a reprehensible action, that the country would condemn such an attitude, and that it was desirable that the government should have full authority in such difficult times," adding that I was convinced that unless the European situation underwent a radical change, the government would not bring the country into a war which would entail such heavy sacrifices in human lives and national prosperity and which was not desired by the vast majority of the nation.

To put a stop to the campaign against me, I asked Peano to publish a letter I had written him in the *Tribuna,* which of its own accord had already protested against these accusations. The letter published is as follows:

Cavour, *January* 24, 1915

Dear Friend,

It is very strange with what ease legends are created, partly in good faith and partly in bad. There are now two taking shape: one concerns my alleged relations with Prince von Bülow, the other the opinion attributed to me that neutrality must be maintained at all costs.

I have known Prince von Bülow for many years and have a high appreciation of his talent and character; I have always found him to be a friend of Italy, although of course he thinks first of all of the interests of his own country, as is his duty.

When he was living in Rome as a private citizen, he used often to come to see me. Now that he has come to Rome as ambassador of his country, we have met casually in the Piazza Tritone, on which occasion he told me he was coming to see me. I replied that as I was at leisure I would come to see him, which I did the next day. Our conversation turned in a general way on the great events of the day, but I was careful to avoid discussing what Italy's attitude should be. To do so would have been a breach of duty on my

part, nor did Prince von Bülow, who has a scrupulous regard for the proprieties, raise this question.

A few days later he returned my call. As I was out, he left his card and I
have not seen him since, for I have left Rome.

Another fable is that of my being in favour of neutrality at all costs.

It is certainly true that, unlike the nationalists, I do not look on war as
desirable, but as a misfortune, which should only be incurred when the hon-
our and the vital interests of the country are at stake.

I do not think it justifiable to precipitate the country into war out of a
sentimental regard for other countries. A man can risk his own life for reasons of sentiment, but not that of his country. If it became necessary, I
should not hesitate to risk war, as I have already proved.

Given the actual conditions in Europe, it is my belief that much may be
obtained without going to war, but only those who are in the government
are fully qualified to judge of this matter.

As for the rumours of conspiracy and crisis, I refuse to give them any
credit. I have supported and continue to support the government and pay no
attention to the insolence of those who profess to be its friends and are, in
fact, its worst enemies.

Yours, etc.,
Giolitti

. . . . In March, when the Chamber re-opened, I returned to
Rome, where I found considerable agitation in political circles, partly
due to the insufficient aid given by the government on the occasion of
the recent earthquake. Many members openly displayed their distrust
of the government and their fear that it would allow the country to be
drawn into war, while not a few of my political friends were in favour
of provoking a crisis. I was not, however, of their opinion, for I knew
that negotiations between the government and Austria were under
way and thought that they should in no way be impeded, being confident that the government would not fail to obtain the greatest concessions possible from Austria and avoid the risk of war. Having convinced my friends, I also endeavoured to persuade those who were
clamouring for war—and who assured me in private conversations in
the Chamber that the war would not last long—of the enormous difficulties and sacrifices which such action would entail. I remember telling them that I was convinced the war was only just beginning and
that there was no hurry.

It was the government's intention to ask for a vote of confidence,
with full liberty of action in regard to the negotiations with Austria,

which were now no longer a secret. A few days before this vote and
the Easter vacation, Salandra came to call on me as he was anxious to
confer with me. He confirmed the report that the government was negotiating with Austria, without, however, entering into details. I told
him that I hoped parliament would give him the means for bringing
pressure on Austria so as to obtain the maximum of concessions. This
conversation further persuaded me of the necessity of letting the government have a free hand and that there was no cause to be alarmed
at the military measures which were being taken, as these were above
all calculated to convince Austria of the necessity of making serious
concessions. In other words, my talk with Salandra satisfied me that
the government did not intend to enter the war, but rather to persuade Austria by every means possible that she could no longer defer
satisfying Italy's just demands, in accordance with Art. VII of the
treaty of the Triple Alliance and the special conventions regarding the
Balkans; nor did I make any concealment of this opinion to my
friends.

There is therefore no ground for the attempted contrast between
my policy of neutrality and so-called concessions, and that of the government, as is also proved by the Green Book, which shows how our
government negotiated for a long while with Austria in order to obtain concessions, being aided therein by Germany, and how up to the
end our claims were moderate (*i.e.*, so framed as to be acceptable).
Even the incorporation of Trieste in the Kingdom of Italy was not insisted upon, despite the justice of this claim. The failure of these negotiations must certainly be ascribed to Austria, which rejected the
moderate and just claims of the Italian government until, apparently,
it was too late.

After my interview with Salandra I spoke to all my friends who
were still hesitating to vote for the government; for a ministerial crisis
at that moment meant for me one of two alternatives: either we
should have a pro-war government, which I could not approve, or one
which was too obviously set on neutrality, in which case Austria
would not make the concessions necessary to avoid war. My friends
were persuaded by my arguments and the government obtained the
vote of confidence which it needed in order to have its hands
free. . . .

In the beginning of May I received other letters from friends in

Rome informing me that there were now certain indications of the government's having decided for war. But up to the last I was in no way informed of the government having given pledges or even negotiated in this sense, and when I left Turin for Rome it was merely to attend the opening of the Chamber and to see for myself what was taking place. On leaving Turin the first attempt at intimidation occurred, having evidently been prearranged: a group of young men began to hoot me and were turned away by my friends. In Rome there were repetitions on a larger scale. At the station I was warned that a crowd of nationalists was waiting to make a hostile demonstration against me, and I was advised to leave by private exit. This I refused to do, declaring that I would go out by the usual way and that if there were to be a demonstration, it was just as well I should see it. A group of demonstrators was, in fact, waiting for me and accompanied me and my friends to my house, hooting and shouting "Abbasso!" Having reached my door, I turned and said to them: "Just for once shout *Viva l'Italia!*"

In the course of the day and the next morning I received more than three hundred cards and letters from members of parliament declaring themselves in agreement with the view I had always openly maintained, namely, that we should not enter the war; there were also many letters and cards from senators. This demonstration of sympathy showed what were the views of the majority of parliament. These deputies and senators were later accused of factious behaviour and of having attempted to take upon themselves the prerogatives of the Crown, with which, according to the Constitution, rests the decision for war or peace. In this connection, I may recall that when Germany declared war on France, Asquith, after having called a cabinet meeting, sent for the French ambassador and made a declaration more or less as follows: "The British government has decided to intervene in the war on the side of France; but while I think it my duty to inform you without delay of this decision, I must remind you that it only becomes effective after the approval of parliament."

Our Constitution has this resemblance to that of Great Britain; that with both nations the decision to make war rests with the Crown, but such decision is of no effect until parliament has voted the necessary credits, which is its prerogative to do. On the morning of the 7th * I re-

---

* Giolitti is in error on this date and several other dates mentioned below. In his memoirs he does not specify the date of his arrival in Rome, which was, in fact,

ceived a card from Carcano, then minister of the Treasury, telling me that he wished to speak with me during the day. I fixed an appointment with him for 4.30 the next day, because in the afternoon I was going to Frascati, where my wife was, and where I intended to stay until the following afternoon. Carcano kept the appointment and we had a long conversation, during which he broadly expounded to me the reasons for which the government deemed it necessary to enter the war. I, however, opposed his arguments at some length, showing him all the dangers which Italy would encounter thereby. Carcano showed some emotion at my words and tears came into his eyes, but he concluded that now the decision of the government to enter the war was definite. He, however, said nothing more, nor even mentioned a treaty which had already been signed, and I understood his silence on this point only some years afterwards, when, the Pact of London having been published by the Bolshevists, I saw that there was in it the formal engagement to keep it secret. Before his silence was explained by this reason, there had even arisen a doubt in my mind that he had known of its existence, because there had been such intimacy between us from the time when he had been my Under-Secretary in 1893, that without an obligation of secrecy I should not have understood why he had not spoken of it to me more openly and confided in me, knowing that he could reckon fully on my silence.

I then received an invitation to visit His Majesty the King, whom I saw on the morning of the next day and to whom I explained all my reasons for opposing war; but in that conversation also, the obligation of secrecy, agreed to in the treaty, prevented my being informed. Later, towards midday, Bertolini who had already informed me of the offers made by Austria with the guarantee of Germany (widely discussed in Italian circles by the Germany deputy, Tozberger, and more or less satisfying Italy's demands, as proved by the publication of the Green Book) came to tell me that Salandra wished to see me. I replied that there was no difficulty. As Salandra, on the last occasion of our meeting, had come to my house, I proposed this time to go to his, and called on him at four o'clock the same day. Salandra told me that he knew of my conversation with the King; I repeated to him my reasons for believing that Italy would commit an error in entering the

---

May 9. His meeting with Carcano occurred not on the 8th but the 9th, and his consultations with the King and Salandra took place on the 10th, not the 9th. Ed. note.

war under present conditions. (I need only repeat that at that time no one imagined that the United States would ever intervene.)

Salandra replied that the government had already decided for war; that it was impossible for him to turn back, and that if he was prevented by parliament from declaring war he would have to resign. He had been informed of the number of deputies who adhered to my point of view and thence deduced the possibility of an adverse vote. Had it not been for Salandra's reticence regarding the existence of the Pact of London, our conversation would have taken another turn. It is evident that the obligation of secrecy prevented him from informing me fully how matters stood. Afterwards I learnt that the government had another very special reason for maintaining absolute secrecy. The second article of the pact, in fact, runs thus:

"Italy on her part engages to wage war with all the means at her disposition in agreement with France, Great Britain and Russia, *against the States which are at war with them.*"

The war, according to the last article, should commence before May 26th. By virtue of this agreement, Italy was to declare war simultaneously against Austria and Germany, whereas the ministry of that period had merely alluded to war with Austria for the liberation of the unredeemed territory. Neither parliament nor the country knew, any more than I did, that we were to fight Germany, nor was war actually declared on that country while the Salandra ministry remained in office. This failure to comply fully with the terms of the pact accounts for the diffidence of the allied countries towards Italy, which ceased only when, more than a year afterwards, the Boselli ministry declared war against Germany. All this explains why no one spoke to me in May, 1915, of the Pact of London.

But to return to the chronology of events. Salandra, evidently appreciating the difficulties of the situation, on the morrow, May 11th,* presented his resignation. I was again sent for by the King for the usual consultations during a ministerial crisis. Ignoring † the formal engagements which Italy had assumed towards the powers of the Entente, I expressed the opinion that a man who was considered averse to Italy entering the war could not accept the responsibility of the

---

* Salandra's government resigned on the 13th, not the 11th. Ed. note.

† The word "ignoring" may be misleading. The original reads "Sempre nell'ignoranza," which would be better translated as "Still ignorant of." Ed. note.

government and I suggested the names of Marcora or Carcano, both being known as men who, in case of necessity, would declare for war. Marcora, after having conferred with the King, wrote that he desired to see me, which he did on the 14th, telling me that he also was convinced of the necessity for entering the war at once. Carcano I did not see again.

The next day * the King declined Salandra's resignation and I, considering my task at an end, departed for Cavour on the 17th. Throughout my stay in Rome, in the interval between the resignation and reconfirmation of the Salandra ministry, demonstrations and meetings took place in the city, directed against me in particular and against the parliament, without the police intervening, however unruly these manifestations became. I remember that at a meeting held at the Costanzi Theatre, close to my house, D'Annunzio incited the mob to kill me, and the crowd, rushing from the theatre, made for my house. The police allowed them to pass, but a squadron of cavalry and a platoon of "carabinieri" stopped them and prevented them from reaching me. The following evening, in view of fresh menace, there was a great display of police forces blocking all the streets which led to the Piazza Esquilino.

In those days I received a great number of anonymous letters from all parts of the country, enough to fill the wastepaper basket twice over. The most curious and characteristic fact about these anonymous letters, coming as they did from places so remote as Venice, Sardinia, Tuscany and Sicily, was that they all formulated the same accusation, namely, that I had taken twenty millions from Austria and Germany in order to try and prevent the war. Some of the anonymous writers, finding, perhaps, the figures too modest, had doubled them. This strange reiteration of the same fantastic and scurrilous accusation was a comfort to me in those troubled days, because I understood that it was not the spontaneous and reasoned expression of the opinion of my fellow citizens, but a campaign organised by the interested advocates of the policy of war at any price.

I retired to Cavour, and as after a declaration of war every citizen, whatever his opinions, is in duty bound to do his utmost to ensure victory, from that day I refrained from all utterances which might cause annoyance or disturb peace at home, this being the first essential in a

* The King declined Salandra's resignation on the 16th, not the 15th. Ed. note.

country at war. For this same reason I ignored all insults, even the most absurd calumnies published by newspapers which sowed discord in the name of patriotism. It was evident that various persons were seeking to exploit the situation for purposes of internal politics, and several of them, posing as "super-patriots," and accusing others, were in reality working for disintegration.

XVIII. THE WAR YEARS, 1915–1919

The interventionist coalition that brought Italy into war began to disintegrate soon after Italy formally entered the hostilities on May 24, 1915, just two days before the one-month limit fixed by the Pact of London of April 26. The heterogeneous interventionist camp had been held together by the one and only goal all interventionists shared: war. But even this goal had not been altogether fulfilled by the declaration of May 24. On that day Italy entered into war only against Austria-Hungary and not against Germany. This step was not only a violation of Article 2 of the Pact of London, it was also a source of discontent for those interventionists who viewed "militarist and autocratic Germany" as the principal antagonist. And so, virtually from the first day of war there began a serious division between Salandra's government—preeminently of the Right—and the democratic interventionists on the aims of the war and the proper means for their realization. Considering that the interventionist coalition consisted of men and parties ranging from the extreme Left to the extreme Right, and in the light of Salandra's determination to keep the conduct of the war essentially in his hands and those of Sonnino at the Foreign Ministry, it was virtually inevitable that so long as Salandra insisted in this intent he would have to face the growing discontent of the democratic interventionists. Had the war ended as quickly as Salandra apparently expected in April 1915, his problems would not have been acute. But by the end of 1915 it became obvious that Giolitti's predictions of a long war were to be borne out. Salandra then proceeded to increase the disaffection of the democratic interventionists by asserting in February 1916 that the credit for initiating and completing Italy's unification belonged to the "monarchist Liberal party." And when, late in May an Austrian offensive in the Trentino threatened to lead to a general Italian withdrawal, Salandra found himself at odds with the Italian Army Chief of Staff, General Luigi Cadorna, at a time when most of the interventionist coalition showed signs of abandoning the government. On June 10, 1916, Salandra was rebuffed in a vote of confidence by a coalition of disaffected interventionists and former neutralists. Two days later he informed the Chamber of his government's resignation and thus left office, never again to return to power.

The document below provides the background to Salandra's fall from power. It is one of capital importance, especially notable for Salandra's frankness in describing the reasons for the political crisis of June 1916.

53. THE CRISIS OF 1916: SALANDRA'S CONFIDENTIAL REPORT TO THE KING, JULY 15, 1916

> Antonio Salandra, *Memorie politiche, 1916–1925.* Giuseppe Salandra, ed. Milan: Garzanti, 1951, pp. 1–11, *passim.* Our translation.

Sire,

I take the liberty of enclosing several notes to whose reading Your Majesty may devote, without urgency, some half hour on a rainy day.

Their aim is to explain, if not to justify, the policy I have followed during these latter times. Inasmuch as I have prepared only one copy, and that for Your Majesty, I speak therein without reticence with regard both to men and events. . . .

The person for whom these notes are intended knows of the subsequent events [after Italy's declaration of neutrality on August 3, 1914] and the reasons for them. Parliamentarism and domestic politics were overwhelmed and dominated by international politics, and from this there followed the miserable failure of the Giolittian attempt at resurgence in May 1915. The whole of the Chamber, except for the Socialists called *Official,* and the Senate unanimously, voted for the war and for the government which had committed itself to declare it, although several days before at least two thirds of the Chamber and three quarters of the Senate had been in favor of the so-called Giolittian *parecchio* thesis.

The protracted duration of the war beyond the most pessimistic predictions and the new and grave financial and economic problems deriving from it did not shake the country's calm. Gradually the country became persuaded of the necessity of its participation in the conflict. In the spring of 1915 this participation had been understood and willed by an active and bold but very small minority which the government could easily have contained were it not for the fact that the government itself was convinced of the inevitable necessity of our participation. But with the passing of time the ties which bound the Chamber to the government—ties which had been more apparent and transient than real and lasting—weakened and finally broke. The government had made some progress in the Chamber and had rallied around itself a considerable number of firm friends, but it was quite far from having the kind of large majority that the times required. In the meanwhile, the government's policies and practices drew ever-growing criticism, in part justified, and two different and largely contrasting currents of opinion converged and undermined the government's efforts:

1) those who had opposed the war and who had only apparently become resigned to it: Official Socialists; Giolittians; and some conservatives who either because of snobbism, fear, material interests, or pettiness of spirit, remained obstinate in their view that our salvation lay only in Italy's subjection to Germany

2) those who had ardently wanted war and who would not admit that it be conducted without their preponderant participation in the government: Reformist or Independent Socialists; militant Freemasons (the Democratic Left); Nationalists; and the Radicals, although in May 1915 a large part of this last group and all its leaders except Pantano favored continued negotiations with Austria.

It was easy for both groups to find reasons or pretexts for opposing the government: the inevitable curtailment of freedom in a state of war (press censorship and internment of suspects); the inadequacy of measures intended to prevent increases in the price of several items of prime necessity (grain, coal); even the deficiencies, in the military establishment and the supply of munitions, which were inevitable since nearly everything had had to be improvised with an effort that has a marvelous quality about it; and finally, no matter how hidden, there was the disenchantment with military successes apparently inferior to expectations.

And so, discontent grew and became organized, and from March [1916] onward there appeared the threat of a ministerial crisis.

The President of the Council could have averted it by causing one himself and by refashioning the Ministry with the inclusion of a large number of *interventionists,* until then excluded from the government. He chose not to do this for a number of reasons. Some of them are subjective in nature, above all the quality and defects of his temperament; others are objective and derive from his way of seeing the real interests of the country and the duties of the government.

The Honorable Salandra found it repugnant to submit to what seemed to him to be an imposition on the part of the interventionist groups. For more than a year he had maintained good relations with them in order to make use of them in the interest of the country, not to be used by them. He found it equally repugnant to be separated from such colleagues as Martini, Cavasola, Ciuffelli * and others. These men had collaborated with him faithfully and usefully for two years, and he held them to be superior to those with whom he would have to replace them. Besides, the Honorable Salandra thought that the government's strength would not be increased by multiplying the number of its component Ministers and by allowing the introduction of parliamentary democracy into the government itself. He saw how much more organic and energetic was the conduct of the war on the part of the Central Powers, directed as they were by a few superior wills, than that of the mammoth-size governments in France and England. Finally, he held (and this was for him the decisive reason) that the so-called democratic parties in Italy, dominated as they were by international Freemasonry, would be induced more or less voluntarily but inevitably to yoke the Italian monarchy to the cart of the French republic, substituting one hegemony for another, and that therefore a truly *Italian* government must be of a kind able to resist also the dangers of the new alliance.

Because of these reasons and others of secondary importance, this past March the Honorable Salandra faced the parliamentary storm with resolution, without giving in an inch and without promising anything. But owing above all to the obvious approval the Ministry found in the country and because of the country's manifest disapproval of mere parliamentary intrigues and ambitions, its opponents and other malcontents did not dare vote against it. But everyone understood that the critical situation of March would repeat itself in an even more bitter form when Parliament would be reconvened on June 6. . . .

It is a fact that after the first days of the Austrian advance in the province of Vicenza the Honorable Salandra became convinced that a situation was developing that required a government which, unlike his, was not forced to fight for its very existence every time the Cham-

* Ferdinando Martini, Minister of Colonies; Giannetto Cavasola, Minister of Agriculture, Industry, and Commerce; Augusto Ciuffelli, Minister of Public Works. All three were excluded from the Boselli government which succeeded Salandra in June 1916. Ed. note.

ber was in session. Consequently he sent a telegram to the Honorable Bissolati (who in March had been elected leader of the "Democratic Alliance" and then had gone to join his unit at the front) asking him to come to Rome. The Honorable Bissolati came and saw the Honorable Salandra, who explained the need that he and some friend of his enter the government, which was to be enlarged. Bissolati appeared disinclined to do so. He observed quite rightly that a crisis prompted by the government itself would increase the alarm already prevalent in the country. He showed little willingness to become a Minister and let it be understood that the position of Salandra's government was perhaps already too compromised and that consequently it might not be convenient to waste new forces for its sake. He concluded by neither accepting nor rejecting the offer and asked to be allowed to go to the combat area to acquire a clear idea of the military situation. He said that he would return soon and see Salandra again. And thus things went. Bissolati went to the front; he witnessed the stubborn but very bloody resistance of the grenadiers at the battle of Mount Cengio; he saw several generals; and he returned encouraged but not free of grave preoccupations. He saw the Honorable Salandra once again and said that he was ready in principle to enter the government as an act of patriotic duty, on condition of an agreement on how to bring about the crisis—better inside the Chamber than outside of it—and on the question of how many new Ministers to bring into the government, their names, and their attributes. Bissolati did not hide his fear that his friends might make too many demands.

Toward the end of May the Supreme Commander [General Luigi Cadorna], upon request of the President of the Council, sent a brief report on the military situation which concluded with the possibility that the army might have to be withdrawn behind the Piave River in the event a report received by the Supreme Command of the arrival of six new Austrian divisions on the Italian front were verified. This possibility, raised as an eventual military necessity to be decided upon by the Supreme Command, was of profound concern to the Council of Ministers.* The Council prayed its president to go without delay to General Headquarters and inform His Majesty the King and the Supreme Command of the enormous gravity of the decision in question

---

* Such a withdrawal would have meant abandoning to the Austrians the whole or part of five Italian provinces in the northeast corner of the country. Ed. note.

with regard to both domestic and international policy; and that, consequently, this decision could not be left to the exclusive judgment of the Supreme Command without the express concurrence of the government.

Consequently, the President of the Council had to leave Rome immediately after his latest conversation with the Honorable Bissolati. He discharged his very painful task, which had become less difficult by reason of an improvement in the military situation, and he returned to Rome early in June, nearly on the eve of Parliament's reconvocation.

On his return the Honorable Salandra immediately perceived that the government's position had worsened rapidly. Taking advantage of the profound concern widespread in the country—and even more in the political circles of the capital—because of recent military events, the government's many open and covert opponents took heart. They no longer feared that the country would react against them and worked speedily for an agreement to overthrow the Ministry immediately. Forgetful of their hatreds, *interventionists* and *neutralists* saw a common ground in a national Ministry. Such a Ministry would make it possible for the first group to satisfy its by now irresistible and perhaps justified desire to participate in the government. On the other hand, by infiltrating itself even in a modest fashion in the new Ministry, the second group would be able to avert the danger of entrusting an even longer electoral preparation to the Honorable Salandra.* The latter had held firm against the *Official Socialists*, checking their overbearing mastery in the numerous local administrations which they had conquered and employed as instruments for new and greater conquests. He had also held firm against the Giolittians, whom he had deprived of the control of the prefectures, on which their electoral strength was based.

These last considerations bear out completely what has been acknowledged almost ingenuously by Senator Rolando Ricci—a man very expert in the backstage aspects of political intrigue on a grand scale—in an article published in the *Tribuna* of July 9 (n. 189), and

---

* This is apparently a reference to the prospect that if the war were to end with Salandra still in office, presumably he would be able to "make" the subsequent elections to the detriment of his neutralist opponents. Ed. note.

that is that the crisis was determined above all by reasons of domestic politics.

In the light of the much worsened situation, the Honorables Salandra and Bissolati did not seek each other out and did not meet again. The Honorable Bissolati certainly knew that by means of skillful and impartial intermediaries agreements were being concluded between his friends and the neutralist groups in the Chamber. He probably did not instigate these agreements, but he neither wanted nor knew how to prevent them. The Honorable Salandra thought that at that time it was not possible usefully to resume negotiations without surrendering unconditionally to the *Democratic Alliance*. The latter would have raised its demands, and because of his temperament and his political views the Honorable Salandra would certainly have not accepted them except in a limited way.

In the meanwhile, the Chamber was convened on June 6 and with clear signs quickly revealed its hostility toward the government. This hostility was directed by several groups particularly against the President of the Council, whom the Official Socialists sought to assail personally and by mandate from the more vehment Giolittians. There took place the conspiracy of blackballing the budgets, especially the budget of the Ministry of the Interior.° After this obscure but significant vote which, however, had not put the government in the minority, the Honorable Salandra could have resigned sure, or nearly so, that the Crown would have given him the mandate to refashion the Ministry. Although urged on by many friends and by several opponents of good faith (especially interventionist Radicals and Reformists), after mature although rapid reflection he decided not to adopt this course, and not only or principally because of disdain. He well knew that in the actual moment of history disdain, even if justified, must give way before the interests of the country. After having pondered over the pro and the contra it seemed to him that he would serve the interests of the country better by withdrawing from the government after an open vote in the Chamber. The reasons which led him to this conclusion are the following:

° This Ministry was held personally by Salandra. The largest number of adverse votes was cast against the budget for the Interior: 120 out of 311 members present and voting. Ed. note.

1) A reduced confidence in his own powers: the long and uninterrupted labors in a state of high tension had diminished his nervous energy and above all his power of self-control. . . .

2) Difficult relations with the Deputies, deriving in part from a certain roughness in his temperament, too different from established parliamentary customs, and in part heightened by frequently and necessarily sharp relations and frictions of two years of power. Besides, it was impossible to achieve a full reconciliation with the neutralist groups, which had not forgiven him for the war, and with the so-called Giolittians, who were dominated by electoral concerns. . . .

3) Difficulties of a certain gravity which arose on a number of occasions in the relations between the President of the Council and General Cadorna. Although these difficulties were smoothed over by the beneficent intervention of a most high person, given the temperament of General Cadorna, who does not forget, and that of the Honorable Salandra, who does not renounce the exercise of his official attributes, it was predictable that these difficulties would be renewed, resulting in the reduction of their already much-shaken mutual confidence. But it is indispensable that this mutual confidence between the head of the government and the head of the army remain intact; it is therefore opportune that General Cadorna live with a head of the government more tractable than the Honorable Salandra.

4) In the light of the irreconcilability of one group [neutralists] and the excessive demands of the other [interventionists], the probable failure of the attempt to refashion the Ministry, with no advantage to the country deriving from the reduction of the Honorable Salandra's personal prestige. . . .

Because of these considerations and others of lesser importance, and perhaps also because of an invincible feeling of annoyance with the parliamentaristic agitation profiting from the unfavorable military situation, the Honorable Salandra chose to face certain defeat in an open vote. Indeed, he hastened it for the sake of cutting short the period of latent crisis and agreed to waive a debate that could have had no result other than to embitter the scene. He deliberately refused to employ any of those expedients suggested to him for the sake of prolonging the life of a weak government. He preferred instead to offer an example of uprightness rather than of petty cleverness.

And thus came the crisis of June 10. Foreseeing it for some time, the Honorable Salandra had prepared for it, as was his duty, the best possible solution by putting forward the name of the Honorable Boselli.

There remains only the doubt that the Honorable Salandra might perhaps have better provided not for himself—this is the least of considerations—but for the interests of the country by undertaking at a more opportune time and with greater desire for success that widening of his Ministry which would have satisfied the best among those who brought about the crisis of June 10. But the reasons which prevailed over his weak desires to refashion the government have already been noted.

The doubt expressed in the last paragraph of this extraordinary document probably stems from the fact that Paolo Boselli, Salandra's successor, found it necessary to include in his "National Union" government a number of men whom Salandra would not consider among the "best." In fact, every party in the Chamber other than the Official Socialist found a place in the new government, and even the Giolittians had an "unofficial" representative in Gaspare Colosimo at the Ministry of Colonies. But the experiences of Boselli's government seem to bear out Salandra's fears of "mammoth-size" Ministries. By including all the parties save one, Boselli achieved not national unity but, instead, a faithful reflection of national disunity. Nor was Boselli's government any more fortunate than Salandra's in its relations with the Supreme Commander. General Cadorna apparently wanted to determine not only the country's military strategy but its domestic politics as well. Just as he maintained a truly iron discipline at the fighting front, he wanted the government to adopt a similar approach on the "home front." Cadorna was especially concerned with the policies of the Minister of the Interior, Vittorio Emanuele Orlando, who had been on cordial terms with both the Giolittians and the Official Socialists before the war and two of whose chief subordinates had even more intimate ties with one or the other of these "neutralist" groups. Increasingly, some of the more intense interventionists called for a military dictatorship to curb the alleged defeatism of the former neutralists and drew unfavorable comparisons between the discipline of the Supreme Commander and the laxity of the Minister of the Interior.

Another source of division among the interventionists and, therefore, within Boselli's government, centered on Sonnino, who remained at the Foreign Ministry. Sonnino was known to view the war in terms of balance of power and national interests, and not as a struggle of ideologies or ways of life. This Sonninian conception was enshrined in the Pact of London, the official statement of Italy's war aims. On the other hand, the democratic interventionists following Bissolati's leadership insisted on the reality of the ideological struggle; and although they were not indifferent to what they considered Italy's just territorial aspirations, they thought the Pact of London too narrow a statement of Italy's war and peace aims. Accepting the principle of self-determination of nationalities, the democratic interventionists were troubled by the clear inconsistency between this principle and the territorial provisions of the Pact of London. The Pact remained secret until made public by the Soviet Russian government toward the end of 1917. Its general outlines, however, were well known enough in Italy to make it obvious that assigning Dalmatia to Italy would mean not only a violation of the principle in question but also difficult relations with the Yugoslav state which would probably issue from the eventual dismemberment of the Austrian Empire.

All the aforementioned divisions, added to immense casualties, economic privations, and growing pacifist sentiment, undermined the prestige of Boselli's government, whose fall became imminent in mid-October 1917. A rallying of Giolittian forces assured the succession to Orlando, who, twenty-two years younger than the seventy-nine-year-old Boselli, promised more vigor in the conduct of the war and greater capacity in reconciling the contrasting groups in Parliament. But at the end of October, precisely when Orlando received the mandate to form a new government, Italy began to reel under the blows of an Austro-German offensive that for a month threatened to drive it out of the war.

54. THE DISASTER OF CAPORETTO

The military disaster which goes by the name of Caporetto began on October 24, 1917, when 37 Austro-German divisions were committed to assault an area of the Julian Alps defended by the Second Italian Army 25 divisions strong. Within two weeks Italian forces withdrew from the whole or part of five Italian provinces in the northeast and suffered losses of 10,000 dead, 30,000 wounded, 293,000 prisoners, and 350,000 missing. Equally staggering losses were incurred in military equipment. There was talk of a separate peace and of Victor Emmanuel's possible abdication. Bissolati wrote in his diary that Italy's very existence was at stake. The tone for these disastrous preoccupations had been set by General Cadorna's military bulletin of October 28: "Lack of resistance on the part of units of the Second Army—cowardly retreating without fighting and ignominiously surrendering to the enemy—has allowed the Austro-German forces to break our left flank on the Julian front." But an heroic Italian defense on the right bank of the Piave River contained the enemy attack, and by the end of December the military crisis was over. The rallying of all political parties to the nation's defense, Cadorna's replacement by General Armando Diaz, and the arrival of Allied reenforcements, all contributed to the successful defense of the Piave. Once the military peril was overcome, there began a search for those responsible for the disaster. This search was entrusted officially to a Commission of Inquiry; a portion of their conclusions is presented below.

The Commission of Inquiry on Military and Political Responsibilities

> *Relazione della Commissione d'inchiesta sugli avvenimenti che hanno determinato il ripiegamento del nostro esercito sul Piave: Dall'Isonzo al Piave, 24 ottobre–9 novembre 1917.* 3 vols. Rome: Stabilimento poligrafico dello Stato, 1919, II, 551–56. Our translation.

CONCLUSIONS

593. The events of October–November 1917 that led to the withdrawal of the Italian army from beyond the Isonzo River to behind the Piave River *have the character of a military defeat.* The determining causes of a military nature, both of technique and of morale, certainly predominated over those other factors, alien to the armed forces, whose alleged influence this report has shown to be exaggerated. Some persons have attempted to deduce from the influence of these other factors that the events in question are to be attributed largely to political causes.

In addition to local and chance causes, the defeat derived also from the confluence of complex factors of a military nature which had been acting upon the army for some time and which, because of exceptional contingencies, were able to exercise a most effective influence, demoralizing the army and destroying its very cohesion.

594. Among those *causes which are judged to have been beyond human control* [forza maggiore], whose presence and influence have been ascertained with certainty by the Commission and which mitigate personal responsibilities, are the following:

The power and capacities of the enemy. The Austro-Germans undertook the offensive animated by a spirit of emulation and sustained by an irresistible impetus deriving from the great military successes obtained against Serbia, Rumania, and Russia. . . . They were perfectly informed not only of our technical military preparation but also of the state of our morale; they were able to exploit every ingenious expedient and every consummate stratagem of war to conceal their very rapid movement of forces as well as the direction of their attack, to allay our vigilance in the sectors of the attack, and everywhere possible to weaken our resistance by means of a debilitating propaganda. . . . With the serenity which may be granted us by reason of our ultimate victory, we must acknowledge that the enemy's plan was the work of genius and most bold and that it was put into operation with energy and intelligence, and with the employment of methods new to us. The result was that the enemy was able to achieve a surprise, not so much with regard to time and place, as to methods employed; and surprise is the principal factor in victory. . . .

The conditions of inferiority of our country and our army. These conditions derived from our geographical situation, . . . from historical events, from the particular circumstances in which the country entered the war, and from the development of operations in the other theaters of war. Among these conditions of inferiority the following seem particularly notable: the strategically most unfavorable nature of *our frontier* with Austria-Hungary; our scant *economic potential* and difficulties in much of our supplies, with the result that we lacked an abundance of certain war materials and thus had to undergo greater sacrifices in the struggle than did other countries and armies; *Italian policy* of the last few decades, resulting in our army being less well prepared than others; the *military collapse* of Serbia, Rumania, and finally and very grave that of Russia, resulting in the concentration of most Austro-Hungarian forces on our front.

Weather conditions quite unfavorable to us, such as, among others, the *bad weather* prevailing during the month of October which made land and air observation more difficult; the *fog*, which notably favored the Austro-German artillery, aimed at known and fixed targets, as well as the advance of enemy infantry in many sectors of the attack, but made difficult and at times impossible our defensive barrages and the adequate maneuver of our support and reserve forces; the *rains* from October 24 to 27 . . . and the *fullness of the rivers*, which obstructed the movement of our very heavy columns in retreat and the crossing of the rivers. . . .

595. The following must be numbered among *the factors which did indeed exercise an influence but only insofar as military conditions* (and particularly the conduct and the results of the war as well as the management of the army's personnel until October 1917) *made possible the growth of these factors and their evil influence*, which other-

wise was no greater than the average evil influence exercised on other armies and people:

The natural and pronounced repugnance felt by many toward sacrifices, harm, and discomforts, as well as family ties that at times were even unhealthy

The confluence of some parties in condoning and favoring the less desirable tendencies and activities of the masses; the refusal on the part of these parties to accept responsibility for the war when fate was unkind to the fortunes of the Entente. (This and the preceding factor constitute the essence of that part of defeatism not nurtured by the enemy.)

The enemy's intelligent and cunningly effective propaganda in the country as well as among the troops

Certain political events, such as the Russian revolution, and public manifestations occurring within a brief span of time, such as the remark made by the Honorable Deputy Treves in Parliament,* the Socialist assemblies attended by Russian emissaries, the Turin riots,† and the Pope's Note on peace ‡

And the attitude assumed by a part of the press which, by directing public opinion toward an exaltation of the High Command, contributed to the weakening of the government's function of control over military operations.

596. The military causes of the defeat may be divided into two categories, in accordance with their influence on the events in question. The first of these categories is of lesser importance and consists of the technical military causes. These are:

Defects in the military apparatus. Although in certain respects these defects were notable at the beginning of the war and exercised an influence on operations in the first several months, they were in time largely eliminated

Errors in the conduct of the war, in operations as well as in the manner in which the troops were employed. Had these errors been

---

* On July 12, 1917, Claudio Treves, Official Socialist, had appealed to all governments of Europe to hearken to "the ultimatum of life to death: by the coming winter, not a man in the trenches." Ed. note.

† Late in August 1917 bread riots broke out in Turin which were repressed by the military with 41 dead, 152 wounded and injured, and over 600 arrests. Ed. note.

‡ Pope Benedict XV's Note of August 1, 1917, appealed to all belligerents to end the "useless slaughter." Ed. note.

avoided, our army would have been able to meet the enemy attack better prepared with men and equipment and with stronger morale

Faults in the deployment of defenses and in the arrangement of reserves

Some improvidence in logistics, especially in the arrangement and deployment of communications and transport. This lack of adequate prearrangement had repercussions in the difficulties encountered and losses suffered during the withdrawal.

597. The second category includes *military causes predominantly of a morale nature. In the judgment of the Commission these causes had a truly efficient effect in the disaster,* but responsibility for them is not limited to the military commanders. In several instances responsibility falls also on the government, which did not always intervene at the opportune moment. In substance, these appear to be the true causes, whereas the ones noted above are revealed as concomitant causes or facilitating circumstances. These true causes are:

Personal defects revealed in the manner of command of several generals, and the repercussions these defects had among their subordinate officers

A deformation in the functioning of the military hierarchy. This deformation was particularly evident in the relief from command of an excessive number of officers and in the relations between superiors and subordinates. These relations had become characterized by fear, suspicion, insincerity, and at times were even spiteful *

Errors in the maintenance of discipline and morale among the troops. These errors were revealed particularly in the inconsistency with which discipline was applied; in the too frequent disregard of the regular procedures of military justice; in the application of not always justified summary executions; and in the scant concern shown for the morale of troops and for adequate indoctrination. . . .

Failure to eliminate certain injustices and disproportions in allotting the burdens and sacrifices of the war; and, on the other hand, failure

---

* General Cadorna had relieved an extraordinary number of senior officers of their commands during the war, and undermined the prestige of others, possibly to eliminate rivals and find scapegoats for his own mistakes. His relations were exceptionally bad with General Luigi Capello, commander of the Second Army whose troops Cadorna charged with cowardice in the military bulletin of October 28, 1917. Ed. note.

to engage in persuasive action to fight the widespread and most exaggerated notions regarding the blight of draft evasion *

Discouragement occasioned by the widespread conviction—no matter whether justified or exaggerated—that the blood sacrifices already performed and those that might come had been and would be fruitless.†

598. With regard to *personal responsibilities* and according to the above-mentioned causes, the Commission holds that responsibility should be assessed against:

General Cadorna, for improper superintendence of the cadres by eliminating an excessive number of general and senior officers, by inspiring measures which were frequently and inopportunely coercive and which in consequence disturbed the morale of the officer corps without, on the other hand, producing the appropriate improvement in military technique that might justify the moral sacrifices incurred; for not taking appropriate care in economizing the physical and moral energies of the troops and, especially, for tolerating unrewarding sacrifices of blood and for inciting frequent disregard of the regular procedures of military justice; and finally for not having attached due importance to the problem of maintaining the cohesion of the several parts in large military units

General Capello, for having employed in the Second Army a system of personal coercion which at times reached the point of vexation and which aggravated the repercussions ensuing from General Cadorna's manner of superintendence; and for having contributed to the depression of the troops' morale by excessively draining their physical and moral energies and by being prodigal with blood in disproportion to the results achieved

General Porro [Carlo, Deputy Chief of Staff of the Army], for not having performed his duties in such a way as to moderate the excessive elimination of officers and for not having inquired into and made known those factors that depressed the morale of the troops, thus

* According to rumors then current there were perhaps as many as a half million deserters and draft evaders by June 1917. Ed. note.

† During the nearly two and a half years of war before the Caporetto disaster the Italian army had suffered 900,000 casualties, with little positive results. Late in the summer of 1917 Italy's eleventh offensive in the area of the Isonzo River cost the Italian army 40,000 dead, 108,000 wounded, and 18,000 missing. The results of the offensive were negative. Ed. note.

being remiss in his duty to provide the Chief of Staff [Cadorna] with that contribution necessary to induce the latter to take measures to prevent degeneration in the functioning of the military hierarchy, to correct the superintendence of the troops, and to maintain the organic cohesion of the armed forces

The Cabinet headed by the Honorable Boselli, for not having performed in a proper measure its high duty of supervision and control of the army's morale and for not having taken the measures appropriate to this end.

The report of the Commission of Inquiry on the Caporetto disaster was not published until 1919, but the essence of its conclusions coincided with the views expressed by a majority of the Chamber during a secret session in mid-December 1917. This session not only liquidated Cadorna as a political power in Italy, it also raised grave questions regarding Sonnino's conduct of foreign policy, particularly his refusal to consider a separate peace with Austria unless the fulfillment of the territorial promises made Italy in the Pact of London were assured. But the Bolshevik revolution in Russia and America's entry in the war rudely shook the foundations of the Pact of London. The new Russian government did not feel bound by the commitments of its predecessors; and the United States, which had never adhered to the Pact, soon announced, in President Wilson's Fourteen Points of January 1918, a number of positions which could not but be of concern to Sonnino. Point IX asserted that "a readjustment of the frontiers of Italy should be effected along clearly recognizable lines of nationality"; Point X said that "the peoples of Austria-Hungary . . . should be accorded the freest opportunity of autonomous development"; and Point XI said that Serbia should be accorded "free and secure access to the sea." The implementation of these points would make difficult if not impossible the implementation of the territorial clauses of the Pact of London. Everyone in Italy concerned with the problem of the eventual peace treaties understood this: Sonnino, who feared the territorial ambitions of a Greater Serbia or an eventual Yugoslav state, stood firmly by the letter of the Pact of London; Bissolati, leader of the so-called democratic interventionists, was prepared to renounce Dalmatia for the sake of his Wilsonian idealism and better relations with the Yugoslav state or states that might issue from the dismemberment of the Austro-Hungarian Empire; and Orlando, apparently undecided in his views, attempted to pacify his two irreconcilable colleagues in the government. So long as the country was at war, Sonnino and Bissolati remained together in the government and muted their dissent; but by the end of December 1918 Bissolati could no longer remain silent, and resigned. Early in January 1919 his views were made public in a newspaper interview and in a speech at the Scala in Milan. Except for his claim to Fiume, Bissolati's position was essentially the same as the one President Wilson would assume during the negotions at the Paris Peace Conference.

55. ITALY AT THE PARIS PEACE CONFERENCE

According to a work by René Albrecht-Carrié,[1] "There was little doubt by this time [January 1919] as to Wilson's position in regard to the Treaty of London.[2] The Armistice discussions had made that clear, while creating at the same time an unfortunate misunderstanding. However, the matter had not yet come before the Conference. The American attitude had been stated again by Miller in his letter of December 13 to Bliss,[3] and once more he now expressed the view 'that any provisions of the Pact of London . . . which may be inconsistent with the agreement [Wilson's Note of November 5, 1918][4] . . . were by that agreement abrogated and are no longer in force.' Wilson adhered to this view throughout the negotiations."

Wilson's unchanging position on this point was predominant in his dramatic confrontation with the Italian delegation at the Peace Conference. The issue which precipitated the clash revolved around Italy's demands for a part of Dalmatia and particularly for Fiume. The nature of this clash and its repercussions on Italy's domestic policies are examined in the following passages from Albrecht-Carrié's work.

Dalmatia and Fiume

René Albrecht-Carrié, *Italy at the Paris Peace Conference*. New York: Columbia University Press, 1938, pp. 100–3. Original footnotes omitted.

In the Adriatic, the claim to a part of Dalmatia, save on the basis of the Treaty of London, could not but appear weak. The military defense of this isolated over-sea possession was likely to be more of a liability than an asset in the event of war. It is difficult to escape the

[1] *Italy at the Paris Peace Conference*. New York: Columbia University Press, 1938, p. 90.

[2] The April 26, 1915, agreement of London is known as both the Pact *and* the Treaty of London. Ed. note.

[3] David Hunter Miller, technical adviser to Colonel Edward M. House, member of the American Mission to the Paris Peace Conference; General Tasker H. Bliss, member of the Allied Supreme War Council and American delegate to the Conference. Ed. note.

[4] Indicates the agreement among the Allied Powers that peace should be effected upon the terms stated in the Fourteen Points. Ed. note.

impression that what Italy really wanted in the Adriatic was not only security but as much as possible a *mare clausum*. That had been the aim of Salandra and Sonnino in 1915, an aim of which the former was still in favor.

But the most striking feature of the Italian claim was the demand for Fiume, specifically allotted to Croatia in the very Treaty of London. This particular provision may well have been the result of Russian influence, and there is no denying that the Russian collapse had put a grievous burden on Italy, as on the other Allies for that matter. Italy did emphasize this fact, but she might well hesitate to put it forward as a justification for further compensation. She did therefore decide to fall back on arguments of nationality and defense.

The facts about Fiume were fairly simple. According to the census of 1910, the city proper had 22,488 Italians and 13,351 Slavs; if, however, the suburb of Sušak were included, there were 23,988 Italians and 24,351 Slavs. Sušak is separated from Fiume proper only by a narrow stream, the Recina (Eneo), and is in every respect part of the same agglomeration. The main port facilities belong to Fiume; Sušak has only a small harbor, Porto Baross, used primarily for the wood commerce of Croatia. . . .

Just why Fiume should have been added to the Italian claims, when Wilson's opposition even to the terms of the Treaty of London was well known, is hard to tell. Before and during the war, the slogan of Italian irredentism had been: Trento and Trieste. It would hardly be an exaggeration to say that Italian opinion had been unaware of the existence of such a city as Fiume. The cry for Fiume was of very recent origin; certainly the Government had done nothing to discourage it and it is worth noting that even Italian moderates, such men as Bissolati and Salvemini, who favored compromise with the Slavs in other places, insisted on the Italian character of Fiume. It is also of interest that Sonnino steadfastly adhered to the written letter of the law and always demanded the terms of the Treaty of London, no more and no less. The responsibility must therefore fall to Orlando for this further demand. Possibly, not to say probably, he had in mind a transaction whereby Italy could secure Fiume in exchange for yielding Dalmatia. Such an arrangement would have made it possible for him to appear before home opinion not to have suffered a defeat at the Conference. The exigencies of politics at home should also be remembered: the cry for Fiume was exploited for purely political purposes by some at least of the Giolittian following. At this time, in fact (second half of January), the situation was still sufficiently fluid so that a compromise might have been successful. Page * reported that the press in Italy was "showing considerable impatience at the prospect of protraction in the Peace Negotiations indicating dangers that will arise from such protraction. . . . The people will follow the Conference now in any firm decision it may make." Later on, Orlando, too, expressed the opinion that all might have been well if a settlement could have been made just after the Armistice, for then "Fiume would never have been injected into the terms by the Italians"; it was perhaps already too late in January to give up Fiume and survive politically, but Fiume for Dalmatia might still have been acceptable. However, this demand for Fiume proved the source of endless complications and difficulties for Orlando, for, as time passed and national feeling became exasperated in Italy, he found it increasingly difficult to retreat from the position which he had originally taken, and when at last he fell back on the written obligation of Great Britain and France, these Powers faced him with the retort that he had been the first to depart from the Treaty.

Unable to resolve the deadlock between his position and that of the Italian delegation, Wilson decided to appeal directly to the Italian people in a Manifesto of April 23, 1919. The next day the Italian delegation, led by Orlando and Sonnino, began its departure from the Peace Conference. The next excerpt examines the content and import of Wilson's Manifesto as well as Italy's reaction to it.

President Wilson's Manifesto and Italian Reaction

Albrecht-Carrié, *Italy at the Paris Peace Conference,* pp. 141–49, *passim.* Original footnotes omitted.

The publication of Wilson's statement naturally created an enormous sensation, not so much on account of its content, as because it signalized an open break in the Conference and a radical departure from its methods. This sudden appeal to public opinion in the midst of nego-

* Thomas Nelson Page, American ambassador to Italy. Ed. note.

tiations, hitherto much criticized for the secrecy in which they had been shrouded, was indeed a novelty.

The Manifesto itself presented no new arguments. It was essentially an earnest appeal to Italy to subscribe whole-heartedly to the new order of things, of which the League of Nations was the embodiment, and, more immediately, to the settlement outlined in the Fourteen Points. Entirely new circumstances, it was pointed out, had come to prevail since the Treaty of London had been signed. That Treaty could not be binding on the non-signatory Powers, who had entered the war subsequently and without knowledge of its existence; moreover, it had been directed in the main against Austria-Hungary, which Power had ceased to exist and whose menace had therefore disappeared. The United States, on the other hand, was bound by definite commitments expressed in the Fourteen Points. These were the basis on which the German peace had been conceived, and Wilson did not feel at liberty to depart from their application in the case of the former Austro-Hungarian and Balkan territories.

Coming to the specific points in dispute, Fiume and Dalmatia, the Manifesto repeated the familiar argument that the former was primarily not an Italian port, and that to give it to Italy would be to put it under a sovereignty alien to its essential economic function. As to Dalmatia, the main reason for its attribution to Italy in the Treaty of London had been strategic, but that argument no longer held, in view of the disappearance of Austria-Hungary and the creation of the League of Nations, under whose auspices, moreover, fortifications would be dismantled in the Adriatic, armaments reduced, and Italian territorial integrity guaranteed, along with that of the other members. The League would likewise insure the safeguard of Italian minorities in Dalmatia.

In view of these considerations and of the advantages already secured by Italy, "it is within her choice," said Wilson, "to be surrounded by friends; to exhibit to the newly liberated peoples across the Adriatic that noblest quality of greatness, magnanimity, friendly generosity, the preference of justice over interest." The appeal concluded with the restatement of America's unyielding adherence to the principles for the defense of which she had gone to war.

The compulsion is upon her to square every decision she takes a part in with those principles. . . . These, and these only, are the principles for which America has fought. These, and these only, are the principles upon which she can consent to make peace. Only upon these principles, she hopes and believes, will the people of Italy ask her to make peace.

With the statements of fact—taken by themselves—regarding Fiume and Dalmatia, little quarrel could be found. But, as the Manifesto clearly recognized, the conclusions arrived at were based on the implicit assumption that the new order would become a workable reality. The issuance of Wilson's Manifesto was a climax in the evolution of the Conference: an issue was joined far transcending the local disputes over Fiume and Dalmatia, or indeed the whole Italian problem, which only the accident of circumstances made the occasion and the symbol about which the opposing ideologies clashed. The first concrete formulation of war aims in the Fourteen Points, the acceptance of his principles by the Allies, the position taken in the debates of the past four months, constituted for Wilson a logical sequence of which his appeal was but a consistent culmination. Clearly and unequivocally, he stood on ground where there could be no compromise, for compromise would mean surrender of principle, and principles could not be surrendered in part.

Nor is it difficult to understand how, despite practical objections and possible consequences, Wilson came to adopt so novel a procedure. To him and the advisers on whom he most depended, the Italian question was a comparatively simple issue. He had definitely recognized the right of the subject nationalities of Austria-Hungary to organize their independent political life; the Fourteen Points had been freely discussed and accepted, save for one reservation, in making the Armistices. He had been generous to Italy in granting the demand for the Brenner frontier and was willing to make reasonable concessions to her in the east at the expense of the Slav population; beyond that, the Italian demands could have but one interpretation: in the words of his experts, "a demand for loot," which could carry no weight against the principle of nationality to which the Slavs made appeal. Even more, it would be to Italy's own future interest to avoid creating a Slav irredentism. The idea of appealing to public opinion was ever-present in his mind; he was thoroughly convinced—and not wholly without reason—that public opinion, if properly informed, would, in general, support him, and that its backing was his greatest source of strength. On the "George Washington," he had expressed the belief to the members of The Inquiry that America was the only disinterested party, the statesmen of Europe did not represent their peoples. The experience of his visit to Rome could only tend to confirm this conviction. He had threatened before, with successful results, to resort to the same device when attacked in the French press. As indicated previously, the news from Italy which reached the American delegation tended to create a picture of a press largely controlled from the source of the Italian delegation in Paris, while it failed to convey the change which had taken place in Italian opinion as the result both of the actual developments in Paris and of the manner in which those developments were presented to it. This impression could not have been more clearly expressed than by Wilson himself when he said that "it had not been possible for him to let the Italian people get their version of what had occurred from a poisoned press." The personal attacks on Wilson hit a sensitive spot. The recurrent mention in Italy, at first, of the Anglo-Saxon block; then, as the issue gradually became more sharply drawn between Orlando and Wilson, the attempt to isolate the United States by insisting that Great Britain and France supported the Italian claims, when, actually, Wilson had the backing of Lloyd George and Clemenceau in the Council; and, worst of all, the endeavor to dissociate Wilson from the United States—all this was psychological preparation for the unexpected procedure adopted by Wilson.

And yet, much as we may understand the background which made this action possible, it cannot be described otherwise than as a capital error in judgment. Without going into the merits of the case presented by Wilson, the fact remains that his Manifesto could be interpreted only as an appeal to Italian opinion, against the Italian delegation. If, as Wilson himself believed, that opinion was molded by a poisoned press, it is difficult to understand his thinking that a mere statement on his part would suffice to put the American position in its true light before Italian opinion.

ORLANDO'S REPLY AND THE REACTION IN ITALY

Be that as it may, the actual appearance of Wilson's Manifesto on the evening of the twenty-third was a complete surprise to the Italians. Under the circumstances, Orlando could hardly let it pass unquestioned, and his answer appeared accordingly on the twenty-

fourth. Whereas Wilson's appeal was earnest and based on high principle, Orlando preferred the lighter touch of irony, which he used not
without skill: such assertions as that Italy must abide by the spirit of
the new order as it was manifested in the German Treaty did, after
all, lend themselves to this sort of treatment. The first part of Orlando's reply is the most interesting and important. It began by expressing surprise at the publication of Wilson's statement, which had
interrupted a promising negotiation, and went on to declare its adherence to this "innovation in international intercourse," which doubtless
"will aid in granting the different peoples a broader participation in
international questions," which participation was "a sign of a newer
era." With a view to his home opinion, Orlando felt that he had to
protest, however, against the derogatory implication toward Italy that
such an appeal might be directed to the Italian people outside, or
even against, the Government which it had elected as its representative. "To oppose, so to speak, the Italian Government and people,
would be to admit that this great free nation could submit to the yoke
of a will other than its own, and I shall be forced to protest vigorously against such suppositions, unjustly offensive to my country."

Coming to the specific issues raised by Wilson, Orlando went on to
repeat and to summarize the customary Italian arguments. He regretted having been unable to convince Wilson of the soundness of his
case, but, at best, that must be set down as an honest difference of
opinion. Once more he insisted on the justice of the Italian demands,
which were moderate by comparison with others; the demise of
Austria-Hungary did not imply a reduction of the Italian aspirations,
for Italy needed security in the east as much as in the north. As to
Fiume, rather speciously, he argued that its size should not prevent
the application to it of Wilson's cherished principle of self-determination. For Dalmatia, "this boulevard of Italy throughout the centuries,"
the precedent of Poland was adduced.

This presentation suffered from the usual weakness of Orlando's arguments, a weakness inherent in the attempt to reconcile the demand
for the Treaty of London plus Fiume, with the Fourteen Points. But if
Wilson's Manifesto was directed to Italian opinion, Orlando's reply
was even more so, and, when the two statements appeared side by
side in Italy, there could be little doubt as to which would arouse the
more favorable response.

The immediate reaction in Italy was violent in the extreme and quite unanimous: an emotional outburst of unreasoning nationalism and injured pride, which joined in heaping maledictions on the head of the American President; and, what was more unfortunate, it put for a moment in the same camp, the most aggressive and irreconcilable annexationists, the type of the followers of d'Annunzio, with those saner elements who, like Bissolati, advocated a just and reasonable peace of compromise with the Yugoslavs. Nor can the outburst be explained away as having been engineered by the Government, though the latter was at least tacitly sympathetic toward it. The dominant note was not so much perhaps anger or disappointment at the prospect of being thwarted in Fiume—the Fiume agitation, as such, was, to a large extent, a comparatively recent and artificial development—as resentment against unfair discimination where Italy was concerned, heightened by touchiness over anything that might seem to raise a question as to Italy's position among the Powers. (Wilson had threatened, but had not used, such methods when Great Britain and France, more powerful nations, were concerned.)

Salvemini, like Bissolati, had, for a long time, been one of the leading advocates of a policy of compromise and of abandonment of the Treaty of London. Yet even he was moved at this time to an impassioned protest. . . . Bissolati also, in a message given to the press on April 25–26, made it clear that his advocacy of renouncing Dalmatia was based on the understanding that Fiume would go to Italy and Zara be made autonomous. . . .

Curiously enough, Wilson's outburst gave the Orlando Cabinet a new lease on life. None too successful at home, it had continued more or less on sufferance, for no one among the politicians in Italy wished to put himself in the invidious position of stabbing the delegation in the back without at least apparently sufficient cause. Orlando had thus been driven more and more into a position of relying on the outcome in Paris to save himself at home. The rather suddenly developed nationalism of the Giolittian element in politics was a maneuver to corner him in that position. But, as the result of the peculiar turn of events in the form of Wilson's Manifesto, these elements found themselves caught at their own game, and could not consistently do otherwise, at the moment, than give Orlando a rousing vote of confidence. Everything then conspired at this time—popular feeling as well as the parliamentary situation—to put Orlando in the position of true champion of a united Italy; even the taciturn Sonnino experienced for a day the unwonted feeling of being a popular hero. But in fact the situation was little changed, for, if Wilson's appeal had failed to achieve its purpose, neither was the reaction in Italy likely to change Wilson's views on the Italian problem.

XIX. THE COLLAPSE OF THE

PARLIAMENTARY REGIME, 1919–1922

Apparently strengthened by public opinion at home, the Italian delegation returned to Paris early in May 1919, and for approximately a month thereafter the English and the French continued in their efforts to achieve a reconciliation between Italian and American points of view. The failure of these efforts was evident in the terms of the draft treaty with Austria, made known in Italy early in June. According to these terms Italy was to receive a favorable frontier on the Brenner, as promised in the Pact of London, but the frontier with Yugoslavia remained unsettled, and authority over the territories in contention was assumed by Allied troops until an eventual resolution of the conflicting Italo-Yugoslav claims. In spite of the favorable Brenner frontier, Italy's attention remained fixed at Fiume and Dalmatia, and Parliament faithfully reflected the country's dissatisfaction with the work of the Italian delegation by giving Orlando an unfavorable vote on his request that a general debate on foreign affairs be conducted in secret session. The last of Italy's wartime governments fell on June 19, 1919, by a vote 78 in favor and 262 against, and thus there began a three-year crisis which shook and eventually destroyed the foundations of representative government in Italy.

The new government was formed by Francesco Saverio Nitti, a Radical who had served as Giolitti's Minister of Agriculture, Industry, and Commerce between 1911 and 1914 and as Orlando's Treasury Minister from October 1917 to January 1919. Nitti's resignation from Orlando's government several months before its fall was interpreted as an expression of his disagreement with Sonnino's foreign policy and as a step designed to free him from sharing responsibility for Sonnino's policies in preparation for his own succession to power. His plan, if such there was, succeeded with the support of the Giolittians and of the *Partito popolare italiano* [Italian Popular Party], newly formed in January 1919 with a domestic program of social reform inspired by Christian principles and a foreign policy harmonious with the idealism of Wilson's Fourteen Points.

The double nature of the enormous problems facing Nitti's government was revealed soon after his accession to power: a general strike began on July 21, 1919, with the aim of preventing Italian intervention against the

Bolshevik revolutions in Russia and Hungary, and was followed by a series of local strikes primarily economic in nature; and on September 12, 1919 d'Annunzio seized the city of Fiume. This seizure, involving as it did groups and individuals on active duty in the regular Italian army and navy, was an act of insubordination which if unpunished would threaten the tradition that in Italy the armed forces did not engage in politics and "always obeyed." D'Annunzio and his "legionnaires" were not punished until December 1920, and then only in a token fashion. After the "radiant days of May" in 1915 when an interventionist minority had imposed its will on the country, the d'Annunzian episode of 1919–20 constituted another precedent and element in the eventual dissolution of parliamentary government.

The whole complex of causes and events that precipitated Italy's crisis of institutions between 1919 and 1922 is seen in two excerpts from a work by the late Federico Chabod, one of contemporary Italy's most perceptive historians. The first excerpt examines the economic and social consequences of the war; the second, the principal political developments in 1919 and 1920.

56. POVERTY AND ECONOMIC RUIN OF THE MIDDLE CLASSES

From *A History of Italian Fascism*, by Federico Chabod. © Copyright 1963 by George Weidenfeld and Nicolson, Ltd. Reprinted by permission of Random House, Inc. Translated from the Italian by Muriel Grindrod. Original footnotes omitted. Pp. 22–26 and 35–43.

The most important of [the domestic changes occasioned by the war] . . . were in the social sphere. What effect had the war had on Italy's social structure? The conduct of the war had called into question the Government's whole economic and fiscal policy. In studying the history of modern Italy it should be borne in mind that this was the first great trial of military strength which the country had experienced. Italy was still a very young State: only four years before her entry into the war, in 1911, the fiftieth anniversary of the constitution of the Kingdom of Italy had been celebrated in Rome and Turin. Fifty years is a short time for a country to develop traditions. The great States of Western Europe, France and Britain, could look back to centuries of national military tradition and participation in large-scale wars. But in Italy for the first time a population of over 36 million found itself plunged into a four-year-long struggle which was not only bloody but also financially ruinous.

Italy is far less wealthy than the other Great Powers, notwithstanding the great advances achieved since the unification. The average diet of an Italian in 1914 corresponded to about 3,200 calories a day, more than a fifth below that of an Englishman. The average income *per capita* in 1911–13 was 549 for the United States, 481 for Britain, 351 for France, 301 for Germany, and only 158 for Italy.

But Italy nevertheless consumed more than she produced: between 1909 and 1913 the excess of imports over exports averaged 1,250 million lire. To put it another way, on a total volume of foreign trade amounting in value to about 5½ milliard lire, Italy had a deficit of 1¼ milliard. How was this gap to be filled? The answer was, largely by income from tourism and emigrants' remittances: for in those years the number of emigrants leaving Italy was sometimes as high as 873,000 in a year, with an annual average of 650,000 over the years 1909–13, and their savings from earnings abroad went back to their families at home.

One of the reasons why the veteran statesman Giolitti disapproved of the Salandra-Sonnino Cabinet's policy in embarking on war in 1915 was because the Italian Government was known to cherish the illusion that it would be a short war. Giolitti, on the contrary, believed that the war would be long and difficult to sustain, especially on the financial side.

From the economic and financial standpoint, a long-term situation should have been envisaged and an organized plan prepared to meet it. But the Italian Government's financial policy provided for no such plan. This point has been clearly brought out by Luigi Einaudi in his book, *La condotta economica e gli effetti sociali della guerra italiana* (The economic conduct and social effects of the war in Italy), published in 1933. In fiscal and financial policy, as in foreign policy, the mistake was made of believing that the war would end quickly. This did not happen, and the Government found itself increasingly under the pressing necessity of finding the means to meet the Treasury's needs by loans or by taxation which, given the system of taxation adopted in Italy, fell very unevenly upon the taxpayer. Budget expenditure rose from 2,501 million lire in 1913–14 (the last normal year) to 10,550 million in 1915–16; 17,315 million in 1916–17; 25,334 million in 1917–18; and 30,857 million in 1918–19. In those same years the deficit rose by stages from 214 million to 23,345 million. Note circulation, which amounted to 2,007 million at 30 June

1914, reached 20,000 million at the end of December 1920. The public debt rose from 14,089 million lire in 1910 to 95,017 million in 1920.

The consequences of all this were extremely serious. The hardest hit were those classes of the population which hitherto had formed the real backbone, in the political sense, of the Italian State—the small and medium *bourgeoisie* (those engaged in the liberal professions, in trade and industry, and owners of property) and the small land-owners who were in the habit of farming-out their estates.

The burden of taxation hit these groups with ever-increasing force. The same was true of property owners living on rents. Rents of land and house-property were blocked, as we shall see later; incomes therefore remained unchanged, or altered only slightly, whereas costs rapidly increased. These are phenomena with which we today are only too familiar, but at that time they were completely novel and un-expected. There was also the plight of those who had subscribed to the public debt or to "victory" loans during the war. Einaudi has cal-culated that between 1916 and 1918 some 30 per cent of the national income went to the Treasury in the form of loans. The rapid devalua-tion of the lira between 1919 and 1920 (in the second half of 1920 it was worth only one-fifth of its 1914 value) spelt impoverishment for many and downright ruin for some.

On the other hand, in contrast to those who saw their economic sit-uation steadily worsening day by day, there were others who experi-enced just the opposite: as always in war, the industrialists were get-ting enormous orders and coining money. Especially in trade, includ-ing the black market (though it never reached anything like the scale of the Second World War), huge fortunes were made from one day to the next. Thus while some were faced with economic ruin, others found themselves suddenly wealthy: in short, a "new rich" society was arising while the old well-to-do *bourgeoisie* collapsed.

In this situation the end of the war was eagerly awaited since it was expected to bring back tranquillity, especially from the financial point of view. This is a fact worth mentioning, for it seems to me to give, better than any other comment, the measure of the mental climate of the times. In the first months of 1919 Italy's trade was so greatly re-duced that even retail trade was affected. Consumers refused to buy in the hope that prices would fall. This seems to me typically indica-tive of the prevailing psychological attitude of much of the country:

the hope that once the war was over the happy days of the past would return.

During the Second World War illusions of this kind were no longer cherished; nobody believed that with the coming of peace prices would revert to their pre-war level, or even that they would be stabized at their wartime maximum. The experience of the First World War had immunized us against such illusions. Peace did not bring serenity in foreign affairs, nor financial tranquillity for most of that *bourgeoisie* which had hitherto constituted the foundation of Italian political life. On the contrary, the cost of living rose steadily. With the end of the war, exchange control, established in July 1918 by agreement with the United States, Britain, and France, also came to an end, on 25 March 1919, and the lira at once collapsed. In June 1914 the dollar was worth 5 lire, 18 cents; in December 1919 it had risen to 13.07 lire; in April 1920 to 22.94; and in December 1920 to 28.57 lire. This meant a rise in the cost of living, since Italy had to import wheat, coal, and oil. She was especially short of wheat. Before 1914 Italy used to produce on an average 50 million quintals a year (the maximum yield per hectare was 12.3 quintals in 1913) and she had to import some 14 million quintals; but during the war production fell to a minimum of 38 million quintals (the lowest yield per hectare was 8.4 quintals, in 1920). In 1920 the total cereal harvest (wheat, maize, rice, etc.) was 18 million quintals below the average of 1909–14. If Italians had not been able to look abroad for supplies they would have starved, for they are a people whose basic diet consists of cereals and especially wheat.

Such were the anxieties preoccupying the Italian Prime Minister, Nitti, in 1919, and therein lies the explanation of his desire to put an end to the exacerbated discussions of foreign policy: if the United States were to stop sending supplies to Italy, what would happen next?

To make matters worse, in July 1919 the populace in the towns, large and small, began to assail the warehouses where supplies were stored. To counter these disorders the authorities imposed a compulsory 50 per cent reduction in prices; this merely had the effect of temporarily arresting the rising curve. The weekly expenditure of a typical Milanese working-class family at this time was 120.05 lire in June 1919; 109.24 in July; and 108.07 in August, rising however in

November to 118.53; to 124.67 in January 1920; and 189.76 in December 1920. In relation to 1914, the rise in the cost of living for a working-class family in the first half of 1921 could be estimated at 560 per cent. The situation of middle-class families was even worse. Salaries of office workers, or at any rate of the civil servants who constitute a considerable part of the Italian lower middle classes, failed to follow the rising curve of prices; owners of house-property and landowners in receipt of rents fixed in cash found themselves saddled with leases blocked by a law which permitted only a ludicrously small increase of rent. On the other hand taxes went up. State taxation has already been mentioned, but to get a correct idea of the situation in 1919–21 communal taxation must also be taken into account. For the communes were at grips with serious financial problems and were pushing up their taxes and supertaxes.

Finally, the plight of the large number of reserve officers must not be forgotten. These men, who had played a prominent part in the war, often suffering for it in their own persons, now had to return to civilian life—for in the summer of 1919 Nitti began to reduce the army cadres, with the laudable aim of bringing down military expenditure and assisting the recovery of the State Budget. But civilian life was extremely expensive for these young men who, once out of uniform, found themselves without jobs and often superceded by others who had not fought but had merely stayed at home looking after their own affairs. These young men, too, came from the middle classes.

The second excerpt from Chabod's work examines the political changes manifest in Italy during 1919 and 1920, with special emphasis on the importance of the newly formed *Partito popolare* [Popular party] and on the "tragedy of Italian Socialism."

57. YEARS OF CRISIS: 1919–1920

Chabod, *A History of Italian Fascism*, pp. 35–43.

In January 1919 a second real political party [in addition to the existing Socialist party] appeared on the scene, one whose aim was to be truly a party and not just a collection of deputies. This was the Partito Popolare, that is to say, the Catholic Party, whose successor today is the Christian Democrat Party. Its animating force was a Sicilian priest, Don Luigi Sturzo, a man deserving of great respect. What did the new party stand for? In certain ways its advent represented a fact of great importance, indeed the most notable event in Italian history in the twentieth century, especially by comparison with the century before: it signified the official return of the Catholics in force into Italian political life. It is difficult for anyone who is not an Italian to appreciate what this meant. We need only recall that after the formation of the Kingdom of Italy the watchword for Catholics was: "No collaboration with the new régime." They could neither vote nor stand for Parliament.

In point of fact it cannot be said that all Catholics abstained from voting. But in practice the ban had meant that up to the end of the nineteenth century Italian Catholicism was officially divorced from the life of the State. Here too Giolitti had tried to blunt the edge of the ban; he had even succeeded in concluding agreements with the Catholics (the Gentiloni Pact of 1913), and twenty-nine Catholic deputies were elected in 1913 (there were 3 in 1904, 16 in 1909). During the war the most important of them, Filippo Meda, had agreed to take part in the Government. That a publicly avowed Catholic should assume the office of a Minister of the Kingdom of Italy, in Rome, the capital still not recognized by the Pope, was a significant fact in itself. But it was not until 1919, with the constitution of the Partito Popolare, that the Catholics emerged into Italian political life as a compact organized mass with a well-defined programme of their own.

In the elections of 1919 they succeeded in sending 100 deputies to the Chamber. The official Socialist Party had 156. This meant that the régime of the old ministerial majorities typical of the Giolittian era was finished for ever. Henceforth it was no longer possible for a Prime Minister to form a Cabinet without the support of either the Popolari or the Socialists. These two parties were the strongest groupings in the Chamber, together representing a majority (256 deputies out of a total of 508). The old groups, the Liberals, Radicals, etc., disappeared.

The Partito Popolare was a "rigid" party which did not permit of the personal agreements typical of the old-style Parliament. The approval of the party secretary, Don Sturzo, had to be obtained. This annoyed Giolitti, who could not bear Don Sturzo or the fact that anyone who was not even a deputy or senator should attempt to have a say in matters of State. Giolitti could not concede that Don Sturzo, a mere party secretary with no parliamentary mandate, should come and discuss with him, the Prime Minister, political questions which, in his view, were purely the concern of Parliament and its members. Giolitti, in fact, had ceased to grasp the terms of the political and parliamentary struggle on its new basis.

The change in the electoral system effected in 1919 was also partly responsible for the revolution in the old parliamentary régime. Proportional representation was introduced, and this had the effect of both reducing the importance of a candidate's personality (and the old parties were still the richest in men of personal prestige) and increasing the importance of the party, the organization.

A rapid glance at some statistics will demonstrate this truth. If voting in 1913 had been by the proportional method, the official Socialist Party would have had 89 deputies instead of the 52 it obtained by the single-constituency method; the Liberals, on the other hand, would have had 242 instead of 270, and the Radicals 60 instead of 73.

Thus the political struggle now became a genuinely inter-party affair; and the strongest parties, in 1919–20, were the two "mass" parties, the official Socialists and the Popolari. Their strength increased thanks to the support of organizations which, while not political in the strict sense, were closely associated with politics: the trade union and social organizations. (It should be noted that the specifically Catholic organization, Catholic Action, did not at this time openly support the Partito Popolare; in this its policy differed from the line it took in relation to the Christian Democrats in 1948.)

We must now consider the Socialist Party. The Socialists had advanced greatly since before the war. In 1919, as has been said, they had 156 deputies as compared with only 52 in 1913. In the 1919 elections they obtained 1,834,792 votes as against 883,409 in 1913. That was a remarkable achievement considering that the Socialist Party had opposed the war; in 1917 it declared that the conflict had lasted long enough and that Italian soldiers should not spend another winter in the trenches. For this the party was accused of having sabotaged the war. I do not propose here to go into the details of this accusation, which was largely false. Italy had sustained some military defeats, notably at Caporetto; but they are not to be explained, as some have maintained, by Socialist propaganda, but by the difficult strategic position in which the Italian army was placed. The mistakes made were military and attributable much more to the High Command than to party propaganda. And these mistakes in turn were due to two causes: the excessive length of the front, and the survival of old prejudices among the army leaders, and in particular their obsession about the importance of every inch of ground gained—a commander felt that he was failing in his duty if he did not advance a hundred yards, even at the risk of landing his troops in a completely untenable position.

Leaving aside these secondary aspects, suffice it to say that at that time the Socialist Party was, in the eyes of the people, the party that had opposed the war. And now, when the war had been won, this "anti-war" party more than doubled its pre-war vote and nearly trebled its representation in Parliament.

Moreover, it is not only the political elections that are important in the life of a country: municipal elections count for something too. And in 1920 the Socialists achieved a majority in 2,022 communes, or in 24 per cent of the total number.

Thus at the end of 1920 the Socialists controlled over 2,000 communes, 156 deputies, 36 provincial councils, and 3,000 party sections, while the CGIL, the trade union organization, also under their control, had 2,150,000 members. They were, in fact, to all appearances, an extremely powerful force.

The Popolari, as we have seen, had 100 deputies. In the local elections of 1920 they won control of 1,613 communes, or around 13 percent of the total. They had 22 daily papers and 93 weeklies. They controlled some of the big banks such as the Banco di Roma, and a number of small local country banks in which the clergy had for decades pursued an interest and which, in such regions as Piedmont, gave them a remarkable hold on the population. They also controlled many local agricultural co-operatives: in 1921, in the Po Valley alone there were 311 such Catholic co-operatives, as against 236 in Socialist and Republican hands. To compete with the CGIL, they created the *Confederazione italiana dei lavoratori*, the Italian Workers' Confederation, allied to the Partito Popolare, which in 1920 had a membership of 1,161,238; of these, 944,812 were farmers, which meant that in the countryside the Catholics—the "Whites"—were stronger than the Socialists, the "Reds," who had only 750,000 members. For this reason the Socialists failed to win over the rural masses as they had done with the urban workers.

Thus the old parliamentary groups found themselves in a position where they could not govern without previous agreement with either the Popolari or the Socialists.

At this point the tragedy of Italian Socialism begins to take shape. It developed for two reasons. First, as we have seen the idea was allowed to grow up—partly with justification because of the attitude of some militant Socialist leaders—that the party was "anti-national." This cost it the votes of the majority of the small *bourgeoisie*. Secondly, Italian Socialism, as visualized by its old leaders, did not want a violent revolution. But at the same time it was torn by a serious internal crisis which paralysed its political action. The prevalent revolutionary fever, exacerbated by what was known and rumored about Russia, made its strongest impact, as was to be expected, on the party of Turati, Treves, and Modigliani. The talk was less of Marx than of Lenin. The extreme Left, which in 1921 was to split off to found the Communist Party, wanted to go all out for a decisive and fundamental struggle against the *bourgeoisie* and display a revolutionary will such as Russia had shown to conquer the State. Such men as Turati were very far from accepting these ideas; they inclined to reformism, not to revolution. Between these two extremes was the revolutionary speechifying, the vehement if sporadic agitation of a considerable part of the party which aimed to attract to itself the masses enticed by the image of Russia. The result was continuous strikes and disorders, which served merely to irritate their opponents without making any real impression on them.

That is not the way to make a real revolution; but, equally, it is not the way to get into the Government. The Socialists could not make up their minds either to conquer power by force or to share it with the *bourgeoisie*. Among the party leaders and in articles in *Avanti!* the same slogan was repeated time and time again: "We must be ourselves!"—we must remain faithful to our great principles, the proletariat, the struggle against the *bourgeoisie*. But often these were only words, with no definite plan of action behind them.

On the other hand there were the Popolari. Theirs was a party that already followed the rules of the same system that we know today: the secretariat kept the direction of the party firmly in its hands and decided on the political line to be adopted. The party secretary was an extremely capable man, but he was to shoulder a heavy responsibility when, in February 1922, he opposed Giolitti's return to power. (This brought about the advent to power of Facta, an honest provincial lawyer without the qualities necessary to lead a Government. He was brought in because the parties vetoed other more eminent candidates.) The Partito Popolare, too, like the Socialists, though numerically strong was also divided within itself. It included sincere democrats such as Sturzo, but also "conservatives" who regarded the new party merely as a means to defend their own positions. There was in fact a bit of everything, from Miglioli, who organized the occupations of land in the Po Valley, to the old-fashioned Catholic conservatives. A party, in short, that was anything but homogeneous; and its political action showed it. . . .

To sum up: with the Socialists in opposition and the Popolari proving difficult allies, the burden of government weighed heavily on the men of the old political groups who still retained the reins of power in their hands. Italian political life was taking on a quite new direction, and the old remedies no longer sufficed. Nevertheless Giolitti, faithful to past methods, dissolved the Chamber and in May 1921 played the great card of calling a General Election, in the hope of breaking the power of the two chief disturbing elements, the Socialist Party and the Popolari, and restoring a Chamber with a majority, on the old lines. It was a mistake. The Socialists lost ground, their representation falling to 123, but at the same time 15 Communist deputies were elected, now representing a party that had detached itself from Socialism. Moreover the Popolari increased their poll, winning 108 deputies instead of 100. In the "national blocs" favoured by Giolitti, the Fascists now made their appearance: they gained thirty-five seats in the new Chamber of Deputies, the first Fascist group to sit there. But the composition of the Chamber as a whole did not permit of the type of parliamentary manoeuvring at which Giolitti was such an adept and which had for years formed the basis of his tactics. The veteran statesman had to retire for the time being.

Between 1919 and 1922 there were five different Governments. Even when no actual crisis arose, the position of the Government was constantly precarious for lack of a solid majority.

All this was taking place in a country which was already profoundly disturbed by the state of confusion and uncertainty described in the two earlier chapters, and which had to face serious difficulties in foreign policy. The Prime Minister, Nitti, resolutely opposed the occupation of Fiume by D'Annunzio.* Giolitti settled the Adriatic problems in 1920, and in November of that year he and his Foreign Minister, Count Sforza, signed the Treaty of Rapallo †—a treaty embodying an agreement which could well have been reached long before but for the errors of the policy of Sonnino and the no less serious mistakes of Yugoslavia. Had it been signed two years earlier, the Treaty of Rapallo might have changed many things not only in the history of Italy but also in the whole post-war political history of Danubian Europe.

Now, however, with the agreement signed, Giolitti as head of the Government had to find a solution for the Fiume question. He therefore ordered D'Annunzio to abandon Fiume, telling him that unless he withdrew Italian troops would be ordered to enter the town. This in fact was what happened in the so-called "Bloody Christmas" of 1920.

On the international plane, the question was settled. But Giolitti's unavoidable action against D'Annunzio provoked fresh outbursts of nationalistic fervour in which the Fascists now joined.

Meanwhile at home strike followed strike in rapid succession. In the first half of 1920 there were probably more strikes in Italy than anywhere else in Europe. The most serious one was in September 1920, following the high-handed action of some Milanese industrialists (it is worth noting that the first provocation came not from the workers but from the industrialist side): a recently published document of the Ministry of Labour gave rise to the suspicion that industrialists had tried to persuade the Government to use force against the workers. The workers replied by occupying the factories in North Italy, and especially in Turin.

This occupation of the factories was the culminating point in the post-war crisis. Was the next stage to be revolution? It is interesting to observe how at this decisive moment a real will for revolution was lacking, at any rate among the great majority of the people. At a

---

* D'Annunzio and about a thousand followers—mostly members of the Italian armed forces acting either independently of their commanders or with their tacit approval—seized Fiume on September 12, 1919. Ed. note.

† This treaty with Yugoslavia gave Italy all of Istria and the city of Zara; Fiume was made a free state; and all of Dalmatia except Zara went to Yugoslavia. Ed. note.

meeting of the National Council of the General Confederation of Labour on 10 and 11 September, the representative of the Socialist Party Directorate rose and, appealing to the revolutionary drive of the working-class movement, called on the Directorate of the Socialist Party, as a political party, to assume the leadership of the movement as a whole and give it a revolutionary character. The CGL gave a negative reply; it considered that this was not the time to risk revolution, both for fear of failure and also for fear of causing famine in a country so dependent as Italy on imports of wheat and raw materials from abroad.

As a matter of fact, at the very moment when the crisis reached its highest point of danger it was already beginning to decline. Giolitti had completely grasped the situation. He did nothing: he was staying in the country at the time, and he never budged. Only when he had to meet Millerand to discuss with him the solution of the Adriatic problem and prepare the ground for what was to be, two months later, the Treaty of Rapallo, did he leave to keep the apointment. When Millerand saw him arrive he said, "I was sure you would put off our talks." "Why?" answered Giolitti. "Because of the situation in Italy? That's nothing to worry about." And the Prime Minister, the man responsible for public order, tranquilly prepared to discuss the agenda with the French Minister.

But Giolitti himself affords us a very clear explanation of the situation as he saw it. He was a past-master in the art of police technique. He had always kept the Ministry of Home Affairs in his own hands, and had had the opportunity to display his great ability during the pre-1914 strike periods. The first General Strike in Italy was in 1904, when Giolitti was Prime Minister. He telegraphed to the Prefects telling them that there were no serious economic causes for the strike and they should therefore keep calm and not worry. His technique lay in disposing the police at a few main strategic points chosen to ensure the maintenance, whatever happened, of the public services. Apart from that, he just let matters ride. He said to the strikers: "You can parade and shout in the streets to your hearts' content: the post offices, the telephone service, the station, the Prefecture, and the Bank of Italy are all in my hands." He did just the same during the occupation of the factories in 1920: "If I use the police and the troops to occupy the factories," he said, "who will there be to guard the really vital places for me?"

This technique, astute as it undoubtedly was, was moreover only one aspect of a much wider political vision: "I wanted the workers to make the experiment for themselves so that they would realize that it is pure imagination to think you can made a factory run without capital, technicians, or bank credits. They'll try it, they'll find out it doesn't work, and that will cure them of their dangerous illusions."

This estimate of the situation proved perfectly correct. The workers, even those of Turin whom I described earlier as the armoured divisions of the extreme Left, had to abandon the factories of their own free will leaving no dead, no martyrs for the cause. They realized that it was not possible to carry out their plan. And that fact was decisive.

From that point onwards the crisis waned. The danger of a revolution had developed during 1919–20 with the pillaging of the shops in 1919 and the occupation of the factories in 1920. That was the culminating point. After that, disillusionment corroded the workers' will and weakened their enthusiasm.

Clear-sighted Italians now felt that the moment for revolution was definitely past. From another very important angle, too, the crisis-curve had reached its highest point. The financial situation, till then wellnigh desperate, began to improve, especially after Soleri, Giolitti's Minister for Supplies, brought before Parliament in February 1921 the law abolishing the bread subsidy. This was an act of great courage. Hitherto people had been paying a good deal less than the economic price for their bread, and the Government had made up the difference between the cost price and the price of sale to the public. Given the rapid devaluation of the lira and the rise in exchange values (for Italy had to pay in dollars for the wheat she imported), this meant a burden on the Budget of some 500 million lire a month.

If this situation had continued the State would have gone bankrupt. The law of 27 February 1921 made it possible to readjust the Budget. There was of course a deficit for some time; but the Budget was saved on the day when Giolitti and Soleri decided to end the bread subsidy.

Thus alike from the purely political and the financial points of view, seen in retrospect, the historian can affirm that between the end of the summer and the beginning of the autumn of 1920 Italy's crisis had reached its culmination; after that the obvious next task was to embark on readjustment. On the other hand, while it is true that historians today are in a position to demonstrate this fact, it is equally clear that it could not be perceived at once by the masses, who certainly did not consist of historians judging the situation from a distance of twenty or thirty years, or indeed of persons of any great perspicacity. This was why, at the very moment when the real danger was waning, anxiety and fear of revolution steadily increased among a large part of the *bourgeoisie.* We all know how it happens that when we have just escaped some physical danger we suddenly feel terrified on looking back at the difficulties we have evaded. Fear can also be retrospective.

Thus, on the one hand, there was widespread apprehension and uncertainty as a result of the constant strikes and unrest, with no immediate prospect of the longed-for day when peace would return; while on the other hand those who felt their interests to be threatened in various ways were beginning to combine together. The General Confederation of Industry had already emerged in 1919 as a counterblast to the General Confederation of Labour: one block of interests was lining up against the other. Faced with the workers' demands and the land occupations, those whose interests were threatened closed their ranks and moved over to the counter-offensive. This happened particularly among the landowners of the Po Valley.

And towards the end of 1920 came a sudden and unexpected upsurge of the movement known as Fascism.

Chabod's examination of the travails Italy experienced after the First World War can be enriched by reproducing a number of documents illuminating some of the themes he expressed. The tragedy of Italian socialism to which he referred began almost immediately after the end of hostilities. On December 22 and 23, 1918, the Executive Committee (*Direzione*) of the Socialist party, the Socialist Parliamentary Group, the General Confederation of Labor, the League of Socialist Communes, and the Railwaymen's Union met in Bologna at the invitation of the *Direzione.* According to Filippo Turati, a leader of the Parliamentary Group and perennial champion of evolutionary socialism, there developed a most lively contrast between the "Leninist" current and the followers of "traditional classical socialism." The former were strong in the Executive Committee and among a number of local party "sections"; the latter predominated in the party's parliamentary delegation and in the General Confederation of Labor. The principal issue at hand was the reaction of the assembled groups to a resolution presented by the Executive Committee. This resolution had been made public in the Milan edition of the party's newspaper *Avanti!* on December 10 and 14, as a statement of the Committee's program and for the information of the party's membership.

After a day of sharp debate, Turati presented an opposing resolution, the first paragraph of which summarizes the Committee's resolution and reproduces textually those portions of it that are most essential and with which Turati's was in strongest disagreement. Turati's resolution was not put to a vote; it is shown not as a statement of the whole party's views but as an indication of the sharp and eventually irreconcilable divisions within Socialist ranks.

58. THE TWO CURRENTS IN THE SOCIALIST PARTY: DECEMBER 23, 1918

Turati's resolution, printed in the *Critica Sociale,* January 1–15, 1919, pp. 5–6. Our translation.* Reproduced by courtesy of the Casa editrice *Critica Sociale.*

The Socialist Parliamentary Group and representatives of the General Confederation of Labor, of the League of Socialist Communes, and of the Railwaymen's Union have been called to assembly in Bologna by the Executive Committee of the Socialist party "to express their views and to insure the solidarity of the proletariat and the means necessary" to the following ends: "1. immediate demobilization of the armed forces; 2. immediate withdrawal of soldiers from revolutionary Russia; 3. the right to the fundamental liberties of civilized life; 4. amnesty for all political and military prisoners." All of this is viewed as the beginning of a "new phase in the struggle." It being held that "the historical moment for Socialism's international realization has arrived," and it being affirmed that "international peace cannot be achieved until after the demolition of the bourgeois capitalist regime," this new phase has as its "objective for immediate action" the *"institution of a socialist republic and the dictatorship of the proletariat"* for the following purposes: socialization of the means of produc-

---

* The resolution follows the traditional format of "Whereas . . . therefore," and thus makes for exceptionally long clauses. For the sake of clarity this format was abandoned in translation, and the one long sentence which comprises the whole resolution has been divided into a number of briefer ones. Ed. note.

tion and exchange with direct management by workers involved; collectivistic distribution of the items produced; abolition of conscription, and universal disarmament; municipalization of all lodgings and hospital services; transformation of the civil services, to be entrusted to the management of the employees; and promise of support without any distinctions to all "those other demands made necessary by circumstances and claimed by proletarian organizations."

Quite apart from the fact that the above-mentioned enunciations are a strange mixture of abstract maximalist socialism and concrete corporativist syndicalism, and therefore antisocialist, there is the fact that the formulation of this complex program (which is indivisible in its parts as well as in its spirit) reveals an incurable theoretical, tactical, and practical contradiction among the separate aims it contains. This program would entail the abdication of socialist-proletarian action both with regard to ends realizable immediately or in the near future and, perforce, with regard to those more remote ends which presuppose the prior realization of the former. This is so because, on the one hand, the alleged impossibility of having international peace before the demolition of the capitalistic regime would exempt the proletariat from what is today its most important and urgent activity. This is the activity designed to help bring about all those conditions which, even under a capitalistic regime, may make the inevitability and danger of new wars as remote as possible and may put an end to the need for those armaments which contribute to the outbreak of wars. Among these conditions for peace are, for example, the juridical federation of nations, the elimination of tariff barriers, the reform of the colonial regime, and general disarmament. These are postulates which formed an essential part of all socialist programs from the very beginning. On the other hand, the [Executive Committee's] program would also tend to create or to strengthen the illusion among the naïve and uneducated that a socialist republic can be created and consolidated anywhere by an instantaneous and prodigious act of will on the part of slight minorities, in spite of the hostility or irresponsibility of the majority, before the gradual preparation of the objectively necessary technical, economic, and moral conditions—and above all before the existence of that proletarian aptitude and organization that would assure the lasting functioning of such a republic. The [Committee's] program depreciates and makes impossible any activity aiming at the realization of the aforementioned conditions, *and thus destroys the possibility of the very realization of socialism's maximum program.*

More particularly, we hold that the announcement of the [Committee's] proposals as aims to be achieved by *immediate* political action . . . and especially the vague and equivocal allusion to a *"dictatorship of the proletariat"* over the majority of the nation . . . are perfectly suited to *make more remote rather than more immediate* the demobilization of the armed forces, the return to a regime of freedom, the influence of the proletariat on international policy, and the very same greater political and military amnesty which it is urged be hastened by any and all efforts. . . .

An attempt at revolutionary violence—even if hidden under the mask of a simple general strike—would not produce results other than *the bloody crushing of the revolt,* with all the disastrous effects of a prolonged and legitimized political reaction, or, in the best of hypotheses, *a purely formal and superficial change of the political structure.* Consequently, if the socialist proletariat were to assume the initiative in such an attempt or were in any way to support it, it would only confirm the opinion of socialism's immaturity and even of its irreparable incapacity to govern society. This would follow from the socialist proletariat's absolute inability to lead the attempted revolt victoriously to socialist ends and also as a result of the failure even to provide the necessities of life for the population and for itself. There would soon follow a revolt against it on the part of all classes of citizens, beginning with the neediest class, and then *the return of a strengthened bourgeois tyranny.* Even worse, such an attempted revolt would have the effect of *exonerating the classes and groups that wanted the war of the terrible responsibility for the inevitable and foreseeable consequences of the war.* These consequences would then be blamed on the Socialist party, which was and must remain absolutely free of such responsibility. . . .

Accordingly, [we] reaffirm the classic and fundamental concept . . . that *the establishment of a socialist regime cannot result either from a* coup de main *or from prodigious anticipations of history.* It can come only from the gradual conquest of power and from the ability of the masses to exercise this power in all fields of social activity, be they technical, economic, political, administrative, national, or international. . . .

[We] firmly renew the purpose of continuing with our great and specific class struggle, making use even of the tragic experience of the war which laid bare all the inner brutality of the bourgeois regime and its impotence in safeguarding civilization. This struggle will be continued not only for the immediate ends of a more prompt and wise demobilization; for the reconquest of basic freedoms; for the respect of the self-determination of peoples in Russia and everywhere; against all forms of imperialism, Italian imperialism not excluded; and for political and military amnesty to the victims of the war; but also and at the same time for the attainment of a peace that is a people's peace and a lasting one. . . . The struggle will continue for all those demands that for so long a time have been found in socialist programs . . . . Not one of them must be abandoned or neglected: universal suffrage with the extension of the vote to the female proletariat; . . . proportional representation; parliamentary control of foreign policy; . . . simultaneous and general disarmament; destruction of tariff barriers and the conversion of colonial possessions into a collective heritage for all humanity; political and administrative decentralization; . . . reform of the civil service; . . . creation of collective agricultural estates; scientific land reclamation; . . . reform of the tax structure in a democratic direction; popular education; control of supplies and consumption in order to eliminate speculation; . . . all the rights of labor, from the eight-hour day and minimum wages to workers' supervision of management, . . . a more comprehensive social legislation, . . . recognition and proper evaluation of the role of union representation in the factories and in legislation, protective measures for emigration, etc. etc. *These reforms constitute the great and strong ladder by which only the proletariat can really achieve his emancipation without deceptions and disappointments. Only these can lead to the end of classes and of rule by a class, to the supreme justice and equality which are the meaning of socialism.*

Accordingly, today more than ever the workers are invited to support with their knowing and active cooperation the unceasing efforts performed to these ends by their representatives in Parliament, in local administration, in the unions, and in the Socialist party.

Filippo Turati

On most of the important economic and social questions, the position defended by Turati and his reformist followers in the Socialist party was remarkably similar to the one adopted by the Popular party in the program it announced upon its foundation in January 1919.

59. PROGRAM OF THE POPULAR PARTY, JANUARY 18, 1919

Reproduced in Vito G. Galati, *Storia della Democrazia cristiana.* Rome: Edizioni Cinque Lune, 1955, pp. 117–18. Our translation.

I. Integrity of the family and its defense against all forms of corruption and dissolution. Safeguard of public morality; assistance and protection of children, and inquiry into their paternity.

II. Freedom of education at every level. Reform of the schools. Struggle against illiteracy. Popular education and culture. Increased professional education.

III. Legal recognition and freedom of class organization in labor unions; class representation—without any exclusions whatever—in all public organs of labor, be they communal, provincial, or national.

IV. National and international social legislation guaranteeing full right to work and regulating the hours, wages, and conditions of labor. Development of systems of mediation and arbitration for all industrial and agricultural labor disputes. Development of cooperatives. Increase and development of small landholdings.

V. Organization of the nation's entire productive capacity through the utilization of hydroelectrical and mineral resources, and by the industrialization of general and local services. Development of agriculture; internal colonization of the *latifundia* on the basis of extensive agriculture. . . . Increase in the merchant marine. A national solution of the problem of the South. . . .

VI. Freedom and autonomy of local public bodies. Recognition of the functions proper to the commune, the province, and the region in the light of national tradition and the developmental needs of local life. Reform of the bureaucracy. Extensive administrative decentralization to be achieved even by means of a collaboration between capital's industrial, agricultural, and commerical organizations and those of labor.

VII. Reorganization of charity and public aid in the direction of social insurance. Respect of the freedom of initiative in charity and aid, as well as of the freedom of institutions engaged in such activities. Widespread measures for the intensification of the struggle against tuberculosis and malaria. Development and improvement of aid to families hurt by the war: orphans, widows, and the maimed.

VIII. Freedom and independence of the Church in the conduct of its spiritual ministry. Freedom and respect of the Christian conscience considered as the foundation and bulwark of the nation's life, the people's freedoms, and the growing triumphs of civilization in the world.

IX. National and local tax reform based on a general and progressive income tax, with exemptions for the lowest incomes.

X. Suffrage and electoral reform with female suffrage, large multiple-member constituencies, and proportional representation. An elective Senate with a prevailing representation of such bodies as academic groups, communes, provinces, and organized classes.

XI. National defense. Protection and appreciation of the importance of emigration. Spheres of influence for the commercial development of the country. A colonial policy related to the interests of the nation and inspired by a program of progressive civilization.

XII. A Society of Nations with the corollaries deriving from a juridical organization of international life; international arbitration; abolition of secret treaties and of compulsory military service; universal disarmament.

The radical transformation that the war had effected in Italian life is to be seen not only in the programs of the two wings of the Socialist party and in the one adopted by the Popular party but also in an event that occurred in Milan on March 23, 1919. On that day, Benito Mussolini and slightly more than one hundred like-minded Italians assembled to approve a number of declarations marking the "birth of Fascism." The *Fasci italiani di combattimento* [Italian Combat Leagues] thus came into existence as an assertion of the necessity of Italy's participation in the war, as an indictment of all neutralists and particularly the Socialists, as a defense of Italian territorial claims in the Alpine and Adriatic areas, and as an expression of the need for revolutionary reforms in the country's basic institutions. This mixture of interventionist, nationalist, and revolutionary but anti-Socialist themes was a composite expression of most of the conditions in the country causing discontent. The very use of the word *Fasci* [1] is suggestive of the movement's

[1] From the Latin *fasces:* a bundle of rods bound around an ax, carried by lictors in ancient Rome as symbols of authority and unity. Ed. note.

varied antecedents. The word came into prominence during the early 1890s when it was adopted by Sicilian peasants in their protest movement led by Socialist-inspired Peasant Leagues (*Fasci siciliani*). It was employed by Mussolini and other interventionists of the extreme Left when, in January 1915, they founded the *Fasci di azione rivoluzionaria* [Leagues for Revolutionary Action] with the purpose of "dragging Italy into war" and thus prepare for the coming revolution. Mussolini himself wrote in his *Popolo d'Italia* in January 1915: "War today, revolution tomorrow." And in December 1917, after the Caporetto disaster, a number of interventionist Deputies formed a *Fascio parlamentare di disfesa nazionale* [Parliamentary *Fascio* for National Defense] with the avowed aim of maintaining the interventionists' supremacy over a Parliament still too much under the influence of Giolittian and Socialist "neutralists."

The declarations approved by the assembly of the *Fasci italiani di combattimento* in Milan on March 23, 1919, and a speech by Mussolini made it clear that the goal of the new *fascista* group was the preservation and augmentation of the power exercised over Italy by the extreme interventionists during the war years.

The following excerpts include Mussolini's three declarations before the assembly at Milan, and a portion of his speech delivered after the approval of the declarations.

60. THE BIRTH OF FASCISM: MILAN, MARCH 23, 1919

Mussolini's Declarations

> Reported in the *Popolo d'Italia*, March 24, 1919; reprinted in Benito Mussolini, *Opera omnia*, Edoardo and Duilio Susmel, eds. Florence: La Fenice, 1951–62, XII, 321–23. Our translation.

First declaration: The assembly of March 23 addresses its first greeting and its grateful and reverent thoughts to Italy's sons who fell for the greatness of the fatherland and the freedom of the world, to the maimed and the invalid, to the ex-prisoners who did their duty, to all combatants. It declares that it is ready to support with energy the material and moral demands that may be made by the veterans' organizations. . . .

Second declaration: The assembly of March 23 declares that it is opposed to the imperialism of other peoples damaging to Italy, and to any eventual Italian imperialism damaging to other peoples. It accepts the supreme postulate of a Society of Nations, presupposing the integration of each one of these. So far as Italy is concerned, this integration must be realized on the Alps and in the Adriatic with the claim and annexation of Fiume and Dalmatia. . . .

Third declaration: The assembly of March 23 commits the Fascists to the sabotage, by any and all means, of the candidacies of neutralists from any and all parties.

Excerpts from Mussolini's Speech Delivered on the Afternoon of March 23, 1919

Benito Mussolini, *Opera omnia,* XII, 325–27. Our translation.

We have no need to propound a revolutionary program because, historically speaking, we have been standing on such a program since 1915. There is no need to state too analytic a program, but we can assert that Bolshevism would not frighten us if it were to prove to us that it assures the greatness of a people, and that its regime were better than others.

It has now been proved beyond doubt that Bolshevism has ruined Russia's economic life. . . . Furthermore, Bolshevism is a typically Russian phenomenon. . . . We declare war against socialism not because it is socialist but because it has been antinational. There may be differences of opinion on socialism's program and tactics, but the Italian Official Socialist Party has been clearly reactionary and absolutely conservative; if its thesis had triumphed, today there would be for us no possibility of survival in this world. It is not the Socialist party that can lead a movement for renewal and reconstruction. By indicting Italy's political life during these recent years, we are the ones who must nail the Official Socialist Party to [the cross of] its responsibilities.

Majorities are inevitably static, minorities are dynamic. We wish to be an active minority; we wish to separate the Official Socialist Party from the proletariat; but the bourgeoisie should not deceive itself into thinking that we are its lightning rod. We must move toward the workers. As early as the time of the armistice I wrote that it was necessary to move toward the workers coming from the trenches, because it would be hateful and Bolshevik to refuse to acknowledge the rights of those who waged the war. Accordingly, it is necessary to accept the postulates of the working classes. Do they want an eight-hour day? Will the miners and night workers demand a six-hour day? Do they ask for disability and old age pensions? Control of the factories? We shall support these requests, both because we wish to accustom the working classes to the management of enterprises and because we wish to convince them that it is not easy to manage successfully a factory or a business.

These are our postulates; they are ours for the reasons I have just given and because in history there are inevitable cycles by which all is renewed and transformed. If the doctrine of syndicalism holds that the capable personnel necessary for the management of economic activity can be recruited from the masses, we cannot oppose this view, especially if the syndicalist movement pays heed to two realities: the reality of production and that of the nation.

With regard to economic democracy, we stand on the ground of national syndicalism and against the interference of the state when the latter seeks to murder the process of creating wealth.

We shall fight against technical and spiritual backwardness. There are industrialists who are not reforming themselves either from the technical or from the moral point of view. If they do not perceive the virtue of changing themselves, they will be overwhelmed. But we should say to the working class that it is one thing to destroy and another to build. Destruction can be achieved in an hour, but creation is the work of years or of centuries.

Economic democracy, that is our banner. And now for political democracy. I have the impression that the present regime in Italy is in a state of crisis. It is a crisis that hits the eye immediately. During the war all of us sensed the inadequacy of the people who govern us, and we know that the war was won by the virtue of the Italian people, not by the intelligence and ability of the ruling class.

The regime is now in a crisis of succession, and we must not be fainthearted. We must run. If this regime is undone, we must be the ones to take its place. It is for this reason that we created the *Fasci*, these organs of creation and agitation capable of going into the streets and shouting: "The succession is ours because we were the ones who pushed the country into war and led it to victory!"

Our program contains a number of political reforms. The Senate must be abolished. Although I write out this death certificate, I must add that in these latter years the Senate has shown itself to be much superior to the Chamber.

(*A voice:*) "It didn't take very much!"

Quite true, but whatever little it took, was done. We want this feudal body abolished. We demand universal suffrage, for men and women. We want regional multimember constituencies and proportional representation. We shall ask the national assembly issuing from the coming elections to decide on the form of government the Italian state is to have. Its answer will be either monarchy or republic, and we who have always had republican tendencies say from this moment on, republic! . . . The present system of political representation is not enough for us. We want a system of direct representation of the various interests because I, as a citizen, may vote according to my ideas, but as a professional man I want to be able to vote according to my professional attributes.

It may be objected that this program means a return to the guild system. No matter. . . .

An examination of our program may reveal similarities to other programs. It may contain postulates similar to those of the Official Socialists; but this does not mean that they are identical in spirit, because we stand on the platform of the war and the victory, and because of this platform we can dare anything. I wish that today the Socialists would experiment with the holding of power in order that they might learn that it is easy to promise heaven on earth, but difficult to bring it into being. No government would be able to demobilize all the soldiers in a few days or increase the food supplies. There just aren't any. But we cannot permit this experiment, because the Official Socialists would want to import into Italy a counterfeit version of the Russian phenomenon, which is opposed by all the thinking minds of socialism . . . because this phenomenon does not abolish classes, it is a ferociously exercised dictatorship. We are firmly opposed to all forms of dictatorship, from that of the saber to that of the three-cornered hat, from the dictatorship of money to that of numbers. We acknowledge only the dictatorship of will and intelligence.

Accordingly, I should like the assembly to approve a resolution accepting the economic demands of national syndicalism.

With this compass to guide us on our journey, our actions should be directed immediately to the creation of the *Fasci di combattimento*. Tomorrow we shall direct their activity simultaneously in all the centers of Italy. We are not static individuals. We are dynamic, and we want to be at our place, which is that of the advance guard.

Mussolini's hatred for his former colleagues who had expelled him from the Socialist party in November 1914 is an undertone recurrent throughout the preceding speech. The Socialists reciprocated the sentiment, and thus the battle between neutralists and interventionists—a battle that should have ended with Italy's entrance into the war—continued even after the war had ended. The chief symbol of neutralism had been and still was Giolitti. During the war he had said or done nothing in public to heighten the antagonisms dividing the country. But his staunchest supporter in the daily press, the *Stampa* of Turin, had warned repeatedly that after the war there would have to be an accounting. The time for the drawing up of accounts had come, and Giolitti chose his moment shortly before the general elections scheduled for November 1919.

On October 12, 1919, he delivered a speech to his constituents in the province of Cuneo in Piedmont. It was an extraordinary speech, both for his searching and bitter indictment of the war and the government that had decided upon it and for the radical economic and constitutional reforms he proposed. The Socialist newspaper, *Avanti!*, still in the hands of the extremists who at the party congress of October 5–8, 1919, had once again triumphed over the moderates, called Giolitti's program "demagogic and false." The Nationalist organ, *Idea Nazionale*, called him a "traitor"; and the moderately liberal but fiercely interventionist *Corriere della Sera* fixed him with the epithet of "Bolscevico dell'Annunziata" [the royal Bolshevik].[2] It is not likely that the King was much pleased by this characterization. As the speech below makes clear, the King could draw little comfort from a statement that indirectly held him responsible in some measure for the "terrible war" and went so far as to propose amending the Constitution to deprive him of control over foreign policy and the declaration of war.

61. GIOLITTI, "THE ROYAL BOLSHEVIK": PROGRAM-SPEECH OF OCTOBER 12, 1919

Giolitti, *Discorsi parlamentari*, III, 1726, 1731–45, *passim*. Our translation.

Because the terrible war has marked the beginning of an entirely new period in history, a period of profound social, political, and economic

[2] As a member of the Order of the Annunziata, Giolitti was an honorary "cousin of the King" and thus also an honorary member of the royal family. Ed. note.

transformations, the new Legislature will have to face the most formidable problems that can be put before a Parliament. . . .

Everyone remembers what happened between May 11 and May 16, 1915. Salandra's Ministry resigned; the resignations were not accepted; and it became clear even to those who were ignorant of the Pact of London that war was inevitable. Its virtual declaration occurred when the King confirmed in office the Ministry that had decided upon it. . . .

Clearly, the conditions imposed on Italy during the diplomatic negotiations [at Versailles] did not live up to the greatness of our victory. Above all, the refusal to acknowledge to the Italian city of Fiume the right to be reunited to the motherland pains the hearts of all Italians. But I still have hope that in the face of the unanimous feeling of all Italians a solution agreeable with the desires of our brothers of Fiume may yet be found.

But in such a painful question it is our duty that we fix responsibility where it belongs. Without doubt this responsibility falls on the government that wrote in the Pact of London of April 26, 1915, the unhappy clause which expressly says that Fiume must go to the Croats. . . . Nevertheless, victory has given us a safe frontier and has united the Italians of Trent and Trieste with the motherland. . . . Geographical necessity has led to the inclusion in our country of a number of people not of our tongue. It shall be our duty to treat them with such cordiality that they will never have cause to regret becoming Italian citizens. . . .

When we compare the enormous sacrifices in blood and treasure incurred during the war with the conditions given us in the peace treaty, and when we compare these conditions of ours with the splendid advantages secured by our allies, we have a proper measure of the terrible responsibility which weighs on those who hurled Italy into war without foreseeing anything, without precise agreements on political and colonial questions, and without keeping in mind the existence of economic, financial, commercial, and industrial needs. . . .

The war has altered all values—political, economic, social, and financial—and thus has marked the beginning of an absolutely new historical period. Woe if we do not take this transformation into account; woe if we were to follow the beaten path of the past! . . . The war altered also profoundly the preexisting political parties, with the effect that the old labels no longer have any real meaning. It is enough to note that representatives of the most reactionary policies have for years unfurled a democratic banner. Consequently, I cannot now point to the road which I believe should be followed by using party labels, but only by examining the problems that Parliament must resolve. The parties undone by the war must refashion themselves not with words, but with deeds. . . .

The mind recoils in horror at the thought of what another war would be like. . . . To follow a policy that may lead to other wars would mean condemning to death, from this moment on, at least 2 million of our children or grandchildren; it would mean condemning Italy to another half century of economic exhaustion in order to enrich another generation of profiteers. . . . Furthermore, failure to achieve a lasting peace would lead not only to the nightmare of a permanent danger of war but also to immediate ruin because of the consequent need to resume the policy of unrestricted armaments. It would mean devoting the principal resources of the state to military expenditures . . . and the renunciation of any policy of labor and social reforms and civilized progress; it would mean the beginning of a period of economic decline ruinous for the working classes, for public order, and for the future of the state.

In the face of such tremendous dangers any means, even the most revolutionary, would be justified in the effort to avoid another war. But a wise policy must seek to reach the same end by legal means and with measures and reforms comprising an effective defense against the spirit of imperialism and against the unwholesome ambitions and shady interests that led to the past war and might lead to another.

These measures and reforms must be of two kinds: one kind relevant to international relations and the other to domestic political institutions. In international relations the first rank should be assigned to the Society of Nations as a guarantee of peace. Unfortunately, the imperialistic spirit that prevailed during the Peace Conference prevented giving to this Society a structure and a formulation that would constitute a sufficient assurance of peace in the way expressed in Wilson's earliest proposals. But the principle has been announced, and the people who must suffer for several decades the terrible consequences of the war will feel the need to do what diplomacy did not know how or care to do. They must force their governments to apply this principle in a thorough fashion by calling on all nations to be a part of the Society of Nations. . . . But all the guarantees of international order will not have sufficient effect unless they are integrated with reforms in domestic political institutions calculated to assure the country's direct control over foreign policy.

There is in our domestic political institutions a most strange contradiction. On the one hand the executive power cannot spend a lira, it cannot alter the administrative structure in any way, it cannot either create or abolish a single magistracy or any other official post without Parliament's prior approval. On the other hand it can assume by means of international treaties and in the name of the country the most terrible commitments that may lead to war. It can do the latter not only without Parliament's approval but even without Parliament and the country being informed, and with no way whereby Parliament and the country could be informed. This state of things will be altered radically by giving Parliament the same powers in foreign policy as it has in financial and domestic policy; that is, by prescribing that no international agreement may be stipulated and no commitment undertaken without Parliament's approval. . . .

This constitutional reform [of Article 5] * is urgently essential so that Parliament may not be denied control of those actions that may be necessary to regulate international relations under the new conditions created by the war in Europe. If Parliament is entrusted with this authority over foreign policy, there follows the necessary corollary that a declaration of war must always be submitted to it for approval. It would be a major guarantee of peace if in all countries it were the people's representatives who conducted foreign policy. In this fashion it would be impossible for rash minorities or governments lacking in intelligence and conscience to succeed in dragging a people into war against its wishes.

In these latter years the reactionary parties have pursued a campaign of defamation against Parliament. They well knew that with the majority of the people against them, they can never have the majority in Parliament, which is the expression of universal suffrage. But they are blind, because they do not see that by now a government that represents chiefly the privileged classes is impossible; and to bring discredit on Parliament, which is the body that represents all classes,

* See p. 67 above for the text of Article 5 of the *Statuto*. Ed. note.

means to favor the advent of a Soviet government, which represents the dictatorship of the proletariat only.

But Parliament's authority cannot be increased solely by increasing its powers through relevant laws. It is necessary that Parliament itself show, by its acts, that it wishes and knows how to exercise these powers. Four years of government exercising full powers had the effect of suppressing, *de facto,* the activity of Parliament in a manner not found in the other Allied states. In our country all discussion of budgets and all controls over the state's expenditures and financial operations were suppressed. Parliament was kept in the dark with regard to financial commitments undertaken, as well as with regard to all military measures and all diplomatic activity. Parliament's legislative activity during the war was absolutely zero. . . . Suppression of all parliamentary activity was matched by the censor's suppression of all public discussion on the country's most vital interests. Thus for four years the country was kept in the dark about the events and the problems that would shape its future, and this was done with a rigidity greater than anything practiced among the other belligerents. With the coming of peace we must put an end to this danger, so deleterious to Parliament's prestige and so harmful to the country. We must begin a new period, one of exceptional activity. . . .

I have already referred to the very grave conditions to which our state finances were reduced by the war. The public debt rose from 13,000 million lire to 94,000 million; we have an annual deficit of at least 4,000 million; and the currency in circulation is at least six times the normal. . . . There are only two ways of balancing a distressed budget without incurring new debts: reduce expenditures and increase receipts. We must have recourse to both measures with the greatest of energy. . . . [But] the only substantial economies that can be made are in military expenditures, and we can have recourse to such economies because the war, which was an enormous disaster for all peoples, is in itself a guarantee of peace. Now that Italy has acquired its natural frontiers, it can have no military aims other than its own defense, and no one has an interest in attacking us. Furthermore, experience has proved that long terms of military service are useless and the old militaristic spirit harmful.

But I would not agree to any economies in benefits for those mutilated and disabled by the war, nor for the families of those who died for the fatherland. Our debt to all these is sacred; indeed, we must make every effort to improve their conditions and show them the country's gratitude in all possible ways.

In addition to a rigid enactment of all possible reductions in expenditures, we much provide for the receipts. On this latter issue there are two explicit political tendencies in our country. One prefers to place the burden of taxes on consumption; the other has in view the imposition of the greater burden on accumulated wealth. There can be no doubt as to my preference because when I was in power I proposed on three separate occasions a two-pronged progressive tax, on total income and on inheritances. But on all three occasions the opposition of the conservative parties prevented the triumph of the principle that more taxes should be paid by those who are not thereby deprived of the necessities of life but simply have their excess wealth reduced. . . .

There is a form of wealth that almost completely evades the burden of a general tax on income and a tax on inheritances. This is the bearer-bonds and securities that represent a large part of personal income. Therefore, for reasons of justice and great financial need, all stocks and bonds of any kind should be registered in the name of the holder. . . . Opposition to the principle that all securities should be registered can have only one serious explanation: the interest of the great capitalists to hide their wealth. . . . And always according to the principle that taxes should tap the truly wealthy, it will be necessary to tax many luxury articles. . . .

But income taxes are not enough to meet the gravity of the present financial situation. It will be necessary, therefore, to secure an immediate relief; and this can be had only by means of a progressive surtax on the larger estates, and with much higher rates for fortunes derived from war profits.

[After specifying a number of proposed economic, educational, and administrative reforms, Giolitti concluded his speech with the following comments:]

The government and Parliament must always tell the country the unvarnished truth. They must give up that empty rhetoric which, by placing facts and judgments under a false light, constitutes one of the most insidious forms of lying. We must remember that governments are made to serve the people, not to dominate them and lead them where they do not wish to go. We must remember that work is a people's only sure source of wealth, of prosperity, and even of glory. Unfortunately, the most narrow kind of conservative spirit and an aversion to all things new are still deeply rooted among us. . . . But these reactionary tendencies can never again prevail because, if the cruel war imposed the greater sacrifices on the lower classes, in compensation it gave them an awareness of their rights and of their strength; and society's privileged classes, which led humanity to disaster, can never again be the only rulers of a world whose destiny henceforth shall be in the hands of the people. . . .

One of the more important noneconomic problems Giolitti had to face during his year in power (June 1920–June 1921) was to dislodge d'Annunzio from Fiume and reassert the authority of the state over mutinous elements in the Italian armed forces that had joined the "Commander" in violation of the most elementary rules of military discipline. When Fiume was taken by d'Annunzio and his "legionnaires" in September 1919, Nitti, then Prime Minister, had ordered a blockade of the territory and threatened to treat as deserters all those members of the armed forces who had joined in d'Annunzio's enterprise. The Nationalists and many other elements of the Right rallied to d'Annunzio and railed against the government. Mussolini, who had been informed by d'Annunzio on September 11, 1919, of his plan to seize Fiume the next day ("My dear comrade, the die is cast. . . . Tomorrow I take Fiume by force"), supported the enterprise with editorials in the *Popolo d'Italia* and with a campaign for financial aid to the "Commander." The seizure went off smoothly. The local Italian commander representing the inter-Allied authorities in the disputed area surrendered the city without resistance; and Nitti, fearing fratricidal strife and apparently impressed by the fact that most of the Right and some elements of the extreme Left supported the Fiume adventure, refrained from energetic steps against d'Annunzio.

Two weeks after the seizure of Fiume d'Annunzio held a plebiscite which led to the victory of the "annexationist" thesis and to the confirmation of his dictatorial authority. During the next fifteen months of his dominion over the territory, the Commander frequently harangued his followers from a balcony. Many of these followers wore black shirts, part of the distinctive uniform worn by Italian shock troops (*arditi:* daring ones) during the war. They replied to his rhetorical questions with the *arditi* battle cry of "a noi" ("to us" or "up and at them"). They chanted the meaningless but intoxicating phrase "eja, eja, alalà"; and there was even some extravagant talk of duplicating the success in Fiume by marching on Rome itself.

D'Annunzio's poses, the uniforms, battle cries, and general manner of his followers were all soon to be copied by a more resourceful leader in a more successful experiment. Another d'Annunzian precedent later to be followed by Mussolini was set in September 1920 when d'Annunzio decided to proclaim a constitution for the territory of Fiume, which was erected into a Regency until its expected annexation to Italy. This constitution, known also as the *Carta del Carnaro,* is of some interest because of its sketch of a political and economic structure erected on the bases of "corporations" representing the various occupational groups in society. This projected "Corporative State" never came into being in the Regency of Fiume because in December 1920, after surviving the crisis of the occupation of the factories and after the conclusion of the Treaty of Rapallo with Yugoslavia,[3] Giolitti decided to deal with d'Annunzio. The Commander refused to acknowledge the validity of the treaty with Yugoslavia and rejected the instructions of the Italian government to withdraw his troops to the limits of the area assigned Italy by the treaty. Several cannonades aimed at the Commander's palace on Christmas Eve persuaded d'Annunzio not to resist. He resigned his dictatorial powers and his legionnaires began to leave the city, eventually to swell the ranks of Fascism.

As Chabod notes (p. 366 above) it was toward the end of 1920 that Fascism, until then not markedly successful in arousing mass support, began to experience a change in its fortunes. One element in this change was the fear aroused among many Italians, property owners and others, by the occupation of the factories and the "Bolshevist peril." In fact, this peril had already reached its crest and had begun to recede by the end of 1920; but the fear aroused by the escape, narrow or otherwise, grew rather than lessened. It grew even though the real revolutionaries in the Socialist party were among the first to admit that they had missed their opportunity. This realization and the consequent acrimonious debate on who should be held responsible for the lost opportunity are exhibited in the proceedings of the XVIIth Socialist party congress, held in Leghorn between January 15 and 20, 1921.

The Socialists were more faction-ridden than ever. Three motions were debated at the congress: one presented by the "pure" Communists, another by left-wing Socialists who called themselves "unitarian Communists," and the third by the reformist faction led by Turati and the principal representatives of the General Confederation of Labor. The pure Communists included the Neapolitan Amadeo Bordiga, leader of the Neapolitan contingent and the most prominent figure in the Communist faction, the Sardinian Antonio Gramsci, the Genoese Palmiro Togliatti, and the Piedmontese Angelo Tasca—all three associated with the Turinese periodical *Ordine Nuovo* [New Order]. The pure Communist motion called for complete adherence to the program of the Communist Third International, preparation for a communist revolution, expulsion of all those not accepting the pure Communist motion (specifically Turati's faction), changing the name of the party from Socialist to Communist, centralization of the party's organization, and greater party discipline.

The unitarian Communists were led by Giacinto Menotti Serrati, editor of the *Avanti!,* and controlled most of the Socialist party's apparatus. Their motion expressed the desire to maintain the "unity of the party" while adhering

[3] For both developments, see the excerpts from Chabod's work, pp. 363–65 above.

to the principles of the Third International and the eventual conquest of political power by a communist revolution. It agreed with the pure Communists' demand for greater party discipline, but refused to abandon the name Socialist. It also insisted that the Twenty-one Points of Moscow, which were the terms for membership in the Third International, should be interpreted according to the needs of the Italian setting.

The motion sponsored by Turati and the leaders of the Confederation of Labor asserted the impossibility of a Russian-style revolution in Italy. It did not exclude the possibility of the Socialists' advent to full political power, but it also did not exclude the possibility of collaboration with bourgeois parties. It was opposed to violence and illegality in the conquest of power except in the last stage of this conquest and only in the case of blind resistance on the part of the bourgeoisie. It rejected the Russian version of dictatorship of the proletariat; it affirmed freedom of discussion within the party and disciplined observance of the party's decisions once these were reached by democratic means. Turati's motion called for unity and denied the need or wisdom of expulsions or secessions.

The three motions were put to a vote on January 20 and the results were announced the next day: pure Communist motion, 58,783; unitarian Communist, 98,028; Turati's motion ("Concentrazione socialista": Socialist concentration) 14,695.[4] The vote marked the definitive eclipse of the Turatian or reformist wing of the party. It revealed also the unusual strength of the pure Communist faction; but marking as it did the victory of the centrist position, it meant that the pure Communists would be unable to remake the party in their image. Accordingly, on the morning of January 21 they carried out their implied threat and seceded from the Socialist party, proceeding to the formation of the Italian Communist Party. A portion of the constitution of this new party is presented below.

62. CONSTITUTION OF THE ITALIAN COMMUNIST PARTY, ADOPTED ON JANUARY 21, 1921

Resoconto stenografico del XVII Congresso nazionale del partito socialista italiano (Leghorn, January 15–20, 1921). Milan: Edizioni *Avanti!*, 1963, pp. 454–58. Our translation.

Article 1. The Communist Party of Italy (a Section of the Communist International) . . . is constituted on the basis of the following principles:

1. There is developing in the present capitalistic regime an ever-

---

[4] These votes represent not the number of delegates present at the congress but the number of enrolled members of the party whose votes were cast by delegates representing the party's Sections. Ed. note.

increasing contrast between the productive forces and the relations of production, resulting in an antithesis of interests and in a class struggle between the proletariat and the ruling bourgeoisie.

2. The present relations of production are protected by the bourgeois state which, based on a democratic representative system, constitutes the organ for the defense of the interests of the capitalistic class.

3. The proletariat can neither shatter nor modify the capitalistic system of production relations, from which arises its exploitation, without the violent overthrow of bourgeois power.

4. A class political party is the indispensable organ for the proletariat's revolutionary struggle. By collecting within itself the most advanced and knowing part of the proletariat, the Communist party unifies the efforts of the working classes. It turns away from struggles for the interests of certain groups and for contingent results, and turns toward the struggle for the revolutionary emancipation of the proletariat. The party has the function of spreading a revolutionary consciousness among the masses, of organizing the material means for action, and of leading the proletariat during the development of the struggle.

5. The world war—caused by those inner and incurable contradictions of the capitalistic system that produced modern imperialism—has initiated the crisis of capitalism's disintegration. In this crisis, the class struggle cannot but end in an armed conflict between the working masses and the power of the bourgeois states.

6. After the overthrow of bourgeois power, the proletariat cannot organize itself into a dominant class except with the destruction of the bourgeois social structure and with the installation of its own dictatorship, that is, by basing the elective representation of the state on the only productive class and by excluding the bourgeois class from all political rights.

7. The form of political representation in the proletarian state is the system of workers' and peasants' councils. This system already exists in the Russian revolution, which is the beginning of the world proletarian revolution and the first stable realization of proletarian dictatorship.

8. The necessary defense of the proletarian state against all counter-revolutionary attempts can be assured only by depriving the bour-

geoisie, and all parties opposed to the dictatorship of the proletariat, of all means of political agitation and propaganda, and by the armed organization of the proletariat for the purpose of defeating attacks from within and without.

9. Only the proletarian state can actuate in a systematic fashion all those measures of intervention in the social economy's relations by means of which there will be realized the substitution of the capitalistic system with collective management of production and distribution.

10. This economic transformation and the consequent transformation of all activities in social life will eliminate the division of society into classes. There will also follow the eventual elimination of the need for the political state, whose workings will be reduced progressively to the rational administration of human activity.

Art. 2. The Italian Communist Party is organized on the basis of personal membership open to both sexes.

The minimum age for enrollment in the party is 21.

Enrollment shall take place only in the Section of the party in the commune, or subdivision thereof, where the member has his permanent residence.

In the event there is no Section of the party in the member's place of residence, enrollment shall take place in the nearest Section.

Art. 5. The minimum number of members for each Section is fixed at 10. Each Section has the duty to belong to the Provincial Federation [of the party].

Art. 6. New members of the party not recruited from the Youth Sections shall undergo a period of candidacy for six months, after which they may remain permanently enrolled in the party. . . .

Art. 7. The period of candidacy which new members must undergo serves to assure the party of the loyalty and spirit of discipline of new members.

Art. 20. Each Section elects from its own membership an Executive Committee . . . which appoints the secretary of the Section and the Control Commission from its own membership. . . .

Art. 22. The Control Commission inquires into the conduct of the members during the period of candidacy as well as after their definitive enrollment.

The Communist party had come into being in large measure as a reaction on the part of the real revolutionaries in the Socialist party to the failure of the occupation of the factories. Another reaction to this failure was the growth in determination on the part of industrial interests to resist the extremism of the Left by supporting the extremists of the Right. This apparently paradoxical decision to resist more strenuously after the passing of the "Bolshevist peril" has been explained by Chabod as resulting in part from ignorance that the peril had passed and in part from a sort of reflex action frequently manifest after escaping a great danger. And when the fears of the landowners of the Po Valley were added to the justified or imaginary fears of the industrialists, there arose a political climate that was to make possible the rapid growth of Fascism's influence. Not at all successful in acquiring mass support during its first year and a half of life, Fascism suddenly made large strides at the end of 1920 and the beginning of 1921. The following excerpt from a work by Ivanoe Bonomi—a leader of the Reformist Socialists expelled from the Official Socialist Party in 1912 and Giolitti's successor as Prime Minister in 1921—provides a perceptive account of the reasons for this abrupt change in Fascism's fortunes.

63. THE SOURCES OF FASCISM'S APPEAL, 1920-1921

Ivanoe Bonomi, *La politica italiana dopo Vittorio Veneto*. Milan: Giulio Einaudi, Editore, 1953, pp. 140–44. Our translation.

According to the opinion of the extreme or Communist elements in the Socialist movement the occupation of the factories was nothing other than the first act of a general expropriation of property. Just as the workers had taken over the factories, the peasants would take over the land; and then the two together would march on Rome and install there a government of the victorious proletariat. But after three weeks of occupation of the factories the tired and disillusioned workers had to acknowledge that they could not operate the factories which had become useless toys in their hands. . . . Under the influence of maximalist propaganda the workers had deceived themselves into thinking that they could install socialism in Italy at one blow. Having taken possession of the factories, they had had to abandon their prey because of the acknowledged impossibility of making use of it; and thus they had experienced the harshest disillusionment possible for a movement to undergo.

But although this defeat had undercut the revolutionary currents in the country nonetheless it produced an increasingly confused and restless situation. Beaten on the economic plane, the extremist elements sought to retrieve their position on the political plane. Political agitation was resumed and violent episodes gave this agitation a tragic prominence. The episode that had the most resounding effect at the time was the one in Bologna on November 21. The Socialist administration was being installed in the town hall when in the disorder of that day a Liberal councilor, the lawyer Giordani, fell victim to a pistol shot in the municipal hall. This tragic event, occurring as it did in the heart of the Po Valley—that is, in the region most fertile in political agitation—was destined to mobilize the agrarian interests and to array them decidedly against the forces of subversion and disorder.

Until then only the industrialists had sought to contain the extremist elements [of the Left]. At first the industrialists had deceived themselves that they could placate them with large concessions, trusting much in Nitti's conciliatory efforts. Then, during the occupation of the factories, they had decided openly to fight the enemy, trusting in the strength of their own wealth. But until then they had found a complete lack of understanding of the situation on the part of the countryside. Not only the large landowners but the medium and small landowners cultivating their own land and the tenant farmers and sharecroppers as well, all seemed indifferent and passive in the face of the avalanche that threatened to bury them all.

The countryside of the Po Valley and especially that of Emilia and Romagna, of lower Veneto and lower Lombardy, had given hundreds of thousands of votes to Socialist candidates and had sent them triumphantly to the Chamber. The terrified industrialists asked themselves what had happened to those agrarians who had been described as hateful conservatives and stubborn defenders of the old order. But now, suddenly, after the tragedy in Bologna, the agrarian classes began to move, to meet, and to organize. In the hamlets of the Po Valley young officers, veterans of the war, convened their friends and relatives among the peasants and told them that it was necessary to defend themselves against those who had opposed the war and who now did not acknowledge the victory, against those who incited to violence and disorder, against the currents that sought to install a dictatorship of the proletariat and repeat the Russian experiment in Italy. An air of battle swept through the countryside. The people of order no longer remained bolted in their homes fearful of disorders during patriotic ceremonies; now they displayed the tricolor flag and went into the squares to shout their "long live. . . ." The writing of slogans on walls—a practice so dear to Italian political habits—was no longer a monopoly of the Communists. The many "Long live Lenin" and "Long live the proletarian dictatorship" were now contrasted by slogans extolling the fatherland and the victory.

The countryside had awakened and precisely at a moment most propitious to a conservative movement. The old landowning class, which had been frequently of an absentee nature and always apathetic and fearful, had considered the Socialist agitations of 1919 and 1920 as the prelude to an expropriation on the Russian model. For this reason it had been induced to sell its land at bankruptcy prices in order to rescue something of its wealth. The tenant and sharecropper class had been more perceptive and took advantage of the situation. It bought with great haste . . . and thus replaced the older, weaker, and exhausted social class. As soon as these new arrivals to landed property acquired their lands they expressed the most determined intentions of preserving and defending them. The very same people who in 1919, swept by the current to the Left, had voted for the Socialists, now that they were landowners began to fight against the men they themselves had helped rise to power. And, as is true of all new classes, these new landowners revealed an unexpected pugnacity in the struggle.

The industrialists appeared incredulous that they had finally found some allies. The episode of the occupation of the factories had terrified them, and they sought comrades in arms to resist against the danger. The agrarians, and especially those of the Po Valley, seemed to them to be a veritable salvation. An agreement was reached between the two elements and the two forces.

Until September 1920 Mussolini had been uncertain as to the road to follow. His movement had issued from a revolutionary matrix; it had inserted itself among the parties of the extreme Left; and at Dalmine it had anticipated events the preceding year by providing an example of a workers' occupation of the factories. Consequently, it should not be surprising to learn that during the early days of September 1920 he had gone secretly to the home of Bruno Buozzi, leader of the metallurgical workers, to offer his support to the workers if these were to initiate a revolutionary movement for the conquest of power and the installation of a Socialist regime in Rome. After receiving a negative reply, Mussolini had returned to his newspaper and his movement, and made a decision which was to place him in power two years later.

By the end of 1920 the forecast of a Social-Communist victory had been discredited. The experiment of the occupation of the factories and their subsequent evacuation had dealt a death blow to the myth of a revolution in Italy according to the Russian model. The Socialist army had appeared close to victory as late as the middle of 1920; now it was in full retreat. It was a beaten army which, even if it were still able to resist the onslaughts of its pursuers, no longer had a chance of recovery. Accordingly, it was necessary [for Mussolini] to choose between revolution and counterrevolution. Given a lack of principles which reached the point of cynicism and moved by his ambition and rancor, Mussolini could not hesitate in his choice.

Toward the end of 1920 the leader of what until then had been a small group of Fascists decided to enter the game of big politics and to become—he who had not been able to be its leader—the pursuer and destroyer of that defeated army which had met its Waterloo in the evacuation of the factories.

Immediately industrialists and agrarians rallied around the fighting journalist who with his *Popolo d'Italia* fought against the excesses of the Red movement. His newspaper was helped in all possible ways; it was distributed in the factories and the countryside. Until then the *Fasci* had been small in number and not at all widespread throughout the country. Now they swelled with new followers recruited primarily from the agrarian classes. Nearly every hamlet of the Po Valley had its *Fascio;* now that its formerly revolutionary whims were put aside, its activity was concentrated on struggle and polemic against Social-Communist extremism. The movement's spread reached the Apennines and crossed them; it spread above all in Tuscany and Umbria, but it stopped at Rome where the competition from the Nationalists blocked its path and whence only a few branches were able to reach to the South.

Mussolini's conversion to the Right was facilitated by the political situation then prevailing. Giolitti had succeeded Nitti in power with a program aimed at the stabilization of financial and public order and the solution of problems still outstanding in foreign affairs. In substance this was a program promising a government of authority and order. Although Giolitti was a man of the Left who had contacts with the Socialists and was not at all from interventionist ranks, it was possible and proper for the Fascists to approach him, if not applaud him. There was no profound bitterness between the Fascist movement and the Giolittian ranks similar to the one that had dug an unbridgeable chasm between Nitti and the Mussolinians chiefly because of the Fiume controversy.

In order to avoid bitter differences it was enough to present Giolitti's government as a transitional one aimed at stability and public order. Mussolini's concern not to tarnish his new appearance with antiministerial attitudes was so great that even after Giolitti's chasing of d'Annunzio from Fiume [December 1920] he avoided assuming any avenging pose or making any gestures of rebellion.

Thus, in expectation of the coming electoral campaign the plan of including the Fascists in the Giolittian majority ripened. This was an event that no one would have been able to foresee in the spring of 1920, and its occurrence crowned the rapid evolution of Fascism. It had evolved from a movement of the extreme Left to one whose self-appointed function it was to restore public order against the excesses of the Reds, and as a new ally of the conservative forces it assumed a place among the parties of the extreme Right.

Naturally, this occurrence was seen in a different light by Giolitti and Mussolini. For Giolitti the inclusion of a small nucleus of Fascists among the ranks of his large army represented only the recognition of their auxiliary function in the reestablishment of that public order already in the process of realization by reason of many and complex forces. But for Mussolini, on the other hand, the inclusion of himself and some 30 of his followers in the ministerial electoral lists was understood to mean that he had won the anticommunist struggle and that he alone had spared Italy the risk of repeating the Russian revolution. It is certain that his boundless pride from that moment on made him believe that he was the awaited saviour and that in this guise he could dare anything.

In reality Mussolini was but the fly which sits on the steering wheel and thinks that it is driving the vehicle. In Italy of 1921 the forces of Red extremism were already in decline and retreat. They were retreating by reason of their clamorous failure in the occupation of the factories, because of the increasing influence of elements of order in the Socialist party itself, because of the natural change in public opinion, by now tired of useless agitation, and not because of the effect of the

"Fascist bludgeon" which in its blind fury struck down on all proletarian institutions, thus destroying even that which could have been
an element of civilization and progress. But this truth could not be
accepted by the ambitious leader of the Fascists to whom it profited
to have people believe that he was the artisan of victory and that Italy
owed its salvation to him.

And thus there began the legend of a Mussolini who was saving
Italy from Bolshevism; and this lie, echoed in a superficial and credu-
lous outside world, paved the way for his coming successes.

On June 21, 1921, Mussolini delivered his first speech in the Chamber of
Deputies. He and 34 of his followers were elected in May as part of an os-
tensibly progovernment bloc of candidates ranging from the extreme Right
to various shades of liberal and democratic tendencies. Giolitti had called
this election and approved of the national bloc in order to reduce the
strength of his opponents among the Socialists, the *Popolari*, and Nitti's personal followers. The results of the elections were not encouraging to the
government. The Socialists dropped from 156 seats to 122, but 16 Communists were returned. The Popular party gained 7 seats, increasing from 100
to 107. Nitti's strength varied slightly.

The election of 35 Fascists proved to be of little comfort to Giolitti, who
has been criticized ever since for helping make possible Fascism's first
electoral success. It seems that he had hoped to render the Fascists more
tractable and less violent by exposing them to the influences of parliamentary environment. Mussolini and his followers had failed to elect a single
candidate in the elections of November 1919; but the fact that their victory
in 1921 owed something to Giolitti did not make them particularly grateful.
The speech reproduced below makes clear that Giolitti could hope for very
little from the Fascists; it also expresses the enormous transformation that
had taken place in Mussolini's views since the day in March 1919 when he
founded the *Fasci italiani di combattimento* with a program of radical social
and political reforms.

64. MUSSOLINI'S FIRST SPEECH IN THE
CHAMBER, JUNE 21, 1921

> *Atti del Parlamento italiano, Camera dei deputati, Legislatura XXVI,
> Sessione del 1921, Discussioni,* June 21, 1921, I, 89–98, *passim.* Our
> translation.

I say to you immediately and with that supreme contempt I have for
all labels that my speech will assert reactionary theses. I do not know

how parliamentary my speech will be in its form; but in substance it will be decidedly antidemocratic and antisocialist. (*Approval from the extreme right.*) And when I say antisocialist I mean also anti-Giolittian (*laughter*), because never before as in these latter days has there been such an assiduous correspondence of loving feelings between the Honorable Giolitti and the Socialist Parliamentary Group. I dare say that between the two there exists only a passing sulkiness common to lovers, and not the irreparable irreconcilability of enemies. . . .

And now to the argument. In the Royal Address to the Chamber you, Honorable Giolitti, had the King say that the Alpine frontier barrier is now all ours. I challenge the geographical and political accuracy of this assertion. We still do not have, a few kilometers from Milan, the Alpine barrier that is the defense of Lombardy and the whole Po Valley. . . .

So long as Count Sforza is in charge of foreign policy in the Giolitti Cabinet, we cannot but be in the opposition. (*Comments.*)

And now for domestic policies. I shall specify Fascism's attitude toward the various parties. (*Signs of attention.*) I begin with the Communist party. . . . I know the Communists. I know them because some of them are children of mine . . . spiritually speaking, of course. (*Laughter; comments.*). . . . And I acknowledge with a candor that may appear cynical that before anyone else it was I who infected these people when I introduced in Italian socialism something of Bergson mixed with much of Blanqui.* . . . These friends or enemies of mine. . . .

(*Voices from the extreme left:*) Enemies! Enemies!

Mussolini: This is settled, then! . . . So long as the Communists speak of proletarian dictatorship, of more or less federal Soviet republics and of more or less idle absurdities, between us and them there can be only combat. (*Interruptions from the extreme left; comments; agitation.*)

The President: Do not interrupt. Let him speak!

Mussolini: Our attitude toward the Socialist party is different. Above all we insist on distinguishing between the labor movement and the political party. . . . We do acknowledge that the General

---

* Reference to Henri Bergson, French philosopher (1859–1941), proponent of doctrines of intuition and of the *élan vital;* Louis Auguste Blanqui (1805–81), French writer and revolutionary, advocate of class struggle and dictatorship of the proletariat, and source of considerable influence on Karl Marx. Ed. note.

Confederation of Labor did not adopt the attitude of hostility to the war as did a large part of the Official Socialist Party. We acknowledge also the fact . . . that by reason of their daily and direct contact with complex economic realities the organizers of the General Confederation of Labor are quite reasonable. (*Interruptions from the extreme left; comments.*) There are witnesses present who can attest to what I say when I declare that we have never adopted *a priori* an attitude of opposition to the General Confederation of Labor.

(*Voices from the extreme left:*) You burned down the Chambers of Labor! (*Comments.*)

The President: Be quiet! You will speak later! You will have the right to speak.

Mussolini: I add that our attitude toward the Confederation could eventually change if the Confederation itself were to break away from the political Socialist party. This is something that the leaders of the Confederation have been considering for some time. . . .

In any case, listen to what I have to say. When you present a bill for the eight-hour day, we shall vote for it. (*Comments from the extreme left; interruptions.*) We shall not oppose, on the contrary, we shall vote for all measures and provisions intended to improve our body of social legislation. Nor shall we oppose experiments in cooperativism. But I say to you immediately that we shall oppose with all our strength any attempt at socialization, collectivization, and state socialism! (*Comments.*) We have enough state socialism already! (*Applause from the extreme right and from other benches; comments at the extreme left; interruptions.*). . . .

We deny that there are only two classes; there are many more. (*Comments.*) We deny that all of man's history can be explained by economic determinism. (*Applause from the extreme right; approval.*) We deny your internationalism because it is a luxury item (*comments from the extreme left*) to be enjoyed only by the upper classes, whereas the people are desperately attached to their native land. (*Applause from the extreme right.*)

Furthermore, we assert, in accordance with a most recent socialist literature that you should not deny (*Comments*) that the real history of capitalism is beginning only now, because capitalism is not only a system of oppression but also a means of selecting values, a coordination of hierarchies, a more amply developed sense of individual re-

sponsibility. (*Approval.*) This is so true that after having established
factory councils, Lenin abolished them and replaced them with dic-
tators. It is so true that after having nationalized commerce he has restored it to a regime of free exchange. And you know, you who have
been in Russia, that after having suppressed the bourgeoisie even in a
physical sense, now he beckons them to come from everywhere, because without capitalism, without its systems of production, Russia
would never again be able to rise to its feet. (*Applause from the extreme right; comments.*)

Allow me to speak to you frankly and tell you the errors you committed immediately after the armistice. These are fundamental errors
destined to weigh heavily on the history of your policies. First of all
you failed to understand and you treated with contempt the surviving
forces of interventionism. (*Approval.*) Your newspaper became ever
more ridiculous, so much so that for months it did not mention my
name, as if in this way it were possible to eliminate a man from the
living or from the news. (*Comments.*) You have grown ever more
roguish in your defamation of the war and of the victory. (*Lively approval from the extreme right.*) You have waved the Russian myth
and aroused enormous messianic expectations. (*Approval from the extreme right.*) And only after you went to see reality as it was, did you
change your attitude by executing a more or less prudent strategic
withdrawal! (*Laughter.*). . . .

And now I come to the Popular party. (*Comments.*) I remind the
Popolari that in the history of Fascism there are no invasions of
churches. . . . I confess that there is a beating here or there (*comments*) and the burning, as a sacred act, of a newspaper that defined
Fascism as an association of criminals. (*Comments; interruptions from
the center; rumblings.*) Fascism does not preach and does not practice
anticlericalism. We can also say that Fascism is not tied to Freemasonry, which in reality does not deserve the dread it seems to
arouse among some members of the Popular party. As far as I am
concerned, Freemasonry is an enormous windshield behind which are
found petty interests and little men. (*Comments; laughter.*)

But let us come to concrete problems. References have been made
here to the problem of divorce. Fundamentally, I am not in favor of
divorce because I believe that problems of a sentimental nature cannot be solved with juridical formulas. But I ask the *Popolari* to con-

sider whether it is just that the rich may divorce by going to Hungary whereas some poor devil is obliged to carry a chain around his neck for a lifetime.

We agree with the *Popolari* on the issue of freedom of the schools. We are very close to them on the agrarian question, on which we feel that where small property holdings exist it would be useless to sabotage them; that where it is possible to create such holdings, it is just to do so; that where it is not just to create them because they would be antiproductive, other forms of holdings should be adopted, without excluding more or less collectivist cooperatives. We are in agreement on administrative decentralization, provided there is no talk of federalism or autonomies, because with provincial federalism and the rest of an infinite chain Italy would become once again what it was a century ago.

But there is a problem that transcends all these other and contingent problems. I call the attention of the representatives of the Popular party to the historic problem of the relations that may intervene not only between us Fascists and the Popular party but between Italy and the Vatican. (*Signs of attention.*)

All of us who from the age of fifteen to twenty-five slaked our thirst with Carducci's * literature have hated an *old vatican and cruel wolf* of which he spoke . . . ; we have heard speak of "a dark pontiff of mystery" as opposed to a poet priest of the august truth, prophet of the future. . . . But although all this may be most brilliant in the field of literature, to us Fascists who are eminently unprejudiced spirits it seems somewhat anachronistic. I affirm here and now that the Latin and imperial tradition of Rome today is represented by Catholicism. (*Approval.*) If, as Mommsen † said twenty-five or thirty years ago, one cannot stay in Rome without a universal idea, I believe and affirm that the universal idea that exists in Rome today is that which emanates from the Vatican. (*Approval.*). . . .

I believe that if the Vatican were to renounce definitively its dreams of temporal power—and I believe that it is already moving in this direction—profane or lay Italy would supply the Vatican with material aid for its schools, churches, hospitals, and the like. . . . I believe this

* Giosuè Carducci (1835–1907), highly influential poet noted for his severe strictures against the Church. Ed. note.

† Theodor Mommsen (1817–1903), German historian noted for his works on ancient Rome. Ed. note.

because the development of Catholicism in the world, the increase in the 400 million men who from all quarters of the globe look to Rome, is of interest and a source of pride also for us who are Italians.

The Popular party must choose: as a friend of ours or an enemy or a neutral. I have spoken very clearly; I hope that someone from the Popular party will speak equally clearly. . . .

I have reached the last part of my speech, and I wish to touch upon a very difficult question that, given the times, should arouse the attention of the Chamber. I refer to the struggle, to the civil war, taking place in Italy. First of all, and with regard to foreign opinion, it is necessary not to exaggerate the vastness and proportions of this struggle. The Socialists have published a volume of 300 pages on this matter. Tomorrow we shall publish our own volume of 300 pages. Besides, all of the nations of Europe have had a little of civil war. It occurred in Hungary, it occurred in Germany, and it is occurring in England in the form of a colossal social conflict. It took place even in France when Jouhaux launched his famous "waves," * which were broken by a government more courageous than the one now in power there. (*Laughter.*)

It is useless for Giolitti to say that he wishes to restore the authority of the state. This is an enormously difficult task because in Italy today there are three or four states in contention for possible or probable power. . . . The function of the state is to provide us with a police force to protect honest men from rogues, a well-organized system of justice, an army ready for all eventualities, and a foreign policy in tune with the nation's needs. All the rest—and I do not exclude secondary education—must be returned to the individual's private initiative. If you wish to save the state, you must abolish the collectivist state (*good!*) we have of necessity inherited from the war, and return to the state of the Manchesterian school.

The civil war is becoming more grave for this additional reason: all the parties are tending to form and organize themselves into armies. There follows a confrontation that was not very dangerous when political parties were in a nebulous state, but has become much more dangerous now that the parties are clearly organized, led, and controlled.

---

* Léon Jouhaux (1879–1954), secretary-general of the French General Confederation of Labor from 1909 to 1947.

On the one hand, it is evident by now that the working masses will be beaten. This was acknowledged quite rightly by Baldesi,* but he did not state the profound reason for it. It is this: the working masses are naturally—I would say saintly—peacemongers; they always represent the static reserves of human society. On the other hand, risk, danger, and the taste for adventure have always been the duty and privilege of small aristocracies. (*Approval from the extreme right.*)

Well then, you Socialists, if you agree and admit and confess that on this score we shall beat you (*rumblings from the extreme left*) . . . then you must conclude that you have taken the wrong road. (*Interruptions from the extreme left.*) For us violence is not a system, it is not a form of aesthetics, and even less is it a sport. It is a hard necessity (*comments*) to which we have submitted. (*Comments.*) And I add that we are ready to disarm if you disarm as well, above all if you disarm your spirit.

In the Milan edition of the *Avanti!* of June 18 it is written:

Unlike our opponents, we do not preach a vendetta. We think of the majestic rise of the masses and the classes in terms of a peaceful and fruitful activity even in the case of inevitable—indeed, necessary—civil strife. Gentlemen, if this is your point of view, it is up to you to enlighten the ignorant and disarm the criminal. We have already spoken and we have already acted.

Now I reply that you too must enlighten the ignorant who believe us to be cutthroats for capitalism and agents of the government. You must also disarm the criminal, because in our list of martyrs we have 176 dead. If you do this, it will then be possible to say the word *end* to the sad chapter of civil war in Italy. You must not think that we are devoid of profoundly humane sentiments. We say with Terence: we are human and nothing human is alien to us.

But if disarmament is to come, it must be reciprocal. If it is reciprocal, the state of things we so ardently desire will come to pass. And we desire it because if things continue as in the past the country will run the risk of falling into an abyss. (*Comments.*) We are at a decisive moment; frankness for frankness; before we lay down our arms, disarm your spirit.

* Gino Baldesi, Socialist Deputy belonging to the right wing of the party and a leader in the General Confederation of Labor. Ed. note.

I have spoken clearly. I await an equally elevated and clear reply from you.

I have finished. (*Very lively and repeated applause from the extreme right; prolonged comments; many congratulations.*)

Two days after Mussolini's speech Giolitti received a scant majority on a vote of confidence in which he was opposed by the extremes of the Right and Left and by Nitti's followers. The parties of the Right thought Giolitti's fiscal reforms too radical; the extreme Left had no confidence in them; and although Nitti, and Don Luigi Sturzo of the Popular party, should have had little objection to these reforms in principle, their personal hostility to Giolitti rendered his parliamentary position unsound. The new government was entrusted to Ivanoe Bonomi, one of the early leaders of the Socialist party who had been expelled with Bissolati in 1912 by the extremist faction then led by Mussolini. Bonomi's government included elements of the Center and the moderate Left, and had the support of the Popular party, three of whose Deputies entered the Ministry. Bonomi's principal aim was to achieve domestic tranquillity, and to this end he promoted a "Pact of Conciliation" between Fascists and Socialists. Mussolini had apparently decided in July 1921 on a less violent course and agreed to the Pact, which was signed early in August. His more violent colleagues in the Fascist movement demurred, and Mussolini retaliated by resigning as a member of the executive group of the *Fasci's* Central Committee, but not from the movement. His resignation was rejected by the Fascist National Council, but the price paid seemed to be the disregard of the Pact of Conciliation. The formal abrogation of the Pact came in November 1921 when the Fascist movement formally converted itself into a party and asserted its right to maintain its armed "squads." Bonomi's efforts thus came to an unsuccessful end; and when, early in 1922, Bonomi found that to his opponents from the Right there suddenly had been added some opponents from the moderate Left because of a minor controversy involving the government's refusal to assure payment to depositors in an insolvent discount bank, he decided to resign. Bonomi's logical successor appeared to be Giolitti; but the opposition of Don Luigi Sturzo, political secretary of the Popular party, to a new Giolittian government excluded this solution; and the final designation fell on Luigi Facta, an old friend of Giolitti and presumably his faithful lieutenant. It was this same Facta that Mussolini displaced late in October 1922 with his famous "march" on Rome.

The background to the fall of Bonomi's government and the consequences of Facta's Ministry of indecision are presented in the following account from a work by Carlo Sforza, Giolitti's Minister of Foreign Affairs in 1920–21 and one of Fascism's earliest and most severe opponents.

65. PRELUDE AND MARCH ON ROME

From the book *Contemporary Italy* by Carlo Sforza. Translated by Drake and Denise DeKay. Copyright, 1944, by E. P. Dutton & Co., Inc. Reprinted by permission of the publishers. Pp. 304–13, *passim.*

An incident at Sarzana on [July] 21, 1921,* showed even to the blindest that Fascism was nothing but a gigantic bluff and that Bonomi could govern with more moral force than the Undersecretary of State Corradini, to whom Giolitti had, unfortunately, left the daily task of the repression of Fascism. At Sarzana, for the first time after months of tolerance, a Fascist "expedition" composed of five hundred armed riff-raff was annihilated by the calm resoluteness of a single captain of the Carabineers supported by only eight Carabineers and three soldiers. . . .

But that was not all. The population of Sarzana had been told by migratory field workers of Fascist columns firing at their train as it approached the city. As soon as the Fascist exploit became known, armed groups from the surrounding countryside, aided by exasperated peasants, hunted down the Fascists, who left half a score of their dead hanged on trees or drowned in swamps, as well as several dozen wounded. The police authorities again intervened, but this time to save the retreating Fascists from popular fury. At the time I was living on an estate belonging to my family not far from Sarzana, and everywhere I saw only delighted peasants wondering, asking, if at last *"la pace"*—peace—had been restored.

After the Sarzana incident Mussolini sent to Bonomi his most abject assurances that he wanted only order and conciliation. He was afraid.

The "Conciliation Pact" was signed August 2, 1921. Mussolini appeared to act in good faith, but the pact was violently attacked by Dino Grandi and his followers who were in the pay of the ferocious landowners of the Po Valley. Grandi had with him a majority of the *squadristi* (combat squads), and Mussolini, as usual, rallied without delay to the side of the strongest. Bonomi failed in his efforts to bring back a modicum of tranquillity to the country.

By their actions the Communists aided Fascism. Not that they were

* The date given in Sforza's work (November 21) is not correct. Ed. note.

not fighting Fascism, but for them everything was Fascism: the State, democracy, the middle classes, even—and especially—the Socialists, who had remained liberal. The Socialists, in a sudden access of common sense and dignity, organized the *Arditi del Popolo*,* the Sarzana incident having proved that only the fear of beatings would make the Fascist *squadristi* flee. The Communist Party forbade its members to join the *Arditi del Popolo*, an organization, it declared, that is "a maneuver of the bourgeoisie." Communism wanted the destruction of Fascism, but on a single condition, that Communism should remain the sole master. Nothing could better serve the Fascist cause.

Mussolini, seeing that the Communists prevented the union of anti-Fascist forces, that the Socialist leaders remained weak and divided, and—above all—that the violent element of Fascism alone had the confidence of the recruiters of *squadrismo*, suddenly decided to become the most violent of all. Having heard the rumor that Bonomi had decided to dissolve the combat squads by a decree, he had the heads of the party vote the following order:

"To all the Sections of the Party! To all the Combat Squads!

"It is rumored in the press that there will be an early offensive of the Government against Fascism. . . . Sections of the Party and Combat Squads form an indivisible whole. Dating from December 15, 1921, all those inscribed in the Sections will become part of the Combat Squads. . . . Dissolution of the Combat Squads will thus become impossible, if the Government shall not have, previously, declared the National Fascist Party as a whole unlawful."

The challenge had been given. The Fascist Party should have been dissolved, since the entire party had joined the combat squads. But the Government dared not accept the challenge. At that period I often saw Bonomi in his modest apartment in the Piazza della Libertà. Personally he was ready to act, to take the risk. But he was head of a Coalition Cabinet and had too few adherents. On February 16, 1922, the Bonomi Cabinet was reversed in the Chambers: Socialists and Fascists united their votes against Bonomi. Federzoni's Nationalists staged demonstrations at Rome and Florence in front of the headquarters of the Army Corps with cries of "Long live the Dictatorship!"

* People's shock troops. Ed. note.

Unfortunately the ministerial crisis, from which the Facta Cabinet emerged, was the longest Italy had ever known since 1848.

The middle classes saw in all this a proof of the failure of Parliament.

The satisfaction evinced by the Fascist leaders after a few days of the Facta Government gave proof that the Bonomi Government had always done its duty or had tried to do it. It was only with the advent of Facta that "justice" began to function in a unique way. It is a matter of record that during the early months of 1922 at Rome, Vercelli, Florence and a hundred other places in Italy all the Fascists accused of murder and "personal violence" were acquitted and carried off in triumph by their friends. In the rare cases in which justice, ashamed, dared not render a verdict of acquittal, the accused were granted provisional liberty to leave for another city where they were safe from any pursuit.

With Facta, Fascism was already tacitly in power everywhere. . . .

I had been Facta's colleague in the same Cabinet * when he was Minister of Finance; but the entire burden of financial problems was borne by Giolitti and by Meda, the Minister of the Treasury. Facta therefore had no opportunity to do well or ill and, with a good bureaucracy helping him, was a good rather than a bad official. I often saw him at the weekly audiences of the ministers at the Quirinal † and at Cabinet councils; yet I have not the least recollection of even a phrase or of any remark whatever of this ever-obliging little bourgeois who was always smiling, always approving. The misfortune of being chosen to preside over a provisional Ministry befell him by reason of a parliamentary situation, which some thought would soon be cleared up by the installation of a new Giolitti Ministry, while others thought the successor would be a Ministry of All the Talents. Events demonstrated that that sort of game is sometimes dangerous. Everyone knows what happened. The Fascists, convinced of the incurable weakness of Facta, met in congress at Naples. It was the occasion for the rallying of their legions.

On October 24, 1922, their leader, Mussolini, left them, going to distant Milan, where he was near the Swiss frontier. It was safer! One

* Giolitti's Cabinet of 1920–21. Ed. note.
† Quirinale palace, the King's residence in Rome. Ed. note.

never knows! On the 27th the Fascists intimated to Facta that he had better resign, which he did the same evening. During the night of the 27th the "march on Rome" was organized, Mussolini remaining at Milan. Meeting that same night, the resigning Ministry decided to resist, not on Facta's motion but on that of three other Ministers, the only resolute members of the entire Cabinet: Amendola, Alessio and Taddei. All the other ministers came over to their opinion and it was decided to proclaim martial law. On the morning of October 28 Facta submitted to the King the decree proclaiming martial law, but returned to the Council, still in session, with the decree unsigned. The ministers insisted on the necessity of martial law and again dispatched Facta to the King. Facta went, but returned a second time without the royal signature. The news that martial law was not to be put into effect spread like wildfire and, naturally, the number of Fascists immediately increased. In fact, Fascist numbers increased so rapidly that on the evening of October 28 Mussolini, who had not left Milan, was summoned to Rome to form a Ministry.

Did Facta, inconsistent as he was, hide some kind of idea under his vacillating attitude? Not one historian of the epoch has given any thought to the Facta element, such a nullity was the man. But how often have men who are nullities done a vast amount of harm!

Sturzo, in his *Italy and Fascismo,* a book which in its honesty and serenity is more like the work of a philosopher-historian than the head of a political party, writes: "The position of the Facta Cabinet (in October, 1922) was not only insecure but had become untenable, and the Prime Minister was only awaiting the reopening of the Chamber to tender his resignation—at least so rumor said. . . . Facta secretly worked for the return of Giolitti, but his efforts bore no fruit."

Sturzo attributes the fact that the King had not signed the decree of martial law "to the fear that worse might happen, to the hope of a possible accord, to the weak and equivocal position of the Cabinet which, after having resigned, was deprived of all authority, to the counsel of certain army leaders."

Facta's responsibilities are far more serious. Not only did he not work for the return of Giolitti, but he did all in his power to prevent it. On that point I have the overwhelming testimony of Giolitti, of Taddei, Minister of the Interior with Facta, and others.

Facta, deputy of an electoral district bordering Giolitti's, had all his life been one of the faithful who silently followed the Piedmontese statesman. His only title was: friend of Giolitti. Nothing was more natural, consequently, than the general belief—shared by Sturzo in his book—that Facta "worked for the return of Giolitti."

When, subsequently, with the respect due his age, I expressed my astonishment to Giolitti that he had not thought it his duty in the autumn of 1922 to go to Rome and seize power, he replied to me: "I see clearly now, after what has happened, that I was wrong; but difficulties and obstacles and objections of all kinds that Facta sent me so that I should not budge from Cavour * were infinite and inexhaustible; he even telegraphed me once, when I had decided to leave for Rome, that floods had made the trip dangerous." Giolitti added that he had not realized, until too late, that Facta had let himself be persuaded by secret proposals of the Fascists, who flashed before his eyes the hope of remaining Prime Minister in a new Ministry composed of Mussolini and other Fascists. As a matter of fact when, on October 28, one of the leaders of his majority advised him to withdraw his resignation, to be in a stronger position, he did nothing about it; and, in the position of having resigned, he kept on negotiating with the Fascists. He thought that by continuing in that status he was placing himself in a better position for a portfolio. I asked Giolitti how a man who ought to have been devoted to him had come to play such a double game. Giolitti replied:

"He was not" (he spoke of the man as of the dead, in the past tense), "he was not a bad man; but vanity had turned the head of the persons of his entourage, and he yielded to the entreaties he heard, day and night, to make his way without me and against me. Poor man. . . ." . . . .

Facta's stupidity and levity became treason the night of October 28, 1922, on the two occasions when the Council of Ministers sent him to the King to have him sign the state of siege that the Cabinet had unanimously voted after listening to the argument of the three Ministers who remained conscientious with regard to their duty, Alessio, Amendola, and Taddei. Both times Facta did submit the decree to the King, but both times adding all kinds of other considerations intended to induce the King not to sign—such considerations as the lack of authority of a resigned Cabinet (and that Facta himself had wished to

* Giolitti's place of residence in Piedmont. Ed. note.

remain in the status of a resigner); horror at the blood that would be shed; reasons for hoping that Mussolini would prove reasonable, and so on.

The King has been culpable of so many faults and criminal complicities that there is no reason to hide that—being what he was—the responsibility for the non-signature of the decree of a state of siege weighs more heavily on Facta than on him.

Being the kind of person I know him to be, I am convinced he would have signed if an energetic prime minister had instructed him that it was his duty, as constitutional king, to sign. . . .

When, several days before the "march on Rome," the Government made the King feel that it would be best to abandon the tranquil refuge of his hunting lodge at Sant'Anna di Valdieri, in the Alps, and return to Rome, the King obeyed, as always. At the Termini station in the capital, where several ministers received him, as he stepped from the train he turned to the Minister of War, Soleri, and muttered in Piedmontese dialect: "If those fellows come to Rome, I'll take my wife and children and I'll go and settle in Savoy or Nice and live tranquilly."

Nice—Savoy—that meant abdication! It was the dream about which he had often in the past spoken to me as of a happy vision of calm days. Why did he stay on? Partly on account of the pressure of all the appeasers who assured him that Mussolini would very soon "normalize," once he had become Prime Minister. That word—normalization—was the illusion and hope of almost everyone, and continually utilized by Mussolini. Yet another and entirely different reason prevailed with the King: his hatred of his cousins, the Aostas, and his fear lest his departure should leave the way open to the throne for the Duke d'Aosta, whom he despised as the Bourbons in France must have despised the Orléans, ever ready to betray the elder branch of the family. The Duke d'Aosta—who as commanding officer of the IIId Army during the war had gained some popularity in Italy—had contracted a bad attack of thronitis: for two years he did not leave me a moment's peace, trying to persuade me to have him appointed King of Poland, King of Hungary. . . . When I mentioned it to the King he used to mutter: "If it were only *that*. . . ."

Guilty as he later became, it cannot be denied that the poor King was most unlucky in his own family: the Aostas, as false and treacherous as the Orléans (whose blood flowed in their veins); the Genoas, near-idiots and deformed; and, later, his own son, more Levantine than Italian; but, above all, on Fascism's attainment to power, the constant and crafty activities of the Queen in favor of the adventure.

PART SIX

THE FASCIST ERA, 1922–1943

XX. THE ROAD TO DICTATORSHIP,
1922–1924

Italy's Fascist era began on October 31, 1922, when Mussolini formed the first of his many Ministries. He had received the royal summons on October 29 and arrived in Rome from Milan the next day. The new government included Mussolini as Prime Minister, Minister of the Interior, and interim Minister of Foreign Affairs. The Ministries of Justice and Finance were assigned to two other Fascists, but all other major Cabinet posts were divided among Nationalists, Social-Democrats, members of the Popular party, a Giolittian, and a Salandrian. On the surface it was a coalition government in the old style, with a Fascist preponderance not in the major Cabinet posts but in the Under-Secretaryships. Apart from the Socialists and the Communists, all major political parties seemed resigned to a Mussolini experiment as the only escape from the political chaos that had prevailed in Parliament and the country during the postwar years. The desire for "normalization" was such that even the truculence of Mussolini's first speech to the Chamber was underplayed in favor of the more responsible remarks made in this formal presentation of the Fascist program of "action, not words." Mussolini's carrot-and-the-stick approach was employed effectively during the two years preceding the crisis brought about by the assassination of the Socialist leader Matteotti in June 1924. When, by the end of 1924, this crisis was resolved in favor of Fascism, Mussolini abandoned all semblance of moderation and embarked definitively on a course of dictatorship.

66. MUSSOLINI PRESENTS HIS GOVERNMENT TO THE CHAMBER, SPEECH OF NOVEMBER 16, 1922

Atti del Parlamento italiano, Camera dei deputati, Legislatura XXVI, Sessione del 1921–1923, Discussioni, November 16, 1922, X, 8390–94. Our translation.

In the brief period of a decade it has come to pass that for the second time the better part of the Italian people has supplanted a Ministry and has given itself a government above and against the wishes of Parliament. The decade to which I refer goes from May 1915 to October 1922.

I leave it to the melancholy zealots of superconstitutionalism to discourse on this matter in a more or less doleful fashion. I assert that revolution has its rights. In order that everyone may know it, I add that I am here to defend the Black Shirt revolution and to bring it to its fullest realization. . . .

I could have abused my victory, but I refused to do so. I imposed limits on myself. I said to myself that the greatest wisdom is the one that does not abandon you after victory. With 300,000 men armed to the teeth,* ready for anything and almost mystically ready to obey my orders, I could have punished all those who have defamed Fascism and have tried to besmirch it. (*Approval from the right.*)

I could have converted this gray and dull hall into a bivouac for my squads. . . . (*Lively applause from the right; rumblings; comments.*)

Modigliani: † Long live Parliament! Long live Parliament!

Mussolini: . . . I could have bolted the Parliament and formed a government exclusively of Fascists. I could have done this but, at least for the present, I have chosen not to do so. . . .

I believe that I express the thoughts of a large part of this Assembly and certainly of the majority of the Italian people when I pay the tribute of a warm greeting to the King, who refused to take part in last minute and uselessly reactionary attempts [to stop us], who prevented a civil war, and who allowed the new and impetuous Fascist current issuing from the war and exalted by victory to enter the weakened arteries of the parliamentary state. (*Shouts of* Long live the King! *The Ministers and very many Deputies rise and applaud long and vigorously.*)

Before reaching this post everyone asked us for a program. Alas, it is not in programs that Italy is lacking. It needs men and the will to apply these programs. All of Italy's problems—I repeat, all—have already been solved on paper. What has been lacking is the will to

---

* An exaggerated statement. The rather badly armed Fascist squads probably consisted of much less than 100,000 men. Ed. note.

† Giuseppe Emanuele Modigliani, a moderate Socialist who with Turati and others finally decided to break with the extremists and form a separate Unitary Socialist Party early in October 1922. Ed. note.

translate them into deeds. Today the government represents this firm and decided will.

What occupies and preoccupies us most, especially at this moment, is foreign policy. I speak of it immediately because I believe that what I shall say will dissipate many apprehensions. I shall not deal with all questions because in this field as in all others I prefer action to words.

The fundamental lines of our foreign policy are these: Treaties of peace, however good or bad they may be, must be executed once they have been signed and ratified. A self-respecting state cannot hold any other doctrine. (*Lively approval.*) But treaties are not eternal, they are not irreparable. They are chapters of history, not history's epilogue. To execute them means putting them to the test. If in executing them they are revealed as absurd, this may be the new fact that opens up possibilities of an eventual reexamination of the respective positions of the parties involved. The Treaty of Rapallo,* as well as the Santa Margherita Agreements deriving therefrom, shall be presented by me to Parliament. . . .

Fascist Italy does not intend to tear up treaties. For many political, economic, and moral reasons it also does not intend to abandon its wartime allies. Rome is in line with Paris and London; but Italy must impose on itself and place before its allies that severe and courageous examination of conscience they have not faced from the time of the armistice to today. (*Lively approval.*)

Does there still exist an Entente in the substantial meaning of the word? What is the Entente's position toward Germany, toward Russia, toward a Russo-German alliance? What is Italy's position in the Entente: that Italy which has lost strong positions in the Adriatic and the Mediterranean, and not only because of weaknesses of its governments; that Italy several of whose fundamental rights are being questioned; that Italy which received neither colonies nor raw materials and is literally crushed by debts incurred for the sake of the common victory?

In the conversations I shall have with the Prime Ministers of France and England I propose to face clearly the whole complex

* Treaty signed by Giolitti and Sforza with Yugoslavia in November 1920 providing for Italy's possession of Istria, Fiume as an independent state, and all of Dalmatia to Yugoslavia except for the city of Zara. The following month Giolitti proceeded to expel d'Annunzio from Fiume. Ed. note.

problem of the Entente and the consequent problem of Italy's position within the Entente. (*Lively applause.*) Two hypotheses will issue from such an examination: either the Entente cures its internal defects and contradictions and becomes a homogeneous, balanced bloc of equal forces with equal rights and equal duties, or its hour is sounded and Italy, resuming its liberty of action, will adopt a new and loyal policy for the safeguard of its interests. (*Lively approval.*) As for me, I wish that the first hypothesis comes to pass for many reasons, including the boiling over of the entire Eastern world and the growing intimacy among Russia, Turkey, and Germany. . . .

A foreign policy such as ours—a policy of national interests, of respect of treaties, of reasonable clarification of Italy's position in the Entente—such a policy cannot be made to pass as adventurous or imperialistic in the colloquial sense of that word. We wish to pursue a policy of peace, but not one of suicide. . . .

Our domestic policy is summarized in these words: economies, work, discipline. The financial problem is a fundamental one, and it is necessary to balance the budget as quickly as possible. We shall follow a policy of misers; we shall spend intelligently; we shall assist all the productive forces of the nation; we shall put an end to all the restrictions remaining from the war. (*Lively approval.*). . . .

Whoever says work means the productive bourgeoisie and the working classes of the cities and the fields. No privileges for the former and none for the latter, but protection for all interests in harmony with those of production and of the nation. (*Lively applause.*). . . .

Increase in the country's prestige before the world is proportionate to the country's internal discipline. The domestic situation is undoubtedly improved, but not as much as I would like. I do not intend to lull myself with easy optimism. I do not like Pangloss. The large cities and all cities in general are calm; acts of violence are sporadic and peripheral, but they must end. All citizens, no matter to which party they belong, may move about freely; all religious beliefs shall be respected, with particular regard for Catholicism, the dominant religion; the fundamental freedoms shall not be impaired; and respect for the law shall be exacted at all costs.

The state is strong and it shall show its strength against all, even against any eventual Fascist illegality because it would be an irresponsible and impure illegality wholly lacking in justification. (*Lively applause; comments.*) I must add, however, that nearly all Fascists have perfectly accepted the new order of things. The state does not intend to abdicate its authority before anyone. Whoever rises against the state will be punished. . . .

So long as it is possible for me, I shall not want to govern against the Chamber, but the Chamber must understand its special situation that makes it subject to dissolution within two days or two years. (*Laughter; applause from the right and the extreme left; comments.*) We ask for full powers because we wish to assume all the responsibilities. You know full well that without full powers we cannot economize on 1 lira—I say 1 lira. This does not mean that we intend to exclude the possibility of willing collaboration, which we shall accept cordially, be it from qualified Deputies, Senators, or private citizens. . . .

We propose to give discipline to the nation, and we shall do so. Let none of our past, present, and future opponents deceive himself on the brevity of our stay in power. (*Laughter; comments; applause from the right.*) This would be a childish and foolish delusion, as were those of the past. Our government has a formidable base in the conscience of the nation; it is supported by the better and fresh Italian generations. Without question, in these latter days a gigantic step has been taken toward the unification of spirits, and the Italian fatherland has found itself once again. . . . Gentlemen, do not shower the country with additional and useless chatter. Fifty-two Deputies scheduled to speak on my communciations are too many. (*Laughter; comments.*) Rather, let us work with pure heart and ready brain to assure the prosperity and greatness of the fatherland. May God help me bring my arduous labors to a victorious conclusion. (*Most lively applause from the right and other benches; prolonged comments; many Deputies congratulate the Honorable President of the Council of Ministers.*)

The new government received a vote of confidence of 306 in favor and 116 against. Among those who voted in favor, in addition to the Fascists and the Nationalists, were leading figures such as Giolitti, Bonomi, Orlando, Salandra, and De Gasperi and Gronchi for the Popular party. The Socialists and Communists voted compactly with the opposition. By the end of the month both the Chamber and Senate accorded Mussolini with unusual speed and large majorities a year of emergency powers to "reform the tax structure . . . reduce the functions of the state [in economic matters], reorganize the public services . . . and reduce expenditures." This is substantially the authority Giolitti had requested of Parliament in 1921, and its refusal had been one of the major reasons for Giolitti's resignation. What it had refused to grant to a genuine parliamentarian, Parliament now accorded to a man who had never concealed his contempt for that institution.

But even with a grant of emergency powers and with the little open opposition to the new government except from the extreme Left, the Fascists did not feel safe enough to abandon their privileged position of being the only political grouping in the country permitted to maintain a private armed force. That Fascism did not intend to be a conventional political formation and its government a body constitutionally responsible to Parliament's non-Fascist majority is evidenced by a number of resolutions adopted by the Fascist Grand Council during 1923.

67. THE "FASCISTIZATION" OF THE STATE

Mussolini's Declaration to the Fascist Grand Council, Meeting of January 12-13, 1923

> Reported in the *Popolo d'Italia*, January 14, 1923; reproduced in Benito Mussolini, *Opera omnia*, Edoardo and Duilio Susmel, eds. Florence: La Fenice, 1956, XIX, 96–97. Our translation.

The Fascist Grand Council, assembled on the evening of January 12, and having heard General [Emilio] De Bono's report on the formation of the Militia for National Security, approves of it in its fundamental features and entrusts the commanding general and his subordinates with the task of completing the necessary steps by February 28.

In homage to the orders of the government prescribing the dissolution without distinction of all paramilitary formations by the end of this month, the Grand Council declares dissolved as of that date the Fascist Party's action squads, which are to become a part of the Militia for National Security. . . .

The Council also affirms that: 1) The character of the Militia for National Security shall be essentially Fascist, this Militia having for its purpose the protection of the inevitable and inexorable developments of the October revolution. . . . 2) The internal character of the Militia for National Security must be guided by a discipline requiring the most difficult renunciations and the most ascetic dedication. Accordingly, the Grand Council urges the Black Shirts of all Italy to be worthy of the highest honor that can be conferred on a Fascist, that of fighting both at home and abroad for the defense of the state and the nation.

Mussolini's declaration was approved unanimously, and thus the extra-legal Black Shirts became a semiofficial body in the country's armed forces. To make sure that all Fascists responded to Mussolini's call, on April 24, 1923, the Grand Council approved another of his proposals to the effect that all members of the Fascist party be enrolled automatically in the Militia. Another resolution adopted at that meeting severely chastised the Popular party, whose congress earlier in the month had revealed that not only had the left wing of the Popular party favored going to the opposition but also that its center faction was prepared to support Mussolini's government only on a conditional basis. Mussolini refused this uncertain support and accepted the resignation of the Popular Ministers in his government the day before the Grand Council's meeting. A proclamation by the Grand Council dated July 1923 spelled out its animus toward the *Popolari* and especially toward their political secretary, the priest Don Luigi Sturzo. It also cast some sharp shafts toward the moderate Socialists, and some democratic and liberal elements, all of which indicated that the truce that had issued from the desire for "normalization" had come to an end.

The Fascist Grand Council Declares War on Erstwhile Supporters: Proclamation of July 1923

> Reported in the *Popolo d'Italia*, August 1, 1923; reproduced in Mussolini, *Opera omnia*, Edoardo and Duilio Susmel, eds., XIX, 412–13. Our translation.

The masks that are falling reveal to us the fearful faces of new enemies who at last declare themselves to be such. The muddled and faint-hearted Sicilian priest and the party he leads must be considered as enemies of Fascism and of the government. The same applies to the Unitary Socialists grouped around old and deteriorated puppets of reformism. And some democratic and liberal factions do not desist from their formalistic opposition. All of this counsels us not to desist and to be strenuously vigilant. . . . The Duce who has led us from 1919 to today is sure and inflexible at his command post. Neither insidious calm weather nor unleashed storms distract him from accomplishing his arduous duty.

In fact, the Fascists had achieved a signal victory early in July when, because of press attacks from Catholic groups favoring unconditional support of the Fascist government, Don Sturzo decided to resign as political secretary of the Popular party. Nonetheless, there were other reasons for concern. A number of dissident Fascists, among whom the Deputy Alfredo Misuri was the most prominent, criticized Mussolini's administration of the Fascist party and the country as full of corruption and inefficiency. Misuri earned a beating for his efforts, foreshadowing the fate to befall Giacomo Matteotti a year later. Another disturbing event was the narrow margin of the government's victory in a test vote on a new electoral law. According to this proposed law, the list of candidates receiving the greatest number of votes would receive two thirds of the seats in the Chamber. Mussolini insisted on a minimum relative majority of 25 per cent for the prize of two thirds of the seats; the *Popolari* proposed a minimum of 40 per cent of the votes cast; and others were willing to settle for 33 per cent. Mussolini presented his proposal as a question of confidence and received a small majority of 178 to 157. And although the electoral law that bears the name of the Fascist Deputy Giacomo Acerbo was finally approved by the Chamber in July 1923 in the form Mussolini desired, his narrow escape in the Chamber and the growing opposition of such major liberal newspapers as the *Corriere della Sera,* the *Stampa,* and *Il Mondo* served to arouse the Fascists against former supporters or until then silent opponents. On July 25, 1923, two days after the Chamber's final approval of the electoral law that seemed to assure the increase of the small Fascist group of 35 Deputies to two thirds of the Chamber's membership of 535, the Fascist Grand Council approved unanimously a declaration expressing its conception of an "integrally Fascist" State.

The "Integrally Fascist" State and the Use of Force: Declaration of the Fascist Grand Council, July 25, 1923

Reported in the *Popolo d'Italia,* July 26, 1923; reproduced in Benito Mussolini, *Opera omnia,* Edoardo and Duilio Susmel, eds., XIX, 334–35. Our translation.

After an ample discussion of the constitution, employment, and relations of the Voluntary Militia for National Security, the Grand Council reached the following conclusions:

1. Until such a time as the state has become integrally Fascist, that is, until we achieve completely in all the state's administrative bodies

and institutes the replacement of yesterday's ruling class by a Fascist ruling class, or a class loyal to Fascism; and until the irremediable decline of idle desires of a return to power on the part of the antinational elements; Fascism, as both a party and a government that made the revolution and assumed all the consequent responsibilities, cannot renounce the armed forces of the Black Shirts.

2. Accordingly, the Black Shirts represent the flower of the party and the faithful, vigilant, and invincible guard of the Fascist revolution culminating in the March on Rome. They represent an inexhaustible reservoir of enthusiasm and faith in the destinies of the country as symbolized in the august person of the King.

3. The [Black Shirt] units are reduced to two with a fixed membership of 300,000 for the first and 200,000 for the second. It is not strictly necessary that all the members of the second unit be armed. The party's membership approaches a million and it can provide the men for these two units.*

4. The Militia is a great political police. Its task, with or without the cooperation of the ordinary police forces, is to make impossible any disturbance of public order and any gesture or attempt at sedition against the Fascist government, and thus assure constant normalcy in the productive and social life of the nation. . . .

6. With its efficiency, organization, and its highly voluntary spirit, the Militia frees the army completely of any operation as a political police . . . and thus the victorious army, from which a large number of the leaders and followers of the Militia are derived and to which Fascism expresses the greatest devotion, can be free to devote itself in perfect tranquillity to its particular duty of preparing for the defense of the fatherland from external threat.

During the last year of his life, Giacomo Matteotti—secretary general of the Unitary Socialist Party formed by Turati and his followers when they finally broke with the Maximalist Socialists in October 1922—prepared an account of Fascism's first year in power. Among the most revealing sections of Matteotti's book is a collection of excerpts from speeches by leading Fascists and articles in the Fascist press. The burden of these excerpts is to show that the Fascists stood condemned by their very own words.

* It was no longer compulsory for all party members to be enrolled in the Militia. Ed. note.

68. "THE FASCISTS EXPOSED"

Giacomo Matteotti, *The Fascisti Exposed: A Year of Fascist Domin-ation*. Translated by E. W. Dickes. London: Independent Labour Party Publication Department, 1924, pp. 74–83, *passim*.

1923

February 11. "The Prime Minister said to me one day that if the Fas-cists want the death penalty instituted, we can allow it, but from now onwards killing must be done in the name of the law and of the State. . . . If, however, the forces of opposition continued their harmful activities, some of the *piazze* [market places] of Italy would soon see the arrival of execution squads." Interview with *Giunta*, sec-retary of the Fascist party.

February 11. "In internal politics there is nothing to discuss; what is happening is happening by my precise and direct will and under my orders, for which, naturally, I assume full personal responsibility. . . . And those who may intend to defame (Fascism) abroad and threaten it at home, must understand that their action entails possible conse-quences of the harshest [kind]. The enemies of the Fascist State must not be surprised if I treat them, as such, with severity. . . ." *Mus-solini*, speech in the Chamber.

February 20. "I do not repent of my action in raising my revolver in the Chamber. . . . We have not formed the National Militia for noth-ing. If these forces of opposition are to spread, we shall plant execu-tion squads in the *piazze* of Italy." *Giunta*, speech at Trieste.

March. "In Russia and in Italy it has been proved that it is possible to govern outside, above and against all Liberal ideology. . . .

"It may be taken as axiomatic that any sort of Government action provokes discontents. How will you avoid the growth of this discon-tent into a flood which constitutes a danger to the solidity of the State? You will avoid it by means of force, by accumulating the maximum of force. By making use of this force, inexorably, when it proves neces-sary. . . . Now, Fascism throws on the rubbish heap all these anti-vital theories. When a group or a party is in power, it is its duty to fortify its position and to defend itself against all comers. . . . Men are, perhaps, tired of Liberty.

"Let it be realised, then, once for all, that Fascism recognises no idols, adores no fetishes; it has already passed, and, if necessary, it will turn again and pass once more, over the more or less decomposed body of the Goddess of Liberty." *Mussolini*, in *Gerarchia*.

June 19. "Let no one abuse our spirit of generosity; otherwise force will be resorted to. If those residual elements of whom I spoke . . . should have any intention of still playing some part on the political stage, they know, and all Italians should know, that I should call out the Black Shirts, many of whom are chewing the bit and growing impatient." *Mussolini*, speech at Cremona.

July 8. "For some days there has been a recurrence of Socialist crimes. Very well! We say candidly that the responsibility for this bloodshed falls on those Liberal leaders who, with their stupid polemics, are putting mistaken ideas into the heads of the lower strata of society as to the possibility of Socialist recovery. . . . Fascism will go inexorably to work, and will reply pitilessly to the shedding of Fascist blood for which the Red band of hooligans is making itself responsible. The responsibility for the disorder falls exclusively on the heads of certain Liberals. We level against them this public accusation and warning. Let them beware of abusing Fascist patience!" *Popolo d'Italia*. (Mussolini's paper.)

October 28. ". . . I beg you, Fascists, to bear in mind that the revolution was the work of cudgels. What have you in your hands now?" (The Fascists shout: "Rifles, bombs, machine-guns!") "If to-morrow the alarm were sounded, the signal for those great days which decide the destiny of peoples, would you respond?" ("Yes, we swear it!") ". . . If to-morrow I told you that you must continue the march to the end, but in other directions, would you march?" ("Yes.") ". . . The Fascist Government will last because we shall systematically scatter our enemies. . . ." *Mussolini*, speech at Milan.

November 30. "Yesterday evening, about 7 o'clock, some 500 Fascists of proved boldness . . . gathered before Signor Nitti's house and commenced a formidable chorus of imprecations. Some hundreds of more exasperated Fascists began to fire at the walls of the house, and two strong groups attacked the railings. Some policemen who came running up were knocked over, and one of them went away to give the alarm at the Police Station. Meanwhile the Fascists had broken into the premises, and, still firing, smashed the ground floor shutters with clubs. . . .

"Owing to the conscienceless and intolerable campaign of certain Nittian newspapers, Fascism has this evening broken the bonds which it has imposed upon itself since the march on Rome, and has returned to the good old legendary days of action. The crafty Opposition has received a warning, and Fascism throughout Italy will learn tomorrow that there are perhaps at hand fresh days of strife, for which everyone is already prepared and resolved. *Corriere Italiano.* (Fascist paper of Rome.)

During their first year in power the Fascists did more than make and execute threats against their opponents. Within several weeks of his rise to office Mussolini revoked by decree the implementation of Giolitti's law of 1920 providing for the registration of all securities in the name of the owner with a view to taxing the income derived from these securities. The revocation was viewed as being especially favorable to the Church, which was a large holder of securities. In January 1923 religious instruction was made compulsory in all public elementary schools; early in March the eight-hour work day was prescribed by decree; and later in the month the state monopoly of life insurance, established under Giolitti in 1912, was abolished and this service was returned to private enterprise. During the same month a fusion pact was reached with the Nationalists who, although absorbed organizationally by the Fascist party, gave it their ideology and thus marked Mussolini's formal abandonment of his leftist origins. In July a decree empowered the government to issue warnings to newspapers for infractions of a wide range of regulations. Upon a second warning, the managing editor of the offending newspaper was to be relieved of his post and the government could exercise the right of approving his successor. During the same month the Acerbo electoral law was passed under threats from the Fascist press that the Chamber would be dissolved unless it acceded to Mussolini's demand for a system granting two thirds of the seats to the list of candidates receiving the highest number of votes and at the same time equal to at least 25 per cent of the votes cast. At the end of August Mussolini ordered the bombardment of the Greek island of Corfu in retaliation for Greece's failure to comply fully with his ultimatum demanding an investigation of and apologies and indemnities for the murder of several Italian members of a mission entrusted with the fixing of the boundary between Greece and Albania. Greece appealed to the League of Nations; Italy denied the League's competence in the dispute; and the League avoided the issue by delegating its solution to a Council of Ambassadors in Paris. Italy was awarded 50 million lire and apologies; Corfu was evacuated by the end of September; and Mussolini had proved his "strong manner" abroad as he had done at home during the preceding months.

The strong manner became even more evident immediately preceding and during the general elections of April 1924. For the purpose of these elections the Fascists prepared a list of 356 candidates (two thirds of the total membership of the Chamber) and invited a number of major Liberal leaders to run as candidates under the Fascist insignia. Salandra and Orlando accepted; Giolitti refused and asserted the historical function and vitality of traditional liberalism in Italy. The elections were conducted in an atmosphere of violence and illegality. Opposition candidates were obstructed at every turn: their campaign meetings were disrupted; their newspapers if not prevented from publishing had their issues destroyed by Fascist bands; and even the candidates themselves were not immune to physical violence.

The results of the election seem to confirm the efficacy of Fascist electoral practices. The Fascist party list received 4,305,936 votes, an absolute majority, and was awarded the prize of two thirds of the seats, 356. The 19 seats and 347,552 votes cast for a separate Fascist-Nationalist list gave the government a total of 375 of the 535 seats in the Chamber and 64.9 per cent of the total popular vote. The Popular party fell from its 107 seats in 1921 to only 39; Turati's Unitary Socialists returned 24 candidates; the Maximalist Socialists, 22; and the Communists rose from 16 seats in the 1921 elections to 19. Even if the latter three parties, formerly united in the once powerful Socialist party, had effected the coalition the Communists had proposed in February 1924, their combined strength could never have approached the 156 seats their united party had won in 1919. Almost completely demolished was the Liberal party. Its faction-ridden but enormous majority of the prewar years was reduced to a mere 15 Deputies, Giolitti among them, campaigning in seven different lists. The Constitutional Opposition, led by Giovanni Amendola, received 14 seats, but Bonomi, one of its other leaders, failed to be elected. The Social Democrats, strongest in Sicily, won 10 seats; the Republicans managed to salvage 7 seats; and the remaining 11 seats went to regional lists and to one and dangerously alone dissident Fascist. It is important to note that in spite of their general success, the Fascists failed to gain a majority of the popular vote in the northern regions of Piedmont, Liguria, Lombardy, and Venetia. The majority was theirs in central and southern Italy, and it was in southernmost Sicily that Mussolini delivered a speech early in May indicating that Fascism claimed Italy not only by right of its electoral victory but also and above all by right of revolution: "We have Rome by right of revolution! Only by another force and only after a struggle that cannot but be fierce can it be taken away from us." By the end of the month the first phase of this struggle began with a speech by Giacomo Matteotti challenging the legality of Fascism's electoral majority. Within eleven days Matteotti was dead, and there thus began a crisis which at first shook the foundations of Fascist power, only to end with the definitive establishment of a Fascist dictatorship.

XXI. THE DICTATORSHIP
ESTABLISHED, 1924–1928

It is impossible to assert with complete certainty whether or not Fascism was inexorably destined to become a dictatorship. Mussolini's overwhelming majority in the Chamber of Deputies should have made it possible for him to govern much as he chose and yet observe the forms if not always the substance of parliamentary government. His own statements during the year and a half of power before the elections of April 1924 are sufficiently equivocal to allow a variety of interpretations as to his probable future course in domestic politics. His autocratic personal qualities clearly inclined him toward arbitrary government; and the influence of certain elements in the Fascist party, such as the extremist Roberto Farinacci, *ras* [1] or party boss of Cremona, spurred this inclination in Mussolini, who might not claim a primacy in physical violence but would not be outdone in verbal excesses. But there were other elements in the party that preferred a more traditional or legalistic course, and although they were in the minority it is not impossible that eventually they might have swayed Mussolini in their direction. The events that seem to have foreclosed this more moderate course were the assassination of the Unitary Socialist leader Matteotti in June 1924 and the ensuing crisis which for a moment appeared to threaten Mussolini's hold on the country.

The prologue to the crisis was provided by Matteotti's speech of May 30, 1924, in the Chamber challenging the legality of the Fascists' majority at the polls and requesting the Chamber not to approve the report of the Credentials Committee validating the election of virtually all Deputies and particularly the entire Fascist list. That Matteotti's charges touched a tender Fascist spot is evidenced by the frequency and violence with which the Fascists interrupted his speech.

---

[1] *Ras* is a colloquial title given to powerful local Fascist bosses and was borrowed from the name of Ethiopian tribal chieftains. It suggests the autonomous power wielded by medieval feudal barons. Ed. note.

69. MATTEOTTI CONTESTS THE LEGALITY OF THE FASCISTS' MAJORITY: SPEECH OF MAY 30, 1924

Atti del Parlamento italiano, Camera dei deputati, Legislatura XXVII, Sessione del 1924–1925, Discussioni, May 30, 1924, I, 57–64, *passim.* Our translation.

[We Socialists] maintain that the government's majority list which received a nominal vote of more than 4 million ballots. . . . (*Interruptions.*)

(*Voices from the center:*) And even more!

Matteotti: In fact this list did not obtain these votes freely and it is therefore doubtful that it obtained the percentage necessary (*interruptions; protests*) for it to receive, even according to your law, the two thirds of the seats assigned to it. . . . We do here and now contest the validity of the election of the entire governmental majority. (*Most lively rumblings.*). . . . No voter was free in this election because everyone knew *a priori* that, even if the majority of the voters dared vote against the government, there was a force at the government's disposal that would annul any contrary results. (*Rumblings and interruptions from the right.*). . . . This intention of the government was reenforced by the existence of an armed militia. (*Most lively and prolonged applause from the right and shouts of* Long live the militia.). . . . About 60 of our 100 candidates were not able to move about freely in their constituencies. . . . In 90 per cent of the cases, and in some regions even in 100 per cent of the cases, the supervisory body at the polling places was wholly Fascist, and the representative of the minority list was not allowed to be present during the voting. Except for a few large cities and in some very few provinces, the representative of the minority list who did go to the polling places was met with the violence that had been promised. . . . We recall what occurred especially in the Milanese and Genoese provinces and in several other places where the results were not very comforting to the Fascist list. Newspapers were destroyed, headquarters were devastated, and beatings were administered. . . . In the Po Valley, in Tuscany, and in other regions cited by the President of the Council for their act of loyalty to the Fascist government and where the peasants had previously been organized under Socialist or Popularist auspices, the electors voted under Fascist party controls. . . . The poor peasants knew that any resistance was useless, and for the sake of their families' safety they had to submit to the law of the strongest, the law of the master, by voting for the candidates assigned them by the local boss of the Fascist union or the Fascist club. (*Lively rumblings; interruptions.*). . . .

It is a fact that only a small minority was able to give its vote freely. . . . For all these reasons and for others that I forgo presenting because of your noisy importunings—you know very well what these other reasons are because each one of you was at least a witness to them (*rumblings*)—for all these reasons we request that the election of the majority be annulled in toto. . . . We request that all elections compromised by violence be deferred to the Committee on Credentials. (*Applause from the extreme left; lively rumblings.*)

Matteotti could not have been surprised by the Chamber's rejection of his motion. Nor, given Farinacci's customarily violent language, could it have surprised Matteotti and other opponents of Fascism to hear Farinacci say on June 3: "Honorable colleagues of the opposition, you must understand that the majority has its rights, and if tomorrow you really wish to provoke us, we shall not be able to limit ourselves to a simple exchange of blows. We shall see, then, what will happen here."

Seven days later, on the afternoon of June 10 Matteotti was assaulted in the streets of Rome, carried off in an automobile and, dying from wounds and injuries, his corpse was buried in a field some miles from the capital. The abduction had been witnessed, and the automobile was traced by the police. On June 12 Mussolini assured the Chamber that the police would make the fullest investigation regarding the presumed crime and that the identity of some of the suspects was known. The next day opposition Deputies from the two Socialist parties, the Communists, the *Popolari*, the Democrats, and the Republicans decided to absent themselves from the Chamber until the uncertainties regarding Matteotti's disappearance were resolved. Thus began the Aventine Secession [2] of the opposition with the aim of isolating the Fascist majority in the Chamber and proving to the country that its Parliament was being led by men who were accomplices of murderers.

[2] The Aventine is one of the seven hills of Rome to which the popular or plebeian party led by the reformer Caius Gracchus repaired in 123 B.C. in its struggle against the Senatorial or aristocratic party. In absenting itself from Parliament the opposition to Fascism retired to the "Aventine of its conscience"; but the historical allusion was unfortunate, since the ancient Aventinians had been crushed by the Senatorial Party. Ed. note.

70. THE BEGINNING OF THE AVENTINE
SECESSION: STATEMENT OF THE OPPOSITION

Reproduced in Alessandro Schiavi, ed., *Filippo Turati attraverso le lettere dei corrispondenti (1880–1925)*. Bari: G. Laterza, 1947, pp. 291–92. Our translation.

Rome, Friday, June 13, 1924

Most Illustrious President of the Chamber of Deputies: *

The meeting just held of representatives of all the Opposition Groups has charged me as the senior member present to convey to you the enclosed resolution adopted by them unanimously.

With all my regards, I am

Most devotedly yours,

Filippo Turati

"The representatives of the Opposition Groups met today in a hall of Parliament Building and agreed that their participation in the work of the Chamber is impossible so long as the gravest uncertainties still reign regarding the sinister episode of which our colleague the Honorable Matteotti has been a victim.

"Therefore, these same representatives are in agreement in deciding that their respective Groups abstain from participating in the work of the Chamber, that they reserve judgment on the government's future action in this matter, and that they will reach further decisions as the situation requires."

As explained by Salvemini in a letter to Turati late the following month, the purpose of the opposition's abstention from the Chamber was to destroy Fascism with passive resistance at home combined with continued revelation abroad of Fascism's misdeeds. Salvemini believed that "the beast has been wounded mortally" and that its end was near. Mussolini's immediate reaction to Matteotti's abduction seemed to confirm Salvemini's judgment, but the prophecy ultimately proved to be wrong. On June 13, the same day of the opposition's statement, Mussolini once again spoke in the Chamber regarding Matteotti's disappearance. The corpse had not yet been found and was not to be found until two months later, but there was a general certainty that the missing Deputy was dead. Mussolini's discomfiture over the presumed murder appeared great and genuine.

* The President of the Chamber of Deputies was Alfredo Rocco, formerly a Nationalist and destined to become the chief theoretician of Fascism. Ed. note.

71. MUSSOLINI ON THE MURDER OF
MATTEOTTI: SPEECH OF JUNE 13, 1924

> *Atti del Parlamento italiano, Camera dei deputati, Legislatura XXVII, Sessione del 1924–1925, Discussioni,* June 13, 1924, I, 328–29. Our translation.

The police have identified all those who participated in the affair. . . . One of them [Amerigo] Dumini, was arrested in Rome yesterday evening; another, [Aldo] Putato, has been arrested in Milan. The other three or four * have been surrounded. . . . The situation is being followed moment by moment, and I believe that by the end of the day at the latest the police will have in custody all those who took part in the misdeed. . . .

If there is anyone in this hall who has more right than anyone else to be grieved and, I would add, exasperated, it is I. (*Lively approval.*)

(*Voices:*) Very true! Very true!

Mussolini: Only an enemy of mine, pondering for many nights something diabolical, could have committed this crime that today strikes us with horror and wrings cries of indignation from us. . . .

The law will take its course; the police will consign the guilty to the judicial authorities which will take up the question and will issue the necessary warrants for arrest. The government cannot be asked to do more. If you authorize me to render summary justice, summary justice will be done. (*Impression in the Chamber.*) But so long as this cannot be asked and must not be asked, it will be necessary to keep our nerves in place and refuse to enlarge a nefarious and stupid episode into a question of the government's general policy. (*Approval.*)

Now the nation shows with a thousand signs that it has confidence in the government's efforts with regard to its duty as the executive power. And I say to you representatives of the nation that this confidence is not misplaced. Justice shall be done, it must be done, because as some one of you has said this crime is a crime against Fascism and against the nation. It is a crime of humiliating bestiality even more

---

* All of the persons involved in the crime were notorious *squadristi* [members of the Fascist "Squads"]. Ed. note.

than it is horrible. In the face of such events we cannot hesitate to distinguish clearly between what is political and what is criminal. (*Approval.*)

An attempt was made to prove to the country that the government was sincere in its protestations of innocence and in its intentions to see to it that the guilty and negligent were punished. Mussolini's Press Secretary, Cesare Rossi, and his Under-Secretary of State for the Interior, Aldo Finzi, resigned on June 14. Two days later Mussolini himself relinquished the Ministry of the Interior to the former Nationalist Luigi Federzoni; and General Emilio De Bono, one of the Quadrumvirs,[3] was relieved of his post as Director General of Public Security. At the end of the month three Ministers were replaced by two Liberals and one former *Popolare* who had become a supporter of the regime. These concessions, which had the air of a certain admission of guilt, did not quiet the opposition. From the middle of June, when the Chamber's meetings were recessed, to mid-November, when Parliament was reconvened, the opposition conducted a press campaign against the regime with the purpose of proving Fascism's moral and legal responsibility for Matteotti's murder. Notable in this campaign were the *Corriere della Sera*, Italy's major newspaper under the direction of Senator Luigi Albertini, one of the foremost protagonists of Italy's intervention in the First World War and a moderate in domestic politics; the *Stampa* of Turin, whose editor was the ever-loyal Giolittian Senator Alfredo Frassati; the whole of the Socialist, Communist, and Republican press; part of the Popular party press, including the *Popolo;* and *Il Mondo* of Rome under the guidance of Giovanni Amendola, who had been one of the *Corriere della Sera*'s principal editorial writers and one of the members of Facta's government most insistent on proclaiming martial law in October 1922 to stop the Fascist march on Rome.

It was an impressive array of journalistic talent, but its concrete influence proved to be insufficient to break the power of the Fascist regime. The vigorous campaign waged by this opposition press in spite of the government's imposition of severe restrictions by decree-laws, and the decision of the opposition Deputies of the Aventine to continue to absent themselves from Parliament, were designed to influence the King and persuade him of his moral obligation to revoke Mussolini's mandate as Prime Minister. The Aventinians may have had some faint hopes at first that the Fascist majority in the Chamber might fall into disarray because of the moral revulsion in the country over Matteotti's murder, and that the government could thus be upset by an adverse vote in Parliament. Although there was genuine confusion in Fascist ranks immediately after the murder, by the end of June the Fascist leaders regained their nerve and at the end of August, even after the rever-

---

[3] The four men who led the March on Rome. The other three were Michele Bianchi, Italo Balbo, and Cesare Maria De Vecchi. Ed. note.

berations occasioned by the discovery of Matteotti's corpse, Mussolini felt secure enough to make a speech openly contemptuous of the opposition. These developments meant that only intervention by the King could overturn the regime. There was no question of trying to oust Mussolini by popular insurrection. In the first place, except for the Communists, the opposition was determined to follow a course of legality and moral pressure. In the second place, the Aventinians had no way of coping with the Fascist Militia. Only if the King took the initiative against the regime and, if necessary, called on the armed forces would it be possible to expel the Fascists from power. But by the end of October Mussolini felt so sure of himself that he had the Fascist Militia swear an oath of loyalty to the King—similar to the oath customarily sworn by the regular armed forces—while retaining operational control of the Militia for himself. Indeed, Mussolini seems to have judged the King correctly. Victor Emmanuel III is reported to have been fond of saying that as a responsible constitutional monarch he was as if deaf and blind and that the two Chambers of Parliament were his ears and eyes. So long as the majority in Parliament supported the regime the King would not move against it. Thus the fundamental assumption underlying the Aventine Secession came to nought. Victor Emmanuel would not be persuaded that the regime's culpability in Matteotti's murder annulled its right to govern the country; nor would he accept Matteotti's own thesis that the Fascist majority was invalid because of the electoral irregularities charged against it. In substance, the opposition asked the King to act on a moral principle and turn out a government that still had a parliamentary majority; or, in other words, the King was being asked to go against the letter of constitutional practice to preserve the spirit of constitutional government. This Victor Emmanuel proved unwilling to do.

As the summer of 1924 wore on Mussolini continued with gestures which were in part conciliatory and in part menacing to the opposition. At the end of August he made a speech assuring his audience of Fascism's desire for domestic peace; and after asserting that Fascism was "most solid," he threatened his opponents: "If the day ever comes when they abandon their annoying vociferation for the sake of more concrete acts, on that day we shall turn them into fodder for the encampments of the Black Shirts." Two months later, on October 28, the anniversary of the "March on Rome" and two weeks before the reconvening of Parliament, the National Directorate of the Fascist party issued a proclamation in which it inveighed against Fascism's "false friends" of earlier days and warned against parliamentary intrigues designed to undo what the Fascists had conquered with their blood. It paid a compliment to the parties that had "openly" arrayed themselves against the regime, but warned them that any provocation on their part would be met with force.

The Chamber was reconvened on November 12, 1924, nearly five months after the recess that followed the murder of Matteotti. The parties of the Aventine opposition continued to absent themselves, save for the Communists, who had concluded that it was useless to forgo the podium provided them by Parliament. The only effective opposition to the regime came from a handful of Liberals who had refused to join the Aventine secession and had chosen to stay in Parliament. Among these were Giolitti and Orlando, both of whom spoke during the debate preceding the approval of the budgets. Giolitti's brief and direct speech branded the regime's domestic policy as illegal and unconstitutional. Orlando's speech of seven days later, November 22, was less direct, almost tortured, and an unmistakable sign of a crisis of conscience in a man whose sense of constitutional proprieties had been offended by a regime he had at first supported.

Outside Parliament the Aventinian opposition continued its agitation against Fascism and insisted on Mussolini's moral disqualification to lead the country. There was still hope that the King would look beyond the Fascist majorities in the two Chambers and judge the regime on the basis not of votes but of morality. This is the appeal implicit in a speech by Giovanni Amendola, the acknowledged leader of the Aventine secessionists and among the most opposed to proposals for accommodation and compromise. Amendola had been the victim of a Fascist beating in 1923; in July 1925 he was to be a victim a second time, and he died in France in 1926 from causes attributed to the violence done him the year before.

72. AMENDOLA SPEAKS FOR THE AVENTINE OPPOSITION: MILAN, NOVEMBER 30, 1924

Giovanni Amendola, *La nuova democrazia*. Naples: Riccardo Ricciardi, 1951, pp. 207–16, *passim*. Our translation.

After two long years of Fascist oppression, here, in this assembly of the Committees of Opposition of Northern Italy . . . there lives once again for the first time the conscious will of the Italian people to resume possession of their rights and to discuss the direction of their lives. . . .

We are the same as in the past: soldiers in a struggle in which passion for an idea is joined to the human concern for our brothers deprived of their rights and oppressed in their daily lives. Before us we have, as always, the unchanged and implacable opponent armed with all his claws, although today these are insidiously hidden. He does not abandon his claim to power; he does not clear the way for our rights, a way that has been closed by his stroke of force. He seeks only to survive the hour of his greatest trial to be able to find another occasion to try his new game with additional experience and better sharpened force. Well now, it may suit others to engage in a tactic of delay that postpones the decisive battle; as for us, we say that our battle is for today. Here we fall or we win; here we lose or secure freedom for Italy. . . .

We are aware that the human need for peace arising from a decade of war and postwar conditions is very important in determining the tendencies of public opinion in our country. We know also that the political battle will be won by those whom the Italians judge as bearers of the quickest and most lasting peace. . . . [But] there can be no compromise between contradictory principles struggling today for the spiritual and political sway over our future. No compromise is possible; something must die. This is the profound meaning, this is the reason for the anxious national travail of the last two years. . . .

The political struggle will continue until either they have annihilated our resistance and have consolidated forever a regime that will erase all of the Risorgimento and reduce a whole century of Italian history into a path taken by mistake by someone bound for another place, or until we have repossessed the Risorgimento by means of a new creation of the Italian spirit. . . .

The key problem of the present situation, a problem on which the Opposition insists with tenacity, is that of the Militia which the Fascists define as "for national safety" perhaps because it is incompatible with individual safety. So long as the Militia exists the saddest and most fruitless of tasks will be that of the Minister of the Interior. Nor did the oath of loyalty sworn [by the Militia] to the Head of the State [the King] and simultaneously devalued by the Head of the Government modify the character of the Militia in the least. This character is defined perfectly by an inscription on the walls of the Roman barracks of Magnanapoli: "The Militia is super-Fascism." We have no need to define the Militia: the definition is found on the bodies and in the memories of innumerable Italian citizens. . . .

For us in the opposition the Militia is the insuperable obstacle to all dreams and wishes of a restoration of peace and order. The Militia is the active demonstration of a criminal intent to oppress; it makes a lie of all lying words; it is the living symbol of the offense that Fascism inflicts on the rights of Italian citizens whose equality is denied in practice and whose civilized existence together is made impossible. It is, in fact, the prison warden of Italian freedom. . . .

But the problem of the Militia is a moral problem as well as a political one. . . . On this point it is necessary that we be precise. There are moral considerations that are worth much more than political success, and it is time that these considerations be established without equivocation. If today there are in Italy industrialists who believe that the Italian people are not worthy of those freedoms that an industrialist of the good old days, Quintino Sella, sought to assure the workers; if these men believe that, on the contrary, the Italian people are worthy of the Fascist bludgeon because Italy is to be considered inferior in comparison to civilized countries; if there are political figures who in spite of the most enlightening revelations on present realities *
show themselves insensitive to the honor and safety of our country,
. . . it is necessary to establish that all these men are fully involved in that very same moral question which by now has inevitably enveloped all of the so-called regime. . . .

All of these considerations lead to this conclusion: the moral question, enveloping as it does the whole regime, stands above the political question itself. Everyone understands the meaning of these words. We assert that the regime is responsible of having committed a crime, of having cultivated criminality.

Early in January 1925 Mussolini publicly took up the challenge of the two oppositions, the one in Parliament and the other outside. Apparently sure that the King would not heed Amendola's plea that he raise the "moral question," Mussolini addressed the Chamber, reconvened after its holiday recess, and revealed his most truculent manner. Even if during the preceding six months he had genuinely considered the adoption of conciliatory moves aimed at "normalizing" the situation, it is clear that by the time he delivered his speech of January 3 he felt sufficiently sure of himself to dispense with any further efforts at compromise with the opposition. It must be added that in demanding that Fascism disband its Militia, the opposition had imposed a condition to reconciliation which Mussolini would most likely never accept unless forced to do so by the King's intervention. This intervention never came.

---

* Probably a reference to: the existence of a memorandum by Cesare Rossi, Mussolini's former Press Secretary, which held Mussolini responsible for the Matteotti murder either for ordering the crime or for approving of it; the resignation of Italo Balbo, interim commander of the Fascist Militia, after the opposition published one of his letters ordering his followers to resume their violences and implying that Mussolini approved of this course. Ed. note.

73. MUSSOLINI CHALLENGES THE OPPOSITION: SPEECH OF JANUARY 3, 1925

Atti del Parlamento italiano, Camera dei deputati, Legislatura XXVII, Sessione del 1924–25, Discussioni, January 3, 1925, III, 2029–32, *passim.* Our translation.

Let it be known that . . . I do not seek a political vote. I do not desire it: I have had too many. (*Good!*)

Article 47 of the *Statuto* says: "The Chamber of Deputies has the right to impeach the King's Ministers and to defer them to the High Court of Justice [the Senate]." I ask formally whether there is anyone in this Chamber or outside who wishes to avail himself of Article 47. (*Most lively and prolonged applause; many Deputies rise to their feet; shouts of* "Viva Mussolini!"; *applause also from the galleries.*). . . .

Gentlemen, it is I who in this Chamber raise the charges against myself. It is said that I have created a *Cheka.** Where? When? How? No one can say! . . . An Italian *Cheka* has never existed. . . . Until now no one has denied me these three qualities: a certain amount of intelligence, much courage, and complete contempt for vile lucre. (*Lively and prolonged applause.*) If I had created a *Cheka* I would have done so according to criteria I have always imposed on that measure of violence which cannot be eliminated from history. I have always said . . . that to resolve anything, violence must be surgical, intelligent, and chivalrous. (*Approval.*) Now the acts of this so-called *Cheka* have always been unintelligent, disorderly, and stupid. (*Very good!*). . . .

Certainly, you do remember my speech of June 7 [1924]. You may find it easy to return to that week of aroused political passions when in this hall the minority and the majority had daily encounters to the point that some despaired of achieving the conditions necessary for a political and civil coexistence between the two opposed parts of the Chamber. There were irritating speeches from both sides. . . .

I then made a speech that clarified the atmosphere completely. I said to the opposition: I recognize your right in principle and even in

* Reference to the Extraordinary Commission for Struggle with Counterrevolution and Sabotage created by the Bolsheviks in Russia in December 1917. Ed. note.

fact. You may disregard Fascism as an historical event; you may subject all the measures of the Fascist government to immediate criticism.

I remember and still have before my eyes the sight of this part of the Chamber where all understood and felt that on that moment I had said profound words of life and had established the terms of that necessary coexistence without which no political assembly of any kind is possible. (*Approval.*)

Now, after a success—allow me to say it without false reticence and ridiculous modesty—after such a clamorous success admitted by the Chamber and the opposition included, by virtue of which the Chamber met the following Wednesday in an idyllic atmosphere resembling that of a living room (*approval*), unless I were struck by complete folly how could I think of ordering the commission of I would not say only a crime but even the slightest and most ridiculous affront against an opponent whom I respected because he had a certain *crânerie*, a certain courage that at times resembled my courage and my obstinacy in upholding my points of view? (*Lively applause.*)

What should I have done? Some petty cricket-brains expected acts of cynicism from me on that occasion. I did not feel up to such acts because they were repugnant to my innermost conscience. (*Approval.*) Or should I have committed some act of force? And what force? Against whom? To what end? . . .

It was at the end of that month—that month which is impressed indelibly in my life—that I said: "I wish that there be peace for the Italian people." I wanted to establish normalcy in our political life.

But what was the reply to this principle of mine? First of all, there was the Aventine secession, an anticonstitutional secession, clearly revolutionary. (*Lively approval.*) Then there followed a press campaign that lasted through June, July, and August; a filthy and wretched campaign that dishonored us for three months. (*Most lively and prolonged applause.*)

The most horrifying, fantastic, and macabre lies were widely asserted in the press! A veritable fit of necrophilia took place! There were inquiries even into what takes place below the ground, in the grave. They invented; they knew that they were lying, but they continued to lie.

And I remained tranquil, calm in the midst of this storm that shall be remembered with a sense of inner shame by those who come after us. (*Approval.*)

In the meanwhile, this campaign bore fruit. On September 11 someone decided to avenge the dead man and shot one of the best of us, who died poor. He had 60 lire in his pocket. (*Most lively and prolonged applause; all the Deputies rise.*)

Nevertheless, I continued with my effort at normalization and normality. I repressed illegalism. It is not a lie. It is not a lie that today there are still hundreds of Fascists in jail! (*Comments.*) It is not a lie that Parliament was convened regularly and at the prescribed date and that all the budgets were debated no less regularly. It is not a lie that the Militia swore an oath [to the King], that generals were appointed to all zonal commands.

Finally, we were seized by a question of great concern to us: the request that the parliamentary immunity of the Honorable Giunta be lifted and that he resign. * The Chamber exploded. I understood the meaning of this revolt; yet, after forty-eight hours, I bent once more, and making use of my prestige and ascendancy I bent this quarrelsome and reluctant Assembly to my will and said: Let the resignation be accepted. It was accepted. But even that was not enough. I performed a last gesture of normalization, I proposed a reform of the electoral law.†

And what was the reply to all this? The reply was a more intense campaign. It was said that Fascism is a horde of barbarians encamped in the country, a movement of bandits and marauders! The moral question was put forth. . . .

Very well, I now declare before this Assembly and before the whole of the Italian people that I assume, I alone, full political, moral, and historical responsibility for all that has happened. (*Most lively and repeated applause; many shouts of* "We are all with you! We are all with you!")

If a few more or less distorted phrases are enough to hang a man, then out with the scaffold! If Fascism has been no more than castor oil and bludgeon, if it is not a proud passion of the best part of Italian

* Francesco Giunta, one of the most violent of the Fascist leaders and Vice-President of the Chamber of Deputies. Ed. note.

† The reform called for the repeal of proportional representation and the return to single-member constituencies. Ed. note.

youth, then the fault is mine! (*Applause.*) If Fascism has been a criminal association, then I am the chief of this criminal association! (*Most
lively applause; many shouts of* "We are all with you! We are all with
you!"). . . .

Gentlemen, Italy wants peace, it wants tranquillity, it wants industrious calm. If possible, we shall give it this tranquillity and industrious calm with love; if necessary, with force. (*Lively approval.*)

You may be sure that within forty-eight hours of this speech the situation shall be clarified throughout the entire area. (*Most lively and
prolonged applause; comments.*). . . .

Mussolini kept his word. During the several days following his speech over a
hundred "suspect" or "subversive" organizations were dissolved or closed;
hundreds of "suspicious" persons were arrested or detained; and the opposition press, especially the periodical press, found its existence more precarious than ever. It was in this atmosphere that the government chose to move
for approval of a law eliminating proportional representation and returning
to single-member constituencies. The most effective and outspoken opposition to the proposed law came from three former Prime Ministers, Orlando,
Giolitti, and Salandra. The first two in particular had always opposed proportional representation and in principle should have favored Mussolini's
proposed law, especially in the light of the fact that a return to single-
member constituencies meant that the Fascists would no longer be assured
the prize of two thirds of the seats simply by gaining a plurality of at least
25 per cent of the votes cast. But, as the resolution sponsored by the three
former Prime Ministers explained, the holding of elections at a time when
"the present methods of government give no assurance that the popular will
may be able to express itself in a free manner . . . without freedom of the
press, of assembly, and of association" is a mockery of constitutional government. In the prewar period the three sponsors of the resolution had represented the three major factions of the then dominant Liberal party. Now,
they were leaders with very few followers, but they did represent in Parliament, as the Aventine secessionists did outside the Chamber, whatever faith
Italy still retained in constitutional government.

In speaking for their resolution, Orlando and Giolitti made more explicit
and emphatic the reasons for which they had joined the opposition during
the debate of the preceding November. At that time Salandra voted for the
government, but his speech of support had been couched in such qualified
and warning language that it foreshadowed his eventual role as opponent
unless Fascism mended its ways. Illness prevented Salandra from participating in the debate of January 1925, but he made it clear through an announcement in the press that he had joined the opposition.

74. THE LIBERAL OLD GUARD IN
THE OPPOSITION

Orlando's Speech of January 16, 1925

> *Atti del Parlamento italiano, Camera dei deputati, Legislatura XXVII,*
> *Sessione del 1924–25, Discussioni,* January 16, 1925, III, 2248–53,
> *passim.* Our translation.

Orlando: You say that the country is calm? Well, if you are willing to be content with that kind of calm! (*Lively comments.*) All the better for you if you think the country is perfectly calm; all the better for you who do not have the anxieties and anguish which we suffer profoundly in our souls. (*Animated comments; interruptions from the right.*). . . .

During these last two and more years of government we have gone through various phases. In some of these there prevailed what I would call the private violence of the [Fascist] party and its organizations. This violence was deplored, even by the government. Then there followed governmental restrictions on personal freedom, with the justification that this was the way to contain the aforementioned violence. And thus pressure from the government replaced that of the party. And then, when this pressure—how shall I call it, authoritarian?—was relaxed in some degree, private violence began once again.

And now we have both; we have both governmental reaction and party violence.

Mussolini: No, it is not true.

Orlando: Honorable President of the Council, how about the events in Pisa? . . . As I said, we have in competition to the other kind of violence, the violence of governmental authority. Let us look at the press. The condition of the press is truly something unprecedented (*comments*); it is comparable to nothing in the history of any other government. At the present moment the press has a constitutional law that is not observed; it has a decree-law which is unconstitutional. . . .

Federzoni (*Minister of the Interior*): Who says so?

Orlando: Without doubt, it is an unconstitutionality that to you may seem necessary, but it is unconstitutional. . . .

The speech of January 3 was an explosion of anger. . . .

(*A voice from the right:*) Of indignation.

Orlando: . . . of rancor, full of dark threats. And we cannot say that these threats have not been carried out! . . .

How can you expect this country to do its work (*Voices:* It is working! It is working!); well, if you prefer, how can it lead a civilized existence, and that is worth more than work . . . (*interruptions*)—of course it is worth more than work—when it oscillates between a mad freedom and a ferocious authority? (*Comments; interruptions.*). . . .

We express the hope . . . that we have not yet reached an irreparable situation and that our country may still have a tomorrow less sad, less painful, and less dangerous than today. (*Applause from the left; comments.*)

Within seven months of this speech Orlando concluded that the time had come for him to resign from the Chamber of Deputies. In his letter of resignation he explained that "for a man of my past and faith there is no longer a place in Italian public life as it is conducted today." Giolitti was more persistent. He remained in the Chamber until a new electoral law in 1928 destroyed completely Parliament's character as a free political and representative assembly.

The reception the Fascists gave Giolitti's speech of January 16, 1925, was even sharper than the one accorded Orlando's remarks of the same day. The reasons for this may be found in the fact that although Giolitti was eighty-two years old, he was still a man of some influence in Piedmont, where the Fascists had failed to gain a majority of the popular vote in 1924. In addition, the old parliamentary warrior had not lost his capacity for direct speech and pointed rejoinder.

Giolitti's Speech of January 16, 1925

Atti del Parlamento italiano, Camera dei deputati, Legislatura XXVII, Sessione del 1924–25, Discussioni, January 16, 1925, III, 2266–67. Our translation.

Giolitti: (*Signs of attention.*) . . . Never during the existence of the Kingdom of Italy has Parliament been called to debate an electoral law in such exceptional circumstances. (*Comments.*)

The Ministry has presented a bill for electoral reform which I would have no difficulty accepting in principle, favorable as I am to the system of single-member constituencies. But the presentation of an electoral law should necessarily imply the intention of allowing the voters freely to express their will. (*Comments.*) On the contrary, several days after the bill was presented, the government's domestic policy became radically exacerbated and there began a more violent repression of public freedoms. (*Comments.*)

I am not debating, I am stating facts. Freedom of the press was suppressed; the right of association and assembly was suppressed; arrests and searches were conducted without warrants and on a large scale against persons charged with no crime, neither then nor now. (*Comments.*). . . . What kind of electoral contest could be conducted under such circumstances?

Mussolini: Elections are not imminent. We are debating a bill.

Giolitti: We also hope that freedom will be reestablished in full.

Mussolini: If not, you will have another reason for being in the opposition. (*Laughter; applause; comments.*)

Giolitti: Honorable President, if you were to wait to reestablish freedom for the very day when the electoral contest were to begin, I would have the perfect right to say that preparation for the elections had been impossible and that the popular will had not been expressed in the electoral contest.

Mussolini: When it comes to elections, I am ready to take lessons from you! (*Laughter; applause; prolonged comments.*)

Giolitti: Honorable President of the Council, you are too modest! The elections you made have brought you a majority in this Chamber the like of which I never dreamt of having. (*Lively laughter; comments.*). . . .

Given the present state of the country, an electoral campaign based on single-member constituencies—where the contest is stronger and sharper by reason of the personal character it assumes—would result in unprecedented violence. . . . The danger of a struggle that might even become a civil war is something that is of concern to all who love the fatherland.

Mussolini: We shall not use cannons!

Giolitti: But it is not a question of cannons, pistols are enough!

Mussolini: You used cannons!

Giolitti: I? Never!

(*Voices:*) Yes, yes, in Fiume! *

Giolitti: I conclude by affirming that whoever were to call an election during the present condition of the country would assume a tremendous responsibility. Inasmuch as I want no part of this responsibility, either directly or indirectly, I shall vote against the electoral law. (*Approval from the left; animated comments.*)

The debate of January 1925 was the last free and meaningful expression of the Italian Chamber of Deputies. In the Senate, where the lifetime tenure of its members made it more difficult for the regime to achieve the almost unanimous consent it enjoyed in the Chamber, the opposition was more persistent, and at times it managed to gather as many as 50 votes against the government. But although strong in moral prestige, the Senate had long since lost effective control over governmental policy. The occasional opposition speech made in its hall and in that of the Chamber could not hide the fact that parliamentary government had come to an end. Fascism's leaders were so sure of themselves that on June 10, 1925, the first anniversary of Matteotti's murder, they denied the 117 members of the Aventine opposition the right to meet in a room of Montecitorio [Parliament Building]. Four months later, on October 28, Mussolini made a speech in Milan marking the third anniversary of the March on Rome. In it he made explicit his notion of the state and his intention of exercising dictatorial power unfettered by parliamentary control.

75. MUSSOLINI DEFINES HIS REGIME: SPEECH OF OCTOBER 28, 1925

Reported in the *Popolo d'Italia*, October 29, 1925; reproduced in Benito Mussolini, *Opera omnia*, Edoardo and Duilio Susmel, eds. Florence: La Fenice, 1956, XXI, 425–27. Our translation.

This is our formula: all within the state, nothing outside the state, nothing against the state. . . . What occurred in October 1922 was not a change of Ministry, it was the creation of a new political regime. I shall be explicit on this matter.

This political regime proceeds from a presupposition that is unassailable and beyond question: the monarchy and the dynasty. (*All present rise and at the shout "Long live the King" engage in a great*

* Reference to Giolitti's use of artillery to dislodge d'Annunzio from Fiume in December 1920. The two situations are hardly analogous, much less similar. Ed. note.

manifestation.) All the rest are institutions that were far from perfect when they arose and today are even less so than before.

Gentlemen! Italy of 1925 cannot dress in that little costume that was suitable for little Piedmont in 1848.* The day after the promulgation of the *Statuto* Cavour himself said that it was something to be reviewed, modified, and perfected.

From what evil have we been suffering? It is the evil of parliamentary supremacy. What is the remedy? Reduction of this supremacy. Great solutions can never be adopted by assemblies unless these assemblies have been adequately prepared beforehand. A battle is either won by a single general or lost by an assembly of generals. You must always keep in mind that modern life is fast and complex, that it presents continuous problems. When modern nations arose under a liberal regime, they had 10 or 15 million inhabitants. Their political classes were small, restricted, and derived from a limited number of families having a special education. Today the environment is radically changed. The people can no longer wait: they are stirred by their problems and urged on by their needs. These are the reasons why I consider the executive power as the first among all the powers of the state: the executive power is the omnipresent and the omnioperating power in the everyday life of the nation. . . .

The government considers itself the general staff of the nation at work on the civil task of peace. The government never sleeps, because it will not allow the citizenry to be lazy; it is hard, because it feels that the enemies of the state have no right of citizenship in the state (*good!*); it is inflexible, because it feels that in these days of trial only inflexible wills can go forward. . . .

During the several years to come Mussolini gave abundant evidence of his inflexible attitude toward his opponents. In addition to introducing a large body of repressive legislation—some of which is given below—Mussolini sought and achieved the dissolution of the Aventine secession by expelling its members from Parliament. Early in 1926 it became clear to many Aventinians that their abstention from Parliament had influenced the King no more than had their petitions, addresses, and manifestoes. During 1925, neither the opposition of the three former Prime Ministers, Giolitti, Orlando, and Salandra; nor a Manifesto of the Intellectuals prepared by Benedetto Croce; nor the violence done to Giovanni Amendola, formerly a King's Min-

---

* A reference to the *Statuto* (Constitution) of 1848. Ed. note.

ister; nor the virtual seizure of the *Corriere della Sera* had been enough to persuade the King to move against Fascism.

The first to break the Aventinian ranks had been the Communists, who returned to the Chamber in November 1924. Early in January 1926 the *Popolari* concluded that their role as opponents of Fascism, reaffirmed at their last party congress in June 1925, could be better performed by returning to Parliament. They chose as the occasion for their return the meeting of the Chamber of January 16 called the commemorate the dead Queen Mother Margherita. Mussolini was incensed by the presence of the Popularist Deputies and insisted that instead of recessing for three days as a sign of respect for the dead Queen, the Chamber be convened the next day, "because there is a moral question that brooks no delay. . . . I insist on it." His insistence was satisfied, and the next day he vented his wrath against the *Popolari* and the whole Aventinian opposition. He demanded that, as a condition for the return of the "Aventinian deserters" to the Chamber, they "acknowledge the accomplished fact of the Fascist revolution"; no less publicly and solemnly acknowledge the failure of their "nefarious and scandal-mongering campaign"; and divorce themselves completely "from those who continue beyond our borders with their anti-Fascist campaign."

The overwhelming majority of the *Popolari* and all of the other Aventinians refused to accept Mussolini's conditions for sitting in the Chamber. The following November the Fascist Chamber approved without debate a motion expelling 123 Aventine Deputies, including the Communists (who had in fact returned in November 1924), because of "subversive activities against the powers of the state." Except for a handful of Liberals who had not joined the Aventine secession, the Chamber was finally "unanimously Fascist." From 1925 to 1928 this truncated Chamber passed a host of laws designed to legalize the dictatorship and sweep away by law the last remnants of free political institutions already eliminated in fact.

76. THE LEGALIZATION OF THE DICTATORSHIP AND ITS INSTRUMENTS

Law on Associations, November 26, 1925

> *Raccolta ufficiale delle leggi e dei decreti del Regno d'Italia*, 1925, IX, 9919–20. Our translation.

Article 1. All associations, organizations, and institutes formed or operating in the Kingdom or its colonies are obliged to communicate to the authorities of public safety their constitution, statutes, and by-laws, their list of officers and members, and all other information regarding their organization and activity every such time this information is re-

quested by the authorities for reasons of order and public safety. . . .
This information must be provided within two days of the time it is
requested. . . .

Art. 2. All civil and military agents and employees of all grades,
whether of the state, or provinces, or communes, or of any entities by
law under the trust of the state, who belong even simply as members
to associations, organizations, and institutes formed in the Kingdom or
outside, and which operate even if only in part in a clandestine or
secret manner or whose members are in any way bound in secrecy,*
are relieved of their rank or removed from their employment or are
otherwise discharged.

All officials, employees, civil and military agents as specified above
are obliged to declare whether they belonged or belong to associations
[as specified] at any time this information is requested of them. . . .

*Law on the Attributes and Prerogatives of the Head of the
Government and Prime Minister, December 24, 1925*

Raccolta ufficiale, 1925, X, 9776–78. Our translation.

Article 1. The executive power is exercised by the King through his
Government. His Majesty's Government consists of the Prime Minister
Secretary of State and Ministers Secretaries of State. The Prime Minis-
ter is the Head of the Government.

Art. 2. The Head of the Government (Prime Minister Secretary of
State) is appointed and dismissed by the King and is responsible to
the King for the Government's general policies. . . .†

The Ministers Secretaries of State are appointed and dismissed by
the King upon the recommendation of the Head of the Government.
They are responsible to the King and to the Head of the Government. . . .‡

Art. 5. The Head of the Government is a member of the Council for

* This article seems aimed particularly against Freemasonry, some of whose
senior members were implicated in Tito Zaniboni's attempt against Mussolini's
life planned for November 4, 1925. The plot was never executed because of the
revelations of a police spy. Ed. note.

† This provision specifically denies the principle of parliamentary responsibility.
Ed. note.

‡ This paragraph gives the Prime Minister a privileged position with regard to
his colleagues in the government and has the effect of reducing the King's
authority. Ed. note.

the safeguard and care of the Royal Family and exercises the functions of notary to the Crown. . . .

Art. 6. All items on the agenda of either of the two Houses of Parliament must have the approval of the Head of the Government. . . .

Art. 8. The Head of the Government designates, from time to time, the Minister to substitute for him in the case of absence or incapacity.

Art. 9. Whoever commits an attempt against the life, health, or freedom of the Head of the Government is punished by imprisonment of not less than fifteen years, and, in the event the attempt is successful, by penal servitude for life.*

Whoever offends the Head of the Government by word or deed is punished by imprisonment or detention ranging from six to thirty months and a fine of 500 to 3,000 lire. . . .

Law on the Discharge of Public Servants, December 24, 1925

Raccolta ufficiale, 1926, I, 7. Our translation.

Article 1. His Majesty's Government is empowered up to December 31, 1926, to discharge from the service officials, employees, and agents of every civil or military rank or grade belonging to any administrative body of the state who, by reason of acts in or out of office, do not give full assurance of faithful performance of their duties or who place themselves in a condition of incompatibility with the general political policies of the Government.

Law on the Press, December 31, 1925

Raccolta ufficiale, 1926, I, 18–19. Our translation.

Article 1. All newspapers and periodical publications must have a legally responsible business manager. . . .

The business manager or managing editor must be listed on the rolls of professional journalists.

The business manager or managing editor must obtain recognition from the Attorney General at the Court of Appeals in the jurisdic-

* This provision may have been the result of the Zaniboni plot against Mussolini's life. Ed. note.

tional district where the newspaper or periodical publication is printed.

The Attorney General may deny or revoke recognition to those who have been found guilty on two occasions of crimes committed through the press.

The Attorney General's denial or revocation of recognition, which may be appealed to the Minister of Justice, is accompanied by a statement of reasons for this step. Appeals against the action of the Minister may be made to the Council of State on questions of law.

Art. 2. No newspaper or periodical may be published until recognition is obtained from the Attorney General.

A newspaper or periodical that is published before the responsible manager receives recognition from the Attorney General must be seized.

Art. 3. At the time request is made for the recognition of the responsible manager, the printer of the newspaper or periodical and the publisher must present to the Attorney General a declaration containing the identity of all owners of the newspaper or periodical, as well as their places of residence and official domicile. . . .

The declaration prescribed by this Article must be renewed annually. . . .

Art. 4. The owners and publisher of a newspaper are financially responsible in civil law for the payment of sums owed in payment of compensation or damages or for expenses deriving from sentences for crimes committed through the press. . . .

Art. 7. An Order of Journalists is created with headquarters in cities having a Court of Appeals. The Order shall prepare its rolls of membership, and these shall be deposited in the chanceries of the Courts of Appeal. The profession of journalist may be exercised only by those listed on these rolls.

Law on Citizenship, * *January 31, 1926*

Raccolta ufficiale, 1926, I, 393. Our translation.

SINGLE ARTICLE

In addition to cases indicated in Article 8 of the law of June 13, 1912, n. 555, a citizen loses his citizenship when he commits or aids in the

* This law was aimed specifically against anti-Fascist exiles (*fuorusciti*). Among

commission in a foreign country of an act intended to disturb public order in the Kingdom, or from which may derive harm to Italian interests or damage to the good name or prestige of Italy, even if this act does not constitute a crime [according to previously existing laws]. . . .

To the loss of citizenship may be added . . . the seizure, and in more serious cases the confiscation, of property. . . .

The efficacy of the provisions for seizure or confiscation is in no way affected by subsequent acquisition of foreign citizenship by the proprietor of the wealth in question.

Loss of citizenship by the terms of this law has no influence on the citizenship of the spouse or children of the excitizen.

In 1926 there occurred three new attempts against Mussolini's life. An elderly Englishwoman, Violet Gibson, succeeded in wounding Mussolini in the nose with a pistol shot; the young anarchist Gino Lucetti, who had emigrated to France, returned to Italy and threw a hand grenade at an automobile in which Mussolini was traveling, with no effect; and a young student, Anteo Zamboni, fired a pistol shot that hit Mussolini's clothes but not his body. Partly as a consequence of these attempts a new law on the defense of the state was introduced on November 9, 1926, the same day the Aventine Deputies were deprived of their parliamentary mandates. The truncated Chamber debated and approved the law in one day, with only a handful of Liberal Deputies voting against it. The Senate proved less remissive and cast 49 votes against the bill.

Law on Measures for the Defense of the State,
November 25, 1926

Raccolta ufficiale, 1926, IV, 4614–15. Our translation.

Article 1. Whoever commits an act against the life, health, or personal freedom of the King or the Regent is punished by death.

The same penalty is applied to acts against the life, health, or personal freedom of the Queen, the Crown Prince, or the Head of the Government. . . .

Art. 3. When two or more persons conspire to commit any of the crimes mentioned in the above Articles, the simple fact of conspiracy

---

the more notable exiles who left Italy from 1924 to 1926 were Nitti, Sforza, Sturzo, Amendola, Salvemini, and Turati. Ed. note.

is punished by imprisonment ranging from five to fifteen years. Leaders, promoters, and organizers are punished by imprisonment ranging from fifteen to thirty years.

Whoever instigates the commission of any of the crimes mentioned in the above Articles, or justifies them, either publicly or by means of the press, is punished by imprisonment ranging from five to fifteen years for the simple fact of instigation or justification.

Art. 4. Whoever reconstitutes, even under different names and forms, associations, organizations, and parties that have been dissolved by order of the public authorities, is punished by imprisonment ranging from three to ten years and by perpetual exclusion from public office.

Whoever is a member of such associations, organizations, or parties is punished for the simple fact of membership by imprisonment ranging from three to ten years and by perpetual exclusion from public office.

The same penalty is incurred by whoever disseminates in any manner the doctrines, programs, and methods of such associations, organizations, or parties.

Art. 5. Any citizen who, while he is outside the territory of the state, spreads or communicates any false, exaggerated, or tendentious news or rumors for the purpose of diminishing the credit or prestige of the state abroad, or engages in any activity such as to harm the national interests, is punished by imprisonment ranging from five to fifteen years and perpetual exclusion from public office. Sentences *in absentia* pronounced on the basis of this article entail by law the loss of citizenship and confiscation of wealth. The trial judge may substitute seizure for confiscation; in that case he establishes the duration of the seizure and the destination of income from such wealth.

Loss of citizenship does not affect the citizenship of the spouse and children of the condemned person.

All transfer of wealth by the condemned person after the commission of the crime and for the year preceding is presumed to be fraud against the state, and the wealth in question is subject to confiscation or seizure. . . .

Art. 7. Legal competence to try the crimes specified by the present law is assigned to a special tribunal consisting of a presiding judge chosen from among the general officers of the Royal Army, the Royal

Navy, the Royal Air Force, and the Voluntary Militia for National Safety, and five judges chosen from among the officers of the Voluntary Militia for National Safety. . . .

The constitution of this tribunal is a function of the Minister of War, who determines its composition. . . .

Legal proceedings for the crimes specified by this law are according to the norms of the Military Penal Code and according to the penal procedures observed in time of war. . . .

Sentences by the special tribunal are beyond appeal, nor may they be impugned in any way; they are subject to review.

Proceedings for crimes specified by this law which are in course at the time of its promulgation, devolve in their existing state to the competence of the special tribunal.*

The last steps in the total elimination of free institutions were taken in 1928. Vested with extraordinary powers verging on a state of martial law, all suspect organizations banned, the press shackled, the public service "purified," local administration "Fascistized," and all Italian citizens in and out of Italy subject to the authority of a special tribunal operating under a law of unusual scope, Mussolini could proceed with a reform of the Chamber of Deputies and the legalization of the Fascist Grand Council. Given the almost unanimously Fascist composition of the Chamber in 1928, it may seem in retrospect to have been unnecessary for Mussolini to reform the manner of its election. But according to the *Statuto* elections had to be held at least every five years, and it was possible that under the prevailing electoral law of 1923 some opponent of the regime might be returned in the elections that had to be held no later than April 1929.

Mussolini had already destroyed all vestige of elective government by means of two laws passed in February and September 1926 which made all communal administrations appointive. These laws ended whatever remained of the thousands of once flourishing Socialist and Catholic local administrations. The aim of the law reforming the Chamber of Deputies was apparently to make the lower house of Parliament virtually as appointive as the Senate and the offices of local government. The bill Mussolini presented in March 1928 proposed reducing the size of the Chamber to 400 members, who were to represent the whole nation as a single constituency. These 400 Deputies were to be designated by the Fascist Grand Council from a list of 1,000 nominees selected by various Fascist organizations, particularly the Fascist Confederation of Syndicates. The 400 designated candidates were then to be presented to the voters who would have the sole option of approv-

---

* A most unusual provision: it meant granting to the special tribunal a retroactive competence over proceedings in course before other legal bodies. Ed. note.

ing or rejecting the entire slate. This bill for the Reform of Political Representation, which became law on May 17, 1928, thus abolishing what little there remained of free political representation on the national level, was "debated" and approved by the Chamber in a single day. The debate consisted of a solitary speech by Giovanni Giolitti. There was something of grandeur in the persistence of this eighty-five-year-old man who was in the last year of his life after more than four decades of parliamentary activity during which he had led five Ministries and conducted four general elections.

Giolitti Speaks against the Law for the Reform of Political Representation, March 16, 1928

> *Atti del Parlamento italiano, Camera dei deputati, Legislatura XXVII, Sessione del 1924–28, Discussioni,* March 16, 1928, IX, 8680–81. Our translation.

Giolitti: By presenting the bill under debate the government has acknowledged that a great civilized country such as Italy must have a national representative assembly among its constitutional organs of state.

But it seems to me that the method proposed for the formation of the new Chamber cannot lead to such representation. In order for an assembly to represent the nation it is necessary that its members be chosen with full freedom by the voters in their electoral constituencies, as is prescribed by Article 39 of the *Statuto.* (*Comments; interruptions.*)

On the contrary, all freedom of choice is excluded in this bill because by law only a single list may be presented to the voters. By assigning the selection of Deputies to the Fascist Grand Council, this law excludes from the Chamber any and all forms of political opposition, and thus marks the decisive break of the Fascist regime from a regime governed by the *Statuto.*

For these reasons, I and several colleagues find it impossible to vote in favor of the bill.

The Political Representation Reform Law of May 1928 contained an unusual anomaly in that it entrusted the designation of the 400 members of the Chamber of Deputies to a body—the National Grand Council of Fascism—which had no standing in law as a constitutional organ of the state.

The Council was an organ of the Fascist party, but not of the Italian Kingdom. This lapse was remedied by an appropriate law of December 1928, excerpts from which follow.

Law of December 9, 1928 Providing for the Structure and Attributes of the Grand Council of Fascism

Raccolta ufficiale, 1928, IV, 3988–90. Our translation.

Article 1. The Grand Council of Fascism is the supreme organ entrusted with the prescription and coordination of all the activities of the regime which issued from the revolution of October 1922. . . .

Art. 2. The Head of the Government and First Secretary of State is by right the President of the Grand Council of Fascism. He convenes it when he thinks it necessary and formulates its agenda.

Art. 3. The Secretary of the National Fascist Party is the Secretary of the Grand Council. In the case of the absence or incapacity of the Head of the Government, or in the event this office is vacant, the Head of the Government may delegate to the Secretary the power to convene and preside over the Grand Council.

Art. 4. The following are members of the Grand Council for an unlimited period of time: 1st. The Quadrumvirs of the March on Rome; 2d. Those who by virtue of membership in the Government have been members of the Grand Council for at least three years; 3d. Secretaries of the National Fascist Party who have left this office after 1922.

Art. 5. The following are members of the Grand Council by reason of offices held and for the duration of these offices: 1st. The President of the Senate and the President of the Chamber; 2d. Ministers Secretaries of State; 3d. The Under-Secretary of State for the Presidency of the Council; 4th. The Commanding General of the Voluntary Militia for National Security; 5th. The members of the Executive Committee of the National Fascist Party; 6th. The President of the Academy of Italy and the President of the Fascist Institute for Culture; 7th. The President of the *Opera nazionale Balilla;* * 8th. The President of the Special Tribunal for the Defense of the State; 9th. The

* Fascist youth organization formed in April 1926. See pp. 471–72 below. Ed. note.

Presidents of the legally recognized Fascist National Confederations of Syndicates [labor organizations]; 10th. The President of the National Corporation for Cooperation. . . .

Art. 11. The Grand Council deliberates on: 1st. The list of Deputies to be designated according to Art. 5 of the Law of May 17, 1928, n. 1019 *; 2d. The constitution, structure, and policies of the National Fascist Party; 3d. The appointment and dismissal of the Secretary, Assistant Secretaries, Administrative Secretary, and the other members of the Executive Committee of the National Fascist Party.

Art. 12. The views of the Grand Council must be heard on all questions of a constitutional nature. Such questions include proposed laws on: 1st. Succession to the throne, and the attributes and prerogatives of the Crown; 2d. The composition and functioning of the Grand Council, of the Senate, and of the Chamber of Deputies; 3d. The attributes and prerogatives of the Head of the Government, Prime Minister Secretary of State; 4th. The power of the executive authority to issue legal norms; 5th. The organization of the Syndicates and the Corporations; 6th. Relations between the state and the Holy See; 7th. International treaties involving a change in the territory of the state and the colonies, or a renunciation to acquire territories.

Art. 13. Upon proposal of the Head of the Government, the Grand Council prepares and keeps up to date a list of names to be presented to the Crown for the appointment of the Head of the Government in the event this office is vacant.

With the passage of the law on the Grand Council of Fascism the machinery of Mussolini's personal dictatorship was complete. No significant structural changes were effected in Italy's Fascist government from 1928 until the end of the regime. Even the creation of the Chamber of Fasces and Corporations in January 1939 involved little substantial change in the regime's governmental structure. First, because it simply replaced a subservient and hand-picked Chamber of Deputies with a body equally subservient; second, because the only truly novel feature in the new Chamber—representation of occupational categories rather than of geographic constituencies—was never put to the test. The coming of the Second World War and the consequent collapse of the Fascist regime left wholly unresolved the related questions of whether the Fascists were sincere in their professions of instituting a new form of representative system and whether this system is indeed superior to the traditional one of geographic representation.

* The *Raccolta ufficiale* identifies this law incorrectly as being of March 17. Ed. note.

XXII. FASCIST ECONOMIC AND SOCIAL POLICIES

After six years of activity in the halls of Parliament and in the country's streets, the Fascists had established by 1928 a firm hold over Italy's political life. This hold was not to be broken until 1943, and then largely because of the disasters of war. But the seventeen years of Fascist rule preceding the Second World War were not devoted exclusively to the solidification and retention of power by the regime; or, rather, precisely because the leaders of the regime realized that political power could not rest solely on laws and decrees, on the Fascist Militia and the political police, this leadership sought to widen and strengthen the bases of its authority by pursuing economic and social policies calculated to foster a favorable national consensus around the regime. The controlling ulterior motive behind these policies may have been preeminently political, but this probability does not invalidate the importance of the policies in question. They deserve attention and examination for their own sake and for what they reveal about the nature of the regime.

The following excerpt by Shepard B. Clough offers a general view of Fascist economic policies from the advent of the regime to the eve of the Second World War.

77. A GENERAL VIEW OF FASCIST ECONOMIC POLICIES, 1922–1939

Adapted from Shepard B. Clough, "Il fascismo in Italia: linee della sua politica economica," *Il Nuovo Osservatore*, VI, Nos. 44–45 (November–December, 1965), 826–33.

Whatever the final judgment of history may be of Italian Fascism, that judgment is likely to be extremely harsh. To be sure, voices will be raised to praise this or that particular aspect of Fascist policy and apologists will certainly contend that if this and that mistake had been avoided the outcome would have been different; but clearly historians whose evaluation of any social process rests on the basic values of Western civilization and on concrete accomplishments rather than hypotheses will condemn Fascism in no uncertain terms.

Probably it is safe also to hazard the guess that historians will conclude that no phase of Fascism was more calamitous than its economic phase. Although Fascism came to power at a time when social stresses were great and the tasks of reconstruction from the First World War were enormous, it fell from power in the midst of a terrible conflict which left Italy in ruins. In the twenty years of its existence, Fascism attempted first to restore the orderly functioning of the economy; then it created, from 1926 to 1934, an elaborate machinery for regulating relations among interest groups and for imposing its authority throughout the economy; and from 1935 to its demise used colonial conquest and wars as a means of furthering the economic well-being of Italians. To be sure, during these two decades it had to contend with enormous problems, one of the greatest of which was the world depression of the 1930s, but even so it made egregious errors of economic policy. It did not stress the importance of domestic economic growth and failed to steer Italian capital, labor, and technology in this direction. It did not emphasize the development of industry, where the possibilities for greatest growth were. It did not recognize the dependence for Italy on foreign trade and even attempted a policy of economic self-sufficiency, an error that many states made in the 1930s. And it did not acknowledge that Italy's population was very large for its resources, but to the contrary encouraged an increase in births.

At the beginning of the Fascist movement, Fascist leaders had no coherent economic policy or program. In the early days, Mussolini's newspaper, *Il Popolo d'Italia,* carried as a subtitle, "Socialist Daily" and in the upper left-hand corner a quotation from Blanqui, "He who has steel, has bread" and in the upper right-hand corner a quotation from Napoleon, "The revolution is an idea that has found bayonets." . . . .

After the March on Rome, Fascists did not have the power to rule alone, and in forming a coalition government, composed of representatives of all parties right of the Socialists, had to accommodate themselves to the views and desires of their colleagues. Then after establishing the dictatorship in 1924, they were not disposed to set out on a revolutionary economic course. They recognized the institution of private property, the incentives to be derived from making private profits, and the effectiveness to be realized from private management.

Italian statesmen before them, however, realized that state intervention in economic matters should be resorted to in order to keep the economic machine in motion. They believed that Italy would be made more economically independent by protecting the home market and by exploiting more fully national resources, even at very high costs. They thought that the country's economic base could be extended by acquisition of colonies. And they were convinced that the state should pursue policies of economic reform and of social welfare. The Fascists' greatest mistake came from carrying some of these notions too far. It seems that they refused to benefit from the country's economic experiences. And they followed Mussolini's economic ideas slavishly, although they realized that his understanding of economic problems was especially limited.

The policies of Fascism's first Minister of Finance, Alberto De' Stefani, seemed to mark not only a continuation of the past but a throwback to a much earlier time of economic liberalism. De' Stefani was an economist trained at Ca' Foscari in Venice, where the tradition of the liberal economist Francesco Ferrara was still strong, and had obtained a not very distinguished teaching post at the Technical Institute of Vicenza. He had come into prominence among Fascists as an *ardito* and leader of bands which had captured the town hall at Bolzano on October 2, 1922 and had carried out a raid on Trent. He at least had convictions about what economic policies the new regime should pursue and thus gained recognition within the party because of a general lack of economic competence among the other leaders.

De' Stefani struck out boldly and courageously in the direction dictated by liberal economic doctrines. Building on the work of his predecessors in office, specifically Filippo Meda, he began unraveling the snarl of wartime taxes, establishing a progressive income tax in 1923 and a general sales tax, which was a forerunner of the IGE, introduced in 1940. He attacked the problem of tax evasion, abolished the rule whereby stocks and bonds had to be registered in the name of the owner, exempted new construction from the building tax, encouraged foreign trade by making commercial treaties, and actually balanced the budget in 1925. De' Stefani's accomplishments were by no means insignificant; and Italy's economic recovery to prewar levels of production was about as rapid as that of other European belligerents.

The economic expansion which accompanied De' Stefani's liberal policies had certain unpopular results, which are not unusual in times of prosperity. Commodity prices began to rise; the value of equity securities began to soar; and the lira began to lose strength in foreign exchange, the rate going from 90.43 lire to the pound sterling in October 1922 to 144.92 in 1925. These developments led De' Stefani to take deflationary measures to restrict expansion, such as raising the discount rate, controlling stock exchange operation, and restricting foreign exchange transactions. These moves had the economic effects which he desired, but they aroused the hostility of certain elements of the business community who convinced Mussolini that a "changing of the guard" was in order. De' Stefani was dismissed rather abruptly.

This sudden end to De' Stefani's term of office marked an important turning point in Fascism's economic history. Henceforth Mussolini was personally to play a much more decisive role in policy formation than had hitherto been the case. This was most unfortunate for *il Duce* had no experience in national economic matters and no competence. In this realm of statesmanship, as in so many others, he allowed his impulses, his emotions, and his sophomoric ideas of national interest to determine what policies should be adopted and executed. When he listened to advice, it was generally the advice of the leaders of big business. More often than not, however, he simply cowed his advisers, his counsellors, and his people with bombastic demagoguery.

Mussolini's subsequent mistakes in economic matters—and in other national affairs which had economic consequences—were so egregious that the state had henceforth to have recourse to a policy of patchwork intervention in order to minimize the consequences of the errors. Indeed, the economic history of Fascism after the departure of De' Stefani from the Ministry of Finance may be characterized as government action to shore up a capitalist economy that was threatened both by the policies of inept political leaders and by a world economic depression.

The first major blunder in policy for which Mussolini could be held personally responsible was the stabilization of the lira at too high an exchange rate (December 21, 1927) for the welfare of the economy. *Il*

Duce was of the opinion that Italian national honor was at stake in the previously mentioned decline of the lira in foreign exchange, and that the lira should be fixed at all costs at a high rate. . . .

Mussolini's advisers were aware of the deflationary effect that a high rate for the lira would have on the economy, but their leader would not listen to them. In fact, he made a real fetish of the *quota novanta* (a rate of 90 lire to the pound sterling) and let its slogan-like appeal drown out all criticism. When the rate of 92.46 lire to the pound was adopted, it began to make Italian goods and services expensive in foreign markets, brought prices down within Italy, and made the paying off of domestic debt more difficult. Exports dropped from 18.2 billion lire in 1926 to 15.2 in 1927; the price of wheat fell from 200 lire a quintal in 1926 to 140 lire in 1927; the official unemployment figures rose from 181,439 in 1926 to 414,283 in 1927.

This "stabilization crisis" added to the unrest of the labor element within the Fascist movement. Workers had already begun to be uneasy and to go out on strike because of the rise in prices in 1925. Such lack of "discipline" could hardly be tolerated by Mussolini, for Fascism had come to power on a wave of revulsion against labor disorders and social disturbances, and it now contended that it had restored social order. Furthermore, *il Duce* had told representatives of labor and of capital in a confrontation at the Chigi Palace as early as December 1923 that workers and employers must get along better than they had in the past and that he would see to it that they did. Thus the new threat of labor agitation, prolonged by the policy of monetary deflation, required action.

The action taken in these circumstances was the creation of the Corporative State. The Rocco Law of Corporations (April 3, 1926) * created a highly schematized organization of both employers and employees by which the dictatorship could exercise its authority over them. Secondly, Mussolini promulgated the Labor Charter of April 21, 1927 which enunciated Fascist principles by which labor and management were to be brought to heel.

These principles were that the life and aims of the state were supe-

* This had been preceded by the so-called Pact of the Vidoni Palace (October 2, 1925) which spelled the doom of all non-Fascist labor organizations. [See p. 461 below.]

rior to the individual and that labor in all forms—intellectual, technical, and manual—is a social duty and is under the guardianship of the state. Here was a doctrine which was directly opposed to Western civilization's ideas of individualistic and personal liberty. It was a doctrine that allowed the dictatorship to intervene in all matters economic. For purposes of intervening in and of controlling the economy, Fascism created elaborate "corporative machinery." This, the first organ of the corporate state, was soon expanded to provide controls of and plans for the economy and to establish a new "corporate" mechanism for governing the body politic. This machinery was created primarily by the law of February 5, 1934, which brought into being the twenty-two corporations based on categories of economic activity, and by the law of January 19, 1939, which envisaged the establishment of a governmental structure representing corporate bodies—and Fascist authority.

Not only did the sudden rise of prices during the economic expansion of De' Stefani's regime and then the depression which followed the stabilization of the lira in 1927 create problems which led to the adoption of the Fascist brand of capitalism, they also led to massive state intervention in economic affairs. Interventionism was nothing new and had been practiced by all organized societies when some major branch of their economy was in trouble. In the present case, however, Fascists carried interventionism much further than had their predecessors at the helm of the Italian liberal state. They went so far as they did, in part, because the trouble in which the economy found itself was so grave, in part, because wealthy industrialists who were Fascist supporters wanted to benefit from state aid, and, in part also, because Fascist leaders had great ambitions which could only be satisfied by a politically controlled economy.

In a real sense, Fascist state interventionist policy fed upon itself. For example, the need to improve the nation's balance of trade and payments led to an effort to increase the production of wheat, which Mussolini lamentably dubbed the "Battle of Grain." The Battle of Grain led to a campaign of draining swamps and other land projects in order to have more hectares for wheat. Then growing of grain on land unsuitable for it contributed to the high price of flour, which could be maintained in the face of falling international grain prices only by rigid price fixing. And once price fixing was resorted to for grain, it was extended rapidly to many other products and services.

In spite of what was done to keep prices up, Italian prices did decline, and these declines, as well as generally depressed economic conditions, threatened many business concerns with bankruptcy. To save them, the Fascist government established the Istituto per la Ricostruzione Industriale (January 23, 1933), provided it with some capital from the treasury, and allowed it to raise more by the sale of its own bonds. This institution came to the rescue of the great commercial banks—the Banca Commerciale, the Credito Italiano, and the Banca di Roma—by buying depressed industrial securities in the portfolios of these institutions. Subsequently it obtained large holdings in productive plants by granting assistance to ailing establishments. Thus the state acquired whole or partial ownership of a vast empire which neither the Fascists nor their successors were able to sell to private interests.

Such efforts to keep the economy going by state action were not without effect, but Italy's foreign trade and balance of trade and payments continued to be depressed, especially after the devaluation of the English pound and the American dollar (1934). With the lira in December 1934 at 58.07 to the pound in place of the *quota novanta* and with the dollar at 11.73 instead of 18.60, Italian goods and services had a harder time than ever finding foreign buyers. Yet confronted with the obvious need to devalue the lira, Mussolini delayed action until October 5, 1936, when he joined in the "alignment of currencies."

In the meantime, *il Duce* embarked upon a course which was to be disastrous. In spite of the fact that Italy's colonial adventures initiated by the liberal Italian state had been far from economically rewarding, Mussolini believed that the country's economic ills could be relieved by the acquisition of new colonial lands. He thus launched the military campaign to conquer Ethiopia (1935) without having any precise ideas of what the economic potentialities of that land were and without apparently giving thought to the fact that the tide of European imperialism was already receding.

The war in Ethiopia led to economic sanctions, which were not vigorously enough applied to halt military operations but which were serious enough to worsen Italy's economic predicament. Mussolini's answer to this new situation was to increase his program of making his country more completely economically self-sufficient and to prepare for war in a collaboration with Germany which was consummated by the offensive-defensive alliance known as the Pact of Steel (May 22, 1939). Both of these policies were foolhardy, for Italy, with its limited national natural resources, could only prosper with a high level of international trade and did not have total resources adequate for the conduct of a large scale war. And how could Italy have benefited economically—or politically—from helping Hitler establish a German-dominated Europe? In fact, Italy's economic strength was sapped by the Ethiopian War, participation in the Spanish Civil War, and in preparation for the war to come. From 1934 to 1939 the nation's public debt rose from 102.2 billion lire to 145.8 billion lire largely because of military expenditures—an amount of capital which could have been used more effectively for the building of productive industrial plant. Yet in spite of everything Italy was lamentably ill-prepared for war, as Mussolini's chief economic advisors for the economic preparation, Carlo Favagrossa and Felice Guarneri, have so bitterly testified.*

If one tries to judge the results of Fascist economic policies from the seizure of power in 1922 to the arrest of Mussolini on July 25, 1943, one can only conclude that the dictatorship left the nation in ruins. If one takes the period 1922 to 1938 and makes suitable allowances for the world-wide depression, one's judgments are, however, less severe, but they are severe enough.† Italian national income at 1938 prices rose from 102,209 million lire in 1922 to 137,877 million lire in 1938, but on a per capita basis went only from 2,703 lire at the former date to 3,201 at the latter. Moreover, total private consumption rose from 97,196 million lire at 1938 prices as an annual average for the period 1921–30 to only 106,009 million lire for the period 1931–40; and between these two periods there was an actual decline in private consumption of food and beverages. Lastly, the rate of growth of value added from 1894 to 1913 was 2.44 per cent per year whereas from 1920 to 1939 it was 1.40 per cent per year; and the re-

* Carlo Favagrossa, *Perchè perdemmo la guerra* (Milan, Rizzoli, 1946), and Felice Guarneri, *Battaglie economiche tra le due guerre* (2 vols.; Milan, Garzanti, 1953).

† A Communist judgment is to be found in Ernesto Rossi, *I padroni del vapore* (Bari, Laterza, 1957).

spective rates of increase of national income were 2.49 per cent and 1.82 per cent per year.

No matter what criteria one employs, the record of Fascism was poor. The regime squandered in gaudy showmanship and in destructive war what should have been invested in industry. Undoubtedly the chief reasons for Italy's post-Second World War economic miracle have been exactly the recognition and implementation of these principles. And what is more, responsible economic leaders in Italy have recognized that economic progress is feasible and have worked to achieve it. Fascists had other and more risky goals.

78. THE CORPORATIVE STATE: MYTH AND REALITY

In January 1939 there occurred the last nominally important change in the Fascist regime's governmental structure by the creation of the Chamber of Fasces and Corporations, designed to replace the more traditionally named Chamber of Deputies. The appearance of the new body was supposed to be the capstone of the "corporativist" reorganization of Italian political and economic life, a reorganization whose first tentative steps had been taken in October 1925 with the signing of the Pact of the Vidoni Palace between representatives of the Fascist labor unions (called "corporations" from the Italian word for medieval craft guilds) and of the employers' General Confederation of Industry. This Pact affirmed, with the government's blessing, that the Fascist corporations and the General Confederation of Industry were the only organizations legitimately entitled to represent labor and capital in industry. Fascism's monopoly control over organized labor became definitive when, in 1926, the once flourishing Catholic labor organizations dissolved themselves and, in 1927, the once formidable Socialist General Confederation of Labor transferred the remnants of its leadership abroad. But Fascism's control of capitalist or managerial groups was never to be so complete as its dominance over Fascist-sponsored labor organizations. As a result, the theory of a corporative state as expressing the cooperation between capital and labor, and in which the very instruments of this cooperation were to become the supreme directing political and economic organs of the state, was destined to remain in the realm of myths and never become a reality. True, the Law for the Reform of Political Representation of May 1928 provided that the National Confederations of Fascist Syndicates [labor organizations] would nominate 800 of 1,000 candidates from whom the Grand Council of Fascism would select the 400 designees for election to the

Chamber of Deputies by means of a vote in which the country could either accept or reject the entire slate of designees. But this reform was a far cry from the theory of corporative syndicalism that would place the direction of the state in the hands of categories of individuals organized along economic lines. Nor did the creation of the Chamber of Fasces and Corporations in January 1939 enhance the effective control that the rank-and file membership of the National Confederations were supposed to exercise over their leaders and over the policy-making authorities of the state. The net effect of the entire corporative structure was to give Mussolini and the Fascist hierarchs a tight control over a domesticated labor movement and a somewhat less sure control over management. But in no sense did the corporative state constitute that new sociopolitical system that theorists of syndicalism, such as Edmondo Rossoni, had envisioned.

The first stone in the building of the corporative structure was set on April 3, 1926, with the Law on the Legal Regulation of Collective Labor Relations, excerpts from which are translated below.

Law on the Legal Regulation of Collective Labor Relations,
April 3, 1926 (Alfredo Rocco, Minister of Justice)

> *Raccolta ufficiale delle leggi e dei decreti del Regno d'Italia*, 1926, II, 1324–28. Our translation.

TITLE I. ON THE LEGAL RECOGNITION OF SYNDICATES AND COLLECTIVE
LABOR CONTRACTS

Article 1. Syndical associations of employers and of employees, either intellectual or manual, may be legally recognized when they show that the following conditions exist: 1. In the case of employers' associations, that the employers voluntarily enrolled therein employ at least one tenth of the workers in enterprises of the kind for which the association is formed and within the geographic area of the association's activity; and in the case of associations of workers, that the workers voluntarily enrolled therein comprise at least one tenth of the workers in the category for which the association has been formed and within the geographic area of the association's activity; 2. That, in addition to the ends of defending the economic and moral interests of the membership, the associations in question propose to pursue and do in fact pursue ends of assistance, instruction, and of moral and national education of the membership; 3. That the leadership of the asso-

ciation give assurance of their ability, morality, and sure national loyalty.

Art. 2. When the conditions prescribed in the preceding article are
met, associations of persons exercising an art or profession may [also]
be legally recognized. . . .

Art. 3. The associations referred to in the preceding articles may
consist of only employers or only workers. . . .

Art. 4. Recognition of the associations referred to in the preceding
articles takes place by Royal Decree and upon recommendation of the
relevant Minister in concert with the Minister of the Interior and after
having heard the views of the Council of State. The same Decree approves the constitution and bylaws of the association. . . .

The constitutions must contain a precise statement of the ends of
the associations, of the manner of choosing their social organs, and of
the conditions for admission of members. Among these conditions
must be good political conduct from the national point of view. . . .

Art. 5. Legally recognized associations are invested with a legal personality; they represent by law all the employers, or workers, or artists, and professionals of the category for which they are formed and
in the territorial circumscription in which they operate, whether or not
they are members of the said associations.

Legally recognized associations have the right to impose annual
dues on all employers, workers, artists, and professionals they represent, whether or not they are members of the said associations. In the
case of employers, dues are not to exceed a day's compensation for
each worker they employ; for workers, artists, and professionals dues
are not to exceed a day's compensation. . . .

Art. 6. Associations may be communal, district, provincial, regional,
interregional, or national in organization.

Under the conditions provided for by the present law, federations
or unions of several associations, and the confederation of several federations may also be legally recognized. . . .

One and only one association may be legally recognized for each
category of employers, workers, artists, or professionals . . . [and]
only one federation or confederation of employers, workers, or artists,
or professionals for each category and within the territorial limits assigned to it. . . .

In no case may recognition be extended to associations which, without authorization from the government, have any ties of discipline or dependency with associations international in character. . . .

Art. 10. Collective labor contracts stipulated by legally recognized associations of employers, workers, artists, and professionals apply to all employers, workers, artists, and professionals in the category to which the collective contract refers and whom they represent according to the provisions of Article 5. . . .

Art. 11. The rules of the present law on the legal recognition of syndical associations do not apply to associations of employees of the state, of provinces, of communes, and of public charitable institutions. . . .

TITLE II. ON THE LABOR COURTS

Article 13. All controversies relative to the regulation of collective labor relations, which concern the application of collective contracts or other existing rules, or the request of new conditions of labor, are within the competence of Courts of Appeal acting as Labor Courts.

Before rendering a decision, an attempt at conciliation is compulsory on the part of the President of the Court. . . .

Art. 14. In order that the Courts of Appeal may function as Labor Courts, a special Section of three magistrates is constituted in each of the sixteen Courts of Appeal. . . .

Art. 15. In the application of existing agreements the Court of Appeal functioning as a Labor Court renders its judgment according to legal rules on the interpretation and execution of contracts; and in the formulation of new conditions of labor, according to equity, striking a mean between the interests of the employers and those of the workers, and in all cases protecting the superior interests of production. . . .

Decisions of the Court of Appeal functioning as a Labor Court may be challenged by petition for reversal according to the provisions of Article 517 of the Civil Code of Procedure.

Art. 17. . . . Only legally recognized associations may represent in judgment all the employers and all the workers of a category. . . .

TITLE III. ON LOCKOUTS AND STRIKES

Article 18. Lockouts and strikes are forbidden.

Employers who, without justified motives and solely for the purpose of obtaining modifications of existing labor agreements from their employees, suspend work in their plants, concerns, or offices, are punished by a fine ranging from 10,000 to 100,000 lire.

Employees or workers three or more in number who on the basis of a prior agreement abandon their work or continue with it in a manner calculated to disturb its continuity or regularity in order to obtain different labor agreements from their employers, are punished by a fine ranging from 100 to 1,000 lire. . . .

Art. 19. Employees of the state and of other public agencies, and employees of enterprises providing a public service or a service of public necessity, three or more in number who on the basis of a prior agreement abandon their work or continue with it in a manner calculated to disturb its continuity or regularity, are punished by imprisonment ranging from one to six months and by exclusion from public office for six months. . . .

Managers of enterprises providing a public service or a service of public necessity who without a justified motive suspend work in their establishments, concerns, or offices are punished by imprisonment ranging from six months to a year and by a fine of 5,000 to 100,000 lire, in addition to temporary exclusion from public office.

Art. 21. When the suspension of work on the part of employers or the abandonment or the irregular performance of work on the part of employees takes place with the purpose of coercing the will or of influencing the decisions of a body or agency of the state, the provinces, or the communes, or of a public official, the leaders, promoters, and organizers are punished by imprisonment from three to seven years and by permanent exclusion from public office; all other participants in the act are punished by imprisonment from one to three years and by temporary exclusion from public office.

Art. 22. . . . Employers and workers who refuse to execute the decisions of a Labor Court are punished by imprisonment ranging from one month to one year and by a fine of 100 to 5,000 lire.

The managing personnel of legally recognized associations which refuses to execute the decisions of a Labor Court is punished by imprisonment from six months to two years and by a fine of 2,000 to 10,000 lire, in addition to dismissal from office. . . .

On April 21, 1927 the Fascist Grand Council announced the issuance of a Labor Charter designed to specify the rights and duties of labor in the emerging corporative state. Much of the impetus that had led to the issuance of the Charter came from labor-oriented elements in the Fascist movement, and from Edmondo Rossoni in particular. But although the Charter was much publicized as a *magna carta* of labor, it is clear from the following excerpts that the emphasis in the Charter is more on the duties of labor toward the state than on labor's rights with regard to the state. The dominant tone of the Charter recalls the ideology of the Nationalists, who had been absorbed into the Fascist party in 1923, and whose doctrines provided a ready-made body of ideas to the previously un-ideological Fascist movement.

The Labor Charter (Carta del lavoro), *April 21, 1927*

Text of the Charter reproduced in Confederazione fascista dei lavoratori dell'industria, *I 10 anni della carta del lavoro.* Rocca S. Casciano: Stab. tip. L. Cappelli, 1937, pp. 11–18. Our translation.

ON THE CORPORATIVE STATE AND ITS ORGANIZATION

I. The Italian nation is an organism having ends, life, and means of action superior, by virtue of its power and duration, to those of the separate individuals or groups of individuals which compose it. It is a moral, political, and economic unity that is realized integrally in the Fascist state.

II. Labor in all its forms, intellectual, technical, and manual, is a social duty. By right of this fact, and only by this right, it is safeguarded by the state. The whole of the process of production is unitary from the national point of view; its aims are unitary and are summed up in the welfare of individuals and in the growth of national power.

III. Syndical or occupational association is free, but only those syndicates that are recognized by law and subjected to the control of the state have the right to represent legally the whole category of employers or employees for which they are established. . . .

IV. The solidarity between the various factors of production finds concrete expression in the collective labor contract, by means of the conciliation of the opposed interests of employers and employees and their subordination to the higher interests of production.

V. Labor courts are the organs with which the state intervenes to regulate labor disputes. . . .

VI. The legally recognized occupational associations assure legal equality between employers and employees; they maintain the discipline of production and labor and promote their increasing perfection.

The corporations constitute the unitary organization of the forces of production and integrally represent its interests. By virtue of this integral representation, and inasmuch as the interests of production are national interests, the corporations are recognized by law as organs of the state. Representing the unitary interests of production, the corporations may impose compulsory rules on the conduct of labor relations. . . .

VII. The corporative state considers private enterprise in the field of production as the most effective and useful instrument in the promotion of national interest. Inasmuch as private organization of production is a function of national interest, the organizer of an enterprise is responsible to the state for the direction its production takes. . . .

IX. State intervention in economic production takes place only when private initiative is lacking or insufficient, or when the state's political interests are at stake. Such intervention may take the form of controls, encouragement, or direct management.

ON COLLECTIVE LABOR CONTRACTS AND LABOR GUARANTEES

XI. Occupational associations have the duty of regulating by collective contracts the labor relations between the categories of employers and workers they represent. . . .

XIV. . . . Night work not included in regular periodic shifts is to be compensated by a percentage in addition to the rate for day work. . . .

XVI. After a year of continuous service, workers in steadily operating firms have the right to paid annual vacations.

XVII. In case of termination of employment by dismissal without fault, workers in steadily operating firms have the right to a severance pay proportionate to their years of service. Such indemnity is due also in the case of a worker's death.

XVIII. . . . Illness of a worker not beyond a specified period does not terminate the labor contract. Call to arms or service in the Militia shall not be cause for dismissal of a worker.

XIX. Infractions of work rules and acts that disturb the normal operation of an enterprise committed by employees shall be punished, according to their gravity, by a fine, suspension from work, and, in more serious cases, by immediate dismissal without compensation. Cases in which the employer may impose fines, suspension, or immediate dismissal without compensation will be specified.

ON INSURANCE, AID, EDUCATION, AND INSTRUCTION

XXVI. Social insurance is another manifestation of the principle of collaboration. Employers and employees shall share the burden of its costs proportionately. . . .

XXVII. The Fascist state resolves to enact: (1) the perfecting of accident insurance; (2) the improvement and extension of maternity insurance; (3) insurance against occupational diseases and tuberculosis as a step toward general insurance against all sickness; (4) the perfecting of insurance against involuntary unemployment; (5) the adoption of special forms of endowment insurance for young workers. . . .

XXX. One of the principal duties of occupational associations shall be the education and instruction, especially the occupational instruction, of those they represent, be they members or nonmembers.

On the basis of the Rocco Law of 1926 and in harmony with the principles enunciated in the Labor Charter, thirteen occupational associations were established. Six consisted of associations of employers (Confederations of Agriculture, Industry, Commerce, Marine and Air Transportation, Land Transportation and Inland Navigation, and Banking); six corresponding employee groups (Syndicates); and one Confederation of intellectuals and professional men. Over-all supervision of this entire structure was entrusted to a Ministry of Corporations, which replaced the Ministries of National Economy and of Labor and was held by Mussolini until 1929. In 1930 a National Council of Corporations, envisaged by the Decree Law of July 1, 1926, was established, only to be radically reformed by the Law of February 5, 1934. This last important organic law of the corporative system provided for the reduction of the original 13 National Confederations to 9 and for the creation of 22 Corporations, 1 for each of the 22 occupations into which the national economy was divided. These Corporations were grouped under three "production-cycles" (agricultural industries and trades, industry and related commerce, and public services) and consisted of representatives from among the leaders of the Confederations of employers and of employees, of technicians, workers, members of cooperatives, and Fascist party representatives. The Corporations were to regulate and plan for the activity of their respective branches of the national economy; and when in 1939 the National Council of Corporations was made the nucleus of a Chamber of

Fasces and Corporations, the Corporations ceased to be purely economic in nature and became in theory a part of the state's directing political organs. The corporative system thus reached its structural completion, but the advent of the Second World War put aside whatever "normal" implementation and development the Fascist leadership may have intended for this "novel" creation.

79. FASCIST SOCIAL POLICIES

Some of the Fascist regime's most publicized policies were in the field of health, social welfare, and leisure-time activities of the Italian people, particularly of young people. There is much controversy on the questions of whether Fascist social policies were the product of an undiluted interest in the people's general welfare, and whether these policies were executed with the greatest efficiency, equity, and economy. Many writers have ascribed these policies more to the regime's partisan political concerns than to its preoccupation with the country's well-being; others have criticized the manner in which these policies were implemented.

The first major Fascist innovation in the area of social welfare legislation was the creation of the *Opera nazionale del dopolavoro* [National Institute for After-Work Activities] brought into being by the decree-law of May 1, 1925. The *Dopolavoro* agency is estimated to have provided opportunities for recreation to about 3 million members by 1938. Certainly, one of the purposes of *Dopolavoro* was to occupy the membership's leisure time in a manner deemed "safe" by the regime; but this fact does not exclude the possibility that the recreational services provided had intrinsic and politically neutral merits of their own.

The selection reproduced below includes the more important portions of the decree-law instituting the *Opera nazionale del dopolavoro.*

Decree-Law Instituting the Opera nazionale del dopolavoro,
May 1, 1925

> *Raccolta ufficiale delle leggi e dei decreti del Regno d'Italia*, 1925, V, 4737–40. Our translation.

Article 1. There is instituted with headquarters at Rome the *Opera nazionale del dopolavoro,* having the following ends: a) the promotion of the healthy and profitable employment of the workers' leisure time through agencies aiming at the development of the workers' physical, intellectual, and moral capabilities; . . . . d) the dissemination, by means of the press and in other ways, of the advantages afforded by such agencies and of the measures employed by them for the elevation of the working classes. . . .

Art. 2. The *Opera nazionale del dopolavoro* is a corporate legal entity; it may receive and administer subsidies, offers, legacies, and donations of any kind or value; it may acquire and possess property; and it may perform all other legal acts necessary for the execution of its ends. . . .

Art. 5. The administration of the *Opera nazionale* is entrusted to a President, an Administrative Council, and an Executive Committee. [Except for two members of the Executive Committee, who were to be elected by the Administrative Council, all other members of the *Opera's* administration were to be appointed by the Prime Minister, Head of the Government.]. . . .

Art. 12. The *Opera nazionale del dopolavoro* is placed under the supervision of the Ministry of National Economy. . . .

In the same year a comprehensive law was passed providing for the protection and assistance of maternity and infancy. Excerpts from this law are reproduced below.

Law for the Protection and Assistance of Maternity and Infancy, December 10, 1925

> *Raccolta ufficiale*, 1926, I, 22–27. Our translation.

Article 1. There is instituted with headquarters in Rome a corporate entity to be called the *"Opera Nazionale per la protezione della maternità e dell'infanzia"* [National Institute for the Protection of Maternity and Infancy]. . . .

The National Institute is subjected to the supervision of the Ministry of the Interior, which approves its budgets and accounts. . . .

Art. 4. Either directly or by means of its provincial and communal organs, the National Institute . . . provides for the protection and assistance of needy or abandoned pregnant or nursing mothers, of physically or psychically abnormal children, of minors materially or morally abandoned, astray, or delinquent, up to the age of nineteen. With measures directed to these ends, the National Institute integrates the activity of already existing agencies for the protection of maternity and infancy, and assists their initiatives. . . .

Art. 5. The National Institute is invested with the power of supervision and control over all public and private institutions for the assistance and protection of maternity and infancy. . . .

Art. 23. The administration to, or use by, children and adolescents of alcoholic beverages, including wine, is forbidden in schools, boarding schools, and all institutes for education and asylum. . . .

Art. 24. It is forbidden to sell or administer tobacco in any form to children or adolescents. . . .

Children and adolescents below the age of fifteen may not smoke in a public place.

Although the laws on *Dopolavoro* and the protection of mothers and children could conceivably have been turned to political ends, the recreational and welfare services they provided were in themselves nonpolitical. The same cannot be said of the purpose and operation of the youth organizations (*Balilla* and *Avanguardisti*) created in 1926. Even the circumspect language of the law providing for these organizations makes abundantly clear the regime's purpose of "moral and spiritual" indoctrination. It also makes explicit the material advantages accruing to those who chose to become a part of "Fascist youth."

Law Establishing the Opera nazionale "Balilla" *for the Assistance and the Physical and Moral Education of Youth,*
April 3, 1926

Raccolta ufficiale, 1927, I, 173–74. Our translation.

Article 1. There is instituted with headquarters in Rome a corporate entity to be called the *"Opera nazionale Balilla* for the Assistance and the Physical and Moral Education of Youth."

This Institute is subjected to the high supervision of the Prime Minister, Head of the Government.

Art. 2. The right to enjoy the assistance provided for by the present law is extended to all minors of both sexes below the age of eighteen, without prejudice to the rights of those who, having obtained the benefits specified in Article 7, may enjoy these benefits until the completion of their studies.

Art. 3. The aforementioned National Institute realizes its ends by means of the institutions of the *Balilla* and the *Avanguardisti.*

The institution of the *Avanguardisti* shall have a special concern with the training and preparation of youth for military life.

Art. 4. Membership in the *Balilla* is extended to children from the ages of eight to fourteen, and in the *Avanguardisti* to young people from the ages of fifteen to eighteen.

Art. 5. . . . A body of regulations to be approved within two months of the publication of the present law . . . shall provide these institutions with an appropriate technical-disciplinary structure and with suitable central and local organs.

This body of regulations shall also provide for the organization of chaplains to be attached to the two institutions. . . .

Art. 7. In discharging the function of integrating the activity performed through the institutions of the *Balilla* and the *Avanguardisti,* the National Institute shall have the power to: a) establish or promote the establishment of agencies for the assistance of youth; b) subsidize those agencies lacking adequate resources, provided they follow the directives of the National Institute; c) encourage the competent authorities in institutions having the task of conferring appointments and scholarships to enact reforms establishing the procedure of competition in assigning such appointments and scholarships, with preference to children and young people belonging respectively to the *Balilla* and the *Avanguardisti.*

Art. 8. No change is made in existing legislation relative to governmental tutelage and supervision over public and private institutions of all kinds . . . having as their end the promotion of the instruction, moral and physical education, preparation for a profession, art, or craft, or the moral and spiritual education of youth in any other fashion. But the National Institute may nevertheless prompt the competent authorities to take those measures necessary for the above-mentioned institutions to adapt their activities to the ends of the present law. . . .

Art. 10. The National Institute is administered by a Central Council consisting of a president, a vice-president, and twenty-three councillors appointed by a Royal Decree upon the recommendation of the Prime Minister, Head of the Government.

The political purposes of the *Balilla* were clear but circumspect. In 1937 a decree-law uniting all Fascist-sponsored youth organizations into one unit, *Gioventù italiana del Littorio* [Italian Fascist Youth], cast aside all circumspection and explicitly asserted the G I L's "unitary and totalitarian" Fascist character.

Decree Law Instituting the Gioventù italiana del Littorio, *October 27, 1937*

Raccolta ufficiale, 1937, IV, 3127–29. Our translation.

Article 1. The *Gioventù italiana del Littorio* [G I L], a unitary and totalitarian organization of all the youth forces of the Fascist regime, is instituted within the fold of the National Fascist Party. . . .

The motto of the *Gioventù italiana del Littorio* is: "Believe—obey—fight" (*Credere—obbedire—combattere*).

Art. 2. . . . The *Opera nazionale Balilla,* instituted by the law of April 3, 1926 . . . is absorbed by the *Gioventù italiana del Littorio.* . . .

Art. 4. Membership in the *Gioventù italiana del Littorio* is extended to all young people of both sexes from the ages six to twenty-one who belong to the organizations of *Giovani fascisti* [Young Fascists], *Avanguardisti , Balilla, Figli della lupa* [Sons of the She-Wolf] and [to the corresponding organizations for girls]. . . .

Young people enrolled in the organizations of the *Gioventù italiana del Littorio* are bound by the following oath: "In the name of God and Italy, I swear to follow the orders of the DUCE and to serve the cause of the Fascist revolution with all my might and, if necessary, with my blood."

Art. 5. The tasks that the *Gioventù italiana del Littorio* performs on behalf of youth are: (a) spiritual, athletic, and premilitary preparation.

80. RELATIONS BETWEEN CHURCH AND STATE

The brief samples of Fascist social legislation shown above suggest the possibility of serious controversy between the Fascist regime and the Catholic

Church. After-work activities, the care of mothers and infants, and the moral and spiritual education of youth were all areas of particular interest to the Church. The regime's insistence that all these activities, whether conducted by public or private agencies, be coordinated and supervised by governmental authorities made for an immediate and pressing concern on the part of the Church even before the 1937 law creating the *Gioventù italiana del Littorio*. This concern was heightened by the anticlerical and even antireligious past of a number of Fascist leaders, including Mussolini himself. Mussolini had long since ceased to make agnostic and anticlerical utterances. His first speech in Parliament as Prime Minister, November 16, 1922, had ended with an invocation for divine assistance in bringing his "arduous labors to a victorious conclusion"; and Article 5 of the April 3, 1926, law creating the Fascist youth organizations specifically provided for a body of chaplains to be attached to these organizations. But in the intervening years there had been a number of bitter moments, particularly with regard to the anti-Fascist attitude of the Church-supported Popular party. The first concrete sign of the Church's desire to disengage itself from the anti-Fascist position of the Popular party's leadership came in July 1923 with the thinly veiled forced resignation of the priest Don Luigi Sturzo as political secretary of the party. Although a number of dissidents in the party openly favored supporting the Fascist regime, the new wholly lay leadership of the Popularists joined the Aventine opposition to Fascism, with the result that the more violent Fascists threatened war against Catholic organizations, particularly Catholic Action,[1] and physical violence against members of the clergy hostile to Fascism. On the other hand, the government itself made authoritative overtures to the Church suggesting negotiations toward an eventual solution of the "Roman question." The regime's policy of "the carrot and the stick" was well displayed in 1925 when, well on its way to dictatorial power, the Fascist leadership alternately collaborated with the Church in the festivities of the Holy Year and outlawed the Freemasons and, on the other hand, allowed its "squads" to practice violence on Catholic organizations.

Entrenched solidly in power by 1926, the Fascist regime began serious negotiations with the Papacy for a solution of the Roman question. The basis for this solution was a compromise in which in return for the Church's recognition of the Kingdom of Italy, the Italian government would recognize the Papacy's rights of temporal sovereignty over a territory eventually to be known as the Vatican City and would also agree to a Concordat on religious

[1] Catholic Action consisted of a grouping of Catholic lay organizations of men and women for the purpose of collaborating with the Church's hierarchy in the promotion of Christian principles. The growth of these organizations was promoted by Popes Pius X (1903–14) and Benedict XV (1914–22). The direction of Italian Catholic Action was entrusted to a *Giunta direttiva* [Executive Body] in 1915, and four years later the secretary of this *Giunta*, Don Luigi Sturzo, took the initiative in forming the *Partito popolare*. This tie between the leaders of Catholic Action and the founders of the *Partito popolare* made Catholic Action particularly suspect in the eyes of the Fascist regime.

questions. Negotiations proceeded fitfully, frequently interrupted by renewed Fascist violence against Catholic organizations after the Anteo Zamboni attempt on Mussolini's life, in October 1926, and by increased Fascist
hostility toward Catholic Scouts organizations (*Esploratori cattolici*) after
the creation of the Fascist youth organizations in the same year. Early in
1927 the regime offered the Church a compromise on the question of youth
organizations by prohibiting all such organizations except those enrolled in
the *Balilla* and the Catholic Scouts groups. But continued protests on the
part of Pope Pius XI (1922–39) against the regime's attempt to monopolize the physical and moral education of youth prompted the regime to
counter with a law in April 1928 outlawing all those semimilitary groups for
the training and education of youth that were not under the direction of the
Opera nazionale "Balilla." In spite of new protests from the Papacy, negotiations between Church and state continued and were concluded on February
11, 1929, with the signature of a treaty, a financial agreement, and a concordat between Italy and the Holy See. Portions of these agreements, known
collectively as the Lateran Accords, follow.

Treaty between the Holy See and Italy, February 11, 1929 (Effective June 7, 1929)

> *Treaty and Concordat between the Holy See and Italy: Official Docu-
> ments.* Washington, D.C.: National Catholic Welfare Conference, 1929,
> pp. 37–51, *passim.* English translation of the official Italian text repro-
> duced by courtesy of the National Catholic Welfare Conference.

His Holiness, the Sovereign Pontiff, Pius XI, and His Majesty, Victor
Emmanuel III, King of Italy, have resolved to make a treaty. . . .

Art. 1. Italy recognizes and reaffirms the principle set forth in Art. 1
of the Constitution of the Kingdom of Italy of March 4, 1848,
whereby the Roman Catholic and Apostolic Religion is the sole religion of the State.

Art. 2. Italy recognizes the sovereignty of the Holy See in the field
of international relations as an attribute that pertains to the very nature of the Holy See, in conformity with its traditions and with the
demands of its mission in the world.

Art. 3. Italy recognizes full possession and exclusive and absolute
power and sovereign jurisdiction of the Holy See over the Vatican, as
at present constituted, with all its appurtenances and endowments.
Thus the Vatican City is established for the special purposes and with
the provisions laid down in the present Treaty. The confines of the

Vatican City are indicated on a plan which constitutes the first appendix to the present Treaty of which it forms an integral part. . . .

Art. 4. The sovereignty and exclusive jurisdiction which Italy recognizes on the part of the Holy See with regard to the State of the Vatican implies that there can be no interference on the part of the Italian Government therein, nor any other authority than that of the Holy See. . . .

Art. 8. Italy, considering the person of the Sovereign Pontiff as sacred and inviolable, declares that any and every attempt against him, as well as any incitement to commit such, to be punishable by the same penalties as attempts against the person of the King or incitement to commit the same.

Public offenses or insults committed in Italian territory against the person of the Sovereign Pontiff, whether by deed or by spoken or written word, are punishable by the same penalties as similar offenses and injuries against the person of the King.

Art. 9. In conformity with the provisions of international law, all persons having a fixed residence within the State of the Vatican are subject to the sovereignty of the Holy See. . . .

Art. 10. . . . Ecclesiastics who, in the performance of the duties of their office, are occupied in the execution of the acts of the Holy See shall not be subjected on account of such execution to any hindrance, investigation or molestation on the part of the Italian authorities.

Every foreigner invested with ecclesiastical office in Rome shall enjoy the same personal guarantees as belong to Italian citizens by virtue of the laws of the Kingdom of Italy.

Art. 11. The central corporate entities of the Catholic Church are exempt from all interference on the part of the Italian State (except for the provisions of Italian law concerning the acquisition of moral entities) and also from expropriation with regard to real estate.

Art. 12. Italy recognizes the right of the Holy See to send and receive diplomatic representatives according to the general provisions of international law. . . .

Art. 17. Contributions of whatever kind due to the Holy See from the other central organizations of the Catholic Church and from the organizations directly managed by the Holy See, even outside Rome, as also those due to dignitaries, functionaries, and employees, even when not fixed, beginning with the first of January 1929, shall be exempt in Italian territory from any tax whatsoever on the part of the State or of any other entity. . . .

Art. 23. For the execution within the Kingdom of Italy of sentences pronounced by the tribunals of the State of the Vatican the principles of international law will be applied.

On the other hand, sentences and decisions pronounced by ecclesiastical authorities, which have to do with ecclesiastical or religious persons in spiritual or disciplinary matters and are officially communicated to the civil authorities, will have full juridical efficacy immediately in Italy even so far as the civil effects are concerned.

Art. 24. With regard to the sovereignty pertaining to it in the field of international relations, the Holy See declares that it wishes to remain and will remain extraneous to all temporal disputes between nations, and to international congresses convoked for the settlement of such disputes, unless the contending parties make a joint appeal to its mission of peace; nevertheless, it reserves the right in every case to exercise its moral and spiritual power.

In consequence of this declaration, the State of the Vatican will always and in every case be considered neutral and inviolable territory. . . .

Art. 26. The Holy See maintains that with the agreements signed today adequate assurance is guaranteed as far as is necessary for the said Holy See to provide, with due liberty and independence, for the pastoral regime of the Diocese of Rome and of the Catholic Church in Italy and in the world. The Holy See declares the "Roman question" definitively and irrevocably settled and, therefore, eliminated; and recognizes the Kingdom of Italy under the dynasty of the house of Savoy with Rome as the Capital of the Italian State.

Italy, in turn, recognizes the State of the Vatican under the sovereignty of the Supreme Pontiff.

The Law of May 13, 1871, No. 214, is abrogated, as well as any other decree or decision contrary to the present Treaty. . . .

The treaty between the Holy See and Italy was accompanied by a financial settlement and a concordat. The Holy See accepted the sum of 750 million Italian lire in cash and Italian 5 per cent State bonds to the nominal value of 1 billion lire as "a final settlement of its financial relations with Italy resulting from the events of 1870." Some of the provisions of the concordat are given below.

Concordat between the Holy See and Italy, February 11, 1929

> *Treaty and Concordat between the Holy See and Italy*, pp. 60–64, 67–69, 72, 76–82, *passim*. Reproduced by courtesy of the National Catholic Welfare Conference.

Article 1. Italy, according to the terms of Art. 1 of the Treaty, guarantees to the Catholic Church free exercise of spiritual power, free and public exercise of worship, as well as jurisdiction in ecclesiastical matters, in conformity with the provisions of the present Concordat; and, where it shall be necessary for the carrying out of their spiritual ministry, grants to ecclesiastics protection on the part of its authorities.

In consideration of the sacred character of the Eternal City, episcopal see of the Sovereign Pontiff, center of the Catholic world, and goal of pilgrimages, the Italian Government will take precautions to prevent the occurrence in Rome of everything that might be contrary to this sacred character.

Art. 2. The Holy See may communicate and correspond freely with the Bishops, the clergy and the whole Catholic world, without any interference on the part of the Italian Government.

Bishops, likewise, in everything that concerns their pastoral office, may communicate and correspond freely with their clergy and with all the Faithful. . . .

Art. 5. No ecclesiastic may be employed or remain in the employment or service of the Italian State or of any public departments subordinate to the same without the express permission of his diocesan Bishop.

The revocation of this permission deprives the ecclesiastic of power to continue exercising the duty or office assumed.

In any case apostate priests or those who have incurred censure cannot be employed or retained in a teaching post, or in an office or an employment in which they are brought into immediate contact with the public. . . .

Art. 7. Ecclesiastics may not be requested by magistrates or other authorities to give information regarding persons or matters which may have come to their knowledge through the exercise of their sacred ministry. . . .

Art. 9. As a general rule, buildings open for worship are exempt from confiscation or occupation. . . .

Except in cases of urgent necessity, the police cannot in the exercise of their duties enter buildings used for worship without having given previous notice to the proper ecclesiastical authority. . . .

Art. 11. The State recognizes the holy days established by the Church. . . .

Art. 19. The selection of Archbishops and Bishops pertains to the Holy See. Before proceeding to the nomination * of an Archbishop, a Bishop, or a Coadjutor with the right of succession, the Holy See will communicate the name of the person chosen to the Italian Government in order to be sure that the latter has no objection from a political standpoint against the nomination. . . .

Art. 20. Bishops before taking possession of their diocese shall take an oath of loyalty at the hands of the Head of the State according to the following formula:

"Before God on the Holy Gospels, I swear and promise, as becomes a Bishop, loyalty to the Italian State. . . ."

Art. 21. The awarding of ecclesiastical benefices pertains to ecclesiastical authority. . . .

Art. 22. Ecclesiastics who are not Italian citizens cannot be appointed to Italian benefices. Moreover the Bishops of the dioceses and rectors of parishes must speak Italian. . . .

Art. 28. In order that their consciences may be at ease, the Holy See will grant full condonation to all those who hold ecclesiastical property as a result of the Italian laws by which the patrimony of the Church was dispersed. . . .

Art. 30. . . . The Italian State, until some other arrangement is made by mutual agreement, will continue to meet the deficits in the revenues of ecclesiastical benefices by granting allowances corresponding at least to the actual value of the subsidy established by the laws now in force. . . .

Art. 34. The Italian State, desirous of restoring to the institution of marriage which is the foundation of the family, the dignity that be-

* "Nomina" should be translated as "appointment." Ed. note.

longs to it according to the Catholic traditions of its people, recognizes the civil effects of the sacrament of matrimony as administered according to the regulations of the Canon Law. . . .

Questions having to do with the nullification of marriage and with the dispensation of a marriage "ratum et non consummatum" are reserved to the jurisdiction of ecclesiastical tribunals and courts. . . .

As regards cases of personal separation, the Holy See is willing that the same shall be judged by the civil judicial authorities. . . .

Art. 36. Italy considers the teaching of Christian doctrine, according to the form handed down by Catholic tradition, as the foundation and capstone of public education. Therefore, Italy agrees that the religious instruction now given in the public elementary schools shall be further developed in the secondary schools according to a program to be agreed upon by the Holy See and the State.

This instruction is to be given by teachers and professors who are priests or religious approved by ecclesiastical authority and who will be aided by lay teachers and professors holding for this purpose proper certificates of fitness and capacity, these certificates to be issued by the diocesan Bishop.

Revocation of the certificate by the Bishop immediately deprives the individual of the right to teach.

No texts will be adopted for this religious instruction in the public schools except such as are approved by ecclesiastical authority. . . .

Art. 43. The Italian State recognizes the auxiliary organizations of the *"Azione Cattolica Italiana"* inasmuch as these, according to the regulations of the Holy See, carry on their activities independently of all political parties and under the immediate direction of the Hierarchy of the Church for the teaching and practice of Catholic principles.

The Holy See takes occasion on the signing of the present Concordat to renew its prohibition to all ecclesiastics and religious to enroll or take part in any political party.

Art. 44. If, in the future, any difficulty should arise with regard to the interpretation of the present Concordat, the Holy See and Italy will proceed with mutual understanding to an amicable solution.

Serious difficulties arose within two years of the ratification of the concordat and precisely with regard to the *Azione Cattolica* [Catholic Action] mentioned in Article 43 of the Concordat. The nature of the dispute is simple when presented in abstract terms. The anticlerical wing which had always existed in the Fascist movement, particularly among its recruits from the extreme Left, was not altogether satisfied with the concessions made the Church in the concordat. In the opinion of this wing, the existence of Catholic social and youth organizations independent of or, at least, not under the direct control of the regime, compromised the regime's total control of Italian life. Furthermore, Catholic Action in particular had always remained suspect in the eyes of many Fascists because of its close association with the defunct Popular party. With a view to discrediting and eventually absorbing or destroying the organizations affiliated under Catholic Action, influential elements of the Fascist press began a campaign early in 1931 aimed at proving that these organizations had political and economic aims contrary to the regime and the country's welfare. Late in May the campaign culminated in physical violence directed particularly against the youth groups in Catholic Action, and in a formal dissolution of all youth organizations not under Fascist control. A reply to the violence and dissolution came from the Pope himself in an encyclical letter to all bishops of the Catholic world dated June 29, 1931, and commonly known by the Italian phrase "Non abbiamo bisogno" [We have no need]. Excerpts from the encyclical are reprinted below.

Encyclical Letter from Pope Pius XI Concerning Catholic Action ("Non abbiamo bisogno"), *June 29, 1931*

> "Encyclical of Pope Pius XI on Catholic Action," in *Sixteen Encyclicals of His Holiness Pope Pius XI, 1926–1937*. Washington, D.C.: National Catholic Welfare Conference, 1938, pp. 1, 7–8, 15, 21–22, 24–25, 27, 30–31. Reproduced by courtesy of the National Catholic Welfare Conference.

We must needs speak to you, Venerable Brethren, about events which have recently occurred in this, Our Episcopal City of Rome, and throughout Italy, that is to say, in the very territory of which We are Primate—events which have had such a vast and such a strong repercussion everywhere, conspicuously so in all of the dioceses of Italy and throughout the Catholic World.

These occurrences are summarized in a very few and very sad words. There has been an attempt made to strike unto death that which was and that which always will be dearest to Our heart as Father and as Shepherd of Souls; and We can, We even must, subjoin "and the way in which it was done offends Us still more." . . . .

Already on several occasions, Venerable Brethren, in the most

solemn and explicit manner and assuming entire responsibility for
what We were saying, We have protested against the campaign of
false and unjust accusations which preceded the disbanding of the associations of the young people and of the university students affiliated
with Catholic Action. It was a disbanding which was carried out in a
way and with the use of tactics which would give the impression that
action was being taken against a vast and dangerous organization of
criminals. And the proceedings were directed against young men and
young women who are certainly some of the best among the good and
concerning whom We are happy and paternally proud to pay them
tribute still once more. It is noteworthy that even among the officers
of the law charged to carry out these orders of suppression, there
were many who were ill at ease and showed by their expressions and
courtesies that they were almost asking pardon for doing that which
they had been commanded. We have appreciated the delicate feelings
of these officers, and We have reserved for them a special blessing.

However, in sad contrast to the manner of acting of these officials,
there were how many acts of mistreatment and of violence, extending
even to the striking of blows and the drawing of blood! How many
insults in the press, how many injurious words and acts against things
and persons, not excluding Ourself, preceded, accompanied and followed the carrying into effect of this lightning-like police order which
very frequently, either through ignorance or malicious zeal, was extended to include associations and organizations not contemplated in
the orders of the superiors, such as the oratories of the little ones and
the sodalities of the Children of Mary. And all of this sad accompani-
ment of irreverences and of violences took place in the presence of
and with the participation of members of a political party some of
whom were in uniform, and was carried into effect with such a unison
of action throughout all Italy and with such a passive acquiescence on
the part of the civil authorities and the police as to make one necessarily think of some uniform directions received from some high authority. It is very easy to admit, and it was also equally easy to have foreseen, that the limits of these directions could and would have almost
necessarily been exceeded. . . . We cannot—We, Church, religious,
faithful Catholics (and not alone We)—We cannot be grateful to one
who, after putting out of existence socialism and anti-religious organizations (Our enemies and not alone Ours), has permitted them to be

so generally readmitted, as all see and deplore, and has made them even more strong and dangerous inasmuch as they are now hidden and also protected by their new uniform. . . .

And here We find Ourselves in the presence of a contract between authentic affirmations on the one hand and not less authentic facts on the other hand, which reveal, without the slightest possibility of doubt, the proposal, already in great part actually put into effect, to monopolize completely the young, from the tenderest years up to manhood and womanhood, and all for the exclusive advantage of a party, of a regime based on ideology which clearly resolves itself into a true and real pagan worship of the state, which is no less in contrast with the natural rights of the family than it is in contradiction to the supernatural rights of the Church. To propose and promote such a monopoly, to persecute for this reason Catholic Action, as has been done for some time more or less openly or under cover, to reach this end by striking Catholic Action in the way that has recently occurred, is truly and actually to prevent children from going to Jesus Christ, since it impedes them from going to His Church and even arrives at the point of snatching them with violence from the bosom of both, because where the Church is, there is Jesus Christ. . . .

A conception of the state which makes the young generations belong entirely to it without any exception from the tenderest years up to adult life cannot be reconciled by a Catholic with the Catholic doctrine nor can it be reconciled with the natural right of the family. It is not possible for a Catholic to reconcile with Catholic doctrine the pretense that the Church and the Pope must limit themselves to the external practices of religion, such as Mass and the Sacraments, and then to say that the rest of education belongs to the state. . . .

With everything that We have said up to the present, We have not said that We wished to condemn the party as such. We have intended to point out and to condemn that much in the program and in the action of the party which We have seen and have understood to be contrary to Catholic doctrine and the Catholic practice and therefore irreconcilable with the name and with the profession of Catholics. And in doing this, We have fulfilled a precious duty of Our Episcopal ministry toward Our dear sons who are members of the party, so that they can rest tranquil with the proper consciences of Catholics.

We believe, then, that We have thus at the same time accomplished a good work for the party itself, because what interest and success can the party have in a Catholic country like Italy in maintaining in its program ideas and maxims and practices which cannot be reconciled with a Catholic conscience? . . .

You Bishops of Italy know that no mortal man—not even the head of a state or of a government—but the Holy Ghost—has placed you there in places which Peter assigned to you to rule the Church of God. These and so many other holy and sublime things that concern you, Venerable Brethren, are evidently ignored or forgotten by him who thinks of you and calls you, Bishops of Italy, "Officials of the State," from which the very formula of the oath, which it is necessary for you to make to the sovereign, clearly distinguishes and separates you, for the oath especially states, "as is convenient for a Catholic bishop." . . . .

Everything is definitely promised in answer to prayer. . . .

And since from so many prayers We must hope for everything, and since everything is possible to that God Who has promised everything in answer to prayer, We have confident hope that He will illumine minds to Truth and turn wills to Good, so that the Church of God, which wishes nothing from the state that belongs to the competence of the state, will cease to be asked for that which is the Church's competence—the education and the Christian formation of youth—and this not through human favor, but by Divine mandate, and that which therefore she always asks and will always ask with an insistence and an intransigeance which cannot cease or waver because it does not come from human desire or design, or from human ideas, changeable in different times and places and circumstances, but from the Divine and inviolable disposition.

After two additional months of controversy a compromise solution was reached early in September whereby the governing structure of Catholic Action was decentralized and placed in the hands of local bishops. Political activity was prohibited, as was any organization or agitation along trade-union lines. The existence of Catholic Action was thus preserved, but its apostolate was restricted to purely religious and recreational activity. After this agreement, the substance of which must be viewed as a victory for the regime, relations between the Church and the Fascist state became more tolerable until the beginning of a deterioration late in the 1930s owing to Mussolini's pro-German foreign policy.

XXIII. FASCIST FOREIGN POLICY:
THE ROAD TO WAR

It is clear in retrospect that the least successful Fascist policy was in the field of foreign affairs. Yet for most of the thirteen years preceding the Ethiopian War this policy was not radically different from the one followed by pre-Fascist governments: balance of power in Europe, security in the Mediterranean based on the "cardinal point" of friendship with England, interest in the Adriatic and Danubian areas, and alternating cold and warm relations with France. The outlines of this policy were stated by Mussolini in his first speech to Parliament as Prime Minister on November 16, 1922. But this speech also raised an issue that was genuinely new: the revision of the treaties concluding the First World War. Although a victor in the war, Italy was among the "dissatisfied" powers, and as such it could and did play an important role in efforts to revise the treaties. This role was made to fit Italy's traditional interest in the Balkans by assuming the position of leader and defender of the revisionism of defeated countries such as Hungary, Bulgaria, and Austria. Revisionism also served Italy's concern with balance of power. A beaten and disarmed Germany and a Russia troubled with domestic problems meant that France, linked by alliances with Poland and the states of the Little Entente (Czechoslovakia, Rumania, and Yugoslavia) was by all appearances the dominant continental power. This real or imagined French dominance restricted Italy's freedom of maneuver in the game of balance of power; and inasmuch as France and its allies were all "satisfied" powers with an interest in preserving the *status quo* established by the postwar treaties, it suited Italy's interests very well to champion the cause of revisionism. But this cause did not necessarily mean a policy of aggression. In fact, except for the Corfu incident in August 1923, Fascist foreign policy did not involve recourse to war until the Ethiopian crisis of 1935.

During the first years of his regime Mussolini seemed bent on settling peacefully a number of irritating problems of foreign relations. In January 1924 he resolved Italy's dispute with Yugoslavia over Fiume by reaching an agreement whereby Italy would annex the Free State of Fiume created by the Rapallo Treaty of 1920 and accept in turn all the other provisions of this treaty favorable to Yugoslavia. In 1925 Italy was a signatory to the Locarno Pacts guaranteeing the frontiers between France and Belgium on the one hand and Germany on the other. The same year Italy reached a number of agreements with England regarding each other's interests in East Africa and the Sudan, respectively. But soon Mussolini became more aggressive. Relations with France in 1926 entered one of the many difficult phases characteristic of the history of the two "Latin sisters." The Fascist press inveighed against French asylum to anti-Fascist Italians plotting against the regime and once again raised the problem of the treatment of Italians in Tunisia. The same year Italy signed a pact with Albania making of that country virtually an Italian protectorate, and the next year a treaty was concluded with Hungary, the most revisionist of the Danubian states. Yugoslavia and its protector, France, replied with a treaty of friendship. Relations between Italy and France were not improved by France's refusal to accede to Mussolini's demand for naval parity with France at the London naval conference in 1930. But with the advent of the Nazis to power in Germany in 1933, Franco-Italian relations continued the improvement begun in 1932, and were further strengthened after the assassination of the Austrian Chancellor Engelbert Dolfuss by Austrian Nazis on July 25, 1934. Mussolini had assumed the role of protector of the Dolfuss Neo-Fascist regime, and, fearing a German-inspired Nazi *coup* in Austria after the latter's assassination, he ordered four Italian divisions to the Brenner as a warning to Germany.

Throughout 1934 relations with France continued to improve, and in January 1935 Mussolini and the French Foreign Minister Pierre Laval reached a number of accords. France ceded to Italy some African territories adjoining Libya and Eritrea, seemed to give Italy a free hand in Ethiopia, agreed on consultations regarding the preservation of Austrian independence, and confirmed their agreement against unilateral alteration of disarmament commitments. The last two provisions were clearly directed against Germany, which in fact proceeded to announce in March 1935 its intention of rearming in disregard of the provisions of the Treaty of Versailles. In April Italy, France, and England replied to this German step by meeting at Stresa and there establishing a "front" against Nazi Germany. But as is made clear in a speech below, Mussolini predicated his collaboration with England and France against Germany on the premise that the two Western powers would not obstruct his ambitions in Ethiopia.

By 1934 Mussolini had apparently decided on a course toward empire building. Many reasons have been advanced for this decision: the need to prove the virility and martial virtues of the Fascist regime; the desire to avenge the defeat at Aduwa in 1896; the notion that a truly great power had to have "a place in the sun" and "a window to the world"; the "call of Rome," that is, the urge to imitate the imperial achievements of the ancient Romans; and the presumed economic advantages of a large and potentially rich colony. Ethiopia seemed the most logical place in which to satisfy these ambitions. A pretext for action against Ethiopia had offered itself in December 1934 when Ethiopian forces attacked an Italian outpost at Wal-Wal, a place on the border between Italian Somaliland and Ethiopia which the latter claimed to be its territory forcefully occupied by the Italians. The Franco-Italian agreements of January 1935 seemed to give Italy a free hand in the matter, and England's attitude in the past toward Italian expansion in Ethiopia seemed encouraging.

Mussolini's speech of May 25, 1935, touched on most of these considerations, and it left no doubt that if the Stresa front against Germany were to operate England and France would have to show their benevolence toward Italy by concrete acts and not just words. The speech also suggested that Italy's hostility toward Germany was not an immutable feature of Italian foreign policy. This hostility derived from Italy's concern for Austrian independence and its preference for a weak Austria on the Brenner frontier rather than an Austria incorporated into Germany. But this policy could change, and in fact did change, as a result of England's and France's negative attitudes toward Italy's determination to absorb all or nearly all of Ethiopia. It is in this sense that the Ethiopian War marks a radical change in Fascist foreign policy culminating in a formal alliance with Nazi Germany in May 1939 and participation in the Second World War in June 1940.

81. ETHIOPIA TO THE FOREFRONT: MUSSOLINI'S SPEECH TO THE CHAMBER OF DEPUTIES, MAY 25, 1935

> Senato del Regno, Camera dei deputati, *Bollettino parlamentare*, Anno IX, No. 2, July 1935, Legislatura XXIX. Rome: Segreteria generale del Senato del Regno, Segreteria generale della Camera dei deputati, 1935, pp. 14–18. Our translation.

Mussolini (*Head of the Government, Minister of Foreign Affairs*): Political "realism," that is, the precise consideration of international forces, of their relations of interests and their inevitable mutations, must be the foundation of our actions. Besides, this is true of other states worthy of the name as it is of us. With this premise established, I shall limit myself to speaking to you of the most recent events. . . .

After the Franco-Italian agreements of January, the governments of France and England met in London in February and fixed several fundamental points regarding the political rearrangement of Europe. The Anglo-French London Conference may be considered as a projection of the Franco-Italian Conference in Rome. Optimists were foreseeing a normal development of the European situation when, on March 16, this development was suddenly shattered by Germany's unilateral denunciation of part V of the Treaty of Versailles regarding disarmament.

The world was presented with an accomplished fact which was noted by three diplomatic protests. All this happened during the course of explorations [regarding disarmament problems], and everyone was immediately convinced that the accomplished fact could not be undone.

It is of some interest—even if only retrospective—to make known at this point that in January 1934 Germany was inclined to accept an arrangement infinitely more limited than its rightful parity, an arrangement that consisted in an army of 300,000 men which, at least for a period of years, would have only a defensive armament to be supervised along the lines of the Italian memorandum.

But that which did not happen is not subject matter for history, and recrimination is useless, just as it is useless to continue talking about disarmament. (*Lively applause.*) It is very difficult for us to believe in the possibility of a limitation of armaments or in the prohibition of certain methods of war. Nevertheless, if something concrete is done, we shall not be the ones to create difficulties.

Waters were very troubled, as were the spirits of peoples, when the Stresa Conference was convened in April. Without exaggerating its intrinsic import, it must be said that this Conference was quite conclusive in that, facing several urgent problems, it determined a unified position on the part of the three Western powers. It is a fact that with such an effective, constant, and omnipresent solidarity it is possible to conduct a policy in the grand style aiming at the elimination of the principal obstacles to the peaceful coexistence of the European peoples. This is an exigency ever more necessary for the existence and future of our continent. (*Lively applause.*). . . .

With regard to Italo-German relations, it is true that one problem only compromises them—the Austrian problem—but it is one of fundamental importance. But, having come to this argument, it is timely to say a few words to those who would rivet our attention to the Brenner in order to prevent us from moving in any other part of the land and waters of the vast globe. (*Enthusiastic acclamations. Shouts of*: Duce! Duce!)

With regard to this matter as well it is necessary to say once and for all and in the most explicit manner that the problem of Austrian independence is an Austrian and European problem and, as a European problem, it is also a particularly Italian problem, but not an "exclusively" Italian one. (*Most lively applause.*) In other words, Fascist Italy does not intend to limit its historic mission to one political problem only (*approval*), to one military sector only (*approval*), such as the defense of one frontier, even a most important one such as the Brenner. All frontiers, the continental and the colonial, are equally sacred and must be guarded and defended against any threat, even if only potential. (*New, most lively, and repeated acclamations.*)

Comrades, I have reached the point I am sure you have been waiting for. The set of problems I have put before you must be considered in relation to what may happen in East Africa and in relation to the attitude the several European states may assume, thus offering us the occasion to show us their concrete and not only superficial and wordy friendship. (*Most lively applause.*) But we must count on ourselves above all. (*Prolonged applause.*)

Now, the threat to our East African frontiers is not potential; it is effective; it is actual; its proportions grow every day, and they are such as to present the Italo-Ethiopian problem in the most raw and radical terms. (*Applause.*) This problem is not of today; it is not of January 1935; * rather, as is clear from documents to be published in time, it dates from 1925. It was in that year that I began to examine the problem. Three years later it seemed that a political treaty † would be a suitable instrument for the advancement of our peaceful expansion in that vast world still encased in its primordial armor and yet susceptible to great progress.

The treaty has remained a completely dead letter, except for Article 5,‡ upon which Ethiopia latched after its aggressions in December 1934.

It is from 1929—I say 1929—that Abyssinia began the reorganization of its army, making use of European instructors. It is from 1930 that certain European factories began supplying modern war material

---

* Time of the presentation by Ethiopia of a request to the Council of the League of Nations for a debate by the Council of Italy's alleged act of aggression at Wal-Wal in December 1934. Ed. note.

† Reference to the twenty-year treaty of friendship and commerce signed by Italy and the heir to the Ethiopian throne, the future Haile Selassie. Ed. note.

‡ Article 5 of the treaty provided for conciliation or arbitration of disputes and excluded recourse to arms. Ed. note.

on an imposing scale. The clash of Wal-Wal was the warning signal of a situation maturing for a long time, and this situation imposes upon Fascist Italy the task of carrying out duties that cannot be disregarded.

Now, for the simple defense of those two modest strips of territory called Eritrea and Somaliland, Italy must face logistic and strategic difficulties of enormous complexity. . . . Only men of bad faith, only covert or open enemies of Fascist Italy can feign astonishment or simulate protests over the military measures we have taken and those we shall take. (*Most lively and repeated applause. Shouts of:* Duce! Duce!)

All this not withstanding we have agreed to the procedure of conciliation and arbitration—limited, naturally, to the Wal-Wal incident—and in spite of certain abnormalities of the Commission, such as for example the representation of the opposing side by non-Abyssinians. (*Laughter.*) But no one, especially in Italy, should entertain excessive illusions in this matter.

No one, therefore, should hope to make of Abyssinia a new pistol pointed permanently toward us and which, in case of European troubles, would make our position in East Africa untenable. (*Approval.*) Let everyone know well that when it comes to the safety of our territories and the life of our soldiers we are ready to assume all, even the supreme responsibilities.

In June England attempted to compromise the dispute by proposing that Ethiopia cede a strip of territory to Italy adjoining Italian Somaliland. The Italian government replied that it already had a large supply of deserts and insisted on a virtual protectorate over Ethiopia. Pressed by a concern with public opinion regarding the effectiveness of the League of Nations in protecting the sovereignty of a member state, England refused to support Italy's demand. The arbitration commission appointed by the League to investigate Ethiopia's charge of Italian aggression at Wal-Wal in turn avoided the issue by submitting a report which appeared to absolve both sides of responsibility. Italy strengthened its apparent determination to have recourse to arms by rapidly increasing its forces in East Africa during the summer. This determination was not weakened by an Anglo-French proposal in September 1935 to arrange a form of League of Nations mandate over Ethiopia with Italy as a principal participant among the supervising powers. Mussolini refused to accept the proposal, and on October 2 announced his decision for a war of conquest.

82. MUSSOLINI'S SPEECH ON THE EVE OF HOSTILITIES AGAINST ETHIOPIA, OCTOBER 2, 1935

Reported in the *Popolo d'Italia,* October 3, 1935; reproduced in Benito Mussolini, *Opera omnia,* Edoardo and Duilio Susmel, eds., XXVII, 158–60. Our translation.

Black Shirts of the revolution! Men and women of all Italy! Italians spread throughout the world, beyond the mountains and beyond the seas! Hear me!

A solemn hour is about to sound in the history of the fatherland. At this moment 20 million men occupy the public squares of all Italy.

Never in the history of mankind has there been seen a more gigantic spectacle. Twenty million men, but one heart, one will, one decision.

Their demonstration must and does show the world that Italy and Fascism constitute a perfect, absolute, and unalterable identity. . . .

For many months the wheels of destiny have been moving toward their goal under the impulse of our calm determination. In the latter hours their rhythm has become more swift and by now cannot be stopped.

It is not only an army that strives toward its objectives but a whole people of 44 million souls against whom an attempt is being made to consummate the blackest of injustices—that of depriving us of some small place in the sun.

When in 1915 Italy exposed itself to the risks of war and joined its destiny with that of the Allies, how much praise there was for our courage and how many promises were made! But after the common victory to which Italy had made the supreme contribution of 670,000 dead, 400,000 mutilated, and a million wounded, around the hateful peace table Italy received but a few crumbs from the rich colonial booty gathered by others.

We have been patient for thirteen years, during which the circle of selfishness that strangles our vitality has become ever tighter. With Ethiopia we have been patient for forty years! It is time to say enough!

In the League of Nations there is talk of sanctions instead of recognition of our rights.

Until there is proof to the contrary, I shall refuse to believe that the real and generous people of France can support sanctions against Italy. . . . Similarly, I refuse to believe that the real people of Great Britain—who have never had discords with Italy—are prepared to run the risk of hurling Europe along the road to catastrophe for the sake of defending an African country universally branded as a country without the slightest shadow of civilization.

We shall face economic sanctions with our discipline, our sobriety, and our spirit of sacrifice.

Against military sanctions we shall reply with military measures.

To acts of war we shall reply with acts of war.

Let no one think that he can make us yield without a hard struggle.

A people jealous for its honor may not use other language nor may it assume a different attitude.

But let it be said once more and in the most categorical manner—and at this moment I make before you a sacred pledge—that we shall do all that is possible to prevent this conflict of a colonial character from assuming the nature and import of a European conflict.

On October 3, 1935, Italy began hostilities against Ethiopia justifying them as a defensive response to Ethiopia's mobilization at the end of September. Four days later a Committee of the League's Council declared that Italy had had recourse to war in violation of the Covenant of the League. By October 11 fifty-two states in the League (all of the League except Albania, Austria, Hungary, and Paraguay) voted for sanctions against Italy on the basis of Article 16 of the Covenant. The nature of these sanctions was specified early in November for implementation by November 18. All imports from Italy were prohibited; no arms, munitions, and other specified war matériel were to be exported to Italy; and no credits were to be extended to Italy. But the vital question of an embargo on oil shipments was left unresolved and, in fact, petroleum was never put on the list of prohibited goods.

In spite of the League's decision to impose economic sanctions on the aggressor nation, the governments of England and France still hoped for a face-saving compromise that would satisfy both Italy and that part of public opinion in their countries that championed the principle of collective security under the auspices of the League of Nations. The result was the Hoare-Laval plan, presented by the Foreign Ministers of England and France, proposing the cession to Italy of a portion of Tigre province in northern Ethiopia and the creation of an Italian sphere of influence and colonization in southern Ethiopia under League auspices and with the retention of nominal sovereignty by the Ethiopian emperor. Mussolini appeared to reject the plan, but before further persuasion could be tried on him, Sir Samuel Hoare felt obliged to resign owing to differences within the British Cabinet and to the popular clamor aroused by publication of the essential points of the plan in the London *Times*. The plan was dropped and Sir Samuel's replacement at the Foreign Office, Sir Anthony Eden, decided on a less compromising policy toward Italy. But contrary to some expectations, Italian military operations in Ethiopia, which were very much a campaign of transportation and supply, proved to be conducted with much skill and success. After a partial lull from November 1935 to February 1936, major operations were resumed and concluded with the capture of the Ethiopian capital, Addis Ababa, early in May. Economic sanctions against Italy had been spottily enforced and did not prove to be a major obstacle to the country's war effort. The United States was not a party to the League-imposed sanctions; and although the American government disapproved of Italy's aggression, the Neutrality Acts imposed on the administration by the American Congress in August 1935 and February 1936, banning shipments of war matériel and loans to belligerents, worked more hardship on needy Ethiopia than on better prepared Italy. Oil continued to come freely into Italy and the Suez Canal remained open to Italian ships. Under these circumstances, the futility of sanctions was officially recognized by the League when it put an end to them in July 1936.

It must be acknowledged that when, on May 9, 1936, Mussolini proclaimed the annexation of Ethiopia and assigned to Victor Emmanuel III an imperial title he put a seal on a war that had been genuinely popular among many and perhaps most Italians. The patriotic fervor aroused by the war undoubtedly strengthened the regime, and this was one of the important immediate effects of the conflict. But far more important were the long-range effects. Of these, the bond established between Italy and Germany was the most significant, because it meant the definitive end of the Stresa front. As something of an outcaste state, and no longer a member of the League, which it had abandoned in October 1933, Germany did not abide by the League's decision to impose economic sanctions against Italy. Moreover, taking advantage of Europe's concern with the Ethiopian conflict, Germany announced the remilitarization of the Rhineland in March 1936, thus violating not only the Treaty of Versailles but also the Locarno Pacts. Italy joined the other Locarno signatories in censuring this German violation, but, still incensed with England and France for their support of the policy of sanctions, Mussolini refused to consider stronger measures against Germany. During the summer of 1936 his annoyance with the Western powers grew at their delay in recognizing the Italian empire in Ethiopia. As Mussolini moved away from his former partners in the Stresa front he moved closer to Germany, promoting a reconciliation between Austria and Germany in July 1936 and coming to an agreement with Germany during the same summer regarding a common front in support of the cause of General Franco in Spain. The growing community of views between Fascist Italy and Nazi Germany was formalized in an agreement reached in October between the Italian Foreign Minister, Count Galeazzo Ciano, and his German counterpart, Konstantin von Neurath. The agreement specified a community of views on the Bolshevik peril, decided on military support of Franco in the Spanish Civil War, confirmed Germany's intention of recognizing the Italian empire in Ethiopia, and reaffirmed the desirability of better relations between Germany and Austria.

In November Mussolini made public the spirit behind these agreements with Germany when in a speech at Milan he announced that the understanding reached with Germany was "an axis around which all European states moved by the desire for collaboration and peace could collaborate." But in spite of signs of a willingness by France and England in mid-1937 to enter into close collaboration with Italy, Mussolini chose instead to visit Germany in September and there make a speech (excerpted below) confirming the solidity of the ties between the two "Axis" powers.

83. MUSSOLINI RECONFIRMS THE ROME-BERLIN AXIS: SPEECH IN BERLIN, SEPTEMBER 28, 1937

> Reported in the *Popolo d'Italia*, September 29, 1937; reproduced in Benito Mussolini, *Opera omnia*, Edoardo and Duilio Susmel, eds. Florence: La Fenice, 1959, XXVIII, 248–53, *passim*. Our translation.

Comrades! My visit to Germany and to its Führer and the speech I am about to make before you are important events in the life of our two peoples and also in mine. . . . I have come among you not only in my capacity as head of the Italian government, but it is above all in my capacity as head of a national revolution that I have wanted to give proof of open and clear solidarity with your revolution. And although the course of the two revolutions has not been the same, the objective that both of them sought to reach and have reached is the same: the unity and greatness of the people.

Fascism and Nazism are two manifestations of that parallelism of historical positions that join in common the life of our two nations, risen to unity in the same century and by the same actions. . . . We have in common many elements of the *Weltanschauung*. Not only do Fascism and Nazism have everywhere the same enemies, in the service of the same master (the Third International); but they have in common also many conceptions of life and history. . . .

Germany and Italy follow the same course also in the field of economic autarchy: because without economic independence the very political autonomy of a nation is compromised and a people of great military prowess may be subdued by an economic blockade. We experienced this danger in all its immediacy when fifty-two states congregated at Geneva voted the criminal economic sanctions against Italy. These sanctions were rigorously applied, but did not achieve their end. On the contrary, they provided Fascist Italy with the occasion to show its mettle to the world.

Although Germany was much urged to join in the sanctions, it did not do so. We shall not forget this. On that occasion there appeared for the first time in the clearest manner the existence of a necessary solidarity between Nazi Germany and Fascist Italy. That which by now is known as the Berlin-Rome Axis was born in the fall of 1935; and during the last two years it has functioned magnificently for an ever greater drawing together of our two peoples and for a more effective policy of European peace. . . .

This community of Italo-German ideas has found its expression in the struggle against Bolshevism. . . . We have conducted this struggle in Spain, where thousands of Italian Fascist volunteers have fallen to save Western civilization, a civilization which may still experience a renaissance if it abandons the false and lying gods of Geneva and Moscow and draws nearer to the shining truths of our revolution.

Comrades! My speech draws to a conclusion. Beyond our frontiers you and we do not conduct propaganda in the banal sense of the word of seeking to make new converts. We believe that truth has a great power of penetration and ends up by triumphing. Tomorrow Europe will be Fascist not so much because of our propaganda but because of the logical development of events.

The "logical development of events" led Germany to march into Austria on March 12, 1938, and effect its annexation the next day. Three days later Mussolini explained to the Italian Chamber of Deputies that Italy had accepted and supported the *Anschluss* of Austria by Germany because the preservation of the Axis was a necessity superior to the defense of the independence of a people the greater part of whom desired union with Germany.

Mussolini's acquiescence to the *Anschluss* constituted a reversal and in large part the undoing of his former policy aiming at an Italian sphere of influence in the Danubian area.

Another event in 1938 which manifested Fascist Italy's increasingly close ties with Nazi Germany was the official adoption of an anti-Semitic policy in defense of "the Italian race," a phenomenon without precedent in modern Italy. Pre-Fascist and Fascist Italy up to 1938 was remarkably free of anti-Semitic sentiments and practices. In 1933 Mussolini's *Popolo d'Italia* had poked fun at Nazi Germany's pretensions to racial purity, and as late as February 1938 a semiofficial announcement denied that the Fascist regime had any intentions of persecuting Jews. But by the end of the year, pressure from Nazi-inclined elements within Italian Fascist ranks led to the adoption of a number of anti-Semitic decrees, portions of which follow.

84. ANTI-SEMITIC LEGISLATION IN FASCIST ITALY: DECREE-LAW OF NOVEMBER 17, 1938: "MEASURES FOR THE DEFENSE OF THE ITALIAN RACE"

Raccolta ufficiale delle leggi e dei decreti del Regno d'Italia, 1938, IV, 2946–49. Our translation.

CHAPTER I. MEASURES REGARDING MARRIAGE

Article 1. Marriage between an Italian citizen of the Aryan race and a person belonging to another race is prohibited.

A marriage contracted in violation of this prohibition is null and void. . . .

CHAPTER II. ON MEMBERS OF THE JEWISH RACE

Article 8. With respect to this law: a) a person is of the Jewish race if born of parents both of the Jewish race, even if he belongs to a religion other than Jewish; b) a person is considered to be of the Jewish race if he is born of parents one of whom is of the Jewish race and the other of foreign nationality; c) a person is considered to be of the Jewish race if born of a mother of the Jewish race and of an unknown father; d) a person is considered to be of the Jewish race if, although born of parents of Italian nationality only one of whom is of the Jewish race, he belongs to the Jewish religion, or is enrolled in a Jewish community, or has in any other fashion made manifestations of Jewishness [*"ebraismo"*].

A person born of parents of Italian nationality only one of whom is of the Jewish race, and who belonged to a religion other than Jewish as of October 1, 1938, is not considered to be of the Jewish race.

Art. 9. Membership in the Jewish race must be declared and entered on the public registers.

All extracts from these registers and related certificates must make express mention of the entry regarding members of the Jewish race. . . .

Art. 10. Italian citizens of the Jewish race may not: a) render military service in time of peace or of war; b) exercise the function of guardian or custodian of minors or disabled persons not of the Jewish race; c) be proprietors or managers in any capacity of enterprises declared to be related to the defense of the country . . . and of enterprises of any nature employing a hundred or more persons; . . . d) be proprietors of lands which altogether have an appraised valuation of more than 5,000 lire; e) be proprietors of urban buildings which altogether have a tax value of 20,000 lire. . . .

Art. 11. A parent of the Jewish race may be deprived of his parental authority over his children if they belong to a religion other than the Jewish and if it is shown that he is giving them an education not corresponding to their religious principles or to national ends.

Art. 12. Members of the Jewish race may not employ Italian citizens of the Aryan race as domestics. . . .

Art. 13 The following agencies may not employ persons of the Jewish race: a) the civil and military Administrations of the state; b) the National Fascist Party and the organizations subordinate to it or under its control; c) the Administrations of provinces, communes, public institutes of assistance and welfare, and those entities, institutes, and enterprises . . . administered or supported by the provinces, communes, public institutes of assistance and welfare or their trusts; d) the Administrations of municipal enterprises; e) the Administrations of para-statal entities; . . . f) the Administrations of enterprises auxiliary or directly subordinate to the entities mentioned under letter *e;* . . . g) the Administrations of banks of national interest; h) the Administrations of private insurance companies.

Art. 14. Upon the documented request of interested persons, the Minister of the Interior may in individual cases declare the provisions of Articles 10 and 11, and of Article 13, letter *h*, inapplicable in the cases of: a) members of the families of those who fell in the Libyan War, the World War, the Ethiopian War, the Spanish Civil War, and of those who fell in the cause of Fascism; b) persons who meet one of the following conditions:

1. persons who were multilated, disabled or wounded, war volunteers, and recipients of decoration for valor in the Libyan War, the World War, the Ethiopian War, and the Spanish Civil War;

2. combatants in the Libyan War, the World War, the Ethiopian War, or the Spanish Civil War who received at least the War Cross for Merit;

3. persons who were mutilated, disabled, or wounded in the Fascist cause;

4. persons enrolled in the National Fascist Party during the years 1919, 1920, 1921, 1922, and the second half of 1924; *

5. Fiumean volunteers; †

6. persons who are exceptionally deserving [of the nation]. . . .

The benefit provided for under letter *b* above may be extended to the families of the persons listed thereunder, even if such persons are dead. . . .

Art. 15. With respect to the application of Article 14, in addition to the spouse, a family shall be considered to include all ancestors and descendants up to the second degree. . . .

Art. 17. Foreign Jews may not establish permanent residence in the Kingdom, Libya, and the Aegean possessions. . . .

CHAPTER III. TEMPORARY AND FINAL PROVISIONS

Article 20. Employees of the agencies indicated in Article 13 who are members of the Jewish race shall be discharged from their service within three months of the date of this decree's application.

Art. 21. Regular employees of the state who are discharged from the service according to Article 20 are acknowledged the right to claim retirement benefits due them according to law.

As an exception to existing regulations, those who have not reached

---

* The second half of 1924 is an especially significant addition: it was the time of the Matteotti crisis and of a drop in Fascist party enrollment. Ed. note.

† Followers of d'Annunzio in his Fiume enterprise, 1919–20. Ed. note.

the prescribed period of time in service are accorded a minimum pension provided they have performed at least ten years of service. In other cases there is accorded an indemnity equal to as many one twelfths of the latest salary as they have years of service.

Art. 22. Insofar as they are applicable, the provisions of Article 21 are extended to the agencies indicated under letters *b, c, d, e, f, g,* and *h* of Article 13. . . .

Art. 23. All grants of Italian citizenship to foreign Jews after January 1, 1919, no matter however made, are considered in all effects revoked.

Art. 24. Foreign Jews and those to whom Article 23 applies who began their stay in the Kingdom, Libya, and the Aegean possessions after January 1, 1919, must leave the territory of the Kingdom, Libya, and the Aegean possessions by March 12, 1939. . . .

Art. 25. The provisions of Article 24 shall not apply to Jews of foreign nationality who before October 1, 1938: a) were over 65 years of age; b) had contracted marriage with Italian citizens. . . .

Art. 27. Nothing new is introduced with regard to public worship and activities by Jewish congregations according to existing laws, except for modifications eventually necessary to coordinate these laws with the provisions of the present decree.

A decree-law of November 15, 1938 provided for the exclusion of all persons defined as of the Jewish race from "any office or employment in schools of any kind or grade" attended by Italian students. A similar exclusion was made to apply to Jewish membership in academic and other educational associations, and to the enrollment of Jewish students in schools "attended by Italian students." Exceptions were made for "students of the Jewish race who professed the Catholic religion" and who could be enrolled in elementary and secondary schools within the jurisdiction of the ecclesiastical authorities. Elementary and secondary schools could be established by Jewish congregations for Jewish students, and Jewish students could remain enrolled in "universities or institutes of higher education of the Kingdom . . . on a temporary basis." On December 22, 1938 another decree-law provided for the discharge of all Jews from the Italian armed forces and the Fascist Militia. As in the other two decrees noted above, this measure also had a touch of humanity. The discharged officers and noncommissioned officers were allowed to keep their uniforms, and the officers could continue to use the title of their rank. There were also provisions for pensions and other benefits.

The adoption of anti-Semitic policies toward the end of 1938 was but one sign of Mussolini's fatal bent toward Germany. Another such sign became evident at the time of the Munich crisis over Germany's claims to the Sudetenland. Heeding an appeal from the British Prime Minister, Neville Chamberlain, Mussolini aided in the convening of a four-power conference at Munich at the end of September which decided on the dismemberment of Czechoslovakia as the price of peace. But while ready to pay the price of the Sudetenland for peace with Germany, France was not willing to assure its peace with Italy by acceding to mounting Italian requests for territorial or commercial concessions at the expense of French interests in French Somaliland, Tunisia, and the Suez Canal Company. France proving obdurate, Mussolini had need to register some success elsewhere, especially after Germany's absorption of the rest of Czechoslovakia in March 1939. He decided on Albania, an Italian protectorate for more than a decade, and occupied it early in April, conferring on an unwilling Victor Emmanuel III the new title of King of Albania. Sporting this new title, his Majesty's Italian government concluded a formal alliance—the "Pact of Steel"—with Germany, in part hoping thereby to apply pressure on France to make the desired concessions to Italy. Portions of this Italo-German offensive-defensive alliance are translated below.

85. PACT OF FRIENDSHIP AND ALLIANCE BETWEEN ITALY AND GERMANY, BERLIN, MAY 22, 1939 (PACT OF STEEL)

> Regio Ministero degli affari esteri, *Trattati e convenzioni fra il Regno d'Italia e gli altri Stati.* Rome: Tipografia del Ministero degli affari esteri, 1941, LIV, 252–55. Our translation.

His Majesty the King of Italy and Albania and Emperor of Ethiopia, and the Chancellor of the German Reich, hold that the moment has come to confirm with a solemn Pact the intimate ties of friendship and solidarity existing between Fascist Italy and National Socialist Germany. . . .

Art. 1. The two Contracting Parties shall keep in permanent contact with each other for the purpose of agreeing on all questions regarding their common interests or the general European situation.

Art. 2. In the event the common interests of the two Contracting Parties were to be put in danger by international events of whatever nature, they shall without delay enter into consultation on the measures to be adopted for the safeguard of these interests.

In the event the safety or other vital interests of one of the Contracting Parties were threatened by an outside danger, the other Contracting Party shall give the menaced Party its full political and diplomatic support for the purpose of eliminating this threat.

Art. 3. If in spite of the desires and hopes of the two Contracting Parties it were to happen that one of them were to become involved in complications of war with one or more Powers, the other Contracting Party shall immediately come to its aid as ally and shall support it with all its military forces on land, on the seas, and in the air.

Art. 4. The governments of the two Contracting Parties shall increase ever more deeply their collaboration in the military field and in the field of war economy for the purpose of assuring, in the case provided for, the rapid application of the duties of alliance assumed in Article 3.

Analogously, the two governments shall keep in permanent contact with each other for the adoption of other measures necessary to the practical application of the dispositions of the present Pact.

For the purposes indicated in the above-mentioned two paragraphs, permanent Commissions shall be formed and placed under the direction of the respective Ministers of Foreign Affairs.

Art. 5. In the event of a war conducted in common the Contracting Parties are committed from this moment on not to conclude an armistice or peace without full agreement with each other.

Art. 6. The two Contracting Parties, conscious of the importance of their common relations with Powers friendly to them, are decided to maintain and to continue to develop these relations by common agreement and in harmony with the consonant relations that bind them with these Powers.

Art. 7. This Pact becomes operative immediately after its signature. The two Contracting Parties agree to fix the first period of its validity to ten years. Before the expiration of this term they shall come to an agreement at an opportune time regarding the extension of the validity of this Pact. . . .

Signed: Galeazzo Ciano   Joachim von Ribbentrop

Italy's basic premise in the discussions preceding the signature of the Pact of Steel was that for a period of at least three years the two allies would take no step likely to lead to war. The need to insist on this premise arose from Italy's military weakness after the exertions in Ethiopia and Spain. But when, toward the end of August 1939, it became clear that Germany's demands on Poland raised the risk of a general European war, a memorandum stating Italy's position was prepared by officials of the Italian Foreign Ministry. This memorandum makes it clear that a certain sense of independence and realism with regard to national interests was still to be found among officials of the Fascist regime.

86. MEMORANDUM PREPARED FOR THE FOREIGN MINISTER, CIANO, JUSTIFYING ITALY'S OPPOSITION TO WAR, AUGUST 21, 1939

> Ministero degli affari esteri, Commissione per la pubblicazione dei documenti diplomatici, *I documenti diplomatici italiani, ottava serie: 1935–1939* (August 12–September 3, 1939). Rome: La Libreria dello Stato, 1953, XIII, 85–89. Our translation.

The conclusion of the Treaty of Alliance between Italy and Germany was preceded by an examination in depth of the political and military situation of the two countries in relation to the international situation. This examination revealed in a precise manner that the two countries felt that they could not expose themselves to war without an adequate period of preparation. This point was maintained precisely by the German government. Since March 1939 the Führer had made it known to the Duce that Germany did not consider it convenient to the interests of the Axis to engage in a war for which Germany would need two or three years of preparation. . . .

Italy declared that it was in agreement with Germany on the need for a period of peace, and the conversations preceding the conclusion of the Alliance were guided by this notion.

During the Milan meeting [between Ciano and German Foreign Minister Joachim von Ribbentrop, May 6–7, 1939], when the alliance between the two countries was decided upon, Count Ciano informed Minister Ribbentrop of the contents of the memorandum of instructions given him by the Duce. This memorandum explained the reasons why Italy and Germany needed a period of peace of *not less than* three years. The principal reasons were these: 1) the need to complete the military and naval preparation, and above all the equipment of the artillery and the readiness of the fleet; 2) the development and completion of plans for economic self-sufficiency; 3) the military preparation of Libya, Albania, and Ethiopia; 4) the need to deepen the relations between [our] two peoples.

These ideas were discussed by Count Ciano and Minister Ribbentrop during the Milan meeting. The latter said that he was in complete agreement on the need for a period of peace of *not less* than four or five years. . . . Ribbentrop then said that Germany was ready to make war even before then, *if forced* to do so. Ribbentrop said in Milan that the Führer had decided to march along a road of conciliation; that Germany's program was one of not taking the initiative; that Germany did not consider the door to negotiations to be closed, and intended to allow the Danzig question *to ripen,* ready to react in the event that Poland were to assume an offensive policy.

The alliance was concluded on these bases.

In other words, it was clearly understood that for a period of *not less than* three years (indeed, Ribbentrop said not less than four or five years) no action would be taken that could lead to war, and that every effort would be made to preserve peace. This was a necessity stated not only by Italy but by Germany as well. It was the very basis of the agreement on which there was complete understanding between the two governments.

Once the Treaty of Alliance was signed, General Cavallero [Ugo, Vice-President of the Executive Committee of the Pact of Steel] delivered to Ribbentrop for the Führer (May 30) a memorandum from the Duce fixing the points of understanding with Germany. First on the list was the necessity of a period of peace of not less than three years—as had been acknowledged by both parties in Milan—and the need to foresee *a long war of exhaustion* for which it was indispensable to be prepared.

On June 6 Ribbentrop informed Attolico [Bernardo, Italian ambassador to Germany] that the Führer had had knowledge of the document sent him and was "in complete agreement with the considerations therein expounded."

It was therefore understood in an unequivocal manner that the two countries would follow—*at least for a period clearly defined*—a policy of peace and of preparation. This was not only the understanding that preceded the treaty, but represented also its application. In fact, Article 1 of the treaty fixes the obligation of consultation and agreement as necessary premise of the reciprocal aid the two Powers owe each other; and this agreement was complete and absolute in the common intention of the two Powers to avoid war. . . .

It was Italy that took the initiative for a consultation which in practice Germany sought to avoid after having repeatedly acknowledged it as imperative according to the Treaty of Alliance.

No consultation took place between Germany and Italy until the meeting at Salzburg [between Ciano and Ribbentrop, August 11]. Until that moment only one agreement existed between the two countries: the agreement *not* to make war for a period of at least three years. This agreement was not to be modified except by common agreement.

At Salzburg Italy was not faced by a German proposal to examine the situation in order to reach an understanding on a common policy; rather it was faced by a decision already taken unilaterally by the German government.* This decision was communicated by Ribbentrop as definitive and irrevocable. Ribbentrop expounded to Count Ciano the reasons for Germany's decision, but chose not to enter into a discussion on the situation of the two countries in the event of war and, therefore, on the very premises of a common action as these premises had been fixed in the Treaty of Alliance.

The exposition of the Italian point of view and the proposal to make, before having recourse to arms, an attempt toward a peaceful solution to be announced in a final communiqué, were countered by the Führer and by Ribbentrop with the categoric determination to make war. Proceeding from the hypothesis of a localized conflict, Ribbentrop did not admit the eventuality of a general war.

Count Ciano had to lead the discussion to this plane to arrive at a clarification. Italy's position was fixed by Count Ciano in open and unequivocal terms: 1) Italy does not believe that the conflict can be localized, and holds French and English intervention to be certain; 2) in such a case Italy with its empire would be the country most exposed to enemy attacks; 3) the conditions that last May counseled the avoidance of a conflict—and on which the two governments were in complete agreement—have not changed; 4) Italy judges that under such conditions one would face a European war in least favorable circumstances; 5) Italy thinks that the German-Polish controversy may be susceptible to a solution such as Germany has the right to expect without recourse to force.

In the face of these arguments Ribbentrop held firm in his positions

---

* The decision to use force in solving the "Polish question" of Danzig and the Polish Corridor. Ed. note.

that the conflict would certainly remain localized and that Germany would take care of the Polish question [all] by itself [that is, without the need of Italian military intervention].

From Salzburg there followed, therefore, an essential disagreement between Italy and Germany on the evaluation of the situation. The Germans rejected out of hand the Italian proposal to attempt a peaceful negotiation before recourse to arms, and this fact in turn made impossible the formulation of a final communiqué on the talks, as proposed by Italy.

Instead, there was issued from the German side a unilateral communiqué which declared that there was 100 per cent agreement between Italy and Germany, and this [alleged] agreement was made to be dependent upon the Treaty of Alliance.

As a consequence of this communiqué, Ambassador Attolico, upon instruction from the Duce and in his name, reconfirmed to the German government the Italian point of view as expounded by Count Ciano.

On August 19 Ribbentrop replied to this communication by confirming to Attolico Germany's decision to act. But instead of emphasizing—as he had done at Salzburg—Germany's intention of considering the conflict as a question of direct action by Germany alone, he felt bound to emphasize that it would be the case of a common action by the Axis Powers. With this—and in disregard of the essential disagreement existing with Italy—Germany made itself exclusive judge of the interests and the action of the two countries by assuming that Italy was obliged to follow Germany in that whatsoever action it chose unilaterally to take.

On August 23, 1939, two days after the preparation of the above memorandum, there came the news of the ratification of a Russo-German nonaggression pact. The German Foreign Office, and Foreign Minister Ribbentrop in particular, apparently believed that the pact with Russia would discourage an Anglo-French military intervention on behalf of Poland. But on August 25 there came two surprises for Germany. First, England announced the conclusion of a defensive alliance with Poland; second, Mussolini informed Hitler that because of military unpreparedness—owing to the efforts made in Ethiopia and Spain—Italy would be unable to enter a war in the event Germany attacked Poland and were counterattacked by the latter's allies. Mussolini reminded Hitler that in their previous conversations they had foreseen a war after 1942 and that Italy could not be ready before then unless

Germany were able immediately to provide Italy with necessary war matériel. The initiation of German hostilities against Poland, planned for August
26, was temporarily deferred; and in the subsequent five days international
diplomacy made futile efforts to ward off the catastrophe. On August 30
Mussolini urged Hitler to consider Chamberlain's proposals for negotiation
of the Polish controversy; and when, on September 1, Germany chose to
march into Poland, the Italian government announced its nonbelligerence in
the developing conflict. Hitler received the news of Italy's decision "without
enthusiasm," but sent Mussolini a telegram expressing his appreciation of
Italy's position. After declaring war on Germany, France and England made
it a point to convey their gratitude to Italy for its nonbelligerence. Unofficial
German sources, on the other hand, made known their displeasure, which
grew with the knowledge that Italy was negotiating for increased exports to
the Western Allies. Hitler informed Mussolini early in October that although
he agreed that Italy's nonbelligerence had been more useful to Germany
than an immediate intervention, he nonetheless felt that Italy could not remain out of the war indefinitely without compromising its imperial ambitions
in the Mediterranean.

These ambitions eventually persuaded Mussolini of the inevitability of
Italy's intervention in the conflict. He expressed this conviction in a meeting
with Ribbentrop on March 11, 1940, adding that Italy would enter the war
only when it was ready to do so without being a burden to its German ally.
The same view was expressed by Mussolini in a meeting with Hitler at the
Brenner on March 18. He explained that Italy could not sustain a long war
and that, therefore, it would enter the conflict when Germany's military action created a favorable situation for Italy's intervention.

At the end of March Mussolini conveyed these decisions in a memorandum prepared for the King, Ciano, and the Chiefs of Staff of the armed
forces. The memorandum is candid in asserting that inasmuch as Italy could
not make war *against* Germany, it would have to make war against England
and France. Mussolini had apparently concluded that "honor" and national
interests demanded Italy's entry into the conflict.

87. MUSSOLINI'S DECISION ON EVENTUAL PARTICIPATION IN THE WAR: MOST SECRET MEMORANDUM TO THE KING, FOREIGN MINISTER CIANO, AND THE CHIEFS OF STAFF OF THE ARMED FORCES, MARCH 31, 1940

I documenti diplomatici italiani, nona serie (1939–1943), III, 576–78.
Our translation.

In a situation such as the present, which could be called one of extreme fluidity, it is difficult if not impossible to make predictions on

the development of events and future phases of the war. A large role must be assigned to the unforeseen (see Russo-Finnish War). . . .

If the most improbable of eventualities were to occur—that is, a negotiated peace during the next few months—in spite of its nonbelligerence Italy could have a say and not be excluded from the negotiations. But if the war were to continue it would be absurd and impossible to believe that Italy could remain out of it until the end. Italy is not situated in a corner of Europe as is Spain; it is not semi-Asiatic as is Russia; it is not distant from the theaters of operation as is Japan or the United States. Italy is in the midst of the belligerents, on land as well as on the seas. Even if Italy were to change its attitude and were to move bag and baggage to the side of the Anglo-French, it would not avoid immediate war with Germany, a war that Italy would have to endure *all alone*. It is only the alliance with Germany, that is with a state that does not yet have need of our military participation and is content with our economic aid and our moral solidarity, which allows us our present state of nonbelligerence. Excluding the hypothesis of an about-face—which, moreover, the Anglo-French themselves do not contemplate (and in this they show that they understand us)—there is left the other hypothesis, that is, a war parallel to that of Germany for the purpose of reaching our objectives. These objectives are summarized in this statement: freedom on the seas, a window to the ocean. Italy will not be a truly independent nation so long as Corsica, Bizerte, and Malta are the bars of its Mediterranean prison and Gibraltar and Suez its walls. Once the problem of its land frontiers is solved, Italy, if it wishes to be a true world power, must solve the problem of its sea frontiers. The very security of its empire is tied to the solution of this problem.

Italy cannot remain *neutral* for the entire duration of the war without resigning from its role, without disqualifying itself [as a world power?], without reducing itself to the level of a Switzerland multiplied by ten.

Accordingly, the problem is not that of knowing whether Italy will enter the war, because Italy cannot avoid entering the war. It is only a question of knowing when and how; it is a question of delaying our entry into the war as long as possible and as is compatible with honor and dignity. This delay is necessary: a) so that we may prepare ourselves in such a way that our intervention determines the outcome; b) because Italy cannot wage a long war, that is, it cannot spend hundreds of billions as the present belligerent countries are obliged to do.

But at the Brenner meeting [between Hitler and Mussolini, March 18, 1940] it was clearly established that the *when*, that is, the *date*, is a matter that regards Italy and Italy alone.

On the premise that war is inevitable and that *we cannot* march with the Anglo-French, that is, we cannot march against Germany, it is a question of fixing from this moment on the lines of our strategy.

The condition to Italy's participation in the war that Mussolini had expressed to Hitler in their meeting of March 18, 1940—the creation of a favorable situation by German military action—apparently came sooner than Mussolini had expected. Early in April German arms swept through Denmark and Norway; the Netherlands, Luxemburg, and Belgium fell by the end of May; the British Expeditionary Force and Allied contingents escaped from the Dunkirk trap early in June; and on June 5 the battle for France began. After about nine months of neutrality—as in 1914–15—Italy decided for war with the prospect of a quick victory. But once again the Italian government made the wrong prediction; only this time the outcome was not a costly victory, it was a disastrous defeat.

The decision for war was announced by Mussolini to the Italian people on June 10, 1940. In his speech of that day, he characterized the war he had declared on Great Britain and France as being directed against "the plutocratic and reactionary Western democracies that [had] always hindered the advance of the Italian people and frequently plotted against its very existence." And indeed, the long series of almost uninterrupted military disasters following upon Italy's intervention in the war did threaten Italy's very existence; but this threat came not from prewar plots of the Western democracies, it came from Mussolini's disregard of the views he had held in 1939 that Italy could not be ready for a major war before 1942.

Mussolini's evaluation of Italy's military position in 1939 was based on purely military considerations of equipment and training of the armed forces; it did not take the matter of morale into account. Soon after Italy's intervention it became clear that the Italian people had no enthusiasm for the war. Indeed, this fact but confirmed the sentiment prevailing in Italy during the period of its nonbelligerence; and this sentiment was shared by the King, who had never shown much enthusiasm for the German alliance, and by the more realistic and responsible members of the military and foreign service establishments.

When properly equipped and commanded, Italian fighting men fought well and did not deserve Mussolini's growing contempt of them. But these requirements were rarely met, with the result that Mussolini's haste in trying to match Germany's military successes exposed Italy to adventures whose end was easy to foresee.

The collapse of France by mid-June 1940 convinced Mussolini that an immediate attack by Italy was imperative if it were to share in the glory and spoils of war. An armistice reached with France on June 24, after four days of battle, produced insignificant Italian territorial gains on the Franco-Italian frontier, whereupon Mussolini sought greater rewards elsewhere. In the summer and early fall he ordered offensives against English positions in East Africa and in coastal Egypt adjacent to Libya. Inadequate equipment brought the offensive from Libya to a halt in October after some successes; in East Africa Italy was obliged to go on the defensive by the end of the year.

In spite of some opposition from the Chiefs of Staff of the Italian armed forces and an earlier disapproval by Hitler, Mussolini ordered an attack on Greece late in October 1940 on the grounds that Greece was aiding the English; but the principal motive for the attack was the expectation of an easy victory. Inadequate preparation brought the Italian offensive to a halt within ten days; within a month the Italians were in retreat toward their bases in Albania. The failure of the Greek campaign was followed quickly by an English counteroffensive in western Egypt and eastern Libya. Italy's major bases in the latter area were captured with enormous Italian losses in men and matériel.

The situation in the Balkans and North Africa was altered dramatically in the spring of 1941 by Germany's direct intervention. Yugoslavia and Greece were invaded and beaten by combined German-Italian forces in April, and in the same month the Axis forces under the leadership of General Erwin Rommel reconquered the lost positions in eastern Libya. But there was no way of saving Italian East Africa, which fell to the English by the middle of 1941.

Throughout 1941 Italian military operations in the Balkans and North Africa fell increasingly under German control, and even Italy itself acquired the appearance of a German-occupied country. Mussolini's pride rebelled at this subservience and expressed itself in his insistence on sending an Italian expeditionary corps to Russia after Germany's invasion of that country in June 1941. These units could have been employed more profitably in North Africa, where the Italo-German forces registered a major victory in May–June 1942. But the difficulty of supplying the Axis forces across the Mediterranean compromised their position and led to the disaster of October–November 1942 at El Alamein. There followed soon thereafter the Anglo-American landing in Algeria and Morocco, assuring the destruction of the Axis forces in North Africa by May 1943. During the earlier part of the year the Italian expeditionary corps in Russia had been all but destroyed at about the same time that Germany suffered the disaster at Stalingrad.

In May 1943, after the doom of the Axis forces in North Africa, the Anglo-American command decided that, assuming the successful invasion of Sicily scheduled for July, they would thereafter proceed to overrun the Italian peninsula. American military leaders would have preferred to concentrate Allied efforts on the invasion of France across the English Channel; inasmuch as such an invasion seemed no longer feasible in 1943, they reluctantly agreed to the Italian peninsular campaign, but rejected Churchill's suggestion of an Allied operation in the Balkans through Italy. The men and equipment committed to the Italian campaign were limited primarily by the overriding priority given to the invasion of France scheduled for the spring of 1944. As a result it proved impossible to achieve a rapid victory over determined and resourceful German resistance, and Italy was thereby doomed to become a battlefield for the last two years of war.

The Allied invasion of Sicily began on July 10, 1943. The fall of the capital city Palermo, in less than two weeks, provided convincing proof of Italy's incapacity to resist even in defense of its homeland. The stage was thereby set for the fateful session of the Fascist Grand Council on July 24, 1943, which ended the morning of the next day with a virtual vote of no confidence in Mussolini and his dismissal and arrest upon the orders of the King. The Fascist regime had come to an end, but the war was to continue and Italy's travail was not yet done.

PART SEVEN

FROM THE FALL OF MUSSOLINI
TO THE PRESENT, 1943–1966

XXIV. FROM THE FALL
OF MUSSOLINI
TO THE END
OF THE WAR, 1943–1945

88. THE FALL OF MUSSOLINI

The successful Allied invasion of Sicily, begun on July 10, 1943, precipitated the development of two parallel movements designed to oust Mussolini and disengage Italy from a war it could no longer hope to win. One group of plotters consisted largely of military men and royal advisers close to Victor Emmanuel III. The other group was composed of Fascist leaders who either opposed the war from the beginning or had lost their enthusiasm for it. The principal royal agents were Duke Pietro Acquarone, Minister of the Royal Household; General Vittorio Ambrosio, Chief of the General Staff; and Marshal Pietro Badoglio, who had been relieved of his post as Chief of the General Staff in December 1940 after the failure of the Greek campaign. The Fascist opposition to a continuation of the war was led by Dino Grandi, former ambassador to London, and Galeazzo Ciano, Mussolini's son-in-law, who had been Foreign Minister from 1936 to February 1943.

The leaders of the two parallel movements were convinced that as long as Mussolini remained in power his ties with Hitler would make difficult if not impossible a disengagement from the war. The two parallels met when after a meeting of the Fascist Grand Council lasting ten hours, July 24–25, 1943, a resolution by Grandi was adopted which in effect voted no confidence in Mussolini and asked the King to assume his full constitutional powers. A brief account of the meeting and the text of Grandi's resolution are presented below. The laconic statement from the *Stefani* News Agency reveals nothing of the intense emotions and views expressed during the meeting. Mussolini and Grandi exchanged violent words, as did others; and after nearly ten hours of exhausting debate, Grandi's resolution was put to a vote and carried by a large majority.

The Fascist Hierarchy Votes No Confidence in Mussolini:
Meeting of the Fascist Grand Council, July 24–25, 1943

Summary account of the meeting of the Fascist Grand Council on July 24–25, 1943, reported by the *Stefani* News Agency and reprinted in the *Osservatore Romano*, Vatican City, July 28, 1943. Our translation.

On July 24, 1943, the Fascist Grand Council, which had not been convened since December 7, 1939, that is from before Italy's entry into the war, met at Palazzo Venezia. . . . The meeting began at 5:00 P.M. with a report by the Head of the Government on the military situation. Thereafter the President of the Chamber [of Fasces and Corporations], Grandi, presented and explained the following resolution bearing his signature and those of Federzoni, De Bono, De Vecchi, De Marsico, Acerbo, Pareschi, Cianetti, Ciano, Bottai, Balella, Gottardi, Bignardi, De' Stefani, Rossoni, Marinelli, Alfieri, Albini, and Bastianini: *

"Meeting in these days of supreme trial the Grand Council wishes above all to address its thoughts to the heroic fighters of all the armed forces who, shoulder to shoulder with the proud people of Sicily among whom shines most brightly the single-minded faith of the Italian people, renew the noble traditions of strenuous valor and indomitable spirit of sacrifice of our glorious armed forces.

"Having examined the domestic and international situation and the political and military conduct of the war, it proclaims the sacred duty of all Italians to defend at all costs the unity, independence, and liberty of the fatherland, the fruits of sacrifices and efforts by four generations from the Risorgimento to today; it asserts the need for the moral and material union of all Italians in this grave and decisive hour for the destiny of the nation; it declares that for the sake of this unity it is necessary immediately to restore all the functions of the State by attributing to the Crown, the Grand Council, the Government, Par-

---

* Most of the nineteen Fascist leaders who supported Grandi's resolution managed to escape Mussolini's vengeance; but five of the six who fell into his hands were executed on January 11, 1944, after a trial for treason at Verona, in German-occupied Italy. The five executed were Emilio De Bono, Galeazzo Ciano (Mussolini's son-in-law), Luciano Gottardi, Giovanni Marinelli, and Carlo Pareschi. Tullio Cianetti was sentenced to thirty years' imprisonment. Ed. note.

liament, and the Corporations the duties and responsibilities established by our statutory and constitutional laws; it invites the Head of the Government to pray His Majesty the King—toward whom the heart of the entire nation turns in faith and confidence—that for the honor and safety of the country he [the King] assume, with the effective command of all the armed forces on land, at sea, and in the air (and according to Article 5 of the Constitution of the Kingdom), that supreme initiative in making decisions which our institutions attribute to him and which [institutions] have always been in all our national history the glorious heritage of our august dynasty of Savoy."

The President of the Chamber, Grandi, requested a roll-call vote on the resolution. . . .

The discussion that followed lasted without interruption until 3:00 A.M. of July 25. At the end of the discussion the resolution presented by Grandi was approved by 19 votes in favor, 7 against, and 1 abstention.

The following answered in the affirmative: Grandi, Federzoni, De Bono, De Vecchi, Ciano, De Marsico, Acerbo, Pareschi, Cianetti, Balella, Gottardi, Bignardi, De' Stefani, Rossoni, Bottai, Marinelli, Alfieri, Albini, Bastianini.* The following answered in the negative: Scorza, Biggini, Polverelli, Tringali-Casanova, Frattari, Buffarini, Galbiati. Abstention: Suardo.

The King and Badoglio Assume Control in Italy

The action by the Grand Council had shaken Mussolini's authority but not his power. Constitutionally, Mussolini was responsible to the King and not to the Grand Council, which was a purely advisory organ. And in spite of earlier information to the effect that the King and his advisers were planning to replace him, Mussolini continued to have faith in the King's loyalty to him. This faith was shattered when in the afternoon of July 25 he was received by the King and was told that he had been relieved of his office and had been replaced by Marshal Badoglio. On the pretext that it was necessary to safeguard his person, Mussolini was placed in the protective custody of the *carabinieri* and after shunting him about to four different hiding places, at the end of August he was finally situated on a mountain top at the Gran Sasso in the Abruzzi from where he was freed by glider-borne German troops on September 12. No effort was made by Mussolini's Italian followers

* All the men who had signed the resolution voted for it. Ed. note.

to free him, and no resistance was offered when Badoglio assumed power and proceeded to shatter the entire apparatus that had kept Mussolini and the Fascists in power for more than twenty years. The ease with which Mussolini's overthrow was consummated proves beyond question how thoroughly the war had undermined the regime.

The following proclamations were issued on the evening of Mussolini's ouster and arrest.

ROYAL PROCLAMATION OF JULY 25, 1943. Reproduced in the *Messaggero* of Rome, July 26, 1943. Our translation.

Italians,

From today I assume command of all the armed forces. In the solemn moment that weighs over the destinies of the fatherland everyone is bound to resume his place of duty, of faith, and of combat: no deviation is to be tolerated, no recrimination may be allowed.

Let every Italian bow before the grave wounds that have lacerated the sacred soil of the fatherland.

By virtue of the valor of its armed forces and the determined will of all its citizens Italy shall once again find the way to recovery in the respect for the institutions that have always encouraged its ascent.

Italians,

Today more than ever I am indissolubly united with you in an unshakable faith in the fatherland's immortality.

Signed: Victor Emmanuel

Countersigned: Badoglio

BADOGLIO'S PROCLAMATION OF JULY 25, 1943. The *Messaggero* of Rome, July 26, 1943. Our translation.

Italians,

By order of His Majesty the King-Emperor I assume the military government of the country with full powers.

The war continues. Although severely hit in its invaded provinces and destroyed cities, Italy remains loyal to its pledged word [to continue the war on the side of Germany] in proud defense of its millenary traditions.

Let the ranks be tightened around His Majesty the King-Emperor, living image of the fatherland and an example for all.

The charge given me is clear and precise. It shall be scrupulously discharged; and whoever deceives himself in thinking that he can obstruct its normal development or attempts to disturb public order shall be struck down inexorably.

Long live Italy!

Long live the King!

Signed: Pietro Badoglio,
Marshal of Italy

In spite of the reference in Badoglio's proclamation that the war would continue, the basic premise underlying Mussolini's ouster was Italy's rapid disengagement from the war. To this end Badoglio's government was erected into an actual military dictatorship, not only dissolving Fascist organizations but prohibiting also the organization of any other political party. While it proceeded with the pretense of continuing the war on the side of Germany, Italy prepared for an armistice with the Allies in the hope that the latter would be able to land sufficiently large forces on the mainland to help the new government rid itself of the presence of impressive German units in the peninsula. But this hope came to nought because of divided counsels among the Allies and because of logistic difficulties in executing so large an operation. In consequence, when the terms of an armistice concluded on September 3 between Italy and the Allies were made public on September 8, the Germans proceeded to occupy all of Italy except for the southernmost portion of the peninsula.

The terms of the armistice of September 3, 1943, called for a suspension of hostilities, but in fact were tantamount to Italy's unconditional surrender. By the end of the month a final Instrument of Surrender was prepared by the Allies and accepted by Italy. The excerpts below are from this final instrument, which goes beyond the purely military terms of the preliminary armistice of September 3 and inlcudes certain provisions dealing with the Italian domestic situation.

89. INSTRUMENT OF SURRENDER OF ITALY, MALTA, SEPTEMBER 29, 1943

U.S. Department of State. Treaties and other International Acts, Series 1604. *Armistice with Italy, 1943.* Washington, D.C.: Government Printing Office, 1947, pp. 3–4, 7–12, *passim.*

1. (a) The Italian Land, Sea and Air Forces wherever located, hereby surrender unconditionally.

(b) Italian participation in the war in all Theaters will cease immediately. . . .

2. The Italian Supreme Command will give full information concerning the disposition and condition of all Italian Land, Sea and Air Forces, wherever they are situated and of all such forces of Italy's Allies as are situated in Italian or Italian occupied territory.

3. . . . The Italian Supreme Command will take the necessary measures to insure Law and Order, and to use its available armed forces to insure prompt and exact compliance with all the provisions of the present instrument. . . .

4. Italian Land, Sea and Air Forces will within the periods to be laid down by the United Nations withdraw from all areas outside Italian territory notified to the Italian government by the United Nations and proceed to areas to be specified by the United Nations. . . .

18. The forces of the United Nations will require to occupy certain parts of Italian territory. . . .

22. The Italian government and people will abstain from all action detrimental to the interests of the United Nations and will carry out promptly and efficiently all orders given by the United Nations.

25. (a) Relations with countries at war with any of the United Nations, or occupied by any such country, will be broken off. . . .

26. Italian subjects will pending further instructions be prevented from leaving Italian territory except as authorized by the Allied Commander-in-Chief and will not in any event take service with any of the countries or in any of the territories referred to in article 25 (a) nor will they proceed to any place for the purpose of undertaking work for any such country. Those at present so serving or working will be recalled as directed by the Allied Commander-in-Chief.

29. *Benito Mussolini,* his Chief Fascist associates and all persons suspected of having committed war crimes or analogous offences whose names appear on lists to be communicated by the United Nations will forthwith be apprehended and surrendered into the hands of the United Nations. Any instructions given by the United Nations for this purpose will be complied with.

30. All Fascist organizations, including all branches of the Fascist Militia (MVSN), the Secret police (OVRA), all Fascist youth organizations will insofar as this is not already accomplished be disbanded in accordance with the directions of the Allied Commander-in-Chief.

The Italian government will comply with all such further directions as the United Nations may give for abolition of Fascist institutions, the dismissal and internment of Fascist personnel, the control of Fascist funds, the suppression of Fascist ideology and teaching.

31. All Italian laws involving discrimination on grounds of race, color, creed or political opinions will insofar as this is not already accomplished be rescinded, and persons detained on such grounds will, as directed by the United Nations, be released and relieved from all legal disabilities to which they have been subjected. . . .

32. (b) Persons of whatever nationality who have been placed under restriction, detention or sentence (including sentences in absentia) on account of their dealings or sympathies with the United Nations will be released under the direction of the United Nations and relieved from all legal disabilities to which they have been subjected.

37. There will be appointed a Control Commission representative of the United Nations charged with regulating and executing this instrument under the orders and general directions of the Allied Commander-in-Chief.

43. The present instrument shall enter into force at once. It will remain in operation until superseded by any other arrangements or until the voting into force of the peace treaty with Italy. . . .

Signed at Malta on the 29th day of September, 1943

Badoglio   Dwight D. Eisenhower

The immediate effect of the preliminary armistice of September 3 was to divide Italy into two: Sicily and the southern portion of the peninsula fell under Allied control; the rest of the country, from the Neapolitan provinces northward, was in effect surrendered to the Germans. The size of the two areas into which Italy was thus divided changed with the progress of the war; but the division itself lasted for twenty months, with Badoglio's royal government nominally in control of the southern area and Mussolini's Social Republic nominally sovereign in the North. This division was destined to have profound effects on political developments during the remaining months of the war and in the immediate postwar period.

Immediately after the announcement of the armistice on September 8, the King and government, expecting Rome's fall to the Germans, left the capital and went south, settling eventually at Brindisi, which was free of Germans and soon to be taken by the Allies. The fate of the Italians who remained in

German-occupied Italy was less fortunate. Equally unhappy was the fate of the Italian soldiers in southern France, Greece, and the Balkans. The failure to take measures to safeguard these soldiers from German retaliation is frequently cited as a grave lack on the part of Badoglio's government and the Allies. The King and Badoglio were also objects of denunciation by Mussolini who, freed by the Germans on September 12, was taken to Germany where on September 18 he made his first public announcement since his liberation. Excerpts from his radio address are presented below.

90. MUSSOLINI INDICTS THE MONARCHY: RADIO ADDRESS FROM MUNICH, GERMANY, SEPTEMBER 18, 1943

Reported in the *Corriere della Sera,* September 19, 1943; reproduced in Benito Mussolini, *Opera omnia,* Edoardo and Duilio Susmel, eds. Florence: La Fenice, 1960, XXXII, 2–4, *passim.* Our translation.

While we recognize our responsibilities, we wish also to specify the responsibilities of others, beginning with the Head of the State who, having exposed himself and not having abdicated—as the majority of Italians expected—can and must be called directly to account.

It is his dynasty that throughout the entire period of the war—and a war which the King declared—has been the principal agent of defeatism and of anti-German propaganda. His disinterest regarding the course of the war, his prudent and not always prudent mental reservations lent themselves to all sorts of speculations on the part of the enemy. As for the heir to the throne [Crown Prince Umberto], although he had insisted on assuming command of the Armies of the South, he never appeared on the fields of battle. Now more than ever I am convinced that the house of Savoy willed the preparation and organization of the *coup d'etat* in its smallest details, with Badoglio as an accomplice and executor, and with the complicity of some faint-hearted and war-shirking generals and some cowardly Fascist elements. There can be no doubt that immediately after my capture the King authorized negotiations for an armistice, negotiations which perhaps may have been already begun between the dynasties of Rome and London [before my arrest]. It is the King who counseled his accomplices to deceive Germany in the most miserable fashion by denying that negotiations were in progress even after these negotiations had been concluded. It is the dynastic establishment that prepared and executed the demolition of Fascism, the very Fascism that had saved it twenty years ago. . . .

It is not the regime that betrayed the monarchy, it is the monarchy that betrayed the regime. . . . When a monarchy fails in its duties, it loses all reason for existing. As for traditions, Italy has more republican traditions than it has monarchical ones. The freedom and independence of Italy were willed more by the republican current and by its purest and greatest apostle, Giuseppe Mazzini, than by the monarchists. The state that we wish to establish will be national and social in the highest sense of the word, that is, it will be Fascist by going back to our origins.

While we wait for the movement to develop until it becomes irresistible, we expound the following postulates:

1. Take up arms once again at the side of Germany, Japan, and the other allies. Only blood can erase so shameful a page from the history of the fatherland.

2. Prepare without delay the reorganization of our armed forces around units of the Militia. . . .

3. Eliminate the traitors, particularly those who until 9:30 P.M. of July 25 were members of the Party—and in some cases for many years—and who have joined the ranks of the enemy.

4. Annihilate the parasitic plutocracies and finally make of labor the object of the economy and the unbreakable foundation of the state. . . .

By the end of September 1943 Mussolini changed the name of the National Fascist Party to the Republican Fascist Party, and thus began the process of converting the part of Italy under German military control into what was eventually to be known as the Italian Social Republic or, more colloquially, as the Republic of Salò, after the town of Salò in northern Italy on Lake Garda where Mussolini had his headquarters. The country's division was further accentuated on October 13, twelve days after the Allied entrance into Naples, when Badoglio's Italy declared war on Germany and was granted cobelligerent status by the Allies. It now became both morally and legally right for those Italians not loyal to Mussolini to fight against the German military occupation and Mussolini's shadow Social Republic. During these days there grew in intensity an armed struggle known as the Resistance, which became an epic enterprise in the years 1943–45, but whose antecedents date from the years when Mussolini solidified his dictatorial rule in the mid-1920s.

When after Matteotti's murder in 1924 and the failure of the Aventine secession it became clear that legal opposition to Fascism was no longer possible, a number of anti-Fascists began to emigrate in order to continue the struggle from abroad. Others, principally members of the Communist party apparatus, remained in Italy to conduct a clandestine activity against the regime. By 1927 the emigrés in France formed an anti-Fascist Concentration (*Concentrazione antifascista*) including the two factions of Italian socialism, the Republicans, and a number of anti-Fascist Liberals. Two years later the "Giustizia e Libertà" group was formed under the influence of Carlo Rosselli with a program of anti-Fascist propaganda outside Italy and direct action within Italy. The next year the reformist Socialists under Turati and the maximalists under Pietro Nenni restored the unity broken in 1922 and confirmed the united party's participation in the Concentration. In 1931 the Giustizia e Libertà group joined the Concentration under an agreement which assigned it the conduct of anti-Fascist activity within Italy. But by 1934 the efforts on the part of the Giustizia e Libertà group to make an end of the old Socialist and Republican formations and to create a new party under its hegemony led to a break with the Concentration. On the other hand the Concentration was strengthened by the conclusion of a "unity of action pact" between the Socialist and Communist parties.

The patriotism aroused among many Italians by the Ethiopian War had some adverse effects on the fortunes of the anti-Fascist resistance, but the Spanish Civil War rallied the emigré anti-Fascists around the Spanish Republic, not without some disagreements between Communist and non-Communist elements in the anti-Fascist movement. The fall of the Spanish Republic and the outbreak of a general war in Europe in 1939 shifted the center of emigré anti-Fascist activity from France to the United States. By 1942 the unfavorable course of the war led to the resurgence of old anti-Fascist elements within Italy and to the appearance of new groups, such as the moderately socialist *Partito d'Azione* [Action party]. At the time of Mussolini's ouster in July 1943 the various anti-Fascist organizations were already linked by Committees of National Liberation (CLN), and the stage was set for a large-scale operation aiming not only at the liberation of Italy from German and Italian Fascist influences but also at a radical reform of the country's political and social life. Although the role played by the Resistance in the eventual liberation of Italy is of large importance, it is nonetheless true that this role was played principally because the disasters of war had undermined the Fascist regime. It is also true that although the prewar opposition had not been lacking in deeds of heroism and sacrifice, nevertheless it had not succeeded in seriously threatening the stability of the Fascist regime.

The development and fortunes of the armed Resistance movement during the last two years of war are examined in excerpts below from an article by Mario Niccoli in the *Enciclopedia italiana*.

91. THE ITALIAN RESISTANCE MOVEMENT

Mario Niccoli, "La Resistenza italiana," *Enciclopedia italiana, Seconda appendice (1938–1948)*. Rome: Istituto della Enciclopedia Italiana, 1949, pp. 686–91, *passim*. Our translation.

In other countries the outbreak of war and the resulting feeling of a common danger and a common duty brought about an instinctive movement of unity among the people that transcended all possible disagreements. In Italy, on the other hand, given the manner in which the war began, many experienced a spontaneous negative reaction which divided the whole of the Italian people from the moment war was declared on June 10, 1940.

At first this reaction was a moral revolt on the part of those who considered the war not only an unforgivable political and military mistake but, even more, an unjustified act of aggression and therefore a brutal violation of basic human and moral laws. But this reaction could not for long avoid becoming also more specifically "political" and thus be expressed in concrete acts. . . . At first there was a form of passive resistance, of the kind entertained by those who hope against hope for a sense of justice stronger than is warranted by facts. . . . But soon many moved from passive resistance to practical action; and it was the war itself which, quickly showing its true nature to most Italians, created a common front against it on the part of all. The spread of distress among all classes prompted a wide sense of rebellion in civilians; the chain of military failures dispelled all hopes of victory among those who had entertained such hopes; and the soldiers "experienced more directly than others, by means of continuous and painful comparisons with [our] allies and the enemy, the depressing spectacle of our lack of preparation [for war]" (R. Cadorna).[*] In the meanwhile, the political parties and especially the Communist party (which during the preceding two decades had not halted its activities, although they had been clandestine and limited) could not fail to consider the possibility that the war could become an avenue toward the achievement of their programs. The Spanish [Civil]

[*] Raffaele Cadorna, *La riscossa. Dal 25 luglio alla liberazione* (Milan, Rizzoli, 1948). Ed. note.

War—in this respect also a "dress rehearsal" of the Second World War—for the first time had converted the ideological conflict into an armed encounter and had offered [anti-Fascists] the opportunity of finally facing the enemy in open battle. In spite of the reluctance on the part of Catholic forces to engage in an alliance with communism, [the Spanish Civil War] . . . had confirmed above all the suitability of a union of all anti-Fascist parties in their action against the common enemy. On the other hand, the new political forces represented by the Giustizia e Libertà formations—the liberal socialist currents that were to give birth to the Action party—had performed the important function of breaking the passivity of a large part of the Italian cultural world, of breaking the barrier that divided the bourgeoisie from the working class, and of leading the bourgeoisie to overcome, on the terrain of battle [against Fascism], its anticommunist prejudices.

As early as October 1941 there was formed in Toulouse an "Action Committee for the Union of the Italian People" [*Comitato d'azione per l'unione del popolo italiano*] consisting of Communist, Socialist, and G. L. [Giustizia and Libertà] representatives. The Committee prepared an "appeal" to the Italian people based on the following points: "Denunciation of the pact of alliance with Germany; immediate separate peace with the countries attacked by Fascism; withdrawal of Italian combat and occupation troops; freedom of the press, of association, and of speech; restoration to the Italian people of their sovereign prerogative to choose for themselves a government responsive to their needs and interests." In October and November 1942 a first "National Front Committee" [*Comitato di fronte nazionale*] was formed in Turin, and for the first time representatives of the Christian Democrats joined the above-mentioned parties. Although in this instance, as in other similar instances taking place in Italy, the unity of purposes and programs did not always correspond to the [announced] formal unity, the war had finally made allies of Catholic and Marxist currents on the same plane of struggle against Fascism.

The first instance of active resistance came from workers. On February 20, 1943, the Communist party instructed the workman Leo Lanfranco (ordered arrested by Badoglio later in August and executed by the Germans in 1945 as commander of a "Garibaldi" partisan division) to organize a strike in the Fiat-Mirafiori plant in Turin. The movement began on March 15 and spread quickly to Milan and to all the principal centers in Piedmont, Lombardy, Emilia, Liguria, and Venetia. Whatever may have been its proportions, it is certain that this movement—the first of its kind in Nazi-oppressed Europe—was also the first collective blow struck at the Fascist state's apparatus after twenty years of prevailing conformism and acquiescence. . . .

Even more than on the morrow of July 25 [date of Mussolini's ouster] . . . the Resistance was born on September 8 * as a spontaneous popular movement without distinctions of social classes and political parties. . . . The Italian people felt alone in the complete absence of all order and law other than the brutal might of an invading [German] army. And the law for which the Italian people yearned they gave to themselves through the Resistance, which was the great moral force from which they drew the means for a struggle without quarter, a struggle waged with disciplined and knowing action. Through suffering the like of which they had never before in their history experienced, the Italian people once again asserted themselves individually and collectively as the determining element of their fate.

The government's abandonment of the capital had created the moral basis of the Resistance. On the other hand, the Germans made a great mistake by promoting the Fascist Social Republic, because they thereby made acute to the point of exasperation those elements of internal differences already present in Italy since the outbreak of war. These elements became irreconcilable, and their struggle gave to the Resistance the form, bitterness, and cruelty of a civil war. . . .

The Resistance was born in Rome between September 9 and 10 [1943]. While the last units of the regular [Italian] army were withdrawing into the city from the Ostian Way (after having fought heroically and unsupported by the authorities who, instead of coordinating the action of these units, were negotiating their surrender), at Porta San Paolo a small group of common people supported by elements of the intellectual bourgeoisie made a last generous effort at defense of the city. This extreme effort was as militarily ineffective as it was morally meaningful. . . . Two weeks later, at two o'clock in the afternoon of September 28, disarmed and starving Naples—after

* Date the armistice with the Allies was made public and of Badoglio's government's flight from Rome to avoid capture by the Germans. Ed. note.

months of unprecedented privation and suffering, after about 120 Anglo-American bombardments, one of which occurred after the signing of the armistice—rose against the Germans in a spontaneous popular movement above all as a reaction to a proclamation for the recruiting of forced labor. (Only 150 of the 30,000 expected workers complied with the proclamation.) Armed in a "truly chance manner," without any prepared or coordinated plan of action, during four days of struggle Naples gave birth to an episode among "the most worthy to be remembered in our national history, worthy of a place alongside the [five] days of Milan in March 1848, with which it has a striking similarity" (C. Barbagallo).* Little more than a thousand fighters (who suffered 300 dead), belonging to all social classes "without political distinctions" (L. Longo),† supported by a goodly number of soldiers almost all junior officers, and in agreement as to means and ends, succeeded in forcing the surrender of the German garrison. This was the first time that the most rigidly militaristic army in the world had surrendered to civilian fighters. When, at 11 o'clock in the morning of October 1, the first Allied units entered Naples they found the city completely liberated. And if this fact told the Italian people that Naples' example could and should be imitated (as it was), it also told the Germans that by now Italy was for them an enemy country ready to answer violence with violence, and ready to accept a war and wage it. . . . [Italy's] formal declaration of war on Germany on October 13 was no more than a legal recognition of a struggle which the people had already undertaken without waiting for orders.

Thus from its very beginnings the Resistance appeared as a truly national movement in that it was fed by a common anti-German ‡ feeling linked to the traditions of the Risorgimento and of the First World War. It was a popular movement in that it recruited or involved all classes of citizens—the clergy and the army, the bourgeoisie and the nobility, the urban and rural proletariat—with a most marked participation by the working classes which thus for the first time took part in the nation's history in a large and organized manner. . . .

* Corrado Barbagallo, *Napoli contro il terrore nazista, 8 settembre–1 ottobre 1943* (Naples, Maone, 1944?) Ed. note.

† Luigi Longo, *Un popolo alla macchia* (Milan, A. Mondadori, 1947). Ed. note.

‡ The original reads "antitedesco," and thus refers to the German-speaking Austrian empire as well as to Germany proper. The traditions of the Risorgimento were more anti-Austrian than anti-German. Ed. note.

Among those who participated in the Resistance there were men who saw Fascism as a contingent evil, an incidental fact that in a certain set of circumstances had forced itself into Italy's political life and, once removed as a malignant "tumor," "would never return" (B. Croce).* On the other hand there were those who thought of Fascism as the "natural outcome of the very manner in which our country was constituted; [as the outcome] not only of the momentary deficiencies of the other postwar period but of the historical deficiencies in the country's regime" (R. Battaglia) † ; and as proved inability, characteristic of Italy's pre-Fascist ruling class, "to grant the desire for a new and greater justice and the right of the larger and more popular classes to share in the management of the public welfare" (M. Delle Piane).‡ But whereas one of the latter views would make a *tabula rasa* of the past, the other would refashion the links with the past "by introducing in it a new leaven of life based on Christian ideas which the old liberalism had opposed or neglected." In substance, it is in this disagreement that there is interwoven and expressed the history of those Committees of National Liberation which were the political organisms that came out of the Resistance and guided it. . . . The Committees of National Liberation [CLN] began with a revolutionary program, above all because of pressure from the parties of the Left, specifically and first of all the Action party and the Communist party. Then they retreated to a position of compromise. And finally, when they dissolved themselves with the election of the Constituent Assembly [in June 1946] "they were already politically dead." We shall seek to present several of the conditions that seem identifiable as causes of this historical process.

From its very beginnings the partisan struggle arose as a meeting of minds between anti-Fascists whose opposition to the war was a conscious political act, and representatives of the army who in most cases had waged the Fascist war and, considering the means available to them, had waged it well. The latter were still moved by a deep feeling of loyalty to the oath they had sworn to the King. In fact, this

---

* Benedetto Croce, "Quando l'Italia era tagliata in due (settembre 1943–giugno 1944)," *Quaderni della Critica*, No. 6 (November 1946), pp. 108 ff. Ed note.

† Roberto Battaglia, "Il problema storico della resistenza," in *Società*, IV (1948), 64–87. Ed. note.

‡ Mario delle Piane, *Funzione storica dei Comitati di Liberazione nazionale* (Florence, Le Monnier, 1946). Ed. note.

feeling of loyalty was the idealistic motive for their actions, which
they understood and felt exclusively on the basis of national and patriotic notions. For them the King was still the personification of the
state—indeed, of the only legal state—and in a certain sense they considered themselves its representatives in the areas occupied by the
"Fascist traitors" who disobeyed the [King's] legitimate government.

On the other hand, the elements which in the beginning had flocked
"to the hills" were of heterogeneous origins. Beside a minority moved
by a sincere ideal (which often was, however, no more than an enthusiastic moral reaction to the overbearing manner of the traditional
German enemy), there were elements without clear, or even any, political views. The latter group included disbanded soldiers who, unable
to reach their homes, had taken to the hills moved by feelings which
often did not go beyond violent reaction against the military leaders
by whom they thought themselves "betrayed." There were young men
in whom the events of September [1943] had created the feeling of a
world in ruins "which had to be made to collapse altogether in order
that it might rise to life once again." Others had taken to the hills only
in order to escape from the Germans and the Fascists, that is, to save
themselves from an immediate danger in the hope of a rapid end to
the war. And there were elements who calculatingly concluded that
partisan activity would be indispensable as condition and credentials
for future positions. But this very same qualitative heterogeneity and
complexity of motives made it possible for the parties of the Left to
initiate a vast program of persuasion on the political level in order to
help the disbanded soldiers rediscover what these political parties
considered the idealistic bases of the struggle. It made it possible for
them to give to the partisan movement a moral and spiritual leaven
conforming to their own ideals and with political and social intentions
clearly in the sense propounded by them and synthesized in two
words, "democratic revolution.". . . .

A circular issued at the end of March 1944 by the political office of
the Giustizia e Libertà group in the second sector of Cuneo province
[Piedmont] read in part as follows: "Drive it well into the heads of
the partisans 1) that they are soldiers in a new and revolutionary
army . . . not to be identified with . . . the old royal army; 2)
that . . . the CLN is the true and authentic national government in
invaded Italy and that only from this government and not from Bado-

glio's government may partisan formations receive orders and instructions; 3) that the soldiers of this army are not only champions of a
general sort of patriotism who aim at 'chasing the foreigner from the
fatherland's sacred soil,' but rather the armed fist and the resolved
vanguard of a movement for renewal, of a revolutionary process that
envelops the country's entire political and social structure."

In contrast to this political and revolution-directed approach given
the partisan war, and the also political approach (but only in the
direction of reforms) advocated by the Christian Democrats, who also
participated actively in the liberation movement, there was a purely
"military" approach. . . . The latter was expressed in the activity of
the military commands that had remained in contact with Brindisi
[seat of Badoglio's royal government in the South]. This activity reflected equally clear interests and approaches and was itself, therefore,
the expression of a "political" position, if for no other reason than that it
aimed at neutralizing if not eliminating the political activity of the
parties of the Left. (See the circular from the Supreme Command, no.
3333/op. of December 10, 1943.)

This is the setting for the failure of an attempt sponsored in Naples
by Benedetto Croce and General Giuseppe Pavone in September and
October 1943 to organize a corps of volunteers. The attempt had the
consent of Allied authorities through the American general Donovan.*
Croce attributed its failure (in a letter of November 18, 1943, to Walter
Lippmann) † to the King's open activity and "insidious maneuvers." It
is also the setting for the mission to the North of General R. Cadorna
(who was a general in the regular, that is, the royal army, and at the
same time a firm and convinced anti-Fascist and anti-Nazi) and the
designated commander of the Corps of Volunteers of Liberty. Cadorna found himself in sharp disagreement with the leaders of the
CLNAI [*Comitato di liberazione nazionale per l'Alta Italia:* Committee of National Liberation for Northern Italy] on the definition of his
functions and above all on the nature of the action [to be performed
by the Corps of Volunteers of Liberty]. Having left "liberated" Italy
on August 11, 1944, he was able to reach an agreement with representatives of the CLNAI [in German-occupied Italy] only by February

* Major General William J. Donovan, director of the Office of Strategic Services.
Ed. note.
† A noted American journalist. Ed. note.

28, 1945, and after frequently sharp discussions and arguments. The Committee attempted to belittle the mandate given Bonomi's government * and to reserve for the CLNAI the political and organizational control of the Volunteers. Cadorna referred energetically to the "clear oral instructions given by the Italian government, and the written ones from the Allies, aiming at the militarization of the partisan movement and at preventing political interferences from hindering the development of the partisan war." In spite of these disagreements, the unification of partisan forces in a Corps of Volunteers of Liberty was accomplished. And although this unification was not really effective with regard to the partisan bands, it did have a political importance. According to a partisan in the Giustizia e Libertà formations (G. Bocca), "it represented the official appearance of harmony," a harmony which was confirmed in a sense negative to the stated revolutionary aspirations of the CLNAI.

The Cadorna episode is, therefore, not to be separated from the attitude assumed by the Allies, and above all the English, with regard to the Resistance. Ferruccio Parri † relates that "our partisan movement had assumed from the very beginning a direction which was not the one the Allies wanted. . . ." The "difficulty in reaching agreement and understanding with the Allies" lay in the fact that "we were swayed by a great and preeminent political end: to establish and promote a war of liberation and redemption, a war coming from the people and fed by the people's blood. We wanted an insurrection." And insurrection was precisely what the Allies did not want. In this respect a significant agreement was signed on December 7, 1944, between General H. Maitland Wilson, Supreme Allied Commander, and representatives of the CLNAI who had come to "liberated" Italy [from the North]. . . . This agreement was defined by the Executive Committee of the Socialist party of the CLNAI (which had not been able to send a representative because of transporation problems) as "a strangling agreement" [*un accordo capestro*] in that it subjected all initia-

---

* Marshal Badoglio resigned after the liberation of Rome in June 1944 and the new government was entrusted to Ivanoe Bonomi, a pre-Fascist moderate Socialist Prime Minister who was the designee of the CLN in liberated Italy. Ed. note.

† An early opponent of Fascism and one of the founders of the Action party. He engaged in underground opposition to the regime after the murder of Matteotti in 1924 and was arrested twice, in 1927 and 1942. In 1944 he became a deputy-commander of the Corps of Volunteers of Liberty under General R. Cadorna. He served as Prime Minister between June and December 1945. Ed. note.

tive on the part of the CLNAI and the very political development of the Resistance to the control of the Allied Command and of the Allied Military Government (when the latter was established in the liberated areas) acting on the basis of rigid observance of the armistice terms signed (it is to be noted) by the royal government. But, comments R. Cadorna, "we had no other alternative in Rome and it was necessary to sign." . . . .

There can be no doubt that the attitude of the Allies—firm in an uncertain position of hostility toward the "Fascist" King, whose abdication they demanded, but at the same time tied to that government which seemed to them to be the only legal one and the one that had accepted unconditional surrender and guaranteed the observance of the armistice terms (see Churchill's speech to the House of Commons, February 22, 1944)—was influential in determining the failure of the development of the Resistance's political program as propounded by the three parties of the Left. . . .

The partisan war [itself] underwent a number of alternate phases, also in connection with the Allied campaign in Italy. The first groups of disbanded soldiers began a sporadic activity of attacks on isolated German outposts and vehicles, frequently with the aim of securing for the patriots arms and supplies they lacked. During the course of the Allied campaign in 1944 the activity of bands in central Italy assumed notable importance. They exploited to the maximum the Germans' need to bring an enormous quantity of supplies across the long and vulnerable lines of communications running along the length of the peninsula. Tuscan partisans brought an end to their intense activity with an active role in the liberation of Florence (August 3–September 1, 1944). Aligi Barducci ("Potente") fell at the head of the Garibaldian "Arno" division. The partisan war to the north of the Tuscan-Emilian Apennines was more complex, more varied and intense. . . . The height of activity was reached in the summer of 1944 and it was related to the certainty of a rapid conclusion of the Allied campaign in Italy after the fall of Rome and Florence and the landings in France. Vast areas in the Alps and Apennines, in Piedmont, Liguria, Venetia, and Emilia were completely freed of Germans and Fascists. . . . The Resistance experienced a moment of crisis after the [enemy's] search-and-seizure operations of the summer and fall of 1944, when the expected Allied offensive did not materialize. But heedless of the famous invitation by Marshal [Harold] Alexander (end of 1944) and then by General Mc Clark * on January 23, 1945, to suspend activities; and deaf to numerous and frequent enticing offers from the Germans to reach a compromise in the light of the surrender in sight; during the winter of 1944–45 the Resistance strengthened its forces for the final insurrection which at the end of April 1945 crowned its efforts. It is impossible to present here a detailed account of the part played by partisan formations in the final phase of the war in Italy, as illustrated by the already cited [British] *Report on No. 1 Special Force Activities During April 1945*. The report is a full, faithful, and explicit acknowledgment of the decisive contribution made by the partisans in the struggle. All of Italy's northern cities were occupied by the patriots. . . .

The price paid in blood by Italians in their war of liberation was quite high. . . . "Provisional" data published by the Italian Ministry of Foreign Affairs . . . in October 1945 provide the following figures on "losses incurred by permanent partisan organizations: 27,000 dead and 17,000 wounded in battle; 20,000 dead and 986 wounded in acts of reprisal"; victims of "crimes consequent to Nazi-Fascist atrocities and acts of reprisal": 19,204 (709 of whom were hanged and 506 burned alive), plus 33 groups of people massacred. A total of 66,204 dead.

The King's and Badoglio's decision, upon assuming power on July 25, 1943, not to allow a resurgence of the old pre-Fascist political parties was probably motivated in part by fear that these parties would question the King's right to rule Italy after Mussolini's fall. In spite of the prohibition, these parties continued to organize in Committees of National Liberation during the second half of 1943, and in January 1944 met in a congress at Bari. Assembled were representatives of the Action, Christian Democratic (successor to the Popular party), Liberal, Labor Democrat (Bonomi's followers), Socialist, and Communist parties. A resolution was adopted calling for the King's immediate abdication, formation of a government representing the parties in the CLN, and the calling of a constituent assembly at the end of the war to decide on Italy's future institutions. England in particular was opposed to the King's immediate abdication because it feared for the stability of the southern Italian political situation. Support for the King came from an unexpected quarter when the leader of the Communist party, Palmiro

* Apparently a reference to the American general Mark W. Clark who in December 1944 became commanding general of Allied armies in Italy. Ed. note.

Togliatti, returned to Italy in March 1944, after spending the war years in the Soviet Union, and announced his party's willingness to support and participate in a transitional government, postponing the institutional question until after the war. In April Badoglio heeded the cue and formed a new government including representatives of the six parties in the CLN as Ministers Without Portfolios. On June 5, the day after the liberation of Rome, the King kept the promise he had made on April 12 and delegated his powers to the Crown Prince, Umberto; but he did not abdicate. Badoglio resigned, and at the request of the CLN the government was entrusted to the prewar Reformist Socialist leader Bonomi, who included representatives of all six CLN parties in his cabinet.

Bonomi's government managed to survive during a most difficult year, until June 1945. The slow Allied drive up the peninsula exposed Italy to the most painful months of wartime experience. In Rome, the anti-Fascist coalition was wracked by charges of inadequate "purification" of Fascist elements from the country's life, by criticism that the war effort was not vigorous enough, and by demands for immediate land reform. In the North Mussolini's shadow Social Republic, kept in existence only by the grace of German arms, diminished in size with the advance of Allied troops. His efforts to rally the support of northern Italians by appealing to republican traditions and by promising a socialized workers' state gained him few followers. The life of the Fascist Social Republic and his own were close to an end.

By March and early April 1945 major partisan risings in Italy's northern cities preceded or coincided with the arrival of Allied troops. During the last week of April the Committee of National Liberation for Northern Italy (CLNAI) gained effective control of much of what had been the Social Republic, and Mussolini himself was in flight toward Switzerland. On April 27 he was discovered and taken captive by a partisan band near Dongo; on the following day he and his faithful mistress, Clara Petacci, together with a number of Fascist officials were shot in order to prevent their escape to Switzerland or eventual surrender to the possibly more lenient Allied forces. On April 29 the commander of the German forces in Italy signed the unconditional surrender of his troops, finally bringing an end to the war in the peninsula. The same day Mussolini's and Clara Petacci's bodies were taken to Milan and, after much abuse, were exposed hanging head down from a girder in a public square. The city that had seen the birth of the Fascist movement thus paid its final insult to the movement's founder, as if to symbolize the utter and brutal disgrace into which the man and the movement had fallen. And yet, for more than twenty years Mussolini and Fascism had ruled the country.

How were Fascism and the man who personified it able to remain in power for so long, to fall only after military defeat had destroyed the regime's physical resources and moral prestige? Ineptitude and shortsightedness on the part of pre-Fascist parliamentarians, a weak king, a fearful bourgeoisie, a disoriented proletariat, a discontented young generation, all manipulated by an unscrupulous and unprincipled demagogue—these are the reasons usually cited as elements in Fascism's successful climb to power. But all these reasons identify the weakness of others, not the strength of the man who triumphed. They help explain why the pre-Fascist political order failed, not why Fascism succeeded. They help us to understand why the Fascist "experiment" was tried, not why it lasted for two decades.

It has been said that the man Mussolini was the essence of the movement, and that with his fall the movement fell with him. But the man survived for two years after 1943, and yet Fascism was already dead even before his fall. It had died when a disastrous war proved the emptiness of the Fascist promises of greatness, order, and prosperity; but until then the promises had been believed by some and acquiesced to by others. The regime's instruments of coercion are frequently cited as the mainstays of its power. Coercion was indeed employed to silence and eliminate the active dissidents, who were few in number; it was used to intimidate the potential dissidents, whose number was certainly greater; but it does not explain the collaboration the regime received from all strata of the population; nor does it explain the genuine enthusiasm Fascism was able to arouse, as at the time of the Ethiopian War. A captive press and a virtual monopoly over other means of indoctrination go far in explaining the outward uniformity of Italian public opinion under Fascism, but they account for neither the widespread cynicism of private opinions nor the fact that this indoctrination did strike a responsive chord at certain times and in certain persons. Both the cynicism and the responsiveness were assets to Fascism not of its own making. The cynics who judged the Fascist regime as no better but probably no worse than what they considered to be Italy's traditionally bad governments, became accomplices or at least passive supporters of that which they scorned in private. Those who responded to the lure of Fascism did so for noble or ignoble ends, but, in either case, they revealed that there was something in many Italians to which Fascism could appeal. Perhaps only a disastrous war could work the cure of dispelling this appeal.

XXV. FROM THE END OF THE WAR
TO THE PROCLAMATION OF THE
REPUBLICAN CONSTITUTION,
1945–1947

The end of the war created an irresistible demand that the northern Committee of National Liberation inject its cold "wind from the North" into the government and thus achieve the general purification not yet realized by the Southerners, who had been stifled by royalist influences and Allied pressure. In a sense, never was Italy more divided: the South had been liberated, the North had liberated itself. However partial this truth, it was felt keenly by those who wanted the end of the war to mean not only the end of Fascism and of German occupation but also the beginning of a new Risorgimento that would accomplish the social transformation the old Risorgimento had hardly attempted. The champions of the "wind from the North" were most numerous in the Action party, a political formation composed largely of men not doctrinaire enough in their socialism to be in the Socialist or Communist party but on the other hand determined to effect a radical social change.

In June 1945 Bonomi resigned and a leader of the Action party, Ferruccio Parri, replaced him. An early opponent of Fascism, Parri became in 1944 one of the two deputy-commanders of the Volunteers of Liberty in northern Italy and revealed exceptional gifts for partisan warfare. He was not equally prepared for the kind of warfare conducted in government councils, especially in a cabinet where the Christian Democrats and the Liberals found themselves frequently at odds with the Socialists and the Communists. The first two parties shared a concern for the authority of the state, and were particularly alarmed by the existence of large armed bands under the control of political parties, but outside the control of constituted public authority. Both parties believed in political democracy, but the Liberals were non-denominational whereas the Christian Democrats openly espoused Christian principles without being thereby a clerical party. On economic questions the Liberals tended to favor a free-trade approach, but were not opposed to some economic reforms. The Christian Democrats, on the other hand, were radical by comparison, as is seen in a resolution passed by the party's National Council on August 3, 1945, demanding the elimination of large and undeveloped land holdings, laws against industrial monopolies, workers' participation in management, progressive taxation, and a comprehensive social security system. Apart from not always clear references to revolution, the socioeconomic program espoused by the Communists and Socialists was not unalterably irreconcilable with that of the Christian Democrats. Even the question of nationalization of the economy was not an insuperable obstacle between Christian Democrats and the parties at the extreme Left. Much depended on how far nationalization was to go and on the manner of its implementation, and on these two issues the Socialists and Communists were not completely explicit or categorical.

What most concerned the Christian Democrats and the Liberals toward the end of 1945 was precisely the manner the parties of the extreme Left would employ in realizing their stated ends; in short, the politics they would follow. And considerations of politics meant, on the domestic scene, the retention or disbanding of military bands loyal to certain parties; on the international scene they meant the attitude Italy should adopt toward the latent but not yet public cold war between East and West.

Parri's government could not contain the divisions affecting its component parts and was forced to resign in December 1945. A new six-party coalition cabinet was formed under the leader of the Christian Democratic party, Alcide De Gasperi, who had been Sturzo's successor as secretary of the Popular party and a leader in the Aventine opposition to Fascism. The fate of this first of De Gasperi's eight cabinets (he led the Italian government without interruption from December 1945 to August 1953) did not seem promising. In addition to the problem of preserving public order, De Gasperi had to face the problems of economic reconstruction, the negotiation of a peace treaty with the Allies, and the solution of the institutional question of monarchy or republic.

The destruction caused by the war was especially heavy in housing, transportation, and industry. More than one sixth of the housing available before the war had been either completely destroyed or seriously damaged. Only 600,000 gross tons remained of the merchant marine's prewar 3.5 million gross tons. One fourth of all rail lines had been destroyed, 60 per cent of the locomotives, 50 per cent of the freight cars, and 40 per cent of the utilities. Comparably heavy losses had been suffered by tramway and autobus services, and nearly 90 per cent of all trucks were destroyed. An estimated 35 per cent of national roads, 90 per cent of port buildings, and 50 per cent of other port facilities were destroyed or damaged. In industry 67 per cent of the pig iron capacity was destroyed, as was 34 per cent of steel, and 50 per cent of shipbuilding. Electrical production was reduced by 25 per cent, and the whole of the country's industrial output was about one half of that of 1938. Agricultural production was reduced by about 40 per cent as compared to 1938 and the available food supply, measured in calories, had fallen by almost the same amount. The problem of inflation is revealed by the fact that the general index of prices (1938 = 100) reached 2,392 in 1945, whereas real wages in the various parts of Italy ranged from 50 to 75 per cent of 1938 levels.

Italy's immediate economic needs were met in part by aid from the United States through the United Nations Relief and Rehabilitation Administration (UNRRA) and other governmental and private agencies. This aid was both a cause and effect of Italy's close ties with the United States, and this fact became an issue in the formulation of Italy's postwar foreign policy particularly with regard to settling Italy's frontiers with Yugoslavia, Austria, and France. The excerpts below from a report by the Italian Communist party's Secretary, Palmiro Togliatti, raise the question of Italy's international alignment. They also refer to the need for the rapid convocation of a Constituent Assembly to formulate the country's new institutions, and for the implementation of a bold policy of national renewal. In addition, the report makes clear that the six-party coalition, in which the Communist party participated, was an unstable structure that could not last for long.

92. TOGLIATTI'S REPORT TO THE 5TH NATIONAL CONGRESS OF THE ITALIAN COMMUNIST PARTY, ROME, DECEMBER 29, 1945—JANUARY 6, 1946

Palmiro Togliatti, *Rinnovare l'Italia* (*Rapporto al V congresso nazionale del Partito comunista italiano*). Rome: Società editrice "L'Unità," 1946, pp. 37–75, *passim*. Our translation.

The first conclusion we have reached, and which I believe the congress will reach in agreement with the Directing Committee of the party, is that we cannot for long continue with the present regime. It is no longer possible to continue with a regime in which there is an actual paralysis of government. . . . It is therefore necessary to proceed to the election of the Constituent Assembly, and it is necessary that in this election we lay the foundations of a bolder and more harmonious enterprise of renewal. . . .

We have need of a Constitution that buries forever a past of social conservatism and reactionary tyranny and that will never allow this past to rise again. We need therefore a Constitution whose originality will consist in being in a certain sense a program for the future. For this reason the Constituent Assembly will have to face problems not only of a political but also of an economic and social renewal, even if it is not possible to expect that all this enter directly in the Constitution inasmuch as in the Constitution there may appear only general principles that orient subsequent governmental activity. All this may be done only if the strictly constitutional activity is accompanied by the preparation and approval of legislative measures which at least sketch out the solution of great and urgent economic and social questions: the question of land and land reform, the question of industry and industrial reform, the guarantees to and rights of labor, and the principles of social legislation. . . .

What is to be the foreign policy of the new democratic Italy? . . . . It is our opinion that in general the orientation of the country's public opinion and above all the opinion of certain groups directing our foreign policy has not been right.* There have come to the surface in this orientation several fundamental distortions, but principally two, which to the degree that they have asserted themselves and have influenced the concrete acts of the government have compromised our country's cause and especially the cause of Italy's independence.

The first distortion stems from the conviction that in order to assert ourselves once again as an independent nation and to acquire once again a place in the world we should exploit the disagreements among the great Allied powers. The second distortion is a preconceived hostility against the Soviet Union. Both errors derive from Fascism and both must be liquidated, if as a government and as a country we wish to carry on a correct foreign policy. . . . I do not believe it to be in the interest of our country to side with or to foster even in a restricted way one bloc of powers of any kind, be it Mediterranean or Western or whatever else it may be called. . . . I hold that a country that has reached our point of economic destruction and collapse cannot conduct a policy of blocs, because no matter which bloc it might join it would become someone's vassal in this bloc. . . .

For national and international reasons we reject any policy of hostility toward the Soviet Union and its peoples, and we denounce this policy as a direct cause of the worsening of our international situation. . . .

But we do not believe that Italy should conduct a policy of friendship toward the Soviet Union for ideological reasons. In general,

* De Gasperi, Christian Democrat, had been Foreign Minister since December 1944. Ed. note.

ideologies are not taken into account when it comes to foreign policy. We should conduct a policy of friendship toward the Soviet Union for national reasons and to remain faithful to a tradition of defense of our interests. . . .

We Communists are in solid agreement with all other Italian democratic parties in the struggle to obtain for our country just conditions of peace. And although as is inevitable these conditions will take into account the tragic heritage of Fascism, they should also take into account the real and effective contribution we made to the defeat of Fascism and to the common victory. . . .

And now we come to the question of [our national] unity which includes first of all the definition of our frontiers. It is not easy to go into details because many things are not yet clear. . . . We must consider as particularly serious among all others any request for the modification of our northern frontiers [Alto–Adige]. . . . As for the eastern frontiers, our position has been falsified artfully by enemies and opponents with the aim of unleashing a nationalistic campaign with which it was hoped to embarrass us. This maneuver has failed by now. We have always asserted the Italian character of Trieste; but at the same time we have asserted and do so again that the eastern frontier must be fixed in agreement with the Yugoslav people, and in any case avoid making it the object of nationalistic agitation. . . . After the First World War there were workers' movements that cut short their development and lost their struggle against reaction because they neglected the national element. One cannot deny the national element, nor can one fail to recognize that the majority of the people consider Italy's retention of Trieste a vital question for the nation. The working class cannot think of solving the question of democracy's victory nor even of socialism's victory by detaching itself from the national community. . . .

The question of unity is also strictly linked to the question of the structure of the new Italian state. . . . We are not federalists; we are against federalism; we hold that Italy should be organized politically as a unitary state with the necessary degree of centralization. This does not mean that we disregard the regions and that we do not wish to grant them their necessary autonomy. . . . But we say it clearly that our regionalism has its limits. . . . A federalist Italy would be a country in which all the local egoisms and particularisms would rise again and would end by triumphing, and thus the solution of national problems in the interest of the entire community would be obstructed. . . .

If we wish to provide solid foundations for democracy in Italy we must solve problems that are reduced essentially to three: the problem of the monarchy, that of relations with the Church, and that of the economic content of our democratic regime. . . . It is not politically possible that the monarchy survive Fascism; its complicities are too numerous and too serious. . . . If we wish to free ourselves completely of Fascism we must free ourselves of the monarchy. . . . By declaring that we are republicans we are gathering and continuing the heritage of the most noble current of the Risorgimento. . . . To those who ask us for the sake of political clarity what kind of republic we want, we answer without hesitation that we want a democratic workers' republic, we want a republic organized on the basis of a representative parliamentary system, that is, a republic that remains within the limits of democracy and in which all reforms of a social nature are realized in accordance with the democratic method. . . .

If much depends on the rapid elimination of the monarchy, much also depends on a proper definition of the relations between a democratic state and the Church. . . . It is true that the leaders of the Catholic Church at certain moments assumed a position against Fascist tyranny; but we know that at other times which, alas, were times of great importance for the life and destiny of our country, their attitude was aimed at favoring the rise and advance of Fascism and its stay in power. . . .

Inasmuch as the organization of the Church will continue to have its center in our country and inasmuch as a conflict with the Church would disturb the consciences of many citizens, we must therefore order with care our attitude with regard to the Catholic Church and the problem of religion. With regard to this matter our position is also consequentially democratic. We claim and demand that the Italian Constitution sanction freedom of conscience, of religion, of worship, and of religious propaganda and organization. . . . But in addition to this there are questions that interest the Church and that have been regulated by the Lateran Pact. As far as we are concerned the solution given the Roman question is something final; it has closed and liquidated the problem forever. But indissolubly linked to the Lateran Pact is the Concordat, and the latter is for us an instrument of an international character besides being national. We understand perfectly well that it cannot be revised except by bilateral agreement, except for violations that might lead one or the other party to denounce it. This position of ours is clear and precise. . . .

But, having specified this point, it becomes our duty to denounce any intervention by ecclesiastical authorities that may exasperate and poison the terms of the political struggle with a propaganda of the "Red devil" variety, or things of that sort. We have never been anticlericals in the pejorative sense of the term, but we do not admit that the Church become an electoral agency in a political struggle among democratic parties. . . .

When we say that we want a republican democratic regime there are many who think they can embarrass us by asking us what sort of democracy we aspire to and, especially, what reforms of an economic nature we intend to achieve. They would have people believe that we wish to achieve certain economic and social demands of ours even at the cost of democracy. But this is a petty game. In fact, not only do we affirm that we want a democratic workers' republic; not only do we demand a Constitution that guarantees freedom of speech, of the press, of conscience, of economic and political organization; but we also want that these democratic achievements be seriously guaranteed. It is precisely because of this that we struggle for the enactment of several economic reforms aiming at the destruction of reaction and Fascism. . . .

Industry must be reorganized not on the basis of an old-style parasitic principle nor on the basis of the Fascist principle of autarchy. Some branches of industry must be reduced in scope or must disappear altogether; others, and above all those that are intimately tied to agricultural development and to the needs of the domestic market, must be given a new impetus. This cannot be done without state intervention; it cannot be done without the introduction of organizational elements on the part of the democratic state in all our industrial life. The state must, therefore, take into its hands the large monopolistic industry and make effective its own control of the entire banking system.

The ends which we place before us in the countryside are the elimination of large parasitic property; a limitation of large capitalistic property in order to ease the way to forms of collective management for which in certain regions, such as the Po Valley, our workers are already particularly mature; and finally a radical reform of agricultural contracts * in order to make them more modern, more just, and more suited to the country's new situation and to the aspirations of the masses. An essential element in this program is the defense of small- and medium-sized property against the greed of large-landed proprietors, of the banks, of the usurers, and of the fisc. . . .

All of our policy aims at a close collaboration with all democratic forces. . . . We are particularly interested in three parties or groups of parties with regard to the definition of a tactic toward them: the Socialist party, the Christian Democratic party, and the truly democratic parties that are neither socialist nor demochristian. We have with the Socialist party a pact of unity of action formed in 1934, which was subsequently renewed to adapt it to new needs in the struggle. This pact has already given such beneficial fruits to the working class and the Italian people that it would be criminal to think of putting it in doubt, of questioning it, of limiting its import. It is evident to us that the pact should be developed in the sense of arriving at the formation of a single workingmen's party. (*Most lively applause.*) We shall discuss in this congress the ways toward a possible concrete realization of this new unity. We do not, however, have the slightest intention of creating difficulties or of prompting dangerous discussions within the bosom of the Socialist party. We consider the Socialist party as a fraternal party; we consider its unity and its solidity as a bulwark of Italian democracy. (*Applause.*). . . .

As for Christian Democracy, we have conducted toward it a policy defined in a coherent manner, offering to collaborate with it on the political as well as on the trade-union plane. We wish to continue this policy, but it is not easy. Speaking of the relations between our party and the Socialist party, friend De Gasperi asked in a polemic with me if we and the Socialist party were one in two or two in one. The answer was easy to give. It seems to me more difficult to answer the question whether the Christian Democractic party is one or two. (*Applause.*) The other day I was speaking with a political leader of note who said to me that the trouble with the Christian Democratic party consists in being like a bat: one does not know whether it is a bird or

* Tenancy, sharecropping, and similar agreements. Ed. note.

a mouse. In fact, there are in this party two contrasting souls. On the one hand we read resolutions from directing organs where we find notions and proposals that go in the same direction as we do, and as do the Socialist party and other democratic forces. We know that these proposals correspond to the democratic will for renewal that prevails among a large part of the members of Christian Democracy. But on the other hand it is clear—and we have reached this conclusion also because of experiences in the government—that it is difficult to reach concrete agreement with Christian Democratic leaders for the realization of these common objectives. It is even more difficult to obtain from this party proof of a real push in the struggle against Fascism and for democracy. . . .

As for the sincerely democratic forces that belong neither to the Socialist party nor to Christian Democracy, that is, the Action party, the Labor Democrats, and the left wing of the Liberal party . . . , I believe that the request to be made of them is that they advance more boldly on the field of political battle. There is room for these parties in Italy, not in the sense that they should put themselves to the task of drawing the working class from what are its traditional parties, but in the sense that they unite to form a great bloc of democratic forces belonging to all social groups and with which the working class may collaborate for a long period of time. . . .

The task of building a new Italy was entrusted to a Constituent Assembly elected on June 2, 1946. This was the first free expression of the whole Italian nation since the advent of the Fascist dictatorship, with the voters being asked to choose the men who would write a new Constitution and also answer the question of whether Italy was to remain a monarchy or become a republic. The referendum on the monarchy produced a margin in favor of the republic, 12,717,923 to 10,719,284, with 1,498,136 other votes declared invalid. The division of the country in two was apparent geographically as well as numerically. The monarchy gained a majority in none of the northern provinces but carried all the provinces from the area around Rome to the south, including Sicily and Sardinia. The vote for the Constituent Assembly shows the following results: Christian Democrats, 207 seats and 35.2 per cent of the vote; Socialists (PSIUP), 115 seats and 20.7 per cent of the vote; Communists, 104 seats and 19.0 per cent of the vote; Liberals, 41 seats and 6.8 per cent of the vote; Common Man's Movement (UQ), 30 seats and 5.3 per cent of the vote; Republicans, 23 seats and 4.4 per cent of the vote; National Monarchists (PNM), 16 seats and 2.8 per cent of the vote.

On May 19, 1946, less than two weeks before the referendum, Victor Emmanuel III had formally abdicated in favor of his son, Umberto, who pledged to accept the verdict of the referendum. But after the preliminary results were made known Umberto raised questions about the transfer of his powers prior to the final certification of the results by the Supreme Court of Cassation (Appeals), and on June 13 he left Italy without a formal abdication and without acknowledging the results of the referendum. The results were confirmed with minor modifications by the Court on June 18, and at the end of the month the Constituent Assembly elected Enrico De Nicola Provisional Head of the Italian Republic.

As leader of the largest party in the Assembly, De Gasperi was asked to form a new cabinet, in which he included representatives of his own party and of the Socialist, Communist, and Republican parties, but not the Liberals, who refused to enter the cabinet because they considered the outcome of the referendum doubtful. The Action party had disappeared from the political scene, its amorphous nature leading its members to satisfy their preferences by joining the Socialist, Communist, or Republican parties. Bonomi's Labor Democrats also disintegrated. There was no question of including the Monarchist party in the government, nor was much thought given to the new formation called *Uomo Qualunque* (Common Man's Movement), conservative in tendencies, but popularist in language, and opposed to the excesses of the armed partisans' "purification" of Fascist elements in the country.

De Gasperi's second cabinet was torn apart by disagreements between the Christian Democrats and the Socialist-Communist bloc, whose "unity of action" was confirmed in a pact signed on October 27, 1946. The text of this pact is translated below.

93. THE UNITY OF ACTION PACT BETWEEN THE SOCIALIST AND COMMUNIST PARTIES, OCTOBER 27, 1946

Reported in the *Nuovo Corriere della Sera*, Milan, October 27, 1946, n. 147. Our translation.

The Italian Socialist Party of Proletarian Unity and the Italian Communist Party, expounders of the unitarian aspirations and the interests of the working classes—determined to achieve the concentration of all popular forces in the struggle against the conservative reactionary forces and for the conquest of power on the part of the working classes; convinced that the workers will not be able to reach their fundamental objectives and perform their function as leaders and renewers of Italy's political and social life without the concentration and unification of the efforts of the two parties—do now hereby agree in full independence and autonomy on the need to specify and strengthen the unity of action pact already in existence between the two parties.*

The objectives in the unity of action pact are:

1) liquidation of all the residues of Fascism and of any attempt at resurrecting the old regime;

2) defense and consolidation of the democratic Republic and of public freedoms;

3) industrial reform based on the realization of an organic plan of industrial reconstruction and renewal; nationalization of monopolistic industries, of large banks, and of public services; the creation of workers' management councils;

4) agrarian reform based on the liquidation of the *latifundia* and large landed estates, with an increase of cooperatives in the production and processing of agricultural goods; improvement in agricultural contracts †; aid to be given to all forms of small private holdings [*coltivazione diretta*];

5) improvement of the standard of living of those who work with their brawn or brain, by means of a defense of wages, salaries, pensions, and welfare allowances, and by their adjustment to the cost of living and to improvement in the actual and general economic conditions of the country;

6) defense of the worker's human personality and dignity by means of social legislation that guarantees work to all and assures them the indispensable minimum for life, for housing, schools, medical services, and insurance against sickness, accidents, and old age;

7) defense of the value of workers' real wages and of pensions and small incomes by the defense of the currency, to be achieved by rigorous taxation of the income of the affluent classes, by extraordinary taxes on property, by reform of the tax structure, and by increases in the entire productive activity of the nation;

8) peace, with a foreign policy which—by allowing us to reacquire as quickly as possible the political and economic independence of the

---

* Unity of action pacts had been signed by the two parties in 1934, 1943, and 1945. Ed. note.

† Tenancy, sharecropping, and similar agreements. Ed. note.

country, that is, the freedom to produce, trade, and emigrate—is based on the principle of international organization of collective security, and on the principle of solidarity among all peoples and among workers' and democratic associations of all countries.

In order to achieve these objectives the unity of action pact aims at the democratic conquest of the majority of the votes and at the closest collaboration of the two parties with all other democratic forces.

94. DE GASPERI VS. TOGLIATTI

The unity of action pact was followed by renewed charges from Communists and Socialists that Italy's foreign and domestic policies were insufficiently independent of Vatican and American influences. De Gasperi replied to these charges during a speech in Rome a week before the city's municipal elections. This speech, excerpts from which are reproduced below, is especially significant as an indication of De Gasperi's relations with his Communist and Socialist colleagues in the cabinet. It is also of interest for the personal data it reveals regarding both De Gasperi and Togliatti.

De Gasperi's Speech in Rome, November 3, 1946

Alcide De Gasperi, *Discorsi politici*, 2 vols., Tommaso Bozza, ed. Rome: Edizioni Cinque Lune, 1956, I, 109–19, *passim*. Our translation.

A leaflet published by the Communists says: Do not take orders from Vatican State, it too is a foreign state. Signed: Italian Communist Party. The most interesting part of this manifesto is the "it too." It says also: "When De Gasperi goes to the Vatican to get his orders, he takes orders from a foreign power." . . . .

Yes, Hon. Togliatti, the Vatican is a foreign city, but it is also the city of Raphael and Michelangelo, the greatest geniuses of Italian art. . . . Yes, but it has also the remains of the Fisherman of Galilee. . . . Yes, but this foreign city lodges the Vicar of Christ, Bishop of Rome. Remember that in past and present history, in the most critical moments the Bishop of Rome extended his hand of protection over the city; it was because of him that Rome was saved in the war; and it was because of his generous direction and charity that thousands of political refugees of all faiths and political parties found refuge and protection in monasteries and convents.

No, dear friend Togliatti, between you and me there is a great difference. You were an emigré in Russia and there you became one of the heads, one of the Secretaries General of the Comintern. I do not mean this to be in any way a reproach. I say that he had the opportunity to serve his political convictions, to receive and give political orders that concerned not only Italy but the whole world. I on the other hand was a poor devil reduced to penury after prison and given refuge among some old books in the Vatican Library. I neither received nor was given any political appointment, no political responsibility by him, who, in any case, had none to give me because this foreign city, this foreign state that is compared to the other [Russia?] has neither artillery nor ships nor fortresses nor bombs nor any diplomatic agreement to divide up the world. And while he had the opportunity to perform his propaganda and organizational efforts throughout all of Europe, I had to seek refuge among ancient books to free at least my spirit from the then prevailing tyranny. And so, finding refuge among these books I found a wealth of documentary evidence of the history of Italy, of the Latin world whose history became joined and fused with the history of Christian civilization. . . . I felt then and feel again today, through Christian interpretation, that which ancient Greeks and Romans before and after Cicero felt: that governing a state creates an intimate tie with God our Father and that governing a state creates a responsibility which is immediate toward the people, but toward a people seen as a mediator of the divine will that governs us.

This my friends is my tie with the Vatican. It is a tie not of political instructions; it is a tie of intimate thoughts; it is a tie that illuminates our conscience. We have need of no orders whatsoever from the Vatican. It is our conscience which, illuminated by the religious faith that has its headquarters in the Vatican, leads us to the defense of Christian traditions and Italian civilization. . . .

There has been injected in this political campaign also a pact of action between Socialists and Communists. . . . In the manifesto outlining the basic points of this pact it is said that the Socialists and the Communists unite for the "conquest of power." This is their right, but I find both the pact and the proclamation of the conquest to be a little premature. It was not necessary to do this just now, when political elections are still quite distant, when on the contrary the pact may disturb [political] collaboration at an extraordinarily serious moment, when we have need of solidarity, harmony, and collaboration to save the economy of the country and meet the vital needs of our people.

Mind you, I do not mean to say that this pact may disturb the collaboration of the members of the government. There are good Communist and Socialist Ministers who try to do their best and Christian Democrats who do still better. . . . But as an anticipated mortgage on the future, this pact has the effect of influencing the press of the parties in the government, and this press behaves in such a manner so as not to compromise itself with this cabinet, for which it has almost always criticisms and warnings and never or rarely a favorable comment. We may well be unanimous in the Council of Ministers, but this does not count: the government is always wrong and the Prime Minister is always the target. . . .

The pact means that we are faced with a Marxist bloc, and it is to this bloc that we must reply as follows: We hold and we have always held that the Marxist approach leads inevitably to collectivism, that is, to an excessive intervention of public organs in private activity. We believe that in politics it leads inevitably to dictatorship and therefore to the denial of democracy. And for these reasons we shall not accept Marxism and we shall fight it.

Many of our followers felt closer to the Socialists because they hoped and expected of the Socialists a greater and more realistic gradualism and a sense of the dangers of dictatorship. . . .

It is not that I fail to acknowledge to the Communist party the positive contribution it made to the solution of several of our country's problems. I also acknowledge that after the war—in which it participated effectively—it did make an effort to become a part of the democratic structure of the state. But it seems to me wrong that it should claim to be the synthesis-party in Italy, the directing party par excellence concentrating in itself the controlling representation of the ideas and interests of the Italian people. The Communist party lacks something basic: because of its doctrines it is a party that has cut the umbilical cord that ties us of the 1945–46 generation to the other generations of Italian and Christian civilization. It is for this reason that, although we may be able to collaborate usefully with the Communist party in the tasks of the day, we cannot entrust it, by means of a ballot, with everything, with the representation of the Italian people, body and soul.

And yet the pact of unity aims at this end, and from his point of view Togliatti deserves my congratulations because he has succeeded in his task with much patience and skill. But he is an acute man, and he cannot think that we have failed to understand the purposes of the bloc. The battle [of the general elections] is still quite distant, but it is best to say immediately that we shall not lend ourselves to a policy which after it is prepared, condensed, and formulated according to the pact is then placed before us so as to say: Eat this soup or jump out of the window [*mangia questa minestra o salta dalla finestra:* take it or leave it]. We shall not eat this soup!

95. SARAGAT'S SECESSION FROM THE SOCIALIST PARTY

Togliatti's success in tying the Socialists to the Communists was too complete; it smacked too much of subservience by the former to the latter. The result was a schism in Socialist ranks. At the Socialist party congress held early in January 1947 a faction led by Giuseppe Saragat, a socialist in the tradition of Filippo Turati and President of the Constituent Assembly, formally seceded and formed the Italian Workers' Socialist Party in opposition to the pro-Communist "fusionist" tendencies of Nenni's majority faction. The break in his party led to Nenni's resignation as Minister of Foreign Affairs, a post he had held briefly since October 1946. And although several members of his party were included in De Gasperi's third cabinet, formed early in February, their stay was to be brief and lasted only until May 1947, when they and their Communist colleagues were excluded from De Gasperi's fourth cabinet. The Communists never returned to the Italian government; Nenni's Socialists made their return only as late as December 1963; but Saragat's Socialists were admitted as early as December 1947, and since then have remained in most subsequent cabinets as a permanent feature of the kind of government De Gasperi conceived to be most fruitful for postwar democratic Italy—a coalition of Center parties committed to reforms within the limits of orderly constitutional government.

The reasons for Saragat's secession from Nenni's party and for his eventual willingness to accept De Gasperi's approach are stated or implied in the following speech.

Saragat's Speech at the Palazzo Barberini, Rome,
January 12, 1947

Reported in *L'Umanità* of January 19, 1947; reproduced in Piero Malvestiti, *I socialdemocratici.* Rome: Edizioni Cinque Lune, n.d., pp. 103–
18, *passim.* Our translation.

What was our situation in the fusionist * party? Two years ago we
saw rise in Italy a wave of hopes leading men and women of our
country toward the socialist idea. Large masses of people looked toward us; but alas this movement toward socialism—which, if it had
been supported and organized would have created the possibility of
a satisfactory solution of the great problems of the nation—went
aground on the sands of the fusionist party. And thus we have come
to the present situation in which the currents that serve the socialist
ideal with the greatest fervor found themselves strangers in their own
house. There were only two solutions: either give up fighting for the
idea that is dear to us or do what we have done. . . .

Comrade Calosso has well said that those who think that our movement may in one way or another become oriented toward a form of
anticommunist struggle deceive themselves. Whatever may be the
radical differences that separate us from the Communists, we know
that in Italy the Communist party represents large sectors of the working class. One of the profound reasons for the rebirth of our movement is precisely this: the possibility of bringing the word of true socialism to the heart of the working class without being necessarily
constrained to claim this right by means of a polemic that could expose itself to the charge of anticommunism. Within the bosom of the
fusionist party we were constrained to fighting for its autonomy [from
the Communist party], and in fighting for its autonomy we had to put
the emphasis on the elements which characterized us, thus exposing
our flank to demagogic speculation on the part of those whose interest
it was to isolate us from the working class. . . .

* Saragat's way of characterizing the pro-Communist or fusionist-led party from
which he and 43 others had seceded to form the Italian Workers' Socialist Party
(PSLI). Ed. note.

Comrades, what is the ideological disagreement that separates us from the Communists? And above all, comrades, what is democracy? Democracy is nothing other than the fervid and continuous participation of a whole people in political life. It is the same thing within a party. Democracy is the participation of all comrades in the life of the party. The difference between us and the Communists is this: while the Communist comrades have their militants participate in the internal affairs of their party with regard to all that refers to organization—and on this level we must acknowledge that they are truly admirable—they on the other hand exclude them from the formulation of the general lines of policy, which are always dictated from the top. . . . We understand democracy to mean the participation of all militants not only in the organization of the party but also in the elaboration of the fundamental policies that guide the common action. . . .

Certainly, [proletarian] unity is a thing sacred to all socialist hearts, but of what unity are we speaking? If this unity is the result of the confluence of all unities, we shall welcome it with fraternal impetus. But if this unity is to be realized on the basis of the destruction of democratic principles, we shall reject it. One of the essential purposes of our party is the creation of the premises for the true unity of the working classes. This unity cannot be achieved except on a democratic plane where all currents may harmonize with each other in a fertile collaboration.

Never has there been a more radical reversal of traditional socialist concepts [than has occurred in communist countries]. Never has there been a more radical denial of those principles on which our ideals rest. The notion of the means has overwhelmed that of the ends. Class struggle as instrument for the overthrow of capitalism and for the establishment of a free and associative society is in fact resolved into a struggle for the establishment of omnipotent states. Capitalism dies but socialism is not born. Adoration of the state is born, totalitarianism is born, social coercion is born, but not social freedom. And the curve of evolution tends to give to these new organizations not a temporary character but rather a definitive one in which are aggravated all the aspects of conformism, and the elements of true socialism that they do contain vanish ever more. The separation between the bureaucracy and the people becomes aggravated, and limitations on the human personality become exasperated. . . .

What have we seen in our country in the course of the last quarter of a century? We have seen that always when the proletariat has linked to itself the workers of the middle classes by means of a truly democratic policy, there has been progress; and it is precisely when the proletariat has rebuffed them that there have been catastrophes. Fascism was born of this laceration of the workingmen's forces and of the consequent polarization of the middle class around monopolistic capitalism. . . .

It is objected that if the party were to accept into its ranks nonproletarian forces it would lose its character as a class party, it would lose its reason for existing, and above all would become the center of an anticommunist action. I have already replied to the first part of the objection; as for the second part I say that if I do not intend to treat the problem of relations with the Communist party it is because only our Directing Committee can do so. I do, however, have the duty of addressing a fraternal appeal to the Communist comrades inviting them, in their own interest, not to allow themselves to be deceived by ghosts that do not exist. The party that comes into being today is a party that calls together on a democratic plane all the Italian working classes. The Communist party entertains the same end. Very well, there will be a contest of emulation between us. We shall meet in the factories, in the fields, and in the offices; each of us will expound its beliefs and its program before the conscience of the workers; and I am sure that it is in the interest of democracy that such a comparison of experiences, doctrines, and programs take place in an atmosphere of serenity. . . .

On February 10, 1947, soon after the formation of De Gasperi's third cabinet, Italy signed the Peace Treaty of Paris. Under pressure from the Soviet Union, Italy was obliged to cede Fiume, Zara, Pola, and most of the rest of Venezia Giulia to Yugoslavia; Trieste and its hinterland were constituted into a Free Territory under United Nations' auspices; Briga and Tenda were ceded to France and the Dodecanese Islands to Greece. All of Italy's African colonies were entrusted to the Allies for eventual disposition; Italy was largely disarmed and had to pay reparations to the three major Allied powers and to Yugoslavia, Albania, Greece, and Ethiopia. Russia received $100 million and the four smaller powers a total of $260 million, but the United States and England renounced their share of reparations. After the

Italian Constituent Assembly ratified the Peace Treaty in July 1947, the United States and England proposed Italy's admission to the United Nations, but the proposal was vetoed by the Soviet Union and continued to be vetoed until December 1955.

The Western Allies' benevolence toward De Gasperi's policies, reciprocated by the latter's manifest pro-Western preferences, prompted much dissension between the Christian Democratic and Socialist-Communist members of De Gasperi's third cabinet. This dissension led to the cabinet's fall in May 1947 and to De Gasperi's exclusion of Socialists and Communists from the one that followed. During the second half of 1947, while the Constituent Assembly continued to write the Constitution, the contrasts between De Gasperi's fourth cabinet—formed exclusively by Christian Democrats and some Independents—and the Socialist-Communist opposition were accentuated by a debate over Italy's participation in the Marshall Plan for European economic recovery. The Communists and their Socialist allies followed the decision reached by a congress of European Communist parties at Bialystok, Poland, opposing participation in the Marshall Plan. The other major Italian parties favored the Plan. The Communist-dominated General Confederation of Labor staged a number of political strikes, culminating in a general strike in December 1947. Under these circumstances and in the light of the fact that the embattled De Gasperi had received support from Monarchists, the Common Man's Movement (*Uomo Qualunque*), and even from the Neo-Fascist Italian Social Movement founded in December 1946, Saragat for the PSLI and Pacciardi for the Republicans decided to take their parties into De Gasperi's fourth cabinet. The following manifesto explains the reasons for Saragat's and Pacciardi's decision to enter De Gasperi's cabinet as Deputy Prime Ministers.

96. MANIFESTO OF THE SARAGAT SOCIALISTS (PSLI) UPON THEIR ENTRY IN THE GOVERNMENT, DECEMBER 15, 1947

Reported in *L'Umanità* of December 16, 1947; reproduced in Piero Malvestiti, *I socialdemocratici*. Rome: Edizioni Cinque Lune, n.d., pp. 141–44. Our translation.

Workers,

The Italian Workers' Socialist Party [PSLI] enters a democratic government in order to contribute with all its energy to the economic reconstruction of the country, to the struggle against misery, to the defense of public freedoms, and to the safeguarding of peace.

The Republican party has reached the same decision. The presence of our two movements in the Ministry, while it avoids the danger latent in the preceding government of a slide toward forces of political and social reaction, also determines a new situation in our country. This new situation breaks with the uncertainties that troubled the recent period of our national life and opens to the working classes sure prospects of a better future.

If the great hopes that animated the working class during the period that saw the dawn of freedom for the fatherland have not been realized, this is due not only to the stubborn resistance of the forces of social privilege, not only to the objective difficulties deriving from the immense economic and moral ruin brought about by the Fascist dictatorship and the war, but to the errors of some of the parties that have as their task the safeguarding of the interests of the poorest part of the Italian people.

The forces of social privilege, principally responsible for the dictatorship and the war, were not faced by parties determined to apply against them the just sanction of a profound reform of one of the structures of the country. Consequently, these forces not only have regained their supremacy in the economic field but, according to more than one sign, have attempted and still attempt to give new life to movements of a Fascist or monarchist character designed to assure them dominion in the political field as well. . . .

Above all during these latter months, the errors of some parties of the Left have seriously jeopardized the situation and have endangered the immediate future of the working class.

In a world dominated by the Russo-American antagonism which threatens to break the family of peoples in two, Italy's supreme interest is to preserve a most rigorous autonomy with regard to the two contrasting blocs, although not renouncing those economic aids that America is in a position to make available to us and which are indispensable to our renaissance. By giving its active support to one of the rival blocs and by adopting the theses of a great continental power, the Communist party has put itself in a most difficult situation with regard to effective collaboration in the reconstruction of the country. This reconstruction presupposes our autonomy with regard to all and friendship with all. Hence the absurdity of the Communist party's policy which, by closing its eyes in the face of the most obvious needs of the working classes and by subordinating them to ideological preoccupations of an extra-national origin, threatens to obstruct the economic assistance coming from the West without being in a position of assuring us in the least corresponding assistance from the East.

The paralysis in which the Communist party has willingly placed itself constitutes not only a dead weight among the forces of the Left but, because of a misconstrued sentiment of class solidarity, also immobilizes those forces that place themselves under its lordship. This is particularly the case of the PSI [Italian Socialist Party].* Under the influence of an apparatus largely controlled by Communist infiltrations both at the base and at the summit,† which suffocates the will to autonomy on the part of the majority of its followers, this party condemns itself to the most absolute sterility. For the constructive action which socialism must perform every day, it substitutes the fallacious mirage of an already too much compromised victory in the coming elections.

Conscious of this situation, and after vain attempts to bring the Communists back to reality, our party has oriented its efforts to freeing as many as possible of those who still serve in the ranks of the PSI from the paralysis to which they are condemned. . . .

With the PSI installing itself in this state of paralysis under the pseudo-revolutionary but essentially electoral mask of the popular fronts, the only active and autonomous forces remaining at the Left are our party and the Republicans. In consequence, it is incumbent on us to accept the weight of the most grave decisions. The absence of the Communist party and of the PSI produced a situation of unstable equilibrium in the governmental policy dominated by the Christian Democratic party; and so only our party and the Republicans were left with the possibility of preventing a definitive landslide to the right of the country's entire political system.

The recent Christian Democratic congress offered, by the efforts of the left wing of that party, the important indication that a useful attempt could be made to foreclose the way to the forces of social conservatism and to give a new orientation to the country's policies.

This attempt was made today and it becomes concrete by our par-

* Nenni's party dropped the words "Proletarian Unity" from its title after Saragat's secession and became simply the Italian Socialist Party (PSI). Ed. note.
† There were persistent rumors that much of Nenni's party's finances came from the more affluent Communist party. Ed. note.

ticipation in a new government in fraternal agreement with our Republican friends.

On December 22, a week after Saragat and Pacciardi entered the government, the Constituent Assembly approved Italy's republican Constitution by a vote of 453 to 62. Five days later it was signed by De Nicola who thereby became the first President of the Italian Republic. The Constitution went into effect on January 1, 1948; thus Italy, sovereign once again after the ratification of the Peace Treaty and now provided with a new instrument of government, could continue on firmer ground the reconstruction of its political and economic life. Basic in this reconstruction was the continuation of De Gasperi's formula of collaboration with all "sincerely democratic" parties.

XXVI. THE ERA OF DE GASPERI: FIVE YEARS OF DEMOCRATIC CENTER GOVERNMENTS, 1948–1953

The test of De Gasperi's conviction that Italy's political and economic reconstruction could best be achieved by a policy of collaboration among all "sincerely democratic" parties came after the elections of April 18, 1948. These elections were conducted under the provisions of the new Constitution and resulted in an absolute Christian Democratic majority in the Chamber of Deputies and a plurality in the Senate. Two hundred thirty-seven Senators were elected and 96 were eventually appointed for special merits, the Christian Democrats gaining 131 of the elected seats and 15 of the appointive ones. Possession of a majority of the Senate's elected seats and a substantial majority of 304 of the 574 seats in the Chamber of Deputies could have made it possible for De Gasperi to form an essentially one-party government. But consistent with his principle of collaboration with the parties of the democratic Center and aware that his own party was not thoroughly homogeneous and therefore prone to factionalism, De Gasperi chose instead to include representatives of Saragat's Italian Workers' Socialist Party, of the Republicans, and of the Liberals. Although not always successful in securing the active collaboration of all three "lay" democratic parties, he never abandoned his policy of "centrism" except for his brief and last cabinet in the summer of 1953. This policy remained dominant even after De Gasperi's death in 1954 and was modified either to the right or to the left only by the end of the decade and the early 1960s.

To understand the nature of De Gasperi's centrism and the outcome of the April 18 elections it is necessary to have some knowledge of the Constitution approved in December 1947. Accordingly, there are below a number of excerpts from the Constitution, with emphasis on its unusual features or those aspects of particular relevance to the Italian scene.

97. THE CONSTITUTION OF THE ITALIAN REPUBLIC

Reproduced in *Ten Years of Italian Democracy, 1946–1956.* Rome: Presidency of the Council of Ministers, Information Office, Documentation Centre, 1956, pp. 5–34, *passim.*

BASIC PRINCIPLES

Article 1. Italy is a democratic Republic based on work.

Sovereignty belongs to the people who exercise it in the manner and within the limits of the Constitution.

Art. 2. The Republic recognizes and guarantees the inviolable rights of man, both as an individual and in the social groups in which his personality finds expression, and imposes the performance of unalterable duties of political, economic, and social solidarity.

Art. 3. All citizens are invested with equal social dignity and are equal before the law, without distinction of sex, race, language, religion, political opinions, and personal or social conditions.

It is the task of the Republic to remove all obstacles of an economic and social nature which, by limiting the freedom and equality of citizens, prevent the full development of human personality, and the participation of all workers in the political, economic, and social organization of the country.

Art. 4. The Republic recognizes the right of all citizens to work, and promotes such conditions as will make this right effective. . . .

Art. 5. The Republic, which is one and indivisible, recognizes and promotes local autonomies; in the services dependent on the State it applies the fullest measure of administrative decentralization and adjusts the principles and methods of its legislation to the requirements of autonomy and decentralization.

Art. 6. The Republic safeguards linguistic minorities by means of special provisions.

Art. 7. The State and the Catholic Church are, each within its own ambit, independent and sovereign.

Their relations are regulated by the Lateran Pacts. Such amendments to these Pacts as are accepted by both parties do not require any procedure of Constitutional revision.

Art. 8. All religious denominations are equally free before the law.

Religious denominations other than the Catholic are entitled to organize themselves according to their own creed provided that they are not in conflict with Italian juridical organization.

Their relations with the State are regulated by law on the basis of agreements with their respective representatives. . . .

Art. 11. Italy condemns war as an instrument of aggression against the liberties of other peoples and as a means for settling international controversies; it agrees, in conditions of equality with other States, to such limitation of sovereignty as may be necessary for a system calculated to ensure peace and justice between Nations; it promotes and encourages international organizations having such ends in view. . . .

[SPECIFIC PROVISIONS]

Article 27. . . . The death penalty is not admitted, save in cases provided for by military laws in time of war. . . .

Art. 29. The State recognizes the family as a natural association founded on marriage.

Marriage is based on the moral and legal equality of husband and wife, within the limits laid down by the laws for ensuring family unity.

Art. 30. It is the duty and right of parents to support, instruct, and educate their children, even those born out of wedlock.

Should the parents prove incapable, the law states the way in which these duties shall be fulfilled.

The law ensures for children born out of wedlock full legal and social protection, consistent with the rights of the members of the legitimate family. . . .

Art. 33. . . . The Republic lays down general rules for education and establishes State schools of all kinds and grades.

Organizations and private citizens are entitled to create schools and educational institutions, which do not involve charges on the State.

Art. 34. Schools are open to all.

Elementary education, imparted for at least eight years, is compulsory and free.

Capable and deserving pupils, even if without financial resources, are entitled to attain the highest grades of study. . . .

Art. 36. The worker is entitled to wages in proportion to the quantity and quality of his work, and in any case sufficient to provide him and his family with a free and dignified existence. . . .

Art. 37. Women workers enjoy the same rights at the same wages for the same work as males. . . .

The Republic prescribes special measures for safeguarding the labour of minors, and guarantees them equal pay for equal work.

Art. 38. Every citizen unable to work and unprovided with the resources necessary for existence is entitled to maintenance and social assistance. . . .

Art. 39. The freedom of the organization of trades unions is affirmed.

No compulsion may be imposed on trades unions except that of registering at the local or central offices according to the provisions of the law.

A condition of registration is that the statutes of the unions sanction an internal organization on a democratic basis.

Registered trades unions have a legal personality. They may, being represented in proportion to the number of their registered members, negotiate collective labour contracts having compulsory value for all persons belonging to the categories to which the contracts refer.

Art. 40. The right to strike is exercised within the sphere of the laws regulating the subject.

Art. 41. Private economic enterprise is free.

It cannot, however, be applied in such a manner as to be in conflict with social utility or so as to prove prejudicial to security, freedom and human dignity. . . .

Art. 42. . . . Private property is recognized and guaranteed by laws which prescribe the manner in which it may be acquired and enjoyed and its limitations, with the object of ensuring its social function and of rendering it accessible to all.

Private property, in such cases as are prescribed by law and with provisions for compensation, may be expropriated in the general interest. . . .

Art. 43. For purposes of general utility the law may reserve in the first instance or transfer, by means of expropriation and payment of compensation, to the State, to public bodies or to communities of workers or consumers, certain undertakings or categories or undertakings operating essential public services, sources of power or exercising monopolies and invested primarily with a character of general interest.

Art. 44. With the object of securing a rational utilization of the soil and of establishing equitable and rational social relations, the law imposes obligations and limitations to private landed ownership, fixes limits to its extent which vary in the different parts of the country and according to the different agricultural areas. . . .

Art. 46. With a view to the economic and social progress of labour and in conformity with the requirements of production, the Republic recognizes the rights of workers to collaborate in the management of businesses in the manner and within the limits prescribed by law. . . .

Art. 48. All citizens, male or female, who are of age [twenty-one] are entitled to vote. . . .

Art. 52. The defense of the country is the sacred duty of the citizen. Military service is compulsory. . . .

Art. 53. All are called upon to contribute to public expenditure in proportion to their resources.

The system of taxation is graded. . . .

Art. 55. Parliament consists of the Chamber of Deputies and the Senate of the Republic. . . .

Art. 56. The Chamber of Deputies is elected by direct universal suffrage, with one Deputy for every 80,000 inhabitants or fraction of more than 40,000.

All voters who are twenty-five years of age on the day of election may be elected Deputies.

Art. 57. The Senate of the Republic is elected on a regional basis.

Each Region is entitled to one Senator for every 200,000 inhabitants or fraction of over 100,000.

No Region shall have less than six Senators. The Valle d'Aosta has only one Senator.

Art. 58. Senators are elected by direct universal suffrage by voters over twenty-five years of age.

Voters over forty years of age are eligible for the Senate. . . .

Art. 60. The Chamber of Deputies is elected for five years, the Senate of the Republic for six. . . .

Art. 70. Legislative duties are carried out jointly by the two Chambers.

Art. 71. Legislative initiative pertains to the Government, to each member of the two Chambers, and to those organs and bodies on whom it is conferred by Constitutional law.

The people exercise initiative in legislation through a proposal, backed by not less than 50,000 voters, of a bill drafted in the form of articles. . . .

Art. 75. A popular referendum is held to decide on the total or partial repeal of a law or of a measure having legal validity if it is demanded by 500,000 voters or by five Regional Councils.

Referenda are not allowed in the case of fiscal or budget laws, amnesties or pardons, or laws authorizing the ratification of international treaties. . . .

Art. 83. The President of the Republic is elected by Parliament in a joint session of both Chambers. . . .

The Presidential election takes place by secret ballot with a majority of two thirds of the Assembly. After the third ballot an absolute majority is sufficient.

Art. 84. Any citizen of fifty years of age enjoying civil and political rights is eligible for the Presidency of the Republic. . . .

Art. 85. The Presidential term is for seven years. . . .

Art. 86. Should the President prove unable to fulfil his duties, these will be carried out by the President of the Senate.

In case of permanent incapacity or death or resignation of the President of the Republic the President of the Chamber of Deputies provides for the election of a new President of the Republic within fifteen days. . . .

Art. 87. The President of the Republic is the Head of the State and represents the unity of the Nation. . . .

Art. 89. No act of the President is legal unless it is countersigned by the Ministers who have submitted it and are responsible for it.

Measures having the value of law and such others as are laid down by law shall also be countersigned by the President of the Council of Ministers [Prime Minister]. . . .

Art. 92. The Government of the Republic consists of the President of the Council of Ministers and of the Ministers jointly constituting the Council of Ministers [Cabinet].

The President of the Republic appoints the Prime Minister and, following the proposals of the latter, the Ministers. . . .

Art. 94. The Government must enjoy the confidence of the two Chambers.

Each Chamber grants or refuses its confidence by a motion in which it gives its reasons and which is voted by roll call. . . .

The hostile vote of one or of both Chambers on a Government proposal does not necessitate resignation. . . .

Art. 95. . . . Ministers are jointly responsible for the acts of the Cabinet as a whole, and individually for those of their own particular departments. . . .

Art. 101. Justice is administered in the name of the people.

The judges are subject only to the laws.

Art. 102. The duties of the judiciary are carried out by permanent magistrates appointed and governed according to the provisions of the judiciary organization.

No extraordinary or special judges may be appointed. . . .

Art. 114. The Republic is divided into Regions, Provinces, and Communes.

Art. 115. The Regions are constituted as autonomous bodies with their own powers and functions according to the principles fixed by the Constitution.

Art. 116. Particular forms and conditions of autonomy, in accordance with special statutes adopted by constitutional law, are attributed to Sicily, Sardinia, Trentino-Alto Adige, Friuli-Venetia Julia, and the Valle d'Aosta. . . .

Art. 134. The Constitutional Court decides: on controversies concerning the constitutional legitimacy of the laws and acts having the force of laws, emanating from the State and the Regions; on controversies arising over constitutional assignment of powers within the State, between the State and the Regions, and between Regions; on impeachment of the President of the Republic and the Ministers, according to the norms of the Constitution.

Art. 135. The Constitutional Court is composed of fifteen judges, a third of whom are nominated * by the President of the Republic, one third by Parliament in joint session, and one third by the supreme magistracy both permanent and administrative. . . .

Art. 136. When the [Constitutional] Court declares a norm of law, or an act having the force of law, to be unconstitutional, the norm

* Should read "appointed." Ed. note.

ceases to have effect from the day following the publication of the decision. . . .

Art. 137. . . . The decisions of the Constitutional Court may not be contested.

Art. 138. Amendments to the Constitution and other constitutional laws are passed by the Chamber of Deputies and the Senate in two successive sessions at an interval of not less than three months and are approved by an absolute majority of the members of each Chamber after a second ballot. . . .

Art. 139. The Republican form [of government] is not subject to constitutional amendment.

TRANSITORY AND FINAL PROVISIONS

XII. Reorganization of the former Fascist Party, under any form whatsoever, is prohibited.

Notwithstanding article 48, temporary limitations are established by law, for a period of not over five years from the effective date of the Constitution, on the suffrage and eligibility of the responsible heads of the Fascist regime.

XIII. The members and descendants of the House of Savoy are not electors and may not hold any public office or elective position.

Former kings of the House of Savoy, their wives and their male descendants may not enter or remain in national territory.

Property within national territory belonging to the former kings of the House of Savoy, their wives and their male descendants, reverts to the State. Transfers and the establishment of royal rights on such properties, which took place after June 2, 1946, are null and void.

XIV. Titles of nobility are not recognized.

The predicates of those existing before October 28, 1922, serve as part of the proper name.

98. THE ELECTIONS OF APRIL 18, 1948

In addition to providing for the machinery of government, the Constitution is also a document of social promises and expectations. There is no necessary contradiction between its purely political provisions and the social promises stated under the "Basic Principles" and in specific Articles dealing with economic relations. But there is a problem of realizing the social promises while always remaining loyal to the Constitution's political provisions. In a political structure that provides for majority rule but also facilitates and protects the rights and political expression of minorities, it is not always easy to achieve the social reforms foreseen by the Constitution without injuring the very minorities the Constitution seeks to protect. Furthermore, and perhaps more serious, in the event the majority were to oppose or for long delay the implementation of the Constitution's social promises, disaffected minorities could conclude that they had to choose between obedience to the Constitution's political provisions and loyalty to its social promises. Such a situation would divide not only the Constitution but the whole country in two by opposing the Constitution's social expectations to its political provisions.

De Gasperi's policy of centrism was designed to mitigate the probable contrast between the two faces of the Constitution—which faithfully reflected the two attitudes prevailing in the country—by promoting the greatest possible consensus around the government, even if it meant denying deserving Christian Democrats of Ministerial posts assigned to members of other parties. Hence the inclusion of a party of the Right but nonetheless democratic—the Liberals—and parties of the moderate Left, Saragat's Socialists and the Republicans. Centrism did not even exclude the collaboration of Nenni's Socialists and the Communists, provided these two parties proved their national loyalty and their devotion to the political as well as the social provisions of the Constitution. But in 1948 De Gasperi was convinced that these two parties did not meet the minimum requirements. It is this conviction that motivated the language of the "appeal" reproduced below, launched by the Christian Democratic party on the eve of the April 18, 1948, elections.

Appeal by the National Council of the Christian Democratic Party

Democrazia cristiana, *Orientamenti programmatici della Democrazia cristiana*, 2d ed. Rome: S.P.E.S. Centrale, D.C., 1950, pp. 79–80. Our translation.

Italians!

On April 18 you will be able to save or destroy your freedom, not only the freedom of Parliament and of democratic institutions but of all of man's elementary freedoms: the freedom to think and to express one's own ideas; the freedom to choose one's own field of work; the freedom to educate one's children according to one's own ideas; the freedom to profess the faith of one's fathers.

By now the choice is between an inhuman totalitarianism that concentrates and suffocates everything within the state, and a human conception of political life in which citizens, associations, and parties may collaborate in free competition for the achievement of the common good.

The choice is between Bolshevik totalitarianism hidden behind the mask of the so-called Popular Front, and the "array" of "sincerely democratic" parties.

The recent tragic experiences of the Eastern European countries show that wherever communism comes to power, there the mask falls and the "fronts" are broken; all parties, none excluded, are suppressed; and freedom dies.

But the affirmation of freedom is not resolved in a purely defensive position, nor does it exhaust Christian Democracy's program. We firmly believe that defense of freedom is not possible without social justice, and social justice demands the preeminence of labor.

Christian Democracy feels that its task coincides with the historical task of our times, that is, Christian Democracy must and can contribute in a decisive manner to the economic, social, and political ascent of the workers, the peasants, and the middle classes. It is to this end that Christian Democracy wishes to commit itself in the concrete realization of the innovating principles on property and economic life as sanctioned by the new Constitution.

Let no one disregard or forget that these principles have received constitutional recognition principally because of Christian Democratic initiative in strictest loyalty to the commitments assumed by the party on June 2, 1946. This loyalty is a pledge for the future, as is our work of two years in the government.

In the government's efforts, which surmounted difficulties and obstacles of all kinds, Christian Democracy was the guide to the restoration of order and the authority of the state, to the defense of the economy, and to social progress. Above all it has made a decisive contribution—which is perhaps its greatest merit and which it alone could have achieved in the present circumstances—to the reintroduction of Italy in full independence and dignity within the framework of peaceful collaboration among peoples. In this fashion it has assured particularly to the Italian working classes the advantages of international economic solidarity. . . .

Christian Democracy believes that in this fashion it is performing a work of national recovery and among other things is creating the best conditions for a revision of the peace treaty.

Italians!

Christian Democracy commits all its forces against totalitarianism, whose logic leads inevitably to war, and for the assurance to the Italian people, in a democratic manner and in the spirit of Christian civilization, of that peace which after so much grief and misery the new generations await with full right.

The Christian Democrats, and all the other parties opposed to the Popular Democratic Front of Communists and Nenni Socialists, fought the elections as a struggle between freedom and tyranny; and in this contest they had the advantage of being able to point to the fate of "sincerely democratic" Czechoslovaks who had collaborated with the Communists only to find themselves overwhelmed by a Communist *coup* in February 1948. They could also point to a statement by Togliatti in November 1946 which apparently acknowledged Communist Yugoslavia's right to Gorizia and to the fact that in March 1948 England, France, and the United States proposed the return of Trieste to Italy, only to meet Russia's refusal to consider the proposal.

The Communists and Nenni Socialists contested the election as a Popular Democratic Front with a single list of candidates and a program essentially the same as the one stated in the unity of action pact of October 1946. The Front received 31.0 per cent of the votes cast and 183 seats in the Chamber of Deputies, a sharp drop from the 39.7 per cent of the vote and 219 seats gained in the elections for the Constituent Assembly in June 1946. The Christian Democrats increased their totals from 35.2 per cent and 207 seats to 48.5 per cent and 304 seats. Saragat's PSLI and an allied group of Socialists (Unità Socialista)received 7.1 per cent of the vote and 33 seats, indicating that if they had remained loyal to the unity of action pact the Popular Democratic Front parties would have held their own in votes and seats. The Liberal party led a National Bloc coalition with the Common Man's Movement and followers of Francesco Saverio Nitti, Prime Minister in 1919, and the whole Bloc received 3.8 per cent of the vote and 19 seats, a sharp drop for all the Bloc's component parts. The National Monarchist party and various small allies received 2.8 per cent of the vote and 14 seats, registering a small decline. The Republicans declined sharply from 4.4 per cent and 23 seats to 2.5 per cent and 9 seats. The Neo-Fascist Italian Social Movement contested its first national election and gained 2.0 per cent of the vote and 6 seats. Roughly comparable results were registered in the elections for the Senate; but the eventual appointment of 96 Senators (including a number of Communists and Socialists) for meritorious service in the anti-Fascist cause and for other reasons as provided for by the Constitution gave the Christian Democrats only a plurality in the Senate.

In May 1948 Italy's first republican National Assembly proceeded to the election of the Independent Liberal Luigi Einaudi, a noted economist, as President of the Republic. Later in the month Einaudi entrusted De Gasperi with the formation of his fifth cabinet, which included representatives of his own party and of Saragat's Socialists, the Republicans, and the Liberals. The parliamentary strength of this four-party coalition was so great that the Communist-Socialist opposition shifted the center of its agitation from Parliament to the streets and factories, precipitating a general strike of forty-eight hours after an attempt on Togliatti's life on July 14, 1948. In consequence of this explicitly political action on the part of the General Confederation of Italian Labor (CGIL), the Christian Democratic elements broke away from the unitary or single national organization of Italian labor and in August formed the Free Italian General Confederation of Labor (LCGIL), subsequently renamed as the Italian Confederation of Workers' Unions (CISL). By 1950 labor elements associated with Saragat's Socialists, the Republicans, and independent groups also broke away from the CGIL and formed the Italian Labor Union (UIL).

99. THE DEBATE OVER FOREIGN POLICY

Checked in the streets by the severe methods employed by De Gasperi's Minister of the Interior, Mario Scelba, and weakened in its almost total control over organized labor, the Communist-Socialist opposition mounted a major offensive against Italy's projected participation in the North Atlantic Treaty. A marathon debate, with one sitting in the Chamber of Deputies lasting more than fifty consecutive hours on March 16–18, 1949, led to the approval of the Treaty by a vote of more than 2 to 1. Early the next month representatives of Italy and eleven other countries formally signed the Treaty in Washington.

For the sake of clarity the normal chronological order is inverted and the text of the Treaty (usually called a Pact by Italians) is presented first, to be followed by a portion of the debate preceding its ratification by the Italian Chamber.

North Atlantic Treaty, April 4, 1949

> U. S. Senate, 81st Congress, 1st Session, Doc. No. 123, *A Decade of American Foreign Policy: Basic Documents, 1941–1949.* Washington, D.C.: U. S. Government Printing Office, 1950, pp. 1328–30.

The Parties to this Treaty reaffirm their faith in the purposes and principles of the Charter of the United Nations and their desire to live in peace with all peoples and all governments.

They are determined to safeguard the freedom, common heritage and civilization of their peoples, founded on the principles of democracy, individual liberty and the rule of law.

They seek to promote stability and well-being in the North Atlantic area.

They are resolved to unite their efforts for collective defense and for the preservation of peace and security.

They therefore agree to this North Atlantic Treaty:

Article 1. The Parties undertake, as set forth in the Charter of the United Nations, to settle any international disputes in which they may be involved by peaceful means in such a manner that international peace and security, and justice, are not endangered, and to refrain in their international relations from the threat or use of force in any manner inconsistent with the purposes of the United Nations.

Article 2. The Parties will contribute toward the further development of peaceful and friendly international relations by strengthening their free institutions, by bringing about a better understanding of the principles upon which these institutions are founded, and by promoting conditions of stability and well-being. They will seek to eliminate conflict in their international economic policies and will encourage economic collaboration between any or all of them.

Article 3. In order more effectively to achieve the objectives of this Treaty, the Parties, separately and jointly, by means of continuous and effective self-help and mutual aid, will maintain and develop their individual and collective capacity to resist armed attack.

Article 4. The Parties will consult together whenever, in the opinion of any of them, the territorial integrity, political independence or security of any of the Parties is threatened.

Article 5. The Parties agree that an armed attack against one or more of them in Europe or North America shall be considered an attack against them all; and consequently they agree that, if such an armed attack occurs, each of them, in exercise of the right of individual or collective self-defense recognized by Article 51 of the Charter of the United Nations, will assist the Party or Parties so attacked by taking forthwith, individually and in concert with the other Parties, such action as it deems necessary, including the use of armed force, to restore and maintain the security of the North Atlantic area.

Any such armed attack and all measures taken as a result thereof shall immediately be reported to the Security Council. Such measures shall be terminated when the Security Council has taken the measures necessary to restore and maintain international peace and security.

Article 6. For the purpose of Article 5 an armed attack on one or more of the Parties is deemed to include an armed attack on the territory of any of the Parties in Europe or North America, on the Algerian departments of France, on the occupation forces of any Party in Europe, on the islands under the jurisdiction of any Party in the North Atlantic area north of the Tropic of Cancer or on the vessels or aircraft in this area of any of the Parties.

Article 7. This Treaty does not affect, and shall not be interpreted as affecting, in any way the rights and obligations under the Charter of the Parties which are members of the United Nations, or the primary responsibility of the Security Council for the maintenance of international peace and security.

Article 8. Each Party declares that none of the international engagements now in force between it and any other of the Parties or any third state is in conflict with the provisions of this Treaty, and undertakes not to enter into any international engagement in conflict with this Treaty.

Article 9. The Parties hereby establish a council, on which each of them shall be represented, to consider matters concerning the implementation of this Treaty. The council shall be so organized as to be able to meet promptly at any time. The council shall set up such subsidiary bodies as may be necessary; in particular it shall establish immediately a defense committee which shall recommend measures for the implementation of Articles 3 and 5.

Article 10. The Parties may, by unanimous agreement, invite any other European state in a position to further the principles of this Treaty and to contribute to the security of the North Atlantic area to accede to this Treaty. Any state so invited may become a party to the Treaty by depositing its instrument of accession with the Government of the United States of America. The Government of the United States of America will inform each of the Parties of the deposit of each such instrument of accession.

Article 11. This Treaty shall be ratified and its provisions carried out by the Parties in accordance with their respective constitutional processes. The instruments of ratification shall be deposited as soon as possible with the Government of the United States of America, which will notify all the other signatories of each deposit. The Treaty shall enter into force between the states which have ratified it as soon as the ratifications of the majority of the signatories, including the ratifications of Belgium, Canada, France, Luxembourg, the Netherlands, the United Kingdom and the United States, have been deposited and shall come into effect with respect to other states on the date of the deposit of their ratifications.

Article 12. After the Treaty has been in force for ten years, or at any time thereafter, the Parties shall, if any of them so requests, consult together for the purpose of reviewing the Treaty, having regard for the factors then affecting peace and security in the North Atlantic area, including the development of universal as well as regional arrangements under the Charter of the United Nations for the maintenance of international peace and security.

Article 13. After the Treaty has been in force for twenty years, any Party may cease to be a party one year after its notice of denunciation has been given to the Government of the United States of America, which will inform the Governments of the other Parties of the deposit of each notice of denunciation.

The Socialists against the Atlantic Pact: Speech by Pietro Nenni in the Chamber of Deputies, March 12, 1949

> *I deputati socialisti contro la politica di guerra: Discorsi e dichiarazioni di voto nella discussione sul patto atlantico alla Camera dei deputati,* Sedute del 12, 14, and 16–18 marzo 1949. Rome: Tipografia della Camera dei deputati, 1949, pp. 11–12, 13, 15, 16–17, 25–26, 29, *passim.* Our translation.

Gentlemen, it cannot escape either the President of the Council or his Ministers or the parliamentary majority that by signing the Pact we renounce in a definitive manner our national independence. By signing the Pact there comes into being a state of things by virtue of which if tomorrow in Asia, the Arctic zone, in Scandinavia, or in Berlin there were to arise any reason whatever for a conflict between the United States of America and the Soviet Union, we are in the conflict, we are belligerents, we are bound with America without having the

least possibility of influencing its decisions. To speak of national independence when we create a relation of subjection without precedents,
of the kind which did not exist even within the ambit of the Pact of
Steel, is an incommensurable absurdity for us who in comparison to
the United States are what the Republic of San Marino is in comparison to Europe. (*Comments from the center.*). . . .

By signing the Atlantic Pact you, gentlemen of the government, will
surrender the independence of the nation. You will make of us vassals
of other states. (*Lively applause from the left.*). . . .

The Atlantic Pact has a clearly aggressive and offensive character
with regard to the country that precisely six years ago these very days
bled itself white at Stalingrad, and in defending itself defended all
Europe, all the world! (*Most lively and prolonged applause from the
extreme left. Shouts of:* Long live Russia! Long live Stalingrad!
Shouts from the center and the right: Long live Italy! *The Deputies
from the center and the right rise to their feet; most lively and prolonged applause. Commotion and comments at the extreme left.*). . . .

I have heard it said—and the argument deserves some thought
—that a disarmed neutrality is a neutrality at the mercy of whoever
is moved to aggression or invasion. But gentlemen, if a disarmed neutrality may be of some danger to us, what must we think and say of a
disarmed aggressive policy? You are putting the country in this amazing situation, that in the very act with which you commit it to an
aggressive policy you confess that you do not have the means for it. I
do not like to raise up ghosts, but Hon. De Gasperi your case is worse
than that of Mussolini (*comments from the center*) when he signed
the "Pact of Steel". . . .

De Gasperi (*President of the Council of Ministers*): I am not an
aggressor like Mussolini! (*Lively applause from the center and the
right; rumblings at the extreme left.*)

Nenni (Pietro): Hon. De Gasperi, there will be someone who will
be an aggressor on your behalf, and you will be at his service. (*Applause from the extreme left.*). . . .

Gentlemen, in a recent speech that suffered the fate of being completely misconstrued I asked myself whether or not it is still possible
for us to follow a national policy.

(*A voice from the right:*) The Russian [national policy]. (*Comments
and interruptions from the extreme left.*)

Nenni (Pietro): In the field of foreign policy a national policy means for us freedom from political and military commitments; that is, to put it more concretely, a policy of peace and neutrality. We assert that if on the basis of such a policy of peace and neutrality it were to come to pass (as some of you think possible) that our country were the victim of aggression, the aggressor, whoever it might be, would be the enemy of our people. (*Applause from the extreme left.*)

In the field of domestic policy a national policy means an effort aimed at eliminating the poisons in the relations between the majority and the opposition, and the abandonment of the methods of reprisals being used against the partisans and workers' and peasants' unions. (*Applause from the extreme left.*). . . .

If the majority backs Italy's participation in the Atlantic Pact it knows that by doing so it aggravates both Europe's objective situation and conditions at home. If it authorizes the government to sign the Pact it knows that we shall not retreat from the opposition we have undertaken and that we shall employ all means. . . .

Giacchero [Enzo, Chr. D.]: Which? (*Comments from the extreme left.*)

Nenni (Pietro): . . . that the Constitution makes available to us. (*Comments from the center.*)

There is a way not provided for in the Constitution but one, given the exceptional nature of the case, you could use if you were moved by a desire for a relaxation of tensions. This means is the submission of the Pact to a popular referendum so that not only our voters but yours as well could say that if by giving you the parliamentary mandate they also authorized you to commit the country to an adventure of war.

If you do not do this, you will assume your responsibilities and we ours. This means that we shall wage against the Atlantic Pact the same intense struggle that Italian democrats waged against the Triple Alliance from 1882 to 1914, the same struggle we waged with some of your men against the Pact of Steel. It means that we shall do all we are able so that the signature the government may affix to the Atlantic Pact may be torn up and protested by the Italian people. (*Most lively and prolonged applause from the extreme left; many congratulations; comments from the center and the right.*)

Perhaps the most effective rebuttal to Nenni's criticism of Italian foreign policy was given not during the debate on the North Atlantic Treaty but in October 1949 when Foreign Minister Carlo Sforza replied to another critical speech by Nenni.

Sforza Defends Italy's Policy of European and Atlantic Solidarity: Speech before the Chamber of Deputies, October 25, 1949

> Carlo Sforza, *Le direttive della politica estera italiana.* Rome: Tipografia del Ministero degli affari esteri, n.d., pp. 18–20, 26, 28–30, *passim.* Our translation.

I now come to the principal opposition speech, that of the Hon. Nenni. If I had to cite a fact that astonished me profoundly it would be that the Hon. Nenni did not accuse me of renouncing our rights [*rinunciatarismo*]—one of the facile slogans employed by the Communist and nationalist opposition—but instead accused me of conducting a policy of megalomania. On the contrary, if I were to characterize the policy we have followed I believe that I instead would use two words: firmness with prudence. A policy that appreciates the displacements which have occurred in the world-wide power equilibrium and which working for interdependence (this is a new word to which we must become accustomed) (*interruptions from the extreme left*) makes all forms of isolation impossible, such a policy is not one of renunciation. A policy of neutrality or one of tacit, underhanded draining of the Atlantic Pact, that would be a policy of renunciation. In fact, such a policy can spring only from a profound lack of confidence in an Italy that is conceived to be only a small entity with limited interests, sleepy and indifferent toward a new world in the making. It is not megalomania to wish to assign Italy the function—and why not say, as did Mazzini, the mission?—(*interruptions from the extreme left*) that its history and its numbers assign it. We have not pursued a vain dream of bygone greatness; but in the most grievous moment of our history we did not despair, we did not renounce the development of a Western policy along with the other nations of Europe. While many, even abroad, thought that we would remain motionless, we have sought to show Italy a new road, the only one it could travel without material power. And in doing so we know that we have also contributed to showing this new road to Europe. . . .

The Hon. Nenni has spoken of inconsistency. No! Ours has been a constant consistency summarized in three fundamental notions: not to break the unity of the West; assure Italy's presence in the plan for an African renaissance; and make of Italy not an old and declining lady but a young and open-minded country which forces itself upon history's stage (*comments*) with other vital peoples not by reason of old genealogical trees but because of its vitality. (*Comments from the extreme left.*)

With this as the fundamental fabric of our policy, you can easily see that all of the Hon. Nenni's theses are without foundation. For example, how can he assert that an independent Libya is equivalent to a British trusteeship over it when in fact England would have to withdraw from a united Libya? * . . . Proceeding to the Adriatic, how can he assert that the appointment of a governor over the Free Territory of Trieste would have been a better guarantee for Italy when it is clear that such an appointment would have strengthened a peace treaty that we seek to revise and that we have succeeded in revising to a large extent?

As for the Atlantic policy, our position is so clear, our aims are so obvious, our safety within the Pact has been guaranteed in so sure a manner that there is need to draw attention to only one point among what the Hon. Nenni has said. Proceeding from the supposed failure of America's economic policy in the world (an assertion completely lacking any basis in fact), the Hon. Nenni has inferred therefrom reasons for a change of course. Rather, to be more exact, he reasons that we should make believe that we continue along this course, but in reality should turn our backs on our course's guiding star, which is the freedom, independence, and future of the country, of this Italy that wishes to live as an equal among equals and that wishes at all costs not to fall under Eastern lordships. . . .

* After the end of the war Italy had sought to retain some presence in its former colonies of Libya, Eritrea, and Somaliland. By 1948 Italy was willing to settle for a trusteeship over the three areas, but failing to secure even this concession, Sforza proposed early in October 1949 at the United Nations that the administrative areas of Libya (Cyrenaica, Fezzan, and Tripolitania) be united as soon as possible into an independent state. Libya eventually became independent in 1952; Eritrea was federated with Ethiopia; and Italian Somaliland was placed under an Italian trusteeship for ten years until 1961, when it became independent. Ed. note.

The Hon. Nenni has smiled skeptically with regard to European Union. It is strange that it should be precisely the so-called extreme parties that in this matter associate themselves with the most stale fixed ideas of the past. . . . Many who today shout Europe! Europe! think also of the development their industries and commerce will have the day when the stupid customs barriers that separate Europe every five minutes are destroyed. (*Applause from the center; interruption from the Deputy Giuliano Pajetta* [Communist].) Dear young man, you scoff at customs unions? Do not deceive yourself, they will come to pass.

The Hon. Nenni has accused us of having conducted for almost three years a foreign policy that lacks a clear direction. It seems to me I have shown that one may perhaps insinuate that my ideas have been too decided, that they have always excluded any attempt whatever at tightrope walking for the sake of those immediate demagogic successes which always cost dearly; but it is impossible to say that our foreign policy has not always followed a clear and precise idea. The inner essence of our ideas has always had one name, peace.

In fact, let us summarize. We sacrificed ourselves by signing a peace treaty containing unjust conditions because it strengthened the peace of Europe. We sacrificed ourselves in signing that treaty because it assured domestic peace to the Italians, who otherwise would have suffered the unhappy fate of the Germans.

After the signature of the treaty, having become free to act and negotiate as we pleased, we fought successfully for all the ideas that strengthened European solidarity. This was the case with regard to the Marshall Plan, which made it possible for us to improve our conditions in the North and the South; this was the case with regard to the Organization for European Economic Cooperation, an agency which has made us take a new step toward European Union; this was the case with regard to the European Union itself, a Union of which we are the leading pioneers and which having begun at Strasbourg has laid foundations that no one can ever destroy, and on which foundations we shall build a structure of peace and European solidarity. The same is the case with regard to the Atlantic Pact, which has now asserted its defensive character, and is truly and strongly defensive of all its members. (*Approval from the center.*)

We shall continue this policy of ours without hesitation because it is the only one that guarantees peace and free trade in the world. These are two essential conditions if the Italians are to be free to become once again what we were in Flanders and England during the fourteenth century, when we were called the fifth element of the world.

100. SUMMARY OF DEVELOPMENTS BETWEEN 1949-1953

While Sforza was preparing for the October 1949 episode of his prolonged "dialogue" with Nenni, De Gasperi was continuing his public dialogue with Togliatti. Early in June, as the Christian Democrats met in a party congress in Venice, Togliatti spoke in Rome and referred to dissension within Christian Democratic ranks. He accused the right wing of the Christian Democrats of seeking to revive Fascism ("anticommunism is Fascism") and to reestablish a regime of reactionary violence. De Gasperi rejoined that when some members of the audience attending the Christian Democratic congress in Naples in November 1947 had demanded the banning of the Communist party, he had replied by asserting that freedom had to be safeguarded even for the "anticonstitutionals, so long as our freedom and all of the freedoms of the Italian people are safeguarded."

Togliatti's reference to dissension within the Christian Democratic camp was not unfounded. Not only were there Christian Democrats who continued to demand the outlawing of the Communist party, there was also dissent at the left of the party. Although the Venice congress of June 1949 approved De Gasperi's centrist formula of firm opposition to communism, a dissatisfied left wing of the party led by De Gasperi's Minister of Labor, Amintore Fanfani, and labor leader Giuseppe Dossetti gained some support. The principal issue in contention was the speed of the country's economic reconstruction and of social reforms. The left wing favored greater state intervention, which was opposed not only by the Christian Democratic right wing but also by the Liberals in the government. Also dissatisfied with the government's economic policies were Saragat's Socialists, who resigned from the cabinet in November 1949.

Another reason for Saragat's resignation was the imminent formation of a new Socialist party by Giuseppe Romita, a dissident member of Nenni's Italian Socialist Party (PSI) seeking to establish a unified party free of intimate ties with the Communists. The new political formation came into being in December 1949 as the Unitary Socialist Party (PSU), and its attraction of some of Saragat's followers forced him not only to resign from the cabinet but also to waver in his support of it. There followed a political crisis resulting in the exclusion of the Liberals from De Gasperi's sixth cabinet and the return of Saragat's Socialists, but not of Saragat himself.

The discontent within the Christian Democratic party and among Saragat's Socialists stemmed in large part from the fact that by 1949, in spite of considerable efforts by all postwar governments to reconstruct the economy through state intervention, only some of the foundations had been established for what was to become known as Italy's "economic miracle." [1] The results of this miracle (which raised per capita income from 303,600 lire in 1951 to 478,000 for northwest Italy, from 184,000 to 319,400 for northeast and central Italy, and from 110,300 to 172,000 for southern and insular Italy) were not yet manifest in 1949.

Apart from the need to provide emergency relief to the homeless and the poor, the most pressing problem facing Italy's postwar governments was the stabilization of the currency. Between the time of Mussolini's ouster in July 1943 and the end of the war uncontrolled prices rose to forty times what they had been in 1938. After a decline in inflationary pressures between the spring of 1945 and the spring of 1946, the price rise resumed, to be curbed only after De Gasperi formed his fourth cabinet in May 1947 excluding the Communists and Socialists and introducing Professor Luigi Einaudi as Deputy Prime Minister and Minister of the Budget. The Independent Liberal Einaudi followed a policy of "sound money" by restricting credit and government spending, and by 1949 the continuation of this policy had stabilized the currency. But it had also disaffected those elements in the Christian Democratic party and among Saragat's Socialists who were devoted to a more "positive" governmental intervention in the economy. In addition to monetary stability, Italy's economic recovery required the importation of large quantities of capital goods for the reconstruction of its productive facilities and raw materials for domestic consumption and for export after processing. A considerable part of the finances necessary for Italy's imports came from United States assistance, through the European Recovery Program and other arrangements, with a total of $1,955.4 million made available to Italy between 1946 and 1949.

The rapidity of Italy's economic recovery is seen in the fact that by 1950 agriculture's gross output in fixed prices exceeded that of 1938. In the first four years of the postwar period considerable government expenditures, made possible in part by American aid, were devoted to reequipping agriculture with buildings, machines, livestock, fruit trees, and the like, and reestablishing an agricultural credit system. Small farmers were aided by legislation in April and June 1947 raising the percentage due sharecroppers from the traditional 50 per cent to a minimum of 53 per cent and requiring that a sum equal to 4 per cent of the landowner's share go to improvements on the land. But the much demanded land reform aimed at the breaking up of large estates and the increase of the number of small landowners did not begin until 1950. In the same year the *Cassa del Mezzogiorno* [Southern Development Fund] was created as the principal agency for the economic development of the South.

---

[1] See pp. 608–15 below for an excerpt dealing with the "economic miracle."

Industrial recovery was even more rapid than that in agriculture. The index of industrial production rose from a catastrophic 25 per cent of what it had been in 1938 to 102 in 1948 and continued to climb steadily. The physical destruction visited by the war occasioned a boom in the building industry strongly promoted by state intervention, as in the Fanfani Plan of February 1949 of reducing unemployment through building low-cost housing.

In short, De Gasperi's governments had been neither so "do-nothing" as its critics both in and out of his party charged nor so bold as they desired. Nevertheless, De Gasperi could not remain indifferent to this criticism without jeopardizing his policy of collaboration with the Center democratic parties and the unity of his own party. The composite or "interclass" nature of the Christian Democratic movement meant that it held within its fold men who shared the economic and social views of the moderately conservative Liberals and others who inclined toward the moderate socialism of Saragat's party. The preservation of his party's unity posed for De Gasperi substantially the same problems as the preservation of the Center coalition he had espoused since 1947. Whereas party discipline could succeed in keeping the various factions in his own party in line, the same instrument could not be employed to curb the differences on economic questions that divided the Liberals from Saragat's Socialists.

In January 1950 De Gasperi shifted his course to the left by welcoming Saragat's Socialists into his fifth cabinet and excluding the Liberals. There followed a productive year of legislation including the laws for land reform and for the economic development of the South. But in 1951 De Gasperi's thesis of government by coalitions of the Center parties received several hard blows. Saragat's Italian Workers' Socialist Party and Romita's Unitary Socialist Party became convinced that for the time being there was little hope of weaning Nenni's Socialists away from their alliance with the Communists. Accordingly, they decided to fuse their two parties and in May 1951 formed a united party eventually known as the Italian Democratic Socialist Party (PSDI). In preparation for this formal union, Saragat's followers resigned from the cabinet in April, leaving only the small Republican party as De Gasperi's ally. In May and June local elections held in northern and central Italy produced results discouraging to all parties of the democratic Center except the Liberals, and registered a rise in the fortunes of the Monarchists and the Neo-Fascist Italian Social Movement. This trend to the Right was confirmed by the May 1952 elections in the central and southern provinces, where the Christian Democrats lost heavily to the Monarchists, whereas the Socialists and Communists held their ground as they had done in the local elections of the year before.

To meet the crisis threatening the whole concept of government by Center parties, late in 1952 the Christian Democrats, Democratic Socialists, Republicans, and Liberals agreed to prepare for the general elections of 1953 by supporting the passage of a law clearly aimed at securing a stable parliamentary majority for a four-party coalition of the Center. The law provided that two or more parties running separate lists of candidates could group the results obtained by the separate lists, and if the grouped results reached the minimum of 50 per cent plus 1 of the votes cast the "grouped" parties would receive the "majority prize" of 65 per cent of the seats in the Chamber of Deputies. If no group of parties obtained the specified majority of votes cast, the prize would not be awarded and the distribution of seats would be made according to the system of proportionality employed in the 1948 elections. The law was passed in March 1953 and, inasmuch as no party or group of parties other than the four-party coalition sponsoring the law could hope to win a majority of the votes cast, the Socialist-Communist opposition in particular branded the law a "swindle" (*legge-truffa*) reminiscent of the Fascist Acerbo electoral law of 1923.

Although the Socialist-Communist campaign preceding the elections made much of the "swindle" character of the new electoral law, it also presented a positive program of its own as stated in the eight points of the unity of action pact of October 1946. In a speech, portions of which follow, Nenni affirmed his loyalty to the pact with the Communists and also presented his view of the "socialist alternative" open to the Italian people.

101. NENNI ON THE "SOCIALIST ALTERNATIVE": REPORT TO THE 30TH CONGRESS OF THE ITALIAN SOCIALIST PARTY, JANUARY 8, 1953

> Direzione del Partito Socialista Italiano, *Davanti al paese, l'alternativa socialista* ("Politica del partito": Testi e documenti, 1). Rome: Direzione del PSI, 1953, pp. 33–36. Our translation.

It is in the spirit of a relaxation of tensions that the Directorate of the party places before the congress, and beyond the congress to the nation and the people, the socialist alternative to the present clerico-moderate-social-democratic policy.

It is necessary to be very clear on this point to avoid confusion that would be cause for many errors. We do not offer the socialist alternative in the sense of an alternative to the present government and least of all as an alternative to the present power. We do not offer it even as an alternative to the present parliamentary majority. We know in what way 1953 differs from 1946, when we had the socialist unity that others have betrayed and broken, and from 1948, when the front [of the Left] was conceived by us as an offensive function. International events even more than domestic ones have placed not only us but all of the Western workers' movement on the defensive from which, however, we can already see the possibility of escaping.

The socialist alternative is the political formula of the new equilibrium we propose to make possible. It is a political formula which by its very nature is neither a party nor a class formula, it is a people's formula. From this angle the socialist alternative is offered as a national and popular necessity, as an exit from the present contradictions, as a large and steady bridge thrown over a political and social cleavage that tends to become irreparable. The foreign policy content of the socialist alternative is the overthrow of the Atlantic [Pact]-policy-at-all-costs, to create the premises for our country's disengagement from military alliances and for neutrality in case of war, excepting the hypothesis of a direct aggression against our frontiers which would automatically create the need and duty to defend the fatherland.

In domestic politics the socialist alternative requires the strict defense and application of the Constitution, and the realization of the economic reforms therein defined by Article 43 on nationalization, Article 44 on agrarian reform, Article 45 on the function of cooperation and its growth, and Article 46 on workers' management councils.

The social and economic policy of the socialist alternative is expressed in the demand for the liquidation of large landed estates and in the subjection of industrial monopolies to the common interest by nationalizing them. The two running sores of Italian society have been made fully evident by recent investigations and statistics which, although they show some small decline in unemployment—from 2 to 1.8 million—owing to the fact that these figures are of a time of greater employment, on the other hand point to an appalling fact. This fact alone explains the general low standard of living which for many strata of the population is much lower than the minimum for life and for civilized existence. The fact to which I refer is the number of Italians who have some employment, 19.4 million out of a population of 47.1 million. This means that 59 per cent of our population does not work, with the unemployment curve touching the maximum in the depressed regions of the South and the islands. In the North an employed person has to support another person, and in the South two. Only by ending this situation of inevitable stasis can we conquer misery, which is the most dangerous enemy of democratic behavior.

In fact, in a society that has not yet solved the elementary problems of bread, work, and education for all, freedom and democracy are the luxuries of the few and lies for the many.

In raising the banner of the socialist alternative the Italian Socialist Party assumes the political pledge of promoting not only the unity of all socialists behind this banner but also the agreement of all democratic and popular forces.

Nenni's emphasis on the "socialist" nature of the alternative he offered the Italian people seemed to imply a certain disassociation of his party from the Communists. De Gasperi denied the validity of this implication and insisted that although the Socialist and Communist parties were contesting the election in separate lists, they continued to share the same ends as before.

102. DE GASPERI REJECTS NENNI'S SOCIALIST ALTERNATIVE AND DEFENDS THE RECORD OF THE CENTER COALITION: SPEECH IN MILAN, APRIL 26, 1953

Alcide De Gasperi, *Discorsi politici,* II, 145–53, 158–60, 165–67, *passim.* Our translation.

Five years have actually passed from the time we began a program of collaboration, from the time we and representatives of other groups appeared before the nation to ask its vote of solidarity with and confirmation of a policy that had already been begun by the government of that time. I should like to remind the forgetful and those who accuse us of not being aware of the course we are following that the alliance of the democratic forces is not a thing of yesterday. We chose this course, which is still our course with regard to the electoral campaign, not through the artifice of an electoral law nor for transient reasons of mere expedience. . . .

Today as in the past this electoral law is but the manifestation of this tendency [of democratic alliance]; it is an instrument for its confirmation; and the relations between our party and the democratic parties are based as always on tolerance and freedom. We must say to these allies of ours, above all petty disputes, a word of frankness and friendship. We ask for neither total support of our program nor, even less, a relation of servility to us. Service is for all, it is common to all groups, and it is offered to the nation. We ask only for loyalty in our relations, for mutual understanding, for competition in large ideas and not in petty matters. And we ask that there be no insinuations and that no shadow be cast on our banner and our good will.

Now, having said this for our collaborators and our friends, let us see who our opponents are today. They are the same as those of yesterday, they are identical. But we shall see that their deployment, their marching orders are somewhat different from those in 1948.

For Togliatti the principal theme in 1948 was fear of war, and he proclaimed this theme in February 1948 in his Pescara presentation: "Christian Democracy wants war, and the danger is imminent. There is need for a union of all sincerely national forces and for unity . . . around the Italian motherland. Italians, defend peace." On March 27, 1948, Togliatti said: "The Italian people knows that if the Popular Democratic Front were not to win, it would see appear once again at its streets corners and under the protection of the Crossed Shield * the death-head insignias of those who once before led us to catastrophe." † He added: "If the Democratic Front were not to win, the most terrible economic crisis would strike our industries and our whole country."

Inasmuch as you are able to determine what has happened during the last five years, I ask you whether you are prepared to honor the Hon. Togliatti's power of prophecy.

But he does not acknowledge the facts to the effect that instead of war there has been a period of peaceful development, instead of our industries being struck by ruin there has been economic reconstruction. He does not acknowledge this and repent; he does not admit that he was mistaken. No, these days Togliatti in his speech of April 17, 1953, repeats the same things. . . .

But it is true that if the opponents are the same—and I have wanted to document the identity of these opponents—and if the ideas of 1948 are the ideas repeated today, they present themselves in a different fashion. The Socialists are divided from the Communists, that is, they march separately. I speak of Nenni's Socialists, of course. But I should like to offer some documentation regarding the reality of

* Reference to the Christian Democratic symbol: a cross on a shield. Ed. note.
† Reference to the death-head insignias of the Fascist action squads of the early 1920s. Ed. note.

this division and difference in the line of march. On April 17, 1953, in announcing that the Communists were presenting themselves [to the voters] separate from the Socialists,* or, better, the Socialists separate from the Communists, Togliatti said: "We have a unity of action pact with the Socialist party. This pact is a fixed political necessity of the Italian situation; it is the result of the history of the entire Italian workers' movement and in particular of the struggle conducted for the liberation from Fascism and from foreign invasion. This unity is one of the basic points of our policy and we shall never depart from it."

It follows that the relations between the Socialist and Communist parties mean temporary separation, separation in movements, but unity of action, unity of chiefs, unity of gains. The unity of action pact—whose text is almost forgotten because neither he nor others wish to speak of it—is a pact concluded on October 27, 1946,† and it foresees that each of the two parties may follow its own road. But it says clearly that when it comes to going on the offensive for the conquest of power, that is, when it comes to taking over the government, then the two parties must be absolutely together in taking power.

In that case what does it matter that they offer themselves separately when in reality at the decisive moments they are united and assume the responsibility of power in unison? We cannot accept this modification of deployment as a fundamental difference, and we must say: It is a tactical maneuver having as its chief aim the drawing toward Nenni of all those souls in anguish who call themselves half socialists and half social-democrats and who would not easily vote for Nenni if he were visibly tied to the Communists even in political symbols.

Nenni would have us believe that this new deployment seeks to create a new situation which he calls the socialist alternative. But he forgets what he said at the Socialist party congress in January 1947 when, in disagreement with Saragat and others, he asserted that unity with the Communists was made necessary by the demands of life and that a front for liberty and democracy without the Communists would be inconceivable, impossible. He said: "A Socialist party could perhaps do without the pact of unity of action if it were in a phase of

---

* Reference to the dissimilarity of the general elections of 1948, when the Socialist and Communist parties ran a single list of candidates, in 1953 the two parties contested the election with separate lists. Ed. note.

† For the text of the unity of action pact see pp. 544–46 above. Ed. note.

propaganda and opposition; but a Socialist party in power which must remain in power in order not to expose the working class to terrible reprisals, such a party absolutely must have the unity of action pact." We may be allowed to reply that the other deployment cannot be interpreted as anything other than a tactical move. There is no socialist alternative. There is only the democratic alternative on the one hand and the social-communist alternative on the other. The Hon. Nenni is an artist when it comes to presenting things with a certain smoothness. I would say that he is a professional lubricator, a varnisher. I speak only of politics and therefore without any intention of offense. He justified the Prague trials * ; he has praised Stalin, forgiving him the elimination of his competing comrades, who were nonetheless old socialists. He has even had words of understanding for the gallows in Prague. Never has he uttered a word of censure or of disassociation that would imply independence or autonomy of thought. . . .

In Italy Nenni accuses us of not making all the organic laws and all the implementations of the Constitution that should have been made. . . . I say to you that we have done much; I know that we have done much. But I must also confess that there is one thing we have not done enough: we have not been in a position to conduct a propaganda explaining all we have done.

The democratic government's principal achievements from 1947 to today may be summarized as follows: 1) reconstruction of the country's most vital property damaged by the war; 2) stabilization of currency and prices, and the end of the inflationary spiral that threatened to throw the entire nation into chaos. This is an achievement to be acknowledged to all the Ministers and especially to the Hon. [Giuseppe] Pella, who is with us today; 3) solution of the major economic problems, such as the reequipment of industry, the development of power supplies, the reorganization of the steel industry, agricultural development, and the development of the merchant marine and other means of transportation. . . .

Well! says Togliatti, it is not the government that did these things, it is the Italian people. What a discovery! Obviously, our people's contribution of work and intelligence is the decisive factor; but the laws

* Reference to the trial and execution of leading Communists and collaborators with the Communist government in Czechoslovakia during the years after the Communist seizure of power with the help of the Czech Socialist party in February 1948. Ed. note.

we made had precisely the aim of promoting this work, of rendering it easier by supporting its financing and in certain cases by having the state intervene directly either by promoting savings or by providing direct financial aid.

In the latter case there are objections to the state intervening in the economy. But it is nonetheless undeniable that there are certain things which individuals or small entities such as the family or the municipality cannot do by themselves. In such cases there is need of aid from the state. It is necessary to create a condition of monetary stability and to supply aid and encouragement.

Now we come to the "depressed areas." It would be difficult for me to understand if you Milanese were to complain that we have spent and are spending billions of lire for the South. You would be wrong, if for no other reason than because the sums being spent down there in time become also an advantage for industry in the North. But [on the other hand] it is absurd that in the South there should be conducted a propaganda against us because we have made these great investments there with money that came from the northern provinces. . . .

I do not say that we have done everything. We have begun to do things, and we have begun well. And it is for this reason that we ask to stay in power for another five years. . . .

And now I should like to say something about foreign policy. What is the meaning of recent events in foreign affairs? They confirm the wisdom of our Atlantic policy. The situation has become attenuated; war has been avoided because war has become too serious a risk both because there is an atomic bomb and because the Atlantic organization is by now a great and solid European force.

It has been said to us in the Senate: "You want this swindle-law in order to pass the European Defense Community treaty." * But we have no need for special legislation to approve the Defense Community treaty. . . .

Let us come to the question of Europe. . . . Nenni says: "There you are, you wish to put this Federal Germany of Bonn with the other states of Europe, make a single Europe of six states, and share both

---

* Reference to the movement in Western Europe, after the beginning of the Korean War in 1950, to create a Western European army with the participation of West Germany. The Italian government favored the Defense Community, but in August 1954 the French National Assembly refused to ratify France's participation, causing the collapse of the scheme. Ed. note.

military and political responsibilities. In reality, you provoke war, you move in the direction of war." It is true that there is a problem; but we on the other hand believe that a Federal Union including France, Italy, the Benelux countries, and Bonn Germany is better able to avoid any adventure, any error, and above all to forgo any aggressive tendency than to leave Germny alone to arm itself, because in the latter case nationalism might once again push the Germans to war.

It is not true, as Lussu [Emilio, Socialist] said in the Senate, that in this European Union there are "papists." * There are the best of socialists, there are Protestants, there are other people. What unites us is not this [alleged papalism]; it is need, and by now the awareness that there is no safety other than in this union.

That is our conception of a European policy. But from this transient conception there follows another hope: that from this policy there may issue a federalist development and that finally Europe's frontiers may be lowered and we may have one single Community and a free movement of peoples and things, and above all of work.

* Probably a reference to the influence of the Catholic parties in Western Europe in favor of European Union. Ed. note.

XXVII. THE CRISIS OF CENTRIST GOVERNMENT AND THE "OPENING TO THE LEFT": POLITICAL AND ECONOMIC DEVELOPMENTS FROM 1953 TO THE PRESENT

103. THE CONSEQUENCES OF THE ELECTIONS OF JUNE 1953

The results of the 1953 general elections were exceptionally close. The four major parties of the Center coalition and three allied small regional parties received 13,488,813 of the total 27,087,701 valid votes cast, thus failing of a majority by a scant 55,038 votes. In consequence, the "majority prize" provision of the new electoral law was not operative, and the distribution of the Chamber of Deputies' seats according to the earlier electoral law resulted in sharp losses for all four parties in the coalition. As compared to the results of the general elections of 1948, the Christian Democrats dropped from 304 to 261 seats, losing and never again regaining the absolute majority they had enjoyed since 1948. The Democratic Socialists declined from 33 seats to 19; the Liberals from 19 to 14; and the Republicans from 9 to 5. Apart from the Christian Democrats, who gained in popular vote in comparison to the provincial elections of 1951–52, the parties of the Center coalition showed a constant decline after 1948. The Communists and Socialists, on the other hand, improved their position with regard to the 1948 general election and the 1951–52 provincial elections. The Communists won 143 seats and the Socialists 75 seats, a gain of 35 seats when compared to their combined total of 183 in 1948, when they contested the election with a single list of candidates. The National Monarchist party rose from 14 seats in 1948 to 40, and the Neo-Fascist Italian Social Movement from 6 to 29.

The June election's adverse effect on De Gasperi's centrism was manifested immediately in the refusal of the other three Center parties to join the Christian Democrats in fashioning a new cabinet. De Gasperi was obliged to form his eighth and last cabinet in July 1953 with men exclusively of his own party (a *monocolore,* or "single-color," government). The Chamber of Deputies refused him its confidence and he resigned early in August, never again to return to office before his death in August 1954.

De Gasperi's resignation opened a period of prolonged crisis during which a caretaker government led by the Christian Democrat Giuseppe Pella lasted five months (August 1953–January 1954) with Liberal and Monarchist support, and a Fanfani government less than a month (January–February 1954). Fanfani's successor, Mario Scelba (De Gasperi's perennial Minister of the Interior from February 1947 to July 1953), succeeded in regrouping the Center coalition behind a political policy of opposition to the extremes of both Right and Left and an economic development program (Vanoni Plan) for full employment. But a number of factors operated to shake Scelba's political position. De Gasperi's death in August 1954 led to the election of Fanfani, not an ally of Scelba, as secretary of the Christian Democratic party. In October Scelba acceded to a compromise agreement whereby the Free Territory of Trieste was partitioned, Zone A (including the city of Trieste and adjacent areas) being returned to Italy and the remainder of the Territory (Zone B) acknowledged to Yugoslavia, already in *de facto* possession of the area. The agreement was not popular in Italy and weakened Scelba further. Finally, his position became untenable when, after the expiration of Einaudi's term as President of the Republic in April 1955, Scelba opposed unsuccessfully the election of Giovanni Gronchi, a left-of-center Christian Democrat. Scelba's resignation led to a cabinet headed by Antonio Segni, who managed to hold the coalition together until the withdrawal of the Democratic Socialists forced his resignation in May 1957 on the issue of the government's alleged lack of drive (*immobilismo*) in socioeconomic reforms. Segni's fall pointed once again to the parliamentary weakness of Center-coalition government constantly exposed to crises by the possible defection of a small but numerically indispensable party in the coalition. The only apparent solution for this state of permanent political crisis was an abandonment of centrism by veering either to the Right or to the Left. Collaboration with the Monarchists and especially with the Neo-Fascists was difficult because of the country's republican institutions and the still strong feelings against Fascism. Moreover, such collaboration, when it was tried by Segni in 1959 and Fernando Tambroni in 1960, proved only a cause for violent dissension among the Christian Democrats and this made for even greater governmental instability. The conviction began to grow from the mid-1950s onward that only a movement or opening to the Left (the *apertura a sinistra*) calculated to draw Nenni's Socialists from the Communists could provide a stable parliamentary majority under Christian Democratic leadership. Associated with the opening to the Left was the never-abandoned hope of reuniting the two Socialist parties on condition that Nenni break his ties with the Communists. This same condition applied to Nenni's possible collaboration with or participation in the government, which meant that an opening to the Left had as a necessary and companion development the eventual unification of the two Socialist parties.

Socialist unification had a bright moment in 1956, the year the First Secretary of the Communist party of the Soviet Union, Nikita Khrushchev, delivered a speech to the 20th Congress of the party denouncing Stalin's ruthless methods and his "cult of personality." After the Democratic Socialists' decision in June to collaborate with Nenni's Socialists in several municipal administrations, Saragat and Nenni had a "cordial" meeting late in August in Pralognan, France, to discuss the unification of their parties. Saragat's public insistence in October that Nenni's party free itself of its Communist ties occasioned a sharp reply from one of Nenni's left-wing colleagues that marked the suspension of all efforts at unification. Soon after, early in November, Russian armed forces suppressed the Hungarian revolution, augmenting the disarray afflicting the Communists and their allies since Khrushchev's speech denouncing Stalin. The excerpt below from a speech by Togliatti is an important episode in both the movement for Socialist unification and the opening to the Left; for although it was not Togliatti's intention to promote the former development, his speech did implicitly support the latter by advocating "an Italian road to socialism."

104. TOGLIATTI ON AN ITALIAN ROAD TO SOCIALISM: REPORT TO THE 8TH CONGRESS OF THE ITALIAN COMMUNIST PARTY, DECEMBER 1956

Palmiro Togliatti, *Nella democrazia e nella pace verso il socialismo, Rapporti all'VIII, IX e X Congresso del PCI.* Rome: Editori Riuniti, 1963, pp. 13, 74–77, *passim.* Our translation.

The congress is the last act of a great process that already contains within itself the elements of a profound renewal. Renewal does not mean either rejection or revision, with the purpose of destruction, of the great and new ideal political and organizational principles which we asserted with the creation of the Communist party and from which we have striven never to depart in all our subsequent activity. Renewal means to define with the greatest clarity the bases and the content of the activity we conduct in Italy for democracy, for peace, and for socialism. It means underscoring once more the national and democratic character of our party; it means the elimination of all open or covert resistance to this activity and this character and to their translation into daily practice; it means breaking and destroying the bureaucratic incrustations and organizational schematics that limit or deform relations with the working classes, that compress the inner life of the party and therefore obstruct its development. Renewal and reinforcement are therefore strictly linked objectives. Indeed, they coincide. . . .

When we speak of a congress that is to reinforce and renew the party and put the emphasis on these two tasks, linking the former strictly with the latter, do we mean only to say that we must extend our criticism and self-criticism to the point of uncovering all the defects and asking the party to correct them? No, we do not mean only to say this. . . . The manifold criticism of all aspects of our work must be made and shall be made also here. But when we speak of a renewal it is clear that we mean something more.

In order to understand what we mean it is not bad to refer to events of the last few years. After the great success registered against the swindle law * a new situation opened before us and the country. It cannot be said that this was not understood at the center of the party. We have only to refer to our decisions of October 1953. These asked that the party, strong in the victory that had been achieved, should enter with impetus into a varied and wide action toward all categories of the working population, an action hinged upon their immediate interests and on the generally felt need for a new policy of basic reforms. The party did not lack for direction; it did lack impetuosity in the realization of this policy. Here and there or in some individuals there was perhaps also lacking the deep conviction that this policy was right. There followed an evident uncertainty which augmented the delay in the evaluation of the changes then taking place in the economy and in the political policies of others. The period of Scelba's government [February 1954–June 1955] was full of initiatives and struggles of great importance, and it came to a close with a success for the democratic forces and for us. But it cannot be denied that after 1953 the whole of our political initiative was more limited, and the party became somewhat shut up within itself.

It is quite clear from this criticism what we mean by the renewal we ask for today. The movement for the party's renewal is essentially

* Reference to the electoral reform law sponsored by the Christian Democrats and their allies in 1953. Ed. note.

a movement which looks to the outside world that conditions the party's political activity and its way of operating. Renewal is not then a simple lash of the whip. It is above all a more complete and better elaboration of our political platform as derived from a deeper search for an Italian road to socialism. It consists in a richer analysis of the propelling forces of democratic renewal and socialist revolution. It consists in a wider and freer search for the allies of the working class in the struggle against the power of the great monopolies. It consists in the definition of the structural reforms we demand, in the definition of their value and of the way to snatch them into being. It consists of the place in the first rank that we still assign to the general agrarian reform for which both the working class and the peasants are fighting. It consists of a better understanding of the democratic method of our activity, in a better understanding of the value which the achievement of democracy has in the advance toward socialism.

Accordingly, at the center of the party's renewal task there is the struggle for the party's line and for an Italian road to socialism. What can prevent us from proceeding along this road? Two principal obstacles: maximalist sectarianism and reformist revisionism. The first shuts itself up within itself in expectation of the great day; the second bends its knees before capitalism in expectation that the latter become converted to socialism by itself. Both of them renounce revolutionary action for the conquest of socialism. The second has made itself felt somewhat among some of our comrades in their evaluation of the new things there are in the world today. The first is more profoundly rooted in our ranks because of our movement's past and its old traditions. The harm that reformism can do within the working class is the most serious because it extinguishes revolutionary impetus and induces passivity. But a party that is closed within itself, not fully convinced of the rightness of its political line and not fighting for its realization, such a party cannot fight effectively against reformism. The struggle to remove one of these obstacles is linked therefore with the other struggle and conditions it. The search for the way in which this struggle appears and should be conducted is to be linked therefore with a correct understanding of the party's tasks and with their realization. This linkage has not been given proper prominence in all the recent regional congresses, and where this [lack] has occurred it has been a serious defect.

It is clear from all that I have said what is the great prominence assumed by questions of the party's internal life and the party's functioning. The partial incapacity of realizing a correct policy and that certain tendency to sectarian shutting within oneself which I have denounced, in fact express themselves within the party by the manifestation of a bureaucratic stiffening and by the restriction of the forms of activity and democratic life. It is clear then why the fire must be concentrated in this direction if we wish to increase all of the party's political capacity and its capacity for work. Accordingly, this becomes the principal task within the party itself. . . . .

Our French comrades have directed a friendly criticism toward us because we were supposed to have made unnecessary and improper concessions to those who assumed erroneous positions. We have made no concessions whatsoever. We realized the gravity of the problems being raised; we condemned the acts of factionalism and lack of discipline and had these acts condemned by the very ones who had committed them; and we have freely debated with those who were in disagreement with us in order to convince them and have them with us on a correct political position. Until now the results have been positive, and the method employed has been correct because it is the normal method of leading a party that wishes to base the unity and solidity of its ranks on reasoned and knowing consensus, and not only on obedience.

105: "THE OPENING TO THE LEFT"

The movement for an opening to the Left and eventual unification of the two Socialist parties received a push forward in January 1959 when Nenni succeeded in having his party's congress approve a motion in favor of "autonomy" from the Communist party. There were immediate repercussions within both the government, then led by Fanfani, and in the Christian Democratic party. Ezio Vigorelli, Democratic Socialist Minister of Labor, resigned from the cabinet to influence the situation in favor of Nenni's eventual collaboration in government. Vigorelli's resignation further undermined Fanfani's slender parliamentary majority already shaken by "snipers" from the right wing of Fanfani's own party. In February, upon Fanfani's resignation, his opponents in the Christian Democratic party fashioned a cabinet around Segni, who had to depend on the votes of the Liberals, the Monarchists, and the Neo-Fascists to stay in power. Italy had thus, for the first time since the end of the war, a government of the Center-Right, radically reversing De Gasperi's thesis of centrist democratic rule. The Christian Democrats could not but feel the consequence of this change. In March 1959 the National Council of their party removed Fanfani from his post as secretary and replaced him with the less controversial Aldo Moro, who, although a member of Fanfani's own *Iniziativa Democratica* [Democratic Initiative] faction, was not close to him. Further troubles came for the party when in July Silvio Milazzo, leader of a Catholic splinter group (the Sicilian Christian Social Union), succeeded in being reelected head of the autonomous Regional government in Sicily by accepting Socialist and Communist support in defiance of Christian Democratic directives. The Christian Democrats fell to open squabbling at their national congress in October, shaking Segni's cabinet which fell in February 1960 after the Liberals withdrew their support. A long crisis ensued, leading to a wholly Christian Democratic government headed by Fernando Tambroni, whose first test before the Chamber of Deputies was successful only because 24 Neo-Fascists gave him their votes. Three left-wing Christian Democratic Ministers resigned immediately, and the crisis deepened when the exultant Neo-Fascists decided to convene a congress of their party on July 2 in strongly anti-Fascist Genoa. There followed violent encounters between Neo-Fascists and anti-Fascists during late June and early July, resulting in several deaths and more than a thousand injuries throughout Italy. These "July disturbances" convinced the leadership of the Christian Democratic party that a move to the Right was a dangerous course to follow and that Tambroni's resignation was necessary. Tambroni's successor was Fanfani who formed in August a cabinet composed of all the factions in the party and supported in Parliament by the votes of the Center parties and the abstention of Nenni's Socialists and the Monarchists. Only the Neo-Fascists at the extreme right of the Chamber and the Communists at the extreme left voted against the new government.

The decision of Nenni's Socialists to abstain from the vote of confidence was the first explicitly political sign that Nenni's collaboration with the Christian Democrats was practicable and that there were fair prospects for an "opening to the Left." Additional proof of this practicality came when, after the local elections of November 1960, the two parties collaborated in the formation of municipal administrations in Milan, Genoa, and Florence, to the discomfiture of the right wing of the Christian Democratic party and the left wing of Nenni's party. This collaboration continued in March 1961 when Nenni's Socialists supported the election of the Christian Democratic candidate for the presidency of the Sicilian Regional government.

The following excerpt reveals the reasons for Nenni's decision to collaborate with the Christian Democrats and to assert his party's autonomy from the Communists.

Nenni Defends His Policy of Collaboration with the Christian Democrats and Autonomy from the Communists: Report to the 34th Congress of the Italian Socialist Party (PSI), March 15, 1961

> Partito Socialista Italiano, *Resoconto stenografico del 34° congresso nazionale,* Milan, March 15–20, 1961. Milan: Edizioni *Avanti!,* 1961, pp. 32–33, 36–37, 40–42, *passim.* Our translation.

The July adventure * has shown that the Right has a plan, an organization, and a technique of its own. Urged on by circumstances and by the ambition of its leaders it perhaps played its card too hastily.

The meaning of the events of July is by now sufficiently clear to us. It was a case not of sporadic events but of a first attempt to create disorder so as to restore order, and to restore it under conditions that would remove Tambroni's government from normal parliamentary control and from the control of the very Christian Democratic party of which it was an emanation if not an expression. The provocations committed in Genoa, at Porta San Paolo in Rome, in Reggio Emilia, in Catania, and Palermo—leaving eight dead in the streets—were directed at feeding the political and press campaign on [alleged] insubordination and rebellion, on the danger to public order and the need to defend the state.

The provocation was rapidly cut short by the people. The old unitary spirit of the Committees of National Liberation burst forth once again among the Resistance organizations; the young people fought with surprising spontaneity; and the general strike found much support among intellectuals and white-collar workers. For its part, our party was equal to its duty in Genoa and throughout the country.

But there comes a time when a movement of the people either succeeds in imposing a political solution or is in turn exposed to the risk of an adventure. We experienced many such situations in 1921–22. That time came after the general strike of July 8 [1960] when it became imperative that the government of provocation fall from power.

* Reference to the disturbances following the projected congress of the Neo-Fascist Italian Social Movement in July 1960. Ed. note.

In order to make it fall our Central Committee was for once unanimous in crediting full faith in the aired proposal for a truce [offered by the Christian Democrats]. In order to make it fall our parliamentary delegation took the initiative in raising questions in the Chamber the results of which made it clear that Tambroni and the extreme Right were isolated, and made it possible for the Christian Democrats to open the crisis [leading to Tambroni's fall]. In order to make this government fall it proved necessary to urge the Republicans, the Social Democrats, and the left-wing of the Christian Democratic party to find a solution that disregarded political formulas and to which the prevailing circumstances would give the character of an open disavowal of the adventure toward the Right. And thus there came into being Fanfani's government toward which the Central Committee decided to adopt a policy of abstention.

I believe now, as I did then, that there was nothing else to do if we wished to avoid falling into the fatal error—for which we paid dearly forty years ago—of making impossible any solution but the worst. The Socialists are in Parliament not only to protest, not only to say no when it is necessary to say no. They are there to use their votes according to the interests of the workers and of democracy. . . .

Whoever recalls the atmosphere prevailing in July, when all of the Right was arrayed in a posture of challenge and provocation toward the anti-Fascists, will agree that it was a time of test for the party's sense of democratic responsibility and for its practical and political effectiveness. That occasion was the first political success in the dialogue with the Catholics.

The second political occasion wherein the dialogue with the Christian Democrats entered the phase of executing dealings and agreements of a local nature is the one that followed the elections of November 6. . . . It is a fact that five years ago, after the local elections of May 1956, the agreements proposed by the Socialists were all rejected; in 1961 they have not been rejected. . . .

But if the party is not thereby in the position to sing songs of victory, it may nonetheless note with satisfaction the breaches opened in the conservative ranks. Everything is still in doubt, in question, in a state of gestation. But a point has been gained, and it is that today the party and the country know that a turn to the Left is possible. Such a turn entails a meeting on the basis of immediate programs and things, and not transformist amalgamations or confusions on the plane of general ideas and programs, nor contaminations of our personality, which remains unaltered. . . .

The Communists' criticism of the dialogue is perhaps more pertinent than the one that comes from the opposition within our own ranks because the former is less generic and closer to the heart of the debate, when it does not end up in haughtiness and slander, as frequently it does.

In this regard, comrade Togliatti has asked two questions. . . . First, "Does Socialist autonomy mean a democratic or a social-democratic policy?" Answer: Socialist autonomy means a democratic policy. It is a democratic policy (as opposed to a social-democratic policy): because it entails neither renunciations nor attenuations of the ends proper to the class struggle and to socialism; because it does not lose the sense of difference between bourgeois and socialist democracy; because it does not postulate insertion into bourgeois society but looks to the creation of civil instruments for democracy's conquest of the state and for socialism's conquest of democracy.

It is a democratic policy different also from the Communist policy because it is not an instrumental policy. It is valid when the Socialists are in the opposition and valid when they will be at the management of society and of the state. It is not burdened by hegemonic liens and by party dictatorships; it is based on those rights to freedom which we consider a permanent acquisition of civilization.

Togliatti's second question: "Does Center-Left mean a government such as the present one or does it mean something different, and what will it be in practice?" Answer: It may be that in parliamentary jargon Center-Left means nothing and is a label for damaged goods. . . . But a Center-Left composed with the Socialists (something for which there exist today neither the national nor international conditions) or which were constituted with our support (something which is neither probable nor impossible) would be something completely different from the present majority and the present government. It would be a Center-Left for struggle against the Right; a Center-Left committed not only to a program but to a program with precise features and due dates. . . .

Nenni's offer of closer collaboration with the parties of the democratic Center was unmistakable even if couched in guarded terms. He was not the undisputed master of his party, as is revealed by the Socialist congress' approval of his "autonomist" position with 269,576 votes in his favor and 205,148 votes [1] for the left-wing opposition groups led by Tullio Vecchietti and Lelio Basso. On the other hand, it was almost as difficult for the Christian Democratic leaders to bring their party into more than transient and local alliances with Nenni. Fanfani favored an opening to the Left on the national level but was opposed by such party stalwarts as his Ministers of the Interior and of Justice, Mario Scelba and Guido Gonella. The decision of the party's secretary, Aldo Moro, to support Fanfani swayed the balance in favor of a Center-Left coalition, and this thesis was approved by the party's congress held at the end of January 1962. A statement by Moro to newspapermen some days later provides a brief summary of the decisions reached by the congress.

The Christian Democrats Accept the Opening to the Left: Aldo Moro's Statement of the Party's Objectives, February 12, 1962

> Reported in the *Corriere della Sera*, Milan, February 13, 1962. Our translation.

1. Firm defense of freedom against all totalitarian forces, against the extreme Right as well as the Communists; 2. security of the country within the ties of the Atlantic Alliance and at the same time a pursuit in and with the Alliance of objectives to relax tensions for peace—a frank orientation toward autonomy; 3. harmonious cultural and socioeconomic development of the nation by means of a stronger commitment to a program and a more organized action on the part of the government.

We propose to resolve the crisis [attending the formation of a new cabinet] with the political forces really available in the light of these objectives. But we wish also to set the conditions for the enlargement, so to speak, of the democratic area, that is, the engagement of new forces—those represented by the Socialist party—in supporting and enriching democratic life in Italy. We plan to pursue these objectives without withdrawals, excesses, or confusion and with a positive action,

---

[1] These figures reflect not the number of delegates at the congress but the votes they cast for the party members they represented. Ed. note.

with a courageous initiative that will lead not to steps backward but to steps forward in the defense and development of democracy in Italy.

The reference to a frank orientation toward autonomy could not but displease those members of the Christian Democratic party who had begun to call Fanfani a neutralist in the cold war, especially after his visit to Moscow in August 1961 to try his hand at relaxing tensions between East and West. The reference was apparently intended to appeal to Nenni, who was an outspoken protagonist of neutralism. The majority in Nenni's party was sufficiently satisfied with the program Fanfani eventually presented to Parliament on March 2 to judge it "largely in harmony with the programmatic approach of the Socialist party." Accordingly, the Central Committee of Nenni's party approved a resolution on March 3 which granted Fanfani its support in the form of abstention by the Socialist parliamentary delegation. The resolution explained that such support would on the one hand avoid the semblance of a general alliance with the government but on the other would also assure Fanfani a majority. The Socialists kept their bargain during the Chamber of Deputies' vote of March 10 and thus made it possible for the 295 votes given Fanfani by his own party, and the Democratic Socialists, Republicans, and some Independents to constitute a large majority over the 195 negative votes cast by the Liberals, the Communists, and the Neo-Fascist Italian Social Movement.

The Socialists' position was clearly one of judging Fanfani's policies on their merits and supporting only those which coincided with the Socialists' "programmatic approach." This approach included as its immediate goals the nationalization of the electrical power industry, decentralization of local government by giving greater power to the regions, further reforms of agricultural contracts, more economic planning by the government, and abolition of the secrecy of bank accounts to curb tax evasion. The first of these demands was met in September 1962 with the nationalization of electricity, arousing considerable opposition among some Christian Democratic elements who were to be further aroused the following month by the introduction of a bill on regional governments. On the other hand, left-wing elements in Nenni's party thought Fanfani's pace of reforms too slow, and still resisted a complete end of cooperation with the Communists in labor organizations and in local administrations. Their resistance was probably strengthened by Togliatti's extraordinary report to the Communist party's congress in December 1962. Much of Togliatti's report is devoted in substance to a rebuttal of Nenni's charge, made at the Socialist party congress of March 1961, that the Communist parties of the world still persisted in the "identification of the class struggle with the victory of the USSR" and in "the consequent need to subordinate or even sacrifice everything to this victory."

*Togliatti Elaborates on His Thesis of a Peaceful Italian Road to
Socialism: Report to the 10th Congress of the Italian Communist Party, December 1962*

> Palmiro Togliatti, *Nella democrazia e nella pace verso il socialismo*, pp.
> 186–88, 192–93, 224–28, *passim*. Our translation.

It is often said that after the liberation the determining factors in the
Communists' policy was the foreign occupation of the national territory which made the success of a popular insurrection militarily impossible. In fact our policy was guided and dictated by much more
profound reasons. In the Resistance there had been created a unity of
democratic forces that reached even to the point of including, socially,
groups of the progressive middle bourgeoisie and politically a large
part of the Catholic mass movement. We were in the first rank among
the promoters, organizers, and leaders of this unity which possessed
its own program of renewing the whole life of the country. This program was put on paper only partially, but it was oriented toward the
establishment of a regime of advanced political democracy, toward
profound reforms of the entire economic and social order, and toward
the advent of a new bloc of progressive forces in the leadership of society. Our policy consisted in fighting openly and coherently for this
solution, which allowed for a democratic development and a social renewal oriented in the direction of socialism. . . .

This political orientation of ours was proclaimed and explained
openly in all the documents, writings, and speeches of the time. In
these there are found the principal elements of what we later called a
search and affirmation of an Italian road for advance toward socialism.

In the first speech of a programmatic nature, made in Naples on
April 11, 1944, it was said openly: "Today Italian workers do not have
to face the problem of doing what was done in Russia."

In September of the same year it was specified in the [periodical]
Rinascita: "The working class knows that it is not its task today to
fight for the immediate establishment of a socialist regime." . . . .

The concept . . . that has now become current in our movement was repeated in 1947, on the eve of our 6th congress. The party's review wrote: "It is by now acknowledged and accepted that in the conditions created by Fascism and from the decisive contribution made by the Soviet Union and by the popular masses of Europe to the victory of the democracies, new roads have been opened to the struggle for freedom on the part of the workers and peoples." But it is immediately added in the same context: "There cannot be any doubt, however, that it is the duty of the Italian people to travel along this road with a method of its own, a method that holds into account all the peculiarities of our country's situation, its international conditions, its economic and political structure, its possibilities and needs for progress." . . . .

The prospect that guided us during the Resistance and in giving birth to the present republican regime is not closed to us. On the contrary, it is more than ever open to us. It is the prospect of a political struggle and of a democratic and peaceful mass movement to transform the present order of things, thrusting all of society in the direction of socialism. I have said peaceful in the sense that it wishes above all to prevent war; but in the sense that it considers civil war also a misfortune to be avoided and maintains that today there exist the conditions that make it possible to avoid it. . . .

For some time there has been talk in our movement of peaceful coexistence between socialist and capitalist countries. After the period of armed imperialist intervention against the young Soviet Republic, it was Lenin who first maintained that such peaceful coexistence was possible. Subsequently, this policy was always upheld and inspired all the peace policy on the part of the Soviet Union and the socialist countries. But today to speak of the possibility of a peaceful coexistence is to say little. In the face of the catastrophic prospects of an atomic conflict we must affirm that peaceful coexistence is, not only for socialist countries but for capitalist ones and for the whole of humanity, a necessity that cannot be postponed. The alternatives are these: either peaceful coexistence or the atomic destruction and therefore the end of our civilization or a major part of it. In the face of these alternatives there can be no doubt as to the choice that must be made. . . .

We have followed with satisfaction the ripening in other political parties and currents of the awareness that new developments in our democratic order are necessary for the good of all our country. Even in the ranks of the dominant party, in meetings promoted by it or by other Catholic organizations there has been noted a certain ripening of new attitudes and orientations. This was manifest at the Naples congress [of the Christian Democratic party, January 1962], and we have considered this to be a positive fact. At least as early as 1960 the Christian Democratic party and its traditional allies have, further-more, found themselves faced by the practical necessity of abandon-ing the old political formulas of a centrism having in fact a parliamen-tary majority oriented toward the Right. The country's democratic and anti-Fascist consciousness, impending new and acute problems, the exhaustion of the old forms of propaganda, all of these imposed a change. From the confluence of these diverse elements there issued a new parliamentary formation called Center-Left, which has brought into being a government supported by the [Nenni] Socialists. But to evaluate this development correctly we must keep in mind the limits and conditions of the new order of things issuing from the Christian Democratic congress at Naples. By declaring itself in favor of a larger intervention of the state in the economy the congress took a step for-ward. But the question remains unanswered whether this intervention is to limit and break the power of large monopolistic capital or whether it is to be conceived solely as an instrument of economic ra-tionalization which does not cut into this power. In fact this second interpretation has been accepted in the statements of the major part of Christian Democratic leaders, and even after the congress their ori-entation has been in this direction. . . . Whatever the present Chris-tian Democratic leaders have been forced to accept that is new they justify as a continuation of their old orientation or as a contingent necessity for the conduct in greater depth of the anticommunist strug-gle until now crowned with very few successes. They have accepted it to unfold a more effective action aimed at breaking the popular forces and to make subservient to their purposes even the Socialist party, which until now has rebuffed them. . . .

Every improvement, even if only limited, of the conditions of the working classes, every blow struck at the system of privilege and ex-ploitation is a positive fact. Nothing is more foolish and harmful than the policy of the worse the better. We have always rejected this pol-icy. Even during the days of the centrist governments we asked for concrete measures we thought necessary, and we approved all that meant improvement and accomplishment. But beyond these contingent measures there unfold two questions of substance: the question of the economic structure of society and that of its political direction. These questions must be invested with proletarian and popular demands to the end of diminishing and possibly breaking the absolute dominion of the bourgeois ruling groups. And in this regard we must take into consideration structural reforms, various nationalizations, a plan for democratic economic development, and the like.

At this point there is advanced what is in appearance the most serious objection. The struggle for these objectives unfolds within the limits of the existing state, which retains its nature as a bourgeois state until such a time as there is a leap in quality. Very well. The class nature of the state is known to us, nor is it modified by the approval of one or more nationalizations. Our very Constitution—which is not a socialist Constitution—has not changed the nature of the state. But this reasoning remains abstract. In order to make it concrete we must come down to an examination of how the present power bloc of the ruling classes is formed and organized, and of the possibility and the manner of transforming it by an advance of a political nature. Did the popular front governments of the prewar period change the nature of the state? In the abstract, no; in the concrete they opened a new political and social prospect. It is a question of seeing if by proceeding from the present structure of the state, if by moving on the terrain of that democratic organization in which the great popular masses participate today, if by realizing the profound reforms foreseen by the Constitution it is possible to develop a movement and obtain results such as modify the present power bloc and create the conditions of another bloc of which the working classes are a part and in which they may conquer the function that is their due. It is clear that in accepting this prospect—which is that of an advance toward socialism in peace and democracy—we introduce the notion of a gradual development in which it is quite difficult to say when precisely the qualitative change takes place. What we foresee in countries having a developed form of capitalism and a rooted democratic organization is a struggle that may go on for a long period of time and in which the working classes fight to become the ruling classes and thus open for themselves the road to the renewal of the entire social structure. Besides being ingenuous, it would be unreal to reduce this struggle to electoral contests for Parliament and await the conquest of 51 per cent of the votes. A dominant bourgeois class can always succeed in preventing this conquest. But also and even more naïve is the proposal made by those who say to us that the task is one of organizing "power committees" without more ado, thus, by decision from those on the top, and then forward!

In this fashion the idea of the conquest of power is reduced to a banality. When the working class has reached the numerical and organized force, when it has the labor union and political movement abilities such as it has in a country like Italy, it tends to assert its power in forms that are much more complicated and articulate, but also much more effective. It asserts its power by defending the institutions of democracy—even parliamentary democracy—by demanding regional and local autonomy, by fighting for substantial reforms, by advancing new proposals for grass-roots control and direct democracy. Is the working class able to find in an advanced capitalist society that mass force that comes from the agreement, the collaboration, and the alliance with nonproletarian strata of the population, such strata as were for instance in other countries the great undifferentiated masses of poor and landless peasants?

This is the decisive problem, and the answer we give to the question is explicitly affirmative.

It is difficult to assess the effect of Togliatti's "collaborationist" report, but the fact stands that in the general elections of April 1963 the Communist party received 25.3 per cent of the votes and 166 seats in the Chamber, the highest totals in its history and a considerable advance from 22.6 per cent and 143 seats in 1953, and 22.7 per cent and 140 seats in 1958. The Christian Democrats suffered heavy losses, from 42.3 per cent of the popular vote in 1958 to 38.3 per cent, and from 273 seats to 260. The opposition Liberals doubled their percentage of the popular vote and won 39 seats, a gain of 22 over 1958, largely at the expense of the Christian Democrats and the rapidly declining Monarchists. Nenni's Italian Socialist party rose slightly from 84 to 87 seats, but Saragat's Democratic Socialists rose from 22 seats in 1958 to 33. The Neo-Fascist Italian Social Movement made some small gains and the Republicans remained stationary with only 1.4 per cent of the vote.

The election's results were interpreted as a defeat for Fanfani's administration, but they nevertheless confirmed that to continue to govern the country the Christian Democrats had either to secure the votes of the moderate and extreme Right by following suitable policies, or to assure themselves of Nenni's continued and more explicit support. The first course, meaning acceptance not only of the Liberals' 39 votes but also the Neo-Fascists' 27 votes, would probably disrupt the unity of the Christian Democratic party. The second course would also divide the Christian Democrats unless Nenni were to give guarantees of his support of the Atlantic foreign policy satisfactory enough to allay the fears of those Christian Democrats who were more concerned with Nenni's neutralism than with his economic program.

In order to allow Nenni time to prepare himself and his party for a fuller collaboration with the Christian Democrats, a caretaker cabinet was formed after an exceptionally long crisis following upon Fanfani's resignation at the end of April 1963. In October 1963 Nenni succeeded in persuading a majority of his party's congress to accept participation in a Center-Left government committed to the Atlantic Alliance and a policy of domestic reforms. The caretaker Prime Minister, Christian Democrat Giovanni Leone, thereupon resigned and Aldo Moro proceeded to form a new cabinet with Nenni as Deputy Prime Minister and Saragat as Minister of Foreign Affairs. The opening to the Left was thus fully consummated, but not without strong opposition from some Christian Democrats such as the group led by Mario Scelba. A pointed reminder by the Vatican City Osservatore Romano of December 14, 1963, on the need for party unity among Christian Democrats subdued some of this opposition, but did not dispel it completely. Nenni also had his troubles. After his decision to join Moro's government, roughly 40 per cent of his parliamentary followers broke away and, led by Tullio Vecchietti and Lelio Basso, formed a Socialist Party of Proletarian Unity (PSUP).

On November 25, 1963, the four parties prepared to enter Moro's cabinet issued a statement explaining the reasons for their coalition and the program they proposed to follow.

Nenni's Socialists Enter the Government: Statement by the Four Parties in Aldo Moro's Center-Left Coalition, November 25, 1963

> Reported in the *Corriere della Sera*, Milan, November 26, 1963. Our translation.

The Christian Democratic, Socialist, Democratic Socialist, and Republican parties—fully aware of the needs attending this decisive political moment which requires a firm and authoritative governmental action on a large democratic and popular base for ends of justice and freedom—and while retaining their full ideological autonomy and in the light of their diverse traditions, inspirations, and political experience, do now commit themselves to the formation of a Center-Left government with the participation of all the contracting parties. . . .

The country's progress is to be achieved in the integrity of free institutions, and the economic, social, and political uplifting of the workers is to be promoted in justice and liberty for all. To these ends it is essential to have the contribution of the Democratic Socialist, Republican, and Socialist parties side by side with the party having the relative majority [in Parliament]. . . .

In fact, in order to achieve the above-mentioned objectives we have sought not any majority whatsoever but a determinate and defined majority, that is, of Center-Left. . . .

Accordingly, there remain excluded from this majority . . . the forces of the Right and also the Liberal party on the one hand, and the Communist party on the other. The forces of the Right are excluded because of the reactionary and illiberal content of their policies; the Liberal party because of its different view of the objectives and methods of a policy of democratic development and of uplifting large masses of the people; the Communist party because of a difference in programs and above all because of its strongly opposed view on the great themes regarding freedom in society and in the state.

106. TOWARD THE UNIFICATION OF ITALIAN SOCIALISM

The specific points outlined in the coalition's statement included a wide range of reforms in regional, provincial, and local administration, in education, labor-management relations, and the legal system. The statement confirmed that foreign policy would remain "based on loyalty to the Atlantic Alliance—with the political and military obligations it entails—and on European solidarity." The coalition's economic and social policy included economic planning for the solution of the still existing imbalances in the "geographic, structural, and distributive" aspects of the economy, and with the purpose of assuring "a progressive drawing nearer to the permanent objectives of a policy of economic development: full employment, propagation of well-being, and elevation of the standard of living."

The Center-Left coalition fashioned by Moro late in 1963 was still in existence in 1966. It has tried to cope with serious economic problems occasioned by inflationary pressures resulting from the speed of Italy's economic expansion, and with political problems caused by the dissension afflicting both Moro's Christian Democrats and Nenni's Socialists. The resignation of President Segni in December 1964 because of ill health (elected in May 1962) led to much dispute when the four-party coalition failed to rally around either of the two Christian Democratic candidates, Giovanni Leone and Amintore Fanfani. The eventual election of Democratic Socialist Giuseppe Saragat, after thirteen days of balloting in Parliament, was achieved with Communist votes and against the opposition of at least 100 Christian Democrats.

Saragat's position as President of the Republic was certainly a factor in strengthening the drive for unification of the two Socialist parties already allied by their joint participation in the cabinet. On July 29, 1966 a committee consisting of representatives of Saragat's Democratic Socialists (PSDI) and Nenni's Italian Socialist Party (PSI) issued the following statement.

Statement by the PSDI—PSI Committee on Unification, July 29, 1966

Reported in the *Messaggero*, Rome, July 30, 1966. Our translation.

On July 28 and 29 there met the joint committee on Socialist unification under the chairmanship of the Hon. Pietro Nenni. . . .

The committee concluded its meetings with a recommendation that the two parties, the PSI and the PSDI, approve the following proposals: a statement of the new unified party's principles, political action, and organization; the party's proposed constitution and the temporary rules to obtain until the first ordinary congress of the unified party; and the rules for the convening of a Socialist constituent assembly.

It was agreed in principle to convene the Central Committees of the two parties on September 16–17, their respective congresses on October 19–21, and on October 22–23 the Socialist constituent assembly to be ratified by delegates of the national congresses of the two parties, PSI and PSDI, and by representatives of groups already in existence or about to be formed, which intended to join in the formation of the new unified party.

Comrades Lombardi, Giolitti, and Balzamo voted against the text of the statement on policies and principles,* and reserved a full presentation of the PSI's minority's opinion for the meetings of the party's Central Committee and the congress.

At the end of the meetings of the joint committee, the chairman

---

* Riccardo Lombardi, Antonio Giolitti, and Vincenzo Balzamo were leaders of those on the PSI's left wing who accepted their party's participation in Moro's cabinet at the end of 1963, but subsequently disagreed either with what they considered to be a too pro-American foreign policy or with a not sufficiently "democratic" economic policy. Ed. note.

Hon. Pietro Nenni expressed a deep satisfaction with the positive results reached by the committee which from this moment on mark the beginning of the final phase of Socialist unification, an event destined to introduce a new factor in the workers' movement and in the country's public life.

The persistent political crisis extending from the mid-1950s to the present, the eventually successful agitation for an opening to the Left, and the current hopes for Socialist unification are all intimately connected with Italy's "economic miracle" and its attendant problems. As long as Italy remained economically dependent on the United States and as long as there appeared to be little hope for Nenni's break with the Russian-oriented Italian Communist Party, it was deemed necessary by Italy's leaders that they follow a policy of political centrism in defense against the external threat from Russia and the internal threat from domestic communism. But the rapid economic recovery not only of Italy but of most of Western Europe, the efforts at a relaxation of international tensions, and the apparent loosening of Russia's "monolithic" control over Europe's Communist parties had the effect of diminishing Italy's sense of dependence on the United States. The resulting greater freedom of political choices open to Italy was facilitated also by Nenni's separation from the Communists. Furthermore, and by no means unimportant, the fact that the Italian Communists themselves could not automatically be adjudged incapable of following an "Italian road to socialism" helped reduce somewhat the fears both at home and abroad of those who had been concerned more with the Communists' subservience to a major foreign power than with the Communists' economic views. A final consideration is that the degree of economic prosperity the "miracle" brought to Italy was in some measure the function of wide governmental intervention in the economy, thus creating in practice an economic policy acceptable at least in part to Socialists such as Saragat and eventually even to Nenni.

The nature and scope of the economic "miracle" are examined in the following excerpts from a work by Giuseppe Scimone.

107. ITALY'S ECONOMIC "MIRACLE"

Giuseppe Scimone, "The Italian 'Miracle,'" in *Economic 'Miracles.'* Introduction by J. Enoch Powell. London: Andre Deutsch, for The Institute of Economic Affairs, 1964, pp. 174–83, 185–86, 191–94, 201–5, *passim.* Tables and some of the original footnotes deleted.

Some of [the] factors of growth were common to other countries after the war (West Germany and Japan); others were peculiar to Italy. In the first group is the assistance through American aid plans. The Italian governments which succeeded the fascists were able to reject the many claims for war damage on the grounds that they had not started the war. At the same time, they qualified for the assistance provided particularly by the USA which supplied consumer goods, machinery, industrial equipment, raw material, finance, and know-how to a value of $2,000 million in the seven years 1945 to 1952, equal to about 3.5 per cent of the national income during that period.*

The loss of colonial possessions overseas and the demobilisation of the armed forces yielded a further large saving. The expenses for defence, the colonies, and the service of debts accounted between 1948 and 1959 for about 25 per cent of the "above the line" total against 66 per cent in the three years before the Second World War.

The discovery in 1949 of large reservoirs of natural gas made Italy the largest producer in Europe. The reserves were within easy reach of the great manufacturing areas of the North, and this proximity reduced processing costs and helped the chemical industry to achieve rapid expansion. There was also a natural oil strike showing an increase of 1,800,000 tons between 1950 and 1962. The production of fuel oil rose from less than a million tons in 1950 to 6.6 million in 1962. In varying degrees these factors combined to create the conditions which made the "miracle" possible. But other technical circumstances assisted and helped to maintain its tempo: mainly the changes in the industrial structure from labour-intensive to capital-intensive, the high yield on investments, and the freedom of private investment to concentrate on the most profitable line of business.

In the years 1957 to 1962 the percentage of GNP † going into gross investment rose from 23.5 to 25.9 per cent and the return on capital invested rose from 2.1 per cent in 1951 to 1957 to 2.4 per cent in 1957 to 1961. This rise was caused by a sharp upsurge in fixed investment in the private sector and by state investment in the development of the southern region. . . .

---

* This figure is given by Dr. R. Tremelloni in his essay "The Last 100 Years of Italian Industry," in *The Italian Economy, 1861 to 1961*, Giuffrè, Milan, 1961. According to other estimates, Italy got as much as $3,500 million from the USA. See "Italy's Booming North," in *Time*, January 12, 1962.

† Gross national product. Ed. note.

INDUSTRIAL GROWTH

Between 1950 and 1958, against an annual average rate of growth of 3.3 per cent in agriculture, forestry and fisheries, the rate for industry was 9 per cent. The difference was larger in the following four years: from 1958 to 1961 1.5 per cent against 10.9 per cent. Agriculture's contribution to the GNP fell from 20 per cent in 1956 to 16 per cent in 1962. Labour was released for non-agricultural work; the latter's share of the labour force rose from 65 per cent in 1957 to 71 per cent in 1962.

Against an increase of 121.6 per cent at the end of 1962 (1953 = 100) in the index of national production, the increase in manufacturing was 125.7 per cent. But even amongst manufacturing industries there have been wide differences in development rates. In cellulose and artificial fibres the rise was as much as 319.9 per cent. Other important gains occurred in chemicals (235.5 per cent), petroleum and coal by-products (203.6 per cent), and vehicles (201.3 per cent). During the same period two older industries—textiles and food—expanded by only 35.5 per cent and 68.4 per cent respectively.

The durable consumer goods industries are a symbol of the "boom years." The best advances were made by household appliances, motor vehicles (cars and scooters), office equipment and some clothing items such as shoes and stockings. The expansion of all these sectors was influenced by diverse causes. In particular, production was stimulated by selling in foreign markets where goods "made in Italy" benefited from the expansion in general demand, from their competitive prices, and characteristic style and design. Italian industries were quick to draw on the experience gained by producers of other countries. Labour was plentiful and, although lacking specific qualifications, was prepared to be more mobile and adaptable than it was, for example, in England. It was also possible to make the large investments necessary to carry out far-reaching plans for technical improvement which in turn helped to reduce prices in spite of some increases in costs.

Household appliances may be regarded as typical. In little more than ten years they have produced one of the largest domestic electrical industries in the world, both in production and exports. Much of this expansion is due to the contribution of firms which only a few years earlier were still no more than artisan workshops. Before the war the industry was almost non-existent, with Fiat producing a small quantity for a market which preferred to import the bulk of its needs from Sweden. In 1962 output reached £77 million, which is the more remarkable in view of the relatively small domestic market. . . .

The "miracle" has produced a new race of business men. The Italian phenomenon had much in common with the development in the United States during the so-called "Roaring Twenties" when many small traders reached the tycoon class in a few months. The case of Signor P., a person I met in Milan and who in a short time rose from the position of sales representative of an aperitif to the proprietor of at least half-a-dozen factories employing 1,000 workers and selling in more than 50 countries, is a good example of the new freedom for entrepreneurs. Probably the worst aspect of self-sufficiency of the Fascist régime had been the confinement which inhibited effort and retarded innovation not sponsored or favoured by the government.

After the war, besides being willing to work hard for expansion, Italian business men exhibited a commendable resolve in investing most of the higher profits realised and also what could be borrowed from national credit institutions and from the stock market.

LABOUR—SURPLUS AND SHORTAGE

What part did labour play in all this? A market with more than enough applicants to meet the needs of production helped industrialists to keep their costs competitive. At the end of the war Italy had a population of 45.7 million with a density of 165 inhabitants per sq. kilometre, almost double the European ratio. This concentration of population combined with the destruction of plant and equipment during the war produced a surplus in the labour market. The complete demobilisation of the armed forces and the repatriation of numerous prisoners of war swelled the numbers wanting work, as did the suspension of emigration during the war years. The end of the war brought back many settlers from the former Italian colonies in Africa, increasing the number of people competing for jobs. Though the official number of unemployed did not rise much above the average of two million, there were also many under-employed, especially in the agricultural South.

The effective level of wages received by the Italian workers has given rise to controversy. The employers have argued that if it is true that in some industries wages are lower than in other European countries, their share of the "indirect burden" (social security contributions, taxes of a social character, and training expenses) is higher in Italy. The Confederazione Generale dell'Industria Italiana (known as CONFINDUSTRIA) calculated that it amounts to between 30 and 37 per cent of total labour costs, while in France the proportion is between 25 and 28 per cent and in the remaining EEC countries lower still. Even so, an investigation in 1959 by the Social Affairs Commission of EEC showed that Italy had, in comparison with the other European partners, the lowest labour costs in most of the 14 industrial sectors examined. However, as from 1962, with a shortage of skilled labour beginning to appear, and a more flexible approach by the centre-left government towards trade union demands, wages in Italy showed a tendency to rise faster than in other industrial countries. . . .

GOVERNMENT ACTION

The policy adopted by successive governments after the fall of Fascism was mainly liberal. At the end of the war the authorities decided to meet the scarcity of goods by facilitating their production and marketing instead of tightening state regulations. The abolition of price control and rationing ended the "black market." The disadvantage was a rapid increase in internal prices with obvious drawbacks for the less well-off. But there were also some advantages, such as an end to the excessive issue of banknotes, together with the elimination of the disparity between artificial and market prices.

In 1946 export trade was liberated, and the imbalance between the exchange rates of the lira and its purchasing power on the international market was ended. This stimulated sales to overseas markets. The state also played an important part in the reconstruction of the national economy and the elimination of deficit spending in the national budget. Spending on "economy and productivity" was higher than on anything else (including defence), followed by expenditure on education and training.

In addition, large investments were made by public corporations under direct state control, which integrated the funds received from the government with the issue of bonds in home and foreign markets, or by obtaining loans from international credit institutions. . . .

FOREIGN INVESTMENT

In the last few years foreign investments have sustained the expansion of the Italian economy. The increase in foreign investment had been non-stop from 1948 when the government had brought in a law allowing the transfer abroad of the profits of foreign capital even though it forbade the repatriation of the funds before the end of five years from the date of the investment. Better conditions were introduced a few years later. With the Decree Law of February 1956, a more liberal policy was adopted and the result was that the L.85 billion invested in productive enterprises from March 1948 to the end of December 1955 rose steeply to L.539 billion in the following five years. A new regulation at the beginning of 1962 practically ended all restrictions on the free movement of funds on "capital account" and so made it possible for foreigners to transfer profits and capital abroad. . . .

THE IMPACT OF EEC

The effect of the establishment of the European Economic Community on Italy's economic growth is of particular interest. Italy, in spite of the size of her territory and population (25 per cent and 30 per cent respectively of the EEC total) had a gross national income only a little over one-sixth of that of the Community. The economy was protected by high tariffs which were regarded as essential for the maintenance of a large part of the local industries. When the idea of joining other countries to create a large community with a free circulation of merchandise, capital and personnel was first raised early in the 1950s, it was received with hostility. The industries which stood to benefit most from high tariffs, individuals infected by "folie de grandeur," and highly placed bureaucrats who feared for their authority, agreed in forecasting disaster if the Community came into being. Even more objective observers expressed the fear that membership with partners who enjoyed high development rates in their own national economies would be at the expense of Italy. Nonetheless, European unification began and Italy joined the European Coal and Steel Community at the end of 1952.

Italians, thinking that their steel industry was doomed, insisted on writing in all sorts of special clauses, none of which proved to be necessary in the end. On the contrary, the steel industry of the country has trebled its capacity in the ten years of the existence of the ECSC—double the rate of Germany—and production has grown from 3.5 million tons in 1953 to 9.4 million in 1962.

Similarly, Italy's GNP rose by 30 per cent in real terms between 1958 and 1961 as against 21 per cent in the Community as a whole. It would, of course, be wrong to attribute the outstanding growth of Italian business activity solely to the establishment of the EEC, but on the whole it represented the main driving force behind the economic "miracle." . . .

The description has so far been concentrated on the more attractive side of the "miracle." But there is another face to the coin. Italy is a country of striking contrasts and conflicts: a young country still in search of national unity. The diversity of sectional interests is most obvious in the proliferation of political parties of which there are ten with nation-wide support.

The antagonisms arise from a lack of confidence and trust. That industrialists are uncertain of trade unionists is not so unusual but that the taxpayer does not trust the impartiality of the tax office, that the efficiency of the bureaucracy is in question, and that fraud and dissimulation are common, is more serious. The lack of information on matters of vital public concern does not help. (For instance, a parliamentary committee of enquiry which has been investigating the extent of competition in Italian industry since 1960 has not so much as published interim findings.) It is therefore important in any discussion of Italy to realise that behind the over-publicised "Dolce Vita" façade lie the simple, primitive lives of millions of working-class people.

AGRICULTURE

While industry during the "miracle" had spectacular gains, agriculture expanded at a modest rate. It suffered from obsolete management structures like the *mezzadria,* a kind of crop-sharing system long since vanished from the rest of Europe, a climate of political instability generated by communist threats to abolish large private estates, and the emigration of enterprising young men which left many rural areas inhabited only by children and elderly people.

In the North the average yield per hectare is much higher than in the South. Against an average increase of 2.7 per cent in the annual rise in added value in Italy as a whole, the rate in the South was only 1.2 per cent, or less than half. The less favourable position of southern agriculture has been the subject of many surveys and long discussions. Most of the experts agree that much of the South could with advantage be turned into pasture-land, but local peasants are forced to grow their own food because of the pressure of population growth. Soil fertilisation is inadequate and there is little modern farm machinery. . . .

In the decade 1950 to 1960 the money poured into agrarian reform had reaced L.1,450 billion. The state also provided L.1,300 billion for general assistance to agriculture, including the so-called "Piano Verde" which among other things aimed to encourage a wider use of mechanical devices. But while the first of these two figures refers to 800,000 hectares, the second had to be spread over about 27 million hectares.

Such a comparison might justify the criticism that has been levelled at state intervention in agriculture: that public investment has been primarily dictated by political considerations. Under heavy communist competition in the rural districts, the ruling Demo-Christian party created organising bodies led by their supporters. The outcome was not a happy one, for it led to the misuse of public funds. . . .

The greatest obstacle to development in the South is the mentality of the landowners who do not want to dirty their hands with manual work. Working on a farm is considered an ungentlemanly occupation. Between 1958 and 1963 the number of tractors increased by some 175,000 units, but the rise was proportionately higher in the North than in the South where landowners cried out against the economic "miracle" responsible for spiriting away their peasants, leaving them to decide between manual work and dignified decline.

It would, however, be inaccurate to generalise about the backwardness of the South. For instance at the Conca d'Oro di Marzameni, in the southern part of Sicily, the world's largest hydroponic cultivation system was established a few years ago. The station has an average daily yield of 35 truck-loads of tomatoes all the year round, and the plant covers an area of 50,000 sq. metres, more than four times the size of its largest American counterpart. Thus alongside primitive agriculture one can find the most modern techniques.

BIBLIOGRAPHY

BIBLIOGRAPHY

Acton, Harold M. *The Last Bourbons of Naples* (*1825–1861*). London: Methuen, 1961.

Albertini, Luigi. *Venti anni di vita politica, 1898–1914*. 5 vols. Bologna: Zanichelli, 1950–53.

Albrecht-Carrié, René. *Italy at the Paris Peace Conference*. New York: Columbia University Press, 1938.

—— *Italy from Napoleon to Mussolini*. New York: Columbia University Press, 1950.

Amendola, Giovanni. *La nuova democrazia*. Naples: Riccardo Ricciardi, 1951.

Ansaldo, Giovanni. *Il ministro della buona vita: Giolitti e i suoi tempi*. Milan: Longanesi, 1950.

Antoni, Carlo, and Raffaele Mattioli, eds. *Cinquant'anni di vita intellettuale italiana, 1896–1946: scritti in onore di Benedetto Croce*. 2 vols. Naples: Edizioni scientifiche italiane, 1950.

Anzilotti, Antonio. *Gioberti*. Florence: Vallecchi, 1922.

Arangio-Ruiz, Gaetano. *Storia costituzionale del Regno d'Italia, 1848–1898*. Florence: G. Civelli, 1898.

Askew, William C. *Europe and Italy's Acquisition of Libya, 1911–1912*. Durham, N.C.: Duke University Press, 1942.

Atti del Parlamento italiano, Camera dei deputati, Discussioni. Rome: Tipografia della Camera dei deputati.

Badoglio, Pietro. *Italy in the Second World War*. Translated by M. Currey. New York: Oxford University Press, 1948.

Balbo, Cesare. *Della speranze d'Italia*. 2d ed. Paris, 1844.

Barbagallo, Corrado. *Napoli contro il terrore nazista (8 settembre–1 ottobre 1943)*. Naples: Maone, 1944?

—— *La questione meridionale*. Milan: Garzanti, 1948.

Barberi, Benedetto. *The Growth of National Income of Italy, 1861–1956*. Rome: Central Institute of Statistics, 1957.

Barberis, Corrado. *Teoria e storia della riforma agraria*. Florence: Vallecchi, 1957.

Barr, Stringfellow. *Mazzini: Portrait of an Exile*. New York: H. Holt and Co., 1935.

Barzini, Luigi. *The Italians*. New York: Atheneum, 1964.

Battaglia, Roberto. "Il problema storico della resistenza," *Società*, Vol. IV (1948).

Beales, Derek E. D. *England and Italy, 1859–1860*. London: T. Nelson, 1961.

Berkeley, George F., and Joan Berkeley. *Italy in the Making, 1815–1848*. 3 vols. Cambridge, Eng.: The University Press, 1932–40.

Bellini, Fulvio, and Giorgio Galli. *Storia del partito comunista italiano*. Milan: Schwarz, 1953.

Bianchi, Nicomede. *Storia documentata della diplomazia europea in Italia dall'anno 1814 all'anno 1861*. 8 vols. Turin: Unione tipografica editrice, 1865–72.

Binchy, Daniel A. *Church and State in Fascist Italy*. London and New York: Oxford University Press, 1941.

Blakiston, Noel, ed. *The Roman Question: Extracts from the Dispatches of Odo Russell from Rome, 1858–1870*. London: Chapman and Hall, 1962.

Blanc, Louis. *The History of Ten Years, 1830–1840: France under Louis Philippe*. 2 vols. Translated by Walter K. Kelly. Philadelphia: Lee and Blanchard, 1848.

Bonomi, Ivanoe. *La politica italiana dopo Vittorio Veneto*. Milan: Einaudi, 1953.

—— *From Socialism to Fascism*. London: Martin and Hopkinson, 1924.

Borgese, Giuseppe A. *Goliath: The March of Fascism*. New York: Viking, 1938.

Brady, Joseph H. *Rome and the Neapolitan Revolution of 1820–21*. New York: Columbia University Press, 1937.

Bulferetti, Luigi. *Introduzione alla storiografia socialistica in Italia*. Florence: Olschki, 1949.

Cadorna, Raffaele. *La riscossa. Dal 25 luglio alla liberazione*. Milan: Rizzoli, 1948.

Cammett, John M. *Antonio Gramsci and the Origins of Italian Communism*. Stanford: Stanford University Press, 1967.

Candeloro, Giorgio. *Storia dell'Italia moderna*. 3 vols. Milan: Feltrinelli, 1956–60.

Cantimori, Delio, ed. *Giacobini italiani*. Bari: Laterza, 1956.

Cappelletti, Licurgo. *Storia di Vittorio Emanuele II*. 3 vols. Rome: Enrico Voghera, 1892–93.

Carocci, Giampiero, ed. *Il parlamento nella storia d'Italia: antologia storica della classe politica*. Bari: Laterza, 1964.

Carrillo, Elisa A. *De Gasperi: The Long Apprenticeship*. Notre Dame, Ind.: University of Notre Dame Press, 1965.

Case, Lynn M. *Franco-Italian Relations, 1860–65: The Roman Question and the Convention of September*. Philadelphia: University of Pennsylvania Press, 1932.

Catalano, Franco. *Filippo Turati*. Milan: Avanti!, 1957.

—— *Storia del C.L.N.A.I.* Bari: Laterza, 1956.

Cavour, Camillo. *Discorsi parlamentari.* 11 vols. Turin: Tipografia della Camera dei deputati, 1863–72.

Chabod, Federico. *A History of Italian Fascism.* Translated by Muriel Grindrod. London: Weidenfeld and Nicolson, 1963.

—— *Storia della politica estera italiana dal 1870 al 1896.* Vol. I, *Le premesse.* Bari: Laterza, 1951.

Chiala, Luigi, ed. *Lettere edite ed inedite di Camillo Cavour.* 6 vols. Turin: Roux e Favale, 1883–87.

Ciano, Galeazzo. *Diario, 1937–38.* Bologna: Cappelli, 1948.

—— *Diario, 1939–43.* 2 vols. Milan: Rizzoli, 1946.

Ciasca, Raffaele. *Storia coloniale dell'Italia contemporanea da Assab all'impero.* 2d rev. ed. Milan: Hoepli, 1940.

Cilibrizzi, Saverio. *Storia parlamentare politica e diplomatica d'Italia da Novara a Vittorio Veneto.* 8 vols. Vols. I–VI: Naples, S.T.E., 1939–1943. Vols. VII–VIII: Rome, Tosi editore, n.d.–1951.

Clough, Rosa Trillo. *Looking Back at Futurism.* New York: Cocce Press, 1942.

Clough, Shepard B. *The Economic History of Modern Italy.* New York: Columbia University Press, 1964.

—— "Il fascismo in Italia: linee della sua politica economica," *Il Nuovo Osservatore,* Vol. VI, Nos. 44–45 (November–December, 1965).

Cognasso, Francesco. *Vittorio Emanuele II.* Turin: Unione tip-editrice torinese, 1942.

Confederazione fascista dei lavoratori dell'industria. *I 10 anni della carta del lavoro.* Rocca S. Casciano: Stab. tip. L. Cappelli, 1937.

Corbino, Epicarmo. *L'economia italiana dal 1860 al 1960.* Bologna: Zanichelli, 1963.

Corriere della Sera, Il. Milan, February 13, 1962; November 26, 1963.

Crispi, Francesco. *Discorsi parlamentari.* 3 vols. Rome: Tipografia della Camera dei deputati, 1915.

—— *Memoirs of Francesco Crispi.* 3 vols. London: Hodder and Stoughton, 1912–14. Translated by M. Prichard-Agnetti from Vols. I–III of *Memorie e documenti,* edited by Tommaso Palamenghi-Crispi, 5 vols., Milan, Treves, 1911–14.

—— *Scritti e discorsi politici, 1849–1890.* 2d ed. Turin-Rome: Roux e Viarengo, n.d. (189?).

Critica Sociale, Milan, Socialist semimonthly.

Croce, Benedetto. *History of Europe in the Nineteenth Century.* Translated by Henry Hurst. New York: Harcourt, Brace, 1933.

—— "Quando l'Italia era tagliata in due (settembre 1943–giugno 1944)," *Quaderni della Critica,* No. 6, November 1946.

—— *Scritti e discorsi politici (1943–1947).* 2 vols. Bari: Laterza, 1963.

—— *Storia d'Italia dal 1871 al 1915.* 13th ed. Bari: Laterza, 1964. English translation by C. M. Ady: *A History of Italy, 1871–1915.* Oxford: Clarendon, 1929.

D'Azeglio, Massimo. *Degli ultimi casi di Romagna*. Florence, 1846.

Deakin, F. W. *The Brutal Friendship: Mussolini, Hitler and the Fall of Italian Fascism*. London: Weidenfeld and Nicolson, 1962.

Debidour, Antonin. *Histoire diplomatique de l'Europe, 1814–1878*. 2 vols. Paris: F. Alcan, 1891.

De Cesare, R. *The Last Days of Papal Rome, 1850–1870*. London: Constable, 1909.

De Felice, Renzo. *I giornali giacobini italiani*. Milan: Feltrinelli, 1962.

—— *Mussolini, il rivoluzionario, 1883–1920*. Turin: Einaudi, 1965.

De Gasperi, Alcide. *Discorsi politici*. 2 vols. Edited by Tommaso Bozza. Rome: Cinque Lune, 1956.

Delle Piane, Mario. *Funzione storica dei Comitati di liberazione nazionale*. Florence: Le Monnier, 1946.

Delzell, Charles F. *Italy in Modern Times: An Introduction to the Historical Literature in English*. Washington, D.C.: American Historical Association Service Center for Teachers of History, Publication No. 60, 1964.

—— *Mussolini's Enemies: The Italian Anti-Fascist Resistance*. Princeton: Princeton University Press, 1961.

Demarco, Domenico. *Una rivoluzione sociale, la repubblica romana del 1849*. Naples: M. Fiorentino, 1944.

Democrazia cristiana. *Orientamenti programmatici della Democrazia cristiana*. 2d ed. Rome: S.P.E.S. Centrale, D.C., 1950.

Depretis, Agostino. *Discorsi parlamentari*. 8 vols. Rome: Tipografia della Camera dei deputati, 1888–92.

Einaudi, Mario, and François Goguel. *Christian Democracy in Italy and France*. Notre Dame, Ind.: University of Notre Dame Press, 1952.

Favagrossa, Carlo. *Perchè perdemmo la guerra*. Milan: Rizzoli, 1946.

Fermi, Laura. *Mussolini*. Chicago: University of Chicago Press, 1961.

Finer, Herman. *Mussolini's Italy*. New York: Henry Holt, 1935.

Fonzi, Fausto. *Crispi e lo "Stato di Milano."* Milan: A Giuffrè, 1965.

Fossati, Antonio. *Lavoro e produzione in Italia dalla metà del secolo XVIII alla seconda guerra mondiale*. Turin: Giappichelli, 1951.

Fried, Robert C. *The Italian Prefects: A Study in Administrative Politics*. New Haven: Yale University Press, 1963.

Galati, Vito G. *Storia della Democrazia cristiana*. Rome: Cinque Lune, 1955.

Galizzi, Vincenzo. *Giolitti e Salandra*. Bari: Laterza, 1949.

Garibaldi, Giuseppe. *Autobiography of Giuseppe Garibaldi*. 3 vols. Authorized translation by A. Werner, with a supplement by Jessie White Mario. London: Walter Smith and Innes, 1889.

Gazzetta Piemontese, Turin, Vol. XVI, No. 674 (1848).

Germino, Dante L. *The Italian Fascist Party in Power*. Minneapolis: University of Minnesota Press, 1959.

Gerschenkron, Alexander. *Economic Backwardness in Historical Perspective: A Book of Essays*. Cambridge, Mass.: Belknap Press, 1962.

Ghiron, Isaia, ed. *Annali d'Italia, 1861–1870.* 3 vols. Milan: Hoepli, 1888–90.

Ghisalberti, Alberto Maria. *Gli albori del risorgimento italiano (1700–1815).* Rome: P. Cremonese, 1931.

—— *Massimo d'Azeglio, un moderato realizzatore.* Rome: Edizioni dell'Ateneo, 1953.

Gioberti, Vincenzo. *Del primato morale e civile degli Italiani.* Brussels, 1843.

Giolitti, Giovanni. *Discorsi parlamentari.* 4 vols. Rome: Tipografia della Camera dei deputati, 1953–56.

—— *Memoirs of My Life.* Translated by Edward Storer. London: Chapman, 1923.

Gladston, E. W., *et al. The Unification of Italy.* Oxford: Blackwell, 1955.

Gobetti, Piero. *Risorgimento senza eroi.* Turin: Edizioni del Baretti, 1926.

Gramsci, Antonio. *Opere di Antonio Gramsci.* 10 vols. Turin: Einaudi, 1947–60.

—— *Il Risorgimento.* Turin: G. Einaudi, 1949.

Greenfield, Kent Roberts. *Economics and Liberalism in the Risorgimento: A Study of Liberalism in Lombardy, 1814–1848.* Baltimore: The Johns Hopkins Press, 1934.

Grew, Raymond. *A Sterner Plan for Italian Unity: The Italian National Society in the Risorgimento.* Princeton: Princeton University Press, 1963.

Griffith, Gwilym O. *Mazzini: Prophet of Modern Europe.* London: Hodder and Stoughton, 1932.

Grindrod, Muriel. *The Rebuilding of Italy's Politics and Economics, 1945–1955.* London: Royal Institute of International Affairs, 1955.

Guarneri, Felice. *Battaglie economiche tra la due guerre.* 2 vols. Milan: Garzanti, 1953.

Guichonnet, Paul, *L'unité italienne.* Paris: Presses Universitaires de France, 1961.

Hales, Edward E. Y. *Mazzini and the Secret Societies: The Making of a Myth.* New York: Kenedy, 1956.

—— *Pio Nono: A Study in European Politics and Religion in the Nineteenth Century.* New York: Kenedy, 1954.

—— *Revolution and Papacy, 1769–1846.* Garden City, N.Y.: Hanover House, 1960.

Halperin, S. William. *Diplomat under Stress: Visconti-Venosta and the Crisis of July 1870.* Chicago: University of Chicago Press, 1963.

—— *Italy and the Vatican at War: A Study of their Relations from the Outbreak of the Franco-Prussian War to the Death of Pius IX.* Chicago: University of Chicago Press, 1939.

—— *Mussolini and Italian Fascism.* Princeton: D. Van Nostrand, 1964.

—— *The Separation of Church and State in Italian Thought from Cavour to Mussolini.* Chicago: University of Chicago Press, 1937.

Hancock, William K. *Ricasoli and the Risorgimento in Tuscany.* Faber and Gwyer, 1926.

Hazard, Paul. *La Révolution française et les lettres italiennes, 1789–1815.* Paris: Hachette, 1910.

Hentze, Margot. *Pre-Fascist Italy: The Rise and Fall of the Parliamentary Regime.* London: George Allen and Unwin, 1939.

Hibbert, Christopher. *Il Duce.* Boston: Little, Brown, 1962.

Hilton-Young, Wayland. *The Italian Left: A Short History of Political Socialism in Italy.* London: Longmans, Green, 1949.

Hostetter, Richard. *The Italian Socialist Movement.* Vol. I: *Origins (1860–1882).* Princeton: D. Van Nostrand, 1958.

Hughes, H. Stuart. *The United States and Italy.* Cambridge, Mass.: Harvard University Press, 1953.

I deputati socialisti contro la politica di guerra: Discorsi e dichiarazioni di voto nella discussione sul patto atlantico alla Camera dei deputati, Sedute del 12, 14, e 16–18 marzo 1949. Rome: Tipografia della Camera dei deputati, 1949.

I documenti diplomatici. See Ministero degli affari esteri.

Jacini, Stefano. *Un conservatore rurale della nuova Italia.* 2 vols. Bari: Laterza, 1926.

—— *La crisi religiosa del Risorgimento. La politica ecclesiastica italiana da Villafranca a Porta Pia.* Bari: Laterza, 1938.

Jamison, Evelyn M., et al. *Italy, Medieval and Modern.* Oxford: Clarendon, 1919.

Jemolo, Arturo C. *Church and State in Italy, 1850–1950.* Translated by David Moore. Oxford: Blackwell, 1960.

Johnston, R. M. *The Napoleonic Empire in Southern Italy and the Rise of the Secret Societies.* 2 vols. London: Macmillan, 1904.

—— *The Roman Theocracy and the Republic, 1846–1849.* London: Macmillan, 1901.

King, H. Bolton. *A History of Italian Unity, being a Political History of Italy from 1814–1871.* 2 vols. London: Nisbet, 1912.

King, Bolton, and Thomas Okey. *Italy Today.* London: Nisbet, 1909.

Kirkpatrick, Sir Ivone. *Mussolini: A Study in Power.* New York: Hawthorn, 1964.

Kogan, Norman. *The Government of Italy.* New York: Crowell, 1962.

—— *Italy and the Allies.* Cambridge, Mass.: Harvard University Press, 1956.

—— *A Political History of Postwar Italy.* New York: Praeger, 1966.

—— *The Politics of Italian Foreign Policy.* New York: Praeger, 1963.

Lama, Ernesto. *Antologia del Risorgimento italiano.* Rome: V. Bianco, 1961.

La Palombara, Joseph. *Interest Groups in Italian Politics.* Princeton: Princeton University Press, 1964.

Lederer, Ivo J. *Yugoslavia at the Paris Peace Conference.* New Haven: Yale University Press, 1964.

Lemmi, Francesco. *L'età napoleonica.* Milan: Vallardi, 1938.

—— *Il Risorgimento: Guida bibliografica.* Rome: Fondazione Leonardo per la cultura italiana, 1926.

Lémonon, Ernest. *L'Italie économique et sociale, 1861–1912*. Paris: F. Alcan, 1913.

Longo, Luigi. *Un popolo alla macchia*. Milan: A. Mondadori, 1947.

Lutz, Vera C. *Italy, a Study in Economic Development*. London: Oxford University Press, 1962.

Luzzatto, Gino. *Storia economica dell'età moderna e contemporanea*. 2 vols. Padua: Cedam, A Milani, 1955.

MacGregor-Hastie, Roy. *The Day of the Lion: The Life and Death of Fascist Italy, 1922–1945*. London: Macdonald, 1963.

Mack Smith, Denis. *Cavour and Garibaldi, 1860: A Study in Political Conflict*. Cambridge, Eng.: University Press, 1954.

—— *Italy: A Modern History*. Ann Arbor: University of Michigan Press, 1959.

Malvestiti, Piero. *I socialdemocratici*. Rome: Cinque Lune, n.d.

Mammarella, Giuseppe. *Italy after Fascism*. Montreal: Mario Casalini, 1964.

Margonari, Vittorio. *"Il Comandante" (Gabriele d'Annunzio): Episodi fiumani*. Milan: Luigi di Giacomo Pirola, 1926.

Mario, Jessie White. *The Birth of Modern Italy*. London: T. F. Unwin, 1909.

Marraro, Howard R. *American Opinion on the Unification of Italy*. New York: Columbia University Press, 1932.

Marriott, Sir John A. R. *The Makers of Modern Italy: Napoleon–Mussolini*. Oxford: Clarendon, 1931.

Martinengo-Cesaresco, Evelyn. *Cavour*. London: Macmillan, 1898.

—— *Italian Characters in the Epoch of Unification*. London: T. F. Unwin, 1890.

—— *The Liberation of Italy, 1815–1870*. London: Seeley, 1902.

Matteotti, Giacomo. *The Fascisti Exposed: A Year of Fascist Domination*. Translated by E. W. Dickes. London: Independent Labour Party Publication Department, 1924.

Maturi, Walter. *Interpretazioni del Risorgimento: Lezioni di storia della storiografia*. Turin: G. Einaudi, 1962.

Mazzini, Giuseppe. *Life and Writings*. 6 vols. London: Smith, Elder, 1890–91.

—— *Politica*: Vol. LIX of *Scritti editi ed inediti*. Edizione nazionale. Imola: Paolo Galeati, 1931. Vol. XX.

Megaro, Gaudens. *Mussolini in the Making*. London: G. Allen, 1938.

—— *Vittorio Alfieri, Forerunner of Italian Nationalism*. New York: Columbia University Press, 1930.

Messaggero, Il. Rome, daily, July 26, 1943; July 30, 1966.

Minghetti, Marco. *Discorsi parlamentari*, 8 vols. Rome: Tipografia della Camera dei deputati, 1888–90.

Ministero degli affari esteri, Commissione per la pubblicazione dei documenti diplomatici. *I documenti diplomatici italiani, ottava serie: 1935–1939*, Vol. XIII. *Nona serie: 1939–1943*, Vol. III. Rome: Libreria dello Stato, 1953, 1959.

Momigliano, Attilio. *Alessandro Manzoni.* 3d rev. ed. Milan: G. Principato, 1933.

Monelli, Paolo. *Mussolini: The Intimate Life of a Demagogue.* New York: Vanguard, 1954.

Monti, Antonio. *Vittorio Emanuele II.* Milan: Garzanti, 1941.

Moscati, Ruggero. *Il ministero degli affari esteri, 1861–1870.* Milan: A. Giuffrè, 1961.

Mussolini, Benito. *Opera omnia.* 36 vols. Edited by Edoardo and Duilio Susmel. Florence: La Fenice, 1951–63.

Natale, Gaetano. *Giolitti e gli italiani.* Milan: Garzanti, 1949.

Nelson, Lowry. *Land Reform in Italy.* Washington, D.C.: National Planning Association, Planning pamphlets, No. 97, 1956.

Nenni, Pietro. *Davanti al paese: l'alternativa socialista. Relazione introduttiva e conclusioni congressuali del XXX Congresso nazionale del P.S.I.* ("Politica del Partito": Testi e documenti, No. 1.) Rome: Direzione del P.S.I., 1953.

—— *Relazione di Pietro Nenni, PSI, 34° Congresso nazionale, Milano, 15–20 marzo 1961.* Milan: Edizioni *Avanti!,* 1961.

Neufeld, Maurice F. *Italy, School for Awakening Countries: The Italian Labor Movement in its Political, Social, and Economic Setting, from 1800–1960.* Ithaca: School of Industrial and Labor Relations, Cornell University, 1961.

—— *Labor Unions and National Politics in Italian Industrial Plants.* Ithaca: Institute of International Industrial and Labor Relations, Cornell University, 1954.

Niccoli, Mario. "La Resistenza," *Enciclopedia italiana, Seconda appendice (1938–1948).* Rome: Istituto della Enciclopedia Italiana, 1949.

Noether, Emiliana P. *Seeds of Italian Nationalism, 1700–1815.* New York: Columbia University Press, 1951.

Nuovo Corriere della Sera, Il. Milan, daily, October 27, 1946.

Omodeo, Adolfo. *Difesa del Risorgimento.* 2d ed. Turin: G. Einaudi, 1955.

—— *L'opera politica del conte di Cavour.* 2 vols. Florence: La Nuova Italia, 1945.

Orlando, Vittorio Emanuele. *Discorsi parlamentari.* 4 vols. Rome: Tipografia della Camera dei deputati, 1965.

—— *Memorie (1915–1919).* Edited by Rodolfo Mosca. Milan: Rizzoli, 1960.

Orsi, Pietro. *Cavour and the Making of Modern Italy, 1810–1861.* New York: Putnam's, 1914.

—— *Modern Italy, 1748–1898.* New York: Putnam's, 1900.

Osservatore Romano, L'. Vatican City, daily, July 28, 1943.

Pacifici, Sergio. *A Guide to Contemporary Italian Literature.* Cleveland: World Publishing Co., 1962.

Packe, Michael St. John. *Orsini: The Story of a Conspirator.* Boston: Little, Brown, 1957.

Paléologue, Maurice. *Cavour*. Translated by Ian F. D. Morrow and Muriel M. Morrow. New York: Harper, 1927.

Pane, Luigi dal. *Antonio Labriola: la vita e il pensiero*. Rome: Edizioni Roma, 1935.

Passerin d'Entrèves, Ettore. *La giovinezza di Cesare Balbo*. Florence: Le Monnier, 1940.

—— *L'ultima battaglia politica di Cavour*. Turin: ILTE, 1956.

Perticone, Giacomo. *L'Italia contemporanea dal 1871 al 1948*. Milan: Mondadori, 1961.

—— *La politica italiana nell'ultimo trentennio*. 3 vols. Rome: Edizioni Leonardo, 1945–47.

—— *Storia del socialismo*. Rev. ed. Rome: Edizioni Leonardo. 1946.

Pius XI, Pope. "Encyclical of Pope Pius XI on Catholic Action," in *Sixteen Encyclicals of His Holiness Pope Pius XI, 1926–1937*. Washington, D.C.: National Catholic Welfare Conference, 1938.

Quazza, Guido. *La lotta sociale nel Risorgimento: classi e governi dalla restaurazione all'unità, 1815–1861*. Turin: Tip. Coggiola, 1951.

Raccolta ufficiale delle leggi e dei decreti del Regno d'Italia. Rome: Libreria dello Stato.

Ramm, Agatha. *The Risorgimento*. London: Routledge and Kegan Paul, 1962.

Rath, R. John. *The Fall of the Napoleonic Kingdom of Italy (1814)*. New York: Columbia University Press, 1941.

Regio Ministero degli affari esteri. *Trattati e convenzioni fra il Regno d'Italia e gli altri Stati*. Rome: Tipografia del Ministero degli affari esteri.

Relazione della Commissione d'inchiesta sugli avvenimenti che hanno determinato il ripiegamento del nostro esercito sul Piave: Dall'Isonzo al Piave, 24 ottobre–9 novembre 1917. 3 vols. Rome: Stabilimento poligrafico dello Stato, 1919.

Resoconto stenografico del XVII Congresso nazionale del partito socialista italiano (Leghorn, January 15–20, 1921). Milan: Edizioni *Avanti!*, 1963.

Rodolico, Niccolò. *Carlo Alberto*. 3 vols. Florence: Le Monnier, 1936-48.

Romani, George T. *The Neapolitan Revolution of 1820–1821*. Evanston, Ill.: Northwestern University Press, 1950.

Romano, Aldo. *Storia del movimento socialista in Italia*. 3 vols. Milan: Fratelli Bocca, 1954–56.

Romano, Salvatore F. *Momenti di Risorgimento in Sicilia*. Messina: G. d'Anna, 1952.

Romeo, Rosario. *Breve storia della grande industria in Italia*. 2d ed. Bologna: Cappelli, 1963.

—— *Risorgimento e capitalismo*. Bari: Laterza, 1959.

—— *Il Risorgimento in Sicilia*. Bari: Laterza, 1950.

Rossi, A. [pseud. for Angelo Tasca] *The Rise of Italian Fascism, 1918–1922*. London: Methuen, 1938.

Rossi, Ernesto. *I padroni del vapore*. Bari: Laterza, 1957.

Rossi-Doria, Manlio. *Dieci anni di politica agraria nel Mezzogiorno*. Bari: Laterza, 1958.

Rota, Ettore, ed. *Il 1848 nella storia italiana ed europea*. 2 vols. Milan: F. Vallardi, 1948.

—— *Le origini del Risorgimento (1700–1800)*. Rev. ed., 2 vols. Milan: F. Vallardi, 1948.

—— *Questioni di storia contemporanea*. 4 vols. Milan: Marzorati, 1952–55.

—— *Questioni di storia del Risorgimento e dell'unità d'Italia*. Milan: Marzorati, 1951.

Saitta, Armando. *Filippo Buonarroti: contributi alla storia della sua vita e del suo pensiero*. 2 vols. Rome: Edizioni di "Storia e letteratura," 1950–51.

Saladino, Salvatore. "Italy," in *The European Right: A Historical Profile*. Edited by Hans Rogger and Eugen Weber. Berkeley and Los Angeles: University of California Press, 1965.

Salandra, Antonio. *L'intervento (1915): Ricordi e pensieri*. Milan: Mondadori, 1930.

—— *Memorie politiche, 1916–1925*. Giuseppe Salandra, ed. Milan: Garzanti, 1951.

—— *La neutralità italiana, 1914*. Milan: Mondadori, 1928.

Salomone, A. William. *Italy in the Giolittian Era: Italian Democracy in the Making, 1900–1914*. 2d ed., 1960. Originally published as *Italian Democracy in the Making: The Political Scene in the Giolittian Era, 1900–1914*. Philadelphia: University of Pennsylvania Press, 1945.

—— "The *Risorgimento* between Ideology and History: The Political Myth of 'Rivoluzione Mancata,'" *American Historical Review*, LXVIII (October 1962), 38–56.

Salvadori, Massimo. *Cavour and the Unification of Italy*. Princeton: Van Nostrand, 1961.

Salvatorelli, Luigi. *A Concise History of Italy*. New York: Oxford University Press, 1940.

—— *Pensiero e azione del Risorgimento*. 6th ed. Turin: G. Einaudi, 1960.

—— *Il pensiero politico italiano dal 1700 al 1870*. Rev. ed. Turin: G. Einaudi, 1949.

Salvatorelli, Luigi, and Giovanni Mira. *Storia d'Italia nel periodo fascista*. Turin: G. Einaudi, 1957.

Salvemini, Gaetano. *The Fascist Dictatorship in Italy*. New York: Oxford University Press, 1927.

—— *Mazzini*. Translated by I. M. Rawson. Stanford: Stanford University Press, 1957.

—— *Under the Axe of Fascism*. New York: Viking Press, 1936.

Sartori, Giovanni, et al. *Il parlamento italiano, 1946–1963*. Naples: E.S.I., 1963.

Schiavi, Alessandro, ed. *Filippo Turati attraverso le lettere dei corrispondenti (1880–1925)*. Bari: Laterza, 1947.

Schmidt, Carl T. *The Corporate State in Action: Italy under Fascism.* New York: Oxford University Press, 1939.

Schneider, Herbert W. *The Fascist Government of Italy.* New York: D. Van Nostrand, 1936.

—— *Making the Fascist State.* New York: Oxford University Press, 1928.

Schneider, Herbert W., and Shepard B. Clough. *Making Fascists.* Chicago: The University of Chicago Press, 1929.

Scimone, Giuseppe. "The Italian 'Miracle,'" in *Economic 'Miracles.'* Introduction by J. Enoch Powell. London: Andre Deutsch, for the Institute of Economic Affairs, 1964.

Scott, Walter Giorgio. *Gli investimenti stranieri in Italia.* Milan: Feltrinelli, 1961.

Sella, Quintino. *Discorsi parlamentari.* 5 vols. Rome: Tipografia della Camera dei deputati, 1887–90.

Senato del Regno, Camera dei Fasci e delle Corporazioni. *Bollettino delle assemblee legislative,* XXXa Legislatura, Anno XIV. Series 2a, No. 1 (July 1940). Rome: Senato del Regno, Camera dei Fasci e delle Corporazioni, 1940.

Senato del Regno, Camera dei deputati. *Bollettino parlamentare,* Anno IX. No. 2 (July 1935). Rome: Segreteria generale del Senato del Regno, Segreteria generale della Camera dei deputati, 1935.

Settembrini, Domenico. *La Chiesa nella politica italiana, 1944–1963.* Pisa: Nistri-Lischi, 1964.

Sforza, Carlo. *Contemporary Italy: Its Intellectual and Moral Origins.* Translated from the French by Drake De Kay and Denise De Kay. New York: E. P. Dutton, 1944.

—— *Le direttive della politica estera italiana: Discorso del 25 ottobre 1949 alla Camera dei deputati.* Rome: Tipografia del Ministero degli affari esteri, n.d.

Sonnino, Sidney. *Discorsi parlamentari.* 3 vols. Rome: Tipografia della Camera dei deputati, 1925.

—— (Un deputato). "Torniamo allo Statuto," *Nuova Antologia,* CLI (January 1, 1897), 9–28.

Spellanzon, Cesare. *Storia del Risorgimento e dell'unità d'Italia.* 7 vols. Milan: Rizzoli, 1933–60.

Spini, Giorgio. *Risorgimento e protestanti.* Naples: E.S.I., 1956.

Spreafico, Alberto, and Joseph La Palombara, eds. *Elezioni e comportamento politico in Italia.* Milan: Edizioni di Comunità, 1963.

Sprigge, Cecil J. S. *The Development of Modern Italy.* New Haven: Yale University Press, 1944.

Sturzo, Luigi. *Italy and Fascismo.* London: Faber and Gwyer, 1926.

—— *Il partito popolare italiano.* Rev. ed., 3 vols. Bologna: Zanichelli, 1956–57.

Tarlé, Evgenii V. *Le blocus continental et le royaume d'Italie.* 2d ed. Translated from the Russian. Paris: F. Alcan, 1931.

Tarrow, Sidney G. *Peasant Communism in Southern Italy.* New Haven: Yale University Press, 1967.

Taylor, A. J. P. *The Italian Problem in European Diplomacy, 1847–1849.* Manchester, Eng.: Manchester University Press, 1934.

Ten Years of Italian Democracy, 1946–1956. Rome: Presidency of the Council of Ministers, Information Office, Documentation Centre, 1956.

Thayer, John A. *Italy and the Great War: Politics and Culture, 1870–1915.* Madison: University of Wisconsin Press, 1964.

Thayer, William R. *The Dawn of Italian Independence: Italy from the Congress of Vienna to the Fall of Venice, 1849.* 2 vols. Boston: Houghton Mifflin, 1893.

—— *The Life and Times of Cavour.* 2 vols. Boston: Houghton Mifflin, 1911.

Togliatti, Palmiro. *Nella democrazia e nella pace verso il socialismo: Rapporti e conclusioni all'VIII, IX, e X Congresso del Partito comunista italiano.* Rome: Editori Riuniti, 1963.

—— *Rinnovare l'Italia: Rapporto al V Congresso nazionale del Partito comunista italiano, Roma, 29 dicembre 1945–6 gennaio 1946.* Rome: "L'Unità," 1946.

Toscano, Mario. *Il patto di Londra.* Bologna: Zanichelli, 1934.

—— *Le origini diplomatiche del patto d'acciaio.* Rev. ed. Florence: G. C. Sansoni, 1956.

Treaty and Concordat between the Holy See and Italy: Official Documents. Washington, D.C.: National Catholic Welfare Conference, 1929.

Tremelloni, Roberto. *Storia dell'industria italiana.* Vol. I: *Dalla fine del settecento all'unità d'Italia.* Turin: G. Einaudi, 1947.

—— *Le strade del benessere in uno stato efficiente.* Milan: Istituto lombardo di studi sociali, 1958.

Trevelyan, George Macaulay. *Garibaldi and the Making of Italy: June–November 1860.* London: Longmans, Green, 1911.

—— *Garibaldi and the Thousand.* London: Longmans, Green, 1909.

—— *Garibaldi's Defence of the Roman Republic.* London: Longmans, Green, 1907.

—— *Manin and the Venetian Revolution.* London: Longmans, Green, 1923.

U. S. Department of State. Treaties and other International Acts, Series 1604. *Armistice with Italy, 1943.* Washington, D.C.: Government Printing Office, 1947.

U. S. Senate, 81st Congress, 1st Session, Doc. No. 123. *A Decade of American Foreign Policy: Basic Documents, 1941–1949.* Washington, D.C.: Government Printing Office, 1950.

Urban, Miriam B. *British Opinion and Policy on the Unification of Italy, 1856–1861.* Scottdale, Pa.: Mennonite Press, 1938.

Valeri, Nino, ed. *La lotta politica in Italia dall'unità al 1925: idee e documenti.* Florence: Le Monnier, 1945.

—— *Storia d'Italia.* 5 vols. Turin: Unione tipografica editrice torinese, 1959–60.

Valiani, Leo. *Gli sviluppi ideologici del socialismo democratico in Italia.* Rome: Opere Nuove, 1956.

—— *Questioni di storia del socialismo.* Turin: G. Einaudi, 1958.

Valsecchi, Franco. *L'alleanza di Crimea: il Risorgimento e l'Europa.* Milan: Mondadori, 1948.

—— *L'Italia nel settecento, dal 1714 al 1788.* Milan: Mondadori, 1959.

Vidal, César. *Charles-Albert et le Risorgimento italien (1831–1848).* Paris: E. de Boccard, 1927.

Volpe, Gioacchino. *Italia moderna, 1815–1915.* 3 vols. Florence: Sansoni, 1943–53.

—— *L'Italia nella Triplice alleanza (1882–1915).* 2d ed. Milan: Istituto per gli studi di politica internazionale, 1941.

Wallace, Lillian P. *The Papacy and European Diplomacy, 1869–1878.* Chapel Hill, N.C.: University of North Carolina Press, 1948.

Webb, Leicester C. *Church and State in Italy, 1947–1957.* Carlton: Melbourne University Press, 1958.

Webster, Richard A. *Christian Democracy in Italy, 1860–1960.* London: Hollis and Carter, 1961.

—— *The Cross and the Fasces: Christian Democracy and Fascism in Italy.* Stanford: Stanford University Press, 1960.

Whyte, A. J. B. *The Early Life and Letters of Cavour, 1810–1848.* London: Oxford University Press, H. Milford, 1925.

—— *The Evolution of Modern Italy.* Oxford: Blackwell, 1944.

—— *The Political Life and Letters of Cavour, 1848–1861.* London: Oxford University Press, H. Milford, 1930.

Wiskemann, Elizabeth. *The Rome-Berlin Axis: A History of the Relations between Hitler and Mussolini.* London: Oxford University Press, 1949.

Zanardelli, Giuseppe. *Discorsi parlamentari.* 3 vols. Rome: Tipografia della Camera dei deputati, 1905.

INDEXES

CHRONOLOGICAL INDEX

OF DOCUMENTS AND READINGS

GENERAL INDEX